Explorations across Languages and Corpora

ŁÓDŹ
STUDIES IN LANGUAGE

Edited by
Barbara Lewandowska-Tomaszczyk

Vol. 24

PETER LANG
Frankfurt am Main · Berlin · Bern · Bruxelles · New York · Oxford · Warszawa · Wien

Stanisław Goźdź-Roszkowski (ed.)

Explorations across Languages and Corpora

PALC 2009

PETER LANG
Internationaler Verlag der Wissenschaften

Bibliographic Information published by the Deutsche Nationalbibliothek
The Deutsche Nationalbibliothek lists this publication in the Deutsche Nationalbibliografie; detailed bibliographic data is available in the internet at http://dnb.d-nb.de.

ISSN 1437-5281
ISBN 978-3-631-61677-2

www.peterlang.de

Table of Contents

Introduction

Ever since corpus linguistics entered the mainstream, it has become increasingly difficult to keep track of its most recent developments due to the sheer volume of corpus-based, corpus-driven or corpus-informed studies. For twelve years, the conferences known as PALC (Practical Applications in Language and Computers) and organized at the University of Łódź in Poland have served the international community of corpus and computational linguists by providing a useful forum for the exchange of views and ideas on how corpora and computational tools can be effectively employed to explore and advance our understanding of language. The conferences and the ensuing volumes have attempted to reflect the widening scope and perspectives on language and computers. The present volume is no different in that it documents new developments and explorations in these areas encompassing an array of topics and themes, ranging from national corpora and corpus tools through cognitive processes, discourse and ideology, academic discourse, translation, and lexicography to language teaching and learning. In keeping with the PALC tradition, it is our policy to publish contributions from both seasoned researchers as well as from colleagues who are recently initiated members of the corpus linguistics community.

The contributions are drawn from papers presented at the 7th *Practical Applications in Language and Computers PALC* conference held at the University of Łódź in 2009. The plenary speakers were Khurshid Ahmad (Trinity College, Dublin), Mark Davies (Brigham Young University), Ken Hyland (then at University of London), Terttu Nevalainen (University of Helsinki) and Margaret Rogers (University of Surrey).

This volume is divided into nine Parts, each Part being further subdivided into chapters.

Part One NATIONAL CORPORA provides overviews of three national corpora. First, Mark Davies (Brigham Young University) in his plenary paper *Semantically-Based, Learner-Oriented Queries with the 400+ Million Word Corpus of Contemporary American English* demonstrates the unique ways in which language learners can use the new Corpus of Contemporary American English to carry out and use semantically-based queries. František Čermák (Charles University, Prague) in *The Case of the Czech National Corpus: Its Design and History* introduces readers to the methodological issues of data acquisition and corpus design involved in creating the Czech National Corpus. The next two contributions are related to the National Corpus of Polish. Rafał L. Górski (Institute of Polish Language, Polish Academy of Sciences) in *The Design of the National Corpus of Polish* describes the proposed design of the National Corpus of Polish arguing that the corpus should reflect the perception of the language by the Polish linguistic community. Finally, Adam

Przepiórkowski (Polish Academy of Sciences) and Piotr Bański (University of Warsaw) in *XML Text Interchange Format in the National Corpus of Polish* describe and provide rationale for employing the XML encoding of texts within the National Corpus of Polish.

Part Two CORPUS TOOLS, INFORMATION AND TERMINOLOGY EXTRACTION comprises eight contributions. The first paper of this part is a contribution from Natalia Kotsyba (Warsaw University), Andrij Mykulyak (A. Sołtan Institute for Nuclear Studies, Warsaw), Igor V. Shevchenko (ULIF NANU, Kyiv) *UGTag: Morphological Analyzer and Tagger for Ukrainian Language* in which the authors describe the UGTag, a programme for morphological analysis and tagging of Ukrainian texts developed within the Polish-Ukrainian Parallel Corpus (PolUKR) project to support morphosyntactic annotation for the Ukrainian part of the corpus. The authors of the next seven papers which follow are Michal Křen (Charles University, Prague) and Martina Waclawičová (Charles University, Prague), who in their contribution *Database Framework for a Distributed Spoken Data Collection Project*, look at the main features of database system that is used in the Czech National Corpus for collecting recordings and transcriptions of authentic spoken Czech used in informal situations, Adam Przepiórkowski (Institute of Computer Science, Polish Academy of Sciences) and Grzegorz Murzynowski: *Manual Annotation of the National Corpus of Polish with Anotatornia* present the procedure of the manual annotation of a 1-million-word subcorpus of the National Corpus of Polish using a purpose-built tool, Anotatornia, Danuta Karwańska (University of Warsaw) and Adam Przepiórkowski in their paper *On the Evaluation of Two Polish Taggers* discuss the results of the comparison of two Polish taggers and the implications they carry for future taggers of Polish, especially the tagger, developed within the National Corpus of Polish, Tomas By (Centro de Linguística da Universidade Nova de Lisboa) in *Additional Comments on the Prolog Version of the Tiger Dependency Bank* updates information and provides more details on some of the methods used to verify that the word order disambiguation produces accurate results, Marcin Miłkowski (Polish Academy of Sciences) in his contribution *Automating Rule Generation for Grammar Checkers* decribes several approaches to automatic or semi-automatic development of symbolic rules for grammar checkers from the information contained in the corpora, Piotr Pęzik (University of Łódź) in *Providing Corpus Feedback for Translators with the PELCRA Search Engine for NKJP* introduces the PELCRA search engine for the National Corpus of Polish (PSEN) focusing on the usefulness of the tool in verifying the phraseology of translated texts, and finally Ewelina Kwiatek, Pius ten Hacken (Swansea University) in *Evaluating the Efficiency of MultiTerm Extract for Extraction of English and Polish Terms* investigate the efficiency of MultiTerm Extract, a component of SDL Trados 2007 to extract terms from English and Polish specialized corpora.

Part Three CORPUS-BASED LANGUAGE STUDIES includes the papers by Janusz Badio (University of Łódź), who in *What's in a "Duck"? A Corpus-based Study of Salience and Attention within Animal-Related, Denominal Verb,* attempts to find evidence for the claim that three processes of indexing, deriving affordances and meshing are used simultaneously in language understanding, Łukasz Grabowski (Opole University) in *Application of Parallel Corpora in Typological Investigations: the Case of Using English-Russian Parallel Subcorpus of the National Russian Corpus in Typological Study of Motion Verbs*, uses the English-Russian Parallel Subcorpus of the National Russian Corpus to explore the applications of this type of corpora in typological investigations, Milena Herbal-Jezierska (University of Warsaw) in *Corpus-based Morphology in the Czech Language* looks at various ways of using corpora in morpohological (especially inflexion) research in Czech; finally María Pérez Blanco (University of León) in her contribution *The Language of Evaluation in English and Spanish Editorials: A Corpus-based Study* discusses some of the linguistic features of newspaper editorials in English and Spanish.

Part Four COGNITIVE LINGUISTICS (Barbara Lewandowska-Tomaszczyk, University of Łódź and Paul Wilson, University of Łódź), *Culture Based Conceptions of Emotion in Polish and English* compares emotional dimensional structure of Polish and English native speakers and discusses the cultural bases to the findings.

Part Five groups papers which adopt A CORPUS-ASSISTED PERSPECTIVE ON DISCOURSE ANALYSIS AND IDEOLOGY. Cinzia Bevitori (University of Bologna at Forlì) in her paper *The Meanings of Responsibility in the British and American Press on Climate Change: A Corpus-Assisted Discourse Analysis Perspective* examines the ways in which the lemma 'responsibility' is used in a corpus of British and American press coverage of climate change in 2007. Mikołaj Deckert (University of Łódź): *Towards an Axiological Picture of the EU – Evidence from a Polish TV News Corpus* uses Polish broadcast news data to explore the axiological constructions of the personified European Union and its metonymic discursive forms. Katarzyna Fronczak (University of Łódź) in her contribution *Keywords and the Discourse of the Northern Ireland Peace Process, 1997–2007. A Case Study in the Election Manifestoes of the Democratic Unionist Party and Sinn Féin* adopts a keyword approach to carry out a textual analysis of language used in the election manifestoes focusing on the development and changes in the usage of words significant for the peace process. Joanna Kaim-Kerth (Jagiellonian University) in *Correspondence Analysis in Discourse Studies* employs multidimensional statistical analysis to demonstrate how such methods, particularly correspondence analysis, can be used in researching discourses focused on similar subject, i.e. values and authorities as well as visions of the family as perceived by different parliamentary fractions (understood as different discourses). Finally, Inga Massalina (Kaliningrad State Technical University) in her study *Selected Cognitive and Discoursal Aspects of the LSP of the Navy* touches upon the cognitive and discourse aspects of the LSP of Navy.

ACADEMIC DISCOURSE is the topic of Part Six, which comprises three contributions. The first paper is a plenary contribution by Ken Hyland (University of Hongkong) *Corpora and EAP: Specificity in Disciplinary Discourses* in which the author draws on his own work conducted over several years into student and research genres to show how some familiar conventions of academic writing are employed by different fields. Silvia Cacchiani (University of Modena and Reggio Emilia) in her paper *Keywords and Key Lexical Bundles as Cues to Knowledge Construction in RAS in Economics* attempts to characterize disciplinary discourses by examining discourse signalling devices, and focussing on lexical bundles and keywords. In the last contribution of this Part *Conceptualising Spatial Relationships in Academic Discourse: A Corpus-Cognitive Account of Locative-Spatial and Abstract-Spatial Prepositions*, Christoph Haase (Chemnitz University of Technology) and Josef Schmied (Chemnitz University of Technology): investigate distributional properties of prepositions as heads of prepositional phrases that negotiate a mapping function between direct/literal and extended/metaphorical meaning when dealing with abstract concepts.

Part Seven deals with the theme of TRANSLATION and it includes eight contributions. It opens with a plenary contribution by Margaret Rogers (University of Surrey) *Translation Memory and Textuality: Some Implications*, who explores the use of computer-based tools in the translation of LSP (language for special purposes) texts and considers whether this has any implications for the nature of textuality. In the next paper, *Corpus Encoding and Integration for English-Spanish MT*, Alejandro Curado Fuentes (University of Extremadura) and Martin Garay Serrano (University of Extremadura) describe the compilation and encoding of the Spanish corpus and its integration on the database with the bilingual dictionary with a view to enhancing the Context-Based Machine Translation of English into Spanish. Dimitra Anastasiou (University of Limerick) in *Localisation, Centre for Next Generation Localisation and Standards* focuses on the description of a project called "Centre for Next Generation for Localisation" which currently runs in Ireland and she describes standards in terms of localization, especially the XLIFF standard. Hanne Eckhoff (University of Oslo), Dag Haug (University of Oslo) and Marek Majer (University of Oslo) in their contribution *Making the Most of the Data: Old Church Slavic and the PROIEL Corpus of Old Indo-European Bible Translations* report on ongoing work on the PROIEL corpus of old Indo-European New Testament texts, consisting of the New Testament in its Greek original and its earliest translations. Cécile Frérot (Université Stendhal Grenoble 3) in *Parallel Corpora for Translation Teaching and Translator Training*

Purposes explores the use of parallel corpora in designing a corpus-based translation course that is relevant from a translational standpoint and that is best suited to future professional translators, especially in terms of corpus-based translation tools. In the next paper, *The Combination of Comparable and Translation Corpora and How Translators May Benefit from it*, Marlén Izquierdo (University of Cantabria) continues the theme of parallel corpora by dealing with the combination of comparable and parallel corpora in the descriptive, functional analysis of languages in contrast and its positive impact for extending applications to translation. Marta Kajzer (Adam Mickiewicz University, Poznań) in *Translation of Eurojargon as a Source of Neologisms in Polish. A Corpus-based Study* presents a corpus-based analysis of Eurojargon translation as a potential source of neologisms in Polish. The last contribution in this section by Maria Tymczyńska (Adam Mickiewicz University, Poznań) *Community Interpreting in a Blended Environment – Student and Teacher Assessment* presents and discusses the application of Moodle, a free open-source online course management system, in the creation and implementation of practical interpreting courses in the Post-Graduate Programme in Community Interpreting offered at the Adam Mickiewicz University in Poznań, Poland.

Part Eight explores the theme of LEXICOGRAPHY. In the first contribution, Piotr Bański (University of Warsaw) and Beata Wójtowicz (University of Warsaw) in *New XML-encoded Swahili-Polish Dictionary: Micro- and Macrostructure* describe the structure of a new Swahili-Polish dictionary and some of the insights resulting from testing its electronic format. This is followed by Piotr Burmann's critical appraisal of a range of technical disctionaries in terms of their usefulness in the translator's work in *Insights into Selected Scientific and Technical Dictionaries Currently Available on the Polish Publishing Market.* Mirosława Podhajecka (University of Opole) in her contribution *Research in Historical Lexicography: Can Google Books Collection Complement Traditional Corpora?* demonstrates that the Google Books collection, a non-specialized textual resource can be applied successfully for research in historical lexicology and lexicography. The last paper in this section authored by Igor V. Shevczenko (ULIF NANU, Kyiv), Natalia Kotsyba (University of Warsaw), Kiryl Kurshuk (Hrodna University) *Towards the Creation of a Belarusian Grammatical Dictionary*, describes the process of creating thc Belarusian grammatical word-inflexion dictionary, the first tool of the kind for this language, on the basis of linguistic similarities with the existing Ukrainian grammatical dictionary.

The last section in the volume, Part Nine LANGUAGE TEACHING AND LEARNING contains four contributions. First, Alex Boulton (CRAPEL–ATILF/CNRS, Nancy-Université) in his paper *Data-Driven Learning: the Perpetual Enigma* traces the evolution of DDL through the work of Tim Johns from 1984 up until his death in 2009, as well as in DDL studies by other researchers. Then, Carmen Dayrell (University of São Paulo (USP) in *Anticipatory 'IT' in English Abstracts: A Corpus-based Study of Non-native Student and Published Writing,* explores the use of anticipatory *it* patterns (such as *it is found that* and *it is necessary to*) in English abstracts written by Brazilian graduate students from the disciplines of physics, pharmaceutical sciences and computing as opposed to abstracts of published papers from the same disciplines. Stefano Federici (University of Cagliari) in his contribution *Automatic Question Generation for E-learning* describes the "E-generation in E-learning" project that aims to evaluate and improve automatic question generation methodologies by means of analogy-based techniques to implement an automatic question generation system that best suites the needs of today e-learning platforms such as Moodle. Finally, Przemysław Krakowian (University of Łódź) in his paper *WEBCEF – The Project, Deliverables and Status Quo* looks at some of the issues and research questions which arose during the completion of WebCEF, a Socrates Minerva project in which web-based environments can be used for assisting the teacher in the process of evaluating spoken performance of language learners.

Acknowledgements

This volume and the preceding PALC conference would not have been possible without the support and encouragement from professor Barbara Lewandowska-Tomaszczyk. Special thanks are also due to dr Anna Cichosz, dr Piotr Pęzik, dr Jacek Waliński, Mr Mikołaj Deckert and Mr Łukasz Dróżdż for running the special workshops and sessions and for the overall efficient organization of the entire event.

Finally, we wish to acknowledge the financial support of the COST office (and personally dr Thekla Wiebusch of the CNRS, Paris), which enabled us to organize a COST Action A31 workshop at PALC 2009.

Stanisław Goźdź-Roszkowski

Part One

NATIONAL CORPORA

Semantically-Based, Learner-Oriented Queries with the 400+ Million Word Corpus of Contemporary American English

Mark Davies

Abstract: The architecture and interface for the Corpus of Contemporary American English (COCA) allow learners of English to carry out a wide range of semantically-oriented queries, including: 1) quick and easy collocates searches 2) comparison of collocates of two words (e.g. small/little) 3) comparison of collocates in different genres (e.g. collocates of "chair" in fiction and academic) 4) use of integrated thesaurus (entries for 60,000+ words) to see frequency of all synonyms (including by genre) and to create more powerful queries (e.g. all synonyms of "beautiful" + a synonym of "woman") and 5) customized wordlists (including hundreds or thousands of words in a semantic domain).

Keywords: English corpus, semantic acquisition.

1. Introduction

One of fundamental problems facing language learners is of course to acquire the semantic and pragmatic knowledge shared by native speakers of the target language. This involves such things as knowing:

- what words co-occur with a given word or phrase, which of course relates to native speakers' knowledge of what the word means and how it is used (i.e. "you can tell a lot about a word by the other words that it hangs out with")
- how the meaning and use of a word differs between genres
- the difference between related words, in terms of meaning and use
- how all of the words in a particular semantic field are related, in terms of frequency and distribution in different genres
  (See Schmitt 2000, Nation 20001, and Gardner 2007).

Corpora architectures and interfaces differ widely in terms of how much attention they pay to providing tools to answer questions such as these. It seems that sometimes these architectures and interfaces are oriented much more towards the interests of computer scientists and computational linguists than they are towards language learners.

In this paper, we will focus on how language learners can use the new Corpus of Contemporary American English (COCA)[1] to carry out and use semantically-based queries such as those listed above. As we discuss COCA[2], we will compare it to the four other architectures for large corpora that are currently available online for language learners:

1. Corpus Query Processor (CQP), as exemplified by its implementation in Sketch Engine (www.sketchengine.co.uk) (hereafter Sketch Engine)
2. Corpus Query Processor (CQP), as exemplified by its implementation in BNCweb (bncweb.lancs.ac.uk) (hereafter BNCweb)
3. VISL / CorpusEye (corp.hum.sdu.dk) (hereafter VISL)
4. Phrases in English (pie.usna.edu) (hereafter PIE)

BNCweb and PIE have only one corpus available – the British National Corpus (BNC), while Sketch Engine and VISL have several corpora – although no large corpora from the United States.

As we will see, both Sketch Engine and BNCweb offer fairly rich semantically-oriented queries. However, the range of semantically-oriented queries that are available with the architecture used for COCA is unique, and it is the only architecture that allows language learners to answer all of the types of issues shown above.

2. The composition of the corpus

Before discussing how the COCA architecture and interface can address this wide range of semantically-oriented queries from a learners' perspective, we should first briefly discuss the composition of the corpus, since of course the corpus data is only as good as the textual corpus on which it is based. For example, if we create a corpus that is based on just web pages and/or newspapers (the easiest types of materials to collect), then we will get a very skewed view of a given language. Ideally, we would want equal samplings from a number of widely divergent genres and registers, from genres as informal as

---

1 www.americancorpus.org

2 In this paper we refer to the "COCA" architecture and interface, as though it were particular to that one corpus. In reality, this architecture and interface have also been applied to a number of other textual corpora, such as the BYU-BNC, the TIME Corpus of Historical American English, the Corpus del Español, and the Corpus do Português. In this paper, however, we will focus on just the Corpus of Contemporary American English, and all of the examples are taken from that one corpus. Those who are interested in the more technical aspects of the corpus architecture and interface might consult Davies (2005) and Davies (2009a) for descriptions of earlier versions, and Davies (2009b) for a technical discussion of the current version.

spoken to genres as formal as academic, with a number of genres in between (cf. Biber *et al*. 1998).

In the Corpus of Contemporary American English (COCA), the corpus is divided almost equally between spoken, fiction, popular magazines, newspapers, and academic journals (see Davies 2009b for a more complete overview of the textual corpus). This composition holds for the corpus overall, as well as for each year in the corpus. As of August 2009, there are more than 160,000 texts in the corpus, and they come from a variety of sources:

- Spoken: (83 million words) Transcripts of unscripted conversation from more than 150 different TV and radio programs (examples: *All Things Considered* (NPR), *Newshour* (PBS), *Good Morning America* (ABC), *Today Show* (NBC), *60 Minutes* (CBS), *Hannity and Colmes* (Fox), *Jerry Springer*, *Oprah*, etc.).
- Fiction: (79 million words) Short stories and plays from literary magazines, children's magazines, popular magazines, first chapters of first edition books 1990-present, and movie scripts.
- Popular Magazines: (84 million words) Nearly 100 different magazines, with a good mix (overall, and by year) between specific domains (news, health, home and gardening, women, financial, religion, sports, etc.). A few examples are *Time*, *Men's Health*, *Good Housekeeping*, *Cosmopolitan*, *Fortune*, *Christian Century*, *Sports Illustrated*, etc.
- Newspapers: (79 million words) Ten newspapers from across the US, including: *USA Today*, *New York Times*, *Atlanta Journal Constitution*, *San Francisco Chronicle*, etc. There is also a good mix between different sections of the newspaper, such as local news, opinion, sports, financial, etc.
- Academic Journals: (79 million words) Nearly 100 different peer-reviewed journals. These were selected to cover the entire range of the Library of Congress classification system (e.g. a certain percentage from B (philosophy, psychology, religion), D (world history), K (education), T (technology), etc.), both overall and by number of words per year.

There is no corpus of any language that is this large and which allows for a genre distribution this diverse. The British National Corpus has very good genre distribution, but is less than one fourth the size of COCA. The Cobuild / Bank of English corpus is somewhat larger than COCA (about 520 million words), but it is heavily weighted towards easily-available newspapers and contains very little spoken, fiction, or academic. The Oxford English Corpus is even larger, but it is based mainly on material from websites. In order to provide the best semantic and pragmatic information, we should have texts from a wide range of genres.

For a corpus this size, this range of genres is uniquely available in the Corpus of Contemporary American English.

3. Collocates: the size effect

As we will see, BNCweb and Sketch Engine provide useful insight into word meaning via powerful collocate-based queries of the BNC, as does COCA. At 100 million words, the implementation of the BNC in these two architectures seems like it would be quite adequate in terms of size for just about any collocate-based query. However, while 100 million words was huge when it was released in the early 1990s, it is beginning to look increasingly small, especially for collocate-based queries with lower-frequency words. Let us briefly look at just a few examples.

The following compares the collocates sets for given words in COCA and the BNC. The bolded number in the [BNC] and [COCA] columns shows the number of collocates that have a frequency of at least five tokens, within the specified span of words (e.g. 2 left, 0 right). The number in parentheses shows the overall frequency of the node word in the two corpora (e.g. the noun lemma *click* occurs 445 times in the BNC and 3145 times in COCA).

Table 1. Number of collocates in COCA and the BNC

node word (PoS)	collocate PoS / span	BNC # **collocates** (node freq)	COCA # **collocates** (node freq)
click (n)	adj 2L / 0R	**5** (445) double, sharp, loud	**26** (3145) loud, audible, double, sharp
nibble (v)	noun 0L / 3R	**2** (244) ear, bait	**28** (1194) edges, grass, ear, lip
crumbled (adj)	noun 0L / 3R	**0** (27) ---	**25** (446) cheese, bacon, bread, cornbread
serenely (adv)	verb 4L / 4R	**0** (83) ---	**30** (308) smile, float, gaze, glide

The node words were not selected on the basis of those that looked particularly good in COCA as opposed to the BNC. We simply looked for words with an overall frequency at a particular range in COCA, and then searched to see how many different collocates had a frequency of at least five tokens (within the specified span of words) in COCA and the BNC. As one can see, the difference is quite striking. Even though the 400+ million word COCA only has a little more than four times the number of words at the 100 million word BNC, it provides much richer collocational data for these lower frequency words. For example, a word like *serenely* occurs only about four times as frequently in COCA as the BNC (which is to be expected in a corpus about four times the size), yet when one looks at moderately frequent collocates (five tokens or more), the difference is much more striking. In a smaller corpus like the BNC, the raw frequency of a node word might appear to be quite robust, but when it comes to finding collocates, the data often is too meager. As a result, in order to gain insight into the meaning and use of these lower frequency words, it seems clear that we need more than the standard 100 million word corpora of past decades.

4. Collocates: basic queries

Turning now to query types, perhaps the most basic type of information that a corpus architecture ought to be able to provide – in terms of meaning and usage – is collocational information. As the well-known saying in corpus linguistics points out, "you can tell a lot about a word by the other words that it hangs out with".

The VISL and PIE architectures can produce collocates for specific sequences of words (e.g. two word strings like *fast* [noun]), but they cannot find, for example, all nouns "near" *fast*. Sketch Engine and BNCweb are the two architectures, in addition to COCA, that do allow quick and easy access to full collocational information. With all three architectures, it is possible to define the collocates span (e.g. 2 words left or 5 words to the right of the node word), and to limit the collocates to a particular part of speech. In all three cases, the architectures are also quite fast – 1–3 seconds for a moderately frequent word like *catch* in the BNC (~15,000 tokens).

With COCA, for example, to find the most frequent nouns within three words after the verb *catch*, users would enter *[catch].[v*]* into WORD(S) (all forms of *catch* as a verb), *[nn*]* into COLLOCATES, and set the span to [0]–[3] (0 words to the left of *catch*, but up to three words to the right). They would then see results like the following:

Table 2. Collocates display (noun collocates of the verb *break*)

COLLOCATE	TOTAL		SPOK	FIC	MAG	NEWS	ACAD
HEART	1718		482	736	235	219	46
LAW	1478		739	134	196	335	74
NEWS	1379		616	211	224	225	103
SILENCE	992		174	540	119	91	68
RECORD	975		199	35	218	512	11
RULES	957		181	184	227	225	140
GROUND	884		114	96	228	325	121
STORY	786		519	54	94	94	25
TIME	780		164	248	193	115	60
WAR	710		206	87	153	153	111

The chart shown here is somewhat more complicated than a typical collocates chart. We see the frequency for each collocate in each of the five genres (and users can also see the frequency in each five year block since the early 1990s), but it is possible to also just see the overall frequency. The differences in collocates between different genres is something that we will return to in Section 7. In addition, we see here the raw frequency in each genre (color-coded by frequency per million words), but it also possible to see the actual normalized frequency in the chart as well.

COCA, Sketch Engine, and BNCweb also allow users to sort the collocates by "relevance" using Mutual Information score (MI) or other statistical tests. In addition, with each of these architectures it is possible to limit the results to just those collocates with a certain frequency or above a certain Mutual Information score. For example, the following are the most frequent collocates of the verb lemma *break* from COCA where the collocate occurs in the span [4 left / 4 right] at least 20 times, and the results are ranked by Mutual Information score.

Table 3. Collocates display: sorted by Mutual Information score

COLLOCATE	TOTAL		ALL	%	MI
LOGJAM	74		178	41.57	8.04
DEADLOCK	122		464	26.29	7.38
MONOTONY	70		346	20.23	7.00
COLLARBONE	74		445	16.63	6.72
STRANGLEHOLD	42		280	15.00	6.57

TABOOS	52		545	9.54	5.92
IMPASSE	78		881	8.85	5.81
SCUFFLE	30		354	8.47	5.75
BURGLARS	34		419	8.11	5.69
STALEMATE	61		806	7.57	5.58
LEVEES	64		861	7.43	5.56
BARRIER	394		5543	7.11	5.49

[TOTAL] shows the number of times that the collocate appears within the indicated span, [ALL] is the total number of tokens for that word in the corpus (e.g. 114 total occurrences of *red-handed* in the corpus, with or without *catch*), [%] is the percentage of tokens that occur in the span near *catch*, and [MI] is the Mutual Information score.

5. Collocates: more advanced queries

As we have seen, COCA, Sketch Engine, and BNCweb all allow for basic collocates functionality. What is the difference, then, between these architectures? The first difference is the range of node word and collocates pairs that the architectures allow. While Sketch Engine and BNCweb allow users to limit by part of speech and word form for the collocates, they are somewhat more limited than COCA, which allows all of the following:

Table 4. Types of collocate-based searches with COCA

NODE	COLLOCATES	SPAN (L/R)	EXPLANATION	SORT BY GROUP BY	EXAMPLES
LAUGH.[N*]	*	5/5	Any words within five words of the noun *laugh*	Percentage Collocates	hearty, scornful
[THICK]	[nn*]	0/4	A form of *thick* followed by a noun	Frequency Collocates	glasses, smoke
[LOOK] INTO	[nn*]	0/6	Nouns after a form of *look* + *into*	Frequency Collocates	eyes, future
[EYE]	clos*	5/5	Words starting with *clos** within five words of a	Frequency Both words	closed // eye closing // eyes

			form of *eye*		
[FEEL] LIKE	[*vvg*]	0/4	A form of *feel* followed by a gerund	Frequency Collocates	crying, taking
FIND	time	0/4	*Find* followed by *time*	Frequency Collocates	time
WORK/JOB	hard/tough/difficult	4/0	*Work* or *job* preceded by *hard* or *tough* or *difficult*	Frequency Both words	hard // work tough // job
[=PUBLISH]	[n*]	0/4	Nouns after a synonym of *publish*	Frequency Both words	publish // book issue // statement print // money
[=EXPENSIVE]	[[jones:clothes]]	0/5	Synonym of *expensive* followed by a form of a word in the *clothes* list created by *jones*	Frequency Both words	expensive / shoes, pricey // shirt
[=BOY]	[=happy]	5/5	Synonym of *happy* near a synonym of *boy*	Frequency Both words	happy // child, delighted // boy

With COCA, it is basically possible to look for "anything near anything else", including all synonyms of a given word, or any word in large "customized lists" that are created by the users via the web interface. The ability to look for "anything 'near' anything else" allows for very complex collocate-based queries, and the range of queries is unique to the COCA interface.

6. Collocates: word comparisons

COCA and Sketch Engine are the two architectures that allow for a powerful variation on regular collocates-based queries, one which involves comparison between words. Researchers have recognized the value of corpora in using collocates to tease apart slight differences between near-synonyms (e.g. *small* and *little*), or to provide insight into culturally-defined differences between two terms (e.g. *girls* and *boys*) (see, for example, Sinclair 1991 or Stubbs 1996). The architecture of COCA allows users to carry out searches such as this quickly and easily, by comparing the collocates of two contrasting words or lemmas. For example, to compare the collocates of the adjectives *utter* and *sheer*, a user would simply select COMPARE WORDS, then enter *utter* in one search field and *sheer* in the other, and then select [nn*] as for CONTEXT. Finally, s/he might specify that the first word (*utter* or *sheer*) should occur at least 20 times with the given noun. The user would then see the following:

Table 5. Word comparisons (*utter / sheer* [NN*])

WORD 1 (W1): **UTTER** (0.30)

WORD	**W1**	**W2**	**W1/W2**	**SCORE**
DARKNESS	42	0	84.0	276.8
FAILURE	30	0	60.0	197.7
DESTRUCTION	26	0	52.0	171.3
DISREGARD	23	0	46.0	151.6
CONTEMPT	35	1	35.0	115.3
ABSENCE	15	0	30.0	98.8
AMAZEMENT	25	1	25.0	82.4
FOOL	12	0	24.0	79.1
DESOLATION	11	0	22.0	72.5
SILENCE	63	3	21.0	69.2

WORD 2 (W2): **SHEER** (3.29)

WORD	**W2**	**W1**	**W2/W1**	**SCORE**
NUMBER	226	0	452.0	137.2
VOLUME	187	0	374.0	113.5
FORCE	144	0	288.0	87.4
SIZE	241	1	241.0	73.1
WEIGHT	64	0	128.0	38.8
SCALE	62	0	124.0	37.6
LUCK	53	0	106.0	32.2
MAGNITUDE	51	0	102.0	31.0
AMOUNT	37	0	74.0	22.5
PLEASURE	73	1	73.0	22.2

This table shows that *sheer* occurs about 3.29 as common overall in the corpus as *utter*, and therefore all other things being example, it ought to occur about 3–4 times as frequently with any collocate than does *utter*. Conversely, *utter* should only occur about .30 times for each occurrence of *sheer*. In the case of *amazement*, however (#7 on the left side of the table), the collocate occurs 25 times as frequently with *utter* as with *sheer*, which is about 79 times as frequent as we would otherwise expect (taking into account its overall frequency, discussed above). In the case of *pleasure*, on the other hand (the last entry for *sheer*), it occurs about 22 times as frequently with *sheer* than we would otherwise expect. As one can readily see, the collocates for *utter* tend to be much more negative than those for *sheer*, and this points out an interesting semantic distinction that most non-native speakers of English would not otherwise be aware of (and perhaps not many native speakers either).

The following table provides a few additional examples of word comparisons that can be done with the corpus. [A] and [B] refer to the two words being compared, [Collocate PoS] shows the part of speech of the collocates, and the rightmost two columns show the collocates that occur with either [A] or [B] much more than the overall frequency of either of these two words would suggest.

Table 6. Examples of word comparisons

[A]	[B]	Collocate PoS	Collocates with [A]	Collocates with [B]
[BOY]	[GIRL]	[j*]	growing, rude	sexy, working
DEMOCRATS	REPUBLICANS	[j*]	open-minded, fun	mean-spirited, greedy
CLINTON	BUSH	[v*]	confessed, groped, inhale	assure, deploying, stumbles
SMALL	LITTLE	[nn*]	amount, fee	while, luck
[ROB].[V*]	[STEAL].[V*]	[nn*]	bank, store	cars, money

In summary, the simple yet quick word comparisons that are possible with COCA would be of value to many different types of users (and similar word contrasts are possible with Sketch Engine as well). Linguists can quickly contrast synonyms and language learners can move beyond simple thesauruses to see more in-depth differences between words. And using COCA, even those interested in using corpora to investigate cultural studies, political science, and other social sciences (cf. Stubbs 1996) can quickly and easily compare how contrasting words (*Bush/Clinton*, *Democrats/Republicans*, *men/women*, *Christians/Muslims*) are used in contemporary American English.

7. Collocates: register differences

There is one type of collocates-based search that is possible only with COCA, and that is the comparison of collocates in two different sections of the corpus (such as genres or time periods) to see how word sense is a function of genre, or how a given word is changing in meaning over time. In this section, we will focus on genre-based differences.

Sketch Engine, BNCweb, and COCA all allow users to limit the query to one section of the corpus, such as Fiction or Newspapers-Sports. In COCA, however, it is possible to compare across two different sections. For example, the following table compares the collocates of *chair* in FICTION and ACADEMIC, and clearly shows the very different word senses in the two sections:

Table 7. Comparison of collocates by section

SEC 1: ACADEMIC

WORD	SEC1	SEC2	PM1	PM2	RATIO
DEAN	25	2	0.34	0.03	11.91
BOARD	76	8	1.04	0.11	9.05
COLLEGE	25	3	0.34	0.04	7.94
SECTION	39	5	0.53	0.07	7.43
COUNCIL	14	2	0.19	0.03	6.67
CONFERENCE	19	3	0.26	0.04	6.04
COMMITTEE	145	23	1.99	0.33	6.01

SEC 2: FICTION

WORD	SEC1	SEC2	PM1	PM2	RATIO
KITCHEN	197	2	2.83	0.03	103.35
LEATHER	209	3	3.00	0.04	73.10
LAWN	185	3	2.66	0.04	64.70
EYES	107	2	1.54	0.03	56.13
WINDOW	156	4	2.24	0.05	40.92
SWIVEL	137	4	1.97	0.05	35.94
ARMS	170	5	2.44	0.07	35.67

As can be seen, the collocates of *chair* that occur much more in ACADEMIC than FICTION are *dean*, *board*, *college*, etc., while those in FICTION but not ACADEMIC are *kitchen*, *leather*, *lawn*, etc. The tables show the frequency of each collocate with *chair* in the two sections (e.g. 197 tokens of *kitchen* near *chair* in fiction but only 3 tokens of *kitchen* near *chair* in academic). These then are converted to tokens per million words in the two sections (2.83 in FICTION, .03 in ACADEMIC), and the ratio figure (103.35) is the ratio of the normalized tokens per million figures for the two sections. As can be seen in this table, the data clearly show that in academic texts, *chair* refers to the position on a committee, whereas in fiction texts it refers to the piece of furniture.

With some modifications, the implementations of the BNC in BNCweb and Sketch Engine could conceivably allow for the same type of cross-genre comparisons, because of the way in which the BNC has been carefully constructed and annotated for genre and sub-genre. On the other hand, it would likely be very difficult to do this with "UK Web as Corpus" (ukWaC) corpus on Sketch Engine, because the architecture does not distinguish as clearly which web "genre" the texts belong to. Of all of the different corpus architectures, COCA is unique in the way in which it shows the relationship between genre and word sense.

8. Basic synonyms-based queries

To this point we have focused on collocates, which are of course one of the best ways of getting some sense of the meaning and use of words and phrases. However, there are two other powerful tools that are part of the COCA architecture and interface, and which are unique to this corpus.

The first feature relates to the integrated thesaurus in COCA. A standard printed thesaurus would show the following synonyms for *fast*: *quick*, *immediate*, *sharp*, *brief*, *sudden*, *rapid*, *swift*, *high-speed*, *abrupt*, *brisk*, *short-lived*, *speedy*, *fleeting*, *momentary*, *hasty*, *prompt*, and *hurried*. Obviously, however, some of these words are more frequent than others, and they would have a different distribution in different genres. Without this information, however, inexperienced language learners might end up sounding strange if they use *fleeting* or *momentary* much more than *fast* or *quick*. Language learners might also sound strange if they over-use a synonym in a genre where it is not appropriate, such as academic writing or in conversation.

COCA has an integrated thesaurus with entries for more than 60,000 synsets, which allows for powerful synonym-based queries. For example, users can enter a simple query like *[=fast].[j*]* (*fast* as an adjective), and then see the following (this is just a partial listing of all of the synonyms):

Table 8. Synonyms list (partial listing for the adjective *fast*)

	SYNONYM	TOTAL	SPOK	FIC	MAG	NEWS	ACAD
1	QUICK [S]	29005	6820	8057	6997	4993	2138
3	IMMEDIATE [S]	15606	2497	1445	3105	2948	5611
5	BRIEF [S]	15206	1845	3600	2790	2371	4600
7	FAST [S]	12713	1960	2524	4131	2736	1362
8	SUDDEN [S]	11345	978	5569	2125	1321	1352
10	RAPID [S]	10394	756	890	2377	1558	4813
14	SWIFT [S]	2817	393	907	714	510	293
15	HIGH-SPEED [S]	2671	269	124	1064	787	427
17	ABRUPT [S]	1886	115	610	408	278	475
18	BRISK [S]	1702	86	563	594	365	94
19	SHORT-LIVED [S]	1467	78	151	457	342	439
20	SPEEDY [S]	1388	184	196	493	353	162
21	FLEETING [S]	1330	93	472	366	191	208
22	MOMENTARY [S]	1068	51	504	185	92	236
24	HASTY [S]	940	77	346	182	160	175
27	PROMPT [S]	709	80	70	152	117	290

This table (which is about the most complex one that the user might see – most tables would be much more simple) contains a wealth of information. It shows all of the matching synonyms for the adjective *fast* in the thesaurus, along with their overall frequency and the frequency in each of the five main genres. Sketch Engine also has a "thesaurus-like" feature, but there are at least three important differences. The most basic difference is that the list of words are not really synonyms per se, but rather words with shared collocates. For example, in Sketch Engine for the adjective *fast* it shows *slow*, *quiet*, *dangerous*, etc.

9. Comparison of synonyms across genres

A second difference between COCA and Sketch Engine is that COCA is the only corpus architecture that allows learners to see the frequency of all synonyms in the different genres, as are shown in the table above. With this information, users can see which synonyms are more formal or informal, and thus appropriate for different styles of speech. For example, the table above shows that *brisk*, *speedy*, and *hasty* are relatively less common in academic writing, but that *immediate*, *constant*, and *prompt* are relatively more common in that genre. Such information allows language learners to begin to develop some sense of which synonyms are most appropriate for a given target genre.

It is also possible to directly query to corpus to ask "which synonyms are more common in one genre than another?" For example, users could easily compare the synonyms of *smart* in newspapers vs. academic writing, by simply entering *[=smart]* for the word, and then selecting Newspapers for Section 1 and Academic for Section 2. They would then see that *ritzy*, *nifty*, *brainy*, *stylish*, *glitzy*, *chic*, and *trendy* are more common in newspapers, and that *intelligent*, *keen*, *clever*, and *shrewd* are more common in academic. Another example would be synonyms of *strong* in fiction and academic. In fiction, the synonyms are *beefy*, *burly*, *strapping*, *spicy*, *brawny*, and *pungent* (relating to people and foods), whereas in academic they are *effective*, *deep-seated*, *clear-cut*, *compelling*, *robust*, and *persuasive* – most of which refer to arguments.

10. Comparing collocates across a range of synonyms

A third and final difference with Sketch Engine, and one that adds real power to the synonyms feature in COCA, is the ability to include synonyms as part of more complex queries. For example, users can enter a query like *[=fast].[j*] [nn*]*, which would yield the following results. (These are just a handful of the more than 400 matching strings, and they are grouped by lemma (e.g. *fix* = *fix* and *fixes*), and include the frequency of that lemma string).

Table 9. Collocates of all synonyms of the adjective *fast*

SYNONYM	collocate	frequency
FAST	food	1178
QUICK	break	679
FAST	track	648

SYNONYM	collocate	frequency
IMMEDIATE	impact	224
RAPID	expansion	221
FAST	facts	205

QUICK	look	637
QUICK	question	529
QUICK	fix	511
BRIEF	moment	465
BRIEF	period	363
HIGH-SPEED	Internet	333
FAST	lane	275

IMMEDIATE	threat	195
SUDDEN	change	192
RAPID	pace	191
RAPID	succession	188
SHARP	decline	185
SHARP	increase	149

The power of a list like this is that users can quickly see which collocates occur with each of the synonyms. For example, language learner would see that native speakers talk and write about *brief moments*, *rapid succession*, *high-speed Internet*, *fast lane*, *sharp decline*, *immediate impact*, and *quick look*, but probably not *fast moments*, *brief succession*, *rapid Internet*, *sharp lane*, *quick impact*, or *rapid look*. Sketch Engine also allows users to click on words in the list of synonyms and to compare two words at a time, but COCA is the only corpus architecture that allows users to see all collocates with all synonyms at once. Such functionality allows users to move far beyond a typical thesaurus to compare competing words.

11. "Synonym chains"

Before leaving the topic of synonyms, we might mention one other very useful feature that is uniquely available via the COCA architecture and interface. As one can see in Table 8 above, each of the synonyms of a given word have an "[S]" after the word. Users can click on this to go from one synonym set to another, via a "synonym chain", and thus see an entire web of related words. For example, if users search for *beautiful*, they will see 18 synonyms, including *exquisite*. They can then click on the [S] after *exquisite* to see the synonyms of that word, including *delicate*, and from there to *sensitive*, and then to *mild*. And as before, for each of these synonym sets (as in Table 7), they can see a frequency-ranked listing of the synonyms, as well as see in which genre they are most common. All of this allows users to quickly and easily investigate a "web" of interrelated concepts and meanings, via a few clicks of the mouse.

12. Customized lists

One last feature of note related to semantically-based searches with the COCA architecture and interface is the ability to create one's own customized wordlists, and then seamlessly integrate these into the query syntax. There are two ways of creating these lists. First, users can save a subset of the words or phrases from an existing search. For example, they could search for the synonyms of *beautiful*, or *crash*, or *money*, and then save just the synonyms that are of interest to them. Similarly, they can find the collocates of a given word, and then save some of these collocates in their own wordlist. They could simply create from scratch a wordlist, such as emotions (*sad*, *happy*, *worried*, *ecstatic*, etc.), colors (*blue*, *green*, *red*, etc.), or parts of clothing (*shirt*, *blouse*, *suspenders*, *hat*, etc.). In any of these cases, they simply create a name for the list and store it via the web interface under their chosen username.

These customized wordlists are saved in a database on the server, and can then be used a day, week, or year later as part of another query. For example, if a user *lingprof* creates a list for words related to emotions, s/he can then use these words as part of the query: *[r*] [lingprof:emotions] that*, to retrieve strings like *pretty worried that*, *quite sad that*, *extremely perturbed that*, etc. Likewise, these customized lists can be used as part of a collocates search. For example, the user *lingprof* might create a second list named *familyMember* (with *mother*, *mom*, *brother*, *uncle*, etc.), and then search for any *familyMember* within six words of one of the *emotions* words, e.g. *her aunt was quite happy to see that*, *when Dad is as angry as that*, *they were excited that Mom could be there*, etc. Again, the ability to incorporate user-defined lists as part of the query, as well as the basic corpus architecture, allows users to carry out quite complex semantically-oriented queries on the corpus. And again, this feature is not available with any other corpus architecture and interfaces.

13. Conclusion

As mentioned, one of the fundamental problems for language learners is the acquisition of the meaning and use of words and phrases. In order to do this efficiently, learners need to be able to quickly and easily find the collocates for a given word or phrase, see how the meaning and usage differs across registers, compare sets of collocates for two words to see differences in meaning between the words, compare collocates across a wide range of synonyms (hopefully all at one time), and see how the word compares in frequency and genre distribution with all related synonyms. Many corpus architectures – which are created by computational linguists or computer scientists – are oriented much more towards syntactic structure (parsing, complex regular expressions, etc.). Relatively few have semantically-oriented features like these, which are of real use to language learners. As we have seen, BNCweb does simple collocates quite well, Sketch Engine adds in a number of other features, but the COCA architecture and interface is perhaps the most advanced in terms of all of these different types of semantically-oriented queries.

References

Biber, D., Johansson, S., Leech, G., Conrad, S., and E. Finnegan (1999). *Longman Grammar of Spoken and Written English*. London: Longman.

Davies, M. (2005). "The advantage of using relational databases for large corpora: speed, advanced queries, and unlimited annotation". *International Journal of Corpus Linguistics* 10: 301–28.

- (2009a). "Relational databases as a robust architecture for the analysis of word frequency". In: D. Archer (ed.). *What's in a Wordlist?: Investigating Word Frequency and Keyword Extraction*. London: Ashgate: 53–68.

- (2009b). "The 385+ Million Word Corpus of Contemporary American English (1990–2008+): Design, Architecture, and Linguistic Insights". *International Journal of Corpus Linguistics* 14: 159–190.

Gardner, D. (2007). "Validating the construct of Word in applied corpus-based vocabulary research: A critical survey". *Applied Linguistics* 28: 241–265.

Nation, I.S.P. (2001). *Learning vocabulary in another language*. Cambridge: Cambridge University Press.

Schmitt, N. (2000). *Vocabulary in language teaching*. Cambridge: Cambridge University Press.

Sinclair, J. McH. (1991). *Corpus, Concordance, Collocation*. Oxford: Oxford University Press.

Stubbs, M. (1996). *Text and Corpus Analysis*. Oxford: Blackwell.

The Case of the Czech National Corpus: its Design and History

František Čermák

Abstract: A brief survey of needs and problems that led to establishment of a corpus institute and, subsequently, to the build-up of Czech National Corpus project are offered. These are followed by a presentation of a strategy adopted, data acquisition and their division, later on, into a number of corpora. Along the way, a number of problems had to be dealt with, out of which some attention is paid here to that of methodology, specifically such that would enable a representative shape of the contemporary corpora. Finally, a survey of existing corpora is presented and some open questions noted.

Keywords: Czech National Corpus, language data, methodology, corpus design, corpus representativeness.

1. General Remarks

Linguists have always suffered from data insufficiency, although they have only rarely admitted that this was the case. Reliable language data are a prerequisite and usual precondition for any information and subsequent conclusions that linguists are likely to draw, just as in any other science. Working with data has always been the mainstream in linguistics and Chomsky's stubborn and irrational contempt for any data hardly invalidates this general data necessity, a fact generally acknowledged. Despite of what he has mistakenly thought ("corpus data are skewed") it has always been quite clear that no one is able, for example, to write a dictionary from introspection only, i.e. the only approach he has subscribed to.

However, linguists may not have always been aware that they lack more data and reliable information being satisfied with what they had, a fact which is being gradually revealed only now, with new and better linguistic output based on and supported by better data. The old illustrious linguists like Otto Jespersen, a grand old man of English linguistics before the war, had been able to collect some 300 000 manual citation slips that he based all his grammars and books on. Today there is just no one willing to follow in his steps: having a corpus he/she does not have to. It used to be prohibitively expensive and time-consuming to collect large amounts of data manually, an experience familiar to anyone who has worked with citation slips from lexical and other archives trying to compile a dictionary or even, in the case of a student trying to write an essay required by his/her professor. To create such an archive of some 10–

15 million slips took many decades and many people (which was the case of Czech, too). Thus, there seemed to exist a natural quantitative limit that was difficult to reach and that was almost impossible to cross. Yet, the amount of information that could be acquired from such a limited archive was used for compilation of all dictionaries of the past, grammars and other reference books, including school textbooks we are still using today, all of them, seen from the contemporary perspective, sadly lacking in many respects, as they are neither contemporary, nor based on sufficient and convincing data. To sum up briefly: if you see one's language as a mirror of what is going on around us and compare the picture with old handbooks, then one did not have very good glasses looking at the language.

All of this has suddenly changed with the arrival of computers and modern very large corpora. For the first time in his/her personal life and in the history of the discipline as well, the linguist has multiples of previous amounts of data now, their flow being, in fact, so overwhelming and even staggering that he/she still has not got used to it and feels like a drowning person feeling a kind of embarassment as to how to handle the enorrmous amount of data one is facing. It is just beyond imagination, both for an old-timer as well as for a modern would-be lexicographer, to have to face, for example, some 83 000 occurrences of the word *člověk/lidé* (man/people) in Czech, a task neither of them has ever faced before. It is, to cool off some of the unwarranted enthousiasm, just not easy to properly use, almost a billion of words (as in Czech) since a lot of specialized work has to be done yet and many areas explored. This is just an illustration of how dramatically the data situation has changed for a linguist, while not all the consequences of this are fully grasped yet and solutions how to handle this found. It has become obvious now that the information to be found in this kind of data is both vastly better and representative of real usage than anything before and that the quality of information is proportionate to the amount of data amassed. Of course, this information has to be drawn from contexts, where it is usually coded in a variety of ways, implying that both the relevant texts and ways have to be found how to get at the information needed. Today, any concentrated work with a large corpus does cast a shadow over the quality and reliability of our present-day dictionaries and grammars making them problematic and dated. Obviously, there is a need for better resources and linguistic outputs based on these.

With modern corpora in existence, it is easy to see that these might be useful for many other professional and academic disciplines and quarters of life, including general public and schools, not only linguistics. After all, we are now living in the *Information Society*, as it has been termed, and it is obvious that there is a growing need for information everywhere. As there is, practically, no sector of life and human activity, no profession or pastime, where information is *not* communicated through and by the language, the conclusion seems inevitable: the information needed is to be found in language corpora as the largest repositories of language. Should one fail in finding in corpora what he or she may need, then these corpora are either still too small, though they may have hundreds of millions of words already, or too one-sided and lacking in that particular type of language, as this happens to be the case of the spoken language. It is evident that there is no alternative to corpora as the supreme information source and that their usefulness will further grow. Corpora are an efficient shortcut and alternative to one's lifetime reading and listening the language and perceiving the information transmitted.

It may be also worth considering language in its proper perspective, as the first and most important attribute of a people and its culture: it seems that a corpus enabling to map the culture of its people might and should deserve a nation-wide attention and care of authorities. There is no better way how to spend one's money, in the long run, where culture and national heritage is concerned, since building a corpus amounts to constructing a permanent national monument.

Much of what has been been just said is general and holds for the Czech National Corpus project, too. Just like anywhere else, linguistic research in the Czech language had to be based on a data archive in past, catered for, in the old academic tradition, by the Academy of Sciences, namely through manually collecting language data on citation slips which have, over some eight decades, grown to reach some 12–15 million archive of excerpts. The decades-long excerption has been drastically cut down in the sixties when it was felt, for some reason, that enough data has been accumulated for a new dictionary of Czech, a decision difficult to understand from the contemporary point of view. Since then, most of the major linguistic work done has been based on this lexical archive including the compilation of a new large dictionary of contemporary literary Czech (*Slovník spisovného jazyka českého*) in four volumes (almost 200 thousand lemmas) which came out in 1960–1971. However, no extensive and systematic coverage of the language has been started ever since.

In the early nineties, a vague idea of a new dictionary of the Czech language has appeared in the hope that the new dictionary would capture the turmoil and social changes taking place after the Communist downfall, but the kind of data needed for this has been found to be non-existent. At the same time, it was becoming evident that thc old manual citation slip tradition could not be resumed, especially one that would bridge a considerable data gap of over 30 years. My suggestion early in 1991–1992 was that a computer corpus be built from scratch at the Academy of Sciences to be used for such a new dictionary and for whatever it might be necessary to use it for, but the move was not exactly applauded by some influential people and old-timers at the Academy.

Yet, times have changed and it was no longer official state-run institutions but real people who felt they must decide this and also act upon their decision and determination, no longer relying on problematic bureaucrats. Thus, thanks to the incentive of a group of people, a solution was found which took shape of a new Department of the Czech National Corpus which has been established in 1994 at Charles University in Prague (or rather its Faculty of Philosophy), introducing thus a base for the study subject of corpus linguistics as well (Čermák 1995, 1997, 1998). This solution was supported by a number of open-minded linguists who did feel this need, too. After the foundation of the Institute of the Czech National Corpus, all of these people continued to cooperate, subsequently as representatives of their respective institutions. Having joined forces, they now form an impressive cooperating body of people from five faculties of three universities and two institutes of the Academy of Sciences, altogether from ten institutions and more are still being addressed, especially in the task of oral data collection. Securing this kind of broad cooperation is now viewed as a lucky strike, indeed. Having gradually, though rather slowly at first, gained support, in various forms, from the State Grant Agency, Ministry of Education and from a private publisher, people have been found, trained and the Czech National Corpus project (CNC), being academic and non-commercial one, could have been launched. In the year 2000, the first 100-million word corpus, called SYN2000 has gone public and was offered for general use (Čermák 1997, 1998, Český národní korpus 2000), meeting with an enthousiastic welcome, mostly.

The general framework of the project is quite broad aiming at as broad a coverage of the Czech language as possible. Hence, more than one corpus is planned and subsequently built at the same time. Briefly, its aim is to cover the available bulk of the Czech language in as many forms as are accessible. The overall design of the Czech National Corpus consists of many parts, the first major division following the **III synchrony-diachrony** distinction where an orientation point in time is, roughly, the year 1990, for obvious reasons (the downfall of Communist régime and an enormous development and change of the language). Both these major branches are each split into the **(1) written**, **(2) spoken** and **(3) dialectal** types of corpora, though this partition, in the case of the spoken language, cannot be upheld for the diachronic corpora and there are problems with getting contemporary data from dialects, too. Yet, this is only the tip of the iceberg, so to speak, as this is preceded by much larger storage and preparatory forms our data take on first, namely by the **I Archive of CNC** and **II Bank of CNC**.

Let us now have a look at a brief outline that each language item (form) has to go through, listing main stages that the data go through before reaching their final stage and assuming the form that may be exploited. Of course, everything depends on the laborious zero stage of **(0) Text Acqusition** being finished, in which texts are gained from the providers mainly, which is not really easy and smooth as one would wish, often depending on the whims of individual providers, legal act of securing their rights and physical transport of the data finally obtained. The Czech National Corpus Institute gets some texts either freely or on the basis of a modest fee, which has to be always supported by the consent of the original providers. There is no need stressing the fact that this is actually the easy way how to get the electronic texts. Two other ways, fortunately somewhat smaller in extent but much more laborious, expensive and labour-costly, are those of text-scanning (especially old texts, but also the authors the CNC did not have in its entirety) and of recording combined with manual transcription (the case of spoken corpora).

The first text format to be based on the data when they are acquired, in fact a variety of them, is stored in the **(I) Archive of CNC**. The Archive is constantly being enlarged and contains, at the moment, almost two billion words in various text forms. All of these texts are gradually converted, cleaned, unified and classified and, having been given all this treatment, they flow then into the **(II) Bank of CNC**. Thus, the Bank of CNC is a repository of raw but unified and "clean" texts prepared for any further treatment. A note has to be made about the conversion, however. This has to face the rich variety of formats publishers prefer to use and implies, in many cases, that a special conversion programme has to be developped allowing for this, though this is not always simple and reliable, such as with the popular and problematic pdf format. Of course, the cleaning of texts does not mean any correction of real texts, as these are sacrosanct and may not be altered in any way. Hence, efforts are made to find and extract **(1) duplicate texts** or large sections of them which, surprisingly and for a number of reasons, are found quite often.

Then, **(2) foreign language paragraphs** have to be identified and removed, these being due to large advertisements, articles published in the Slovak language, English, etc.

Finally, **(3) most of non-textual parts** of texts, such as numerical tables, long lists of figures or pictures are taken out, too (eg. stock-exchange columns of figures or sporting events tables).

So treated, each text gets, then, a modified **SGML (XML) format** containing an explicit and detailed information about the kind of the text, its origin, classification etc., including information about who of the staff of CNC is responsible for each particular stage of the process.

It is obvious that to be able to do this and achieve the final text stage and shape in the Bank of CNC, one has to have a master plan designed showing what types of texts should be collected and in what proportions. While more about this will be said later, it is necessary now to mention that this plan has been implemented and recorded in a special **(4) database** the records of which are mirrored in the corpus itself.

At this stage, after an elaborate weighting, selection, tagging and lemmatization (more about that later), some texts meeting the demands are selected and proclaimed to be a **(III) corpus** that is given a name and, usually, made public on the web (www.korpus.cz). At the moment, there is a number of such corpora made available and more are being prepared (see part 6).

Originally, CNC was served by a comprehensive retrieval system called *gcqp*, which is based on the Stuttgart *cqp* programme. This has been considerably expanded (by P. Rychlý, a member of a partner team) and exchanged for a sophisticated graphic interface **Bonito** supported by Windows, although it is Linux-based, of course. Being now part of a client-server (**Manatee**), it offers a rich variety of search functions and facilities, including a possibilty to define one's own (virtual) subcorpus (see korpus.cz). This corpus manager is free and is being used by several universities and institutions.

2. Data and Resources

It is obvious that only the data that were available could be used first, the financial aspects of their acquisition being important, although most data are now given freely to the CNC on the basis of a prior contract with the provider (almost 300, of different nature, including publishers, newspapers, a number of private institutions, etc.); however, there are still some rare cases when the data have to be paid for.

Next to these electronically available texts, some texts that are not available, have to be either scanned into the computer (using OCR programmes, mostly FineReader) or manually recorded in the case of oral data. This means that a broad net of collaborators, mostly students, from virtually all major regional universities are secured and asked to record, for a small fee, their talk which should be as typical and spontaneous as possible involving a generalized cross-section of speakers.

3. Strategies Adopted

Realizing that not all familiar types of language are used in the same degree and that data for them are sometimes difficult to obtain, a decision to arrive at some kind of representativeness of most language types was adopted rather early. Being based on discussions and three subsequent stages of research in the domain of the written language (Čermák 1997, Čermák, Králík, Kučera 1997, Králík, Šulc 2005), the idea of representativeness has been oriented toward a general and broadly used vocabulary with the primary though not the only aim of eventually establishing a basis for a new general dictionary of Czech. With the stress laid only on language reception (i.e. the degree to what passive users have been exposed to the language, i.e. readers only) the reseach has offered a balanced quantified picture, the only one that is available and based on research in any language, in fact. It is impossible here to specifically argue and substantiate every single item, which, after a further research, landed somewhere in a rich network that data have been classified into having now no less than a hundred categories in several strata. Thus, CNC might be now called to be a representative corpus which has been carefully planned from scratch. It is to be realized here that such a corpus becomes a referential and proportionate entity anyone can refer and come back to, a thing which Internet will never be. This also stands in sharp contrast to that type of corpora where any available text, preferably newspapers, is accepted, amassed into an amorphous entity and called a corpus. These rather spontaneous corpora do rely on a seemingly infinite supply of texts and the philosophy of great numbers, hoping somehow that even the most specific and specialized information might find its way into it eventually; a new version of this is to be seen in the blind and problematic reliance on the Internet. For many reasons, this could not be the Czech philosophy. Hence, these figures arrived at by this reaserch, which should be further scrutinized and revised, of course, were then being used for the fine-grained construction and implementation of the synchronic corpus SYN2000. The overall structure is this:

IMAGINATIVE TEXTS	**15%**
Literature	**15%**
Poetry	0,81%
Drama	0,21%
Fiction	11,02%
Other	0,36%
Transitional types	2,6%
INFORMATIVE TEXTS	**85%**
Journalism	***60%***
Technical and Specialized Texts	***25%***
Arts	3,48%
Social Sciences	3,67%
Law and Security	0,82%
Natural Sciences	3,37%
Technology	4,61%
Economics and Management	2,27%
Belief and Religion	0,74%
Life Style	5,55%
Administrative	0,49%

Let me make a single note at least, instead of many that could and should be discussed here. Any comparison with the few available data of this kind from elsewhere is problematic, as it obviously depends on how various subcategories are defined. To give an example, there is no consensus as to what might be viewed as Leisure, for example, the term used by the BNC and represented there by over 15%, which must overlap with what is termed Life Style in CNC (although its representation happens to be three times lower).

However, this general framework has recently been modified by the last research into libraries, data by publishers etc. so that the main division has been slightly shifted in favour of more literature, giving the definite tripartition as:

Literature	***40%***
Journalism	***33%***
Technical and Specialized Texts	***27%***

To give an idea how this is projected, in part, into the data annotation and the database, the following distinctions are used that every text has to fit into:

1 – type of corpus: synchronic, diachronic, spoken; parallel
2 – type of text: informative, imaginative or a mixture of both
3 – type of genre: different in specialized and non-specialized language (made of some 60 different types, e.g. drama, novels..., music, philosophy, industry, sport, ... religion, etc.)
4 – type of subgenre (such as text-book, criticism, encyclopedic, etc.)
5 – type of medium (such as book, newspaper, script, occasional, etc.)
6 – sex of the author if known (including a team)
7 – language (in the case of foreign language texts)
8 – original language (in the case of translation)
9 – year of publication
10 – name of the author if known or that of the translator
11 – name of the text/work
12 – identification of the part of a larger work/text

Somewhat later, it has been realized that the spoken language needs some master plan, too, which, obviously, must be quite different from that used for the written language. This has been based (Čermák 2007, 2008) on the idea of prototypicality of the spoken texts in the sense that protypical means different in all the aspects identified and not found in the written one. At the same time as it is, for example, really very easy to record TV or radio broadcasts that are often nothing more than written texts spoken for the microphone, it has been decided to go first after what is really different and prototypical, namely spontaneous dialogues, usually between friends. Admittedly, these are the most difficult to get, too, so they seem to be a good start. The aspects suggested and used include:

PLUS (+)	**MINUS (-)**
a. Origin of the text:	
1 spoken (i.e. original)	– read
2 dialogue (i.e. original, typical)	– monologue
b. Interpersonal, sociological relationship of partners and physical situation:	
3 proximity of partners (friends, family)	– no proximity
4 equality of partners	– unequality
5 private (non-public)	– public
6 informal	– formal
7 interactive	– unidirectional
8 present	– distant (e.g. phone)
9 non-multiple (one-to-one)	– multiple (one-to-many)
c. Topic/situation approach:	
10 spontaneous (unscripted)	– prepared (more or less scripted, prepared)
11 casual (informal)	– regular/official
d. Awareness of the recording:	
12 not aware	– aware

In this framework, a fully and **prototypically spoken text** has all of the following plus parameters, such as a talk (conversation) between friends:

+spoken(1),
+dialogue(2),
+proximity(3),
+equality(4),
+private(5),
+informal(6),
+interactive(7),
+present(8),
+non-multiple(9),
+spontaneous(10),
+casual(11),
+not aware(12).

Obviously, texts having all 12 plus parameters (PLUS features) may be viewed as the core, hence as a part of prototypical corpus itself.

4. Technical Aspects and Linguistic Treatment of Texts

Those **technical aspects** that are related to acquisition, conversion, cleaning, filtering and unification of data shaping them the way they can be further used have already been mentioned above (in 1). However important and time-consuming, they are performed mostly automatically now and are finished when raw data are ready for further use. However, they do require that a lot of specialized procedures has to take place before this, including tokenization, splitting texts into future units (i.e. very large texts), marking paragraphs in them, sentences and word tokens, within the SGML format. Finally, the SGML head is added in this series of technical steps. Should these texts be now used, one would only get pure textual type information offered by sequences of forms.

However, many linguists wanting more have introduced at least some **linguistic mark-up**, consisting mostly of **tagging** of word forms of texts and a subsequent **lemmatization**, both being automatic procedures that are dependent on a prior existence of a national reliable tagger and lemmatizer. For an inflected language like Czech this is easier said than done, however. Both procedures, based originally on a small training corpus that had been manually tagged, have been fighting ever since with never-ending problems, however. Due to a number of reasons, the limited size of the training corpus, enormous homonymy of forms in Czech, problems with mistaken statistical guessing of morphological values of text forms, etc., a great amount of work and effort is still going into this business requiring efforts of several people. It is now evident that, still being far from any real end (success rate being now around 95%), a combination of both methods will slowly improve the output in both procedures, namely the statistical one and rule-based one. For the latter, a really impressive amount of rules (in fact, thousands) is being developed and partial local programmes written on their basis are constantly applied in an incremental way. This bootstrapping and evolutionary method, in fact a whole bunch of methods, does yield a gradual success. As a consequence of this, there are now several versions of some corpora available, due to their different markup in this way and because of the need to preserve their referential status.

Not all the Czech problems in this are due to the specifically complicated morphology of the language, however. There are general problems in the field no one has satisfactorily and comprehensively solved so far in any language, though the situation varies here considerably, also due to the typological character of the language in question. Among the most serious problems is handling of **multi-word forms**, completely or mostly neglected, usually. It is just not possible to be satisfied with mere text tokens where both grammatical forms (of complex verb tense forms of the kind *have seen*) and complex lexemes (idioms or terms, such as *take for granted* or *nitric acid*) have not been brought together by lemmatization and viewed as single lexemes and lemmas. There are many more idioms in everyday language use than one is aware of, this point being just where technicians and computational linguists do not mind while corpus linguists despair. It is very much a long-term task and programme to set this right. Another perennial problem, to name just one more, is distinguishing between **proper and common names**, not only because of a considerable overlap but also because of a constant influx of foreign surnames coming into one's language, usually through newspapers, and into the corpus. The new foreign names are nowhere to be found and their inflection is far from being always clear. This, too, is one of the major sources of the experience now well established anywhere, namely that the size of text forms recognized by a tagger and lemmatizer is still about fifty percent. The implication is that half of our enormous work is useless having no tag and lemma for this half. Fortunately, the data are still there and one can always query the forms there at least. Obviously, languages with less inflection might have less problems of this kind.

5. Methodology and Research

The study of language, made easier and more reliable by the existence of corpora now, has always been based on identification of **regularities**, **rules and relations** deduced from language data. It seems now, that the time for a dramatic change in linguistics has come, allowing one to study fully the **syntagmatic and combinatory aspects** of language for the first time and to redress the balance and past practice, which has always been bent on **paradigmatics**, categorizing, classification etc., without really having enough data for doing this. However, the obvious part played in this by the researcher's **introspection**, has never been critically questioned and it is only now that one is able to see to what degree this has been applied, contrary to facts one has now. The assumptions made by linguists and teachers about language on the basis of really few examples are staggering. Equally problematic are now past judgements about what is correct and what is wrong in language, a subject dear to hearts of all prescriptivists. There is no such thing as right or wrong, if it is not supported by data from real usage. The abyss between wishful thinking, recommended to and even imposed on the others in some cases, and real language facts is considerable. It is now clear that major revisions of old pre-conceived and unwarranted claims and made-up descriptions are due to come.

The language reality shown by corpora is no longer black and white with fine distinctions and simple truths built on these.

The new emphasis on syntagmatics, contrary to the paradigmatic past, requires new methodologies to be developed starting from the strategy of samples, ways how to handle clines and scales instead of the old pigeon-holing and marrying new statistical methods, these being still far from satisfactory. As these tasks that have to be solved in new pertinent and effective ways touch the very heart of linguistics, revision of all of the past will be necessary: there are first corpus-based grammars and dictionaries available now and these do tell a different story from the old bookshelf manuals. An answer starting with fresh insights is to be seen in corpus linguistics, as a new, unprejudiced study branch.

6. Current Shape of CNC

Aiming at a billion-word synchronous corpus by 2011 at least, the goal being almost attained by now, the current state of the whole Czech National Corpus Project can be described in its main sections as follows:

Type	**Corpus (+year)**	**Size**
Contemporary:		
Written synchronic:		
	SYN 2000	100 mil (balanced)
	SYN 2005	100 mil (balanced)
	SYNPUB 2006	300 mil (i.e. newspapers and magazines)
	SYNPUB2009	700 mil (newspapers and magazines)
Spoken synchronic:		
	PMK (Prague Spoken Corpus)	0.7 mil.
	BMK (Brno Spoken Corpus)	0.5 mil.
	ORAL 2006	1 mil (informal spoken language)
	ORAL 2008	1 mil (informal spoken language sociolinguistically balanced)

Historical:

DIA	1,8 mil (7 centuries from 13th cent.).

Specialized Corpora:

Karel Čapek' Corpus	2.6 mil.
Bohumil Hrabal' Corpus	1.7 mil.
Corpus of Totalitarian times	14 mil.
Hand-written letters KSK	0,8 mil (2000 letters)

Parallel Corpora (Czech vs 20 languages, in progress) manually aligned fiction, total size of the Czech part is currenly 25 mil. tokens

These are only the corpora that have already been published, but there is much more data in the Bank of CNC waiting for a further treatment and eventual release. On the other hand, the data here is constantly growing.

7. Outlook and Open Problems

Though there are, undoubtedly, new entities, phenomena and constructions to be yet discovered, certain things have already been recognized as new and important aspects of the corpus research. With the current, though often a bit fashionable, interest in discourse (whatever that means) a possibility to study language stereotypes and their use in authentic contexts has opened. With respect to their frequent use this will become a vast field of study (including phraseology). Another fact, new and uncomfortable for traditional linguists, is the corpus linguist's insisting on the study of word forms in contrast to the old interest in and description of lemmas only. It is evident that many word forms have a specific meaning bound to it only (eg. to a special personal form of a verb in one tense only, etc.) that are not to be found in the rest of its lexeme. The implication is to basically revise the existing dictionaries, among other things.

The Czech National Corpus project is an attempt at an unprecedented documentation and mapping of a language, reaching increasingly more from the present into the past and, hopefully, into the future as well. It will eventually enhance our understanding of the nature of the language across time, its major trends, core and periphery. As a supreme mirror of our reality and culture it offers an objective knowledge of facts, preventing unwarranted subjective conclusions, based on the introspection of a single man. Bridging different times in its development offers glimpses of the whole, but not only that. As no community and its language lives in isolation, knowledge and research of the links and ties to other languages are necessary, too. A modest start of this may be seen in a rather recent subproject of InterCorp[3], a parallel corpus of some 20 languages linked to Czech, where also small languages such as Latvian, Lithuanian, Finnish, Dutch or Serbian are included. Obviously, to be able to go on, one must not resign and stop, having achieved a corpus of, say, a hundred million words. On the contrary, as the language is in constant flow and change serving the needs of our society that is not going to stop its development one day, it is necessary to upkeep its mapping in a corpus, too. Hence the need for a continuous corpus project and its support that must be firmly institutionalized and financially anchored.

It would be wrong to take a corpus for a general medicine for linguistics and all those disciplines dealing with the language. Today's corpus (let alone Internet) may not have answers for everything one might want to know, but it does offer at least hundred times more than the archives of recent past. Corpora have arrived and are likely to remain here whatever that might mean and imply. Realizing what they can offer and, in terms of human labour, what time they can spare us one must really appreciate the fact that we have them.

References

General

Burnard, L. (1995). *Users' Reference Guide for the British National Corpus*. Oxford U. Press, Oxford.

Burnard, L. (2007). Spoken Corpora Design Revisited
Available at: http://www.corpus.bham.ac.uk/corplingproceedings07/

Burnard, L. (2009). *Spoken Corpora Design: Their Constitutive Parametres*. IJCL 14: 113–123.

Burnard, L. (1995). "Jazykový korpus: Prostředek a zdroj poznání". *Slovo a slovesnost* 56: 119–140 (Language Corpus: Means and Source of Knowledge).

Burnard, L. (1997). "Czech National Corpus: A Case in Many Contexts". *International Journal of Corpus Linguistics* 2: 181–197.

Burnard, L. (1998). "Czech National Corpus: Its Character, Goal and Background". In: P. Sojka, V. Matoušek, K. Pala, I. Kopeček (eds.). *Text, Speech, Dialogue, Proceedings of the First Workshop on Text, Speech, Dialogue-TSD'98, Brno, Czech Republic, September*. Masaryk University: Brno: 9–14.

Burnard, L. (2001). "Language Corpora: The Czech Case" In: *Text, Speech and Dialogue, TSD 2001*. Eds. V. Matoušek, P. Mautner, R. Mouček, K. Taušer Springer Berlin etc.: 21–30.

Čermák, F., Králík, J. and K. Kučera (1997). "Recepce současné češtiny a reprezentativnost korpusu". *Slovo a slovesnost* 58: 117–124 (Reception of the Contemporary Czech and the Representativeness of Corpus).

3 http://ucnk.ff.cuni.cz/intercorp/

Český národní korpus. Úvod a příručka uživatele (2000). Eds. Kocek J., Kopřivová M., Kučera K., Filozofická fakulta KU Praha (Czech National Corpus. An Introduction and User's Manual).

Králík, J. and M. Šulc (2005). "The Representativeness of Czech Corpora". *IJCL*: 357–368.

Kruyt, J.G. (1993). *Design Criteria for Corpora Construction in the Framework of a European Corpora Network*. Final Report. Institute for Dutch Lexicology INL: Leiden.

Kučera, K. (1998). "Diachronní složka Českého národního korpusu: obecné zásady, kontext a současný stav". *Listy filologické* 121: 303–313 (Diachronic Component of the Czech National Corpus: General Principles, Context and Current State of Affairs).

Kučera, K. (2002). "The Czech National Corpus: Principles, Design, and Results". *Literary and Linguistic Computing*. Vol. 17, No. 2: 245–257.

Kučera, K. (2007). "Mapping the Time Continuum: A Major Raison d'être for Diachronic Corpora". In: M. Davies, P. Rayson, S. Hunston, and P. Danielsson (eds.). *Proceedings of the Corpus Linguistics Conference CL2007.* University of Birmingham, 2007, 10 s. http://www.corpus.bham.ac.uk/corplingproceedings07.html

The Design of the National Corpus of Polish

Rafał L. Górski

Abstract: The paper describes the proposed design of the National Corpus of Polish. The corpus shall reflect the perception of the language by the Polish linguistic community. Sources allowing for the reconstruction of the structure of readership in Poland as well the method leading to the final design of the are discussed.

Keywords: text, channel, corpus design, general-reference corpus, National Corpus of Polish, readership, representativeness, text types.

Corpora significantly differ in their design. This is due to two reasons. First of all there is no consent what is the reality which a corpus should represent. Further even if there was such a consent, each corpus represents a different linguistic community. In Górski (2008) we discuss several approaches to the question of the representativeness of a corpus. We suggested to adopt the concept of representation of the perception of the language by a certain linguistic community, as far as the written part of the corpus is concerned (cf. Čermák *et al*. 1997).

1. Balance and representativeness

Although the terms balance and representativeness are used interchangeably, we shall distinguish them for the purposes of the present paper. A *representative* corpus is a corpus which represents a certain reality (at this stage no matter which), a *balanced* one is a corpus which is not dominated by one text type. There is also a number of texts which are scarcely read, however cannot be omitted in a corpus if we expect it to reflect the entire language. These three requirements are often mutually exclusive. If we ask linguists for their preferences probably most of them would rather choose a balanced although not representative corpus than the other way round. Another problem, which never can be resolved is the proportion of the spoken component – measuring the right proportion is hardly feasible. Intuitively however we can say that an average representative of a linguistic community perceives much more spoken than written language, thus the proportions of these two channels in the corpus should favour the former.

Taking it all into account the design of the corpus is always a compromise between the strict requirements of adopted methodology, feasibility and usefulness of the compiled corpus.

2. Text typology

First prerequisite of any work on the design of a corpus is to set an appropriate typology of texts[1]. At the starting point we tried to elaborate a relatively simple and flat text typology, especially because assigning a given text to one of the classes is not always a straightforward task. The bigger granularity of the adopted typology the more difficult and prone to mistakes is the task. What is more we cannot say much about the readership of marginal text types as drama[2]. On the other hand some more detailed information (eg. the distinction between prose and poetry) is important to the end-user of the corpus. Again we tried to meet a compromise: texts are described by a more granular typology, however there is a certain hierarchy of categories: some of them consist of several sub-categories.

The set of text types consists of: fiction (with subcategories: prose, poetry and drama); non-fiction literature; journalism[3]; academic writing and textbooks; instructive writing and guidebooks; unclassified non-fiction book; miscellaneous (written) (with subcategories: legal and official; advertisements; announcements; political marketing; user manuals; letters); Internet (subcategories: interactive (forums, chat rooms, instant messaging, mailing lists); static WWW pages). Three further categories encompass various types of spoken texts: conversational; spoken from the media; quasi-spoken.

This typology requires some comments: it may seem that some texts are defined rather by their channel than strictly by the text type (journalism, Internet). Of course there is a number of literary or legal texts published in newspapers, still most of the content of press is journalism. On the other hand it is very difficult to filter out non-journalistic texts in press. The solution is to treat everything what is published in non-specialised press as journalism[4]. Again Internet is not a specific sort of texts but a channel. There are however texts

1 A detailed description the typology adopted for the corpus will be published elsewhere.

2 Marginal in means of audience not – say – importance for the culture.

3 By journalism we understand both short reports and opinion journalism, which are in fact two distinct (although close) text types. We decided to merge them because of lack of means of automatic sorting texts from newspapers.

4 Strictly speaking the press – with some exceptions – in the corpus is introduced via Internet so as to avoid digitalization of printed material. If one wants to be very precise the channel of these texts should be labeled as Internet. The divulgation of these texts primarily however disseminated as print.

which occur only on the Internet as e.g. dynamic www pages (blogs, forums etc.) thus in these and only these cases the channel defines the text type. It is worth noting that there is a certain hierarchy of text types. The less granular hierarchy is more essential. Thus we care more about the proportions of press, fiction, and non-fiction[5], then – inside the category of non-fiction – the proportions between academic writing and non-fictive literary work. We shall also stress that the more granular categories listed above in brackets serve only for a more precise description of text and play no role in representativeness.

The procedure of assigning a text to a particular class is as follows: what is published in general non-specialised press is assigned to the category journalism. In case of books first we distinguish fictive from non-fictive books. If the book is fictive – no further decisions have to be made. Otherwise the book has to be assigned to one of five remaining categories. Academic writing and textbooks form a clear category – an informative text written by specialist for specialists. The target distinguishes it from a similar category, namely instructive writing and guidebooks. This broad category encompasses: all kinds of instructive writing, as well as how-to books, tourist guides, cookbooks etc. Contrary to the former category its audience consists non-specialists. Another very broad category is non-fiction literature. It includes all non-fictive literary works, as well as biography, memoirs, non-fictive novels etc. The category is defined rather negatively, that is it is non-fictive on the one hand and but still shows some narration. Journalism is published not only in newspapers but also in books – and in principle we do not distinguish them from texts published in press. The last category – "unclassified non-fiction book" encompasses non-fictive books which either belong to a well defined category, however so marginal that it is not worth creating a different category, such as eg. collections of sermons, or belong to more than one category, or – last but not least – it is very hard to classify them. This typology is based basically on the Polish mainstream research on stylistics (cf. Gajda 1995, Klemensiewicz 1982).

The classification of the spoken component is based on different grounds. Note that we do not introduce one category "spoken", because all the three categories differ so much, that simply narrowing a query to it would be useless. Thus we distinguish transcripts of spontaneous dialogs from transcripts of texts spoken in media. The category quasi-spoken is created for texts which are primarily spoken, but are then edited and turned to a written text, as parliamentary transcripts or radio interviews published on the Internet. These texts while being written rather than spoken, still keep features of the spoken language. This means that there is a different rationale behind the typology of

5 Górski and Łaziński (forthcoming) prove that the distinction between fiction and non-fiction is also fundamental as far as intralinguistic features are concerned.

spoken and written texts. In case of spoken texts we take into account the setting (spontaneous vs. formal), but also the method of transcription of the text, or to put it in other words – the faithfulness of the transcript.

Apart from the above mentioned typology we classify texts by a channel with the categories: press (subcategories: daily; weekly; monthly; other press), book; Internet; spoken; leaflets, announcements, ads; manuscript. Every text is characterised by both text type and channel.

So as to assure that the corpus will cover as many topics as possible, we also include in headers the classification done by librarians: Universal Decimal Classification and the classification of the National Library (Biblioteka Narodowa). We shall stress however that we do not want the corpus to be representative according to topic. We use the classification as auxiliary means to check if the topics are covered evenly; it also helps in classifying texts according to the text typology of the corpus.

3. Methods

We decided to reflect in the corpus the reception of the language by the Polish language community (as far as the written component is concerned) rather then the population of texts. The motivation for this choice was discussed in detail in Górski 2008.

This methodology means in practice that we try to reflect the structure of the readership in Poland. To put it simply: the more words of a certain text type an average Pole reads, the larger is the proportion of this text type in the corpus.

3.1. Sources

Ideally we should conduct a pool asking the respondents about the volume of texts of different text types, that they read. However if we expected reliable data such a pool would be expensive and time consuming. Instead we can make use of data which are publicly available.

There are two main sources of the data in question. First: a biannual report of the National Library (Straus *et al.* 1996a, 1996b, 1998, 2000, 2002, 2006, 2008) A specialised department conducts a survey to answer the following questions: how many and what kind of books people read and buy. These surveys are managed by professional opinion poll agency and seem to be reliable. What is also important – the data are quite stable. Although in the nineties one could observe an increase of those who declare reading instructive books, once their readership reached a certain point radical changes are no more observed.

As far as the press is concerned there are two sources available. The first is PBC (Polskie Badanie Czytelnictwa). It is a pool conducted twice a year and its aim is to show how many respondents declare reading a newspaper. In contrast ZKDP (Związek Kontroli Dystrybucji Prasy) controls the circulation of the press. In the latter case we can assume that everybody who bought a newspaper read it. It is not necessarely true in two cases – some people accept free press, just because it is free but do not read it and on the other hand a copy of a teenagers magazine is often read by a couple of readers. This however should not affect very highly the data. On the other hand ZDKP controls a wider range of magazines and for that reason we chose it as a basis for establishing the design of the corpus.

3.2. Methods

We adopted a bottom-up method of establishing the design of the corpus. At the first step we decide about the proportions of books. As we wrote above ideally we should know how many running words did an average Pole read in books belonging to a certain text-type. Instead, the quoted above reports of the National Library tell us how many respondents declare reading a certain type of texts. In fact it is not exactly what we want. Still however it tells us about the audience of a given text type. The larger is the audience the wider is the reception of this text type. Thus what we do is we assign the volume of texts belonging to a certain text type proportionally to the percentage of respondents declaring reading this very text type. Now, we count the average of the percentage of respondents declaring reading each text type in the available reports and normalize it so as to obtain the percentage of certain text types characteristic for books.

The figures in the following table show mean percentage of respondents declaring reading a given text sort. The first column contains Polish labels of text categories the second their English translation[6], and the third the mean percentage of respondents declaring reading this text type. Each respondent could choose as many text types as he wants, so the figures do not sum up to 100. Note that the typology set by the poll differs form the one which we propose. It is however possible to “translate” one to another.

6 One has to be aware of the fact that the English counterparts of the Polish terms do not match exactly. For example Polish *esej* has a narrower meaning than its English counterpart essey – it is a kind of literary work, thus it excludes scientific writing.

	Type (Polish)	Type (English)	Mean percentage of respondents
1.	lektury szkolne i podręczniki	literary set books and textbooks	23%
2.	obyczajowo-romansowe	romantic stories	18%
3.	sensacyjno-kryminalne	detective stories	16%
4.	dziecięco-młodzieżowe	novels for youth and children	10%
5.	encyklopedyczno-poradnikowe	encyclopaedias and how-to books	14%
6.	literatura faktu (wspomnienia, pamiętniki, reportaże, biografie, autobiografie)	non-fiction literary works (memoirs, reportages, biography, authobiography)	13%
7.	powieści grozy, horrory, thrillery	horrors and thrillers	3%
8.	fantastyka (science-fiction, fantasy, litertatura grozy z horrorami)	fantasy	6%
9.	fachowe	professional literature	8%
10.	religijne	religious writing	8%
11.	eseistyka i publicystyka	esseys and opinion	3%
12.	ezoteryka i ufologia	esoterics and ufology	2%

As you can see these categories describe rather the "literary taste" or cultural needs of respondents than text sorts. Especially the row 1 is unclear: it may cover any kind of book which the respondent was forced to read by the school, that is why we do not take this figure into account. If we add rows: 2, 3 4, 7, 8, (which are all various genders of belles-lettres) and treat books as 100% we obtain following figures:

Gender	percentage
fiction	52%
non-fiction literature	19%
journalistic book	5%
academic writing and textbooks	5%
instructive writing and guidebooks	19%

Now let us turn to newspapers. Note however that there are two good reasons to treat books and newspapers separately at this stage: we have quite distinct data, which do not match each other, according to those two channels of text. As far as newspapers are concerned we only know how many copies of each title are bought. The proposed typology of press is a very simple one – we distinguish dailies and magazines. Although there are detailed typologies of press established within media studies, they are useless, because almost every title belongs to several categories at once. On the other hand this rather oversimplified classification has a strong justification. Dailies contain both informative writing and persuasive texts (the former outnumbering the latter), whereas magazines contain predominantly the latter. In fact short news and opinion journalism form two distinct text types. Now, we count the sum of all copies of magazines in a year and again the same for dailies. The proportion between these two sums is the proportion which we obtain for these two channels, that is 52% dailies and 48% magazines.

Having already established the design of the two main components of published texts we pass to the most delicate question of the proportions of books and newspapers. The book readership surveys tell us that an average Pole reads 8 books a year. Assuming that the length of an average book is 70 000 running words (a figure suggested by the corpus), the annual "consumption" of texts read in books is 560 000. Unfortunately the precise amount of text read in newspapers is not monitored so accurately[7]. There is one publicly available source (Makarenko 2001) which states that an average Pole reads the press ca. 25 minutes a day. With the average speed of 200–230 per minute this gives us ca. 1 960 000 words a year (215 x 25 x 365 = 1 961 875). If so, the percentage of words read in press is ca. 78% against 22% read in books.

As stated above, we would like the corpus to *represent* the entire language in its variety. Thus we add a component labelled "other" or "miscellanea". In case of this component we only care about diversity so as to cover all possible kinds of texts. No a priori set amounts of texts are foreseen. In fact it is impossible to state the audience of such texts and probably some of them are hardly ever read (e.g. legal texts), other attract broad public (internet). Thus we arbitrarily assign them a share of 10% of the entire corpus, which breaks down into 7% Internet texts and 3% of "miscellaneus (written)". The other arbitrarily set part of the corpus is the spoken component which is also covers 10% of the corpus.

If we put all of it together we would obtain:

press	62%
books	18%
miscellanea	10%
spoken	10%

4. Final design

Recall however that we assume balance as an equally important feature of corpus design as representativeness. Let us define a balanced corpus as a corpus in which no component forms more than the halve of it. Again we arbitrarily

7 This for an obvious reason – the advertiser cares only about reading a newspaper, what means to him reading also his advertisement. The question how much of the newspaper is really read is of no importance to him.

decide to lower the amount of journalistic texts to 50%. There is also another motivation for this change – in general newspapers are read less carefully than books[8].

Taking this assumption we finally propose following design of the corpus:

journalism	50%
fiction	16%
spoken	10%
internet	7%
non-fiction literature	5.5%
instructive writing and guidebooks	5.5%
miscellaneus (written)	3%
academic writing and textbooks	2%
unclassified non-fiction book	1%

In case of a large corpus there is no need of extracting samples from the texts, because no single text can skew the data. What is the more one should not “waste” text if the corpus is to be very large. Although a random selection of texts should be desired (cf. Biber 1993) it never happens in modern corpora. Each text to become part of a corpus must satisfy two conditions it should be available in electronic form and the agreement of a copyright holder must be obtained. Of course there is a danger of self-selection, for example publishers are not prone to give their permission for best-sellers. This is however the cost of building a large corpus.

References

Biber, D. (1993). “Representativeness in Corpus Design”. *Literary and Linguistic Computing*, 8 (4): 243–257.

Čermák, F., Králík, J. and K. Kučera (1997). “Recepce současné češtiny a reprezentativnost korpusu”. *Slovo a Slovesnost*, 58: 117–124.

Gajda, S. (ed.) (1995). *Przewodnik po stylistyce polskiej*. Opole: Wydawnictwo Uniwersytetu Opolskiego.

Górski, R. L. (2009). “Representativness of the written part of a Polish general reference corpus. Primary notes”. In: B. Lewandowska-Tomaszczyk (ed.). *Corpus Linguistics, Computer Tools, and Applications – State of the Art*. Frankfurt a. Main: Peter Lang: 119–123.

Górski, R. L. and M. Łaziński (forthcoming). „Wzór stylu i wzór na styl. Zróżnicowanie stylistyczne tekstów w Narodowym Korpusie Języka Polskiego”. To appear in: VIII Forum Kultury Słowa, Gdańsk.

---

8 This fact was pointed to me by František Čermak (personal communication). Even if I do not know research on this topic I suggest a simple test – most people remember both the plot of a novel and even some quotations from them but hardly can tell that of a daily read a week ago.

Klemensiewicz, Z (1982). „O różnych odmianach współczesnej polszczyzny". In: Z. Klemensiewicz (ed.). *Składnia, stylistyka, pedagogika językowa.* Warszawa: Państwowe Wydawnictwo Naukowe.

Makarenko, V. (2001). „Nie tylko liczyć, trzeba też rozumieć". *Gazeta Wyborcza*, no 288: 22 Available at: http://szukaj.wyborcza.pl/archiwum/1,0,1599476.html

Straus G. and K. Wolff (1996a). *Czytanie i kupowanie książek w Polsce w 1994 r.* Straus G. and K. Wolff (1996b). *Polacy i książki: społeczna sytuacja książki w Polsce 1992.* Warszawa: Biblioteka Narodowa.

Straus G. and K. Wolff (1998). *Zainteresowanie książką w społeczeństwie polskim w 1996 r.* Warszawa: Biblioteka Narodowa.

Straus G. and K. Wolff (2000). *Czytać, nie czytać..., kupować, nie kupować... sytuacja książki w społeczeństwie polskim w 1998 r.* Warszawa: Biblioteka Narodowa.

Straus G. and K. Wolff (2002). *Sienkiewicz, Mickiewicz, Biblia, harlequiny...: społeczny zasięg książki w Polsce w 2000 roku.*Warszawa: Biblioteka Narodowa.

Straus G. and K. Wolff (2006). *Czytanie, kupowanie, wypożyczanie: społeczny zasięg książki w Polsce w 2004 roku.* Warszawa: Biblioteka Narodowa.

Straus G., K. Wolff, S. Wierny (2008). *Czytanie, kupowanie, surfowanie: społeczny zasięg książki w Polsce w 2006 roku.* Warszawa: Biblioteka Narodowa.

Polskie Badanie Czytelnictwa www.pbczyt.pl

Związek Kontroli Dystrybucji Prasy www.zkdp.pl

XML Text Interchange Format in the National Corpus of Polish

Adam Przepiórkowski and Piotr Bański

Abstract: The aim of this paper is to describe and justify the XML encoding of texts within the National Corpus of Polish. Basic text encoding, rather than linguistic annotation, is considered here: the encoding of the primary data, the structural markup and the metadata. A set of schemata conformant with the Text Encoding Initiative Guidelines P5 is presented.

Keywords: Text Encoding Initiative, TEI P5, National Corpus of Polish, NKJP, metadata, TEI header, structural markup, primary data, XML, Polish.

1. Introduction

National Corpus of Polish[1] (Pol. *Narodowy Korpus Języka Polskiego;* NKJP; http://nkjp.pl/) is a project carried out in 2008-2010, involving 4 Polish institutions: Institute of Computer Science of the Polish Academy of Sciences (coordinator), Institute of Polish Language of the Polish Academy of Sciences, University of Łódź and Polish Scientific Publishers PWN.[2] Each of these instituti-tions contributes texts from their own corpora, and each – apart from the coordinator – acquires new texts for the National Corpus of Polish (NKJP, henceforth): books, newspapers and magazines, blogs, transcripts of spoken data, etc. All these texts are imported into two very different search engines available in NKJP (cf. the "Demo" link at http://nkjp.pl/).

Obviously, before NKJP texts can be indexed or automatically processed by any other tools they must be converted to a common interchange format. Such interchange format should allow for the representation of various types of texts mentioned above, and also for the encoding of various kinds of metadata and structural information. The only text encoding standard sufficiently versatile to meet these requirements is TEI P5, presented in the Guidelines of the Text Encoding Initiative (TEI; Burnard and Bauman 2008; http://www.tei-c.org/). It is not an official ISO standard, but a mature and very specific XML-based *de facto* standard for text encoding in the humanities, with a rich user base and supporting tools.

---

1 Research funded in 2007-2010 by a research and development grant from the Polish Ministry of Science and Higher Education.

2 A programmatic description of the project may be found in Przepiórkowski et al. 2008, and more recent developments are presented in Przepiórkowski et al. 2009.

The reason for continuing this paper beyond the previous paragraph is that TEI is a large treasure trove of solutions, rather than a lean and highly focussed formalism, and a particular text encoding schema must still be designed by choosing the most appropriate mechanisms from the TEI toolbox and – in rare specific cases – by introducing new XML elements or attributes. The aim of this paper is to present and document one such particular schema, developed within NKJP. As there are few well-documented TEI corpora around, and hardly any corpora following the current P5 version of the TEI Guidelines (substantially differing from the previous TEI versions), we hope that this presentation will facilitate the development of other TEI P5 corpora.

The remainder of the paper starts, in § 2, with a presentation of the NKJP corpus header, i.e., an XML document containing metadata pertaining to the National Corpus of Polish as a whole. The representation of text headers, i.e., metadata for particular texts, is described in § 3. The ensuing section, § 4, makes clear the overall structure of a corpus text and the place of both kinds of metadata in that structure. This section also sketches the representation of structural and typographical distinctions within texts. Although, within NKJP, texts are also annotated at various linguistic levels, this paper does not deal with such linguistic annotation – see Przepiórkowski and Bański 2009 for an overview and Bański and Przepiórkowski 2009 for a discussion of some technical issues. Finally, § 5 concludes the paper.

2. Corpus Header

Following the TEI Guidelines, the NKJP corpus header consists of 4 sections contained in the `<teiHeader xml:lang="en" type="corpus">` element: `<fileDesc>`, `<profileDesc>`, `<encodingDesc>` and `<revisionDesc>`.

Two of these have very simple structure. First, `<profileDesc>` identifies the main languages used in the TEI encoding of texts and metadata, and it is cited in its entirety below:

```
<profileDesc>
   <langUsage>
      <language ident="pl">Polish</language>
      <language ident="en">English</language>
   </langUsage>
</profileDesc>
```

The values of `@ident` attributes may be used for any element to specify the language of the content of that element. In fact, the `xml:lang="en"` specification in the <teiHeader> element is inherited by other elements in the header, unless explicitly overridden by xml:lang="pl", thus making English the default language of the NKJP header.

Another simple and homogeneous section is <revisionDesc>: it contains a sequence of <change> statements like the following:

```
<change who="#adamp" when="2009-08-01">
   Added <gi>profileDesc</gi>.
</change>
```

The <fileDesc> section contains 4 subsections. The first, <titleStmt>, specifies the name of the corpus and describes the responsibility of various institutions and persons involved in its creation. One such responsibility statement is referenced by who="#adamp" in the example above, another may look as follows:

```
<respStmt>
   <persName xml:id="bansp">Piotr Bański</persName>
   <resp>initial design of various XML schemata</resp>
</respStmt>
```

The other three subsections of <fileDesc> are: <editionStmt> – a brief statement concerning the stability of the current version of NKJP, <publicationStmt> – defining availability and distribution of NKJP, and <sourceDesc> – specifying the origin of texts in general terms (specific source descriptions are contained in the headers of particular texts).

Finally, <encodingDesc> characterizes NKJP in various ways, e.g., <projectDesc> repeats the description of the project given at http://nkjp.pl/, <samplingDecl> says that *Whole texts are included, whenever possible* and provides some information on text structure, as discussed in § 4, and <editorialDecl> briefly discusses anonymisation of spoken data and other editorial interventions in NKJP texts.

While these subsections contain free-text statements, many other <encodingDesc> subsections are more structured. Perhaps the most important are <classDecl> subsections, which specify text classifications referenced in particular text headers. For example, one of the ways in which NKJP texts are classified is according to the Universal Decimal Classification, so the following declaration is present in the corpus header:

```
<classDecl>
   <taxonomy xml:id="ukd">
      <bibl>
         <title xml:lang="pl">Uniwersalna Klasyfikacja
         Dziesietna</title>
         <title xml:lang="en">Universal Decimal
         Classification</title>
         <edition>UDC-P058</edition>
      </bibl>
   </taxonomy>
</classDecl>
```

Within a text header (cf. § 3 below), a reference to this classification may be made as follows:

```
<classCode scheme="#ukd">821.162.1-3</classCode>.
```

Similarly, in order to control the good balance of the corpus with respect to genres, a taxonomy of text types is defined; its fragment is presented below:

```
<classDecl>
   <taxonomy xml:id="taxonomy-NKJP-type">
    <! -- ... --->
      <category xml:id="typ_lit_proza">
         <desc xml:lang="pl">proza</desc>
         <desc xml:lang="en">prose</desc>
      </category>
      <category xml:id="typ_lit_poezja">
         <desc xml:lang="pl">poezja</desc>
         <desc xml:lang="en">poetry</desc>
      </category>
      <category xml:id="typ_lit_dramat">
         <desc xml:lang="pl">dramat</desc>
         <desc xml:lang="en">drama</desc>
      </category>
    <! -- ... --->
   </taxonomy>
</classDecl>
```

Again, the type of a particular text may be defined by referencing one of the categories defined in such a classification.

The final `<encodingDesc>` subsection in the NKJP header to be mentioned here[3] is `<nkjp:fsLib>`. As the namespace prefix `nkjp` suggests, this element is not defined by TEI but introduced within NKJP for a specific purpose.

TEI specifications contain the ISO standard on the XML representation of feature structures (ISO:24610-1 2005) and, within NKJP, feature structures are used for representing various types of linguistic annotation (Przepiórkowski and Bański 2009). The standard makes it possible to define feature structure libraries containing, e.g., feature structures representing complex morphosyntactic information. Such feature structures may subsequently be referenced from an appropriate linguistic layer by their identifier, thus simultaneously increasing readability and compactness of linguistic representations. Curiously, according to TEI specifications it is not possible to define such feature structure libraries in a header, which seems to be the most natural place for such libraries: once they are in the corpus header, they may be referenced in a way analogous to how particular categories defined within `<classDecl>` are referenced for classification. Hence the need for the project-specific element `<nkjp:fsLib>`.

The presence of such nkjp:... elements and attributes is what makes the NKJP schema TEI conformant in a weaker sense: it is a TEI Extension rather than TEI Conformant (with a capital 'C'), as defined in Burnard and Bauman 2008, § 23.3. Nevertheless, there are only a few conservative and well-justified modifications of this kind in the NKJP schema presented here, so it may be regarded as a "nearly" TEI Conformant TEI Extension.

3. Text Header

Each NKJP text is represented as a number of XML files, two of which are relevant here: `header.xml` and `text_structure.xml`.[4] The structure of the latter will be presented in § 4. The structure of text headers, `header.xml`, is similar to that of the corpus header: the `<teiHeader>` element, implicitly marked as `type="text"` here, contains three sections: `<fileDesc>`, `<profileDesc>` and `<revisionDesc>`. The last section, `<revisionDesc>`, is fully analogous to that of the corpus header and

---

3 Two other such subsections present in the NKJP header are <tagsDecl> and <refsDecl>; see appropriate links in http://www.tei-c.org/release/doc/tei-p5-doc/en/html/ref-encodingDesc.html for a description of their role in <encodingDesc>.

4 Other files contain various layers of linguistic annotation, as described in Przepiórkowski and Bański 2009.

contains a sequence of <change> elements describing modifications to any of the files representing the text and its annotation.

On the other hand, <profileDesc> differs from that of the corpus header and it comprises one element, <textClass>, which contains classifiers of the text, referencing appropriate taxonomies posited in the corpus header. For example, the content of <profileDesc> for Manuela Gretkowska's novel *Namiętnik* may look as follows:

```
<profileDesc>
   <textClass>
      <classCode scheme="#ukd">821.162.1-3</classCode>
      <keywords scheme="#bn">
        <list>
         <item>Opowiadanie polskie -- 20 w.</item>
        </list>
      </keywords>
      <catRef scheme="#taxonomy-NKJP-type
      "target="#typ_lit_proza"/>
      <catRef scheme="#taxonomy-NKJP-channel"
      target="#kanal_ksiazka"/>
   </textClass>
</profileDesc>
```

References to 4 classification schemes are made here: two external to the project (the Universal Decimal Classification mentioned above and the classification of the Polish National Library, cf. #bn), and two internal (text type: `#typ_lit_proza`, i.e., prose, and text channel: `#kanal_ksiazka`, i.e., book).

Finally, <fileDesc> contains a variety of information about the text: its title in NKJP (e.g., "`TEI P5 encoded version of "Namiętnik"`"), bibliographic information about the source of the text (title, author, publisher, etc.), a note about the origin of the text in NKJP (e.g., "<note type="text_origin">IPI PAN Corpus</note>"), the original header, if available, of the text as it was defined in the corpus from which the text is inherited, as well as a <publicationStmt>, exemplified below:

```
<publicationStmt nkjp:subcorpus="balanced">
   <availability status="restricted">
     <p>For all NKJP purposes.</p>
   </availability>
</publicationStmt>
```

The `@nkjp:subcorpus` attribute shown above is another example of a non-conformant modification of TEI, needed here in order to represent the information about the target NKJP subcorpus for which the text was acquired.

For transcripts of spoken data, the text header may also contain information about the person responsible for transcription (encoded as `<respStmt>` within `<fileDesc>`), various kinds of information about the source of the text (different from written texts, because here the source is a recording rather than a publication), as well as another element from the nkjp namespace, `<nkjp:topic>`, describing the topic of the conversation. Moreover, apart from `<textClass>`, `<profileDesc>` also contains a `<langUsage>` element specifying the level of formality of the conversation, `<particDesc>`, containing background information about participants in the conversation, as well as `<settingDesc>`, mentioning when and where the conversation took place; some of these elements specific to transcripts of spoken data are exemplified below:

```
<langUsage>
   <language ident="pl-x-formal"/>
</langUsage>
<nkjp:topic xml:lang="pl">Rozmowa o immunitecie Zbigniewa
   Ziobro, sytuacji w Gruzji i reakcji unii europejskiej na
   nią.</nkjp:topic>
<particDesc>
   <!-- ... --->
   <person xml:id="sp2" role="speaker">
      <persName>Zbigniew Ziobro</persName>
      <sex value="1">male</sex>
      <education xml:lang="pl">wyższe</education>
      <age>40</age>
      <residence>unknown</residence>
   </person>
   <!-- ... --->
</particDesc>
   <settingDesc>
      <setting>
      <name type="place">TVP Info</name>
      <name type="voivodship" xml:lang="pl">mazowiecki
      </name>
      <date type="recorded" when="2008-09-02"/>
   </setting>
</settingDesc>
```

4. Text Structure

For any corpus document, `text_structure.xml` contains the actual text, as well as the structural markup of the document.

It is often considered best practice to have a read-only pure text file referenced by a stand-off file containing structural information. The main justification for this requirement is the need for an immutable text level. While stand-off annotation is used for all other NKJP layers, it has turned out to be impractical to separate primary data and structure. The reason for that is that corpus data are virtually never acquired as pure text, but almost always come with some markup already present: XML, HTML, or even implicit markup in Microsoft Word and OpenOf-fice files. Separating this markup from text for the sake of stand-off annotation (rather then converting it *in situ* into the appropriate TEI markup), and then logically combining them again for processing at later stages, would only generate unnecessary work. Hence, for the purposes of NKJP, it is `text_structure.xml` that is considered immutable.

The outline of `text_structure.xml`, containing a single text and any structural annotation, is as follows, with the `<front>` and `<back>` matter elements optional (always absent in transcripts of spoken data):

```
<teiCorpus
   xmlns:xi="http://www.w3.org/2001/XInclude"
   xmlns="http://www.tei-c.org/ns/1.0">
   <xi:include href="NKJP_header.xml"/>
   <TEI>
   <xi:include href="header.xml"/>
   <text xml:id="struct_text">
      <front><!--     front matter      --></front>
      <body><!--      main text body    --></body>
      <back><!--      back  matter      --></back>
   </text>
   </TEI>
</teiCorpus>
```

It should be noted that each text is a `<teiCorpus>` and logically includes not only the text header (`<xi:include href="header.xml"/>`), but also the entire corpus header (`<xi:include href="NKJP_header.xml"/>`).

For `<front>` and `<back>`, any structural elements defined in TEI P5 are allowed. Typically, within front matter there will be a title statement, possibly distinguishing between the main title and the subtitle, as in the following example:

```
<docTitle>
   <titlePart type="main">Pieśni nędzy i zagłady
   </titlePart>
   <titlePart type="sub">Twórczość Mordechaja Gebirtiga w
   Salonie Poezji</titlePart>
</docTitle>
```

On the other hand, in NKJP, the content of <body> is constrained with respect to the range of possibilities offered by TEI P5. For spoken texts, only a sequence of <u>tterances (and perhaps <incident>s between them) may occur within <body>, as in the following fragment:

```
<body xml:id="txt_body">
   <u who="#sp3" xml:id="u1">ale zostaw to w ogóle dajcie
   buziaka przepraszam was laski</u>
   <u trans="overlap" who="#sp1" xml:id="u2">no dałyśmy sobie
   buziaka no</u>
   <!-- ... -->
</body>
```

For written texts, the main blocks are <p> (paragraph), <ab> (anonymous block, i.e., a paragraph-sized chunk of text exceptionally used for texts without division into paragraphs) and <head> (for headings starting a textual division at any level, e.g., for chapter and section titles). These blocks can be grouped into chapters, sections, subsections, etc., using the – possibly nested – <div> elements, e.g.:

```
<body>
   <!-- ... -->
   <div type="chapter" n="1">
      <head>Rozdział 1 Skąd się biorą paradygmaty?</head>
      <p><!-- ... --></p>
      <p><!-- ... --></p>
      <p><!-- ... --></p>
   </div>
   <div type="chapter" n="2">
      <head>Rozdział 2 Świat według Pszczółki Mai</head>
      <p><!-- ... --></p>
      <p><!-- ... --></p>
      <p><!-- ... --></p>
   </div>
   <!-- ... -->
</body>
```

The content of the elements `<u>`, `<p>`, `<ab>` and `<head>` is (almost) pure text; the only XML elements which may appear there are: `<gap>` (to mark places where tables, pictures, etc., were removed from text), `<hi>`, with the obligatory attribute `@rend` specifying how the highlighted text is rendered (in written texts only), `<lb>` (always empty, to mark line breaks in poetry or in a motto; only in written texts) and two elements used in spoken texts for marking non-verbal events, `<vocal>` and `<incident>`.

These restrictions on `<u>`, etc., are caused by the fact that the content of these elements will be further marked linguistically and indexed by search engines, so any additional markup which would complicate the operation of these tools must be well justified. More specifically, the following XPath expressions define the elements to be further processed:

- `//body//(p|ab|u|incident|head)`
- `//front//titlePart`

In other words, the content ofany `<p>`, `<ab>`, `<u>`, `<incident>` and `<head>` elements anywhere within `<body>`, as well as the content of `<titlePart>` anywhere within `<front>` will be marked linguistically and indexed by corpus search engines.

5. Conclusion

Given that TEI P5 Guidelines were released in November 2007, there are still very few publicly available or documented TEI P5 corpora around. One that provided inspiration for some of the solutions presented above is the corpus of the project "Communication in Slovene" (http://nl.ijs.si/ssj/), although currently it does not represent nearly as many different kinds of linguistic and structural information as NKJP.[5]

Because of this lack of a large base of well-documented TEI P5 corpora, and because of the daunting number of choices that TEI makes available in its 1350-page guidelines, the design of the TEI-based NKJP interchange format turned out to be a tedious and time-consuming task. We hope that this paper, together with the accompanying articles cited above, will facilitate the design of similar TEI P5 schemata in other corpus projects.

5 Also, for a minor technical reason (adding new elements to the TEI namespace) it is not TEI conformant in any sense of TEI conformance.

References

Bański, P. and A. Przepiórkowski (2009). "Stand-off TEI annotation: the case of the National Corpus of Polish". In: Proceedings of the third linguistic annotation workshop (LAW III) at ACL-IJCNLP 2009. Singapore, 64–67.

Burnard, L. and S. Bauman (Eds.) (2008). *TEI P5: Guidelines for electronic text encoding and interchange.* Oxford. Available at: http://www.tei-c.org/Guidelines/P5/

ISO:24610-1 (2005). "Language resource management-feature structures-part 1: Feature structure representation". ISO/DIS 24610-1, 2005-10-20.

Przepiórkowski, A. and P. Bański (2009). "Which XML standards for multilevel corpus annotation?". In: Vetulani, Z. (Ed.), *Proceedings of the 4th language and technology conference.* Poznań, Poland, 245-250.

Przepiórkowski, A., Górski, R. L., Lewandowska-Tomaszczyk, B. and M. Łaziński (2008). "Towards the National Corpus of Polish". In: *Proceedings ofthe sixth international Conference on Language Resources and Evaluation, LREC2008.* Marrakech.

Przepiorkowski, A., Górski, R. L., Łaziński, M. and P. Pęzik (2009). "Recent developments in the National Corpus of Polish". In: Levická, J. and R. Garabík (Eds.), *NLP, corpus linguistics, corpus based grammar research: Proceedings of the fifth international conference, Smolenice, Slovakia, 25-27 November 2009.* Brno: Tribun, 302-309.

Part Two

CORPUS TOOLS, INFORMATION AND TERMINOLOGY EXTRACTION

UGTag: Morphological Analyzer and Tagger for the Ukrainian Language

Natalia Kotsyba, Andriy Mykulyak and Igor V. Shevchenko

Abstract: UGTag, a program for morphological analysis and tagging of Ukrainian texts, is developed within the Polish-Ukrainian Parallel Corpus (PolUKR)[1] project to support morphosyntactic annotation for the Ukrainian part of the corpus. The tagger accepts plain, HTML or XML texts and produces XML files structured according to the XCES standard and suitable for search with such programs as Poliqarp.

The process of the analysis consists of three stages: tokenization, tagging and chunking. At the tokenization stage the text is split into tokens (words, numbers, etc). During the tagging all possible morphological and lemma interpretations are assigned to each token (morphological analysis) at first, then the correct interpretation is selected (disambiguation). During the chunking stage tokens are grouped into sentences. The Ukrainian Grammatical Dictionary is used as a source of morphological information for UGTag. It is not restricted to it, however: modular design allows plugging-in additional dictionaries as well as modification of the existing one. Users can interact with UGTag in three ways: console-based, GUI and Web-based client.

Keywords: corpus, grammatical dictionary, morphological analyzer, PolUKR, Slavic, tagger, UGTag, UGD, Ukrainian, XCES.

1. Introduction

UGTag is a set of NLP tools for the Ukrainian language. Its development was inspired by the functionally similar TaKIPI[2] toolset for Polish. There are two reasons for this. Firstly, TaKIPI is a very convenient software package with well thought out design that includes all major NLP tasks to prepare an annotated monolingual corpus. Secondly, UGTag is developed within the Polish-Ukrainian Parallel Corpus project to provide the grammatical annotation for the Ukrainian part of the corpus. Therefore, it is natural to use a unified output format for both language parts of the corpus suitable for search with such programs as Poliqarp[3].

---

1 This project has received financial support from the Ministry of Science and Higher Education of Poland in 2007–2009. URL: http://corpus.domeczek.pl

2 All the code for UGTag was written from scratch.

3 http://korpus.pl/index.php?page=poliqarp.

However, some tasks were implemented in a different way. Namely, UGTag allows for interactive annotation of texts with manual disambiguation and sentencing. Its modular design allows plugging-in additional grammatical dictionaries as well as modification of the existing ones.

2. The program architecture

UGTag is written in Java, which means that it is platform independent, currently tested under Windows and Linux. It comes in a ready-to-use binary form with no need of compilation of source files.

The scheme below represents the main elements of the program.

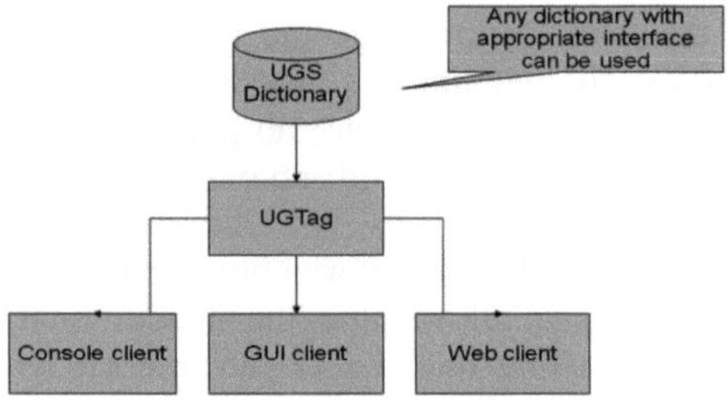

Figure. 1. UGTag architecture

Users can work with the program using the console, GUI or a Web client, each of which gives different possibilities. The command-line client provides the fastest access to the basic functionality and is mainly intended for processing large amounts of data.

The GUI client provides some advanced features such as possibility of manual disambiguation, sentence splitting and editing grammatical dictionaries. The Web interface is used for public access to the functionality of the program. It is planned to provide a possibility for users to tag their own texts through the Internet and suggest new words that were not recognized by the program to the general dictionary.

The logic of the program is concentrated in the UGTag package, which is described in more detail below.

3. Dictionaries

UGTag provides morphosyntactic information to each token in a raw text supplied by the user based on dictionaries that include a list of word forms and their grammatical interpretations. The core grammatical database is an extended version of the UGD (Ukrainian Grammatical Dictionary). Any compatible dictionary can be used instead, partly because the UGD data are subject to copyright law.

The Ukrainian Grammatical Dictionary (UGD) was developed in 1996–2002 at the Ukrainian Linguistic Information Institute of NASU by Ihor Shevchenko. UGD contains detailed information about declension for Ukrainian allowing both morphological analysis and synthesis. The data were initially stored in a relational database and amount to 180 thousand lemmas and 56 thousand endings that can be combined into over 2000 paradigmatic classes.

4. The process of analysis

UGTag is intended to be used for corpora development and includes a number of tasks that can be grouped as follows:

1) pre-processing stage: tokenization and chunking;
2) morphological analysis;
3) disambiguation (leading to proper tagging);
4) sentence grouping.

The following scheme shows in more detail the stages of text processing.

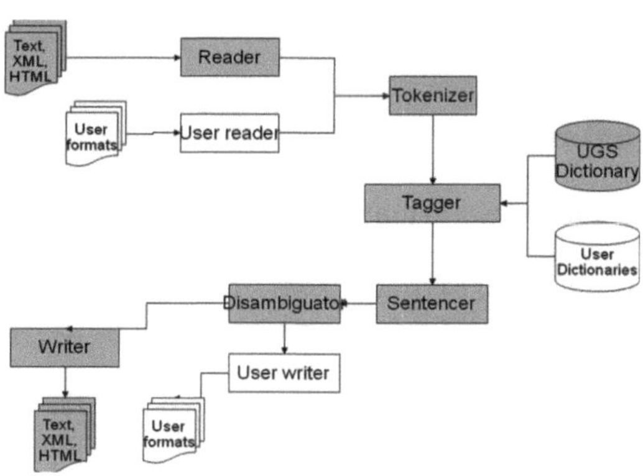

Figure. 2. Sequence of logical analysis of corpus texts

Stage	Role	Input	Output
Reader	Separates (different) external representations of the text from its internal representation (one or more character sequences). In other words, it converts a text to a standard file format.	Texts in different file formats	One or more sequences of characters (usually one sequence per line of the input file)
Tokenizer	Splits sequences into tokens (smallest meaningful pieces of text)	Character sequence	List of tokens
Tagger	Adds morphological information with lemmas to tokens (additionally it can split or group some tokens basing on their meaning – e.g. abbreviations, composite words like *zeleno-červony*)	List of tokens	List of tokens with morphological information and lemmas attached to each token
Sentencer	Groups tokens into sentences	List of annotated tokens	List of sentences
Disambiguator	Selects appropriate grammatical interpretation of the token	List of annotated tokens (optionally augmented with a list of sentences)	List of tokens with a most probable annotation
Writer	Converts list of tokens to the format most appropriate for the user	List of tokens, list of sentences	File with annotations in a specified format

5. Pre-morphological analysis

5.1. Reading phase and input formats

The tagger accepts plain, HTML or XML texts and produces XML files structured according to the XCES standard and suitable for search with such programs as Poliqarp.

By default the program strips all tags from input HTML or XML files and turns them into raw texts. However, users can create, and add on the fly to the program, their own file readers that take into account the logical mark-up of input XML files and incorporate it into the output XML format. A file reader separates the external representation of texts from their unified internal representation fed to the tokenizer. In other words, it extracts the text itself, possibly portioning it into chunks for further processing.

5.2. Tokenization

The pre-morphological analysis presupposes procedures that do not involve the use of the grammatical dictionary.

The tokenizer divides chunks into blocks delimited by whitespace characters. A block can consist of one or more tokens, e.g. a quatation mark and a word with no white space in between ("token"). Then it divides blocks into tokens that are minimal structural units. There are five categories of tokens at the moment, more or less corresponding to those in yhe TaKIPI program, namely: words, numbers, punctuation marks, whitespace characters and unrecognized tokens. The word category is defined as a sequence of alphabetical characters with an optional hyphen. If they contain a hyphen, they are classified as technical composite words that are divided into either proper composite words or word collocations during the morphological analysis depending on the existing corresponding records in the grammatical database.

5.3. Morphological analysis and its conceptual basis in the grammatical database

A grammatical dictionary is the core source for the morphological analysis. There are different ways of arranging and presenting grammatical information and very often some additional work has to be carried out to fit a standard or expected representation of grammatical mark-up.

As was mentioned before, the structure of grammatical information in the UGD was considerably rearranged and further division into finer categories was carried out and implemented to meet the requirements of the intended tagsets. Presently UGTag supports two tagsets.

5.3.1. The IPIC style tagset

One of the tagsets is basically an extended version of the IPIC[4] tagset that also considers Ukrainian language-specific features, see (Kotsyba, Turska, Shypnivska

4 IPIC is a shortcut for corpus developed at the Institute of Computer Science (abbreviated as IPI PAN in Polish), presently the largest publicly available and well-documented corpus for Polish: http://korpus.pl

2008) and (Kotsyba 2009) for details. Some of the changes that were introduced in the arrangement of Ukrainian grammatical information arrangement to bring the original ULIF tagset (roughly supported by the UGD) to conformity with the IPIC one were the following: the category of degree of comparison for adjectives and adverbs was reintroduced; the category of predicatives was regrouped based on the conclusions in (Derzhanski, Kotsyba 2008).

The notation used in this tagset is also based on the IPIC one but includes a few Ukrainian language specific tags like: adjv (adjectival, a common notion for "syntactic" adjectives like proper adjectives, ordinal numerals and adjectival pronouns), nadj (invariable adjectives), kadj (short form of adjectives), fut (future tense), pres (present tense), numcol (collective numerals)[5].

The POS categorization in the database brings together both the original practical solutions of the UGD and IPIC developers and the traditional intuitive division into parts of speech. For example, UGD treats nouns of different genders and nouns denoting family names as different parts of speech. Similarly, the IPIC tagset singles out derogative nouns and gerunds. It also groups forms like infinitives, participles, -no/-to forms, etc., as separate word classes[6]. All these were brought together by the cost of partial information redundancy. The basic categories and the part of the tag which corresponds to them can be seen in the figure below. They are followed by possible attributes that are ticked off if the category possesses this attribute.

5 The Polish grammatical information is slightly altered as well. First of all it concerns the treatment of the so-called predicatives. Secondly, pronouns other than personal were reintroduced as separate categories (in the IPIC they are grouped according to their syntactic features with nouns or adjectives correspondingly without further differentiation). Ordinal numerals are also referred to as a numerals subclass of adjectivals. Atypical adjectives *winien* and *powinien* categorized under "winien" class can be found both by "winien" and "kadj" tags.

6 These classes are called flexemes which are more tight than the traditional parts of speech and are singled out on the basis of common morphological and syntactic behaviour. The term was introduced by Janusz Bień in the 1960's.

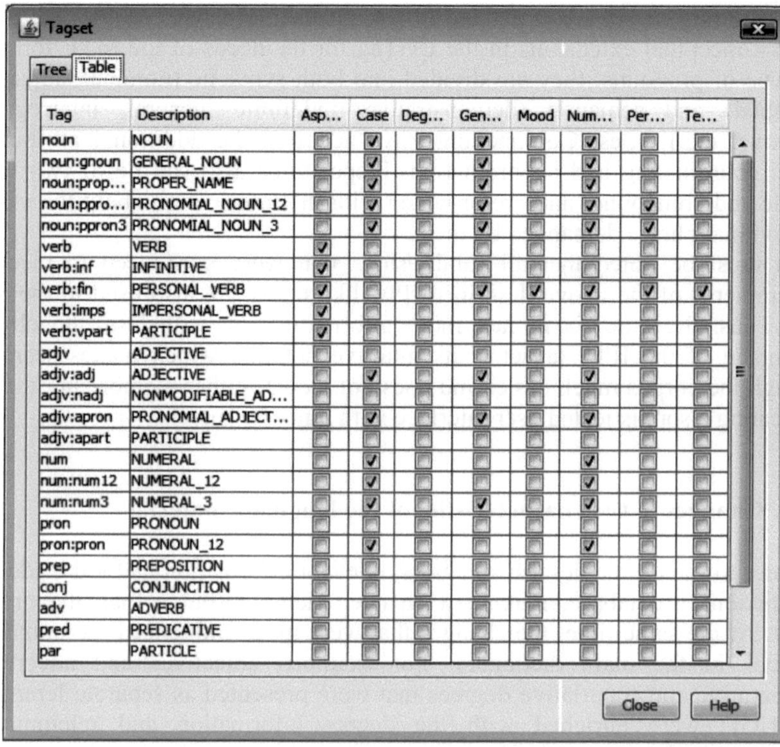

Tag	Description	Asp...	Case	Deg...	Gen...	Mood	Num...	Per...	Te...
noun	NOUN		✓		✓		✓		
noun:gnoun	GENERAL_NOUN		✓		✓		✓		
noun:prop...	PROPER_NAME		✓		✓		✓		
noun:ppro...	PRONOMIAL_NOUN_12		✓		✓		✓	✓	
noun:ppron3	PRONOMIAL_NOUN_3		✓		✓		✓	✓	
verb	VERB	✓							
verb:inf	INFINITIVE	✓							
verb:fin	PERSONAL_VERB	✓			✓	✓	✓	✓	✓
verb:imps	IMPERSONAL_VERB	✓							
verb:vpart	PARTICIPLE	✓							
adjv	ADJECTIVE								
adjv:adj	ADJECTIVE		✓		✓		✓		
adjv:nadj	NONMODIFIABLE_AD...								
adjv:apron	PRONOMIAL_ADJECT...		✓		✓		✓		
adjv:apart	PARTICIPLE								
num	NUMERAL		✓				✓		
num:num12	NUMERAL_12		✓				✓		
num:num3	NUMERAL_3		✓		✓		✓		
pron	PRONOUN								
pron:pron	PRONOUN_12		✓				✓		
prep	PREPOSITION								
conj	CONJUNCTION								
adv	ADVERB								
pred	PREDICATIVE								
par	PARTICLE								

Figure 3. Fragment of the list of categories of the IPIC style tagset

5.3.1. The MULTEXT-East compatible tagset

The other tagset supported by UGTag is MULTEXT-East that currently is becoming an international standard. It is foreseen that starting from version 4, the Ukrainian language will be included into the MULTEXT-East standard[7]. Some theoretical assumptions and decisions that appear in the MTE-4 morphosyntactic specifications for Ukrainian[8] which predefine the

7 For the purposes of the PolUKR, a similar package was developed also for the Polish language. A converter from the IPIC-style tagged XML corpus files into MTE-style ones was written to provide the Polish part of the parallel corpus in the MTE tagging format. See (Kotsyba, Radziszewski, Derzhanski 2009) for details.

8 The draft of the specifications, as well as some of the mentioned papers, are also available at http://domeczek.pl/~natko.

corresponding tagset are explained in (Derzhanski, Kotsyba 2009). One of the major conceptual extensions in the UGTag for the needs of the MTE format is the type of pronouns: they are divided into both syntactic (nominal, adjectival, adverbial) and semantic (demonstrative, indefinite, general, interrogative, reflexive, etc.) types. Conjunctions have acquired the additional attribute of Type: coordinating and subordinating. Prepositions also can be of two types: simple and compound, and are provided with the information about the case of the nominal phrase demanded by them.

It must be noted that all subdivisions that were introduced to meet the requirements of the above described IPIC-like tagset are also used in the MTE one. Thus, the latter is in fact more informative. Nevertheless, the obvious advantage of the IPIC tagset is its intuitive notation which makes searching through the corpus much easier and does not require either memorizing the tags or creating a sophisticated user interface with hints for search.

5.3.3. Changes in the characteristics of the language material

In order to satisfy the described tagsets, relevant information had to be added to the dictionary database, making it an even richer resource than the original UGD. At the same time, the changes that were made influenced the number of lexemes in the main dictionary. For example, adjectives and adverbs of comparative and superlative degrees that were presented as separate lemmas in the UGD were enriched with the degree information and relemmatized accordingly. This led to the decrease of number of adjectives in the dictionary by ca. 2200 words. This procedure was partly automated basing on typical suffixes and prefixes for the comparative and superlative degrees and a list of exceptions. The correct lemmas were deduced on the basis of the similarity of stems and morphological rules of degree transformation. The results were checked manually.

158 prepositions were supplied with the information about the case they govern. Those that govern several cases are treated as homonyms, which increased their general number by ca. 30.

Adjectival participles, treated as verb forms in the UGD, were extracted and modified to present separate lemmas. Ca. 20 new paradigmatic classes were defined for them. The number of newly acquired word forms was quite significant due to the introduced feminine, neutral and plural forms, as well as five new cases for each gender and number, that were absent in the UGD.

Pronouns were divided into semantic types (the Type attribute in the MTE tagset). In cases when more than one semantic feature was presented in one pronoun, the second one was recorded as a Referent_Type. The word *чийсь*

(„somebody's") is an example of a combination of an indefinite and a possessive type[9].

Some other changes concern word splitting. Originally the UGD contains collocations with white-space characters or hyphens treated as individual units. During the tokenization phase, the collocations are split into separate words and they are not recognized by the analyzer as a whole[10]. A highly productive group with a hyphen combining two or more adjectives that is not systematically represented in the UGD[11], is treated in the UGTag space as combinations of separate words. Most of the remaining hyphen-containing words were left intact.

5.3.4. Working with the dictionary filter

Information used for further grammatical mark-up can be sorted for various kinds of queries and correctness control with the help of the dictionary filter. It allows setting restrictions on the category and searching for lemmas with the help of regular expressions, cf. the figure below.

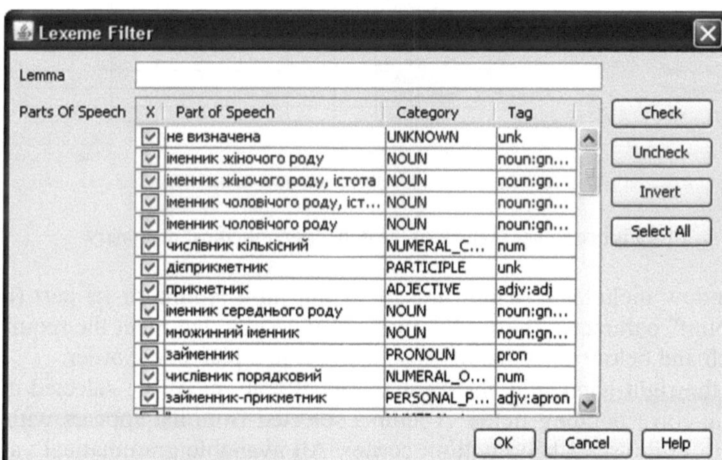

Figure 4. Lexeme and category filter

---

9 This way of representation in the MTE-4 was selected for more conformity with the existing MTE notation for other languages, see (Derzhanski, Kotsyba 2009) for details.

10 However, information about those combinations is preserved and can be used for syntactic analysis in the future.

11 It is practically impossible to cover the whole class as it is highly productive.

The result of search applying the dictionary filter for the class of feminine nouns:

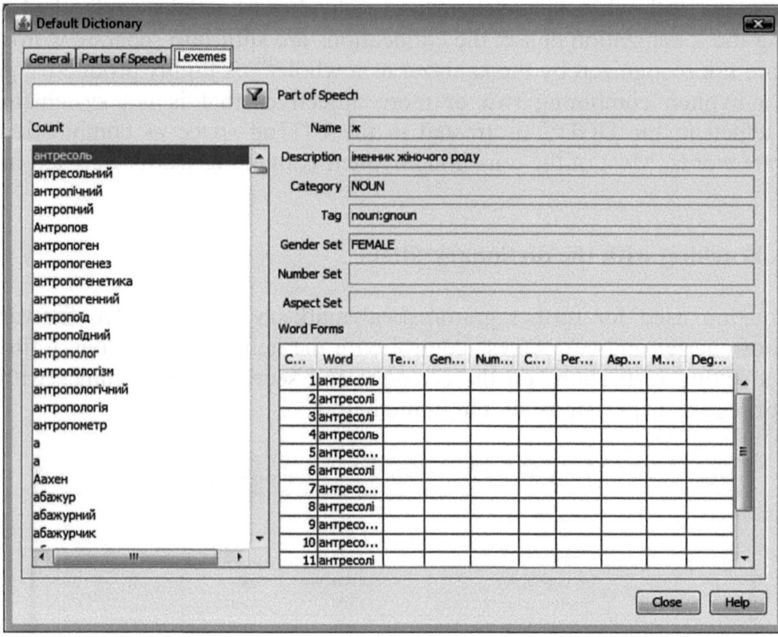

Figure 5. The content of the default grammatical dictionary

The window includes a search line for typing in a lemma or its part (regexp). The "count" parameter shows the quantity of results that meet the requirements of search and below is the list of those lemmas in alphabetical order.

On the right-hand side, the morphological features of the selected class are shown in corresponding fields. A lemma selected from list appears with its full paradigm in the right-hand bottom corner. All available grammatical values for each form are shown as well.

These features of UGTag are mainly useful for grammatical reference and the control of dictionary content.

5.4. Sentencing

Sentence splitting as part of structural text mark-up is done after grammatical annotation because it is rule-based and some of those rules require grammatical information. The implemented so far rules are partially based on Rudolf's work for Polish (Rudolf 2004)[12].

The rules are an interplay of heuristics that use popular abbreviations and words starting with a capital letter, whose meaning is also taken into account. More work on enhancing automated structural mark-up is planned in the nearest future.

5.5. Writing phase and writing format

At the moment we foresee two output tag formats for resulting XML files. The default format is based on the TaKIPI one (version 1.8) for Polish but extended for Ukrainian specific features, see (Kotsyba, Turska, Shypnivska 2008), slightly modified. It retains a maximum of grammatical information that can be provided by the Polish and Ukrainian grammatical dictionaries. The second available format is MULTEXT-East compatible. As well as in the case of file readers, users can define their own writers that produce output files with customized mark-up.

6. Working with texts

The choice of the intended tagset is suggested to the user immediately after loading the text file for analysis and can be changed during the process of work.

UGTag accepts raw texts or structured HTML or XML files. The structural information (division into paragraphs and sentences) can be retained or replaced by UGTag.

The user can watch the progress of tagging as it goes. Tagged tokens of different categories are displayed in a screen colour code[13]. For example, in the window below the colour red[14] marks unrecognized tokens, e.g. "№14", green marks words with only one available grammatical interpretation (this is important because these do not need disambiguation afterwards), blue shows words with multiple grammatical interpretations. They are additionally marked by italics in this case.

12 The implementation of the sentence-splitting algorithm was carried out by Oresta Tymchyshyn.

13 Colour coding can be changed by the user through the configuration menu.

14 The original figure is coloured.

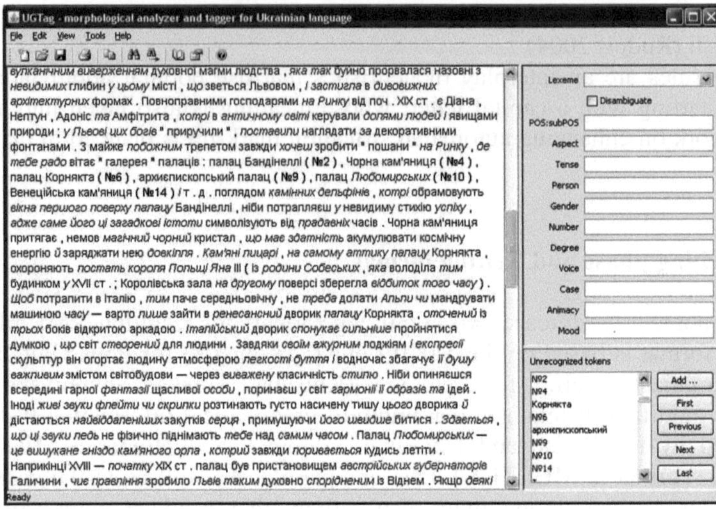

Figure 6. Text processing

The panel in the top right corner displays the grammatical characteristics of the selected item and the possibility of manual disambiguation is given for words with multiple available interpretations.

The bottom right corner displays a list of words that were not recognized by the active built-in dictionary. The user can select a word from this list and add it to the common bulk of words by clicking the "add" button which instantiates a further dialog.

6.1. Automatic disambiguation

Preliminary rules for automatic disambiguation based on statistical analysis were devised for a small but frequently used class of prepositions. For example, the word "do" can have 15 grammatical interpretations, only one of which is the preposition "do" and the rest are all possible interpretations of the invariable noun "do" (a musical note). The tagger chooses the prepositional interpretation at the moment as the most frequent one. Also, the lexeme "na" is most frequently used in the prepositional function, although the colloquial use of it as an interjection is possible as well. The further disambiguation policy foresees combination of rules and statistical analysis of manually disambiguated data as training samples for machine learning.

6.2. Ways of enriching the dictionary database

During annotation UGTag automatically creates a list of words that were not found in the dictionary, displays it to the user and allows adding them to one of custom dictionaries. Custom dictionaries can be used along with the default one or instead of it, enhancing the quality of annotation.

The lemma for a new word should be introduced manually (the selected input word form is prompted by default) and the part of speech should be selected from the drop-down list.

The program gives hints as to the paradigm of the word. A grammatical paradigm class identifier is assigned to the new word based on the answers provided by the user. The most probable grammatical paradigm for the selected part of speech is generated in a table below and the user is prompted to confirm it in case it is correct for the given word. Other declension paradigms can be accessed by navigating if the first one fails, or definition of the word forms can be done manually.

This feature is available through the GUI client and will be also available through a Web client.

Users can also create their own dictionaries by using the embedded dictionary editor.

Other ways of extending the lexical and grammatical database for tagging can be developed based on various heuristics, e.g. for derivational patterns, if this is justified experimentally.

7. Plans for further development

Extensive experimenting with real corpus texts will indicate the directions for further development of the program. One of our priorities is enriching the dictionary database using both manual and automatic ways as well as enhancing the quality of automatic disambiguation. We also plan to concentrate on word grouping for syntactic analysis, including first of all composite words like numerals: "dvadciat' try" (twenty three) currently recognized as separate words ("dvadciat'" and "try"), complex passive structures, prepositional phrases, etc.

References

Broda, B., Piasecki, M. and A. Radziszewski (2008). "Towards a Set of General Purpose Morphosyntactic Tools for Polish". *Proceedings of Intelligent Information Systems, Zakopane, Poland, 2008*. Institute of Computer Science – PAS.

Derzhanski, I. and N. Kotsyba (2008). "The category of predicatives in the light of the consistent morphosyntactic tagging of Slavic languages". *Lexicographic Tools and*

Techniques: Proceedings of the MONDILEX First Open Workshop. Moscow: IITP–RAS: 68–79.

Derzhanski, I. and N. Kotsyba (2009). *Towards a Consistent Morphological Tagset for Slavic Languages: Extending MULTEXT-East for Polish, Ukrainian and Belarusian.* Metalanguage and Encoding Scheme Design for Digital Lexicography: MONDILEX Third Open Workshop, Bratislava, 15–16 April 2009.

Kotsyba, N. (2009). *The Current State of Work on the Polish-Ukrainian Parallel Corpus (PolUKR).* Proceedings of the International Workshop within MONDILEX project "Problems of Slavic Lexicography" Kyiv, 2–4 February 2009.

Kotsyba, N., Radziszewski, A. and I. Derzhanski (2009). *Integrating the Polish language into the MULTEXT-East family: morphosyntactic specifications, converter, lexicon and corpus*. Proceedings of Research Infrastructure for Digital Lexicography: MONDILEX Fifth Open Workshop, October 14, 2009. Ljubljana, Slovenia.

Kotsyba, N., Turska, M. and O. Shypnivska (2008). *Linguistic principles of organizing a common morphological tagset for PolUKR (Polish-Ukrainian Parallel Corpus). Proceedings of the international conference* ."Intelligent Information Systems, 16–18 June 2008, Zakopane, Poland".

Rudolf, M. (2004). *Metody automatycznej analizy* korpusu *tekstów polskich*. Warszawa: Uniwersytet Warszawski – Wydział Polonistyki.

Shevchenko, I. V. (1996). "Algorytmična slovozminna klasyfikacija ukrajins'koji leksyky". *Movoznavstvo*. Vol. 4–5. Kyiv: 40–44.

Shevchenko, I.V., Shirokov, V.A., and A.G. Rabulets' (2005). „Elektronnyj grammatičeskij slovar' ukrainskogo jazyka". *Proceedings of the international conference „Megaling'2005. Prikladnaja lingvistika v poiske novyx putej", 27.VI–2.VII 2005*. Meganom, Crimea, Ukraine: 124–129.

Shevchenko, I. (2008). „Parametryzacija jak osnova hramatyčnoji identyfikaciji slovnykovyx odynyc' ukrajins'koji movy". *Prykladna lingwistyka ta lingvistyčni texnolohiji. Megaling-2007. Zbirnyk naukovyx prac'*. Kyiv: Dovira: 393–402.

Shirokov, V.A., Rabulets', O.H., Shevchenko, I.V., Kostyshyn, O.M., and K.M. Yakymenko, (2007). *Intehrovana leksykohrafična systema „Slovnyky Ukrajiny"*, version 3.1. Kyiv. CD-edition.

Database Framework for a Distributed Spoken Data Collection Project

Michal Křen and Martina Waclawičová

Abstract: The paper describes the main features of database system *Mluvka* (chatterbox) that is used in the Czech National Corpus for collecting recordings and transcriptions of authentic spoken Czech used in informal situations. To record maximum possible variety of speakers, the material is collected in the whole country through a network of local collaborators. The system is a central data storage that reflects distributed character of the project and facilitates its organisation in various ways. In particular, it ensures formal conformance of all the submissions, it supports several levels of read/write access rights based on the collection areas and it enables continuous balancing of the collected material. *Mluvka* is a well-attested system lying behind both recently published corpora of authentic spoken Czech, ORAL2006 and ORAL2008. Their total size is 2 650 000 tokens including punctuation, ORAL2008 is balanced in selected sociolinguistic categories of speakers.

Keywords: corpus design, Czech language, data collection, informal spoken Czech, language resources, regional coverage, representativeness, sociolinguistics, spoken corpora, transcription.

1. Introduction

One of the aims of the Institute of the Czech National Corpus (ICNC) is mapping of authentic spoken language used in informal situations. Attention paid to spoken language has increased in the last decades, as well as its importance for linguistic research and natural language processing in general. It is widely accepted that character of spoken language differs substantially from its written counterpart and this fact increases awareness of many-sidedness of language variation. This is even more distinctive for Czech because of its specific language situation that is sometimes described as close to diglossia: apart from common differences present in every language, there are also differences between spoken Czech and its written standard that include case endings, vowel changes etc. Moreover, there are also regional differences, especially in Moravia, although their influence disappears gradually. While the written standard is fully described in many books and dictionaries and it is covered by large written corpora as well, spoken language is underrepresented and often neglected in many respects (Čermák and Sgall 1997). Divergence of spoken language from the written standard is most remarkable in case of language spoken in informal situations. In order to facilitate its scholarly studies, it is first necessary to overcome the scarcity of resources that are very labour-intensive and thus expensive to build.

2. Overview of the project

The main aim of the project is to collect material that would represent authentic spoken language. This is done by recording maximum possible variety of speakers from various regions in various everyday situations. For practical reasons, such a broad coverage calls for transcription and annotation system that is not only well-grounded linguistically, but also easy to learn for individual transcribers and comprehensible for corpus users (Waclawičová 2007). In other words, it is important to realise the trade-off between required amount of collected material on one side and depth of the annotation on the other. Similarly, it is often not possible to avoid noisy environment that sometimes accompanies authentic language (e.g. conversations in a car or in a pub) and that conflicts with quality of the recording. Therefore, it should be noted beforehand that the collected material is aimed neither at building multi-modal corpora with several levels of detailed annotation, nor at producing high-quality studio recordings for speech recognition. Rather, the material is primarily intended to facilitate studies of morphology, syntax, lexicon and syntagmatics of spoken language in contrast with written language. Therefore, there is only one transcription layer that is manually transcribed and aligned with the recording using Transcriber (Geoffrois *et al.* 2000). Quality of the transcription is verified on several levels it passes through the database system for final approval (cf. below).

In relation to the needs of corpus compiling, sociolinguistic factors that influence character of spoken language can be divided into two groups. Factors of the first group should be observed to ensure authenticity of spoken language and thus constitute suitable selection criteria. The key factor is informality of situation, the other factors are closely related and include private environment, physical presence of speakers that know each other, dialogical character, unscripted speech with topic not given in advance. This means that neither radio broadcasts nor TV political debates are collected because they can hardly be considered suitable for this purpose. Factors of the second group influence character of spoken language on a more detailed scale. These include mainly gender, age, education, occupation, particular type of the recorded situation, as well as various regional factors. In order to create representation of authentic spoken language, these factors should be used as balancing criteria. In practice, the collected data are balanced only according to the factors considered the most important, i.e. gender, age group, education and region of childhood residence (all the regional information used in the project follows the traditional dialectological division described in Bělič 1972 or Balhar *et al.* 1992–2005).

The spoken data collection project coordinated by the ICNC started in 2002 in very modest conditions. It has grown significantly since then, nowadays a network of local collaborators is established and the amount of collected data has been steadily increasing. The material is collected in the whole of Czech Republic in cooperation with universities from Brno, České Budějovice, Hradec Králové, Plzeň, Praha and Ústí nad Labem. ICNC is the main coordinator responsible for project organisation, administration and funding, as well as central data storage, standardisation and overall quality assurance. ICNC also provides local collaborators with computer and other support including updating and dissemination of manuals, holding tutorials, customizing program tools etc. Local coordinators choose, train and administer their collaborators (mostly students) that make the recordings and transcriptions and are responsible for quality of data from their collection area. The distributed character of the project is supported by database system *Mluvka* (chatterbox). The next chapter describes in detail its main features with emphasis on its connection with project organisation in general.

3. Database architecture

Database system *Mluvka* has been used since 2004 for storing all the information about the recording, situation and participating speakers. It has undergone substantial changes and innovations since then (major enhancements in 2007) in order to facilitate organisation of the widening project and to ensure data standardisation at the same time. Technically, *Mluvka* is a set of PHP forms and additional Perl scripts above MySQL database accessible via https protocol. It was developed at the ICNC mainly by Radek Pavlis and Michal Štourač. The current version of the system is more than a simple database, it supports also upload/download of the recordings and their transcriptions that are immediately checked for formal errors, several levels of read/write user access rights, automatic payment calculation, continuous balancing of the material or semi-automatic detection of duplicate speakers. Since all the submissions are made through the database, this ensures specified format of the sound files and the transcription files' formal conformance with the transcription rules.

For the sake of completeness, the basic functions should be mentioned first, as well as the information stored in the database. The PHP forms enable users to create, view, edit and delete individual database records provided they have sufficient rights to do so. When creating or editing a record, it is automatically checked for completeness and consistency of the input data, selected values being generated automatically. Incomplete or incorrect records can be stored, but cannot be passed on for further processing. Naturally, the database can be also easily searched with two possible types of the results that match the input parameters: list of recordings or list of speakers. The input parameters can be arbitrarily combined and the results sorted in various ways.

Every recording is automatically assigned unique identifier in a YYANNNF format where YY denotes year of the recording, A denotes the collection area (proprietary code of the university responsible for the recording, e.g. H is Hradec Králové), NNN is number of the recording within given year and collection area, F denotes formality or non-formality of the recording (obsolete, as only N for non-formal is applicable now). For instance, 07A157N is a non-formal recording recorded in 2007, coordinated directly by the ICNC (letter A) and it is the 157-th such recording in the given year.

The information about the recording stored in the database includes:

- current status of the recording
- name of the corpus the recording has been incorporated into (if applicable, e.g. ORAL2008)
- creation and last modification time of the database record
- name of the person who made the recording and the transcription
- length of the recording
- total number of words and characters in the transcription (counted automatically)
- number of participating speakers
- year and month of the recording
- region and exact place of the recording
- several fields describing the situation in detail
- amount paid for the transcription (counted automatically)

Every speaker is automatically assigned unique identifier that is based on the recording they participate in. It is in a YYANNNFSS format where YYANNNF is the recording ID and SS denotes speaker number within the recording. Speaker number 00 is reserved for the person who made the recording and who was thus aware of it. If the recording person does not take part in the dialogue, the speakers are numbered from 01 onwards. For instance, five speakers with IDs from 07A157N00 to 07A157N04 participate in the recording 07A157N, which means that it was speaker 07A157N00 who has recorded 07A157N.

The information about the speaker stored in the database contains no personal data. It consists of:

- gender
- age

- education
- socio-code; automatically-assigned string of three letters, binary simplifications of the three above mentioned categories: gender, age group (younger/older) and education type (lower/higher). It is a conventional shorthand used mainly for corpus balancing purposes, e.g. MVA is decoded as M – man, V – older (35 and more), A – university education.
- place of birth
- region of birth
- region of childhood residence
- region of current residence
- occupation according to the Czech Statistical Office categorisation
- number of words uttered in the recording (counted automatically).

4. User administration and data flow

Because of the distributed character of the project, user administration issues gain great importance, especially with the possibility to download all the recordings and transcriptions one can access. Every user is assigned to exactly one collection area that corresponds to one university code, i.e. the third letter of the recording ID. With respect to this, there are three levels of read permissions every user has to be assigned to: reading restricted only to the records the users have created themselves, reading restricted to given collection area and unrestricted reading. Similarly, there are corresponding write permissions, further supplemented by another two (rarely used) options: no write permission at all (that allows to create guest accounts) and permission to alter not only all the records, but also some of the interface items. This is reserved only for central administrator and it enables them to customise the interface easily and without programmer's intervention, for instance to add a new collection area or a listbox value that describes situation of the recording.

However, in practice there are basically three widely used combinations of read/write access rights that correspond to the typical data flow in the project. The aim is to implement the delegated responsibilities principle and to restrict access of every user so that they have authorisation to view/modify only the data they have to deal with. The three typical hierarchically-ordered users are:

- *editors* who mostly record and input the data with access restricted only to their own records,
- *local coordinators* who verify the data submitted by the editor and are generally responsible for the whole collection area; they have

unlimited access within the given collection area including also administration of the editors,
- *central administrators* with unlimited access who make final revision, approve the data and eventually authorise the payment.

The data flow typically from the editor to the central administrator. This is reflected by changes of the status of the recording that is indicated in colour to make it easily identifiable. For passing the recording to higher level, all the data including the transcription and the sound file must be complete and formally correct. In case of any imperfections found at any point during the verification process, the data can be either corrected or returned for correction back to lower level and this can be repeated any number of times if necessary.

5. Advanced features

So far, only the database proper and the PHP forms have been discussed. However, the information provided by the stand-alone Perl scripts adds very useful functionality to the whole system. Among them, online checking of the recording and the transcription for formal conformance are of primary importance. Because non-conforming files cannot be even uploaded, individual editors are not able to complete the record and thus to pass it on to their coordinators for further verification. In case of the recordings, formal conformance means simply adhering to the required format of the sound file that is uncompressed 16-bit PCM WAV, mono, 16 kHz. On the contrary, formal conformance of the transcriptions goes far beyond simply checking if the transcription file is XML and its parsing with the Transcriber DTD. It includes basically every automatically-checkable feature laid out in the transcription manual. For instance, speakers defined and used in the transcription must match those defined in the database, only allowed characters can be used in the transcriptions (not e.g. comma, colon, semicolon etc.), pause marks cannot be used in immediate succession, interrupted utterance marks cannot be used in the middle of the utterance etc. More sophisticated features include proper placement of anonymisation abbreviations (this is essential to enable later automatic anonymisation of the recordings), using conventional strings for non-verbal agreement, disagreement or hesitation, proper transcription of some problematic word forms (e.g. "by sme" should be always transcribed as "bysme") etc.

As already mentioned above, *Mluvka* registers also counts of words uttered by individual speakers in every transcription file. This information is important not only to determine the size of the transcription in words (the script counts only words proper, not e.g. punctuation), but also to calculate the payment automatically. The formula takes into account also length of the recording apart from the number of words to account for the administration overhead. Furthermore, the number of words uttered by individual speakers is also linked with their sociolinguistic categories and displayed in a summary form for every transcription and also for every search result. This is an easy and efficient way to provide this information for any user-selected subset of the recordings that consequently enables the central administrator as well as local coordinators to continually balance the data composition.

For instance, the following snapshot shows bottom of the page that resulted from simple search for all recordings with IDs beginning with string "09A" (as of March 26, 2009), i.e. those recorded in 2009 and coordinated directly by the ICNC (letter A). The upper part shows the recordings and their main characteristics in a table, the rows are displayed in colour that reflects current status of the individual recordings. The lower part shows overall statistics for the given sample, i.e. that 42 recordings were found and that the total number of words proper uttered in all these recordings is 119 950. Further down, distribution of this total sum across selected sociolinguistic categories is shown. These consist of the socio-code mentioned in Chapter 3, age of the speakers and region of their childhood residence. The coordinator can thus learn immediately that the sample collected in the first quarter of 2009 is satisfactorily balanced in terms of the binary socio-code values: 63 038 words uttered by men (M) and 56 912 by women (Z), 60 002 words uttered by younger speakers (I) and 59 948 by older speakers (V), 61 951 words uttered by speakers with higher education (A) and 57 999 by speakers with lower education (B). The age decades (*věk*) inform the coordinator about prevalence of speakers in their thirties (37 740) and fifties (32 862). Similarly, the region (*pobyt*) category shows prevalence of speakers who spent their childhood in Central Bohemia (*středočeská* with 29 274 words), but this is natural as the ICNC as a direct coordinator concentrates on this region and the imbalance will be compensated by recordings coordinated by other universities.

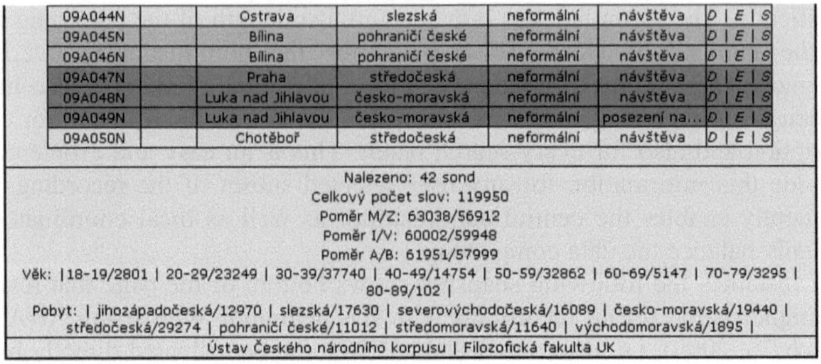

09A044N		Ostrava	slezská	neformální	návštěva	D | E | S
09A045N		Bílina	pohraničí české	neformální	návštěva	D | E | S
09A046N		Bílina	pohraničí české	neformální	návštěva	D | E | S
09A047N		Praha	středočeská	neformální	návštěva	D | E | S
09A048N		Luka nad Jihlavou	česko-moravská	neformální	návštěva	D | E | S
09A049N		Luka nad Jihlavou	česko-moravská	neformální	posezení na...	D | E | S
09A050N		Chotěboř	středočeská	neformální	návštěva	D | E | S

Nalezeno: 42 sond
Celkový počet slov: 119950
Poměr M/Z: 63038/56912
Poměr I/V: 60002/59948
Poměr A/B: 61951/57999
Věk: |18-19/2801 | 20-29/23249 | 30-39/37740 | 40-49/14754 | 50-59/32862 | 60-69/5147 | 70-79/3295 | 80-89/102 |
Pobyt: | jihozápadočeská/12970 | slezská/17630 | severovýchodočeská/16089 | česko-moravská/19440 | středočeská/29274 | pohraničí české/11012 | středomoravská/11640 | východomoravská/1895 |
Ústav Českého národního korpusu | Filozofická fakulta UK

Figure 1. Bottom of the search result page for the "09A" query

Last but not least, the word counts are used as an initial point for semi-automatic detection of duplicate speakers. Since the speaker IDs are unique and no personal information is collected, the database would lack information whether e.g. speakers 08M024N01 and 09M002N01 are the same person or not. Obviously, this may not be possible in case of substantial differences in sociolinguistic data, but even if all the data including e.g. exact age, education and place of birth are the same, the IDs can represent different person. Therefore, a script is run every week that monitors the database growth together with any changes made to the existing data and reports by e-mail any new duplicate speaker candidates. The candidates are then manually verified (listening to the recording is often necessary) and all the duplicate speakers are marked in the database explicitly. This information is used mainly for limitation of the total number of words each individual person utters in the collected material in order to observe variety of recorded speakers.

6. Spoken corpora ORAL2006 and ORAL2008

Mluvka is a well-attested system lying behind both ORAL2006 and ORAL2008, spoken corpora published in 2006 and 2008 respectively. They consist entirely of transcriptions of authentic spoken Czech used in informal situations recorded from 2002 onwards that regionally cover the whole of Bohemia (i.e. not Moravia). The corpora were compiled from the same repository of recordings collected at the ICNC and served by *Mluvka*, and therefore they share a number of features including also the transcription rules and overall annotation scheme. Although both corpora are fully compatible, none of the transcriptions was re-used and they have thus no intersection. Since each of them is sized 1 million words proper (i.e. more than 1.3 million tokens including punctuation), the overall size of the published material is 2 million words.

Composition of both corpora in terms of the selected sociolinguistic categories of speakers can be found in the following tables. Although it was attempted to compile a balanced corpus, ORAL2006 shows prevalence of women, younger speakers and speakers with higher education because there was not enough material at that time. On the other hand, ORAL2008 is fully balanced in the selected sociolinguistic categories of speakers (gender, age group, education and region of childhood residence). Reasons for their selection as well as applied automatic balancing procedure are described in Waclawičová and Křen (2008).

Table 1. Composition of ORAL2006 (words proper)

gender	men 303 783		women 697 015	
age group	younger (18–34) 576 448		older (35 and more) 424 350	
education	lower (elementary / intermediate) 404 554		higher (university) 596 244	
region of childhood residence	central Bohemia 438 129	northeast Bohemia 341 220	southwest Bohemia 109 774	Czech borderland 102 021

Table 2. Composition of ORAL2008 (words proper)

gender	men 499 619		women 500 478	
age group	younger (18–34) 500 199		older (35 and more) 499 898	
education	lower (elementary / intermediate) 499 425		higher (university) 500 672	
region of childhood residence	central Bohemia 247 630	northeast Bohemia 242 199	southwest Bohemia 237 417	Czech borderland 239 511

7. Conclusion and future plans

Experience shows that elaborate database system is essential for coordination of such a large-scale project. The most valuable features include especially delegating responsibilities while retaining control over the entire data collection and enforcing required format of the recording and the transcription. The database obviously cannot be expected to do the whole job and despite its valuable help, the large number of collaborators (currently 170 editors) remains a real challenge. Similarly, manual verification of the transcriptions by trained professionals can hardly be avoided. However, thanks to the guaranteed formal conformance to the transcription rules they can concentrate on more advanced issues with positive impact on the final quality of the transcriptions as well as on larger amount of collected data.

Lemmatisation and morphological tagging will be added to both ORAL corpora in the near future. Unfortunately, it is not possible to use unmodified versions of tools available for processing written language because of their poor coverage of the variation of spoken word forms and different character of spoken language in general. After this will be at least partly resolved, a super-corpus ORAL will be made publicly available. Unlike the individual ORAL-series corpora that are invariable entities once published, ORAL will become their regularly updated unification into one super-corpus with the original corpora processed with state-of-the-art versions of available tools. This will allow for future enhancements of all kinds including lemmatisation and morphological tagging. It will be also easily possible to make subcorpora of ORAL that would correspond to the original ORAL-series corpora.

The amount of collected material is steadily growing for a new corpus of authentic spoken Czech that will join ORAL2006 and ORAL2008 in the future. Although its publication date is still too far to predict even the year, two improvements as compared to ORAL2008 can perhaps be announced. First, it will be hopefully possible to compile a balanced corpus covering not only Bohemia, but also Moravia, so that the whole of Czech Republic could finally be covered. Second, the transcriptions will be manually aligned with the recordings and this alignment will be supported by the search engine to enable users to hear actual realisation of every corpus token.

Acknowledgement

This research has been supported by MSM0021620823 grant.

References

Balhar, J. *et al.* (1992–2005). *Český jazykový atlas 1–5*. Praha: Academia.

Bělič, J. (1972). *Nástin české dialektologie*. Praha: SPN.

Čermák, F. and P. Sgall (1997). "Výzkum mluvené češtiny: jeho situace a potřeby". *Slovo a slovesnost*. Vol. 58, no. 1: 15–25.

Geoffrois, E., Barras, C., Bird, S. and Z. Wu (2000). "Transcribing with Annotation Graphs". *Proceedings from The Second International Conference on Language Resources and Evaluation (LREC)*. Athens: 1517–1521.

ORAL2006 [on-line]. Praha: Ústav Českého národního korpusu.
Available at: http://ucnk.ff.cuni.cz.

ORAL2008 [on-line]. Praha: Ústav Českého národního korpusu.
Available at: http://ucnk.ff.cuni.cz.

Waclawičová, M. (2007). "Spoken Corpus ORAL2006, Information It Provides and General Characteristics of Spoken Text". In: J. Levická and R. Garabík (eds.). *Computer Treatment of Slavic and East European Languages*. Bratislava: Tribun: 283–289.

Waclawičová, M. and M. Křen (2008). "ORAL2008: New Balanced Corpus of Spoken Czech". *Труды международной конференции "Корпусная лингвистика – 2008"*. Санкт-Петербург: Издательство СПбГУ: 105–112.

Manual Annotation of the National Corpus of Polish with Anotatornia

Adam Przepiórkowski and Grzegorz Murzynowski

Abstract: The aim of this paper is to present the procedure of the manual annotation of a 1-million-word subcorpus of the National Corpus of Polish, using a purpose-built tool, Anotatornia. The annotation is carried out at four levels: word-level segmentation, sentence level segmentation, morphosyntax and word sense disambiguation. Some emphasis is put on the quality control of the resulting annotation: each information is introduced by two annotators, and the system implements a sophisticated procedure of resolving annotation conflicts.

Keywords: manual corpus annotation tool, segmentation, morphosyntactic annotation, word sense disambiguation, annotation quality control, National Corpus of Polish.

1. Introduction

Within the National Corpus of Polish[1] (henceforth, NKJP, as in Pol. *Narodowy Korpus Języka Polskiego*; http://nkjp.pl/; Przepiórkowski et al. 2008, 2009), one of the subtasks concerns the manual annotation of a 1-million well-balanced subcorpus of NKJP at various linguistic levels.

The main tool used for this task is Anotatornia, whose early version (Hajnicz et al. 2008) was used in a project concerned with the automatic acquisition of argument structures. Since then, Anotatornia has been extended to new linguistic levels and otherwise adapted to the needs of NKJP, as described below.

The aim of this paper is to describe the process of the manual annotation of NKJP with Anotatornia. § 2 presents the preliminaries, § 3 discusses the levels of linguistic annotation, and § 4 describes the management of annotation conflicts within the system. § 5 concludes the paper.

2. Preliminaries

Each NKJP text contains three general types of annotation: metadata (mainly bibliographical information), structural markup (divisions within texts, e.g., into

---

1 Research funded in 2007–2010 by a research and development grant from the Polish Ministry of Science and Higher Education.

chapters and paragraphs) and linguistic annotation. The following levels of linguistic annotation are distinguished in the project: 1) segmentation into fine grained word-level tokens, 2) segmentation into sentences, 3) morphosyntactic analysis, 4) coarse-grained syntactic words (e.g., analytical forms, construction involving bound words, etc.), 5) named entities, 6) syntactic groups, 7) word senses (for a limited number of ambiguous lexemes).

The first three levels are crucial, as any further linguistic annotation will build on segmentation and morphosyntactic markup. For this reason, any information introduced at these levels must be double-checked. The best practice in such cases is the "2+1" annotation model, where two annotators introduce relevant information independently, and any conflicts are resolved by a referee (or a "superannotator").

Manual annotation is perhaps the most costly task in the development of a corpus, so a tool facilitating this task is needed. It should be ergonomic, it should facilitate work over the Internet, preferably with the use of any browser, and it should handle various linguistic levels. Moreover, it should implement the "2+1" annotation model and have built-in conflict management procedures. No off-the-shelf tool satisfying all project requirements was found at the start of the NKJP project, so it was decided to adapt Anotatornia, a tool whose prototype (Hajnicz et al. 2008) had been developed in an earlier project carried out at the Institute of Computer Science, Polish Academy of Sciences (ICS PAS; the coordinator of NKJP).

The first task of the system is to assign appropriate paragraphs to annotators. This must be done in such a way that each paragraph is annotated by two different linguists. In fact, an annotator at one time fetches a 10-paragraph batch, where 5 of the paragraphs are assigned to another annotator, and another 5 – to a third annotator. The procedure is implemented in such a way, as to avoid "co-learning" of annotation errors; rather, annotators are forced to work with each other in different configurations (virtually all possible), thus increasing the overall consistency of the annotation.

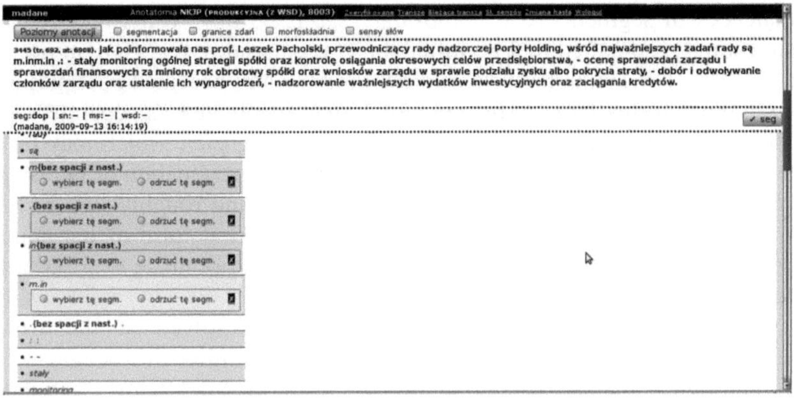

Figure 1. Word-Level Segmentation, annotator's view

3. Levels of Annotation

Anotatornia handles both segmentation levels, the morphosyntactic level, as well as word sense disambiguation. Work at all these levels is currently, in September 2009, well under way in NKJP. For the annotation of syntactic words, named entities and syntactic groups, a tool will be selected from a number of general syntactic annotation tools available.[2]

The following subsections describe the four annotation tasks and their implementation in Anotatornia, in the order in which the tasks are performed by annotators.

3.1. Word-Level Segmentation

By default, word-level segments (henceforth, simply *segments*) are maximal strings of non-delimiter characters, where delimiter characters are white space characters and punctuation. That is, segments are normally "space-to-space" orthographic words, with typical punctuation characters treated as separate segments. Consequently, to a large extent word-level segmentation can be performed automatically.

One exception concerns the hyphen: sometimes words containing a hyphen are best treated as single segments (e.g., *Mercedes-Benz*), and at other times – as

2 Originally, the intention was to implement all annotation levels in Anotatornia, but the complexity of the task and the costs of the system development turned out to be prohibitive.

sequences of segments (e.g., *biało-niebiesko-czerwony* 'white-blue-red'). More interestingly, so-called mobile inflections (agglutinates; e.g., *śmy* in *przyszliśmy* 'came-1PL'), the subjunctive particle *by* and the non-accented post-prepositional pronominal forms (e.g., *ń* in *nań* 'for him') are treated as separate segments. This may lead to segmentation ambiguities, as in *gdzieś*, which may be treated as a single adverb meaning 'somewhere' or as a concatenation of two segments: *gdzie* 'where' and *ś* '2SG', with the overall meaning roughly 'where have/did you. . . ?'. Similarly, *długom* is either a dative plural form of the noun DŁUG 'debt', or the adverbial form *długo* 'long' with the agglutinate *m* '1SG' attached; etc.

Such segmentation ambiguities should be resolved at the word-level segmentation. In some cases, segmentation ambiguities are recognised by the morphological analyser used to preprocess texts (cf. § 3.3 below), and the action to be performed by annotators boils down to the selection of an appropriate segmentation variant. Annotators may also propose to split one segment into multiple segments or to join multiple segments into one segment. This is a sensitive operation, as it amounts to postulating the existence of words which, at the same time, are unknown to the morphological analyser and do not follow the default segmentation rules, so it must always be confirmed by a referee (cf. § 4).

3.2. Sentence-Level Segmentation

Text preprocessing does not involve any sentence-level segmentation, as automatic tools may make mistakes where the full stop apparently ending a sentencje is possibly a part of an abbreviation, as in the fragment na ul. *Stefana*, which may be a part of *Mieszkał na ul. Stefana Batorego*. 'He lived at the Stefana Batorego street', where *ul.* stands for *ulicy* 'street', or a part *of Zbierał na ul. Stefana to jednak nie obchodziło*. 'He collected (money) for a beehive. But Stefan didn't care.', where *ul* means 'a beehive'.

Even though such cases are rare, there are also texts in NKJP which do not follow standard punctuation (transcripts of speech being the extreme case), and on the other hand the task of sentence-level segmentation is inexpensive compared to other annotation tasks, so it is performed fully manually in the project. Technically, a paragraph is presented to an annotator in such a way that each segment is a separate box, and clicking on a given box declares the segment as the last segment in a sentence.

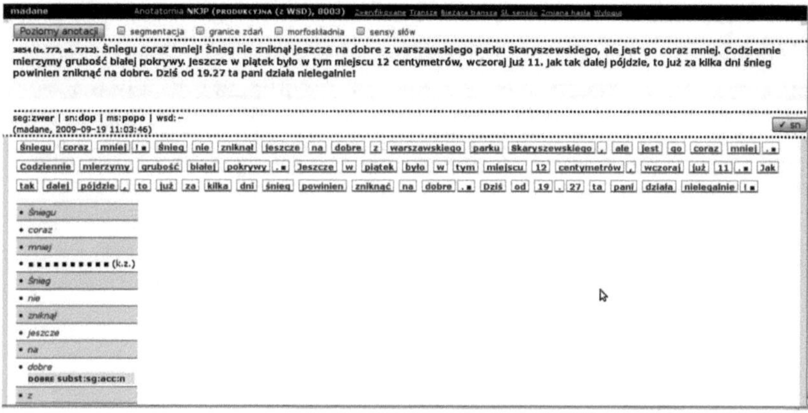

Figure 2. Morphosyntactic annotation, annotator's view. A discrepancy is marked in yellow (shown here as a shade of grey over "DOBRE subst:sg:acc:n").

3.3. Morphosyntactic Annotation

As mentioned above, texts are preprocessed by a so-called morphological analyser (in fact, little more than an appropriately compressed morphological dictionary), Morfeusz (Woliński 2006). This tool tokenises texts into word-level segments and assigns morphosyntactic interpretations to each segment. Morfeusz does not attempt to disambiguate these interpretations according to context; instead, it marks segments with all interpretations present in its dictionary. The dictionary of the version of the tool used in NKJP, Morfeusz SGJP, is essentially that of Saloni et al. 2007, with subsequent improvements, and the interpretations follow the NKJP Tagset (Przepiórkowski 2009a), a conservative modification of the IPI PAN Tagset (Przepiórkowski & Woliński 2003a,b).

The basic task of annotators is to select the appropriate morphosyntactic interpretation from among those known to Morfeusz. Technically, such interpretations are presented in a column, as radioboxes, and morphosyntactic disambiguation boils down to scrolling the page down and clicking appropriate boxes.

It may happen that the morphological analyser does not know a word or does not contain information about some of its interpretations. Anotatornia makes it possible to add a new interpretation to a segment. On the basis of the formal specification of the NKJP Tagset, Anotatornia suggests completions as the annotator types in a new interpretation, thus facilitating and speeding up the process.

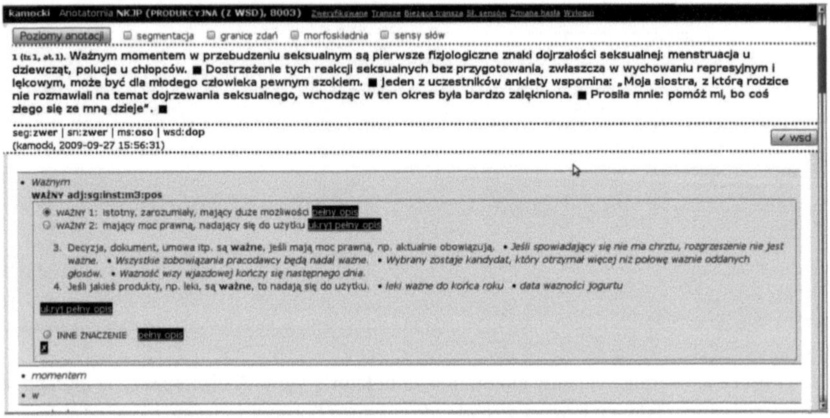

Figure 3. Word Sense Disambiguation, annotator's view, brief description of meaning 1 and full description of meaning 2 are displayed

3.4. Word Sense Disambiguation

In NKJP, word sense disambiguation (WSD) is performed only for a little over 100 lexemes, selected from the most frequent clearly ambiguous (strictly homographic, rather than simply polysemous) Polish lexemes.

If a form of one of these ambiguous lexemes is (automatically) detected in a paragraph, this paragraph is marked as due to be annotated at the WSD level. The presentation of the WSD task is fully analogous to that of morphosyntactic annotation: senses are presented in a column, next to vertically aligned radioboxes, so again annotation boils down to scrolling and clicking.

More specifically, brief (usually, 3–7 words) definitions differentiating senses of a lexeme are presented next to radioboxes, with a button next to each such brief definition for displaying the full dictionary definition of the sense, together with examples. This way annotators may work efficiently relying on the brief definitions, but they may also easily access full definitions in more problematic cases.

Although definitions are based on a relatively comprehensive Polish dictionary (Bańko 2000), situations have arisen where a word is used in a sense not included in the dictionary. For this reason, there is an additional "sense" for each lexeme, for out-of-dictionary uses. However, annotators are asked to make a very sparing use of this artificial "sense".

WSD is dependent on the morphosyntactic level in a subtle way. The word-sense dictionary contains verbal, nominal and adjectival lexemes. There are cases where a given word form is morphosyntactically ambiguous between different grammatical classes, and it should be semantically disambiguated only if it is judged to belong to one grammatical class, but not when it belongs to the other. For example, the form *spraw* may be analysed as a form of the ambiguous noun SPRAWA 'matter, case; trial, hearing', or as a form of the verb SPRAWIĆ 'cause, make'. Only the former lexeme is present in the dictionary of ambiguous lexemes, so the form should be subjected to sense disambiguation only if it was assigned a nominal interpretation at the morphosyntactic level. Anotatornia fully implements this feature.

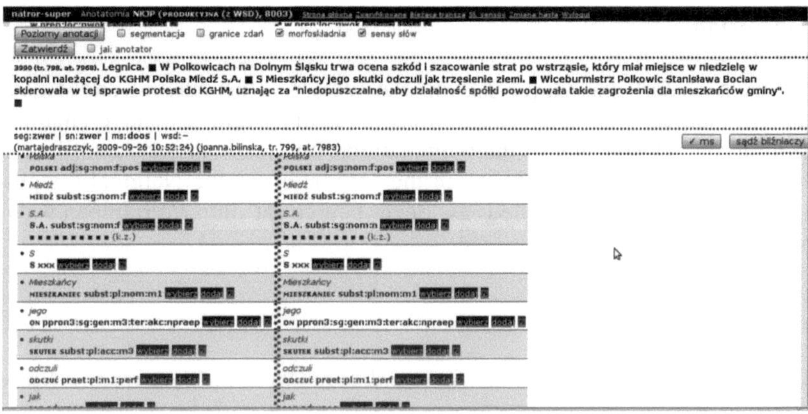

Figure 4. Morphosyntactic annotation, referee's view. A discrepancy is marked in yellow

4. Annotation Management

NKJP sets a careful procedure for controlling the quality of annotation. The two annotators working on the same paragraph do not know each other's identity, and any questions regarding the annotation should be asked on a mailing list to which all annotators subscribe. This way the results of a discussion are known to all annotators, whether or not the discussion gives rise to a modification of annotation guidelines. Even when the two annotators can guess each other's identity, e.g., as a result of such a mailing list discussion, they are forbidden to communicate in private.

Any discrepancy in the annotation of two linguists is registered by Anotatornia. In such a case, the annotators are informed about the fact and place of the disagreement, but not about the other linguist's decision. This way, rather than perhaps blindly accepting the annotation of the other linguist, both annotators are forced to think again about the annotation adduced earlier, and either explicitly confirm it or change it.

In many cases such differences result from simple inattention and are easy to correct. However, when – after the step described in the previous paragraph – a discrepancy still exists, the paragraph is presented to a referee, who makes the final decision. Annotators have read-only access to previously annotated paragraphs, and they can see the results of this refereeing process. Moreover, if the disagreement reflected a genuine weakness of the annotation guidelines, and if a general and precise solution may be formulated, it is added to the guidelines.

5. Conclusion

Anotatornia is perhaps unique among the tools for the manual annotation of corpora in that it implements careful procedures of assigning texts to annotators, controlling the consistency of their annotations, and resolving any conflicts. It is currently employed and fine-tuned in the annotation of the National Corpus of Polish. The code is published as open source at http://nlp.ipipan.waw.pl/ Anotatornia/.

References

Bańko, M. (Ed.) (2000). *Inny słownik języka polskiego*. Warsaw: Wydawnictwo Naukowe PWN.

Hajnicz, E., Murzynowski, G. and M. Woliński (2008). 'ANOTATORNIA – lingwistyczna baza danych'. In: *Materiały V konferencji naukowej InfoBazy 2008, systemy * aplikacje * usługi*. Gdańsk: Centrum Informatyczne TASK, Politechnika Gdańska, 168–173.

Przepiórkowski, A. (2009a). 'A comparison of two morphosyntactic tagsets of Polish'. In: Koseska-Toszewa, V., Dimitrova, L. and R. Roszko (Eds.), *Representing semantics in digital lexicography: Proceedings of MONDILEX fourth open workshop*. Warsaw, 138–144.

Przepiórkowski, A. (2009b). 'Zasady znakowania morfosyntaktycznego w NKJP'. Unpublished manuscript, ICS PAS. Version 1.23 of 27 September 2009.

Przepiórkowski, A., Górski, R. L., Lewandowska-Tomaszczyk, B. and M. Łaziński (2008). 'Towards the National Corpus of Polish'. In: *Proceedings of the sixth international Conference on Language Resources and Evaluation, LREC 2008*. Marrakech.

Przepiórkowski, A., Górski, R. L., Łaziński, M. and P. Pęzik (2009). 'Recent development in the National Corpus of Polish'. In: Levická, J. and R. Garabík (Eds.), *NLP, Corpus linguistics, corpus based grammar research: Proceedings of the fifth international conference, Smolenice, Slovakia, 25–27 November 2009*. Brno: Tribun, 302–309.

Przepiórkowski, A. and M.Wolińnski (2003a). 'A flexemic tagset for Polish'. In: *Proceedings of Morphological processing of Slavic languages, EACL 2003*. Budapest, 33–40.

Przepiórkowski, A. and M.Wolińnski (2003b). 'The unbearable lightness of tagging: A case study in morphosyntactic tagging of Polish'. In: *Proceedings of the 4th international workshop on linguistically interpreted corpora (LINC-03), EACL 2003*, 109–116.

Saloni, Z., Gruszczyński, W., Woliński, M. and R. Wołosz (2007). *Słownik gramatyczny języka polskiego*. Warsaw: Wiedza Powszechna.

Woliński, M. (2006). 'Morfeusz – a practical tool for the morphological analysis of Polish'. In: Kłopotek, M. A., Wierzchoń, S. T. and K. Trojanowski (Eds.), *Intelligent information processing and web mining*. Berlin: Springer-Verlag, 511–520.

On the Evaluation of Two Polish Taggers

Danuta Karwańska and Adam Przepiórkowski

Abstract: The aim of this paper is to discuss different ways in which the performance of morphosyntactic taggers may be compared and to present the results of the comparison of two such Polish taggers. This comparison sets the stage for measuring the performance of future taggers of Polish, including the tagger being developed within the National Corpus of Polish.

Keywords: POS tagger, Polish, morphosyntactic disambiguation, TaKIPI, evaluation, IPI PAN Tagset, National Corpus of Polish.

1. Introduction

The general issue addressed in this paper[1] is how to compare the performance of two different morphosyntactic taggers for a given language. Obviously, the problem has been addressed before, but usually in the setting in which both taggers employ exactly the same tagset, both produce exactly one tag for each token, and also the gold standard contains exactly one tag for each token. As we will see below, all these assumptions are violated to some degree in the current setting.

In cases when these three assumptions hold the standard procedure is as follows:

- the same gold standard corpus is used to evaluate both taggers;
- in the procedure known as 10-fold cross-evaluation, the gold standard is randomly split into 10 portions of the same size, and for each such portion, the tagger is trained on the remaining nine and evaluated on that portion;
- the measure known as accuracy (and its dual, error) is used for the evaluation within each of the ten experiments;
- the final numerical evaluation of the tagger is the average of the ten evaluation results;
- the tagger with significantly higher accuracy is considered better.

---

1 This article is largely based on the unpublished report Karwańska 2009. The authors wish to thank Łukasz Dębowski and Maciej Piasecki for their comments on an earlier version of this paper. Research funded in 2007–2010 by a research and development grant from the Polish Ministry of Science and Higher Education.

Accuracy is commonly understood as the percent of *tokens* (roughly, words; also called *segments* in the following sections) on which the gold standard and the tagger agree (Manning and Schütze 1999, p. 342), although sometimes it is defined as the percent of *tags* on which they agree (Jurafsky and Martin 2009, p. 189). Conversely, *error* is the percent of tokens (or tags) on which the gold standard and the tagger *dis*agree. As we will see below, it is not clear, however, how to interpret these measures in case more than one tag is considered correct for a given token.

Why should ever more than one tag be assigned to a token, whether within a gold standard or by a tagger? As discussed, e.g., in Oliva 2001, there are perhaps rare but linguistically justified cases where it is in principle impossible to tell which of a number of interpretations is the right one, as in (1) below, taken from Przepiórkowski 2004.

(1) Pamiętam ją pijaną.
remember.1ST her.ACC drunk.ACC/INS
'I remember her drunk.'

(2) a. Pamiętam go pijanego.
remember.1ST him.ACC drunk.ACC
'I remember him drunk.'

b. Pamiętam go pijanym.
remember.1ST him.ACC drunk.INS

As shown in (2), the predicative adjective may occur either in the accusative or in the instrumental case in this construction. However, the feminine form *pijaną* in (1) is syncretic between these two grammatical cases, so both interpretations are fully correct and no context or world knowledge can provide any disambiguation clues here.

This reasoning determined the design of the IPI PAN Corpus of Polish (http://korpus.pl/; Przepiórkowski 2004), as well as accompanying annotation and search tools. In particular, a manually annotated subcorpus of the IPI PAN Corpus has numerous instances of multi-tagged tokens, and two taggers trained on that subcorpus, presented in § 3, occasionally disambiguate to more than one morphosyntactic interpretation.

2. Evaluation Measures

Let us assume that the segment pijaną may have three[2] different morphosyntactic interpretations: **ppas** (passive participle), **adj:acc** (adjective in the accusative) and **adj:inst** (adjective in the instrumental), and that in the gold standard (GS) corpus both adjectival interpretations are marked as correct.

Let us consider five different taggers, T1 to T5, making different decisions for the segment *pijaną* in (1), as in Table 1. It is clear that the tagger T1 fares best for this segment, as its decision is identical to the annotation in the gold standard, and T5 clearly performs worst here. But what is the relative value of the other three taggers?

Table 1. Different decisions of five hypothetical taggers

word	tag	GS	T1	T2	T3	T4	T5
pijaną	**ppas**	0	0	0	1	1	1
	adj:acc	1	1	0	1	1	0
	adj:inst	1	1	1	1	0	0

2.1. Accuracy-Like Measures

We will consider three interpretations of the general notion of accuracy:

- **correctness**: word-level accuracy understood as the percent of words for which the tagger and the gold standard agree completely;
- **weak correctness**: the percent of words for which the set of tags selected as correct by the tagger and the set of tags marked as correct in the gold standard overlap;
- **tag-level accuracy**: the percent of tags for which the tagger and the gold standard agree.

The values of these three measures for the single segment *pijaną* annotated as in Table 1 are given in Table 2.

The **tag-level accuracy** seems to be the most useful of the three measures in the tiny artificial example above, but it does not behave gracefully in case of realistic corpora of Polish, where it is not uncommon for a segment to have a dozen or two dozen interpretations, only one of which is correct. In such a case, a tagger that selects a wrong interpretation still has a very high **tag-level**

2 These three interpretations are an illustrative simplification of the real set of interpretations for *pijaną*; in particular, passive participles in Polish bear case, among other morphosyntactic categories.

accuracy, as it agrees with the gold standard on all the interpretations rejected by both. For example, in case of a segment with 10 interpretations, such an erroneous tagger would score 0.8 **tag-level accuracy**, but – more reasonably – only 0.0 **correctness** and **weak correctness**. For this reason we do not consider **tag-level accuracy** in the remainder of this paper.

Table 2. Evaluation of the hypothetical taggers according to the three accuracy-like measures

measure	T1	T2	T3	T4	T5
correctness	1	0	0	0	0
weak correctness	1	1	1	0	0
tag-level accuracy	1	2/3	2/3	1/3	0

Obviously, the other two measures are also not unproblematic: according to their scores, T4 is as good for *pijaną* as either T2 or T3, contrary to the fact that 1) both T2 and T4 got one of the two correct tags right, but for the incorrect interpretation **ppas**, only the former reached the right decision and, similarly, 2) the interpretation on which T3 and T4 differ is marked correctly by the former and not by the latter. Note also that **weak correctness** alone is not a sufficient measure of tagger quality: it is trivial to achieve the maximal value of this measure (by selecting all interpretations as correct). Nevertheless, as these measures have been used in the past, we will retain them also in the current evaluation exercise.

2.2. Information Retrieval Measures

It has also been proposed (van Halteren 1999) that standard Information Retrieval (IR) measures of **precision** and **recall**, as well as their harmonic mean, called **F-measure**, could be used for the evaluation of such partially disambiguating taggers:

- **precision**: the percent of tags selected by the tagger which are correct according to the gold standard;

- **recall**: the percent of correct tags that are selected by the tagger.

The values of these measures for the hypothetical taggers and the artificial 1 segment corpus pijaną are given in Table 3. Note that the **F-measure** reasonably evaluates T2 and T3 as better than T4, but it is not clear that the relative strengths between T2 and T3 are correctly reflected by this measure: which of these two taggers should be preferred is a matter of the relative importance of precision and recall for the further uses of the tagged corpus.

Table 3. Evaluation of the hypothetical taggers according to the IR measures

measure	T1	T2	T3	T4	T5
precision	1	1	2/3	1/2	0
recall	1	1/2	1	1/2	0
F-measure	1	2/3	4/5	1/2	0

3. Polish Taggers

There are two Polish taggers which were trained on the manually disambiguated corpus – of over 880,000 segments – created within the IPI PAN Corpus of Polish project (http://korpus.pl/).[3]

3.1. Dębowski's Tagger

The first of these taggers, probably the first morphosyntactic tagger of Polish[4], is a nameless tagger developed by Łukasz Dębowski at the Institute of Computer Science, Polish Academy of Sciences (ICS PAS; the Polish acronym is IPI PAN, hence the name of the IPI PAN Corpus), described in Dębowski 2004. It is a classical trigram-based statistical tagger, whose error rate was reported as 9.4%, corresponding to the **weak correctness** of 90.6%, although the possibility of multiple correct tags is not discussed explicitly in Dębowski 2004, so it is not fully clear which notion of word-level accuracy was assumed here.

For practical reasons the tagger has never been made publicly available: it is inefficient, it consists of a rather large set of Perl scripts, and it is not easy to install it in a new environment or to maintain it. Nevertheless, this tagger was used for the morphosyntactic annotation of the first version of the 250-million-segment IPI PAN Corpus of Polish.

In the rest of the paper, we will refer to Dębowski's tagger as DT.

3.2. TaKIPI

The second edition of that corpus was tagged with TaKIPI (Piasecki 2007), a tagger originally developed by Maciej Piasecki and his colleagues within a project carried out at ICS PAS, subsequently further developed and maintained

3 Another Polish tagger, which – to the best of our knowledge – has not seen the light of day, is reported in Rudolf 2004. Recently, one more tagger has been constructed by two students of the second author at the Institute of Informatics, University of Warsaw; cf. Acedański & Gołuchowski 2009.

4 An earlier attempt, following a different methodology, is described in Dębowski 2003

at the Wrocław University of Technology.[5] It is a hybrid system based on decision trees, unigram frequencies and manually constructed correction rules, it is rather efficient, partially due to its implementation in C, and it is publicly available as open source under the GNU General Public License.[6]

The weak correctness of TaKIPI reported in Piasecki and Godlewski 2006 is 92.55%, but – as the article hastens to add – *[c]omparison with 90.4% reported by [(Dębowski 2004)] is difficult, as his tagger always leaves the best one tag, and was tested on a very small part of [the manually disambiguated corpus].* For this reason – and also in order to set the stage for the evaluation and comparison of future taggers of Polish, including the tagger to be trained within the National Corpus of Polish project (http://nkjp.pl/; Przepiórkowski et al. 2008, 2009) – an independent comparative evaluation of both taggers is needed, using a variety of measures introduced in the previous section. The results of such an evaluation are presented in § 4 below.

3.3. Common Tagset and Gold Standard

There are many factors which may influence the fairness of a comparison or even make the whole exercise futile. As noted in van Halteren 1999, the size of the tagset and, especially, the average number of interpretations per segment correlate with the difficulty of the tagging task. In case at hand, the gold standard and both taggers in principle assume the same tagset, the IPI PAN Tagset described, e.g., in Przepiórkowski and Woliński 2003a,b, with 4179 potentially possible tags, out of which up to 1642 are used in practice (Przepiórkowski 2006) and with 3.32 tags per segment (Przepiórkowski 2008, p. 44, fn. 32). However, somewhat surprisingly, it turned out that there were subtle differences between the three versions of the IPI PAN Tagset.

Each tag in this tagset has the form **kl:kat$_1$:kat$_2$:...:kat$_n$**, where **kl** is the name of a grammatical class, while each of kati is the value of a grammatical category appropriate for that class, e.g., **adj:sg:acc:f:pos** for the singular accusative feminine positive degree form *pijaną* of the adjective PIJANA 'drunk'. The formal specification of the IPI PAN Tagset makes some categories for some classes optional, for example, in the case of the neutralisation of the rather ephemeral binary-valued categories of accentability and post-propositionally for some 3rd person pronouns. The gold standard and DT sometimes took advantage of this possibility to omit values of these two categories, while TaKIPI always produces maximally specific tags.

---

5 Currently the tagger is co-owned by the two institutions.

6 It can be downloaded from http://nlp.ipipan.waw.pl/TaKIPI/ and http:// www.plwordnet.pwr.wroc.pl/g419/tagger/.

In the current experiments, in order to make the gold standard and tagger results uniform, the abbreviated tags in the gold standard and in the results of DT were expanded by adding all possible values of both binary categories; in case the abbreviated tag was marked as correct (in gold standard) or selected (by the tagger), all expended tags were so marked, and analogously for the opposite marking.

Another difference between the three tagset versions stemmed from the optionality of another ephemeral binary-valued category, accommodability, pertaining to Polish numerals. Both taggers treat this feature as if it were obligatory, while within the gold standard it only appears with human-masculine (**m1**) numerals in the nominative. In this case, because of the peculiarities of the category of accommodability (see the original presentations of the IPI PAN Tagset and references therein), tags were uniformly contracted, by removing the value of accommodability (and retaining the correct / selected status of the tag).

4. Evaluation Results

Both taggers were evaluated using the same version of the underlying morphological analyser, Morfeusz SIAT (Woliński 2006), namely the version for which TaKIPI was optimised, thus giving this tagger a certain competitive edge. TaKIPI has an optional module, a morphological guesser, used for words unknown to Morfeusz, but since there is no similar guesser in DT, we used TaKIPI with the guesser switched off. The evaluation was performed for full morphosyntactic tags, as well as for grammatical classes (roughly, parts of speech; POS) only. In the latter case, all interpretations sharing the same POS were contracted to one tag, marked as correct / selected exactly in cases when at least one of the original interpretations was correct / selected.

Table 4 presents the results of the evaluation. C and WC stand for **correctness** and **weak correctness**, and P, R and F – for the IR metrics of **precision**, **recall** and **F-measure**.

A number of observations may be made about these results. First, note that the **weak correctness** result of DT is slightly higher than reported in Dębowski 2004 (90.59% vs. 90.4%), and the result of TaKIPI is a little lower than reported in Piasecki and Godlewski 2006 (91.30% vs. 92.55%), thus making the two taggers more similar with respect to this measure than originally assumed. Nevertheless, the WC quality of TaKIPI is still significantly better than that of DT.

Table 4. Summary of evaluation results

tagger	C	WC	P	R	F
DT	87.39%	90.59%	84.51%	83.09%	83.80
TaKIPI	86.63%	91.30%	88.83%	93.47%	86.06
DT (POS only)	96.79%	97.11%	96.75%	96.78%	96.77
TaKIPI (POS only)	94.58%	96.81%	94.67%	96.55%	95.60

Second, in case of the strong **correctness**, DT fares better than TaKIPI. We assume that one of the reasons for that is that TaKIPI does not disambiguate between nouns and gerunds, so in case of – relatively frequent – ambiguities of this kind, TaKIPI never produces exactly the same decisions as the gold standard, which specifies either the noun interpretation or the gerund interpretation as correct. This is probably also one of the reasons why, when the tagset is constrained to grammatical classes, TaKIPI produces consistently lower results than DT, for all measures considered here; since noun and gerund are two different grammatical classes, such behaviour of TaKIPI has detrimental effect on **correctness** and **precision**.

Finally, let us note that for full morphosyntactic tagging, the evaluation results as measured by the Information Retrieval metrics are consistently higher for TaKIPI than for DT.

5. Conclusion

Contrary to earlier preliminary results, the quality of both taggers, when trained on the same corpus and using exactly the same tagset, turns out to be similar. One or the other tagger achieves better results depending on the evaluation metrics and the granularity of the tagset. For fine-grained morphosyntactic tagging TaKIPI is clearly better than DT as measured with IR metrics, and a little better in terms of weak correctness, but DT is a little better than TaKIPI in terms of (strong) correctness. For coarse-grained POS tagging, DT is uniformly better than TaKIPI; in case of correctness and precision (and, hence, also F-measure) – clearly so.

So which of the two taggers should be recommended for the morphosyntactic tagging of Polish? While the evaluation results given above do not provide an unqualified answer, practical considerations do: unlike DT, TaKIPI is not only open source and publicly available, but also reasonably efficient, so currently there is no alternative to using this tagger. But as other taggers are being developed, and existing taggers are trained on new manually annotated corpus being developed within the National Corpus of Polish, the need for the comparative evaluation of taggers will grow. We hope that the discussion in the current paper will facilitate such comparison in the future.

References

Acedański, S. and K. Gołuchowski (2009). 'A morphosyntactic rule-based Brill tagger for Polish'. In: Kłopotek, M. A., Przepiórkowski, A., Wierzchoń, S. T. and K. Trojanowski (Eds.), *Advances in intelligent information systems – design and applications*. Warsaw: Akademicka Oficyna Wydawnicza EXIT, 67–76.

Dębowski, Ł. (2003). 'A reconfigurable stochastic tagger for languages with complex tag structure'. In: *Proceedings of Morphological Processing of Slavic Languages, EACL 2003*.

Dębowski, Ł. (2004). 'Trigram morphosyntactic tagger for Polish'. In: Kłopotek, M. A., Wierzchoń, S. T. and K. Trojanowski (Eds.), *Intelligent Information Processing and Web Mining*. Berlin: Springer-Verlag, 409–413.

Jurafsky, D. and J. H. Martin (2009). *Speech and language processing: An introduction to natural language processing, computational linguistics, and speech recognition*. Upper Saddle River, NJ: Pearson Education, Inc., 2nd ed.

Karwańska, D. (2009). 'Porównanie tagerów dopuszczają̨cych niejednoznaczności'. Unpublished manuscript, National Corpus of Polish.

Manning, C. D. and H. Schütze (1999). *Foundations of statistical natural language processing*. Cambridge, MA: The MIT Press.

Oliva, K. (2001). 'On retaining ambiguity in disambiguated corpora: Programmatic reflections on why's and how's'. TAL (Traitement Automatique des Langues) 42(2): 487–500.

Piasecki, M. (2007). 'Polish tagger TaKIPI: Rule based construction and optimisation'.Task Quarterly 11(1–2): 151–167.

Piasecki, M. and G. Godlewski (2006). 'Effective architecture of the Polish tagger'. In: Sojka, P., Kopeček, I. and K. Pala (Eds.), *Text, speech and dialogue: 9th international conference, TSD 2006, Brno, Czech Republic, September 2006*. Berlin: Springer-Verlag, 213–220. (Lecture Notes in Artificial Intelligence, 4188.)

Przepiórkowski, A. (2004). The IPI PAN corpus: Preliminary version. Warsaw: Institute of Computer Science, Polish Academy of Sciences.

Przepiórkowski, A. (2006). 'The potential of the IPI PAN Corpus'. Poznań studies in contemporary linguistics 41: 31–48.

Przepiórkowski, A. (2008). Powierzchniowe przetwarzanie języka polskiego. Warsaw: Akademicka Oficyna Wydawnicza EXIT.

Przepiórkowski, A. (2009). 'A comparison of two morphosyntactic tagsets of Polish'. In: Koseska-Toszewa, V., Dimitrova, L. and R. Roszko (Eds.), Representing semantics in Digital lexicography: Proceedings of MONDILEX fourth open workshop. Warsaw, 138–144.

Przepiórkowski, A., Górski, R. L., Lewandowska-Tomaszczyk, B. and M. Łaziński (2008). 'Towards the National Corpus of Polish'. In: Proceedings of the sixth international Conference on Language Resources and Evaluation, LREC 2008. Marrakech.

Przepiórkowski, A., Górski, R. L., Łaziński, M. and P. Pęzik (2009). 'Recent development in the National Corpus of Polish'. In: Levická, J. and R. Garabík (Eds.), NLP, corpus linguistics, corpus based grammar research: Proceedings of the fifth international conference, Smolenice, Slovakia, 25–27 November 2009. Brno: Tribun, 302–309.

Przepiórkowski, A. and M.Woliński (2003a). 'A flexemic tagset for Polish'. In: Proceedings of Morphological processing of Slavic languages, EACL 2003. Budapest, 33–40.

Przepiórkowski, A. and M. Woliński (2003b). 'The unbearable lightness of tagging: A case study in morphosyntactic tagging of Polish'. In: Proceedings of the 4th international workshop on linguistically interpreted corpora (LINC-03), EACL 2003, 109–116.

Rudolf, M. (2004). Metody automatycznej analizy korpusu tekstów polskich. Warsaw: Uniwersytet Warszawski, Wydział Polonistyki.

van Halteren, H. (1999). 'Performance of taggers'. In: van Halteren, H. (Ed.), Syntactic wordclass tagging, volume 9 of Text, Speech and Language Technology. Dordrecht: Kluwer, 81–94.

Woliński, M. (2006). 'Morfeusz — a practical tool for the morphological analysis of Polish'. In: Kłopotek, M. A., Wierzchoń, S. T. and K. Trojanowski (Eds.), Intelligent information processing and web mining. Berlin: Springer-Verlag, 511–520.

Additional Comments on the Prolog Version of the Tiger Dependency Bank

Tomas By

Abstract: The conversion of the Tiger dependency bank to Prolog format involved disambiguating the word order, which is not represented in the original data format, and a small number of corrections. An earlier publication reporting this work contained some incorrect figures. The present paper updates that information, and provides more details on a couple of methods used to verify that the word order disambiguation produces accurate results, as well as additional benefits of the Prolog representation not described in the earlier paper.

Keywords: dependency format, parser evaluation, corpus conversion, Prolog.

1. Introduction

The Prolog format version of the Tiger dependency bank (By 2009) avoids a number of apparent problems with the original data format. In addition to the absence of an explicit representation of the word order, leading to a token ambiguity of up to 9% in the Tiger dependency bank, these include a spurious distinction between 'full' tokens and attribute tokens, the absence of a distinction between words and empty nodes in the dependency tree, and an unnecessarily distributed representation of the token attributes, which are stored together with the word they belong to in the Prolog version. Since the word order disambiguation is only probabilistic, and 1865 sentence trees[1] are too much to check manually, a couple of automatic verification methods were used. One involved comparing the Tiger treebank token indexes, which are mostly retained in the Tiger dependency bank, with the sequence obtained in the disambiguated data. The other used Prolog code to check the grammatical attributes of pronouns, which are words that are frequently ambiguous in the original Tiger dependency bank. After a short section giving correct figures for the token counts in the Tiger treebank and dependency bank, there is one section on the conversion procedure and two on the methods of verifying its output. Then there is one section on the use of a Prolog interpreter to examine the data, followed by a summary.

1 There are 1867 files, but two pairs are duplicates.

Table 1. Comparison of the tokenisations of Tiger corpora

	Treebank	Depbank	(both)
Identical			26923
Same, except for capitalisation			1220
Morphology			9
Extra punctuation in the Treebank token			45
Space char. in DB, but not TB, token			9
Tokens that correspond directly	28206	28206	28206
Multi-word tokens	2554[a]	262[b]	
Components of multi-word tokens	587	5379	
Tokens with no correspondence	4969	5	
Empty strings (fused words)	–	563	
Total number of tokens	36316	34415	

[a] These are mostly compound words that have been separated in the dependency bank.
[b] Seem to be mainly hyphenated words that are individual tokens in the treebank.

2. Token counts

The table of token counts in By (2009: 124) is incorrect, because 'tokens' that only contained whitespace or an empty string were counted mistakenly. A correct version appears here as Table 1. The difference between the 'empty string' tokens in the table and 'empty nodes'[2] (By 2007: 265) is that the former have a position in the word order since they are parts of the representation of fused words (cf. By 2009: 123, 121).

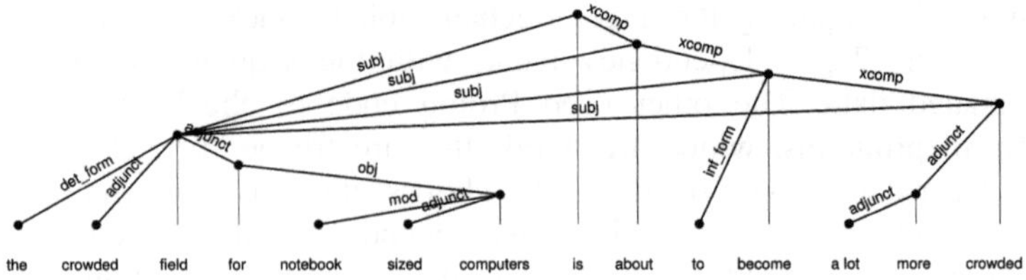

Figure 1. PARC #284

2 Of which there are 1161 in the Tiger dependency bank.

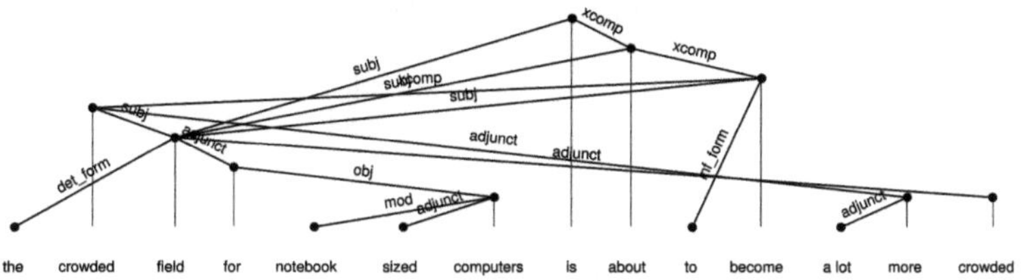

Figure 2. PARC #284 with the word 'crowded' incorrectly disambiguated

3. The conversion procedure

In the original PARC 700/Tiger dependency bank representation (Forst *et al.* 2004: 34), word order is not encoded so that multiple occurrences of the same word type in one sentence are ambiguous. A graphical illustration of the problem is given in Figures 1 and 2 (By 2007: 266). The word 'crowded' occurs twice in the sentence, and without knowing the word order the two tokens are ambiguous. The total number of instances of this problem in the Tiger dependency bank in 9% (By 2009: 120), and in PARC 700 it is 15% (By 2007: 275–7). During the conversion to Prolog format, disambiguating the word order was the main technical challenge. The input is the entire string of the sentence, together with the set of dependency bank tokens whose order is not known, and these tokens are in many cases base forms or otherwise modified words that are not exact substrings of the sentence string. The basic idea of the disambiguation procedure is to find the set of token positions that give the minimum total dependency link distance (By 2007: 268–9; By 2009: 124, 126–7).

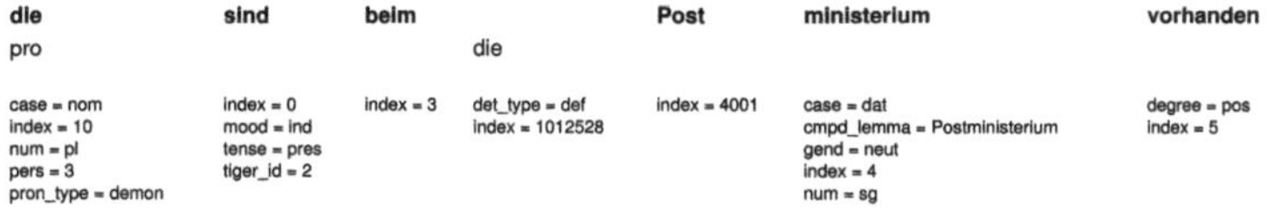

Figure 3. Tiger 8019

Table 2. Token index ordering in the Tiger dependency bank, per sentence

Sentences	1867	
Root word has no `tiger_id` attribute	284	15%
One or more indexes in range but not in order	96	5%
No apparent token index order at all	24	1.3%

Table 3. Token ordering in the Prolog version of the Tiger dependency bank

Word tokens	34415	(100%)
In range and order	27171	79%
Outside range	5293	15%
In range but not order	150	0.4%
New tokens[a]	1801	5%

[a] i.e. Tiger treebank tokens that were not included in the original Tiger dependency bank but have been added during the conversion to Prolog format

4. Tiger treebank token numbering

Since there is no guarantee that the resulting disambiguations are correct, a couple of test were devised to try to discover problems. In the XML version of the Tiger treebank (Forst *et al.* 2004: 34; Brants *et al.* 2002), each token[3] is numbered consecutively starting at one. In the Tiger dependency bank, the root of the tree always get the index zero (Forst *et al.* 2004: 33), and in quite a few cases some systematic rearrangement of the tokens has happened, leading to new token numbers. For the remaining tokens, with a few dozen exceptions (By 2009: 127), the numbering is typically the same in the dependency bank as in the treebank. The idea, then, is to see if the proposed disambiguation of the word order produces token numbers that are ordered. The non-triviality of this comparison is illustrated by Figure 3. In the XML version of the Tiger treebank, this sentence has the following tokens:

Word:	Die	sind	beim	Postministerium	vorhanden	.
Lemma:	der	sein	bei	Postministerium	vorhanden	--
Index:	1	2	3	4	5	6

3 The tokenisations differ somewhat between the Tiger treebank and the Tiger dependency bank, as shown in Table 1.

For this sentence in the Tiger dependency bank (Figure 3), the sequence of index numbers is: 10, 0/2, 3, 1012528, 4001, 4, 5. The root has index zero, but the treebank index (2) is given by the '`tiger_id`' attribute. Two new tokens have been introduced (4001, 1012528), and the first token has been given a new index (10). All of these are outside the range of numbers between one and the length of the sentence. Of all the sentences in the Tiger dependency bank, 95% have all the tokens whose index is in this range, also in order (cf. Table 2; the figures for individual tokens are given in Table 3).

```
pronouns :-
    (member(Attr,[pers,num,case]),
        write('personal pronouns that have the wrong'~w' value',[Attr]),nl,
        (sentence(I,Id,_,_),
            word(I,W,Word,_,As),
            (personal_pronoun(Word,_,_,_) ->
                (member(Attr-Value,As) ->
                    ((Attr = pers, personal_pronoun(Word,Value,_,_)
                        ;Attr = num,  personal_pronoun(Word,_,Value,_)
                        ;Attr = case, personal_pronoun(Word,_,_,Value) ) ->
                        true
                        ;format('~w ~w/~w (~w=~w)~n',[Id,Word,W,Attr,Value]) )
                    ;true )
                ;true ),
            fail
        ;true ),
        fail
    ;true ).
```

Figure 4. Prolog code to check the pronouns

```
personal_pronoun(ich,       '1',sg,nom).
personal_pronoun(mein,      '1',sg,gen).
personal_pronoun(meine,     '1',sg,gen).
personal_pronoun(meiner,    '1',sg,gen).
personal_pronoun(mich,      '1',sg,acc).
personal_pronoun(mir,       '1',sg,dat).
personal_pronoun(wir,       '1',pl,nom).
personal_pronoun(uns,       '1',pl,nom).
personal_pronoun(uns,       '1',pl,acc).
personal_pronoun(uns,       '1',pl,dat).
personal_pronoun(unser,     '1',pl,gen).
personal_pronoun(unsere,    '1',pl,gen).
personal_pronoun(unserem,   '1',pl,gen).
personal_pronoun(unseren,   '1',pl,gen).
personal_pronoun(unserer,   '1',pl,gen).
personal_pronoun(unseres,   '1',pl,gen).
personal_pronoun(du,        '2',sg,nom).
```

```
personal_pronoun(dich,      '2',sg,acc).
personal_pronoun(dir,       '2',sg,dat).
personal_pronoun(dein,      '2',sg,gen).
personal_pronoun(deinen,    '2',sg,gen).
personal_pronoun(deinem,    '2',sg,gen).
```

Figure 5. Prolog data, pronouns and their attributes (subset)

5. Pronoun attributes

Since pronouns and determiners are highly ambiguous in the Tiger dependency bank (partly, or mostly, because many have been 'lemmatised' to a single common form 'die') and a complete list of all those words with their grammatical attributes is relatively easy to obtain, a simple way to find likely problems in the disambiguation is to check the pronoun attributes in the data. The code in Figure 4, together with the data in Figure 5 does that.

```
| ?- pronouns.
personal pronouns that have the wrong 'pers' value
s8484/tiger-db-8486.fdsc wir/6 (pers=3)
s8491/tiger-db-8493.fdsc wir/6 (pers=3)
personal pronouns that have the wrong `num' value
s8586/tiger-db-8588.fdsc seinen/13 (num=pl)
s8615/tiger-db-8617.fdsc seinen/2 (num=pl)
s9441/tiger-db-9444.fdsc es/0 (num=pl)
personal pronouns that have the wrong `case' value
s9612/tiger-db-9612.fdsc sein/15 (case=nom)
```

This procedure verifies that all pronouns have the right person, number, and case attributes. It found dozens of errors in the disambiguation, and the disambiguation of those individual words were then hard-coded. About one hundred individual occurrences of pronouns and determiners have been hard-coded in total. The box below above the output of the program in Figure 4 on the final version of the Prolog version of the Tiger dependency bank. The first four words in the example are errors in the data, but they cause no problems for the token disambiguation. In the fifth case, the 'es,' the pronoun is the subject of a plural verb and co-refers with a plural noun. The last reported error is not in fact a pronoun at all but the verb, or perhaps a nominalisation (it is part of a compound).

6. Examination of the data

A general advantage with storing data in Prolog format is that it can very easily be loaded into a Prolog interpreter, and explored by querying the database. Finding a particular word with a certain combination of attributes and links, for example, (here a subject with genitive case) is easily done with command that fits on a single line.

```
| ?- word(S,W,_,_,As), dependency(S,w(W),sb,_), member(case-gen,As).
S = 1547,
W = 11,
As = [index-'12',cmpd_lemma-'Umweltfirma',gend-fem,pers-'3',num-sg,case-gen] ?
```

The built-in Prolog command 'setof' lets us easily find all dependency link labels.

```
| ?- setof(L,S^W1^W2^dependency(S,W1,L,W2),Ls).
Ls = ['',ams,app,app_cl,cc,circ_form,cj,comp_form,coord_form,da,det,fut,
   gl,gr,measured,mo,mod,name_mod,number,oa,oa2,obj,oc_fin,oc_inf,og,op,
   op_dir,op_loc,op_manner,pass_asp,pd,perf,precoord_form,pred_restr,
   quant,rc,rs,sb,sbp,topic_disloc,topic_rel] ?
```

Finding all attribute names is slightly more complicated because a disjunction (;) is needed since both word tokens and empty nodes can have them.

```
| ?- setof(Nm,S^I^T^V^X^As^( ( word(S,I,T,X,As) ; node(S,I,T,As) ),
   member(Nm-V,As) ),Nms).
Nms = [case,circ_form,cmpd_lemma,comp_form,coord_form,degree,det,det_type,
   fut,gend,index,mo,mod,mood,num,number,numverb,pass_asp,passive,perf,
   pers,precoord_form,pron_form,pron_type,tense,tiger_id]
```

When a command gets too complicated to write on a single line, it can be put in a file instead, like the procedure in Figure 4. This continuous progression from simple database queries to short programs is a Prolog specialty.

7. Summary

In the Tiger dependency bank, and the PARC 700 dependency bank, the combination of lemmatised tokens and the absence of an encoding of the word order means that sentences with more than one ocurrence of token types with the same base form in the same sentence are ambiguous. The number of such ambiguous tokens is about 9% in the Tiger dependency bank. The conversion to Prolog format involved a disambiguation of the word order. In order to verify that this disambiguation produced correct results, a couple of automatic procedures were used, to compare the ordering of the Tiger token indexes, which for about 80% of the tokens were inherited from the Tiger treebank, and to check that pronouns, which were problematic for the automatic disambiguation, have the correct attributes. After manual corrections of problems found by these methods, a high level of confidence is felt that the Prolog data is accurate.

The converted and slightly corrected Tiger dependency bank, in Prolog format, can be downloaded from the following web page.

http://www.basun.net/homepages/tomas/papers/tiger/

There are two files: 'tiger.pl' is the Prolog data, and 'tiger.pdf' contains the graphical trees of all the 1867 sentences.

References

Brants, S., Dipper, S., Hansen, S., Lezius, W. and G. Smith (2002). "The TIGER treebank". *Proceedings of the first workshop on treebanks and linguistic theories*. Sozopol, Bulgaria: 24–41.

By, T. (2007). "Some notes on the PARC 700 dependency bank". *Natural Language Engineering* **13**(3): 261–282.

By, T. (2009). "The TiGer dependency bank in Prolog format". In: M.A. Kłopotek, A. Przepiórkowski, S.T. Wierzchoń and K. Trojanowski (eds.). *Recent Advances in Intelligent Information Systems*: 119–129.

Forst, M., Bertomeu, N., Crysmann, B., Fouvry, F., Hansen-Schirra, S. and V. Kordoni (2004). "Towards a dependency-based gold standard for German parsers – the TiGer dependency bank". *Proceedings of the 5th International Workshop on Linguistically Interpreted Corpora*. COLING 2004.Geneva, Switzerland.

Automating Rule Generation for Grammar Checkers

Marcin Miłkowski

Abstract: In this paper, I describe several approaches to automatic or semi-automatic development of symbolic rules for grammar checkers from the information contained in corpora. The rules obtained this way are an important addition to manually-created rules that seem to dominate in rule-based checkers. However, the manual process of creation of rules is costly, time-consuming and error-prone. It seems therefore advisable to use machine-learning algorithms to create the rules automatically or semi-automatically. The results obtained seem to corroborate our initial hypothesis that symbolic machine learning algorithms can be useful for acquiring new rules for grammar checking. It turns out, however, that for practical uses, error corpora cannot be the sole source of information used in grammar checking. We suggest therefore that only by using different approaches, grammar-checkers, or more generally, computer-aided proofreading tools, will be able to cover most frequent and severe mistakes and avoid false alarms that seem to distract users.

The paper shows that an error corpus generated from Wikipedia revision history can be used to automatically generate error-matching symbolic rules for grammar checkers. Though no error corpora can be considered complete, transformation-based learning (TBL) algorithms deal with small corpora sufficiently well.

Keywords: grammar checking, rule induction, symbolic machine learning, transformation-based learning.

1. Introduction

In this paper, I describe several approaches to automatic or semi-automatic development of symbolic rules for grammar checkers from the information contained in corpora. The rules obtained this way are an important addition to manually-created rules that seem to dominate in rule-based checkers. However, the manual process of creation of rules is costly, time-consuming and error-prone. It seems therefore advisable to use machine-learning algorithms to create the rules automatically or semi-automatically. The results obtained seem to corroborate our initial hypothesis that symbolic machine learning algorithms can be useful for acquiring new rules for grammar checking. It turns out, however, that for practical uses, error corpora cannot be the sole source of information used in grammar checking. We suggest therefore that only by using different approaches, grammar-checkers, or more generally, computer-aided proofreading tools, will be able to cover most frequent and severe mistakes and avoid false alarms that seem to distract users.

In what follows, I will show how Transformation-Based Learning (TBL) algorithms may be used to acquire rules. Before doing that, I will discuss the pros and cons of three approaches to creating rules and show the need to make use of them all in a successful grammar-checking tool. The results obtained seem to suggest that the machine-learning approach is actually fruitful, and I will point to some future work related to the reported research.

2. Three approaches to rule-based grammar checking

It could seem that a *pure empirical approach* is the most advisable way to create rules for grammar checkers. However, it must rely on error corpora, and these are hard to find and costly. Although it is possible to automatically bootstrap the development of such corpora (see Miłkowski 2008), they are still not sufficient to cover all variety of important errors in the language on the proper level of generality. Direct use of smaller error corpora does not seem to lead to useful results (see below), and they must be accompanied with a "clean" corpus that contains no or only minor errors. The rules acquired this way, however, can be a useful addition to the existing base of rules.

Pure a priori approach as based on existing normative prescriptions, such as usage dictionaries, style guides, grammar textbooks etc. offers two significant advantages over the pure empirical approach. First, the justification of the rules seems to be more reliable. It is the job of lexicographers to check if the advice offered is accurate and authoritative, and the authors of grammar-checkers can simply rely on it. Moreover, if the grammar checker is to impose style guidelines, then it is doubtful that any empirical corpus would embody them beforehand. For example, if the style guide requires that dates be written only in a recommended format, it is easier to define the standard format and use the corpus only to find out what deviations seem to occur most frequently. This is why for some uses, the a priori approach cannot be replaced with pure empirical one.

For larger-scale projects, however, pure a priori approach has some disadvantages: it lags behind linguistic development, as dictionaries tend to be outdated (especially the printed ones). In other words, some errors listed in the dictionaries may no longer exist in the language, and some existing errors may be missing from the dictionary. Both factors can negatively affect the recall of grammar-checking rules. For example, Polish dictionaries of usage usually advise against using cliches of Soviet propaganda, including especially bureaucratic borrowings from Russian. It turns out that those cliches are almost extinct nowadays; it makes therefore little sense to develop rules detecting them as contemporary speakers are not likely to use the cliches anyway. At the same time, with the wide adoption of computers for word processing, spell-checkers seem to introduce specific kinds of errors into the text. One of the basic functions in spell-checkers is detecting run-on words but when implemented carelessly, it seems to introduce errors in Polish neologisms (for example, the word "technohumanizm", which is a correct productive neologism, missing in spelling dictionaries, could be automatically corrected to "techno humanizm", which is incorrect but composed of two correct dictionary words). This kind of errors is however completely missing from usage dictionaries and similar resources, so by relying completely on them, we would fail to detect it.

There is also another factor that makes a priori approach hard in practical applications. Culturally-transmitted normative prescriptions for linguistic behavior are vague and tend to lack contextual information needed to disambiguate between correct cases and incorrect ones, even if some examples are given. This is true of usage dictionaries, spelling dictionaries, and grammar textbooks. Moreover, as some prescriptions are on the semantic level, which is not fully reducible to the surface level on which most grammar checkers operate, they need to be (sometimes painfully) adjusted to the Procrustean bed of what is expressible on the surface level. As a result, even authors with a background in linguistics need process a corpus with the newly created rules to make sure that they are not resulting in a very high number of false alarms. Yet, as our research shows, the false alarms can also result from automatic acquisition of rules (which is shown by precision levels of 30%), so the step of processing corpora with the rules and refining them seems unavoidable.[1]

Lastly, minority languages can lack authoritative sources altogether, so in some cases such resources cannot be reused at all. As one of the goals of our research project was to alleviate the process of adding new rules to an open-source proofreading tool, LanguageTool (for a general description, see Naber 2003), and we wanted to include minority languages among the ones supported, using reliable dictionaries could not be a requirement.

It is possible to use the information from both worlds: machine learning algorithms with some existing language resources, such as authoritative usage guides. Although the quality of some automatically-developed rules may be lower in terms of their precision, we may restrict ourselves to the best ones and refine others manually. *The mixed approach* uses therefore both corpora to create rules using real-world data and some prescriptions that lead the process of acquisition of rules.

---

1 However, some automatically-acquired rules can be discarded automatically if they seem to result in a very high number of matches in a substantial corpus that is considered to be relatively free of errors.

3. Machine learning of rules

One of the machine-learning techniques that was used successfully in the mixed approach is, as we already mentioned, Transformation-Based Learning (see Mangu and Brill 1997) but it can also be used in the pure empirical approach, as shown in the section 5. TBL is of course just one of the available machine-learning algorithms that may acquire rules. It is also quite straightforward to use statistical machine translation (SMT), which is already applied in automatic post-editing (Simard *et al.* 2007) and could also be quite easily adopted to add missing words in the text (like determiners or missing parts of common phrases). It might be used for ESL grammar checking (Gamon *et al.* 2008). Here, I will focus on TBL, as it creates rules that can be easily translated into LanguageTool symbolic notation (constructs admissible in TBL rules are a subset of what is expressible in LT notation). One of the interesting properties of TBL is that the training corpus can be relatively small to achieve good results, contrary to most SMT-based methods that are data-intensive.

TBL is most well-known for its application in the Brill tagger (Brill 1995), however, it may be used in a wide variety of NLP tasks that involve classification. The algorithm starts with an initial classification, and tries to find transformations from initial classes to the correct ones. In the case of part-of-speech (POS) tagging, it transforms most frequent POS tags, which were applied first, into correct ones, which are taken from a manually-annotated corpus. To constrain the search space of possible transformations, the TBL algorithm uses a finite list of admissible transformation templates that usually include features (POS tags, surface tokens, lemmas) that precede or follow the feature under consideration.

The application of TBL to the error-detection task is straightforward: we need to find the transformation from incorrect tokens into the correct ones. Brill used TBL to find commonly confused words in English, by simply substituting POS tags in the POS tagging task with confused words.[2] The confused words create (at least two-element) confusion sets such as {*than*, *then*}, {*its*, *it's*}, {*there*, *their*}, {*advice*, *advise*}. For any member of the confusion set, the original word was replaced with other(s) in a clean corpus, and the original word was moved into the place of the correct feature. In a familiar column format of Brill tagger, this could look like this (assuming that POS tags were used in the clean corpus):[3]

NN advice advise

2 The list of words was simply excerpted from a dictionary (Flexner 1983).

3 Note that the POS tag used is the one that corresponds to the confused word.

Next, the standard learning procedure is run. It results in a ranked list of transformation rules. The original paper of Mangu and Brill used a dictionary-based word list, but TBL can be used with confusion sets created in a different way, using additional corpora or without them.

For example, one could use artificially created errors in a clean corpus (Sjöberg and Knuttson 2005). Such approach has been taken in transformation-based learning for punctuation correction in Danish (Hardt 2001). Note that artificial errors should not be just randomly created; otherwise, the rules created will have no recall on normal text, as nobody will actually make mistakes detected by those rules (as Miłkowski 2008 observes, this was the case of automatically created autocorrection rules for early versions of Polish OpenOffice.org). So, the search space of possible errors should correspond to the space of frequent errors typical of the data-entry method used (OCR, standard keyboard, mobile phone on-screen keyboard...). For example, if the error corpus is to contain frequent typos and the grammar checker will operate in a word processor, then the errors should be selected based on distances between letters in the most popular keyboard layout (*c* replaced with *v* more frequently than with *p* in the case of QWERTY keyboards). If the proofreading tool is to be used in a digitalization project on OCRed text, the typos should be selected based on graphical character similarity in typical typefaces (*l* replaced with *1* more frequently than with *k*). Yet, in all those cases the simulated errors are only mechanical rather than cognitive mistakes that result from insufficient linguistic competence. It is much harder to artificially simulate errors involving confused nouns, non-standard versions of idioms, or false-friends in a translated text without any additional language resources.

An obvious source of confusion set is an error corpus. Approaches based on reusing error corpora were often discarded as non-realistic, as creating such corpora is costly. Yet, there are ways to automate building such corpora by observing the frequency of user revisions to the text (Miłkowski 2008). Frequent minor edits tend to be related to linguistic mistakes and textual conventions. They have been used to learn transformation rules that automatically correct machine-translated text and improve its quality (Elming 2008).

It can be noted that for some purposes, automating rules for sticking to a linguistic convention may be desired. So, for example, if Wikipedia editors usually correct some non-adherence to the Wikipedia typographical standards, they could use a proofreading tool to scan the texts for non-compliance with those standards. However, in a general proofreading tool those conventional edits should be filtered out; either by averaging on many different revision histories from various sources (which is not yet realistic), or by manually filtering out such frequent revisions.

4. Approaches to learning from the error corpus

It might seem that one could simply use the corpus of errors (or revisions) directly. But rules created from a corpus tend to have high recall with low precision: there are simply not enough examples for members of the same confusion set to discriminate the cases during learning. Here are the highest-ranked rules created by fnTBL toolkit (Ngai and Florian 2001) on a Holbrook corpus used directly (Holbrook 1964):[4]

```
GOOD:21 BAD:0 SCORE:21 RULE: pos_0=Jame word_0=Jame =>
pos=James
GOOD:20 BAD:0 SCORE:20 RULE: pos_0=dont word_0=dont =>
pos=don't
GOOD:10 BAD:0 SCORE:10 RULE: pos_0=two pos_1=the word_0=two
word_1=the => pos=to
GOOD:10 BAD:0 SCORE:10 RULE: pos_0=yow word_0=yow => pos=you
GOOD:10 BAD:0 SCORE:10 RULE: pos_0=thats word_0=thats =>
pos=that's
GOOD:10 BAD:0 SCORE:10 RULE: pos_0=oclock word_0=oclock =>
pos=o'clock
```

As is easily seen, some of these rules are hardly useful in a normal context. All occurrences of "Jame" are unconditionally transformed into "James" (there are more examples like that, for example "cave" being replaced with "gave"). Moreover, it turns out that the third rule is based on a mistaken tagging[5] in the original corpus (the ERR *tag* contains the suggested correction as the contents of *targ* attribute):

*15 NOVEMBER 1960 The Redex Jack O'Malley: Boss George Green 2 Head John Young 2 head went <ERR targ=**two**> to </ERR> the <ERR targ=pictures> pictyres </ERR> and hit the <ERR targ=manager> maneger </ERR> and he went down the <ERR targ=stairs> stars </ERR> and hit a <ERR targ=woman> women </ERR> and <ERR targ=she> he </ERR> fainted We home.*

This shows that error corpora, which tend to be small, do not offer a sufficient number of examples of features to be learned. Moreover, a slight error in tagging can lead to surprisingly bad results. This is again a question of scale, as in a huge error corpus, a single tagging error could become irrelevant.

However, there is a way to use small corpora as seeds to create artificial errors in a large clean corpus. In other words, we need to extract only confusion

4 I left the original names of features from the Brill tagger to stress the connection between both tasks.

5 During writing of this paper, the error has been fixed in the edition of Holbrook corpus maintained in computer-readable form by Roger Miton.

sets ({*two*, *to*}, {*pictures*, *pictyres*}...) from the error corpus, possibly filter non-dictionary words as they are already flagged by standard spelling checkers, and apply confusion sets to the clean corpus. A bigger corpus will have more examples, and that results with higher precision. Let us look at the result of learning now:

```
GOOD:4845 BAD:0 SCORE:4845 RULE: pos_0=end word:[-3,-1]=, =>
pos=and
GOOD:1443 BAD:0 SCORE:1443 RULE: pos_0=end word:[1,3]=PRP =>
pos=and
GOOD:839 BAD:0 SCORE:839 RULE: pos_0=end pos:[1,3]=. =>
pos=and
GOOD:681 BAD:0 SCORE:681 RULE: pos_0=end word:[1,3]=DT =>
pos=and
GOOD:408 BAD:0 SCORE:408 RULE: pos_0=end word:[-3,-1]=DT =>
pos=and
GOOD:354 BAD:0 SCORE:354 RULE: pos_0=end word:[1,3]=, =>
pos=and
```

The rules concerning the confusion of "end" and "and" make now much more sense: "end" most of the time requires a determiner, so it is quite improbable that it will occur straight after a comma or before a determiner. The rule that suggests that "end" is incorrect before a dot (third one) might be however incorrect and result from a too small learning sample. The Table 1 contrasts results achieved using the (1) naïve learning method and (2) introducing extracted confusion sets to a clean corpus (*mixed learning* for short). The resulting rules were applied to the Brown corpus (Francis and Kucera 1964).

Corpus type	**Measure**	**Naïve learning**	**Mixed learning**
Training corpus	Recall	20.34%	99.43%
	Precision	95.11%	99.97%
Brown corpus	Recall	0.00%	100.00%
	Precision	0.00%	38.00%

The results obtained suggest that rules created directly from Holbrook corpus by naively using it for learning have no practical value for any data sets that were not included in the training. In other words, using the naïve approach, especially with a small error corpus, makes no sense; only the mixed approach offers some interesting results but precision is also relatively low. It means that only some rules could be usefully used for grammar checking.

Yet, Holbrook corpus seems to be too tiny for almost any machine learning task. This is why we evaluated the strategies on a much larger error corpus, i.e., the one we previously created from the whole Polish Wikipedia revision history (Miłkowski 2008). As a baseline, we used the Frequency Dictionary of Polish corpus, which is comparable to Brown (Kurcz *et al.* 1974–1977). The results are:

Corpus type	Measure	Naïve learning	Mixed learning
Training corpus	Recall	33.60%	99.99%
	Precision	80.14%	100.00%
Frequency Dictionary Corpus	Recall	100.00%	100.00%
	Precision	0.34%	34.65%

As can be seen, much bigger a training corpus does not seem to change the situation: the naïve approach has very low precision, and detects almost any occurrence of a confused word as an error (hence, 100% recall). As before, the mixed approach enhances precision significantly but the rules still need human evaluation.[6]

One more thing deserves a mention. The original idea of applying TBL to detect errors focused only on confused words. It is also possible to create rules to detect missing words; the transformation words would simply substitute a missing word for the artificial token "NULL". We tested the idea by removing the word "się", which is required by some reflexive verbs in Polish; the resulting rules cite almost only reflexive verbs. In the case of words that were written separately but sometimes need to be spelled together ("no body" vs. "nobody" in English), the confusion set can simply contain an artificial word "no-body", so that mapping between subsequent features is retained. As long as the error form can be brought into a form of transforming a single feature into a target one (incorrect word into a correct word), TBL can be used. For more complex structural transformations, it could become less viable.

5. Adapting the rules to LanguageTool and future work

TBL rules, as noted, can be easily translated into the notation of declarative symbolic rules used in LanguageTool (the exact description of the notation is outside the scope of this paper). Rules are specified in XML files as patterns of tokens; tokens can be tested for multiple attributes (such as POS tags, lemmas

6 We accepted all possible candidates for rules from the ranked list; we could apply a threshold to filter out the rules that did not have sufficient examples to learn their features from. This would make recall probably lower but could enhance precision.

and surface forms, and preceding white space) and relations (including conjunction, negation, exceptions, conditional skipping of tokens forward, as well as feature unification). The attributes can be specified as regular expressions. For that reason, the rules can be much more general than the ones created by TBL. So, although it could be possible to convert transformation rules automatically to LT notation, human intervention is still advisable to make them more general.

In all cases we observed the same phenomenon as with the test results above in section 4: we were able to enhance the recall of many existing confused words rules in LT by using TBL, but the precision of some of the automatically-acquired rules was too low. Here are some examples of rules acquired using μ-TBL toolkit (Lager 1999) in its Prolog-style notation:

```
wd:they>the <- tag:'DT'@[5] o
wd:they>the <- tag:'NN'@[-2] o
wd:they>the <- tag:'JJ,NN,RB'@[1] o
wd:they>the <- tag:'NNS,VBZ'@[5] o
wd:there>their <- wd:of@[-1] o
wd:they>the <- tag:'JJ,NN'@[1] o
wd:there>their <- wd:'SENT_START'@[3] o
wd:they>the <- tag:'NN'@[1] o
wd:they>the <- tag:'SENT_START'@[-3] o
```

As can be seen in the example, we experimented with rule templates quite freely, and tried to see what would be the result of using the feature which is the 5th one after the current one. Contrary to our expectations, the results in most cases are still somewhat useful, although it is of course safer not to use such controversial templates.

The input text was tagged with the internal LanguageTool POS tagger (which disambiguates only to a very limited degree due to specific requirements of grammar checking) to create rules that may be almost directly translated into LT notation with limited manual changes. Polish and English automatically-acquired rules both seem to be useful and are gradually implemented, while human intervention is limited to enhancing rule precision.

In the future, we want to port the current prototype framework (consisting mostly of AWK scripts and Unix tools) to Java, including bootstraping the error corpus from Wikipedia history dump (see Miłkowski 2008). This would offer more platform-independence. This way, the process of adding a new language to LanguageTool would be greatly facilitated, which is one of the practical goals of the project. We consider also using one of the Java implementations of TBL learning directly in our learning tool, and using automatic translation from TBL rules to LT formalism.

We think that even though automatically-acquired rules not always have a satisfactory level of precision, TBL may actually help with development of rules. If minimizing manual intervention were our goal, we could simply use only the best ranked rules with the best precision and test it on additional corpora to make sure they do not raise an unusually high number of alarms, at the price of lower recall. The best automatically-acquired rules are sometimes simpler than the ones proposed by human linguists, and may become a source of inspiration. Therefore, though we cannot completely rely on the automatically generated results, they seem to alleviate creation of rules in a significant way.

References

Brill, E. (1995). "Transformation-Based Error-Driven Learning and Natural Language. A Case Study in Part of Speech Tagging." *Computational Linguistics*, 21(4): 543–565.

Elming, J. (2008). "Transformation-based correction of rule-based MT." *Proceedings of EAMT 2006*: 219–226.

Flexner S.B. (ed.) (1983). *Random House Unabridged Dictionary*. Second edition. New York: Random House.

Francis, W. and H. Kucera (1964). *Brown Corpus Manual*. Revised 1979. Available at http://www.hit.uib.no/icame/brown/bcm.html.

Gamon, M., Gao, J., Brockett, Ch., Klementiev, A., Dolan, W., Belenko, D. and L. Vanderwende (2008). "Using Contextual Speller Techniques and Language Modeling for ESL Error Correction". *Proceedings of IJCNLP 2008*. Hyderabad, India: Asian Federation of Natural Language Processing.

Hardt, D. (2001). "Transformation-Based Learning of Danish Grammar Correction." *Proceedings of RANLP 2001*.

Holbrook, D. (1964). *English for the Rejected*. Cambridge: Cambridge University Press.

Kurcz, I., Lewicki, A., Sambor, J., and J. Woronczak (1974). *Słownictwo współczesnego języka polskiego. Listy frekwencyjne. Tom I. Teksty popularnonaukowe*. Warszawa: Uniwersytet Warszawski.

Kurcz, I. Lewicki, A., Sambor, J., and J. Woronczak (1975). *Słownictwo współczesnego języka polskiego. Listy frekwencyjne. Tom II. Drobne wiadomości prasowe*. Warszawa: Uniwersytet Warszawski.

Kurcz, I. Lewicki, A., Sambor, J., and J. Woronczak (1976). *Słownictwo współczesnego języka polskiego. Listy frekwencyjne. Tom IV. Proza artystyczna*. Warszawa: Uniwersytet Warszawski.

Kurcz, I. Lewicki, A., Sambor, J., and J. Woronczak (1977). *Słownictwo współczesnego języka polskiego. Listy frekwencyjne. Tom V. Dramat artystyczny*. Warszawa: Uniwersytet Warszawski.

Lager, T. (1999). "The μ-TBL System: Logic Programming Tools for Transformation-Based Learning." *Proceedings of the Third International Workshop on Computational Natural Language Learning (CoNLL-99)*. Bergen.

Lewicki, A., Masłowski, W., Sambor, J. and J. Woronczak (1975). *Słownictwo współczesnego języka polskiego. Listy frekwencyjne. Tom III. Publicystyka*. Warszawa: Uniwersytet Warszawski.

Mangu, L. and E. Brill (1997). "Automatic rule acquisition for spelling correction". *Proceedings of the 14th International Conference on Machine Learning*: 187–194.

Miłkowski, M. (2008). "Automated Building of Error Corpora of Polish." In: B. Lewandowska-Tomaszczyk (ed.). *Corpus Linguistics, Computer Tools, and Applications – State of the Art. PALC 2007.* Peter Lang: 631–639.

Naber Daniel (2003). *A Rule-Based Style and Grammar Checker.* Diplomarbeit, Bielefeld: Universität Bielefeld. Available at:
http://www.danielnaber.de/languagetool/download/style_and_grammar_checker.pdf

Ngai, G. and R. Florian (2001). "Transformation-Based Learning in the Fast Lane". *Proceedings of the Second Conference of the North American Chapter of the Association for Computational Linguistics* (NAACL). Pittsburgh.

Simard, M., Ueffing, N., Isabelle, P. and R. Kuhn (2007). "Rule-based Translation With Statistical Phrase-based Post-editing." *Proceedings of the Second Workshop on Statistical Machine Translation*. Prague: Association for Computational Linguistics: 203–206.

Sjöbergh, J. and O. Knutsson. (2005). "Faking errors to avoid making errors: Very weakly supervised learning for error detection in writing". *Proceedings of RANLP 2005.* Borovets, Bulgaria.

Providing Corpus Feedback for Translators with the PELCRA Search Engine for NKJP

Piotr Pęzik

Abstract: The present paper introduces the PELCRA search engine for the National Corpus of Polish (PSEN). This highly scalable corpus search tool provides access to concordance and collocation search results in a variety of output formats, including downloadable spreadsheets, compressed URL-s, integrated browser plug-ins and web services. Apart from outlining the general functionality of this tool, I demonstrate the usefulness of PSEN slop factor queries in verifying the phraseology of translated texts. This specific example is meant to illustrate the general possibility of ensuring easy and universal access to corpus evidence through the combination of a robust query syntax and compressed Uniform Resource Locators (URLs). The search engine is freely available at *www.nkjp.uni.lodz.pl.*

Keywords: PELCRA search engine, corpora in translation, collocation extraction.

1. National Corpus of Polish

The National Corpus of Polish (NKJP) is a research project funded by the Polish Ministry of Science and Higher Education (project number: R17 003 03). Its main objective is the construction of a 300 million word (MW) balanced corpus of modern Polish. The total pool of texts used to sample the balanced corpus from will reach 1 billion words by the end of 2010. More detailed information on the recent developments in the NKJP can be found in (Przepiórkowski *et al.* 2009) and on the project's web site at *www.nkjp.pl.*

The sheer size of the acquired data as well as the rich Polish morphology pose special challenges for the retrieval engines used in the project. The PELCRA NKJP corpus search engine (PSEN) is one of the two tools used for the NKJP[1]. Based on a combination of Apache Lucene[2] and relational database technologies, it scales well with the size of the corpus; an uncached query for *raczej* matching 85 429 paragraphs in a 500 MW version of the corpus retrieves

1 *Poliqarp for NKJP* is another search tool available for the NKJP data. It supports more complex types of linguistic search at various levels of annotation (http://chopin. ipipan.waw.pl/poliqarp/).

2 http://lucene.apache.org

the first one hundred results in 0.063 seconds. This sort of performance can currently only be achieved in index-based retrieval systems.

2. Exporting and sharing results

For the sake of clarity, it makes sense to introduce a feature of PSEN used throughout the paper to provide a permanent reference to the original result screens obtained for submitted queries. The results of all search operations supported by the engine can be saved and shared in the form of compressed URLs. Having typed in a complex query, the user can click the *URL* button (shown in Figure 1) to generate a compressed reference to the result set. As an example, the query for the noun *prawda*, with additional sorting and grouping options is compressed to the following form:

http://nkjp.uni.lodz.pl/?q=ygtpdvf

Such a compressed link can be easily shared or saved for future reference. Typing in the compressed link in a web browser's address bar should bring up precisely the original result screen together with the completed search form. The reader may find the discussion of the PSEN query syntax easier to follow by typing in the compressed URLs listed next to each of the examples I introduce below. This feature of PSEN also eliminates the need for including space-consuming screenshots. The use of URLs as references to concordance results was previously introduced by (Gaskell and Cobb 2004) and also implemented in the *IFAConc* tool[3].

3. Basic PSEN Query syntax

Given a basic introduction, the PSEN query syntax is relatively easy to learn. Single term queries such as:

rewolucja (http://nkjp.uni.lodz.pl/?q=yz3nckf)

can be expanded both orthographically:

rewolucj* (http://nkjp.uni.lodz.pl/?q=yc4y7r8)

and morphologically, as in:

3 http://ifa.amu.edu.pl/~ifaconc/

rewolucja** (http://nkjp.uni.lodz.pl/?q=yjckk4g).

The morphological expansion of a query term saves a lot of typing in languages such as Polish, where a single verb may have dozens of inflectional variants.

Multi-term queries for phrases can be specified by simply typing a sequence of query terms. It is important to remember that for a term to be morphologically expanded, it needs to be entered as a lemma, even if a phrase query is not intended to retrieve the required base form itself. To illustrate, the query for *Wielka Brytania* (Great Britain), i.e.:

Wielki** Brytania** (http://nkjp.uni.lodz.pl/?q=yz2r3yo)

is clearly meant to match the occurrences of the feminine forms of the adjective *wielka* even though the base masculine base form *wielki* is required by the query syntax.

The pipe symbol | can be used to specify morphological, orthographic or lexical variants of a term. For example, to search for all inflections of the noun *łza* (tear) and its diminutive variant *łezka*, one could formulate the following query:

łza**|łezka** (http://nkjp.uni.lodz.pl/?q=ycvghd2).

The orthographic expansion wildcard can also be prefixed to the search term. For instance, to check the productivity of the *-essa* suffix, which is often used in Polish to create feminine noun variants, the following query could be used:

*essa** (http://nkjp.uni.lodz.pl/?q=ygvfhn5)

resulting in matches such as *stewardessa*, *poetessa* or *hostessa*.

4. Slop factor and term order

The basic query syntax is complemented by a number of options available in the search form. The following screenshot shows the options currently available in the basic search form:

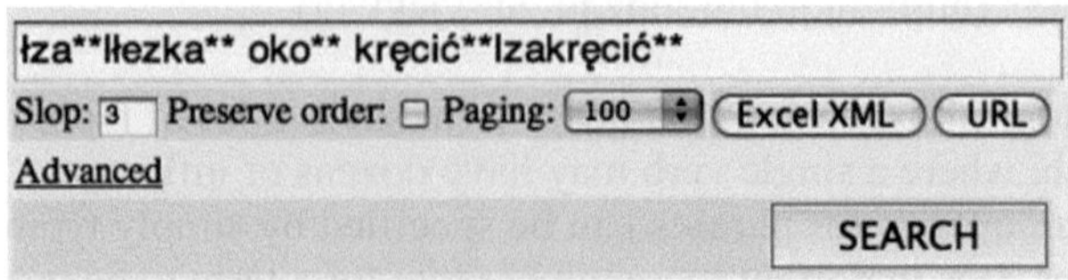

Figure 1. Basic options search form

The first two options, i.e. *Slop* and *Preserve order* can be used to specify the maximum slop factor and the word order restriction respectively. The slop factor indicates how many words may occur between the query terms. Increasing the slop factor generally increases the recall of the result sets when searching for flexible collocations, at the expense of their precision. As an example, the query shown in the screenshot is intended to find collocations of the nouns *łza* (tear) and *oko* (eye) with the verb *zakręcić*, as in "*łza zakręciła się w jej oku*". The phrase would roughly translate into English as "***a tear welled up** in her **eye***".[4]

To further increase the recall of the query, the *Preserve order* box can be unchecked to indicate that the order in which the query terms are entered in the form does not have to be preserved in the matching results. Quite conveniently, a single query such as:

*łza**|łezka** oko** kręcić**|zakręcić***

where the terms *łza*** can be labelled as *1A*, *łezka*** as *1B*, *oko*** as *2A*, *kręcić*** as *3A*, and *zakręcić*** as *3B*, can thus result in a set of permutations of this collocation such as:

kręcą się łzy w oczach (3A 1A 2A)
kręcą się w oczach łzy (3A 2A 1A)
łezka kręci się w oku (1A 3A 2A)
łezka się w oku kręci (1B 2A 3A)
oczach jej zakręciły się łzy (2A 3B 1A)
zakręciła się łezka w oku (3B 1B 2A)

(see: http://nkjp.uni.lodz.pl/?q=37hsds4).

Other options in the advanced search screen include 2-level sorting and grouping of results. The latter option is particularly useful when a large result set is retrieved; a maximum number of results from each register, text or date can be

4 For an example of an equivalent query against the British National Corpus, see http://nkjp.uni.lodz.pl/?q=ya7x6u6.

specified, thus providing an outline of the distribution of the matching words and phrases across registers and time periods. For example, limiting the maximum number of occurrences of the verb *ściemniać* (whose literal meaning roughly corresponds to the English verb *to dim*) to 3 per year (http://nkjp.uni.lodz.pl/?q=yzoezf8) shows that one of the first occurrences of *ściemniać* in the underlying corpus in its relatively recent metaphorical sense of "obfuscating" can be found in a text published in 1996.

It is also possible to search with metadata criteria, including genre, medium, text title and publication date. Particularly useful may be the option of limiting the result set to paragraphs matching a Boolean query specifying contextual keywords. For example, it is possible to search for all the occurrences of the word *połączenie* (connection) as long as it occurs in a paragraph containing at least one of a set of obligatory keywords, such as *kolej* (railway), *pociąg* (train), *autobus* (bus), but none of a set of disqualifying keywords such as *telefon, sieć* (network) or *serwer*:

http://nkjp.uni.lodz.pl/?q=38k8f4a

This option enables basic word sense disambiguation, which comes in handy whenever the user is only interested in one sense of a polysemous word.

5. Collocation extraction module

A separate module of PSEN facilitates the extraction of collocations. In order to retrieve a set of potential collocations, it is necessary to specify the node terms using the query syntax introduced above. As an example, the following definition of a node term:

*bezczelny*** (http://nkjp.uni.lodz.pl/?q=qfrs93)

will be expanded into the set of all inflections of the adjective *bezczelny*. Interestingly, the node of a collocation can be defined as a sequence of terms, thus giving some possibility of extracting multiword collocations, e.g.:

*wymigać*** *się od* (http://nkjp.uni.lodz.pl/?q=pe2q27).

When defining a single term collocate of a given node, it is possible to define its basic part of speech category as well as some positional restrictions, such as the distance from the node. To extract a set of potential adjectival collocations of the noun *zdrada*, the following query could be run:

zdrada** (http://nkjp.uni.lodz.pl/?q=onbdzr)

with the part of speech option set to *adjective*.

6. Application of PSEN in translation teaching

Corpus search software is often claimed to play an important role in a translator's workshop. This claim is based on the generally recognized applicability of corpus tools in the study of lexis and the fact that the job of a translator involves making quick and accurate lexical and phraseological choices. This potential capability of corpus tools is particularly important for beginning translation students, who often find it difficult to break free from the shackles of formal equivalence and develop dynamic equivalence skills at the phraseological level.

Although intuitively, this application of corpora seems reasonable and many translators are indeed frequent corpus users, it is not always obvious how beginning translation students can be encouraged to fully benefit from representative language resources. A general introduction to corpus linguistics is often not enough for translation students to develop a sustained reliance on corpus evidence. Students often lose their interest in corpus resources for a number of reasons. First of all, setting up a desktop corpus application for a large underlying corpus can be a nuisance. Depending on the speed of the computer used and the implementation of the corpus software, it may also be difficult for the software to compete with *Google* in terms of providing instant and universal access to simple examples of word or phrase usage, which is probably the most frequent reason why a translator would refer to a corpus. Moreover, the query syntax of generic corpus tools may offer little advantage over internet search engines when it comes to phraseological queries. Finally, the hassle of reproducing more complex corpus queries and result sets may also discourage both translation students and teachers from a frequent use of corpora. In the remaining part of the paper I address these issues by focusing on two features of PSEN which facilitate the use of corpus evidence in a translation course curriculum.

7. Slop factor phraseological queries

Most translation students are perfectly willing to admit a logical mistake or obvious problems with single-word lexeme equivalence in their assignments. It is usually more difficult to convince them about phraseological incongruities in the target text, and especially so when they are translating into their mother tongue. As native speakers they do not feel less entitled to phraseological judgments about their mother tongue than their teacher.

Although phraseological restrictions are often purely idiomatic, they can equally well be positioned on the grammatical end of the continuum of lexico-grammar (Sinclair 1991). Therefore the difficulty of identifying and explaining phraseological errors in target texts stems not only from purely idiomatic restrictions but also from lexico-grammatical intricacies. Without instant access to a convincing body of evidence, discussing either of the two types of incongruities is often perceived as an exercise in semantic hair-splitting. The advantage of using PSEN in such a situation is that it supports high recall phraseological queries which can be compressed to short URLs, which in turn can be used to annotate a suspicious lexical or phraseological structure.[5] Let us consider the following excerpt from a BBC news article on the recent celebrations of the demise of the Berlin Wall with a corresponding translation provided by one of my translation students:

> ORIGINAL: "History is palpable and alive here. The peaceful revolution of the fall of the Wall 20 years ago ***paved the way*** to an unprecedented transformation of Berlin," Mayor Klaus Wowereit said.

> TRANSLATION: *"Tutaj historia jest wyczuwalna i ciągle żywa. Pokojowa rewolucja związana z upadkiem muru dwadzieścia lat temu niejako* ***wybrukowała drogę do*** *bezprecedensowego procesu przemiany Berlina,' powiedział burmistrz miasta Klaus Wowereit."*

One problematic phraseological item in this translation is the expression *wybrukować drogę*, which is a fairly literal translation of the phrase *to pave the way* used in the original.[6] Most of the native speakers of Polish presented with this translation have found the phrase in question "artificial", but none have attempted a more precise explanation without corpus evidence. One reason why a more definitive explanation is difficult to provide in this case is the fact that the verb + noun collocation *wybrukować drogę* and its variants do occur in Polish[7], and thus it cannot be dismissed as a totally artificial equivalent. A closer look at the examples retrieved from the NKJP data reveals, however, that it is frequently used in the literal sense of "paving a road" and when used metaphorically, it tends to have rather negative prosodies as in *droga do piekła wybrukowana jest dobrymi intencjami* (*the road to hell is paved with good*

5 The use of URL-based concordance references to provide feedback for writing errors was previously discussed by (Cob & Gaskell 2004).

6 Incidentally, in contrast to English, Polish does not distinguish between *droga* as a *way* and *droga* as a *road*.

7 http://nkjp.uni.lodz.pl/?q=yl8wy6n

intentions). Furthermore, another phraseological equivalent *utorować drogę* seems to fit much better in this context[8]. Although based on a slightly different metaphor, it is used almost exclusively in the figurative sense of enabling or facilitating actions and achievements.

Using PSEN it is possible to reference both positive and negative corpus evidence with two compressed URLs. As shown in the screenshot below, the teacher marking up a translation assignment can thus make evidence-based and verifiable comments about the student's phraseological choices:

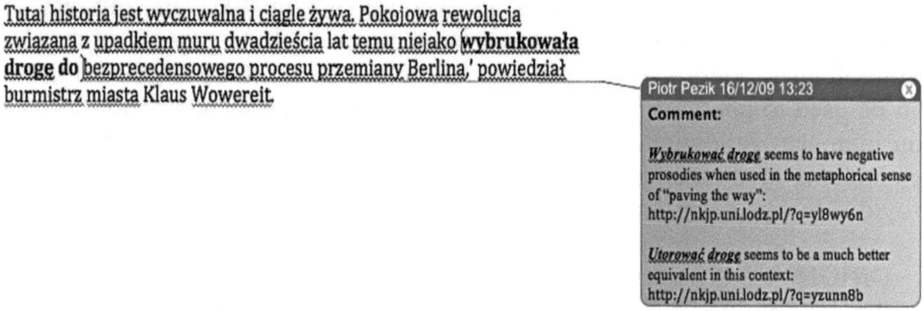

All the students need to do to access the relevant corpus evidence is type the URL provided in their browsers' address bars and hit the enter key. Obviously, a similar sample could be obtained with a few queries sent to a standard concordancer. However, the simplification of tedious search procedures by means of compressed links leaves students with no excuse for ignoring the corpus evidence available.

The collocation extraction module of PSEN can be used in a similar fashion to provide examples of lexico-grammatical restrictions which are difficult to retrieve with a simple concordancer query.

Let us consider an example news article about a space mission aimed at studying the Earth's water cycle. A student's translation of this passage into Polish uses a relative clause based on the verb phrase *mieć na celu*, which can be literally translated as *to have an objective*. Although the choice of the phrase seems to fulfil formal equivalence criteria, it raises difficult to explicate lexico-grammatical suspicions. The problem with *mieć na celu* in this context can be traced to the use of *statek kosmiczny* (spacecraft) as its subject:

ORIGINAL: *The SMOS spacecraft launched on Monday* ***to study the Earth's water cycle*** *has passed a key mission milestone.*

8 http://nkjp.uni.lodz.pl/?q=yzunn8b

TRANSLATION: *Wystrzelony w poniedziałek* ***statek kosmiczny SMOS mający na celu*** *obserwację obiegu wody na Ziemi osiągnął już najważniejszy etap swej misji.*

Somehow, *statek kosmiczny* does not sound right as the subject of *mieć na celu*, but this incongruity can only be fully exposed by examining the subcategorization frames of the idiomatic verb phrase in question. The collocation extraction module of PSEN makes it particularly easy to obtain a list of nouns preceding a word or phrase, have them sorted by statistical significance and saved as a compressed URL:

http://nkjp.uni.lodz.pl/?q=yhamox2

A brief look at the results shows that the great majority of nominal collocates preceding the phrase *mieć na celu* are hyponyms of the notions of *action* or *effort.* There seems to be a semantic restriction on the range of subjects of this lexical item, which would be difficult to identify with a simple concordancer, due to the lexico-grammatical rather than purely lexical nature of the restriction (Biber *et al.* 2008). In other words, the fact that *statek kosmiczny* does not occur in the NKJP corpus as a subject of *mieć na celu* does not convincingly prove that such a combination is impossible. On the other hand, generating a list of typical subjects of the phrase revealing its strong preference to describe the intended purpose of abstract actions rather than physical objects does seem to confirm the seemingly inexplicable intuition signalled by most of the speakers of Polish presented with this translation.

Again, the advantage of using PSEN to bring up the problem is not only the collocation extraction module, but also the possibility of generating direct links to support the teacher's comment with a wealth of corpus evidence. Incidentally, should the teacher misinterpret the corpus evidence available, such a marking procedure may turn out to be a double-edged weapon. An evidence-based discussion of translation choices, however, would be a rather desired development in a university class.

8. Summary

The PSEN syntax supports slop factor and relaxed word order functions, which increase the recall of phraseological queries. In other words, a single query can be formulated to fetch a sample of occurrences of a phrase regardless of the order and position in which its individual constituents and their lexical, orthographic or grammatical variants occur. As illustrated above, such evidence can prove to be indispensable in identifying both lexical and lexico-grammatical incongruities. Together with the collocation extraction module, this functionality can be of real interest to translators, linguists and lexicographers.

The simplification of online search tools sometimes referred to as *googlization* can be defined as an interface design strategy following the assumption that search engine users only need to learn complex syntax and advanced options when absolutely necessary. The familiarity of web-based interfaces also means and that users tend to choose fast and universal browser-based access interfaces over less familiar desktop clients. PSEN follows this philosophy not only by hiding away the advanced options from casual users, but also by providing a way to encode complex searches in compressed URLs, which can be used to reference and share corpus findings.

The present paper shows how the combination of slop factor queries and URL compression can be used to retrieve and share corpus evidence in a way that leaves virtually no excuse for ignoring it. This solution has one application in translation teaching, but it is not difficult to imagine similar applications in other standard use cases of corpus linguistics techniques, such as dictionary making or language teaching. The PELCRA Search Engine for NKJP is hopefully an example of how state-of-art technologies can be used to provide universal access to corpus evidence.

Research funded in 2007-2010 by a research and development grant from the Polish Ministry of Science and Higher Education.

References

Sinclair, J. (1991). *Corpus, Concordance, Collocation*. Oxford University Press.

Biber, D., Conrad, S. and R. Reppen (2008). *Corpus Linguistics: Investigating Language Structure and Use. Cambridge Approaches to Linguistics.*

Gaskell, D. and T. Cobb (2004). *Can learners use concordance feedback for writing errors?* Available at: http://www.lextutor.ca/cv/conc_fb.htm.

Przepiórkowski, A., Górski, R., Łaziński, M. and P. Pęzik (2009). *Recent Developments in the National Corpus of Polish.* In: J. Levická and R. Garabík (eds.). *NLP, Corpus Linguistics, Corpus Based Grammar Research: Proceedings of the Fifth International Conference, Smolenice, Slovakia, 25–27 November 2009*. Slovko 2009: 302–309.

Evaluating the Efficiency of Multiterm Extract for Extraction of English and Polish Terms

Ewelina Kwiatek and Pius ten Hacken

Abstract: The question we investigate in this paper is how efficient MultiTerm Extract is for extracting terms from English and Polish specialized corpora. MultiTerm Extract is a component of SDL Trados 2007, based on statistical methods. The major strength of the statistical approach is its language independence. We carried out term extraction experiments on the basis of small, comparable text corpora taken from English and Polish land surveying textbooks. In order to establish a benchmark, we started by manually extracting the terms from the two corpora. In the experiments, we explore the relation between noise ratio and number of term candidates extracted from corpora as well as the inclusion of terms in the list of term candidates. In order to evaluate extraction outcomes, we use precision and recall measures. The analysis for English uses a stop word list and basic vocabulary, but for Polish these files were not available. We created a stop word list and basic vocabulary for Polish to investigate how the presence of those files affects the size of the list of extracted term candidates.

Keywords: basic vocabulary, land surveying terminology, precision, recall, SDL Trados, stop words, term extraction.

1. MultiTerm Extract

SDL MultiTerm Extract is a component of SDL Trados 2007 used for the computer-assisted extraction of terms. It automatically extracts candidate terms from monolingual and bilingual documents and may also be used for the verification of termbases. There are five types of projects that may be created in MultiTerm Extract, listed in (1).

(1) a. Monolingual Extraction
b. Bilingual Extraction
c. QA Project
d. Translation Project
e. Dictionary Compilation Project

For the identification of terms in monolingual texts, only (1a) is relevant. We do not have access to suitable translation corpora in the domain of land surveying, which excludes (1b), and projects of the types (1c–1e) are used only when a termbase has already been created. In (1c) the goal is to compare a termbase and term use in a text (Quality Assessment), (1d) is concerned with translating a monolingual termbase, (1e) with extracting a bilingual dictionary from a translation memory. The outcome of a monolingual project is a list of candidate terms in a format illustrated in Figure 1.

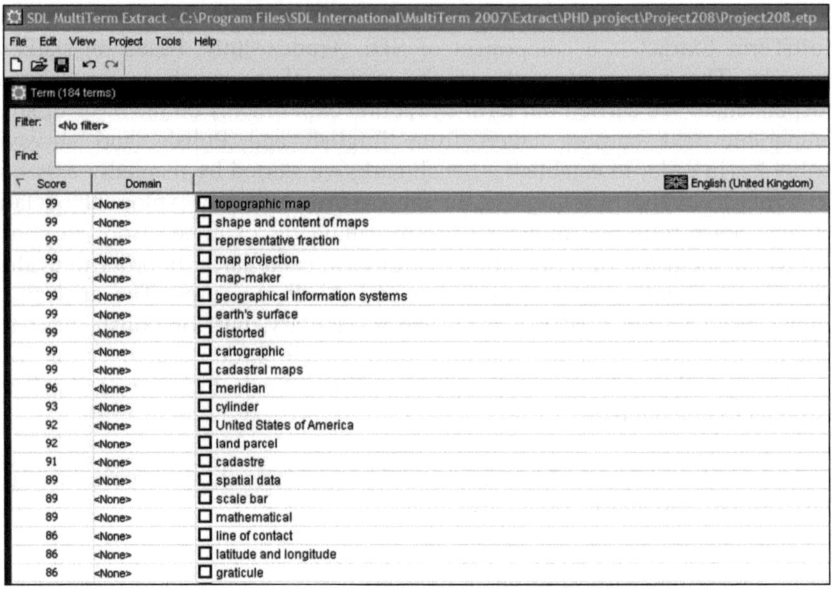

Figure 1. Outcome of monolingual project – Term window

In Figure 1, information is displayed in the main window, called *Term* window, in three columns. The leftmost column in Figure 1 shows the *Score*, which is a value between 1 and 99 generated by the system. It indicates the system's confidence in proposing the term candidate.

The middle column is labeled as *Domain* and contains information about the candidates which is specific for each project. When the list of candidate terms is produced, all candidates have a value of <None>. The user can create a list of possible values and assign one of them to each accepted candidate. This column is intended for a domain specification, e.g. the subfield of land surveying of the term, but it may also be used to specify the part of speech. This information is used in exporting terms to a termbase, not in term extraction, so that it is not relevant to our experiments. Therefore we leave it unspecified.

The rightmost column in Figure 1 includes candidate terms. The column is headed by the language name and each candidate term is preceded by a tick box, which is used to validate a candidate (i.e. to confirm that it is a term).

The *Term* window has filtering and sorting facilities. Items can be filtered according to their validation status: *Only validated* or *Only non validated.* This hides term candidates not fulfilling this condition. Sorting of candidates can be done by each column.

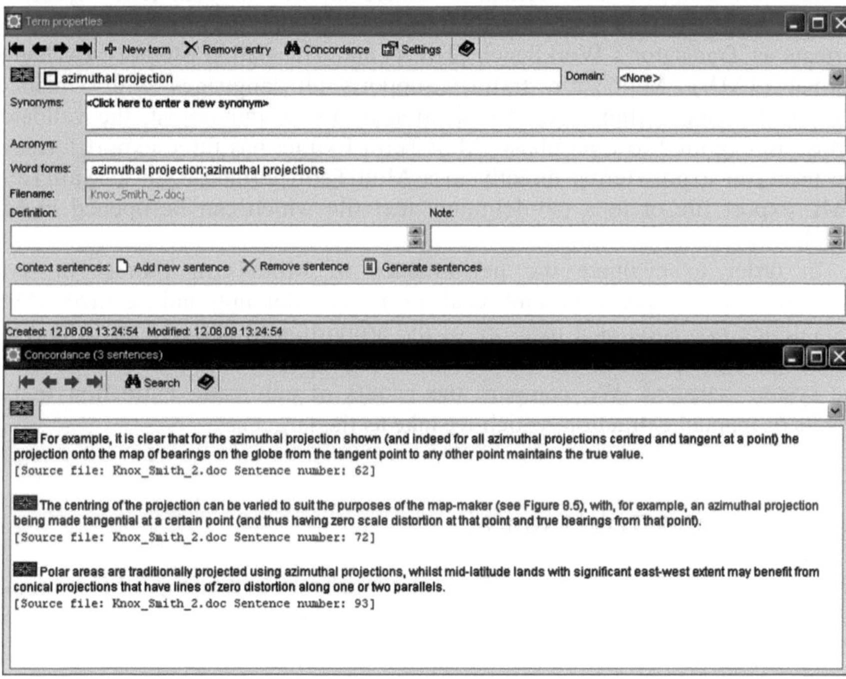

Figure 2. Outcome of monolingual project – Term properties window and Concordance window

Figure 2 shows the *Term properties* window and *Concordance* window for a monolingual project. These windows are opened automatically and appear below the window in Figure 1. By double-clicking on a particular candidate in Figure 1, its specification is displayed in the *Term properties* window. A number of fields are made available for the specification of synonyms, acronyms, definition and notes. The system displays the name of the file the term was taken from and calculates word forms. The system does not include lemmatization rules and guesses a citation form from the set of word forms collected. Thus, it combines *projected*, *projection* and *projections* into a lemma *projected*, whereas *projection* would be more appropriate. The button *Concordance* in the *Term properties* window generates a concordance for the selected item. The result is shown in the lower part of Figure 2.

MultiTerm Extract supports term extraction from a wide range of file formats. The supported file formats depend on the type of project. The monolingual file formats encompass such formats as plain text, reach text format, Microsoft Office: Word, Excel, PowerPoint, HTML, SGML, and XML, whereas the bilingual file formats available in the bilingual term extraction project, translation project and dictionary compilation project cover such formats as Translator's Workbench (TMW) and Translation Memory Exchange Format (TMX). MultiTerm Extract supports all languages with Unicode-compliant scripts. After manual validation by the terminologist, the validated terms are exported to a termbase. MultiTerm Extract has three export formats; the user can export terms directly to a MultiTerm termbase, to a MultiTerm XML export file or to a tab-delimited text file which can be opened in MS Excel.

In order to evaluate the performance of MultiTerm Extract in term extraction, we use precision and recall measures. Manning and Schütze (1999: 267) define *precision* as a measure of the proportion of selected items that the system got right and *recall* as a measure of the proportion of the target items that the system selected. We compare the results of automatic extraction to the results of manual extraction, which we take as the target set.

2. Settings in MultiTerm Extract

The user of MultiTerm Extract can adjust a number of settings in a Monolingual Extraction project. These settings influence the selection of candidate terms. They are listed in (2).

(2) a. Minimum term length
b. Maximum term length
c. Maximum number of extracted terms
d. Silence/noise ratio
e. Stopword lists
f. Exclusion files

These settings may be adjusted in the *New Project Wizard* window shown in Figure 3.

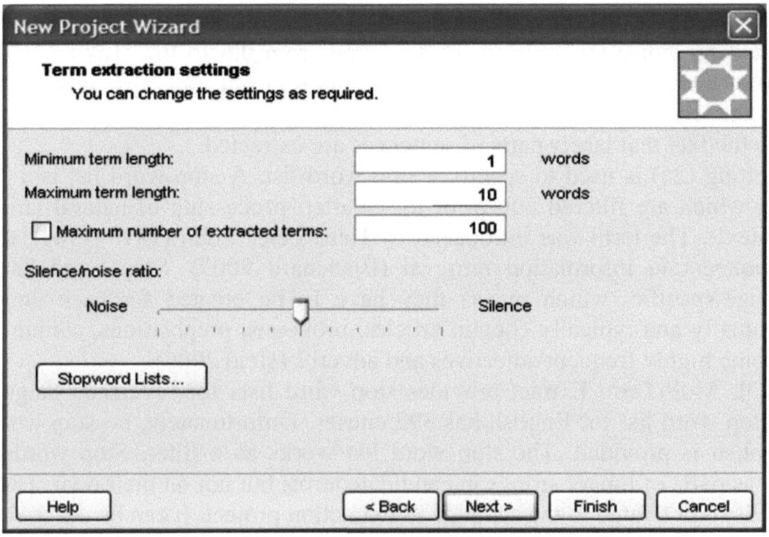

Figure 3. Default settings in MultiTerm Extract

The settings (2a–b) determine the length (in words) of the strings considered as candidate terms. The minimum default term length is 1 and the maximum is 10, but the user can restrict the maximum term length to 3 or 4 to avoid obtaining whole phrases or even parts of sentences as a result of extraction. We did not vary term length settings in our experiment. Whereas the maximum length of the terms in the target set is 4, terms are often components of longer strings of texts, e.g. *large-scale map* can appear in 'maps are often known as large scale or small scale'. We considered such longer strings also as occurrences of the term.

Setting (2c) is used to restrict the maximum number of candidate terms. If this number is set to *n*, no more than *n* candidate terms are returned. The candidates returned are the ones with the highest scores in the total number of candidate terms extracted when this setting is not activated. For example, if the user only wants to obtain 30 candidate terms, the software will extract 30 candidates with the highest scores and remove the remaining part of the list. We did not use this feature in our experiment as we were interested in the whole set of candidate terms.

Setting (2d) has the form of a scale with maximal noise (minimal silence) indicated by the leftmost point on the scale, maximal silence (minimal noise) indicated by the rightmost point on the scale and the default setting just in the middle of the scale. Following Fernandéz Parra and ten Hacken (2008), we will refer to this setting as *noise levels*, ranging from 0 (minimal noise) to 1 (minimal silence). The scale in Figure 3 indicates nine intermediate points between 0 and

1. The outcomes of term extraction proved, however, that the same output was obtained for noise levels from 0.8 to 1 and from 0.6 to 0.7. Taking this into account, there are eight noise levels to choose from. We also observed that candidate terms identified for the highest levels of noise are often very long. It is due to the fact that larger parts of sentences are extracted.

Setting (2e) is used to specify a stop word list. A stop word list is a list of words which are filtered out, prior to, or after, processing of natural language data (text). The term was introduced by Hans Peter Luhn (1896–1964), one of the pioneers in information retrieval (Blanchard 2007). Stop word lists are language-specific, which means they have to be created for each language individually and typically contain articles, pronouns, prepositions, conjunctions and some highly frequent adjectives and adverbs (Heid 2006).

SDL MultiTerm Extract provides stop word lists for seventeen languages. The stop word list for English has 392 entries. Unfortunately, no stop word list for Polish is provided. The stop word list works as a filter. Stop words may occur as parts of longer strings in candidate terms but not on their own. The stop word list is activated in the setup of an extraction project. It can be deactivated if required. It is possible to edit stop word lists or to select other files. Therefore we considered various ways to produce a Polish stop word list (cf. section 4 below). The outcomes of the extraction presented in sections 3 and 4 below will show the influence of the stop word list on the results of term extraction.

The final option, (2f), is not visible in Figure 3 but can be specified elsewhere in the project setup. An exclusion file typically contains basic vocabulary, i.e. frequent verbs, nouns, adjectives, adverbs, pronouns, prepositions, conjunctions as well as geographical names, nationalities, proper names, titles, days, months and their abbreviations. Basic vocabulary is used in a way similar to the stop word list. It is compiled taking into consideration the frequency of general vocabulary known to an average speaker of the language (SDL Trados 2007). SDL MultiTerm Extract provides basic vocabulary for five languages: English, French, German, Spanish and Italian. The English inventory has 4,279 entries. For Polish, no basic vocabulary is provided. In sections 3 and 4, the effect of using basic vocabulary in term extraction will be evaluated.

3. Investigation of the English corpus with MultiTerm Extract

For our experiments, we had to use corpora that are small enough for manual term extraction and for the evaluation of a relatively large number of experiments with alternative settings. At the same time, they have to be dense on terms. Therefore, we decided to take fragments from textbooks in the domain of land surveying. For English, we chose Bannister *et al.* (1992) as our textbook and selected the first two chapters as our corpus. The first chapter, entitled

"Introductory", is 3,337 words long and the second chapter, entitled "Tape and offset surveying", is 2,454 words long. The total size of the corpus is 5,791 words.

Before automatic extraction, we identified terms in the corpus manually in order to obtain the target set. The target set consists of 120 terms. Then, we carried out 32 term extraction projects for the English corpus. We performed automatic extraction with MultiTerm Extract for four sets of projects with 8 different noise settings. These sets of projects are characterized as in (3).

(3) a. Both the stop word list and the basic vocabulary are used
b. Only the basic vocabulary is used, no stop word list
c. Only the stop word list is used, no basic vocabulary
d. Neither the basic vocabulary nor the stop word list are used

Each experiment is characterized by one of the filter settings in (3) and a particular noise level. Our aim is to find out which noise level(s) and which filter setting produce the best recall and precision.

The result of each experiment is a list of candidate terms. In the discussion of the results, we will consider the noise level and the filter settings of the project together. A first measure characterizing the output of the projects is the number of candidate terms returned, presented in Figure 4.

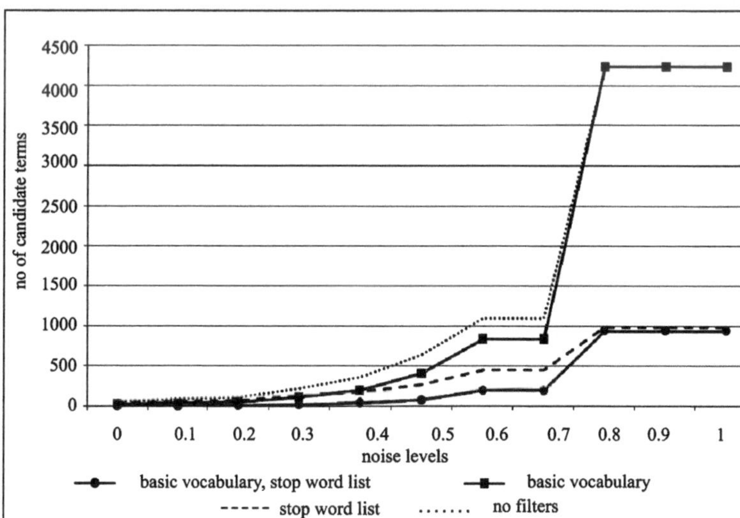

Figure 4. Number of candidate terms for different sets of projects

Figure 4 suggests that the extraction results are comparable for (3a) and (3c) and again for (3b) and (3d). The basic vocabulary does not seem to be as crucial as a filter for extraction as the stop word list. With high noise levels, the influence on the number of candidates is minimal. Nevertheless, for noise levels up to 0.7, the comparison of (3a) and (3c) shows that the basic vocabulary eliminates about half of the number of term candidates. The number of candidate terms for the highest noise levels under settings (3b) and (3d) is almost the same as the number of words in the corpus. It is also quite interesting that there is a significant jump in the number of candidate terms between the noise levels 0.7 and 0.8. As mentioned above, for the noise levels between 0.8 and 1, the same list of term candidates is returned, as well as for 0.6–0.7.

The data in Figure 4 only represent the size of the output, not its quality. We analysed the sets of candidate terms for the different noise levels under filter settings (3a) and (3c) by calculating precision and recall. The results for (3a) are given in Table 1.

Table 1. Precision, recall and F-measure for different noise levels for (3a)

Noise level	**0**	**0.1**	**0.2**	**0.3**	**0.4**	**0.5**	**0.6–0.7**	**0.8–1**
Candidate terms	6	9	14	29	49	86	205	941
No of terms	1	3	7	13	17	25	51	118
Precision (%)	17	33	50	44	35	29	25	12.5
Recall (%)	0.8	2.5	6	11	14	21	43	98
F-measure (%)	0.05	0.59	3.36	5.32	4.80	6.09	14.62	27.07

Table 1 indicates a clear tendency for recall to go up when the noise level is raised. It reaches a maximum of 98% with the highest noise level. Precision goes up till noise level 0.2, where it reaches a maximum of 50%, and then gradually decreases with rising noise level. These inverse tendencies for precision and recall are more or less what we can expect. They complicate the choice of an optimal noise level, because they give contradicting information. Manning and Schütze (1999: 269) propose the *F-measure* as a solution to this problem. The F-measure combines precision and recall into a single value. In our case, the F-measure follows recall and goes up when the level of noise goes up although this tendency is slightly disturbed for noise level 0.4 when the F-measure drops. The F-measure has the highest value for noise levels 0.8–1, the same as recall. This shows that the rise in recall is higher than the expected drop in precision. A similar result for MultiTerm Extract was obtained with a somewhat different research question by Fernández Parra and ten Hacken (2008).

For practical purposes, the highest noise level may not be the most appropriate value, despite its high recall and F-measure. Even with a small corpus like ours, the set of candidate terms is very large. For larger corpora, the output set may soon reach a size that is too large for manual processing. Confidence scores are only a modest help in the analysis. Thus, *optical square* only reaches 51, whereas *see figure* has 99. A compromise may be to settle for noise level 0.6–0.7, which reduces the amount of work (number of candidate terms) by almost 80% while still retrieving 43% of the genuine terms. The very high recall for the highest noise level should be offset against the alternative of manual retrieval without MultiTerm Extract.

A factor that is important in the evaluation of these results is illustrated in the sample of term candidates in (4) and (5).

(4)
a. required
b. located
c. graduated
d. follows
e. observed
f. geographical information system

(5)
a. zone has the same coordinate values as on the central meridian
b. various ellipsoids were recommended for different parts of the world
c. precautions are required when connecting such surveys to control points
d. use in navigation where correct representation of bearings
e. used as a convenient means of reproducing the hard copies
f. versatile little instrument can be used either as a hand

In (4), the complete set of candidates for noise level 0 is given. Only one of these candidates, (4f), is a term, while all others, which are single-word items, are general words. Candidate terms extracted for noise level 0 can be relatively quickly analysed. (5) is a selection from the term candidates returned for the highest noise level. We counted (5a) as a correct case of the retrieval of *coordinate* and *central meridian*, (5b) of *ellipsoid*, (5c) of *control point*, and (5d) of *bearing*. (5e–f) do not contain any terms. As can be seen from these examples, for high noisc levels, the the set of candidates is not only much larger, but the analysis of each candidate also requires more time. Yet this approach is essential to obtain the high recall value in Table 1. It is possible to eliminate such candidates by changing the value for (2b), but then recall also drops. In fact, we found that changing the maximal term length to 4 resulted also in an increase of the number of term candidates. For the highest noise level, we had 1501 term candidates instead of 941, because strings such as (5) tend to be split. In total we found 107 terms among them, i.e. a recall of 89.17%.

In the analysis of a set of candidates including (5), it is not straightforward to keep track of which candidates have already been validated. One term may occur as a part of more than one term candidates and these term candidates may be arbitrarily far apart in the list presented to the terminologist. Validation is therefore a two-stage process. In the first step, each of the term candidates is analysed and evaluated. Then the non-validated term candidates are eliminated and the remaining candidates alphabetically sorted. Then the terminologist eliminates duplicate terms and checks for consistency before exporting the result to a termbase.

In order to explore the exact contribution of the basic vocabulary list, we also analysed the results for (3c). They are summarized in Table 2.

Table 2. Precision, recall and F-measure for different noise levels for (3c)

Noise ratio	**0**	**0.1**	**0.2**	**0.3**	**0.4**	**0.5**	**0.6–0.7**	**0.8–1**
Candidate terms	41	65	76	134	187	269	451	988
No of terms	6	10	11	16	21	47	67	118
Precision (%)	14.63	15.38	14.67	11.94	11.23	17.47	14.86	11.94
Recall (%)	5	8.33	9.17	13.33	17.5	39.17	55.83	98.33
F-measure (%)	0.29	0.61	0.63	0.80	1.13	7.75	11.73	18.78

As Table 2 shows, the basic vocabulary gives a substantial contribution to precision. Deactivating it yields a higher recall at noise level 0.6–0.7, but at the cost of having to go through more than double the number of candidates.

The conclusion is, therefore, that recall can be very high if a large amount of time and effort is invested in the post-editing of a large set of term candidates. Various shortcuts may reduce the effort, but they invariably also reduce recall. The two filters make a significant contribution to reducing the amount of term candidates returned, in particular the stop word list. High recall values were achieved also with these filters activated, so that they are very useful.

4. Investigation of the Polish corpus with MultiTerm Extract

In compiling our Polish corpus, we did an effort to achieve a correspondence with the English corpus, in order to increase the scope for comparison of the results. As a source, we selected a Polish textbook on land surveying, Wołłodko (1973), from which fragments of the following chapters were taken:

- Chapter 1 "Podstawowe wiadomości z teorii błędów" ('Basic information on the errors theory', 300 words)
- Chapter 2 "Pomiary sytuacyjne" ('Geodetic surveys', 1,451 words)
- Chapter 5 "Niwelacja techniczna" ('Technical levelling', 3,139 words)
- Chapter 7 "Pomiar kątów" ('Angle measurement', 760 words)

In the listed chapters, we only selected those parts that are dense in terms and contribute new information to the corpus, omitting tables and some passages with detailed descriptions of measurement processes. The total size of the Polish corpus created by applying such criteria reaches 5,650 words. In manual extraction we identified 139 terms.

The extraction procedure for the Polish corpus followed the same pattern as applied to the English corpus. However, as no stop word list and basic vocabulary for Polish were provided by MultiTerm, we had to develop our own in order to be able to compare the extraction output for English and Polish.

We started by creating a stop word list for Polish. We considered two different approaches: translating the English stop word list into Polish or using an available stop word list taken from the Internet. The first approach was rejected immediately. The English stop word list, which has 427 entries, could be translated into Polish but the proper selection of stop words is language-specific. Some entries in the English stop word list have no direct translation into Polish. For instance, Polish has no articles. In other cases, many translations are possible, but it is not clear which ones should be stop words in Polish, e.g. *of*, *been*, *being*, *don't*, *didn't*, *will*, *would*, etc. Another problem is the large number of inflected forms associated with Polish verbs (including auxiliaries), nouns, and pronouns.

We found a stop word list at Wikipedia (http://pl.wikipedia.org/wiki/Wikipedia:Stopwords, retrieved on 20.03.2009), and a lexeme frequency list based on the demonstration corpus compiled by Polskie Wydawnictwo Naukowe ('Polish Scientific Publishers', PWN). The stop word list available at Wikipedia is language specific but quite limited with only 144 entries. The lexeme frequency list for the PWN demonstration corpus (http://korpus.pwn.pl/stslow_en.php, retrieved on 20.03.2009) proved to be the most reliable solution. It was elaborated for the purpose of the Polish PWN dictionary. The frequency list consists of 571 word forms with a very high frequency. They cover the most frequent inflected forms of auxiliary and modal verbs, pronouns and high-frequency nouns such as *mężczyzna* ('man'), *praca* ('job'), or *rok* ('year'). For example, there are 49 word forms of the lexeme *być* ('be') and 22 of the lexeme *on* ('he'). The list also contains 198 lexeme entries. The frequency of the lexemes was calculated by summing up the frequency of all forms with reference to the proportions of their occurrence in the Polish frequency dictionary SFPW (Kurcz *et al.* 1990).

Whereas a stop word list could be selected in this way, finding basic vocabulary for Polish was a more challenging task. There are a few Polish corpora that could be a basis for creating a basic vocabulary file. They include the *IPI PAN* corpus (Przepiórkowski 2008), the corpus of the SFPW and the PWN corpus of Polish. They are available on-line and provide search engines and concordancers so it is possible to check if a word occurs in a corpus and in what contexts it can be found. The type of access is however constrained to simple search so we could only ask for the occurrences and frequency of a specific expression. What we need for our experiments is a basic vocabulary list. It could be extracted by making a full concordance of the Polish corpora samples if such were available on-line or on CD-ROM and could be in a format that is easy to process with MultiTerm (doc, txt or html files).

Due to the fact that neither a basic vocabulary list nor a full Polish corpus were available for our research, we used the basic vocabulary list for learners of Polish as a second language available at http://www.dicts.info/vocabulary. This site offers vocabulary for a number of languages. Words are sorted by semantic and grammatical categories (e.g. linguistics, mathematics, science, geography, weather, communication, nouns, adjectives, verbs, prepositions) and we collected a total of 1,514 entries. The selection of vocabulary for different languages seems to be based on English as a pivot language, because all lists are bilingual and German and Polish versions have the same English lexemes.

After creating a basic vocabulary file, term extraction was performed for four sets of projects corresponding to (3a–d), as for the English corpus. The results of term extraction are presented in the Figure 5 below.

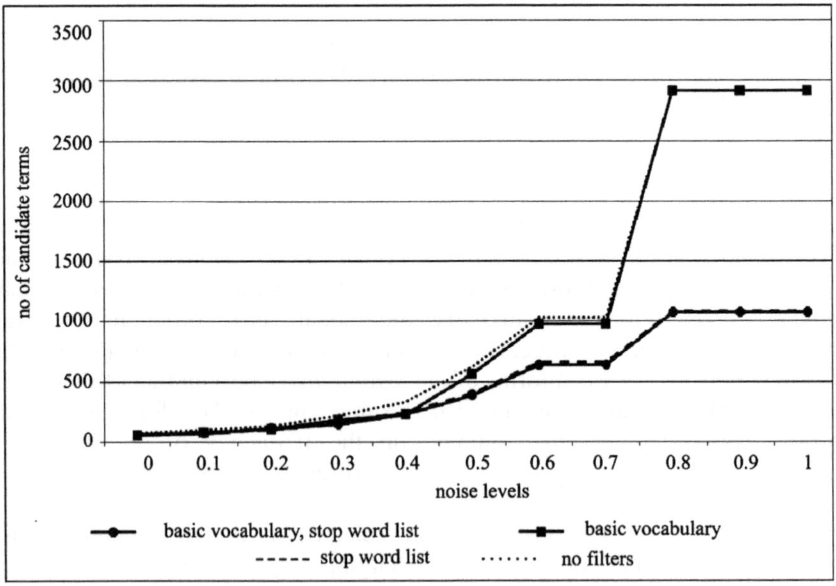

Figure 5. Number of candidate terms for different sets of projects

Figure 5 shows a similar tendency to what we found for the English corpus in Figure 4. There are two pairs of projects sets that produce comparable results. One pair is (3a) and (3c) and the other one is (3b) and (3d). In Polish, the stop word list on its own has a similar influence on term extraction as the use of both filters. Without the stop word list, the number of term candidates rises significantly and we can expect that there is a lot of noise among them. As for English, the noise levels 0.6 and 0.7 produce identical results as do the noise levels from 0.8 to 1.

There are also a number of interesting differences. Whereas in English, high noise levels without the stop word list resulted in a number of term candidates of around 4,200, the same settings produced fewer than 3,000 term candidates in Polish. For setting (3a), with both filters enabled, the highest noise levels resulted in less than twice the number of term candidates to noise level 0.6–0.7 for Polish, as opposed to almost five times as many for English. Another striking point is the reduced influence of the basic vocabulary list. Whereas for English, Figure 4 shows clear differences between projects with and without the basic vocabulary list for noise levels between 0.4 and 0.7, for Polish the effect of the basic vocabulary list is absorbed entirely in the effect of the stop word list. There are two possible explanations for the latter. Either the basic vocabulary is less useful in reducing the number of term candidates in Polish than it is in English or we have not found the right basic vocabulary list yet. This is clearly a question for further research.

Turning now to the evaluation of the sets of term candidates, Table 3 summarizes the number of candidate terms, the number of actual terms and precision, recall and F-measure for each noise level. In view of the results summarized in Figure 5, we only considered projects with both filters enabled.

Table 3. Precision, recall and F-measure for different noise levels

Noise level	**0**	**0.1**	**0.2**	**0.3**	**0.4**	**0.5**	**0.6–0.7**	**0.8–1**
Candidate terms	54	68	108	144	225	384	634	1073
No of terms	14	14	18	26	31	48	81	130
Precision (%)	26	20	17	18	14	12	13	12
Recall (%)	10	10	13	18	22	34	58	93
F-measure (%)	1.87	1.20	1.33	2.20	2.22	3.67	10.71	23.44

The figures in Table 3 are broadly in line with our findings for English. Recall gradually rises to 93% for the highest noise levels. Precision decreases from a maximum of 26% for noise level 0 to about half that figure for noise levels between 0.4 and 1. The F-measure shows that the rise of recall is much more significant than the fall in precision, so that it generally follows recall. As can be expected from the higher numbers of the candidate sets, precision is generally lower in Polish than in English, where all noise levels between 0.1 and 0.7

reached precision levels of 25–50%. Recall figures for Polish are generally much higher, except for the highest noise levels. This cannot be because the system is tuned to Polish so it must be that the language gives more clues about termhood that can be retrieved automatically.

As for the choice of an optimal noise level in Polish, a similar reasoning can be followed as for English. The highest noise levels return impractically large sets of candidate terms. The case for noise levels 0.6 and 0.7 is less convincing than in English, however, because they return a much larger set of candidates than for English and do not show the rise in precision we observed in Table 1. Precision is rather comparable to Table 2, i.e. when basic vocabulary is deactivated. This reinforces the conclusion that a better basic vocabulary list for Polish is needed.

5. Conclusion

In this paper, we described experiments with automatic term extraction by means of MultiTerm Extract. We tried to evaluate the efficiency of the software for the identification of terms in comparable, specialized corpora of English and Polish texts. We tried to find the optimal use of filters and noise level setting. In our experiments we did not use all possible settings, listed in (2), but concentrated on the ones that seemed to us most useful for our research question. The Polish stop word list and basic vocabulary we used were not part of the SDL Trados package and we realize that the basic vocabulary list was not optimal for our purposes.

Our experiments show that the activation of both the stop word list and the basic vocabulary for the English corpus eliminates a great amount of noise compared to projects where these filters are not activated. The tendency for Polish is similar, but compared to English, the basic vocabulary list has less impact on the set of candidate terms returned. The list we used was developed by translation and intended for learners. It remains to be seen whether a better list for use in term extraction can be devised, for instance by further analysis of Kurcz *et al.*'s (1990) frequency dictionary.

In both languages, we found that when both filters are activated the increase of noise levels results in a rise of recall and a fall in precision. However, precision is much higher in English overall and in Polish, recall is higher at all noise levels except for 0.8 to 1. Using Manning and Schütze's (1999) F-measure, we found that for both languages the rise in recall is much more significant than the fall in precision. Nevertheless, given the amount of manual validation work involved, there is a good case to be made for not using these highest noise levels. Even for our small corpora, around 1000 individual candidates have to be analysed. This analysis is not just a matter of assigning yes/no to a candidate, but involves recognizing terms in a longer string. In English, the case for a lower noise level is stronger, because at 0.6–0.7 precision is much higher and the number of term candidates drops by almost 80%. For Polish the effect is less striking and we might explore other means of improving the overall level of help provided by the software, in particular a well-designed basic vocabulary list.

References

Bannister, A., Raymond, S. and R. Baker (1992). *Surveying* (7th ed). Edinburgh: Longman.

Heid, U. (2006). "Extracting term candidates from recursively chunked text". In: ten Hacken, Pius (ed.). *Terminology, Computing and Translation*. Tübingen: Narr: 97–116.

Kurcz, I., Lewicki, A., Szfran, K. and J. Woronczak (1990). *Słownik frekwencyjny polszczyzny współczesnej – SFPW* [A Frequency Dictionary of Contemporary Polish]. Kraków: Instytut Języka Polskiego PAN.

Manning, Ch. and Schütze, Hinrich (1999). *Foundations of Statistical Natural Language Processing*. MIT Press: Cambridge (MA).

Ogrodniczuk, M. (2008). *Polish language of the XX century sixties*: http://www.mimuw.edu.pl/polszczyzna/pl196x/index_en.htm (retrieved on 26.07.2009).

Przepiórkowski, A. (2008). *IPI PAN Corpus* [Polish Corpus developed at the Institute of Computer Science, Polish Academy of Sciences – ICS PAS]: Available at: http://korpus.pl/index.php?page=welcome (retrieved on 26.07.2009).

PWN (2009). *PWN Corpus of Polish*: http://korpus.pwn.pl/index_en.php (retrieved on 26.07.2009).

SDL Trados (2007). *SDL MultiTerm Extract* [Computer program].

Wołłodko, Z. (1973). *Geodezja*. Warszawa: Państwowe Wydawnictwo Rolnicze i Leśne: 7–277.

Part Three

CORPUS-BASED LANGUAGE STUDIES

What's an a "DUCK"? A Corpus Study of Salience and Attention Within Animal-Related, Denominal Verb

Janusz Badio

Abstract: The present article attempts to find converging evidence for the thesis proposed by Kashak and Glenberg (2000: 508–529) that three processes of: indexing, deriving affordances and meshing are used simultaneously in language understanding. The verb *duck* has been used to search the XML BNC. This denominal verb is shown to involve various constructions that arguably provide clues in the interpretation process. So it is not only the denominal verb which contributes its more or less conventional semantic profile, but also constructions in which it is embedded highlight salient portions of our conceptualisations. The categories of analysis that were used were: *DUCK* as VVB, VVI, VVD, VVN and VVG. So what is in a duck? Partly what "is" in this verb is connected with our experiences and interactions with ducks and partly in the constructions that convention has smoothly attached to it. Such a conclusion seems to back up the embodiment thesis endorsed by cognitive linguists.

Keywords: affording, BNC XML, constructions, foregrounding, highlighting, indexing, meshing, profiling, understanding.

1. Introduction

The article undertakes the task of corpus analysis of animal-related, *denominal verb 'duck'* as in:

1 to **duck** into sth/behind sth

More specifically, it is designed to provide additional (corpus), converging data for the thesis endorsed and experimentally researched by Kashak and Glenberg (2000: 508–529) that the interpretation of linguistic utterances is constrained by the extralinguistic context in which an utterance occurs and by the particular syntactic construction employed in an utterance. In other words, meaning emerges in the process of constructing *salience*[1] by instructing verbally against rapidly accessed and processed contextual information and syntactic constraints.

---

1 Rachel Giora (2003) skillfully demonstrates how salient concepts can arise despite and against clear contextual clues and direct verbal instructions that should guide attention properly towards the desired interpretation.

Processes of attention are crucial in coding decisions. By way of example, the utterance:

2 The goal keeper **ducked** his head to avoid the impact, which cost Liverpool a point. (invented example)

uses lexis that can be easily guessed to describe a scene from a football match. The particular order is not haphazard. Sentence (4) is an example of a S+V+O+ADV construction, whose prototypical meaning is shown below:

3 S+V+O+ADV → S acts on O (and circumstances [ADV])[2]

Some other constructions and their hypothesized, though only prototypical meanings are illustrated in the table below (adapted from Kashak and Glenberg: ibid. 509).

Table 1. Syntactic Form and Meaning Pairs

Form	Example	Hypothesized (prototypical) meaning
Mono-transitive ***N-V-O***	Jack pushed the car.	N **acts on** O
Di-transitive ***N-V-O1-O2(C)***	Mum gave Dad the keys.	N **transfers** O2 to O1
Caused motion *N-V-O-OBL*[3]	Mary pulled the cloth off the table	N **causes** O to go to OBL
Resultative ***N-V-O-COMP***	He kicked the door open.	N **causes** O to **become** Comp.

A linguistic expression guides processes of interpretation by highlighting certain aspects of the described *event*. The following sub-processes are said to be critical in verbally pointing to those fragments of the perceived or imagined

2 There can be other non-prototypical semantic extensions such as *John swam the river,* which do not have the meaning component ACT ON. In fact, different extensions from the prototype of this transitive construction have been demonstrated (Taylor 1989) to form a continuum, which construction grammars claim to be necessarily different constructions. So, for example *The children were slowly approaching the stadium* and *He kicked the ball* will differ with regard to the AGENT (singular, plural) or EFFECT (the ball changes position while the stadium does not).

3 Many verbs can be used with an object noun phrase and a prepositional phrase with preposition. This construction is sometimes called transitive oblique. For example: *George handed the bottle to William. She sent an email to him. I taught English to adults,* or with other prepositions as in *He sneezed the foam off his beer* (last sentence adapted from Goldberg 1995, 2003).

event that should be granted appropriate level of attention when people listen or read a sentence. First, words are *indexed*, mapped to their referents in the described scene or their analog mental representations (conf. Barsalou 1999). Words then can be said to set up the content of the scene/event; they express the WHO and WHAT, the participants in a physical scene or an imagined, even abstract one. The second process, *deriving affordances*[4] is responsible for generating possibilities in which people can interact with the environment/object in a given context. Finally, during the third process, *meshing*, affordances get combined into "what amounts to a mental *simulation*" (Glenberg and Kashak 2000: 511) or a mental imagery that involves visual, olfactory, kinetic, auditory and motor information. The three processes act in parallel to achieve the desired interpretation.

The term *construction* is an important one in the discussion of lexical meaning, as the latter is inextricably bound (*afforded from* and *meshed*) by context and syntax. Even in the case of novel uses of a lexeme, one can derive proper *affordances* and reach the *meshing* phase amounting to a simulation because of numerous earlier interactions with a class of objects that are pointed to by the *denominal verb*. In the absence of at least some contextual clues and in the presence of only those that can be inferred from the very utterance, the interpretation process is usually not adequately constrained. In the sentence,

4 *She lamped the butter

one is left wondering who or what is the *she*, what it is that *she* may have done with the butter. Possible interpretations include: *she heated it with a lamp*, *she found it using butter*, *made it into a lamp-shape*, and perhaps some other. The interpretation process is additionally guided by the syntax of the expression, which is SVO, that is SOMEONE or SOMETHING ACTS ON SOMETHING, so the reader is clued to expect some entity has been acted upon in a certain way. In the invented examples [7] and [8],

5 *Their duck lamped last year. (died under a lamp, had small ducks under a lamp, had a nest in an old lamp)

---

4 An affordance is a quality of an object … that allows a person to perform an action. The term was proposed by Gibson (1977) in his article "The Theory of Affordances …". For example, if one says *He telephoned Peter*, by convention we understand he talked with Peter on the phone, rather than hit him. Novel expressions can be understood in context because objects have affordances, possible actions they can put into. E.g. *Tom booked his head because it was raining* induces a scene and the verb *book* used in a novel way is most probably understood as "cover with a book" or some other interpretation because the contex is minimal can emerge. Moreover, **affordances** can become conventional in a language, but in another.

6 *Their dog lamped last year. (jumped so high it touched a lamp, ran into a tree)

two different animal-related denominal verbs impinge on our consciousness the affordances of prototypical nominal profiles of predicates *dog* and *duck* that seem relevant in the interpretation process. Moreover, the structure S+V+Adv makes us assume the denominal verbs in [7] and [8] are intransitive, which invokes a schematic, complex process involving at least three entities.

So constructions are to be understood as learnt pairings of form and meaning (Goldberg 2003: 220) or to use Langacker's (1991) term *symbolic units* with variable: complexity, cognitive entrenchment, schematicity, conventionality, type/token frequency of occurrence and use or productivity. One feature of construction grammar is that it does not propose different senses each time a form points to a different interpretation. Instead, constructions (form meaning pairings) including words have a general meaning with different shades that, apart from context, are also provided by the larger construction in which it participates (Kashak and Glenberg 2000: 510). If one delegates a part of responsibility for meaning construction from words, it must grant it to *syntactic schemas* such as S causes Y to Z. Goldberg (1995) puts forward a hypothesis that argument structure constructions encode basic scenes of human experience such as: *transfer*, *acting on* or *motion*. For instance, the SVOO construction cues the comprehender that the sentence concerns a transfer situation or energetic interaction of some other kind.

Very importantly, the term *construction* is not a synonym of *expression*. In fact, as Goldberg (2003) points out, the latter may and usually does involve half a dozen of constructions at the same time. The skillful, parallel operations of using the *constructions* within a single *clause* is supervised by various strands, features and functions of our attention. The achievement of the desired level of salience of a substructure of a *predication* requires appropriate, skillful use of form. Even the smallest alternation will result in some change in an aspect of attention, for example its *scope* or *intensity*. In other words, the *profile* of a predication and/or *active zone* may change from slightly to greatly.

2. Question and analysis

To repeat, the question that Kashak and Glenberg (2000) researched in a two-factor within subjects design was whether two independent (manipulated) variables (construction type and nonce verb) had some effect on the dependent variable – the proportion of double subject constructions chosen. Using the statistical test ANOVA, they were able to demonstrate that:

> adult participants are sensitive to the meanings associated with particular syntactic forms and that these meanings are not due to previously established meanings of these verbs … constructional meanings can be used to constrain the meaning of innovative denominal verbs … constructional meaning is not enough to ensure felicitous understanding of sentences and denominal verbs.
>
> (Kashak and Glenberg (2000: 542).

This article presents a corpus analysis of the denominal verb *duck* to argue that the interpretations of the meaning of the verb are guided by more *schematic constructions* and the linguistic context (perhaps less obvious but still deducible from corpus) that a text builds and in which the verb is embedded. This, on the other hand, is also a process of constructing *salience* and guiding our *attention processes* to those aspect of our knowledge that agree with the affordances of the word, context and syntax.

Below the reader will find enclosed a screenshot of the dialogue box of Xaira, the BNC related tool for text analysis.

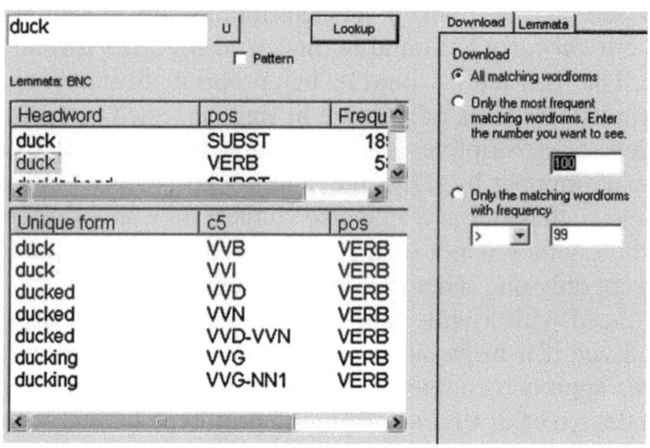

Figure 1. Screenshot of the dialogue box and the results of a search for the denominal verb *duck*

The verb has been found in the corpus with seven different tags, whose list and meanings in the Claws 5 part of speech system of tagging are:

- VVB The finite base form of lexical verbs (e.g. *forget*, *send*, *live*, *return*) [Including the imperative and present subjunctive]
- VVI The infinitive form of lexical verbs (e.g. *forget*, *send*, *live*, *return*)
- VVD The past tense form of lexical verbs (e.g. *forgot*, *sent*, *lived*, *returned*)

VVN The past participle form of lexical verbs (e.g. *forgotten*, *sent*, *lived*, *returned*)
VVG The -ing form of lexical verbs (e.g. *forgetting*, *sending*, *living*, *returning*)

The remaining two tags: VVD-VVN and VVG-NN1 are called ambiguity tags. In the process of automatic parsing it was unclear whether to classify the forms in question to either of the two grammatical classes, but it seems more likely that it is the first category mentioned in each ambiguity tag that should be considered a more plausible interpretation. So, five categories (ambiguity tags were disregarded) were used to produce concordances of the lemma verb *duck*.

2.1. Categories of analysis

The analysis to follow is organized in agreement with the verb categories found in the corpus (see above). First, it seemed appropriate to start with whichever forms of the verb *duck* can be found in the corpus in order for the analysis to be non-reductive. That is, I felt it would be inappropriate to start with a ready made set of basic syntactic patterns of a clause in English. Such patterns are presented in many models of descriptive grammar, such as Quirk (1972) or the more recent functional grammar by (Downing and Locke 1992, 2nd edition). Applying the found data to such patterns would also suggest they are synonymous with the term *construction*, which is not true. Not only that, the so-called basic syntactic patterns represent only one schematic level of representing.

So one is faced with a wide range of linguistic contexts in which the verb *duck* appears. Even if it turns out there is some overlap between the categories of the verb, this approach compels one to deal with every case, regardless of its complexity or degree of divergence from the prototype or analyst's expectations. The search generated the following number of instances of the denominal verb *duck*:

lemma_duck_vvb	110
lemma_duck_vvd	267
lemma_duck_vvn	32
lemma_duck_vvi	106
lemma_duck_vvg	110
lemma_duck_vvd-vvn	ignored
lemma_duck_vvn-vvd	ignored

The above categories will serve the purpose of providing a framework for the analysis of the verb *duck*, its *general meaning* as well as structures constraining the meaning. The linguistic forms that one can find in the corpus shed light on how functions and features of attention guide language users coding of events. At the same time, the author would like to refer the reader interested in the features, functions, definitions and types of attention to appropriate works such as Nęcka *et al.* (2006) or Eysenck and Keane (2002: 363–397).

2.2. VVB – the finite base form including imperative and subjunctive

The search for this category rendered 110 example contexts in the BNC concordance, which I sorted according to the grammatical category (C5) one position right of the word *duck*. The following categories were found, which represent a finite base of the verb duck.

2.2.1. Duck + punctuation mark

The construction embedding the verb is SV, whose meaning is roughly AGENT ACTS ON ITSELF. The verb *duck* specifies how one acts. In a general sense, the action has something to do with physically or metaphorically lowering one's whole body or its part, usually the head. It is the context that further clarifies the actual interpretation and makes the simulation of the scene possible.

7 Eighty per cent of it I **duck**, but people look at the other eighty per cent …

8 – Otherwise she might clout you round the earhole with her ladder.
– You duck?
– Yeah.

9 You duck. When she swings her ladder round you duck. Do you know what it means to duck? (1st sentence – imperative, 2nd sentence infinitive)

10 The first person goes round the outside and pats on the head those sitting saying 'duck' each time. (imperative, quotation)

2.2.2. Duck + adjective, either comparative, superlative or neutral <AJ0, AJC, AJS>

This category is of interest to anyone studying language through corpora. There are a few cases in this class of wrongly tagging the word *duck* to the verb category, where in fact they are nouns.

11 Duck paler and more blotched than Duck Teal …
12 Duck smaller and tenderer than Duck Mallard …
13 Drake has a low moorhen-like weak nasal 'gseee' and in courtship a rather musical c roak, and **duck** a rather hoarse quack. A fast flyer.

The lesson from such an observation should be that automatic corpus tagging results must be accepted with caution. This especially applies to rather fast modern functions of statistical analysis that are available with such software as WS-Tools, Sara or Xaira. The margin of error is not easy to asses. In an analysis like this one, the erroneously tagged examples can be ignored. This important comment also applies to the results of other queries.

2.2.3. Duck + noun, often with a determiner (various tags) in BNC: <NN1, 2, 3, 0, P>

In fact, only one example has been found in this category.

- Then I went into the bathroom and held my head under some cold water for a while. When I ran out of breath I'd come up for another helping, then duck the head again. The water was very cold, and after a while I wasn't feeling so bad.

I presented a larger context so that the reader can construct the whole scene in which the verb is embedded. The verb *duck* is here ellipted; its full finite form is *would duck*. Again, as in many other cases its general meaning of moving something down is here narrowed by the context and the whole scene one can construct as a result. The meaning of the SVO syntactic frame embedding the verb is AGENT ACTS ON AN ENTITY (WHOSE SHAPE, APPEARANCE OR POSITION CHANGES). The particular syntactic frame used is iconic of the type of interaction involved in the scene. Even without such a frame we are dealing with two participating entities: the head and the agent. Further details allowing proper imagery and simulation get provided by context.

2.2.4. Duck + adverb or adverb particle <AV0><AVP>

15 Her answering smile was thoughtful as she watched him duck gracefully through the doorway.
16 He swallowed hard once or twice. His face was drooping into his chest, but Pumfrey saw him half look up at him, then duck sharply down again.
17 … go left to a wall, duck down and crawl under it

18 go right and duck down to go along the conveyor belt
19 'I think I'll just kind of duck down in your pocket if that's OK, chief.
20 Sadly, some parents duck out of both of these.
21 If I've a complicated feature to write, or a problem to solve, I usually duck out and go for a run.
22 I trudge off the platform on to the exit gantry and look below. At the foot of the stairs is the old man. I duck back inside.| He didn't see me.

In [15] and [16] the verb *duck* is used in a subordinate clause that is a complement to the main verbs *watched* and *saw*, so the scene coded by the frame with *duck* is embedded in a larger scene. The scope of attention narrows as the sentences continue. First, it involves the agent of the main clause and then attention is shifted to the other participant; his activity of lowering the head in order to leave a room – *ducking* – is profiled. However, the construal of the scene is objective as both participants are placed in the on-stage region. Only because the sentence proceeds in a word by word fashion, so also the readers' attention follows from one participant and her actions to the other one. The scene could be filmed by first showing the observer who visually attends to the first participant, then it shifts to the other one. Again, the verb *duck* receives proper interpretation only when the whole scene gets integrated into a coherent simulation derived from lexemes, syntax **and** context.

Sentences [17–18] exemplify the use of adverbial particle *down* in the literal sense. With the verb *duck* the combination means LOWER (verb) BODY. One is asked to simulate the whole scene with actual participants, particular perspective, scope, only the selected and verbally coded elements. The process of bending to go under a wall [17] and under a conveyor belt [18] is coded with the verb *duck.* In agreement with the embodiment thesis popular in cognitive linguistics, the iconicity present in many language forms can be attributed to the primary, physical experience with entities and interactions among them. In the case of *duck*, this experience would be watching ducks and their behaviour. But people do not use words in a haphazard way, but they conform to linguistic convention, which means that even if it could be demonstrated that there is some truth in deriving the senses of the verb *duck* from the most prototypical sense of the noun *duck*, the cognitive salience of this sense would be diminished by contextual clues. In other words, understanders would simulate the whole scene of a person going under a conveyor belt, perhaps in a factory, and this would not be obvious from the very reduced context provided in [17–18]. The context, in fact, was much richer than the very text – no matter how big in scope.

Example [19] is metaphorical. It involves two related domains. The source domain is physical and encodes a scene of putting a hand in a pocket to get something (money). The target though encodes a scene of persuading a person to pay for something. Without activating the proper mental model of the world that constitutes the context for interpreting the sentence, one would not be able to achieve proper understanding. It is argued here that this understanding involves mentally simulating a scene. The process described by the verb *duck* is hypothesized to refer to the act of a duck plunging into a river or lake – something we know from experience.

The other particle used with the verb *duck* is *out*. In [20], similarly to [19] it is used metaphorically about parents who avoid responsibility; in [21] *out* is used in a literal sense to leave the flat or house, whereas [22] illustrates how *back* complements the verb *duck* to mean RETURN. I also want to argue that the important component coded by the verb *duck* is FAST, which seems to correspond with our intuitions about the state of the world (or ducks) and serves as another argument for the contention that even simple (one-morpheme) predications are not totally arbitrary. Regardless of the model of mental representation, one can see that with the help of context the same form can help focus attention to one or another entity within a scene and background other entities. Selection is a foundational feature of attentional processes. In the case of [22] one is invited to select a proper ICM (idealized cognitive model), within which the participants are profiled (I, PLATFORM, GANTRY, STAIRS, OLD MAN) and interact. Some models of cognitive-linguistic processing such as Barsalou (1999) show that the process of mental imagery or mental simulation is unavoidable, albait sometimes subconscious. Many would even equate it with understanding. That is, if one can simulate a scene, one understands a sentence. Simulation, however, comes in degrees, varies across individuals and situations.

In this section it is also important to underlie a fact that the syntactic pattern embedding the verb *duck* is SV. As it was posited above, it clues comprehension towards an understanding that some AGENT ACTS ON ITSELF. The very lack of the object (landmark) foregrounds this interpretation and backgrounds tertiary entities that are unimportant in view of the intending speaker-writer. The presence of a linguistic expression positively correlates with the level of salience of the semantic content that this expression profiles.

Adverbs are sometimes used as adverbials of manner: *duck sharply*, *duck gracefully*. In the first example the act of one's head falling as he is sleeping upright sitting on a chair is described and in the other example someone gracefully enters a room and lowers his head as he does so. Both examples involve the SV pattern described above.

One can also find examples that illustrate the use of pronouns:

23 We duck into a gulley and the waves curl around the boat.
24 … so I duck behind the door

which together with their complements form a constituent that specifies the trajectory of the movement and/or the final position of the acting agent-subject.

The trajectories, if focused on, are quite specific due to the almost spontaneous simulations that are triggered on hearing or reading the sentences. The syntactic pattern here is SVAdverbial. It clues the activation of a schematic model with one participant whose intentional act causes her to change position. Although not coded explicitly, the trajectory is recoverable from the simulation and the activated mental model.

So much for the first category of *duck*, VVB. As it was noted, the syntactic patterns that it was used with turned out to be SV, SVC, SVO and SVADV. Each of them contributed semantic content, but was shown to be co-active with important information available in a detailed simulation of the described scene.

3. VVI – the infinitive form of lexical verbs

This concordance rendered 106 examples of the infinitive form of the verb *duck* followed by various grammatical classes, according to which the concordance was sorted. So first came the adjectives, adverbs and so on. In general, the non-finite verb forms of verbs allow one to render the scene or intention less specific with regard to how the verb arguments relate to the verb. Even if one can infer the relations, the arguments of the verb seem less salient. Usually the verb that is used in its infinitive form is not the only verb in the clause or utterance. Interestingly, most examples in this category are metaphorical as the verb *duck* is used in numerous collocations and colligations. As to the latter, the following list features grammatical classes that colligate with the verb *duck.* The highest Z-score is obtained by the category AVP (adverb particle). Examples include the verb *duck* followed by such particles as: *back*, *down*, *in*, *out*, and *through*. As to the back category, it includes both literal senses such as:

25 … and thought he might duck back to the hut and …
26 She was about to duck back into her room when Terry turned.
27 Ace poked her head around the stone with the idea of following, but covering fire from Richmann blasted chunks from the stone and forced her to duck back again.

Neither [25] nor [26] involves a downward movement, but the profiled entity is the simulated speed with which an action is done. This interpretation can be inferred from the ICM that is activated and the active zone of the verb *duck* begins to emerge as a result of parallel cooperation of the used lexemes, grammatical constructions and context. The metaphorical use of *duck back* is shown below:

28 … the assistant should duck back into doing such a worthy … activity

The activity does not probably require any physical action. The *duck* part of the predication foregrounds and profiles the speed and resoluteness. The correspondences that are formed after a proper comparison has been made between the physical domain and the metaphorical one make this construal possible. Namely, physically *ducking* is fast, energetic, involves submerging in water. *Ducking* back into an activity will similarly mean that the action is fast, resolute, and it will be involving to the point where the person performing the activity is almost unaware of his/her surroundings.

Similar explanations can be used in the discussion of other particles. Let us look at the selected examples:

29 … I'd duck down under the covers
30 and had to duck down under the water
31 Gabriel … had to duck down inside the cart
32 … the puppets can duck in and out of the curtained-off side booths to change costumes
33 THERE IS A CREEK in North America which in early summer is overhung with arching fronds of flowers; you have to duck in and out of them as you paddle the canoe.
34 She tried to duck out of his grip, half-succeeding, and he went off-balance.
35 Fortunately he managed to duck out of the way of a lump of glass as it speared towards his neck.
36 Lewis, though, pushing apparent naivety to incredulous proportions, said: 'I couldn't let the WBC down by allowing Bowe to duck out of the commitment he made.

In these and similar examples the interpretation of the meaning of *duck* is different depending on the described scene; Examples [29–31] involve the particle *down*, but only [29] is literal. [33] is interesting because only someone that has ever paddled in a canoe will know what it means to swim through a lake or river overgrown with flowers or other plants. Relatively much context has to be activated for proper understanding or as simulation semantics proponents would say on hearing the sentence one performs detailed mental imagery. The verb duck profiles the moment to moment submerging of the paddle in water in the process of propelling the boat. [34] profiles energetic interaction and attempt to free oneself from a grip (metonymic-metaphoric construal of the act of strongly holding someone by the hand). [35] describes ducking out of the way, so the expression presupposes an imagined but very possible trajectory of a piece of glass flying through air. The sentence profiles the attempt to get out of the way. Although there is no mention of who threw the piece of glass, how big it was, how fast it was flying or what the distance was between the agent and the recipient, all these elements are implied in the simulation. We can see mental imagery provides a natural context for appropriate inferences. The meaning of *duck* is specific only when we can simulate the event. [36] is also metaphorical. It describes an attempt to *duck out of a commitment* (giving up a commitment). This got objectified and is construed as a nominal that can be an argument in our sentence that corresponds to a physical entity that tries to get out of some container that holds it and restricts its freedom. The various particles often profile the direction or end position of entities that participate in the process described by the verb *duck*.

The verb *duck* next colligates with AVP (adverbs). There are two examples in this category, both involving the word *low* as in:

37 I don't think he heard me – due to a very loud explosion a short distance away forcing everyone to duck low into their trenches as lumps of earth and other debris accompanied the flying shrapnel through the trees.
38 … she made her way cautiously around the side of the building, careful to duck low enough under the shattered windows to avoid detection.

Both examples pertain to the physical downward movement of the whole body, here with the element of fear and terror in agreement with the evoked scene. To conclude this section, the infinitive form of the verb *duck* profiles either a literal or metaphorical and fast movement reminiscent perhaps of how ducks behave on a pond or lake.

4. VVD – The past tense form of lexical verbs

The concordance of this category contains many of the cases already discussed in the previous sections. The difference is that the verb *duck* is used in the past simple tense and that it is the largest category in the corpus – a fact that is probably attributable to the more general tendency of talking and writing in the displaced mode, rather than about the here and now. So the verb is used in various linguistic and non-linguistic contexts as well as syntactic patterns. One of these is the SV pattern as in:

40 **Robert** waved briefly, **ducked**, and looked for an alternative means of escape.

Sometimes this pattern is used metaphorically:

41 **The county ducked** and dived throughout the Sixties and Seventies, and got away with it.

Also the SVO pattern is visible in a few examples that are also either literal or metaphorical as in:

42 But **he ducked** and punched **you** and you dropped the bottle.
43 Malcolm hit on helmet as **he ducked another short ball**.
The pattern SVAdverbial is present, too, and this is exemplified by:
44 **I ducked around the corner** of the alleyway and flattened myself against the wall the way a flounder hugs the ocean floor.

Depending on the described situation the different syntactic patterns are used. They exemplify basic types of interactions among objects and people in physical and metaphorical contexts. The verb *ducked* can be positied to have a general meaning that is in agreement with observed scenes of ducks' behaviour on water. This is only a hypothesis that is concordant with the embodiment thesis in CG. The general sense of ABRUPT MOVEMENT becomes more specific as understanders perform mental imagery of the actual scenes guided by linguistic evidence (lexemes, syntax) and details of the extralinguistic context. The very verb *ducked* as it is followed by various other words: *down*, *up*, *low*, *out*, *fast*, *him*, *the issue* and so on clue the understander as regards the direction, force, speed, patient or instrument of the movement. This process is bound up with the functions of our attention. The lingusitic units serve the function of instructing the understanders as to the aspects of their mental imagery that they should foreground or background, whether to select one or another aspect of the scene, whether to enlarge the scope of attention to process information less intensely, or finally whether to look at the pool of long term memory or at an aspect of the surrounding world as in *Look out*! before crossing a busy street.

5. VVN and VVG The past participle form of lexical verbs and the gerund form

This VVN form is used as part of the Present Perfect tense, the Past Perfect Tense, Having Past Participle + Clause. The activity of *ducking* is embedded in a larger situational frame in the case of Past Perfect or Having + ..., constructions, but one cannot find important differences between the behaviour of duck here and in the already described categories. The same applies to the VVN sub-concordance, in which the process of *ducking* is seen to be in progress.

6. Conclusions

The process of understanding discourse, text interpreting is best described with the use of experimental methodology. Corpus analysis, though, can support the observations and conclusions reached there. It is the study of naturally appearing texts that gives access to numerous examples of the denominal verb *duck*. Such an analysis brings an important requirement of ecological validity that experiments may find it hard to achieve.

So what's in a duck? In this study I have hypothesized the possibility that the general meaning of the verb that Goldberg (2003) proposed can be traced back to the experiences one has had with ducks and its particular references are derivable from the linguistic and non-linguistic contexts built up in communication. The process of understanding has been argued by Barsalou (1999) and others to depend on a spontaneous running of mental imagery, the so-called mental simulation. It is not possible to show this by using corpus analysis, but corpus analysis does provide us with rich evidence of actual language use, where one cannot dismiss cases that are difficult to interpret. In this process lexemes, their syntax and imagery are important clues for the understanders to guide their attentional resources in order to achieve important levels of salience of the right aspects of the conceptualisation.

References

Barsalou, L. (1999). "Perceptual Symbol Systems". *Behavioral and Brain Sciences* 22: 577–660.

Downing, A. and P. Locke (2006). *English Grammar, A University Course. 2nd Edition.* London and New York: Routlege.

Eysenc, W.M. and M.T. Keane (2002). "Attention and Performance Limitations". In: D.J. Levitin (ed.). *Foundations of Cognitive Psychology, Core Readings.* Cambridge, Mass.: The Mitt Press.

Giora, R. (2003). *On Our Mind: Salience, Context and Figurative Language.* Oxford: Oxford University Press.

Gibson, J.J. (1977). "The Theory of Affordances". In: R. Shaw and J. Bransford (eds.). *Perceiving, Acting and Knowing.* New York: Lawrence Erlbaum Associates.

Golbreg, A.E. (1995). *Constructions: A Construction Grammar Approach to Argument Structure.* Chicago: Chicago University Press.

Goldberg, A.E. (2003). "Constructions: a new theoretical approach to language". *Trends in Cognitive Sciences.* Vol. 7, No 5: 219–224.

Kashak, P.M. and M. Glenberg (2000). "Constructing Meaning: The Role of Affordances and Grammatical Constructions in Sentence Comprehension". *Journal of Memory and Language* 43: 508–529.

Langacker, R. (1991). *Foundations of Cognitive Grammar. Volumes 1 and 2.* Stanford: Stanford University Press.

Nęcka, E., Orzechowski, J. and B. Szymura (2006). *Psychologia poznawcza.* Warszawa: PWN.

Quirk, R., Greenbaum, S. and J. Svartvig (1972). *A Grammar of Contemporay English.* London: Longman.

Taylor, J.R. (1995). *Linguistc Categorisation: Prototypes in Linguistic Categorisation 2nd edition.* Oxford: Oxford University Press.

Application of Parallel Corpora in Typological Investigations: The Case of Using English-Russian Parallel Subcorpus of the National Russian Corpus in Typological Study of Motion Verbs

Łukasz Grabowski

Abstract: Recently there have appeared numerous research articles dealing with divergence between corpus linguistics and linguistic typology, and more specifically, with the application of parallel corpora and parallel texts in typological investigations (Bickel 2001, Comrie 1998, Cysouw 2003, Cysouw and Wealchli 2007, Diessel and Schmidtke 2008, Stolz 2006). Diessel (2008) postulates that if linguistic typology is focused on grammatical conventions (as grounded in usage) and corpus linguistics is concerned with data usage, then one should find the same principles and tendencies in both linguistic typology and corpus linguistics.

The purpose of this paper is to verify the above observation through application of English↔Russian Parallel Subcorpus of the National Russian Corpus in a cross-linguistic study of selected English and Russian motion verbs. According to Talmy (2000: 102–131) English and Russian belong to two different types as regards signaling path in motion verbs: in English the path is expressed by a preposition bound with the noun phrase following the verb (e.g. *I had almost to* ***carry*** *her* ***into*** *our room*), and in Russian the path is rendered through both a prefix bound with the verb and a preposition bound with a noun (e.g. *Мне чуть ли не на руках пришлось* ***внести*** *ее* ***в*** *номер*). Execution of relevant search in the resources of the ERPS on the example of eight English motion verbs (*carry into*, *crawl into*, *fall down*, *go away (from)*, *put in*, *put into*, *run away (from)*, *run into*), and further analysis of frequency counts of equivalent Russian verbs found in target texts aims to determine the degree to which the assumption proposed by Talmy (2000: 105–107) holds true.

The article concludes with readdressing of issues related to pros and cons of using parallel corpora in typological investigations.

Keywords: corpus linguistics, English language, English↔Russian Parallel Corpus, lexicalization patterns, linguistic typology, motion verbs, National Russian Corpus, parallel corpora, parallel texts, Russian language.

1. Scope of linguistic typology

In the most general sense, typology is the classification or analysis of objects in terms of their common properties (Gak 1983: 8). According to Greenberg (1974: 13, n. 4), the first use of the word 'typology' in linguistic literature dates back to 1928 when the First Congress of Slavonic Philologists was held in Prague, at that time Czechoslovakia. The theses presented at this gathering included the said term in the sense of classification of languages in terms of their structural properties. Nevertheless, such classifications had been already undertaken by A.W. Schlegel, F. Schlegel and W. von Humboldt, members of 19th century German school of comparative linguistics, who attempted to classify languages on the basis of whether language units (morphological ones) have been autonomous – isolating type – or associated with affixes – inflecting or agglutinating types (Hagege 1992: 7), which today would be referred to as linguistic typological study. At that time, however, such classifications were not referred to as typology. Moreover, the date of the Prague Congress (1928) was a milestone in the development of typology in that most classifications of languages undertaken before had been largely of genetic (and diachronic) character and aimed to study development of languages in order to group them into language families on the basis of their origin, and reproduce proto-language(s), or ancestor language(s) which gave rise to particular language families. The first significant genetic classification of this kind was conducted by A. Schleicher (1821–1868) in the *Die Sprachen Europas in systematischer Übersicht (The languages of Europe in systematic perspective)* (1850) in which he proposed a model *(family-tree theory)* of language classification that resembled a botanical taxonomy, tracing groups of related Indo-European languages and arranging them in a genealogical tree.

Throughout the decades following the Prague Congress, development of typological research and resulting changes in understanding of the term *linguistic typology* contributed to multidimensionality of its definitions.

According to Greenberg (1974), the assumption underlying linguistic typology is that "the ways in which languages differ from each other are not entirely random, but show various types of dependencies among those properties of languages which are not invariant differences statable in terms of the 'type'" (Greenberg 1974: 54–55). Pottier (1968: 300) emphasizes comparative dimension of linguistic typology and claims that typology is the characteristics of properties constituting organization of a particular language, which is primarily of descriptive and comparative character.[1]

Thus the linguistic typology is the classification of languages into types (particularly structural ones) in terms of those structural properties that are not shared through their genetic relatedness or areal contact (Comrie 1981: 448). In this context, it is referred to as 'typological classification' (Croft 2002: 1), whereby "a language is taken to belong to a single type, and a typology of languages is a definition of the types and enumeration or classification of languages into those types". According to Shurinskaya (1975: 438), linguistic typology "studies individual types of language, language types and determines the most essential and specific characteristics of natural languages". Moreover, Shurinskaya (1975: 439) claims that linguistic typology pertains to "the typology of language as a structure, referring to the types that appear in language". In this contexts researcher may arrive at a typology of a particular language or specific groups of languages, or a typology of a specific subsystem (i.e. individual levels) or categories of a particular language, so that specific fragments of linguistic system are subject to typological research. The result of such an approach may be, for example, determination of semantic typology, or typology of verbs, or typology of the structure of syllables etc.[2] This view is also supported by Comrie (1988: 450) who claims that "in principle, any structural property of a language could be chosen as the basis of a linguistic typology". Finally, Shurinskaya (1975: 439) sees linguistic typology "as an organizational principle of linguistic material, which makes it possible to give a typological description of a particular language as well as similarities and differences as it is compared with other languages". This organizational character of linguistic typology conforms with the claim made by Uspenski (1965: 10) who represents that linguistic typology comes down to systematization and inventorying of phenomena existing in different languages on the basis of their structural properties". This view is also corroborated and summarized by Arakin (1979: 13) who emphasizes that linguistic typology is also understood as the principle of organization of linguistic material.

Sgall [1984, quoted in Ramat (1987: 4)], on the other hand, proposed threefold approach to typological studies. Firstly, Sgall understands typology "as a study of existing language types and, in particular, as their classification (the

---

1 I paraphrased Pottier's definition quoted in P. Ramat (1984) translated into English and edited by G. Bossong, and B. Comrie (1987: 3): "(…) L'etude typologique se situe au niveau le plus general de la description linguistique. Elle suppose une caracterisation de l'ensemble des phenomenes qui constituent une langue. Elle est en premier lieu descriptive, puis comparative (...)."

2 Arakin (1979: 12) provides an example of the work by M.I. Lekomtseva (1968), "Typology of structure of syllable in Slavic languages". Лекомцева М.И., *Типология структур слога в славянских языках*, Москва 1968.

line of typological studies running from Humboldt up to Jespersen)". Secondly, he adopts Sapir's extension of the classification of typological properties of existing languages with the study of possible combinations of properties. Finally, the distribution of these combinations is subject to the concept of implications as introduced by Jacobson (i.e. if a language has feature A, then it also has feature B, e.g. if a language X has noun declension, then the language X also has adjective declension). As the last observation indubitably refers to the notion of language universals, Sgall defined typology as classification of languages on the basis of possible structural properties (i.e. language universals), which in other words means the determination of limits on the linguistic structures allowed in a system of particular language(s) (comparative typology) as well as a language in general (general typology). If the latter is the case, the typology may be referred to as 'typological generalization', which is the study of patterns that occur systematically across languages.

Therefore, the relationship between linguistic typology and language universals is that the latter one helps set parameters for typological research (i.e. establish significant typological parameter which would characterize a sizeable part of any language system). Thus, linguistic typology assumes that there are differences among languages as in the case of their absence all human languages might be classified in terms of one and the same type (Comrie 1988: 450). According to Comrie, "the overall aim of the combined enterprise of language universals and linguistic typology is the study of the range of possible variation across languages and of the constraints on that variation" (1988: 450). Due to such a conspicuous link between linguistic typology and language universals, it has been commonly referred to in the literature as universalist typology (Bickel 2007), which aims to study differences between world languages in order to classify them, determine limits on their structure, and to explain the very nature of these limits.

Another linguistic definition of typology represents an approach to the study of language which contrasts with prior approaches, such as structuralism (linguistic typology or typological classification) and generativism (typological generalization). It is based on the assumption that linguistic structure should be explained primarily in terms of linguistic function, and hence it is referred to as 'functional typology' or functional-typological approach to language studies (Croft 2002: 2). According to Croft (2002: 3), all definitions of typology (i.e. typological classification, typological generalization and functional-typological approach) correspond to three stages of any empirical analysis. Typological classification is the observation of empirical (linguistic) material and its classification into types on the basis of similarities and differences obtained in the material. Typological generalization (with language universals) is the formulation of generalizations over linguistic facts subject to observation in order to set limits on the possible variation of linguistic structures. Finally, functional-typological approach aims to provide explanations of the observed generalizations. The explanatory models used by functionally-biased typologists include, among others, competing motivations, economy of language use, iconicity, processing of linguistic material, semantic maps in conceptual space, rethinking of syntactic argumentation (Croft 2002: 4).

2. Modern linguistic typology

According to Waelchli (2006a), notwithstanding the fact that language typology dates back to the beginning of 19th century and that classification of languages was thought to be an exhausted topic in the 1970s, typology has been one of the most expansive approaches to linguistics over the last thirty years. This revival of typological studies was made possible due to rapid developments of communication and information technologies (ICT), corresponding advances in computational and corpus linguistics, which together opened up access to multifarious collections of linguistic data in electronic form, as well as to new computational (statistics, multidimensional scaling, semantic maps, scales and hierarchies, implications) and corpus-based methods of data analysis (e.g. inferential and descriptive statistics, such as mean, median, mode, standard deviation, as well as sentence length, frequency counts, type/token ratio etc. (Biber *et al.* 1998, McEnery *et al.* 2006)

According to Waelchi (2005), the most widely (and traditionally) used sources of linguistic data for typological research are reference grammars and fieldworkers' expertise. What these sources have all in common is that therein language is approached in preconceived abstract terms, as it is the usual case with any reference grammar favouring top-down approach to presentation of linguistic data. This type of linguistic data may be referred to (after Waelchli 2005) as 'secondary data', which had been processed and filtered by the researcher (before their presentation) in terms of rules and generalizations included in reference grammars. However, it becomes more and more apparent that for a number of topics in typology, information typically found in grammars is unreliable, insufficient or even absent (it particularly pertains to semantic and pragmatic information and discourse related phenomena). Descriptive grammars often disregard variation in morpho-syntactic patterns, frequencies of their occurrence and rationale behind their choice in actual conversations (Bakker forth.). Waelchli (2005: 1) outlines some more reasons which have made traditional data sources insufficient for contemporary typological studies and thus changed the role and status of linguistic data in typological studies.

Firstly, typologists started to compare more linguistic structures across languages which were not believed to be either comparable or have anything in common before (ibid.). As a result, lack of reference grammars, which would provide researchers with ready-made *tertium comparationis* statable in abstract terms, or insufficient fieldworkers' expertise, called for new data sources and materials, which were not believed to be reliable before, such as questionnaires, responses to non-verbal stimuli, language corpora, parallel texts (pair of source language text and its translation into target language), massively parallel texts (set of texts translated into many languages, e.g. *Universal Declaration of Human Rights*), parallel corpora, typological databases etc. According to Bickel (2005), there are about two dozen research groups in the world which develop typological databases, as well as international collaboration research projects [such as *The World Atlas of Linguistic Structures* by Haspelmath *et al.* (2005) and Haspelmath (forth.)] based on a huge typological database. The aforementioned data sources differ from both reference grammars and fieldworkers' expertise in that they contain neither processed nor filtered abstract data, which means that the data are real and concrete instances of texts in particular languages (Waelchli 2005: 3). Hence such data are referred to as 'primary data'. The two ways of collecting or extracting typological data (e.g. reference grammars vs. corpora) have exerted profound influence upon the role and status of linguistic data in typological studies, and spawned terminological distinction between descriptive typology (which is based on primary sources and exemplars of real language use) and grammar-extraction typology (which is based on secondary sources of data and abstractions of pre-processed linguistic data) (Waelchli 2005: 2). Therefore the data used in grammar-extraction approach is abstract and generalized, whereas the data used in descriptive typology consists of individual exemplars of actual language use in speaking or writing (e.g. speeches, utterances, translations etc.). Due to different character of data sources, grammar-extraction typology provides answers to different questions than descriptive typology. Grammar-extraction typology answers questions such as whether language X is of type A1, A2, A3, or whether category Y exists or does not exist in language X, or whether domain C in language X is encoded by type A1, A2, A3 etc. Descriptive typology, on the other hand, answers questions whether feature Y has low, intermediate, high frequency in language (or text corpus) X, or what is the distribution Z of a feature Y in language X, or what variation Z is exhibited by feature Z in language X etc. (Waelchli 2006: 5).

As a result, over the past decade linguistic typology has started to distance itself from universalist goal of determination of limits of possible human languages (similar to objectives of generative grammar), and developed into a fully-fledged discipline with its own research agenda, theories and problems posed in order to answer the question why linguistic diversity is the way it is by capturing and testing distributions of typological features through developing variables measuring similarities and differences between languages (Bickel 2007). As a result of this transition, contemporary typologists work not with types, but with independently and narrowly defined variables, which follows that instead of typologizing entire languages, modern typology studies individual structural patterns. As a result, linguistic diversity is captured by large sets of variables rather than grand types (ibid.).

With the above aim in mind, modern linguistic typology may be divided into three subfields: qualitative typology (which aims to define variables, or types, capturing cross-linguistic similarities and differences between languages), quantitative typology (which aims to survey these variables with the use of statistical methods in order to explore universal and local skewings in their distribution) and theoretical typology (which aims to explain skewings in distribution of the variables subject to typological study) (Bickel 2001).

3. Interface between corpus linguistics and linguistic typology

Nowadays corpus linguistics is a widely recognized and used methodology of linguistic research with well-developed theoretical and methodological foundations. In simple terms, it can be described as "the study of language based on examples of "real life" language use" (McEnery and Wilson 1996: 1). Therefore corpus linguistics is not a specific aspect of language, which would necessitate description and explanation in a similar vein as syntax, semantics etc, but a methodology or usage-based approach, which may be used in many areas of linguistic enquiry (e.g. corpus-based syntax, corpus-based semantics etc.). Application of corpus-based or corpus-driven methodologies in any area of linguistics requires introduction of research procedures used in that area and their further integration with selected corpus methodologies. Therefore the question arises: is it possible to integrate corpus linguistics with modern linguistic typology?

As it has already been noted, modern linguistic typology aims to define variables, or types, capturing cross-linguistic similarities and differences between languages as made explicit in their grammar, which is grounded in the use of "real" language. According to Diessel and Schmidtke (2008), if the foundation of corpus linguistics is to study "real life" language use (i.e. usage data), and if grammar is grounded in usage, then the same underlying principles and tendencies shall be found in both linguistic typology and corpus linguistics.

Corpus data can thus offer insights into the frequency of occurrence of selected grammatical (typological) phenomena, on the one hand, and its use, on the other, and provide information on the profile, either qualitative or quantitative, of specific variables, or types. As a result, corpus linguistics fits perfectly into the tripartite division of modern linguistic typology, i.e. qualitative, quantitative and theoretical one, as the access to data collected in corpora (parallel corpora, in particular) facilitates both capturing variables, or types, as well as surveying their distribution with the use of corpus-based statistical methods (e.g. type/token ratio, frequency counts, wordlists and keyword analyses). Finally, access to wider context (concordances, collocation and colligation patterns, functional domains, especially in case of corpora annotated with meta-situational information) in which linguistic data collected in the corpora are actually used, facilitates explanation of skewings in distribution of the variables subject to typological study.

4. Application of parallel texts and parallel corpora in typological investigations

While constructing a typology and identifying hypotheses-to-be-tested in cross-linguistic research (which is inescapable in typological investigations), it is a prerequisite to ascertain that empirical basis (i.e. language samples/language data) to be compared is in relation of equivalence, According to Stolz (2006), the easiest way to achieve the said equivalence is translation. As a result, it seems plausible to assume that parallel texts, massively parallel texts and parallel corpora may be applicable in any typological and cross-linguistic investigations (Stolz 2006, Waelchli 2006). Moreover, Stolz (2006) claims that linguistic structure cannot be accessed directly, as it can be investigated only in particular utterances. Therefore linguistic typology is always a typology of texts (ibid.).

The data collected in any parallel corpus consists of source texts and their respective translation into a target language or target languages (if texts translated into many languages are subject to study). Such text and its translation are referred to as 'parallel texts'. According to Waelchli (2006), parallel texts written in different languages can be considered translational equivalents and thus studied and used today in both literary- and computationally-oriented (automatic and machine translation) approaches to translation.

Obviously enough, any parallel text may vary in size (it may be a leaflet translated into many languages, or *acquis communitaire* of the EU) and the number of its translations (a text may be translated into one or more languages). With this division in mind, Waelchli (2007) introduces a term 'massively parallel text (MPT)' which is used for such texts of which many different translations are available, e.g. verbatim reports of the proceedings of European Parliament (translated into 20 languages), *Universal Declaration of Human Rights* (translated into 332 languages), *The Holy Bible* (a collection of the Lord's Prayer is available in more than 1300 languages), movie subtitles etc. Massively parallel texts have gained considerable importance in typological studies aimed to explain universal and local skewings in distribution of selected typological variables, or types, as the access to equivalent data in dozens of languages facilitates production of semantic maps with multidimensional scaling (see Cysouw and Waelchli 2007, Stolz 2006, Waelchli 2007). Two literary MPTs have already been used in typological studies, namely "Le Petit Prince" by A. de Saint-Exupery and "Harry Potter" by J.K. Rowling (Stolz 2006). The breakthrough in the field is the study of comitatives undertaken by Stolz *et al.* (2006), who on the basis of data drawn from 400 languages world-wide identified three types of languages in terms of the morphological treatment of the comitative and its syncretistic association with other concepts.

The decision whether to choose parallel text, massively parallel text or parallel corpus is subject to the type of linguistic study the typologist intends to conduct. Any parallel text in only two languages may be subject to translation study, but such pairwise collection of texts may be of limited value for linguistic typology, as today researchers want to compare large sets of languages. In such a case, the most important issue in a parallel text or parallel corpus investigation is the selection of languages, texts and functional domains[3] to be considered [the idea that functional domains are largely identical across languages is the basis of most work in functional typology (see Croft 2002: 3)]. Defining particular functional domain has the advantage that there is no need to provide any abstract semantic definition as it is sufficient to undertake a selection of semantically similar contexts. It is then an empirical question to what extent there is domain internal variation, a question which is more difficult to address in traditional approaches to functional domains, which tends to assume that semantic domains selected at the beginning of the study are more or less homogeneous. In other words, parallel texts and parallel corpora can be useful for higher semantic resolution of the domains to be considered on condition that there are enough different contexts in the sample of parallel texts or parallel corpus used in the study.

5. Corpus-based typological study of English and Russian motion verbs expressing Path

According to Cysouw (2003), "a typology is always constructed on the basis of a 'tertium comparationis', i.e. by an explicitly formulated subject to be compared in the world's linguistic variation". On the basis of such a tertium comparationis – which has to be formulated extra-linguistically as a language independent parameter or variable – different languages can be categorized in terms of how they formulate that part of linguistic structure. As a result, tertium

---

3 According to Waelchli (2006), translational equivalents across the languages of the world belong to the same functional domain.

comparationis is never theory-independent as it presupposes something to be universally expressible in language. Cysouw (2003) claims that this universal hypothesis originates in theoretical background on the basis of which the typology is made. Therefore, according to Cysouw's (2003) strict interpretation, typology is a hypothesis-testing methodology.

For the purpose of this article, I will conduct a simple test of a tiny fragment of Lexicalization Pattern Theory as proposed by Talmy (2000) [whereby "lexicalization is involved where a particular meaning component is found to be in regular association with a particular morpheme"] on the selected examples of English and Russian motion verbs. Motion verbs, both intransitive and transitive, characteristically express in the verb stem only one of the three semantic entities, which are path, manner, or shape. Moreover, Talmy (2000: 105) claims that path is expressed in a non-verbal element (referred to as a 'satellite') if it is not expressed in the verb (hence, according to Talmy (2000: 106), English and Russian are satellite-framed languages as regards the expression of path). All three semantic entities (i.e. path, manner, and shape) have the same functional domain (defined as the sum of semantically-close associated contexts; hence in this case the functional domain contains all situations which express path of motion event), which means that they occur in the same contexts of use.

According to Talmy (2000: 102–131), who researched typological patterns in the representation of event structure, **English and Russian belong to two different types as regards signaling path in motion verbs**: even though they are both satellite-framed languages, in English (apart from limited number of borrowings from Latin, such as *to descend*, *to ascend*, *to enter* etc.) the path is expressed by a preposition bound with the noun phrase following the verb (e.g. *The platitudinous colonel gallantly offered to* ***carry*** *them* ***into*** *the car*), and in Russian the path is rendered through both a prefix bound with the verb and a preposition bound with a noun (e.g. *Пошляк полковник галантно заявил, что охотно сам* ***пере****несет их* ***в*** *свою машину*). Therefore, satellites expressing path do not overlap in case of English and Russian.

Verification of the aforementioned hypothesis will be conducted through the use of English↔Russian Parallel Subcorpus[4] of the National Russian Corpus[5]

4 The English↔Russian Parallel Subcorpus contains 1,100,000 tokens (English-Russian) and 500,000 tokens (Russian-English) available for online search. For more detailed information on size, structure and annotation of the ERPS, see Добровольский Д. (2005).

(*Национальный корпус русского языка*, henceforth the ERPS and the NRC, respectively). The choice of ERPS as a data source was motivated by the fact that 1) the languages of the sample are independent of each other in terms of their encoding of motion events, 2) parallel text data constitute actual language use and are mutually independent to a large extent, and 3) functional domains may be easily selected in texts making up the parallel corpus due to prior alignment of these texts.

Execution of relevant lexico-grammatical search in the resources of the ERPS on the example of eight English motion verbs (*carry into*, *crawl into*, *fall down*, *go away (from)*, *put in*, *put into*, *run away (from)*, *run into*), and further analysis of frequency counts of equivalent Russian verbs found in target texts enabled to determine the degree to which the assumption proposed by Talmy (2000: 105–107) holds true.

The results of the study conducted in the ERPS confirmed that English and Russian belong to two different types as regards signaling path in motion verbs, whereby in English the path is expressed by a preposition bound with the noun phrase following the verb, and in Russian the path is rendered through both a prefix bound with the verb and a preposition bound with a noun. Six out of eight motion verbs subject to study scored compliance level of 80% and higher (four out of eight verbs scored compliance level of 90% and higher), whereas only one out of eight verbs scored compliance level below 50% [*run away (from)*], which means that only 1 in 8 motion verbs fails to conform with the hypothesis proposed by Talmy.

5 The National Russian Corpus (*Национальный корпус русского языка*; henceforth the NRC) has been compiled since 2001 at V. Vinogradov Institute of Russian Language of Russian Academy of Sciences in Moscow. The corpus, which is available through the website http://ruscorpora.ru, includes 149,357,020 million tokens (recorded as of January 2008) which make up the meta-situationally, meta-textually and meta-linguistically annotated representative collection of Russian texts in the electronic form. (www.ruscorpora.ru; Grabowski 2006).

Table 1. Frequency of occurrence of motion verbs expressing Path in the ERPS, and compliance with Talmy's hypothesis

Motion verb	Overall Frequency	Compliant occurrences	Non-compliant occurrences	Compliance
carry into	6	5	1	83%
crawl into	8	8	0	100%
run away (from)	19	9	10	47%
go away (from)	10	8	2	80%
run into	27	21	6	77%
put in	20	18	2	90%
fall down	19	18	1	95%
put into	28	25	3	90%

The main reasons for non-compliance referred to the choice of different translation strategies in either Russian or English target texts [syntactic strategies, such as structural change (compare: *He, who had* ***run away from*** *women most of his life* vs. *Он, который всю жизнь* ***спасался бегством от*** *преследовавших его женщин*); semantic strategies, such as synonymy (compare: *A weakling and an alcoholic, he had* ***run away from*** *the doctors and the chicken-coop of a city* vs. *Заморыш, пьянчуга, он* ***бросил*** *врачей и курятник, именуемый городом*); pragmatic strategies, such as omission or simplification (*When he has* ***gone away from*** *us?* vs. *Раз он* ***уехал****?*)]. Another reason came down to other typological differences obtained between English and Russian, whereby perfective and imperfective aspect in English is a feature of context and may be rendered through the use of present perfect tense or present perfect continuous tense, respectively, whereas in Russian aspects are expressed by a pair of perfective and imperfective verbs, which means that aspect is not a feature of context, but it is encoded in the verb (compare: *Why,* ***I've been running away from*** *ladies ever since I can remember* vs. *Да я, с тех пор как себя помню, только и делал, что* ***бегал*** *от женщин*).

Therefore, the results of the corpus study indicate that translation strategies may exert considerable influence on testing typological hypotheses with the use of parallel corpora (and parallel texts). It is frequently the case that stylistic decisions made by translators (notwithstanding the fact that the parallel text fragments belong to the same functional domain) result in substitution of the linguistic form compliant with the generalized type with another non-compliant form or structure. However, this effect may be downplayed as typologists use larger multi-million parallel corpus as a source of material for such a hypothesis testing typological study.

Obviously enough, it has to be emphasized that representativeness of the results of this study equals representativeness of data collected in the ERPS, which contains only 1,100,000 tokens (English-Russian) and 500,000 tokens

(Russian-English) included in selection of texts ranging from early 19th century prose to contemporary literature (Dobrovolsky 2005).

6. Conclusions. Advantages and disadvantages of using parallel corpora in typological investigations

Stolz (2006) and Waelchli (2006a, 2006b, 2007) provide an overview of advantages and disadvantages of using parallel texts in typological investigations. In conclusion I will adduce the points which have become relevant as regards the case study presented in this article. According to Waelchli (2007), a strong point of using parallel texts in typological investigations is their direct comparability whereby the same domains are instantiated in the same examples occurring in the same textual and situational contexts. Nevertheless, the corpus study conducted in this article indicated that one of the disadvantages obtained in parallel corpora is the bias towards translational language rather than non-translational language. As a result, the use of various translation strategies (e.g. lexical, syntactic, semantic or pragmatic) may result in considerable skewings in occurrence and distribution of typological variables subject to study. Thus, it has to be emphasized that the sample of a parallel text or parallel corpus subject to study is not a sample of languages; it is a sample of translations of particular texts into particular languages.

Another problem area related to selection of functional domains refers to the bias towards a particular register, e.g. religious, legal, narrative etc. In such a context there arises the question whether the results obtained from restricted register-specific language material retrieved from parallel texts or parallel corpus (e.g. the literary texts used in this study) may be representative for typological generalizations projected upon a language as a whole (ibid.).

The study conducted in this article also indicated that feasibility of using parallel texts and parallel corpora in typological investigations largely depends on how many examples are needed to reach a certain representativeness of the results. It has to be assumed that the number of examples (and number of registers, styles etc.) needed will vary greatly from typological variable to typological variable, which is why it cannot be known beforehand how viable the use of parallel corpus is as regards representativeness of the results of the study conducted on it.

One more problem related to the use of parallel corpora refers to the very selection of languages subject to study. For certain research questions, large and unbiased samples are required in typology, but if typologists are aware of their capability to cover only a small proportion of linguistic diversity by looking at two or three languages only, then such a selection should be viable too. In a similar vein, the ERPS was chosen as the parallel corpus representing two languages only.

Selection of languages is also closely connected with the choice of research methods. As a result, for some research questions the corpus-methods, such as frequency counts, are sufficient (as it is the case with the study presented in this article and conducted on two languages only), especially when one intends to formulate or test hypotheses about markedness or non-markedness values of particular typological variables (Stolz 2006). Nevertheless, corpus methods are not sufficient as regards research questions related to distribution in general whereby analyses are conducted on samples of many diverse languages, which all enables one to produce semantic maps with multi-dimensional scaling (samples in two or three languages are not ideal for this).

In conclusion, given some disadvantages of using parallel texts and parallel corpora as data sources in typological investigations, the results obtained from them are so important for typological studies in linguistics that they have to be conducted even if they are not perfect. As a rule of thumb, parallel texts or parallel corpora should provide typologists with more information than already available from other data sources, particularly filtered and processed reference-grammars.

References

Bakker, D. (forthc). "Language sampling". In: Jae Jung Song (ed.). *Handbook of Linguistic Typology*. Oxford: Oxford University Press.

Biber, D., Conrad, C. and R. Reppen (1998). *Corpus Linguistics. Investigating Language Structure and Use.* Cambridge: University Press.

Bickel, B. (2001). What is typology? – a short note. Retrieved on 14 Apr 2007 from: http://www.uni-leipzig.de/~bickel/research/papers/manifesto.pdf

Bickel, B. (2007). "Typology in the 21st century: major current developments". *Linguistic Typology*. Volume 11, Issue 1: 239–251.

Bossong, G., Comrie, B. (1987). *Empirical Approaches to Language Typology*. Berlin: Mounton de Gruyter.

Comrie, B. (1986). "Contrastive linguistics and language typology". In: D. Kastovsky, A. Szwedek (eds.). *Linguistics Across Historical and Geographical Boundaries*. Vol. 2: Descriptive, Contrastive, and Applied Linguistics. In Honour of Jacek Fisiak on the Occasion of His Fiftieth Birthday: 1155–1163. Berlin: Mouton de Gruyter.

Comrie, B. (1988). "Linguistic typology". In: F. Newmeyer (ed.). *Linguistics: The Cambridge Survey*. Volume I. Linguistic Theory: Foundations: 447–461. Cambridge: CUP.

Comrie, B. (1981/1989). *Language Universals and Linguistic Typology: Syntax and Morphology*. Oxford: Basil Blackwell; 2nd edition 1989.

Comrie, B. (1998). "Translatability and universals revisited". In: L. Kulikov and H. Vater (eds.). *Typology of Verbal Categories*: 283–286. Tuebingen: Max Niemeyer Verlag.

Croft, W. (2002). *Typology and Universals*. Cambridge: Cambridge University Press.

Cysouw, M. (2003). *The Paradigmatic Structure of Person Marking.* (Oxford Studies in Typology and Linguistic Theory). Oxford: Oxford University Press.

Cysouw, M. and B. Waelchli (2007). "Parallel Texts: Using translational equivalents in linguistic typology". Special Issue of *Sprachtypologie und Universalienforschung (STUF)* 60(2). Retrieved on 14 Mar 2007 from: http://email.eva.mpg.de/~cysouw/pdf/STUF.pdf

Diessel, H. and K. Schmidtke (2008). *Converging evidence: linguistic typology and corpus linguistics*. Retrieved on 15 Dec 2008 from: http://www.eva.mpg.de/lingua/conference/08_springschool/pdf/course_materials/Diessel_1_Introduction.pdf

Grabowski, Ł. (2006). "Comparative Characteristics of Polish and Russian Language Corpora". In: B. Німчук (ed.). *Лексикографічний бюлетень: Збірник наукових праць*: 29–33. Kiev.

Greenberg, J. (1974). *Language Typology. A historical and analytic overview*. (Janua Linguarum, Series Minor, 1984). Den Haag and Paris: Mouton.

Hagege, C. (1992). "Morphological typology". In: *Oxford International Encyclopedia of Linguistics*, vol. 3, 7-8. Oxford: Oxford University Press.

Haspelmath, M. (2003). "The geometry of grammatical meaning: Semantic maps and cross-linguistic comparison". In: M. Tomasello (ed.). *The New Psychology of Language* 2: 211–242. Mahwah, NJ: Lawrence Erlbaum.

Haspelmath, M., Dryer, M., Gil, D. and B. Comrie (eds.) (2005). *The World Atlas of Language Structures*. Oxford: Oxford University Press.

Haspelmath, M. (forth.). "The typological database of the *World Atlas of Language Structures*." To appear in: Everaert, Martin and Musgrave, Simon (eds.). *The use of databases in cross-linguistic studies.* (Empirical Approaches to Language Typology, 41.) Berlin: Mouton de Gruyter.

McEnery, T. and A. Wilson (1996). *Corpus Linguistics*. Edinburgh: University Press.

McEnery, T., Xiao, R., and Y. Tono (2006). *Corpus-Based Language Studies. An Advanced Resource Book.* London: Routledge.

Pottier, B. (1968). "La typologie". In: A. Martinet (ed.), *Le langage*: 300-324. Gallimard: Paris. Quoted in Ramat (1987: 5).

Ramat, P. (1987). *Linguistic typology*. Berlin – New York – Amsterdam: Mouton de Gruyter.

Shurinskaya, M. (1975). "Die Sprachtypologie". In: B. Serébrennikow (ed.), *Allgemeine Sprachwissenschaft. Band II: Die innere Struktur der Sprache:* 430-451. München and Salzburg: Fink; Kap. Quoted in Ramat (1987: 5).

Stolz, T. (2006). *Harry Potter* meets *Le petit prince*: On the usefulness of parallel corpora in cross-linguistic investigations. In: Cysouw and Wälchli (forthc.), Retrieved on 24 Jul 2007 from: http://www.atypon-link.com/PublisherAV/doi/abs/10.1524/stuf.2007.60.2.100

Stolz, T., Stroh, C., and A. Urdze (2006). *On Comitatives and Related Categories: A Typological Study with Special Focus on the Languages of Europe*. Berlin: Walter de Gruyter.

Talmy, L. (2000). *Toward a Cognitive Semantics. Typology and Process in Concept Structuring*. Cambridge, MA: MIT Press.

Waelchli, B. (2006a). Descriptive typology, or, the typologists expanded toolkit. Retrieved on 14 Mar 2007 from: ling.uni-konstanz.de/pages/home/a20_11/waelchli/waelchli-desctyp.pdf

Waelchli, B. (2006b). Lexicalization patterns in motion verbs revisted. Unfinished manuscript retrieved on 12 Mar 2007 from: http://ling.uni-konstanz.de/pages/home/a20_11/waelchli/waelchli-lexpatt.pdf

Waelchli, B. (2006/7). Constructing semantic maps from parallel text data. Retrieved on 25 Mar 2009 from: http://ling.uni-konstanz.de/pages/home/a20_11/waelchli/waelchli-semmaps.pdf

Waelchli, B. (2007). "Advantages and disadvantages of using parallel texts in typological investigations". In: Cysouw and Wälchli (eds.). Theme issue in *Sprachtypologie and Universalienforschung (STUF)* 60(2). Retrieved on 14 Mar 2007 from: http://email.eva.mpg.de/~cysouw/pdf/STUF.pdf

Аракин, В. Д. (1979). *Сравнительная типология английского и русского языков*. Ленинград: Просвещение.

Гак, В.Г. (1983). *Сравнительная типология французского и русского языков*. Москва: Просвещение.

Добровольский Д.О., Кретов А.А., Шаров С.А. (2005). Корпус параллельных текстов: архитектура и возможности использования // Национальный корпус русского языка: 2003–2005. М.: Индрик, 2005.

Успенский, Б. А. (1965). *Структурная типология языков*. Москва.

НКРЯ (RKN): Национальный корпус русского языка – http://www.ruscorpora.ru

Corpus-Based Morphology in the Czech Language

Milena Hebal-Jezierska

Abstract: Various ways of using corpora in morphological (especially inflexion) research are presented in the paper. Emphasis is put on the research of Czech language. The aim of the paper is to make a research review especially for Czech. First of all, we are interested in the way of using corpora data: methods of searching linguistic information, the choice of corpora approach, using the statistical tools, creating or not a statistical description, methods of analysis. Then we present some interesting results of the analysis. The author's experience will be also presented.

Keywords: corpora, corpora approach, Czech language, frequency, inflection, statistics, tag errors, variants.

1. Introduction

It is very difficult to present a methodology of using corpora in inflectional research because of the lack of description of conditions of using corpora data. Some approaches to this issue will be presented in the paper. Most of them were used by researchers of teams working on two projects: "Exploring the Core and Limits of Czech Grammar as seen through the Czech National Corpus" and "Studies in Czech Grammar". These projects were carried out in The Czech Department of Grammar in Czech Academy of Society and Arts in Prague in 2003-2008. The head of the projects was doc. PhDr. František Štícha, CSc.

2. Methods of searching linguistic information

There are many ways of linguistic information retrieval from corpora, beginning from automatic to manual, using only one query or many queries. Unfortunately only very few researchers consider the problem as the linguistic one, therefore only very few authors include query notation in their articles. The way of searching linguistic information is the basis of research. If the query is not right, the results are false. If there is no query notation, the readers of article cannot be sure of results. It is more dangerous especially in the studies based on statistics (see Konečná, Prošek 2008)[1]. If corpora have possibilities of advanced automatic search, many researchers use it without checking it. There are many dangers connected with automatic search, for example: errors in query syntax, errors in annotation, editorial mistakes, excerpts written in other languages, reoccurrence of the same concordances. Searching only with one automatic query syntax may cause the following problems: lack of appropriate concordances due to errors in tags, lack of concordances because of unrecognised tags, lack of neologisms.

To avoid these problems searching should be done with several queries, not only one, using a combination of automatic and manual methods, introducing checking procedures (work with concordances containing the searched tags, work with concordances not containing the searched tags).

The author's proposal[2] of how to obtain the optimal number of concordancies will be shown on the example of searching variation of the dative and locative singular (the hard stem paradigms). In this method we use many queries beginning from the most general automatic ways through introducing checking procedures to manual checking. This grammatical issue may be analyzed starting with the syntax query that allow to find masculine animate nouns ending in non-soft consonant and occurring in the dative and locative singular.

[(lemma=".*[bdfghklmnprstvz]")&(tag="NNMS3.*")][3]
[(lemma=".*[bdfghklmnprstvz]")&(tag="NNMS6.*")]

On the basis of this query and the available function (frequency distribution) introductory results can be obtained from the Czech corpus Syn2000.

Apart from the queries shown above, unrecognized words can be extracted with the help of the following groups of regular expresions.

---

1 The authors of the article are not aware of the problems with searching. The whole research is based on the figures retrieved from the corpora but materials of study were received from IT specialists.

2 It was also presented in Hebal-Jezierska (2009).

3 The letters in the first square bracket allow to find lemmas ended in non-soft consonant. Thanks to the symbols in the second bracket we can find masculine animate nouns (M – masculine, M – animate, N – noun) in the dative case (3) (sequency in the first line) and locative case (6) (sequency in the second line).

[(word=".*ovi")&(tag="X@.*")][4],
[(word=".*u")&(tag="X@.*")]

In order to find other needed concordances with the queries with searching after endings (but these endings are not limited only to dative and locative singular).

[(word=".*ovi"]
[(word=".*u"]

Introducing checking procedures can be very useful to find right occurrences. The checking procedures is divided into two groups: work with the concordances including and not including searched tag.

Work with the concordances including searched tag depends on removing mistakenly tagged homonymous forms. In the research on the dative and locative singular this problem concerns the following type of words.

There are often cases when possessive adjectives are tagged mistakenly as the dative or locative singular.

<soupeřovi/soupeř/NNMS3-----A---1> pěšci nejsou ...[5]

There are also vocative forms with erroneous tags as the dative or locative singular.

můžeš mi říkat strýčku, nebo milý
<strýčku/strýček/NNMS6-----A---1>[6].

Other errors are instrumental forms wrongly tagged as the dative or locative singular.

když si nedovedl představit ... zemi [...]
vlastněnou <muži/muž/NNMS3-----A---->[7].

Words with common elements can be the source of problems, for example the feminine word *prémiera* 'premiere' in the accusative singular (*prémieru*) is

4 The masculine animate nouns (in hard-stem paradigms) in the dative and locative singular end in Czech language in *-ovi* or *-u* (but these endings are not restricted to these categories), therefore in the first brackets of these queries there are endings *-ovi*, *-u*. The symbols of the second bracket have the following meaning: X – unknown part of speech, @ – unrecognized word.

5 There are no rival's pedestrians.

6 You can call me, uncle.

7 He could not imagine ... the earth [...] owned by men.

homonymous with the potentially possible dative/locative masculine animate noun *prémieru* (nominative form *prémier*) 'prime minister'.

> *Ale snad tu budeš na <premiéru/NNMS6-----A---1>*
> *našeho filmu!*[8]

The next step is obtaining relevant concordances that do not include a searched tag. It consists in searching needed words in linguistically appropriate for them places, for example the Czech preposition *k* should be followed by the dative form. But the corpora software does not know about it.

> *mystik přirovnával k <papeži/papež/NNMP1-----A---->*[9]

To prove the necessity of after-check in the case of complicated searching we would like to show some results before and after the introducing of checking procedures.

Table 1

Case	Results according to corpora tags	Results after checking them
Variants endings *-i*/*-ové* in the nominative plural of words ending in *-eta*, *-ota*	*-i*/*-ové* = 0%/100%[10]	*-i*/*-ové* = 45%/55%
Orthographic variants of the word *rasismus* 'racism'	*Rasismus/rasizmus*=0%/100%[11]	*Rasismus/rasizmus* =99,98%/0,02%
The variant endings (*-i*/*-ové*) of the word *otec* 'father' in the nominative plural	*Otci*/*otcové* = 70%/30%	*Otci*/*otcové* = 0,02%/99,98%

Another trap connected with the automatic searching without checking is the reoccurrence of the same concordances or word combinations, for example the form *mnichové* 'monks' occurs 53 times, but 43 times in the same text. It concerns also idiomatic collocations, popular names of books, bands and sport teams etc.

---

8 But you will be on premiere of our film.

9 The mystic equates him to the pope.

10 Unrecognized by corpora software ending *-i* has caused the wrong results.

11 The choice of only one lemma (rasizmus) has caused the wrong results. It is especially interesting because the variant rasizmus was codified only in 1993 and it was criticized by not only linguists but many other people as well.

Another problem is presented by excerpts of texts written in other languages, especially Latin and Slovak, can be very confusing.

3. The way of using and interpreting corpora data

There are two main problems with corpora data: too large or too small number of them. If a corpus has statistical tools, the problem of great number of concordances is resolved by using various of mathematical methods availaible in them. In this case there is also a minor problem with interpretation. Large number of concordances most often means that the grammatical future is simply often used. A more significant problem is connected with interpretating zero number of concordances, one concordance or a small number of them. There are a lot of approaches to this issue. In the Czech linguistic society the zero case was broadly discussed in a journal for the theory of language and language cultivation „Slovo a slovesnost". There are two opposing points of view (see Štícha 2004, Uhlířová 2004): zero in corpora is zero in language and zero in corpora does not need to mean a zero in language.

The next matter is to determine the representative number of data on which it is possible to carry out the research. Let us begin with the meaning of one piece of data. In a research on inflection (variants) there is a lot of interpretation of it. The most important are: missprint, grammatical and spelling errors, incidental errors, new tendency in the language. It is very important not to confuse a new tendency in the language with a common grammatical error, especially in cases in a new tendency in language has developed from mistakes.

That can be one of the arguments for not determining number of the dataquantity. According to Hebal-Jezierska (2008), Štícha (2007), sporadic occurence are defined by various conditions. Some researchers try to determine a standard number of the dataquantity. According to Tušková (2006) there should be at least 20 examples, of course provided that they fulfil conditions of representativeness (stylistic conditions, etc.).

4. The choice of corpora approach and using frequency of the data in them

There are two main corpora approaches: corpus-based and corpus-driven. "The term corpus-based is used to refer to methodology that avails itself of the corpus mainly to expound, test or exemplify theories and descriptions that were formulated before large corpora became available to inform language study[12]".

12 Tognini Bonelli 2001: 65.

This one is used by most Slavic linguists. "In a corpus-driven approach the commitment of the linguist is to the integrity of the data as a whole, and descriptions aim to be comprehensive with respect to corpus evidence. The corpus, therefore, is seen as more than a repository of examples to back pre-existing theories or probabilistic extension to an already well defined system. The theoretical statements are fully consistent wit, and reflect directly, the evidence provided by the corpus. Examples are normally taken verbatim, in other words they are not adjusted in any way to fit the predefined categories of the analyst; recurrent patterns and frequency distributions are expected to form the basic evidence for linguistic categories; the absence of a pattern is considered potentially meaningful[13]". The corpus driven is rarely used in Czech linguistics. Fewer of corpora linguists tries using in their any mixed approaches (see below).

The next issue is using of corpora frequency in the description. In spite of the fact that using corpora makes linguists use figures and mathematical methods, papers on the Czech corpora linguistics often simply register the quantity of grammatical features. In most of texts figures are not classified in any groups and there is no mention about the methods of using them. Some papers make attempts to use figures to create some frequency bands.

Let us go through some Czech inflectional papers. Šimandl (2008), who has studied words belonging to the type: *kamen* 'stone', describes words in the alphabetical order but the analysed words are labelled by the following labels: (A, B: variants, f: frequency):

1 – A has f ≤ 5% and is labelled as the marginal variant, B's f > 95,0% and is labelled as the monopoly variant
2 – A has f < 5,1–39,9 > % is labelled the minority variant, B has < 94,5–60,1 > % is labelled the majority variant
3 – A and B has f < 60–40 > % are labelled the equity variants
4 – A has f < 60,1–94,5 > % is labelled the **majority variant**, B has < 39,9–5,1 > % is labelled the **minority variant**
5 – A has f > 95,0% is labelled the **monopoly variant**, B has f ≤ 5% is labelled the **marginal variant**[14]

For example: in the analysis of the genitive singular of the word *ječmen*, one of the possible endings *-e* is described as monopoly. The scale is very useful for its accuracy (precision), when the range of the analysed words in not very wide.

Hebal-Jezierska (2008), who studied the Czech masculine animate variants, used the mixed corpora approach. She describes the grammatical issue in the

13 Ibidem, p. 84.
14 Šimandl 2008: 37.

following order: paradigm, case, semantic categories: animal, people. In the frame of the semantic category the words are analysed in the following frequency categories: words with dominant ending (oscilates between 85 and 100%), words with the variants' endings (are not sporadic or dominant) and words with the sporadic or not found endings. The last category is not defined by numbers but only by the conditions of non-representativeness, for example: strange style, etc. The corpora results are compared with the codification ones. This way of describing grammatical issues allows to avoid repeating conclusions. One of the disadvantages is a very big range of the middle scale band. Very often there is one type of words in different places, for example: the words in *-ik*, which have two endings according to the dictionary, according to corpora is divided into three groups: the ending *-ové*, endings *-ové*, *-i*, ending *-i*, what makes verification complicated.

Tušková (2006), who studied the Czech feminine variants, describes them in the frame of the paradigm and case. The words with one ending, two endings, are analysed separately. The results are also compared with information contained in the dictionary. She does not use any frequency band, but she operates with words "central" and "peripheral" (which are used intuitively). But she does not define them in any way.

The last one is the Bermel's scale. He connects the frequency of corpora data with *acceptability judgments* of native speakers (Bermel 2009). He carried out a pilot research of the Czech genitive singular that tested the relationship between corpus frequency and acceptability[15]. Sporadic occurrences for a frequent morphological feature – correlate with low acceptability for native speakers. Proportions over 50% in the corpus correlates with high acceptability for native speakers. From c. 5% on up to 50% of occurrences, there is no clear correlation between frequency and acceptability.

There is no corpus driven Czech inflection study yet, but in the paper will be present a plan of the research. In this approach the corpora frequency of searched variants can be the superior category, for example:

Words with just only ending *-ové* (~100%)
Words with two endings *-ové,-i* (> 0% < 100%)
Words with just only ending *-i* (~100%)
On the basis of the category new paradigms may be created.

15 It follows study on syntax by e.g. Divjak (2008) and Kempen and Harbusch (2005).

5. Analysed factors in Czech corpora inflectional research

In all the studies many factors have been analysed. The corpora allowed us to analyse many factors affecting choice of one of the endings, for example: frequency, the structure of the word, the ending of the word, existence of homonymous and syncretic forms, the position in the sentence, situational context, semantics of the word, language layer, type of the text, collocations, euphony. The very important is the cooperation of the factors.

Let us look at the influence of some factors on the choice of a variant.

The example of the impact of a word structure, word ending and euphony upon the choice of ending can be seen in foreign words in *-ál*, *-graf*, *-man*, *-sof* in nominative plural, dative and locative plural. In foreign words, because of the lack of appropriate for language users clarity of the lexeme structure, there is a need for an ending that contains a more precise information about the category of animacy[16]. It is also very important that the words end in consonants: *l*, *f*, *m*, which have a tendency to connect with longer endings (*-ové*, *-ovi*) than shorter (*-i*, *-u*). In the nominative plural, with regard for the possibility of occurence of homophony with accusative, there is a tendency to choose ending *-ové*. Another group is represented by words with suffix *-graf*: this suffix can be animate or inanimate, therefore there is a need to signal animacy. Words ending in *-l* also have a tendency to be connected with longer endings not only in this case. There are hardly any occurences with ending *-i* in the nominative plural. Most cases contain ending *-ové*[17].

Referring to the existence of homonymous words, there are many words in Czech language, in which endings depends on it. One of the interesting words is *racek* 'seagull'. According to the corpora data ending *-ové* (*rackové*) is dominant in the nominative plural (83%). The reason of it can be seen in the consonant *-k*. Choice of the ending *-i* brings together two consonants *c*. In the case of uncareful pronunciation and in the Common Czech (obecná čeština) incorrect pronunciation [raci] is possible (Palková 1997: 327)[18]. This way of pronunciation causes the change of meaning. *Raci* is the nominative plural of the word *rak* 'crayfish'. In order to avoid this kind of misunderunderstanding users prefer for this word ending *-ové* to *-i*[19].

---

16 Rusínová also writes about it (1987), p. 74.

17 Hebal-Jezierska 2008: 68.

18 The author of the chapter concerning orthoepia writes about examples of geminate, in which double sound pronunciation is codified (in the Czech language geminates are typically pronounced as one consonant). One of the conditions for exceptions is a difference in meaning. Among the examples is the word *racek*. The pronunciation [*racci*] is codified but the incorrect form [*raci*] is met in the Common Czech.

19 Hebal-Jezierska 2008: 106.

Another example are words in *-ik* in the dative and locative plural. Thanks to connecting with the ending *-ovi* they are not homonymous with the accusative feminine forms ending in *-ika*. The same problem is with the masculine animate word *premiér* 'prime minister' – with the feminine word *premiéra* 'premiere'. It is very important especially in verbs with two rections: the acusative and dative. Homonyms can disturb the process of communication. Sentences **vysvětluju matematiku matematiku*[20], *píšu kritiku kritiku*[21] sound not only unintelligible but also comic. In order to avoid misunderstanding users prefer the ending *-ovi* to *-u*[22].

Other important factors for the choice of the ending are prepositions and attributes[23].

In the masculine animate nouns (in the semantic group of animal) this factor can be often significant (see table 2 and 3).

Table 2

The construction: attribute + noun in dative with the ending *-ovi* or noun in dative with the ending *-ovi* + attribute	The construction: Noun without an attribute in dative with the ending *-ovi*
23%	77%

Table 3

The construction: attribute + noun in dative with the ending *-u* or noun in dative with the ending *-u* + attribute	The construction: Noun without an attribute in dative with the ending *-u*
37%	63%

The influence of the attribute‘s existence on the choice of the noun ending was confirmed especially in the dative and locative singular. The ending -ovi in the construction with an attribute appears in 23% (without it 77%), while the ending -u appears in 37% of cases (without the attribute 63%). But the difference in the results is smaller than it can be expected after analysing grammar description existing before the corpora.

20 I explain mathematics to a mathematician.

21 I write a review for a critic.

22 Ibidem, p. 69.

23 Ibidem, p. 39.

The next factor that can influence upon the choice of ending is the text type. This factor is significant for the group of masculine animate nouns ending in -*asta, -ista, -ita* in the nominative plural. There is a big difference between occurrences of endings in various types of text. In the fiction, the ending *-i* occurs more often (20% in the group of words with sporadic occurrences of the ending *-i* and 30% in the group with the above average occurrences of this ending) than in the press. Using of the ending in this genre is caused by using the Commom Czech[24] in dialogs and in the narration containing expressive vocabulary. The ending *-é* makes only 2% in fiction. A large difference is also seen in the technical and specialised literature, where occurrences of the ending *-é* are typical, while the morf *-i* appears only in 5% in this genre. In the publicistic genre the ending *-é* is also dominant (91%), while the ending *-i* is restricted to quotations or stories containing expressive vocabulary.

The next significant factor can be the language layer. The choice of the ending (*-é* or *-i*) in the masculine animate nouns ending in *-ista*, *-ita*, *-asta* strongly depends on the language layer type. The table below shows that frequency of endings are totally different in particular language layers.

Table 4

	The ending *-é*	The ending *-i*	Total
Standard Czech	97%	3%	100%
Common Czech	2%	98%	100%

Meanings of words and collocations are very important in many cases, for example there are two variants of the nominative plural forms: *čtvrti* and *čtvrtě*. The corpora analysis shows that the word *čtvrti* has often the meaning 'district' while the form *čtvrtě* has the meaning 'quarter'[25].

Collocations are significant in the analysis of variants of the nominative forms *lodi* and *lodě* 'boats'. The first one occurs in the following collocations: *ztroskotané lodi* 'wrecked boats), *potopené lodi* 'sunk boats', while the second one in: *námořní lodě* 'marine boats', *rybářské lodě* 'fishing boats'[26].

Difference between adjectives determining the word *práce* 'work' can also be seen (There is a weak tendency not to use the ending *-em* in the meaning 'manual work'[27] (see Table 5):

24 Common Czech is a language used in informal situation. The ending *-i* is typical for this language layer.
25 Tušková 2006: 55.
26 Ibidem, p. 93–94.
27 Ibidem, p. 47.

Table 5

Pracím (*Work* in the dative plural with the ending *-ím*)	**Pracem (*Work* in the dative plural with the ending *-em*)**
Výkopovým 'excavation'	Výkopovým 'excavation'
Záchranařským 'rescue'	Nuceným 'compulsory'
Prospěšným 'profit'	Stavebním 'building'
Průzkumným 'research'	Domácím 'domestic'
Nuceným 'compulsory'	
Přípravným 'prepare'	
Záchranným 'rescue'	
Ručním 'hand'	
Stavebním 'building'	
Nezbytným 'necessary'	
Domácím 'domestic'	

6. Conclusion

Although the corpus linguistic is a new phenomenon in Czech linguistic society there are already attempts not to use corpora as a repository of examples, but as a database which makes the researcher to change his method of working with language and describing it. Attempts of looking at the inflectional variants problems in the Czech corpora analysis in other way than the precorpora desription was the issue presented. Some facts were validated but some were denied, for example Šimandl's description denied the commonly accepted thesis about some variants of the word *ječmen* 'berley'. The corpora analysis has proved that forms which are described in all the types of Czech grammars, *ječmena* (gen. sg.), *and v ječmeně* (Loc. sg.) *are* obsolete and therefore mistaken. A lot of inflectional variants were also denied in corpora analyses carried out by Bermel, Tušková and Hebal-Jezierska. All those corpora descriptions are first ones where the issue is given such a detailed analysis.

References

Bermel, N. (2004). "V korpuse nebo v korpusu? Co nám řekne (a neřekne) ČNK o morfologické variaci v tvarech lokálu". In: Z. Hladká, P. Karlík (eds.). *Čeština – univerzália a specifika 5. Sborník 5. mezinárodního setkání bohemistů v Brně 13.–15.2003*, Brno: 163–171.

Bermel, N. (2009). "Pilotní studie o vztahu mezi korpusovými daty a hodnoceními přijatelnosti konkurujících tvarů". A lecture given in Brno (in press).

Český národní korpus (Syn2000), www.korpus.cz

Divjak, D. (2008). "On (in)frequency and (un)acceptability". In: B. Lewandowska-Tomaszczyk (ed.). *Corpus Linguistics, Computer Tools and Applications – State of the Art.* Frankfurt am Main: Peter Lang.

Hebal-Jezierska, M. (2008). *Wariantywność końcówek fleksyjnych rzeczowników męskich żywotnych w języku czeskim.* Warszawa.

Hebal-Jezierska, M. (2008a). "Variantnost některých podstatných jmen v mluveném korpusu". In: M. Kopřivová, M. Waclawičová (eds.). *Čeština v mluveném korpusu (Studie z korpusové lingvistiky).* Praha: 89–96.

Hebal-Jezierska, M. (2009). „Praca z elektronicznym korpusem przy wyszukiwaniu wariantów fleksyjnych". In: J. Mindak-Zawadzka, I. Doliński (eds.). *Językowy świat Słowian.* Warszawa: 101–114.

Kempen, G. and K. Harbusch (2005). "The relationship between grammaticality ratings and corpus frequencies: A case study into word order variability in the midfield of German clauses". In: S. Kepser and M. Reis (eds.). *Linguistic Evidence: Empirical, Theoretical and Computational Perspectives.* Berlin and New York: Mouton de Gruyter: 329–349.

Kocek, J., Kopřivová, M. and K. Kučera (eds.) (2000). *ČNK Úvod a příručka uživatele,* Praha.

Konečná, H. and M. Prošek (2008). "Tvary příčestí minulého u sloves typu „tisknout" v korpusech psaného a mluveného jazyka". In: F. Štícha, M. Fried (eds.). *Grammar and Corpora, Gramatika a korpus.* Academia. Praha: 383–390.

http://mam.ujc.cas.cz

Palková, Z. (1997). *Fonetika a fonologie češtiny s obecným úvodem do problematiky oboru.* Praha.

Rusínová, Z. (1987). *K distribuci alomorfů -i/-ové v nom. pl. maskulin životných.* In: J. Pačesová (ed.). *Sborník prací Filozofické fakulty Brněnské univerzity/Studia Minora Facultatis Philosophicae Universitatis Brunensis A 35.* Brno: 71–78.

Štícha, F. (2001). "Kritéria gramatičnosti (korpus jako argument a inspirace)". *Slovo a slovesnost,* 62: 161–175.

Štícha, F. (2007). "Jak posuzovat gramatičnost potenciálních variantních koncovek", online paper prepared for a team working on the project Studies in Czech Grammar, http://mam.ujc.cas.cz/ (17.01.2007).

Šimandl, J. (2008). *Dnešní stav skloňování substantiv takzvaných typů kámen a břímě* (PhD disertation). Available at: http://ktf.cuni.cz/~simandl/trf/dis/1.pdf (in press)

Tognini-Bonelli, E. (2001). *Corpus Linguistics at Work.* Amsterdam/Philadelphia.

Tušková, J.M. (2006). *Variantní a dubletní tvary v současné deklinaci apelativních feminin.* Brno.

Uhlířová, L. (2004). "Gramatika v korpusu, korpus v gramatice: příspěvek k diskusi o vyhledávání gramatické informace v korpuse". *Slovo a slovesnost,* 65: 16–23.

The Language of Evaluation in English and Spanish Editorials: a Corpus-Based Study

María Pérez Blanco

Abstract: This paper deals with some of the linguistic features of newspaper editorials in English and Spanish. Also known as 'leading articles' in the English press, non-bylined editorials articulate the newspaper's voice representing the prototypical type of comment text. As such, editorials are loaded with instances of writer stance or evaluation actualized in texts by different formal resources. The present paper is a multi-level analysis of the linguistic realization of evaluation in leading articles in English and Spanish: 1) a macro-level analysis of text organisation (rhetorical moves); 2) an intermediate level analysis of text organisation in combination with evaluation (illocution types), and 3) a micro-level analysis of the evaluation-loaded lexico-grammatical categories used in newspaper editorials.

A contrastive analysis methodology will unveil the main trends and the similarities and differences between both languages. The comment texts analyzed in this paper have been extracted from a large comparable corpus of English and Spanish editorials from the most widely read British and Spanish quality newspapers. The similarities and differences between both languages revealed in this study will be valuable in the field of translation and will supply the raw material for the building up of applications in the field of professional writing for the press (ESP).

Keywords: attitude, construed reader, contrastive analysis, editorials, evaluation, move structure, illocution types, English, Spanish, stance.

1. Introduction

The present paper deals with evaluation, a complex and relatively new field of research which in these days seems to be stirring the interest of many scholars. In recent years, different conferences have been organized around the study of evaluation and volumes collecting different contributions have been published (Del Lungo and Bonelli 2004; Hunston and Thompson 2000). Many researchers working on this area seem to be concerned with the expression of evaluation in academic texts (Del Lungo and Bonelli 2004; Hyland 1998, 2005). Another area in which evaluation is being studied is opinion journalism (Bednarek 2006; Marín-Arrese 2004), especially editorials or leading articles. Such is the case of the present study.

Why study evaluation in editorials? Editorials describe a current event or problem – political, social or economical – not objectively, but evaluating the possible solutions and the subsequent outcomes. The writer (either the editor or the editorial board) takes up a position about the issue on hand. Therefore, the analysis of the language of editorials implies analyzing the linguistic realization of writer stance or evaluation.

In the attempt of analyzing the different linguistic features expressing evaluation, it must be born in mind that "stance is a meaning, a type of meaning, or several types of meaning, rather than a form." (Hunston 2007: 27). The complex process of identifying all the different resources expressing this semantic function becomes aggravated by the fact that evaluative meanings are "randomly dispersed across a range of structural options shared with non-evaluative functions." (Hunston and Sinclair 2000: 74)

This paper studies evaluation in newspaper editorials from an English-Spanish contrastive perspective.

2. Theoretical background

A number of studies have been published focussing on evaluation under different names: *stance* (Biber and Finnegan 1988, 1989), *evaluation* (Hunston and Thompson 2000), *evidentiality* (Chafe 1986), *metadiscourse* (Hyland 2005), *appraisal* (Martin and White 2005). Such reference works and other small contributions, articles, PhD theses and conference dissertations provide ample proof of the different ways in which the topic of evaluation has been tackled.

The present study adopts an eclectic approach. It is partly rooted in the concepts of *appraisal theory* as presented by Martin and White (2005) and partly on Hyland's (2005) notions of *stance* and *engagement*. Some other ideas have been borrowed from various studies on evaluation by Hunston (1995, 2007).

Evaluation, defined as "the expression of the speaker or writer's stance towards, viewpoint on, or feelings about the entities or propositions that he or she is talking about." (Hunston and Thompson 2000: 5), encompasses a wide range of meanings. These meanings can be distributed along four axes, in other words, four semantic functions can be signalled for the expression of evaluation: 1) ways of feeling or attitudinal meanings, 2) writer stance towards propositional content in terms of truth, source of knowledge or epistemic and evidential meanings, 3) writer-reader relationship or meanings related to addressing readers, 4) degrees of evaluation.

3. Data and working procedure

The data for this case study consists of 10 leading articles from each of the languages in contrast. The English texts have been extracted from *The Times, The Daily Telegraph* and *The Guardian* and the Spanish texts from *El País, ABC* and *El Mundo*, which are the most widely read quality newspapers in the United Kingdom and Spain. Both selections present a virtually identical number of words (English: 5,373; Spanish: 5,400). All leading articles were published in the second half of 2006. The specific dates have been selected at random.

The study follows a top-down approach to the linguistic realization of evaluation in leading articles in English and Spanish. First, texts have been analysed at a macro-level. At the strictly formal level, rhetorical moves and sub-moves (*triads* and *turns*) have been delimited following the *triad* pattern (Bolívar 1994). Moving on to a semantic-pragmatic level of analysis, the different illocution types characterizing these chunks of texts have been identified. In the second stage of the study, at the micro-level of analysis, the evaluation-loaded lexico-grammatical categories have been isolated and classified according to both semantic and formal criteria.

3.1. Stage 1: macrostructure

The first stage of the study is the analysis of the rhetorical structure of editorials, which means the identification of the three main triads or moves in opinion texts classified according to position and function: *Situation*, *Development* and *Recommendation* (Bolívar 1994).

Move 1 or the *situation* triad appears in initial position and introduces the topic of evaluation; move 2 or the *development* triad, in medial position, develops the topic already introduced in the situation; and finally, move 3 or the *recommendation* triad, occupying the final position, closes the evaluation. Triads exhibit usually three turns: *lead-follow-valuate*. The *lead* (L) introduces the topic of the triad and a position towards it, the *follow* (F) keeps the same topic and evaluates the preceding piece of information and the *valuate* (V) closes the triad evaluating the two preceding turns. Triads may present more than three turns, provided the sequence LF is repeated and V is final. In most texts in our study *situation* and *recommendation* triads present a three-turn pattern. However, *development* triads are fairly longer presenting different alternatives to the three turn pattern: LFLFV; LFVLFV; etc. Figure 3.1 below shows a sample text divided in moves and sub-moves:

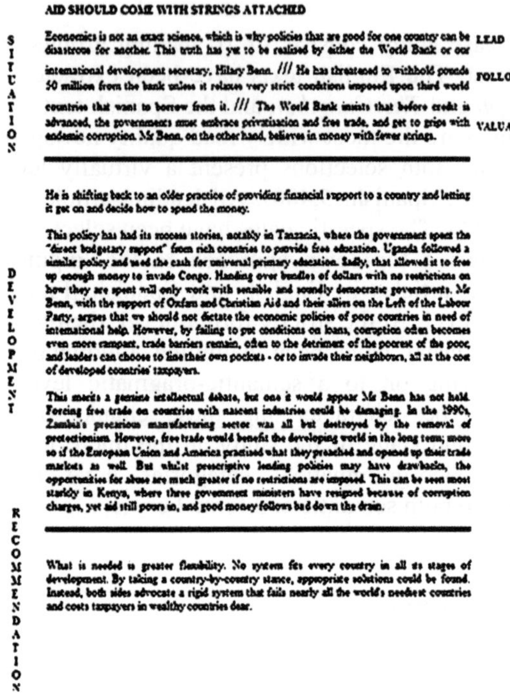

SITUATION

AID SHOULD COME WITH STRINGS ATTACHED

Economics is not an exact science, which is why policies that are good for one country can be disastrous for another. This truth has yet to be realised by either the World Bank or our international development secretary, Hilary Benn. /// He has threatened to withhold pounds 50 million from the bank unless it relaxes very strict conditions imposed upon third world countries that want to borrow from it. /// The World Bank insists that before credit is advanced, the governments must embrace privatisation and free trade, and get to grips with endemic corruption. Mr Benn, on the other hand, believes in money with fewer strings.

LEAD

FOLLOW

VALUATE

DEVELOPMENT

He is shifting back to an older practice of providing financial support to a country and letting it get on and decide how to spend the money.

This policy has had its success stories, notably in Tanzania, where the government spent the "direct budgetary support" from rich countries to provide free education. Uganda followed a similar policy and used the cash for universal primary education. Sadly, that allowed it to free up enough money to invade Congo. Handing over bundles of dollars with no restrictions on how they are spent will only work with sensible and soundly democratic governments. Mr Benn, with the support of Oxfam and Christian Aid and their allies on the Left of the Labour Party, argues that we should not dictate the economic policies of poor countries in need of international help. However, by failing to put conditions on loans, corruption often becomes even more rampant, trade barriers remain, often to the detriment of the poorest of the poor, and leaders can choose to line their own pockets - or to invade their neighbours, all at the cost of developed countries' taxpayers.

This merits a genuine intellectual debate, but one it would appear Mr Benn has not held. Forcing free trade on countries with nascent industries could be damaging. In the 1990s, Zambia's precarious manufacturing sector was all but destroyed by the removal of protectionism. However, free trade would benefit the developing world in the long term; more so if the European Union and America practised what they preached and opened up their trade markets as well. But whilst prescriptive lending policies may have drawbacks, the opportunities for abuse are much greater if no restrictions are imposed. This can be seen most starkly in Kenya, where three government ministers have resigned because of corruption charges, yet aid still pours in, and good money follows bad down the drain.

RECOMMENDATION

What is needed is greater flexibility. No system fits every country in all its stages of development. By taking a country-by-country stance, appropriate solutions could be found. Instead, both sides advocate a rigid system that fails nearly all the world's neediest countries and costs taxpayers in wealthy countries dear.

Figure 3.1. Macrostructure of a sample text

Once the texts were segmented this way, our interest lay in discovering the most frequent illocution types in each of the main moves or triads in English and Spanish. In addition to the three triads identified, attention has also been paid to the type of illocution appearing in the titles of newspaper editorials.

There are a number of illocutions characterizing leading articles which Vestergaard (2000) calls *assesives* and which are defined in opposition to Searle's *representatives* (1976). Here, the notion of truth is irrelevant; it is a matter of human assessment:

- Evaluations: whether things are good or bad, desirable or undesirable: "*That child is lucky to have a determined parent…*" (ENLE3)
- Proposals: what needs to be done to change the present state of affairs: "*The process must also address the grievances…*" (ENLE17)
- Interpretations: ascribing meanings to phenomena: "*It is indeed a global and American tragedy…*" (ENLE17)

- Predictions: Though in due course they may turn out to be true, they are ultimately based on human assessment: *(...) "whatever is done in the short term will not work unless... "* (ENLE30)
- Causal explanations: also a question of assessment, especially when it comes to questions of human actions: "*Economics is not an exact science, which is why policies that are...*" (ENLE6)
- Ascriptions of mental states: ascribing intentions, wishes...They are a matter of human assessment. There is no way of knowing what other people thinks: "*Virtually everyone in the world wants that.*" (ENLE30)
- "Speculations": modalized statements: "He is unlikely to do more than pass on the message" (ENLE30)

In order to provide a full of account of all illocutions in our texts, another four illocution types have been added to this list:

- Attributions: statements originating in an external source: "*Tony Blair (...) said it would be unwise and foolish...*" (ENLE39)
- Questions to readers: questions bringing readers into discourse: "*What of the rest of children in Mr Johnson's constituency (...) who have not choice but to attend...?* (ENLE3)
- Attitudinal representatives: representatives with attitudinal lexis: "*The government made a serious attempt to address some of the shortcomings in yesterday's Green Paper*" (ENLE35)
- Neutral representatives: neutral factual statements: "The PDs were not alone in advocating low taxes, restrained public spending and smaller government" (ENLE33)

This last illocution type presents a small percentage in the texts analyzed and it does not belong to the *assessives* group.

It is possible to draw a correspondence between one or more of the linguistic devices that express subjectivity or evaluation and each of these types of illocution.

3.2. Stage 2: microstructure

The different types of evaluative meanings are realized in texts by an enormous variety of lexico-grammatical resources. The second stage of the analysis consisted in identifying the microlinguistic resources actualizing the different evaluative meanings.

- Attitude: adjectives, nouns, adverbs...
- Stance: epistemic and evidential modal markers, negations, connectors...
- Construed reader: reader pronouns, deontic modal markers, questions addressing readers...
- Degree of evaluation: degree adverbs, comparatives...

The data extracted from both languages were yuxtaposed and compared in order to reach conclusions about the similarities and differences in the language of evaluation in English and Spanish.

4. Description and analysis

4.1. Stage 1: macrostructure

In this section we analyze the number of times each illocution type appears in each move. The aim is to discover the illocution types characterizing each move in each of the languages. The title of editorials will be called move 0.

- **Move 0: title**

Differences between English and Spanish editorials become apparent from the very beginning. Spanish editorials prefer non-evaluative titles, that is, *neutral representatives* as in "El voto de los inmigrantes"[1] or "Israel se defiende"[2]. On the other hand, English editorials quite often select proposals or even questions involving readers already in the title as in "The lessons a helpful minister should learn" or "Who cares?" In other words, there are more cases of evaluation and directives in the titles of English editorials, while more factual statements appear in Spanish titles. In Spanish seven out of ten titles are realized by neutral representatives; two titles are evaluations and one is an attitudinal representative. In English, only three out of ten titles are realized by neutral representatives. There are three proposals, two attitudinal representatives, one question and one case of evaluation.

- **Move 1: Situation**

In move 1, the *situation*, English texts present a lot of evaluation, either in the form of proper evaluative illocutions (21.8%) or representatives reporting facts but sprinkled with some evaluative adverb or noun here and there (25.5%).

1 Translation: "Immigrants vote".
2 Translation: "Israel defends itself".

Attributions are also quite common in this initial move in English (23.6%). By means of attributions the writer places the responsibility of the statement in an external source. Spanish situation triads tend to be more neutral or less evaluative. Although a high amount of attitudinal lexis appears somewhat hidden in what we have called *attitudinal representatives*, *neutral representatives* are predominant in the situation triad (23.2%), in contrast with English (9.1%). Although this study does not reach the level of delicacy of identifying the illocution types appearing in the particular turns within each move, it is noticeable that, in Spanish, evaluations (13%) tend to appear in the valuate, but never in the lead of the situation triad. On the contrary, in English they open the editorial. That initial position in Spanish texts is occupied mainly by factual statements, that is, neutral representatives. These data clearly point towards differences in the conventions referring to the expression of evaluation between the two languages.

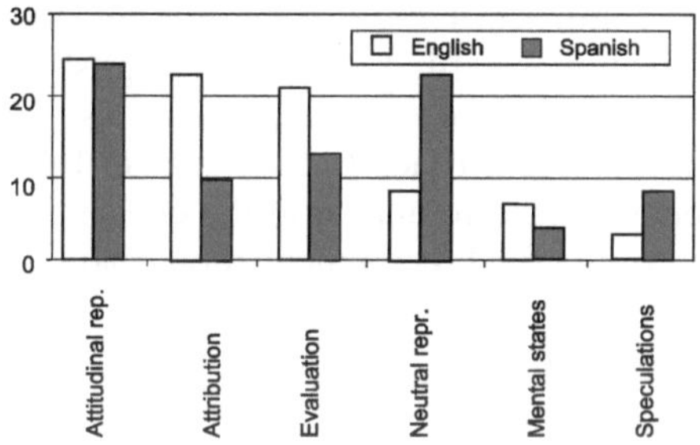

Figure 4.1. Instances of illocution types in move 1

- **Move 2: Development**

It is not easy to select one single illocution type characterizing this triad. Evaluation is important in both languages in the body of editorials, as they are opinion texts *per se*. The development triad develops the topic of the text impregnating the reporting of facts with attitudinal lexis. Attitudinal representatives score really high in English (27.5%). There are also bare evaluations about whether things are good or bad (in this case, scoring higher in Spanish, 15.8%). Nonetheless, the development triad also presents empirical facts and data expressed by neutral representatives. In English this is the move that presents a larger amount of this type of illocutions even if it is not really outstanding (13% vs 9% in situation and even less in the final move).

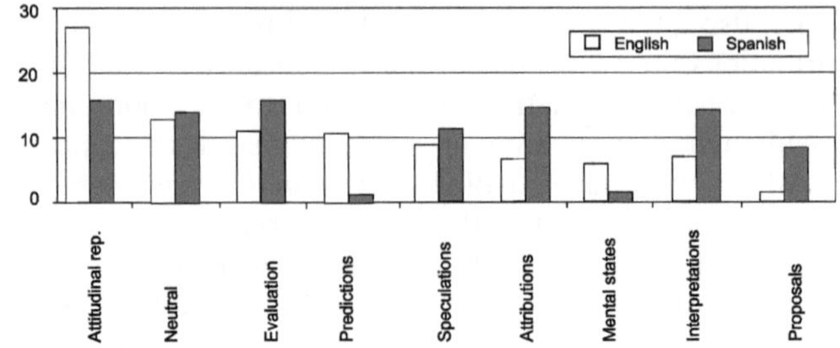

Figure 4.2. Instances of illocution types in move 2: development

Illocution types presenting the most salient differences between both languages are: predictions, interpretations, attributions and proposals. English presents more predictions (11.4% vs none in Spanish) in this position while Spanish clearly favours interpretations (14.7% vs 6.8% in English). In Spanish this move is also the place for attributions (14.7%) while in English they appear more often in the initial triad. The difference regarding proposals is also relevant, scoring higher in Spanish development triads (9.5%) than in English (3%). It must be noted that those proposals tend to appear at the end of this triad, in the valuate turn, paving the way for the final recommendation triad.

- **Move 3: Recommendation**

In Spanish there is a clear illocution type characterizing move 3: proposals (43.2%). As opinion texts, the function of editorials is to persuade the reader to share the writer's viewpoint, and, sometimes, also, to take a particular course of action. It is in this final move in which writers explicitly point out what needs to be done to change the current, usually, unsatisfactory state of affairs described in the text. In English leading articles, proposals also present the highest score in this final triad (14%), even if it is not the most or the only outstanding illocution type in the recommendation move. In English, speculations, attitudinal lexis and even neutral representatives share predominance with proposals in this final triad. Other important differences between both languages is the number of evaluative illocutions in this final move, which is higher in Spanish (20.5%) than in English (12.5%), and a fair amount of representative illocutions in English (8.5%) and none in Spanish.

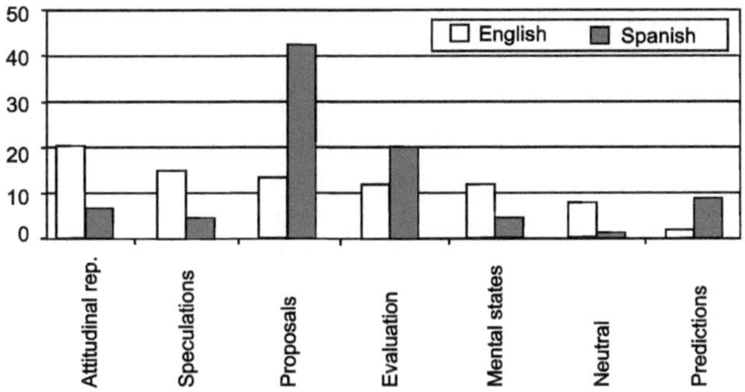

Figure 4.3. Instances of illocution types in move 3: recommendation

To sum up, according to the texts analyzed, it seems that English and Spanish exhibit a kind of reversed *illocutionary* structure. Spanish editorials present first the bare facts, then, they provide interpretations, speculations, and evaluations about the situation presented and finally, recommend what should be done. English editorials start strong with evaluations and, only later come to the facts. This is illustrated in figure 4.4 below.

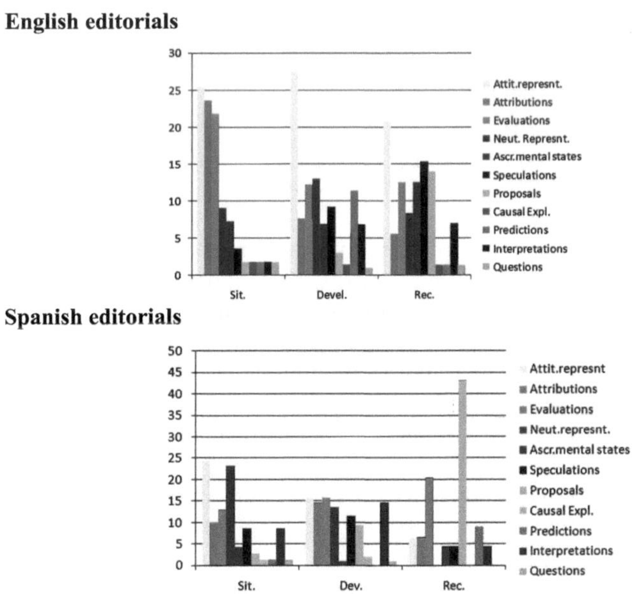

Figure 4.4. Types of illocutions in English and Spanish editorials

4.2. Stage 2: microstructure

The second stage of the analysis consisted in identifying the microlinguistic resources expressing each type of evaluative content. For this analysis, the different types of evaluative meanings or evaluative semantic functions of *attitude*, *stance*, *construed reader* and *degree of evaluation* have been classified into sub-functions. Table 4.1 shows the quantitative differences between both languages with respect to the different types of evaluation.

Table 4.1. Total number of lexico-grammatical units expressing evaluation

English		Spanish	
Attitude	199	Attitude	171
Stance	179	Stance	126
Construed reader	64	Construed reader	63
Degree of evaluation	149	Degree of evaluation	106
Total	591	Total	466
Total nº of words	5,371	Total nº of words	5,400

English shows more instances of evaluation in all types, except in *construed reader* where the number of cases are similar in both languages. For each broad semantic function, the subsequent tables will show in detail how the gross number of instances of evaluation is distributed along two axes: different sub-functions and particular formal resources.

4.2.1. Attitude

This semantic function is concerned with the expression of the writer's emotional reactions or ways of feeling towards the propositional content of the discourse. Martin and White (2005) distinguish three different semantic regions involved in the expression of attitudinal meanings: affect (positive and negative feelings in terms of emotivity) judgement (social and moral judgements) and appreciation (axiological evaluation). The semantic function of attitude is actualized across a range of grammatical structures, as can be seen in Table 4.2.1-1.

Attitude is expressed mainly by adjectives and nouns in both languages. The larger number of attitudinal resources belongs to the appreciation sub-function, (comprehensibility, importance, valuation, etc.), but with many more cases in English (110) than in Spanish (85). English editorials present more appreciative adjectives (75) of the type of *revealing, helpful* or *suitable* than Spanish editorials (52). A few selected examples are provided in (1) to (3).

1. Affect, adjective: *"Even more disturbing than Mr Johnson's atavistic assumption about is (...)"* (ENLE3)
2. Appreciation, adjective: *"Yesterday's shift in Middle East policymaking away from military escalation and towards diplomacy is welcome as far as it goes."* (ENLE17)
3. Affect, adjective, and, appreciation, noun: *Es muy desmoralizador que en lugar de establecer una tregua (...) se busquen motivos para adelantar la bronca.* (SPED30)[3]

Table 4.2.1-1. The grammar of *attitude* in English and Spanish

		English		Spanish	
ATTITUDE	**Affect**	Adjective	17	Adjective	13
		Verb	9	Verb	7
		Noun	8	Noun	12
		Adverb	4	Noun	2
		Total	**38**	**Total**	**34**
	Judgement	Adjective	30	Adjective	30
		Verb	5	Verb	1
		Noun	12	Noun	14
		Adverb	3	Adverb	1
		P.P.	1	Fixed expression	6
		Total	**51**	**Total**	**52**
	Appreciat.	Adjective	75	Adjective	52
		Verb	4	Verb	4
		Noun	23	Noun	19
		Adverb	5	Adverb	5
		Fixed expression	3	PP.	2
		Total	**110**	**Total**	**85**

4.2.2. Stance

As mentioned above, the semantic function of *stance* renders meanings related to authorial positioning or commitment. Writers may present a proposition as highly warrantable (*proclaim*) or as one of a range of possibilities (*entertain*). They can also hold a contrary point of view, rejecting a proposition mentioned previously or inferred from the situational context (*disclaim*). Another option is to present a

3 Translation: "*It is really demoralizing that instead of agreeing to a truce, they are looking for reasons to bring forward a quarrel.*"

proposition as originating in an external voice (*attribution*). Table 4.2.2.1 presents the resources actualizing each of the different sub-types of writer stance.

Table 4.2.2-1. The grammar of *stance* in English and Spanish

		English		Spanish	
STANCE	**Proclaim**	Epistemic adverb	9	Epistemic adv.	7
		Modal verb	1	Epistemic adj.	5
		Ev. Cogn. Verb.	3	Deductive verb	3
		Pseudo-cleft	2		
		Total	**15**	**Total**	**15**
	Disclaim	Adversative connectives	41	Adversative connectives	29
		Denial/negatives	13	Denial/negatives	11
		Concession adverb	2	Concession adv.	1
		Comment adverb	1	Contrastive expression	1
		Total	**57**	**Total**	**42**
	Entert.	Epistemic mod. Vb.	48	Epistemic mo.l vb.	8
		Epistemic adv.	2	Conditional endings	5
		Epistemic adj.	2	Epistemic adv.	3
		Ev. Perceptual vb.	1	Episemic expression	3
		Agentless passive	1	Epistemic adj.	3
		Perceputal noun	1	Future endings	2
				Epistemic noun	2
		Total	**55**	**Total**	**28**
	Attribut.	**Total**	**52**	**Total**	**41**

The *proclaim* semantic function is expressed mainly by epistemic adverbs in both languages and the differences between English and Spanish are minor, almost nonexistent.

English shows a larger number of elements having a *disclaiming* sub-function (57 cases) than Spanish (42 cases). The most common resources actualizing this particular meaning in both languages are adversative connectives followed by structures expressing denial, that is, negatives.

The *entertain* sub-function is also more predominant in English (55) than in Spanish (28). The grammar of *entertain* is expressed in English mainly by epistemic modal verbs. There is a really outstanding difference between both languages regarding this resource: English (48) vs Spanish (8). In Spanish this stance meaning is spread over a wider range of lexico-grammatical resources, including conditional and future endings which are inflections in the Spanish language and nonexistent in English. Examples of *proclaim*, *disclaim* and *entertain* are given in (4) to (6).

4. Entertain, epistemic modal verb: "*Forcing free trade on countries with nascent industries could be damaging*." (ENLE6)
5. Disclaim, adversative connective: "*Despite the party's modest size, it has made an enormous contribution to the economic and social liberalisation of this country*." (ENLE33)
6. Proclaim, epistemic adverb: "Ciertamente, no tienen esa suerte."[4] (SPED9)

Finally, *attributions* present propositions as grounded in external voices rather than in the author's subjectivity. This fact leads to a discussion about whether or not attribution should be considered as belonging to the expression of writer stance (Bednarek 2006). Hunston (1995) claims that "an act of attribution is also an act of evaluation." (1995: 34). The classification of Martin and White (2005) place *attribution* together with *proclaim*, *entertain*, and *disclaim* as meanings assigned to the category of *engagement* (*stance*, in our study). In this study, we subscribe that view. The fact that attribution is presented in a separate table does not mean it is segregated from the rest of sub-functions of stance. It is merely a matter of presenting the results as clearly as possible. In the case of attribution, it is important to distinguish the different kind of third party occupying the role of subject of the attribution, whether they are specific, unspecified or abstract rhetors. There can also be instances of direct quotations.

Employing a *specific rhetor* means the attribution of voices to others with reporting verbs (Neff *et al.* 2004) as in "The Prime Minister has said..." An alternative strategy is to resort to an *unspecified rhetor* such as "Some people think..." Finally, writers may conceal their voices by placing an *abstract rhetor* in subject position, apparently allowing the facts to speak for themselves, for example, "The opinion poll suggests..."

4 Translation: "Certainly, they are not so lucky."

Table 4.3.2-2. The grammar of *attribution* in English and Spanish

	Conceptualizer of proposition	English		Spanish	
ATTRIBUTION	**Other voices**	Ev. Comn. Vb.	23	Ev. Comn. Vb.	20
		Ev. Cogn. Vb.	8	Ev. Cogn. Vb.	7
		Ev. Perceptual vb.	3	Ev. Percep. Vb.	1
		Ev. Ep. Adj.	1		
		Total	**35**		**28**
	Unspecified rhetor	Cognitive noun	4	Ev. Comn. Vb.	1
		Ev. Cogn. Vb.	2		
		Ev. Comn. Vb.	2		
		Total	**8**		**1**
	Abstract rhetor	Ev. Percep. Vb.	2	Ev. Percep. Vb.	3
		Ev. Comn. Vb.	1	Ev. Comn. Vb.	3
		Ev. Cogn. Vb.	1		
		Total	**4**		**6**
	Quotations		5		4

Most times writers of editorials resort to attribution, they choose specific rhetors as the conceptualizers of propositions. The reporting verbs preferred are more or less neutral evidential communicative verbs (*say*, *argue*, *claim*, *suggest*, *agree*) as exemplified in (7). Also evidential cognitive verbs (*think*, *consider*, *realize*, *expect*) and, in fewer cases, evidential perceptual verbs (mainly: *seem*, *show*, *signal*) are used in these reporting constructions.

7. "(…) *about half of children in care said that they were never praised or rewarded if they did well in school.*" (ENLE35)

The main difference between English and Spanish is represented by the number of cases of unspecified rhetors of the type of "Some people think" or "It might be argued" as in example (8), which are much more common in English.

8. *"It could also be argued that she might have resigned sooner."*(ENLE33)

In both languages, editorials present some instances of attribution to the agency of abstract rhetors (Neff et al. 2004) as in (9).

9. *"(...) el comunicado demuestra que ETA no está dispuesta a rebajar un ápice sus objetivos."* (SPED37)[5]

5 Translation: "(…) the communiqué shows that ETA is not willing to lower a bit their goals." (SPED37)

4.2.3. Construed reader

The different resources actualizing this particular semantic function are oriented towards building up a relationship between readers and writers.
Table lists the linguistic resources found in our English and Spanish texts:

The most outstanding differences between English and Spanish editorials are in the number of directives, on the one hand, and reader pronouns, on the other hand. Directives, actualized mainly by deontic modal verbs in both languages (10), are more prevalent in Spanish than in English. On the other hand, English editorials address readers more explicitly by means of second person pronouns or inclusive 'we' (11).

10. "El gobierno no debe dar un paso más hasta que ETA abandone su repugnante chantaje, (…)"[6] (SPED22)
11. *"We should all hope for the best, but we must be prepared for the worst."* (ENLE39)

Table 4.2.3-1. The grammar of *construed reader* in English and Spanish

Construed reader	English		Spanish	
Directives	Deont. mod. verb	17	Deont. mod. verb	25
	Fixed expression	2	Fixed expression	2
	Indirect directive act	1	Indirect directive act	4
	Deontic mod. noun	1	Deontic mod. noun	2
	Deontic adjective	1	Deontic adjective	2
	Imperative	1	Deontic mod. periphrasis	1
			Lexical verb	1
	Total	**23**	**Total**	**37**
Digressions	18		15	
Reader pronouns	15		4	
Questions	5		3	
Shared knowledge	3		1	

6 Translation: "The government should not take any more steps till ETA does not give up their disgusting blackmail." (SPED22)

4.2.4. Degree of evaluation

In Martin and White (2005), graduation (or degree of evaluation, in our terms) is central to the appraisal system. Not only attitudinal meanings are gradable (*extremely* good), but also engagement values or writer stance can be graded to a lower or higher degree (*very* possibly). *Force* implies the intensification or attenuation of a gradable quality, while *focus* refers to bringing attention to a grammatical unit by means of focalizing adverbs. Table 4.2.4-1 lists the linguistic resources in English and Spanish for the expression of degrees of evaluation.

English editorials show a larger number of resources conveying intensification or attenuation meanings. They are actualized in this language mainly by degree adverbs (12) and, also, comparative or superlative structures. In Spanish, this grading function is carried out mostly by comparative and superlative structures (13). There is a very significant difference between both languages with respect to degree adverbs: English (39 cases) vs Spanish (9 cases).

12. "*(...) improvements have been painfully slow and much has already stalled*" (ENLE19).
13. "*Diríase que para algunas de estas personas es más urgente encontrar un culpable de los hechos que acabar con ellos*."[7] (SPED30)

7 Translation: "It could be said that for some of these people is more urgent to find out a culprit for this situation than putting an end to it."

Table 4.2.4.1. The grammar of *degree of evaluation* in English and Spanish

		English		Spanish	
Degree of evaluation	Force	Degree adverb	39	Comparative /superl.	21
		Comparative/ superl.	36	Quantitative ad.	16
		Quantitative adv.	7	Degree adverb	9
		Lex. Adj. (quant.)	6	Lexical adj.	6
		Lex. Noun (quant.)	3	Lexical Vb.	6
		Lex. Adv. (manner)	2	Lexical noun	1
		Emph. Adv. (+ adj.)	2	Quantitative pronoun	1
		Fixed expression	1	Fixed expression	1
		Total	**96**		**61**
	Focus	Additive	26	Additive	30
		Restrictive	15	Restrictive	10
		Emphasis	7	Emphasis	3
		Limitation	5	Limitation	1
		Total	**53**	**Total**	**45**

As regards focusing adverbs, they may convey meanings of addition (*also*, *even*, *también*), restriction (*only*, *sólo*) or emphasis (*indeed*, *simply*) and they behave similarly in both languages.

5. Conclusions

The results of this study reveal some interesting conclusions about the language of evaluation as it is used in English and Spanish editorials. From a semantic point of view, it has been proved that, in general, there are more evaluative markers in English editorials than Spanish editorials in all 4 semantic functions, especially in degree. The study of the macrostructure has spotted noticeable differences regarding their distribution across different moves or triads. Evaluative markers appear before in English editorials than in Spanish, in the title and in Move 1 already, whereas in Spanish they tend to appear later in the text. We have also determined which illocution types can be viewed as characterizing each specific move, and, again, the differences between both languages. In Spanish, more proposals appear in move 3 and even at the end of move 2, whereas in English there are overall fewer, concentrated in move 3.

In the micro-linguistic analysis, the present study shows certain differences regarding the lexico-grammatical resources expressing evaluation. The following lists sums up the findings put forward in the body of this article:

- More appreciative adjectives in English.
- More adversatives and epistemic modals in English.
- More unspecified rhetor structures in English.
- More reader pronouns in English.
- More degree adverbs and comparative structures in English.
- More directives and deontic modal verbs in Spanish.

We can conclude that English editorials convey more explicitly the author's emotional reactions, as they contain more appreciative adjectives and more degree adverbs and comparative structures grading attitudinal meanings. Writers of English editorials also show more openly their position or stance towards the propositional content, using epistemic modals and adversative connectives, and they explicitly address their audience often by means of reader pronouns. On the other hand, writers of Spanish editorials, lower a bit the number of evaluative markers, except for the ones expressing deontic or obligation meanings (advice, suggestions). Spanish editorials can be said to be, to a certain extent, less evaluative, but more directive than English ones.

The data point towards very strict conventions in English and Spanish for distributing evaluative resources across editorials.

The similarities and differences between both languages revealed in this study may be valuable in the field of translation. Also, the findings of this study may supply the raw material for the building up of applications in the field of professional writing for the press (ESP) in both languages.

References

Bednarek, M. (2006). *Evaluation in Media Discourse: Analysis of a Newspaper Corpus*. London: Continuum.

Biber, D. and E.T. Finegan (1988). "Adverbial stance types in English". *Discourse Processes*, 11: 1–34.

Biber, D. and E.T. Finegan (1989). "Styles of stance in English: Lexical and grammatical marking of evidentiality and affect". *Text*, 9 (1): 93–124.

Bolívar, A. (1994). "The structure of newspaper editorials". In: M. Coulthard (ed.). *Advances in Written Text Analysis*. London: Routledge: 276–294.

Chafe, W. (1986). "Evidentiality in English Conversation and Academic Writing". In: W. Chafe and J. Nichols (eds.). *Evidentiality: The Linguistic Coding of Epistemology*. Norwood, NJ: Ablex: 261–272.

Del Lungo Camiciotti, G. and E. Tognini Bonelli (eds.) (2004). *Academic Discourse: New Insights into Evaluation*. Bern: Peter Lang.

Hunston, S. and Thompson, G. (eds.) (2000). *Evaluation in Text. Authorial Stance and the Construction of Discourse*. Oxford: Oxford University Press.

Hunston, S. (1995). "A corpus study of some English verbs of attribution". *Functions of Language*, 2 (2): 133–58.

Hunston, S. and Sinclair, J. (2000). "A Local Grammar of Evaluation". In: S. Hunston and G. Thompson (eds.). *Evaluation in Text. Authorial Stance and the Construction of Discourse.* Oxford: Oxford University Press: 74–101.

Hunston, S. (2007). "Using a corpus to investigate stance quantitatively and qualitatively". In: R. Englebretson (ed.). *Stancetaking in Discourse: Subjectivity, Evaluation, Interaction.* Amsterdam: John Benjamins.

Hyland, K. (1998). *Hedging in Scientific Research Articles*. Amsterdam/Philadelphia: John Benjamins.

Hyland, K. (2005). *Metadiscourse. Exploring Interaction in Writing*. London: Continuum.

Marín-Arrese, J.I., Hidalgo Downing, L. and S. Molina Plaza (2004). "Evidential, epistemic and deontic modality in English and Spanish: The expression of writer stance in newspaper discourse". In: R. FacchinettI and F. Palmer (eds.). *English Modality in Perspective: Genre Analysis and Contrastive Studies.* Frankfurt am Main–New York [etc.]: Peter Lang: 121–139.

Martin, J.R. and White, P. R. R. (2005), *The Language of Evaluation: Appraisal in English.* Basingstoke (England): Palgrave Macmillan.

Neff, J., Ballesteros, F., Dafouz, E., Martínez, F. and J.P. Rica (2004). "The expression of writer stance in native and non-native argumentative texts". In: R. Facchinetti and F. Palmer (eds.). *English Modality in Perspective: Genre Analysis and Contrastive Studies.* Frankfurt am Main; New York: Peter Lang: 141–161.

Searle, J.R. (1976). "The classification of illocutionary acts". *Language in Society*, 5: 1–24.

Vestergaard, T. (2000). "From Genre to Sentence: The Leading Article and its Linguistic Realization". In: F. Ungerer (ed.). *English Media Texts Past and Present: language and textual structure.* Amsterdam; Philadelphia: John Benjamins: 151–173.

Part Four

COGNITIVE LINGUISTICS

Culture-Based Conceptions of Emotion in Polish and English

Barbara Lewandowska-Tomaszczyk and Paul Wilson

Abstract: A comparison was made between the similarities and differences of the emotional dimensional structure of Polish and English native speakers. Participants evaluated 24 prototypical emotion terms on scales representing 144 features that represent activity in all six of the major components of emotion ((a) appraisals of events, (b) psychophysiological changes, (c) motor expressions, (d) action tendencies, (e) subjective experiences, and (f) emotion regulation). The dimensions representing the similarities and differences in the meaning of emotion words showed a different pattern in the two language groups. This was most notably shown by the relative importance of the dimensions of activation-arousal and potency-control, and stands in contrast with the similar emotional structure shown by Fontaine, Scherer, Roesch, and Ellsworth (2007) for English, French and Dutch speakers. The cultural bases to the findings are discussed.

Keywords: conceptualisation, cross-linguistic, cross-cultural, emotion, English, Polish.

1. Introduction

Using the GRID methodology developed by Scherer (2005), we investigated the emotional conceptual structures of Polish-speaking individuals. This methodology is comprehensive in its scope as, in contrast with most early research that identified at least three dimensions (e.g., Osgood, May, and Miron 1975), it allows the multicultural comparison of emotion conceptualisation on all six of the emotion categories that have recently been recognised by emotion theorists (Ellsworth and Scherer 2003; Niedenthal, Krauth-Gruber, and Ric 2006; Scherer 2005): (a) appraisals of events, (b) psychophysiological changes, (c) motor expressions, (d) action tendencies, (e) subjective experiences, and (f) emotion regulation. Each of these six categories were represented in 142 features, which were rated on 9-point scales in an evaluation of 24 prototypical emotion terms.

The major focus of our investigation was to compare the emotional dimensional structure of Polish-speaking individuals with that of English speakers. Using the GRID methodology, Fontaine *et al.* (2007) have recently found a similar emotional conceptual structure for three language-culture groups (English, French and Dutch). Within each of the three language-culture samples, the following four factors were extracted (in order of importance): evaluation-pleasantness, potency-control, activation-arousal, and unpredictability. Our specific aim was to determine whether Polish-speaking individuals produce such a structure.

The application of the GRID methodology to investigate cross-linguistic emotional conceptual structure is a useful tool to investigate the extent to which emotions are biologically endowed vis-à-vis culturally constructed. At the centre of this debate are the opposing universalist and relativist positions, with the more moderate weak linguistic relativity in the middle. The universalists argue that the experience and expression of emotion is largely independent of language (e.g., Ekman 1972; Izard and Buechler 1980). The relativists reason that people who speak different languages have different conceptual representations of emotions (e.g., Rosaldo (1980, 1984) and Lutz (1985, 1987, 1988)). The weak linguistic relativity position theorises that rather than language determining the concepts that individuals form in a rigid way, it has the effect of making certain concepts more salient, which forms default modes of thinking. Supporting evidence for this has come from experiments performed on bilingual individuals (e.g., Stepanova and Coley 2002). If Polish and English-speaking individuals are found to have similar structures for emotional experience, this would suggest support for the universalist position. Any differences in such a structure could point to evidence consistent with the relativist position. However, it is important to note that such differences could also be a consequence of the use of non-equivalent Polish and English terms.

2. Method

2.1. Instrument

The GRID project is coordinated by The Geneva Emotion Research Group at the University of Geneva, The Swiss Centre for Affective Sciences, The Geneva Emotion Research Group, the HUMAINE Association and Ghent University. Our research is part of a worldwide study into emotional patterning across 28 languages and 4 additional varieties (English and Chinese, two each).

The GRID instrument comprises a Web-based questionnaire composed of 24 prototypical emotion terms and 144 emotion features. These features represent activity in all six of the major components of emotion. Thirty-one features relate to appraisals of events, eighteen to psychophysiological changes, twenty-six to motor expressions, forty to action tendencies, twenty-two to subjective experiences, and four to emotion regulation. An additional three features refer to other qualities, such as frequency and social acceptance.

2.2. Procedure

Participants completed the GRID in a controlled Web study (Reips 2002), in which each participant was presented with 4 emotions randomly chosen from the set of 24 and asked to rate each in terms of the 144 emotion features. They rated the likelihood that each of the 144 emotion features can be inferred when a person from their cultural group uses the emotion term to describe an emotional experience on a 9-point scale ranging from *extremely unlikely* (1) to *extremely likely* (9). Each of the 144 emotion features was presented on a separate screen, and participants rated all 4 emotion terms for that feature before proceeding to the next feature.

2.3. Participants

In total, 124 Polish-speaking participants (29 males, 95 females; average age = 23.17 years) and 201 English-speaking participants in the United Kingdom (77 males, 124 females; average age 21.23 years) completed the GRID instrument in their own language.

2.4. Results

Principal component analysis was used to extract factors for Polish and English, treating the 24 emotion terms as observations and the average scores on the 144 emotion features as variables. Following varimax rotation, a five-factor solution was selected. There were both similarities and differences between the Polish and English samples. Factor 1 (evaluation-pleasantness) showed a high level of congruence between Polish and English, and accounted for 48.2% and 53.1% of the variance respectively. The relative salience of factors 2 and 3 was different in Polish and English. For Polish, the second factor was represented by activation-arousal (12.5% of the variance), and the third factor by potency-control (6.9% of the variance). For English, the second factor was potency-control (17.7% of the variance) and the third factor was activation-arousal (8.1% of the variance). The fourth factor was represented by surprise-expectedness for both Polish (5.8% of the variance) and English (4.9% of the variance), but there were some differences. Similarly, despite some differences the fifth factor related to expression-concealment for both Polish (4.6% of the variance) and English (3.3% of the variance).

2.5. Evaluation-Pleasantness

The congruency demonstrated on the evaluation-pleasantness dimension (factor 1) by the two languages was manifested by appraisals of intrinsic pleasure and goal conduciveness. Other features included action tendencies of approach versus avoidance, and pleasant emotions versus unpleasant emotions. Specific examples of the 144 emotion features that loaded highly on this factor included “felt positive”, “wanted to sing and dance”, “in itself unpleasant for the person”, “felt inhibited or blocked”, and “incongruent with own standards and ideals”.

2.6. Potency-Control

The differences in relative saliency between factors 2 and 3 for the two languages means that potency-control is represented by the English second factor and by the Polish third factor (see Figure 1). This dimension includes appraisals of control, leading to feelings of power and weakness. It is also characterised by appraisals of interpersonal dominance or submission. From Figure 1 we can see the specific examples of “assertive voice”, “felt submissive”, and “wanted to take the initiative her/himself”.

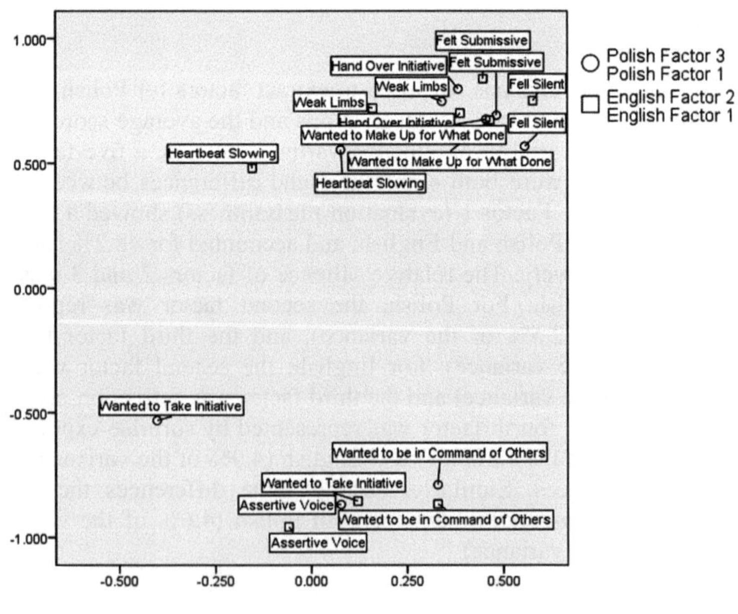

Figure 1. Polish Factor 3 vs. English Factor 2

2.7. Activation-Arousal

Again, as a consequence of the relative saliency differences between the two languages, activation-arousal is represented by the English third factor and by the Polish second factor (see Figure 2). This dimension is mainly characterised by sympathetic arousal (e.g., rapid heartbeat and readiness for action). From Figure 2 it can be seen that specific examples include "breathing getting faster", "felt hot", "sweat", and "spoke faster".

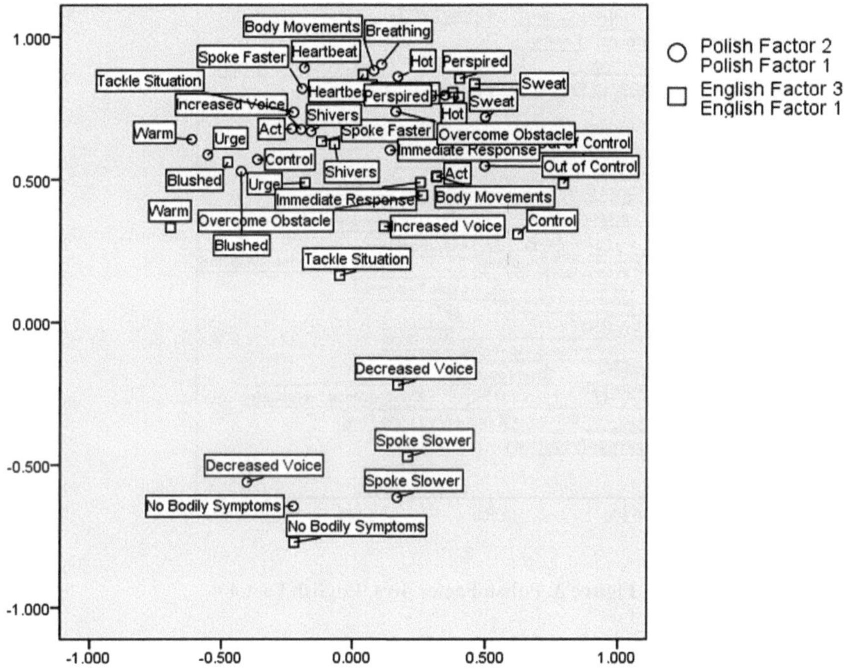

Figure 2. Polish Factor 2 and English Factor 3

2.8. Surprise-Expectedness

The fourth factors of both Polish and English are largely represented by surprise-expectedness. On this dimension appraisals of novelty and unpredictability are compared with expectedness or familiarity. From Figure 3 it can be seen that specific examples include "raised eyebrows", "jaw dropping", and "confirmed expectations".[1] There are some features that show inconsistent loadings between the two languages. For example, it can be seen in Figure 3 that "tears" and "closed eyes" have higher loadings in Polish than English.

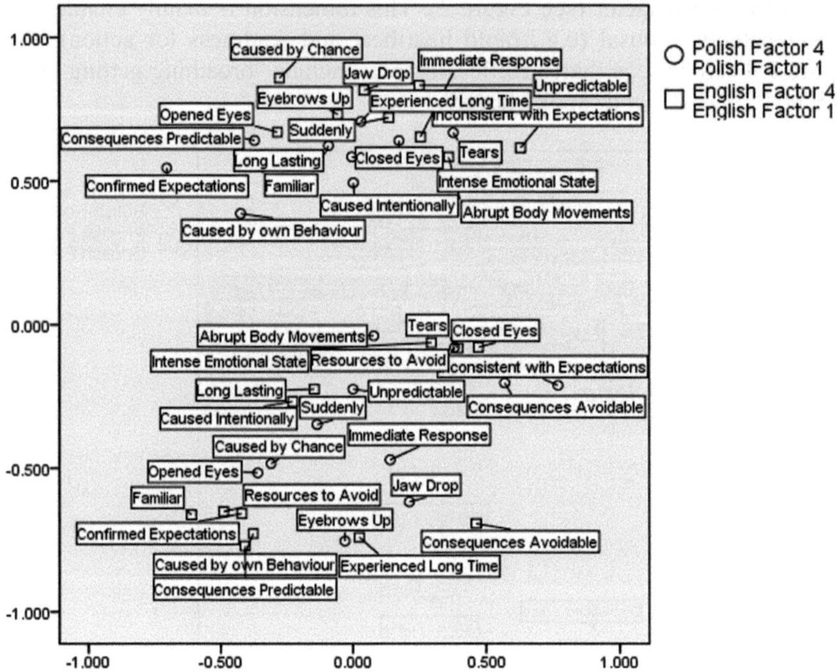

Figure 3. Polish Factor 4 vs. English Factor 4

2.9. Expression-Concealment

The fifth factors for both Polish and English are mostly represented by expression-concealment. This dimension is characterised by the interpersonal expression of emotion. The outward expression of emotion is opposed by the concealment of emotion. Specific examples include "Showed emotion to others more than felt it", "did not show any changes in face", and "changed melody of speech" (see Figure 4). There are some inconsistencies in the feature loadings

1 As a consequence of the rotation procedure employed, equivalent features appear at opposite ends of the scale with opposing positive and negative values. The positive/negative aspects of the values should therefore be ignored.

between Polish and English. For example, Figure 4 shows that "unpredictable" and "suddenly" have higher loadings in Polish than English.

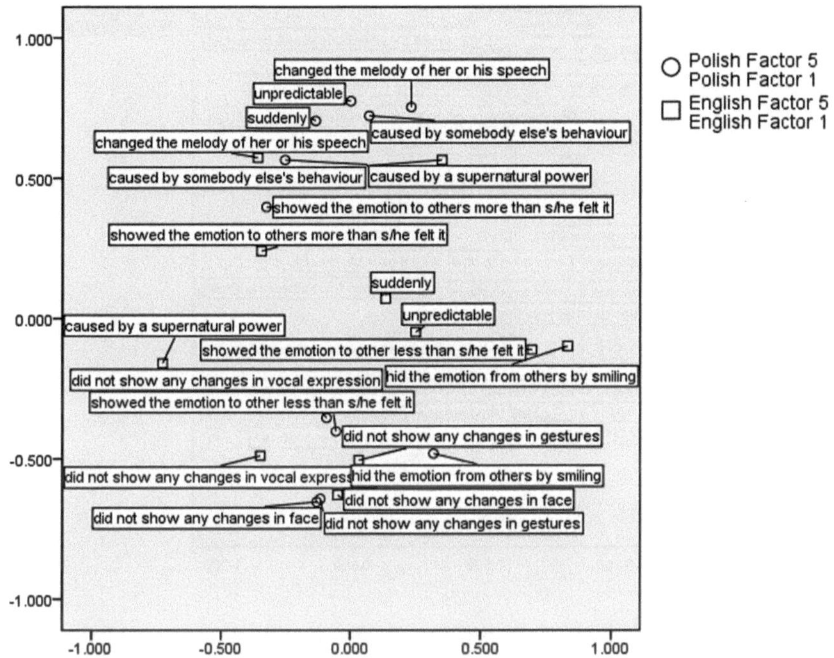

Figure 3. Polish Factor 4 vs. English Factor 4

2.9. Expression-Concealment

The fifth factors for both Polish and English are mostly represented by expression-concealment. This dimension is characterised by the interpersonal expression of emotion. The outward expression of emotion is opposed by the concealment of emotion. Specific examples include "Showed emotion to others more than felt it", "did not show any changes in face", and "changed melody of speech" (see Figure 4). There are some inconsistencies in the feature loadings between Polish and English. For example, Figure 4 shows that "unpredictable" and "suddenly" have higher loadings in Polish than English.

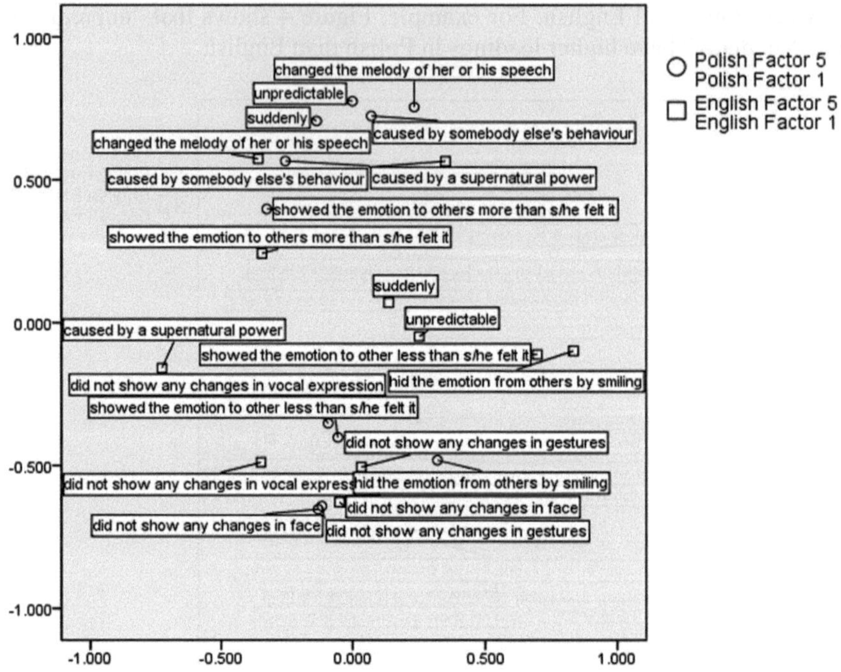

Figure 4. Polish vs. English Factor 5

3. Discussion

The main difference in the emotional structure of the two language samples was the relative salience of the second and third factors. For English, the order of importance of these was potency-control followed by activation-arousal. The opposite order was found for the Polish sample.

The first possible explanation for the difference in relative salience in the structure of the two language samples concerns the use of the emotion terms used in Polish and English. There are often differences between emotion terms that are deemed to be equivalent in different languages. A wealth of research (originating with Quine 1964) shows that translational equivalence is very difficult, if not impossible, to achieve. Further research using the GRID instrument in our own laboratory, for example, has shown that *zdziwienie*, the most commonly used equivalent to *surprise*, is associated with relatively lower physiological arousal, lower physical activity, heightened regulation or control, and more negative evaluations than *surprise*. It is likely that further differences exist between Polish and English in the other 23 emotion terms that are presented in the GRID methodology and that this is a source of the differences in emotional conceptual structure that have been found in the present study.

The second possible explanation for the differences in saliency of the second and third factors of the two samples is based on possible cross-linguistic differences in emotional conceptual structure that might be present in the two language groups. This would offer support for the linguistic relativity position. Wierzbicka (2003) argues that the differences that exist between similar emotion terms in different languages both "contribute to, as well as provide evidence for, differences in the experience itself" (p. 596). The question to be asked here is whether there are any cultural or linguistic differences between Polish and English that might explain the saliency differences that were found for the second and third factors. A culture-based explanation would suggest that the activation-arousal factor was more salient in the Polish-speaking individuals because they generally respond to emotional situations with more arousal than English-speaking individuals. However, even though this cannot be excluded, to our knowledge there is no documented evidence for this. Similarly, English-speakers should show a relatively heightened degree of potency and control than Polish-speakers. Some possible support for this comes from Wierzbicka (1994), who argues that English-speaking individuals are relatively more likely to regulate their own emotions than Polish-speakers. However, this offers only a partial explanation as the potency-control factor extracted using the GRID methodology in the present study represents control features associated with extrinsic situations in addition to those related to intrinsic regulation. Wierzbicka (1994) also argues that one of the main ways in which Polish-speaking and English-speaking individuals differ is in the expression of emotion, with English-speakers being more reserved than Polish-speakers. Closer inspection of the differences between the two language groups on the fifth factor (expression-concealment) does not provide support for this proposal, at least for the examined group of subjects. As noted above, the main differences between Polish and English on the fifth factor is in the sphere of predictability (recall that "unpredictable" and "suddenly" have higher loadings in Polish than English).

The robustness of the pattern of results found in the present study can be questioned as it was found that the structure of the Polish sample was consistent with that of the English sample (i.e., potency-control followed by activation-arousal) when mean-centred data was used[2]. Clearly, further investigation is required to determine the precise differences that exist between the two languages. It is hoped that such research will provide further clues regarding

2 Statistical analyses were also performed on mean-centred data (this is a statistical procedure that is used to standardise datasets).

whether these differences are based more on translational inequivalence or differences in the emotional dimensional structure of Polish and English native speakers. However, it is important to stress that it would be erroneous to consider these positions as mutually exclusive. A key aspect of further work needs to determine the extent to which the discrepancies in the saliency of the second and third factors shown in the present study are based on an interaction between the degree of translational accuracy that is achieved and emotional conceptual structure. It is likely that any translational inequivalences that exist between emotion words for the speakers of two languages are a consequence of differences in the conceptual structure of these words for these speakers.

References

Ekman, P., Friesen, W.V., and P.C. Ellsworth (1972). *Emotion in the human face: Guidelines for research and an integration of findings*. New York: Pergamon.

Ellsworth, P.C., and K.R. Scherer (2003). "Appraisal processes in emotion". In R.J. Davidson, K.R. Scherer, and H. Goldsmith (eds.). *Handbook of affective sciences* (pp. 572–595). New York: Oxford University Press.

Fontaine, R.J., Schere, K.R., Roesch, E.B., and P.B. Ellsworth (2007). "The world of emotions is not two-dimensional". *Psychological Science*, 18 (12): 1050–1057.

Izard, C.E., and S. Buechler (1980). "Aspects of consciousness and personality in terms of differential emotions theory". In R. Plutchik and H. Kellerman (eds.). *60 Emotion: Theory, research, and experience*. Vol. 1 (pp. 165–187). New York: Academic Press.

Lutz, C. (1985). "Ethnopsychology compared to what? Explaining behavior and consciousness among the Ifaluk". In: G. White and J. Kirkpatrick (eds.). *Person, self, and experience: Exploring Pacific ethnopsychologies* (pp. 35–79). Berkeley, CA: University of California Press.

Lutz, C. (1987). "Goals, events, and understanding in Ifaluk emotion theory". In D. Holland and N. Quinn (eds.). *Cultural models in language and thought* (pp. 290–312). Cambridge: Cambridge University Press.

Lutz, C. (1988). *Unnatural emotions: Everyday sentiments on a Micronesian atoll and their challenge to Western theory*. Chicago: University of Chicago Press.

Niedenthal, P., Krauth-Gruber, S., and R. Ric (2006). *Psychology of emotion.* New York: Psychology Press.

Osgood, C.E., May, W.H., and M.S. Miron (1975). "Cross-cultural universals in affective meaning". Urbana: University of Illinois Press.

Quine, W.V. (1964). Meaning and translation. In: J.A. Fodor and J.J. Katz (eds.). *The structure of language: Readings in the philosophy of language* (pp. 460–478), Englewood Cliffs, N.J.: Prentice-Hall, Inc.

Reips, U.-D. (2002). "Standards for internet-based experimenting". *Experimental Psychology*, 49: 243–256.

Rosaldo, M. (1980). *Knowledge and passion: Ilongot notions of self and social life*. Cambridge: Cambridge University Press.

Rosaldo, M. (1984). "Toward an anthropology of self and feeling". In: R.A. Shweder and R.A. LeVine (eds.). *Culture theory: Essays on mind, self, and emotion* (pp. 137–157). Cambridge: Cambridge University Press.

Scherer, K.R. (2005). "What are emotions? And how can they be measured?" *Social Science Information*, 44: 693–727.

Stepanova, O., and J.D. Coley (2002). "The green eyed monster: Linguistic influences on concepts of envy and jealousy in Russian and English". *Journal of Cognition and Culture*, 2 (4): 235–262.

Wierzbicka. A. (1994). "Emotion, language, and cultural scripts". In: K. Shinobu and M.H. Rose (eds.). *Emotion and culture: Empirical studies of mutual influence* (pp. 133–196). Washington, DC, US: American Psychological Association.

Wierzbicka, A. (2003). "Emotion and culture: Arguing with Martha Nussbaum". *Ethos*, 31 (4): 577–600.

Part Five

A CORPUS-ASSISTED PERSPECTIVE ON DISCOURSE ANALYSIS AND IDEOLOGY

The Meanings of *Responsibility* in the British and American Press on Climate Change: a Corpus-Assisted Discourse Analysis Perspective

Cinzia Bevitori

Abstract: The paper aims at investigating the lemma responsibility, an item which proved of some interest for my recent study of a corpus of British and American press coverage of climate change in 2007. Drawing on Gerbig (1997), the semantics of responsibility shall be discussed with reference to our specialized domain of analysis. An examination of the ways in which the lemma is used reveals partially overlapping but distinct senses of the term which, in turn, helps to uncover traces of the diverging or converging ideological positionings of the news outlets under investigation. In particular, the paper aims at exploring which meanings of responsibility in the climate change discussions are construed by the different newspapers, as well as the ways in which "responsibilities" are mediated to their readership. The methodological framework will make use of the tools of corpus linguistics with a discourse analytical perspective grounded on Systemic Functional Linguistics (SFL), whose combination has been proved to be a productive terrain of analysis in previous research on specialised corpora (see, inter alia, Miller 2006, Bayley 2008, Morley and Bayley (eds.) 2009).

Keywords: climate change, corpus-assisted discourse analysis, corpus linguistics, discourse analysis, environmental discourse, global warming, newspapers discourse, responsibility, systemic functional linguistics.

1. Introduction: Aims and purpose

Almost fifteen years after Bell's characterization of climate change as a "high profile issue of the global environment" (1994: 33), his words may sound even more appropriate today. Coverage of climate change both in the UK and US quality newspapers has increased progressively since the late 1980s (Boycoff and Boycoff 2004, Carvalho 2005) reaching, from 2004 onwards, twice as much as any previous peaks (Boycoff 2007). As a crucial arena of debate, lying at the intersection between science and policy-making, reporting on highly controversial scientific issues by mass media can contribute to shape public perception and opinion. However, if at the time of Bell's publication mentioned above, global climate change was primarily concerned with topics such as the hole in the ozone layer, acid rain and global warming (see also Hayer 2005), as well as with the risks associated with it (Carvahlo and Burgess 2005), the debate is partly being shifted into new territories in 2007 (Bevitori forthcoming). To begin with, the year 2007 coincided with a number of key events regarding the issue of climate change, such as the release of the *Fourth Assessment of the Intergovernmental Panel of Climate Change* and the *UN Climate Change Conference* held in Bali on closing of 2007. Moreover, the influential *Stern Review on the Economics of Climate Change*, commissioned by the British Government and published at the end of 2006, gave rise to reactions that were still debated throughout 2007, contributing to an upsurge of reporting on climate change. Besides, 2007 was the year in which the International Panel on Climate Change (IPCC) and the former US Vice-President Al Gore were jointly awarded the Nobel Peace Prize for their commitment to fighting global climate change. All these events, which may be regarded as "critical discourse moments" (Chilton 1987, Carvahlo 2005), have succeeded in getting increased media attention, due to their "newsworthiness".[1]

The present paper, a by-product of research into the representations of climate change in the press (Bevitori forthcoming), explores the meanings of the lexeme responsibility across a corpus of British and American news coverage of climate change and related phenomena in 2007. After a brief overview of the tools and methods used, corpus data will be presented. In the following section, the focus will turn to the analysis of the meanings of the lexeme and their distribution across corpora. Finally, the semantic profiles of the lexeme will be discussed from a corpus-assisted discourse analytical perspective.

2. Tools and Methods

The paper combines the empirical approach of corpus linguistics with the analytical methods of SFL-based discourse analysis. Quantitative approaches provided by corpus linguistics techniques (such as lists of frequency, keywords, concordances and collocates) permit comparison of language patterns across texts and discourse. In the present study, a scanning of all the instances of the word *responsib**, giving all word forms of the lemma, was first carried out through the concordance facility of Wordsmith Tools 4.0 (Scott 2004), the distinct meanings teased out and their frequency compared across the various subcorpora which compose the corpus (see below). Although discourse analysts have commonly regarded quantitative data as a resource of limited value (Fairclough 2003), there is a developing body of work that, starting from the pioneering study by Gerlinde Hardt-Mautner (1995), highlights the potential

1 The notion of 'newsworthiness' relates to a set of criteria, first categorised by Galtung and Ruge (1973 [1981]) in their pioneering study, which defines why news outlets select certain events as news.

benefits of the use of corpora in discourse analysis (see, *inter alia*, Baker 2006, Partington 2004, Baker *et al.* 2008, Morley and Bayley (eds.) 2009)[2].

Within this methodological perspective, the synergic combination of quantitative and qualitative approaches to the analysis of texts and discourse, allows the researcher to investigate how meanings are constructed (and contested) in a given domain by grounding them empirically. I see corpus-assisted discourse studies in this perspective as concerned with mapping connections between the analysis of concordances, their co-textual environment and close reading of texts. In sum, a cross-fertilization of methodological and analytical linguistic and discursive approaches which, of course, needs to be complemented with analysis of how meaning is produced, reproduced and negotiated within social practices (Halliday 1978).

3. Corpus and Data

The Climate Change Corpus (henceforth CC Corpus), which I have personally compiled and categorised, consists of newspaper articles from both daily and Sunday editions of three British quality newspapers, *i.e.* the *Guardian*, the *Independent* and *The Times*, amounting to about 1,900,000 running words, and three American qualities, the *New York Times*, the *Washington Post* and the *Los Angeles Times* corresponding to approximately 1,480,000 running words. Newspapers articles were collected by running a Lexis-Nexis[3] search for the terms *climate change*, *global warming*, *carbon dioxide*, *carbon emissions*, *greenhouse gases*. The search provided a corpus of complete newspapers articles on the issue of global climate change, and related phenomena, over a well-defined period of time. The period covered by the study is the first three months of the year 2007, spanning from January 1st to March 31st, as well as the entire month of December. The articles include a variety of genres and text-types and a broad range of dimensions: scientific, political, social and economic amongst others, emerging in a number of sections. All articles were then categorized into five main sections and their distribution is discussed in Bevitori (forthcoming).

This study, however, draws on a dataset of the daily news section of the corpus. Although the British corpus contains a greater number of articles in

2 Despite agreeing on methodological procedures, the notion of corpus-assisted discourse studies (Partington 2004) has been recently challenged by Baker *et al.* (2008: 274) as the definition of 'corpus-assisted' would seem to privilege the subservience of one method to the other.

3 Except for part of the articles of The *Los Angeles Times* which, due to the databank's terms and conditions, were partly collected through the newspaper archive available online.

comparison to the American one, the number of tokens is higher in the latter. This contrasts with results from the other sections in the whole corpus and may thus lead to the assumption that the average length of the American news articles tends to be longer than the British one. The breakdown of the number of articles, the overall number of running words and the estimated average number of words per article of all the newspapers composing each subcorpus are summarized in Table 1.

Table 1. Data breakdown across UK and US news subcorpora

News sub-corpora (daily ed.)	**No. articles**	**No. of running words**	**Ave no. of words per article (estimated)**
UK News			
Guardian	270	178,185	1,484
Independent	138	83,959	699
The Times	279	167,163	1,393
Overall	**687**	**429,307**	**3,576**
US News			
New York Times	239	212,815	1,773
Washington Post	234	197,712	1,647
Los Angeles Times	163	158,026	1,316
Overall	**636**	**608,239**	**4,736**

It should be pointed out that the news section is a fairly broad category. It contains what in Bell (1991) is treated under two separate categories: "hard news" and "special topic news". The former, or "news as we all recognize it" (Bell 1991: 14), includes tales of accidents, disasters and crimes, as well as political issues such as government announcements, international negotiations and so on. The latter covers all the news which normally appear in separate sections and are overtly selected for their subject matter, such as business/financial or sport pages.[4]

A search for *responsib**, giving all word forms of the lemma, both singular and plural forms of the noun: *responsibility/ies*, the adjective *responsible*, in both predicative and attributive form, and the adverb *responsibly*, yields 140 occurrences in the news subsection of British corpus compared to 108 in the

4 Following Bell's typology of "hard news", White (1997: 104) further characterizes them into two subtypes, "events" and "issues", depending on whether they are grounded in "material" newsworthy events, such as natural disasters and so on, or in "communicative-based events", such as announcements, typically made by authoritative sources.

American one. Its normalized figure per thousand words is 0.3 and 0.1 respectively. The breakdown of the data is given in Table 2.

Table 2. Breakdown of *responsib* across the UK and US news subcorpora

Search Terms	**UK News**		**US News**	
	a.f.	r.f.*	a.f.	r.f.
responsib*	**140**	**0.3**	**108**	**0.1**
Word forms				
responsibility/ies (noun)	**62**		**49**	
responsible (adj.)	76		57	
responsibly (adv)	2		2	

While data from the American corpus are in line with data from a larger reference corpus, the *Corpus of Contemporary American English* (COCA),[5] giving a figure of 0.1 per thousand words, in the *British National Corpus* (BNC), the lemma is comparatively less frequent, corresponding to 0.2 per thousand running words. However, it must be said data from the 100 million word British National corpus are from 1980s till early 1990s and have therefore to be handled with caution.

4. Meanings and distribution of *responsibility*

According to the *Collins Cobuild Dictionary* (see also Gerbig 1997), four distinct, albeit related, meanings of the polysemous lexeme responsibility can be identified. They will be glossed below as meanings 1 to 4. Examples from the CC Corpus shall be provided for each one. Moreover, a fifth specialised meaning (5), *corporate responsibility*, emerges from observation of corpus data and will be also sketchily considered.

Meaning 1. Having responsibility in the sense of having control and authority over someone or something and it is your duty to make sure necessary tasks are carried out.

1. The decision comes after months of lobbying, the intervention of Angela Merkel, the German Chancellor, and an open feud within the European Commission between the top official **responsible** for environment and his counterpart with **responsibility** for industry. (*Independent*, 7 February 2007)

5 The COCA is a 385+ million word corpus of American English from 1990 to the present day. The corpus is freely available online at http://www.americancorpus.org

Meaning 2. Accepting or assuming responsibility for something, that is, having caused and being to blame for it.

2. The president of Brazil, Luiz Inacio Lula da Silva, said Tuesday that wealthy countries were **responsible** for global warming and that they should stop telling Brazil what to do with the Amazon rain forest. (*New York Times*, 7 February 2007)

Meaning 3. Responsibility as the ability to behave properly and make the right decisions (without needing to be controlled by someone else).

3. The former US vice-president Al Gore hit out at the short-termist attitude of corporate executives and fund managers yesterday, urging the British pension fund industry to use its muscle to force companies to take a more **responsible** approach to environmental issues. (*Independent*, 15 March 2007)

Meaning 4. Responsibility as a particular task one has because of one job or position.

4. When asked whether he had let his 96,000 employees down, Lord Browne said: "I have a deep and moral **responsibility** for this company. In that moral responsibility, I always feel that when anything goes wrong, I have let the staff down. I think that's a moral responsibility for any leader." (*Guardian*, 17 January 2007)

As far as meanings 3 and 4 are concerned, a good number of instances in the two corpora show that meanings are indeterminate and tend to overlap, as the following example shows, in which *responsibility* can be interpreted in terms of either behavioural or task-related duty:

5. The Toyota executive said the auto industry "has a **responsibility** to be part of the solution, but these issues cannot be addressed by the industry alone." (*Los Angeles Times*, 15 March 2007)

Meaning 5. Corporate Social responsibility (CSR): the responsibilities a business faces in relation to the social and environmental impact of their operations

6. Companies wanting to demonstrate **corporate social responsibility** by being a member of the FTSE4Good stock market index will be forced to

show they are reducing their carbon emissions. (*Guardian*, 27 February 2007)

From an examination of the distribution of meanings across the UK and US subcorpora (figures 1 and 2) some differences emerge. To begin with, instances of meaning 1 occur with a higher degree of frequency in the American news subcorpus, compared to the British one, 28% of all instances in the former as opposed to 8% in the latter.

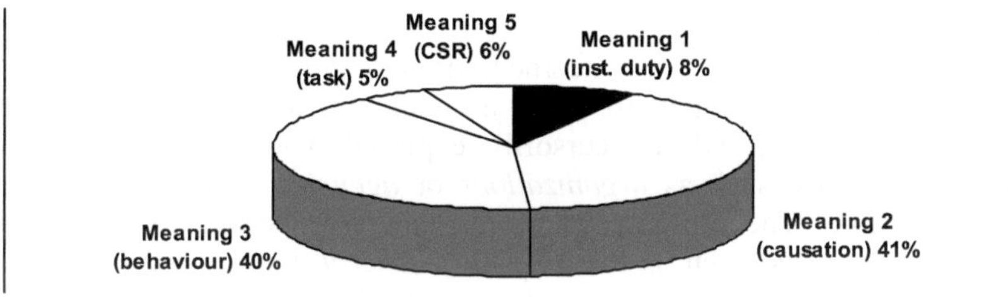

Figure 1. Distribution of meanings across the UK news subcorpus

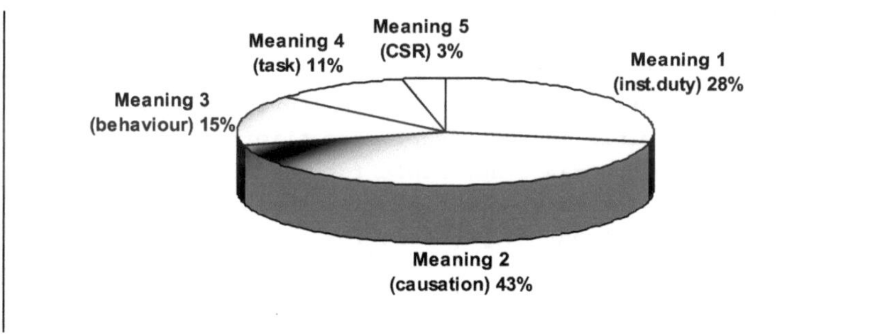

Figure 2. Distribution of meanings across the US news subcorpus

As the figures show, instances of meaning 2 and 3 have almost the same frequency in the British subcorpus, around 40 percent of all instances; in contrast, in the American subcorpus, instances of meaning 2 are the largest group, covering more than 40% of all instances, while occurrences of meaning 3 are the smallest (15%). Furthermore, bringing meaning 3 and 4 together, as they both imply values of moral obligation, gives a figure of 45% in the UK compared to 26% in the US. Finally, instances of meaning 5 are twice as frequent in the UK corpus than in the US.

Bearing in mind the quantitative findings of the lemma, I shall now turn to the investigation of the semantic profiles of each meaning. However, due to space constraints, I will concentrate on those features that emerged as most salient.

5. Discourses of *responsibility* in the UK and US news reports

Discourses of responsibility will be now looked at by starting from the typical patterns in the environment of the concordance lines. The constant movement between instances in the concordance lines and the text is what has guided the analytical process.

As far as meaning 1 is concerned, despite a remarkable difference in frequency, co-occurrence patterns show a rather similar collocational profile in both subcorpora and will be cursorily explored. Grammatical Participants include institutions, such as *organizations* or *agencies*, or people playing an institutional role. The presence of words that are specific to the different institutional contexts, such as the adjectives *federal* and *gubernatorial* or the *California Energy Commission* can be noted. Concordance 1 and 2 give a sample of 10 instances from each one:

ny **organisations** which have	responsibility	for floods
ancial **officer**, will assume	responsibility	for mergers a
regions for which they are	responsible.	And it was far from cle
on between the **top official**	responsible	for environment and his
t Mr Stevenson, **as minister**	responsible	for climate change, "could
of Network Rail and **the man**	responsible	for ensuring the nation's
facing the world". **The man**	responsible	for Honda Racing's new I
The **Government department**	responsible	for tackling climate chan
tavros Dimas, his colleague	responsible	for environment policy.
ronmental quality, which is	responsible	for the draft report, told

Concordance 1. Meaning 1 of responsibility – UK news subcorpus

knowledges that his **public**	responsibilities **as a regent** someti
ic officials with oversight	responsibilities were forced to go to
use, traditionally a **local**	responsibility, in order to meet
he views **his gubernatorial**	responsibilities. Schwarzenegger has
andards, which is a **federal**	responsibility, they argue.
cerning **the authorities** and	responsibilities" of the new
as the **federal government's**	responsibility to establish one
r. Bowles, whose **agency** was	responsible for reviewing the impact
fornia Energy Commission is	responsible for monitoring the progres
Air Resources Board will be	responsible for drawing the blueprints

Concordance 2. Meaning 1 of responsibility – US news subcorpus

An investigation of the semantic domain of causation (meaning 2) proves far more interesting. To begin with, as a causative verbal group, *be responsible* construes processes of "doing and happening" (Halliday 1994). Participants typically involve the Causer, playing the role of the initiator or instigator of a particular event, and the 'entity caused'. The preposition *for* is the right collocate in nearly all instances. In the US subcorpus, three distinct patternings can be traced. Firstly, "global warming" is construed as the 'caused entity', while the Causer is typically one or more industrialized countries or regions, construed as the principal emitter of greenhouse gases:

7. The president of Brazil, Luiz Inacio Lula da Silva, said Tuesday that wealthy countries were **responsible** for global warming and that they should stop telling Brazil what to do with the Amazon rain forest. (*New York Times*, 7 February 2007)
8. Wisconsin's Coal-Burning Plants Pump Out More Greenhouse Gases: Thomas Content and Lee Bergquist of the Milwaukee Journal Sentinel report that Wisconsin is **responsible** for disproportionate contributions to global warming. (*Washington Post*, 16 February 2007)
9. Today, the United States is **responsible** for about a fifth of the world's annual carbon dioxide emissions. Its emissions jumped 20% between 1990 and 2005, according to U.N. figures. (*Los Angeles Times*, 3 December 2007)

Secondly, emissions are construed as the 'caused entity', while the Causers are human activities; especially, the combustion of fossil fuels and transportation. Figures expressing the amount of emission are frequently present:

10. The transportation sector is **responsible for about 40 percent** of the state's carbon dioxide emissions, state officials said, and cars make up about half that amount. (*New York Times*, 10 January 2007)

11. Ships are also **responsible for 3.6 million to 6.5 million metric tons** of nitrogen oxide, another pollutant. (*Los Angeles Times*, 23 March 2007)

Previous research has highlighted the tendency of the US newspapers to represent human activity as the major cause for global warming as highly controversial (Zehr 2000, Boycoff and Boycoff 2004, Antilla 2005). This is mostly due to a politicization of the climate change concern from the 1980s onwards (Trumbo 1996, Carvahlo 2005), often aiming at perpetrating inaction (Demeritt 2001). In brief, it has been argued that by giving roughly equal coverage to both sides of the debate, the media have consistently given increased attention to a small group of climate change "contrarians", which, according to Boycoff and Boycoff (2004: 129), is a result of the application of the journalistic norm of "balance[6]. Further, Boycoff (2007: 474) suggests that an "evolutionary shift" in US newspaper coverage of anthropogenic climate change has taken place since 2005, due to a number of reasons, getting more in line with the scientific consensus. This change of attitude has also emerged from the analysis of my material; however, it can be claimed that in 2007 the release of the *IPCC Fourth Assessment Report (AR4): Climate Change* marks a major turning point. Still, discussions around the nature and the impact of science, where traces of sceptical views may still be found, remain crucial in the American press reports:

12. Less than 40% accept the scientific consensus that human activity, such as burning coal for energy, is **responsible for** the Earth's rising temperatures. (*Los Angeles Times*, 10 March 2007)
13. "They found that it was untenable to be in a position of casting doubt on whether global warming is happening and whether pollution is **responsible for** that." (*Washington Post*, 10 February 2007)

The third pattern relates to weather disasters, deaths and disruption being construed as 'caused entity' and positing global warming as the Causer. This would seem to relate to what can be defined a non-agentive causal sense of responsibility, provoking effects which differ from the moral sense of the term in that it carries no implication of praise or blame. Responsibility in this sense has to do with mere 'happenings' rather than with 'doings', although its typical semantic associations are negative:

6 Balance, one of the four journalistic norms (along with objectivity, fairness and accuracy), is a very thorny concept to define, as the two authors acknowledge.

14. Flooding is the most common weather disaster, **responsible** for the deaths of about 100,000 people and the displacement of 1.2 billion from 1992 to 2001. (*Washington Post*, 17 December 20007)
15. El Nino has been **responsible** for some of Southern California's most destructive storms, flooding neighborhoods in 1998 and toppling piers in 1983. As recently as Jan. 12, NOAA predicted that El Nino would persist through March. (*Los Angeles Times*, 2 February 2007)

A few instances in the US corpus pointing to different discourses may also be documented. In example (16), the semantic sequence "responsible for obstructing progress" is drawn from a speech delivered by the former US vice-president Al Gore at the climate change talks in Bali, and reported by all American newspapers in the corpus, accusing the Bush administration of hindering negotiations in Bali. The main obstacle to consensus in Bali was in fact the refusal of the US and several other developed countries to endorse a non-binding statement saying rich nations would need to cut emissions between 25% and 40% by 2020 to avoid the most severe effects of climate change. As a Nobel prize winner in 2007, for his documentary film *An Inconvenient Truth* in 2007, Al Gore's remarks and interventions received much of the news attention across the year:

16. The escalating bitterness between the European Union and the United States came as former Vice President Al Gore told delegates in a speech that "My own country, the United States, is principally **responsible for** obstructing progress here in Bali" (*New York Times*, 14 December 2007)

Turning to the UK subcorpus, similarly to patterning 1 and 2 above, in which global warming is construed as the 'entity caused', the main patterning shows that the Causer is generally one or more developed nations, principally the US, but the EU and Britain (17–20), as well as certain industrial sectors (21–22), are the main culprits:

17. "If we do 30% alone, the costs for the EU would be too high," they said, noting that the EU was **responsible for** 14% of global emissions. (*Guardian*, 21 February 2007)
18. The US produces about a quarter of the world's carbon dioxide and other gases believed **responsible for** warming the world's atmosphere (*Guardian*, 5 March 2007)
19. Britain is **responsible for** hundreds of millions more tonnes of greenhouse gas emissions than official figures admit, according to a new report that undermines UK claims to lead the world on action against global warming. (*The Times*, 10 December 2007)

20. "The industries that are **responsible for** the other 98.4% of global carbon emissions are not being focused on." (*Guardian*, 2 February 2007)
21. "Food production and processing are **responsible for** three quarters of the total carbon footprint, with the largest proportion – 60 per cent – related to the life cycle of the turkey." (*The Times*, 15 December 2007)

Unlike in the US news subcorpus, however, a discussion of strategies and/or solutions to tackle climate change also appears in the UK subcorpus. The debate on mitigation and adaptation strategies is particularly significant; the former implying a decrease of greenhouse gas emissions, the latter including changes in lifestyle related to people's behaviour. While mitigation is primarily substantiated by international agreements, such as the Kyoto Protocol, which the US did not sign, and the ensuing national public policies, most adaptation is motivated by private interests involving individuals, households, industries and by public arrangements of affected communities. In the *Guardian* and in the *Independent*, special attention is given to underdeveloped countries, which are generally construed as victims of climate change:

22. "A comprehensive range of mitigation and adaptation efforts are needed, including changes in the lifestyle and unsustainable consumption patterns of the richer industrialised nations. They are **responsible for** the pollution causing climate change and must repay their ecological debt to poor communities who are bearing the brunt of its damaging effects. These countries need funds to help vulnerable communities adapt and build resilience against climate change impacts." (*Guardian*, 3 December 2007)
23. Air-freighted fresh flowers, fruit and vegetables from the whole of sub-Saharan Africa accounted for less than 0.1% of total UK carbon emissions, he said. Moreover, while the average Briton **emits 9.3 tonnes of carbon a year**, the average Kenyan **is responsible for 0.2 tonnes**. "European nations must look to reduce their emissions first before penalising African producers. A boycott of Kenyan roses or green beans would be disastrous for many Kenyan farmers, especially smallholders, and would do little to mitigate climate change." (*Guardian*, 10 February 2007)

In example (22), voice is given to a member of *Friends the Earth*, which, alongside other environmental pressure groups, is a long-established news source on environmental issues (Anderson 2004). The attributed voice strongly advocates a change in behaviour and lifestyles of the industrialised world in order to help poor countries through implementation of adaptation strategies (see also Doulton and Brown 2009). Similarly, in the following examples (24–25), individual responsibility of Western citizens is emphasised in terms of culpability, blaming in particular emissions coming from personal travel:

24. Working men earning more than £40,000 a year are **responsible** for the lion's share of climate change emissions from personal travel, according to a Oxford University survey. It found that one in five people are **responsible** for 61% of climate change emissions from private transport and that most of these are well-off men. (*Guardian*, 10 March 2007)
25. The National Express website will be adapted to include a carbon calculator that will work out how much carbon **individual passengers** would be **responsible for** by using different modes of transport. Mr Bowker said that he wanted the scheme **to raise customers' awareness of the environmental benefits** provided by using public transport. (*The Times*, 17 March 2007)

In sum, in the UK news subcorpus, in contrast to the US one, the burden of responsibility for the increase in emissions of gases into the atmosphere is largely attributed to individual lifestyles, involving personal travel and consumption. Interestingly, as example (24) above anticipates, a strong connection is made between meaning 2 and 3, aiming at raising people's awareness and engaging them in more environmentally responsible behaviour. This semantic motif, which could be glossed "engaging responsibility" is frequently associated with another semantic motif, namely that of "taking the lead" in the fight against climate change (for a discussion, see Bevitori forthcoming):

26. Ministers are also set to launch a campaign in Britain **to encourage people to do more to reduce their own carbon emissions,** including a new "carbon calculator" *so that* individuals can work out how much they are personally **responsible for**. Mr Miliband told The Times last night: "The science is moving faster than the politics now. In 2007 we need significant progress at the international level. The **UK is showing leadership** with its Climate Change Bill, the EU **is showing leadership** and we hope that other legislatures across the world will take similar action." (*The Times*, 3 February 2007)

What emerges quite clearly in the analysis of instances of the lexeme in the British corpus is that politically responsible attitudes and behaviour are shifted from institutions to the people, who are typically construed as individually and socially engaged. Co-selection patterns for meaning 3 show that the lexeme typically occurs with the material process *take*; moreover, the personal pronoun *we*, *all of us* and *anyone*, as the Actor, are typically co-selected with modal meanings of obligation/necessity: *have to*, *must*, *should.* Concordance 3 gives 10 selected instances of this:

```
led over who should take responsibility for cutting carbon pollu
picture. We have to take responsibility for the carbon we consum
ccount of who was taking responsibility. "This panel is very kin
ns have to address their responsibilities. Yes, climate change w
 boards must take direct responsibility under a first phase of t
 says: "All of us have a responsibility, actions taken at an ind
 right. We have absolute responsibility to put things right. Wha
ke decisions and take on responsibility." Teaching primary
on all countries to take responsibility for cutting green
ailure of anyone to take responsibility for the Omagh bombi
```

Concordance 3. Meaning 3. Co-selection of *take* and *responsibility* (UK subcorpus)

Pre-modifiers of the noun *responsibility* are typically adjectives, such as *personal, individual* and *social*, as well as adjectives expressing judgement of social sanction, *i.e. moral.*

```
chancellor said personal responsibility needed to be kept in "pr
nal action and "personal responsibility", he stressed. LOAD-D
ert to merit of personal responsibility Greens now urge PM
. I think that's a moral responsibility for any leader." The T
is individual and social responsibility involved," Mr Brown sai
 is big theme of "social responsibility", Mr Cameron said, wher
```

Concordance 4. Meaning 3: Left-hand collocates of *responsibility* (UK subcorpus)

Occurrences of the adjective *global* are also found, although only in *The Times*, most of which relating to the keynote speech of the German Chancellor, Angela Markel, at the World Economic Forum held in Davos at the end of January 2007, calling on all countries to take responsibility for cutting greenhouse gases:

27. "We should ask those with the highest growth rates to share **global responsibility** and to make it their own," she said. (*The Times*, 25 January 2007)

Instances of meaning 3 are rarely found in the US subcorpus. Interestingly, discourses which are seen to dominate the US news agenda are mostly connected to two main controversial issues; the questions of "sustainable energy" though the use of biofuels, particularly through palm oil and cocoa plantations (28), and China, one of the largest emitters of CO2, which, despite signing the Kyoto Protocol, was not bound to meet mandatory reduction targets (29):

28. Yes, there have been bad examples in the palm oil industry," said Arjen Brinkman, a company official at Biox, a young company that plans to build three palm oil electrical plants in Holland, using oil from palms grown on its own plantations in a **manner** that it says is **responsible**. (*New York Times*, 31 January 2007)ù
29. Mr. Wen said China intends to "act in a **responsible manner**" and work toward reducing emissions, even though it does not have to meet mandatory targets for reducing emissions under the Kyoto Protocol to fight global warming. (*New York Times*, 17 March 2007)

5. Conclusions and way forward

This paper has aimed at providing a corpus-assisted analysis of the meanings of one lemma in the semantic area of responsibility across UK and US news reports on the issue of climate change in 2007. The analysis of distribution of patterns of occurrence and co-occurrence of responsibility, synergically combined with a detailed qualitative analysis of longer stretches of text, alongside the recourse to the wider context, has helped emphasize a number of features in the discourse(s) of climate change in both the British and American news reports.

The discussion has highlighted a number of key issues in the attempt to contribute to a deeper understanding of the nuanced meanings of *responsibility* and how these are mediated to the readership. Overall the findings demonstrate that in the British press, in contrast to the American one, meanings of causation (meaning 2) and the ability to behave properly (meaning 3) are strictly connected with a proper relationship of what has been glossed as "engaging responsibility". From the journalistic treatment of these issues, it becomes clear that there is a tendency in the British press to represent the individual as socially engaged in environmentally (and politically) responsible behaviour.

Clearly, a full account of the semantics of "responsibility" has to take into due consideration the analysis of a wider range of lexemes. But we leave this for further research.

References

Anderson, A. (2004). "Source-media relations: the production of the environmental agenda". In: A. Hansen (ed.). *The Mass Media and Environmental Issues*. Leicester, London and New York: Leicester University Press: 51–68.

Antilla, L. (2005). "Climate of scepticism: US newspaper coverage of the science of climate change". *Global Environmental Change*, 15 (4): 338–352.

Baker, P. (2006). *Using Corpora in Discourse Analysis*. London: Continuum.

Bayley, P. (2008). "Weakness and fear; a fragment of corpus-assisted discourse analysis". In: A. Martelli and V. Pulcini (eds.). *Investigating English with Corpora. Studies in Honour of Maria Teresa Prat*. Monza-Italy, Polimetrica International Scientific Publisher: 37–53.

Bell, A. (1991). *The Language of News Media*, Oxford: Blackwell.

Bell, A. (1994). "Climate of opinion: public and media discourse on the global environment". *Discourse and Society*, 51(1): 33–64.

Bevitori, C. (forthcoming). *Representations of Climate Change. A corpus-assisted study of newspaper discourse*. Bologna: BUP.

Boykoff, M. and J. Boykoff (2004). "Balance as Bias: Global Warming and the U.S. Prestige Press". *Global Environmental Change* 14 (2): 125–136.

Boykoff, M. (2007). "Flogging a Dead Norm? Media Coverage of Anthropogenic Climate Change in United States and United Kingdom, 2003–2006". *Area* 39(4): 470–481.

Carvahlo, A. (2005). "Representing the politics of the greenhouse effect. Discursive strategies in the British media". *Critical Discourse Studies*, 2 (1): 1–29.

Carvalho, A. and J. Burgess (2005). "Cultural Circuits of Climate Change in U.K. Broadsheet Newspapers, 1985–2005". *Risk Analysis*, 25 (6): 1457–1469.

Chilton, P. (1987). "Metaphor, Euphemism, and the Militarization of Language". *Current Research on Peace and Violence*, 10: 7–19.

Demeritt, D. (2001). "The construction of global warming and the politics of science". *Annals of the Association of American Geographers*, 91 (2): 307–337.

Doulton, H. and K. Brown (2009). "Ten year to prevent catastrophe? Discourses of climate change and international development in the UK press". *Global Environmental Change* 19: 191–202.

Fairclough, N. (2003). *Analysing Discourse. Textual Analysis for Social Research*. London and New York: Routledge.

Hardt-Mautner, G. (1995). "Only Connect. Critical Discourse Analysis and Corpus Linguistics". UCREL Technical Paper 6. Lancaster, UK: Lancaster University.

Galtung, J. and M. Ruge (1973 [1981, 2nd edition]). "Structuring and selecting News". In: S. Cohen and J. Young (eds.). *The Manufacture of News*. London: Constable: 52–63.

Gerbig, A. (1997). *Lexical and Grammatical Variation in a Corpus. A Computer-Assisted Study of Discourse on the Environment*. Bern: Peter Lang.

Halliday, M.A.K. (1978). *Language as Social Semiotic: The Social Interpretation of Language and Meaning*. London: Edward Arnold.

Halliday, M.A.K. (1985 [1994, 2nd edition]). *An introduction to functional grammar*. London: Edward Arnold.

Hajer, M. (2005). "Coalitions, Practices, and Meaning in Environmental Politics: from Acid Rain to BSE". In: D. Howarth and J. Torfing (eds.). *Discourse Theory in European Politics*. Basingstoke: Palgrave Macmillan: 297–315.

IPCC (2007). *Climate Change 2007. Mitigation. Contribution of Working Group III to the Fourth Assessment Report of the Intergovernmental Panel on Climate Change* [B. Metz, O.R. Davidson, P.R. Bosch, R. Dave, L.A. Meyer (eds.)]. Cambridge, United Kingdom and New York: Cambridge University Press.

IPCC (2007). *Climate Change 2007. Impacts, Adaptation and Vulnerability. Contribution of Working Group II to the Fourth Assessment Report of the Intergovernmental Panel on Climate Change*. M.L. Parry, O.F. Canziani, J.P. Palutikof, P.J. van der Linden and C.E. Hanson (eds.). Cambridge, United Kingdom and New York: Cambridge University Press.

Miller, D.R. (2006). "From concordance to text: Appraising "giving" in Alma Mater donation requests". In: G. Thompson and S. Hunston (eds.). *System and Corpus. Exploring Connections*. London: Equinox: 248–268.

Morley, J. and P. Bayley (eds.) (2009). *Corpus-Assisted Discourse Studies on the Iraq Conflict: Wording the War.* London: Routledge.

Partington, A. (2004). "Corpora and Discourse, a Most Congruous Beast". In: A. Partington, J. Morley and L. Haarman (eds.). *Corpora and Discourse*. Bern: Peter Lang: 11–20.

Scott, M. (2004). *Wordsmith Tools. Version 4.0.* Oxford: OUP

Sinclair, J. (ed.) (1987). *Collins Cobuild English Language Dictionary*. London: Collins.

Trumbo, C. (1996). "Constructing climate change: claims and frames in US news coverage of an environmental issue". *Public Understanding of Science*, 5: 269–283.

White, P.R.R. (1997). "Death, disruption and the moral order: the narrative impulse in mass "hard news" reporting". In: F. Christie and J.R. Martin (eds.). *Genres and Institutions: Social Processes in the Workplace and School*. London: Cassell. 101–33.

Zehr, S. (2000). "Public representations of scientific uncertainty about global climate change". *Public Understanding of Science*, 9: 85–10.

Towards an Axiological Picture of the EU – Evidence from a Polish TV News Corpus

Mikołaj Deckert

Abstract: The paper uses Polish broadcast news data to talk about axiological constructions of the personified European Union and its[1] metonymic discursive forms.

Poland officially became part of the EU in May 2004. Notwithstanding this, it seems uncontroversial but still thought-provoking that the EU and Poland invariably tend to be construed as separate entities. This suggests that while Poland is a component of the EU structures, the sense of membership (or even the European identity) of the Polish people is not well-developed. One of the convictions behind this paper is that axiological insights from a corpus of television news could help account for this. What is more, given the high social prominence of the EU issues in Poland and elsewhere, a discussion about where on the good-bad cline the EU can be located seems needed.

Keywords: axiology, broadcast news, Europe, metaphor, Polish television data, the European Union.

1. Introduction

The principal objective in this paper is to survey instances of axiological marking of the metaphorised European Union as it is discursively represented in selected Polish broadcast news. The data I look into are part of the *IntUne*[2] television corpus. They comprise transcripts and audiovisual recordings of evening news programmes from two Polish channels – TVP 1 (a state channel) and Polsat (a commercial station). The programmes are respectively "Wiadomości" and "Wydarzenia". The data were collected in two waves – from February to April 2007 and throughout March 2009. The 2007 and 2009 subcorpora used here contain a total of 447 384 tokens – 281 526 in 2007 and 165 858 in 2009.

---

1 While the choice of pronoun is problematic, the conventional one shall be used.

2 The "Integrated and United? A Quest for Citizenship in an Ever Closer Europe" project financed by the Sixth Framework Programme of the European Union, Priority 7. The corpus includes also parallel data for English, Italian and French.

The paper first gives a quantitative overview of the EU occurrences and then proceeds with more qualitative semantically-driven analyses. First, however, it seems relevant to address briefly the very fusion of linguistics and axiology.

2. The axiological variable

The shift in linguistic interest from the true-false opposition to that of good-bad is neatly reflected in the distinction between model-theoretic semantics and axiological semantics. The latter, developed mostly by Krzeszowski (1989, 1990, 1997) but also, among others, by Puzynina (1982, 1992), Lakoff (1996), Kalisz (1981, 1993), Kalisz and Kubiński (1993), Bierwiaczonek (1993) or Kleparski (1990) sees the parameter of "axiology" (Gr. "study of value/worth") as no less important than the parameter of truth. Here an exchange between Howard Cosell and Muhammad Ali might serve as an anecdotal illustration[3]:

Ali: I'm gonna whoop him, Howard. You just watch!
Cosell: You're feeling very truculent today, Muhammad.
Ali: Truculent? If that's good, I'm it!

In addition to inferring that Ali's boxing talent is not exactly matched by his linguistic sophistication, one sees that truthfulness might at times be of little significance and its import can be substituted for by that of positivity.

The axiological parameter is being elaborated on also outside the area of axiological semantics as mentioned above – for instance within the Appraisal Theory. Resting on M.A.K. Halliday's Systemic Functional Linguistics, the model looks into "the subjective presence of writers/speakers in texts as they adopt stances towards both the material they present and those with whom they communicate" and "the means by which writers/speakers positively or negatively evaluate the entities, happenings and states-of-affairs with which their texts are concerned" (Martin and White 2005: 2). Crucially for the present paper, "attitudinal evaluations are of interest (...) because their expression can be related to the speaker's/writer's status or authority as construed by the text, and because they operate rhetorically to construct relations of alignment and rapport between the writer/speaker and actual or potential respondents" (Martin and White 2005: 2). It appears broadcast news are one of the venues where such evaluative positioning will be conspicuous.

Coming back to axiological semantics proper, pertinently for this paper, it is argued with respect to the correlation of metaphorisation and axiology that "words have a tendency to be axiologically loaded with 'good' or 'bad'

3 The example is also referred to in Kalisz (2001: 56).

connotations in proportion to the degree of the human factor associated with them" (Krzeszowski 1990: 150). The proposition implies that the more metaphoric a language use instance is the more axiologically-marked it is supposed to be. This dovetails with the occurrences of the EU in the corpus because with the preponderance of uses strongly figurative the positive-negative polarity gains more prominence.

3. Evaluation in the news

While the so-called accessed voices, i.e. legitimated persons and *vox populi*, will often talk about their beliefs or feelings (more openly in the case of *vox populi*), no clues should ideally be given as to what the reporters' or newspresenters' opinions on the relayed topics are. But to assume so would be lacking in realism because, as Stubbs (1996: 197) posits, whenever someone says or for that matter writes something "they encode their point of view towards it" (cf. Bakhtin's 1981, Voloshinov's 1995 notions of "dialogism" or "heteroglossia"). What is more, in part to pander to the growing audience expectations, and keep abreast with other thriving news sources like the Internet, the broadcast news producers adopt novel techniques. As is observed by Scannell (1996: 20) "communicative ethos on radio and television has – over 70 years – shifted from distant and authoritative relationships between broadcasters and audiences to more equal, open and accessible relationships". Similarly, Montgomery (2007: 202) remarks that news "must best be viewed as a fragile attainment, an arena of discursive innovation competing with sedimented discursive practices." Not to mention that newsmakers more and more seldom fight shy of venting their views in jocular or derisive fashions.

Whether the path followed by broadcast news is that of tabloidisation, conversationalisation or democratisation (cf. Fairclough 1995, Winston 2002), the distance between the newscasters and the viewers is shrinking, also viewed through language. And even if newsmakers strived for unbiassedness, they will always favour one interpretation over another and will be imposing a particular set of assumptions on the viewers – be it by the choice of words or the choice of topic to be covered, whereby what is omitted in a particular news bulletin is, by virtue of its concealment, not less telling than what is extensively talked about.

4. The EU *vis-à-vis* Europe

To talk about the EU necessitates making recourse to the concept of "Europe". What poses a problem is that the concept has a huge potential to activate different associations.

For instance, Horolets (2006) analyses press texts and talks of a number of negative depictions of Europe and the EU – domination, exclusion, hostility, coloniality, liberalism, 'reddness', beaurocracy, competition, 'the demon of Europe' – which are countered with positive ones like Christianity, humanistic legacy, democracy, solidarity, love, home, familiarity, stability or normality. Analogously, Libura (2005) discusses the "euro" particle as capable of actuating many different profiles, also those axiological, in addition to the primary locative one.

As regards the EU-Europe configuration, in many cases no clear-cut divisions exist between the two. Because the concept of "Europe" is highly polysemous, in certain settings it will more readily be interpreted as denoting the EU rather than the countries geographically located on the continent (again, not even locatively is there a single incontrovertible delimitation)[4]. A stance favoured by opponents of the EU sees it and Europe as mutually exclusive (cf. Zając 2006). Importantly, this makes it possible to retain the positive connotations of Europe and at the same time portray EU negatively, which often constitutes the starting point for argumentation.

5. Some quantitative findings

With the above in mind, for the purpose of clarity and brevity this paper concentrates on three discursive constructions of the EU as shall be explained below. The aim is to look into the uses of the ontological metaphor of the EU as an animate entity engaging in actions[5] prototypically performed by humans. The choice here is to take under scrutiny selected discursive elements rather than longer stretches or texts which could be useful, for instance, to trace evaluation in material produced by a particular interlocutor. These elements could be exemplified as follows: "Unia Europejska wysupłała pięć miliardów euro" [the European Union shelled out five million euro], "Unia nie zgodziła się na protekcjonizm" [the European Union did not consent to protectionism].

The three basic forms under which the European Union is discursively present in the Polish TV news corpora are "Unia (Europejska)" – the European Union, "Komisja (Europejska)" – the European Commission, and "Bruksela" – Brussels.

While calculating the occurrences of the different "incarnations" of the personified EU one has to remember that they are polysemous. For instance, "Komisja" (the Commission) will not denote exclusively "Komisja Europejska"

4 As was pointed out by Davies (2006, *passim*), the "Europe" category could have as its members only Great Britain, Germany, France plus, somewhat optionally, Spain and Italy.

5 The EU is preponderantly constructed as an agent rather than an experiencer or a patient.

due to the proliferation of commissions whose tasks are to investigate the various politically-motivated scandals. This has significant bearing on the numbers for there are only 21 occurrences of the "European Commission" in the 90 occurrences of "Commission", which amounts to mere 23% in the 2007 subcorpus, and 6 occurrences in 35, i.e. as little as 17%, in the 2009 subcorpus. Even more evidently, rather than denoting an actor, "Brussels" in most cases will quite unambiguously point to a locative profile, often used when a correspondent gives his or her location to end a newsitem.
The statistics are as follows:

Table 1

	2007 subcorpus		2009 subcorpus	
	Frequency	No. of newsitems	Frequency	No. of newsitems
Unia (Europejska)//The European Union	25	18	30	13
Komisja (Europejska)//The (European) Commission	24	14	6	4
Bruksela//Brussels	6	4	4	2
Total	55	36	40	19

Resting on the concept of conceptual metaphor, the distinction between a personified and non-personified EU/Commission/Brussels will be controversial just as problematic will be any attempt at drawing a dividing line between literal and figurative language use. As was noted by Lakoff and Johnson (1980/2003: 4), it is a misconception to see metaphor exclusively as a "device of the poetic imagination and the rhetorical flourish" and as "a matter of extraordinary rather than ordinary language". Crucially, by assuming that the language-mind relation is central to a linguist's inquiries and by viewing language as interrelated with the workings of human cognition, cognitive linguistics confirms the claim that metaphors are grounded in human experience and motivated by people's interactions with the environment.

Still, as regards the metaphoric occurrences of the European Union, the numbers above have been extracted from a total of 29 occurrences of "Unia (Europejska)" in 2007 and 41 in 2009, which shows that "Unia" easily lends itself to personification because there are only 4 instances in the 2007 subset which construct the EU more explicitly as an inanimate political structure, as if suppressing the human being profile. Also, within a particular discursive occurrence of an item there will always be a number of potentially activated profiles and with the multiplicity of variables such as immediate context, the interpreter's knowledge, beliefs and the like, it is at times hard to establish which profile is the more prominent one.

6. Towards qualitative findings

The starting assumption is that rather than being clearly compartmentable as "good" or "bad", the agentive occurrences of the EU, or the features ascribed to the personified EU by the news receptor, could be located along the positive-negative continuum. Any axiological demarcations, if possible to introduce, would thus be radial, the median category being the most dubious once one bears in mind what has already been hinted at – that any linguistic material can *de facto* be viewed as evaluative. The features ascribable to the EU can then be seen as closer to the negative end of the spectrum, for instance when it threatens Poland, or can approximate the positive pole, for example when the EU offers support.

6.1. The European Union

Out of the 25 occurrences analysed, as many as 9 display a discernable aura of negativity. For example, the European Union:[6]

- grozi Polsce finansowymi karami za budowlane inwestycje na terenach chronionych//threatens Poland with fines for building investments in protected areas
- rozlicza kraje członkowskie z jakości wód//is assessing the member states' water quality
- Zapowiedź głosowania w województwie podlaskim nie wpłynęła na plany Brukseli. Unia wciąż chce karać Polskę.//Announcing the voting in podlaskie voivodeship did not influence the plans of Brussels. The EU still wants to punish Poland.[7]

6 The excerpts have been adjusted to meet orthography and punctuation standards since those are treated differently in transcripts; simultaneously the aim is to provide optimal Polish-English renderings of spoken discourse.

7 Notably, the metonyms (in this case "Unia" and "Bruksela") are sometimes used interchangeably. By contrast, with regard to French newspaper data Williams (2008: 505) notices that "politicians tend to use the term *EU* positively (...) while the semantic prosody of Brussels is extremely negative collocating verbs such as *impose*".

- narzuciła tutaj swoją politykę ekologiczną, która nie do końca podoba się Polsce//has imposed here its environmental policy which is not fully to Poland's liking
- chce też uniknąć odpowiedzialności za ewentualny kryzys energetyczny//also wants to escape responsibility for a potential energy crisis
- Jeśli Polska nie zastosuje się do tych żądań, Unia Europejska nałoży na nasz kraj wielomilionowe kary.//If Poland fails to meet the demands, the EU will impose on our country multimillion fines.

The EU is here framed as a powerful entity, superior to others, and thus legitimated to sanction them (in the majority of cases by heavy pecuniary measures), take them to task or impose regulations which need not be perceived as favourable by a the party involved. While the 2009 has only 4 occurrences of the EU that are clearly negatively-marked, analogous constructions are employed:

- Donald Tusk chciał, by Unia złagodziła zasady wejścia do strefy euro. Unia się na to nie zgodziła.//Donald Tusk wanted the EU to temper the eurozone accession requirements. The EU did not consent to it.
- W poniedziałek Unia zdecyduje, czy przedłuży sankcje dla władz w Mińsku.//On Monday the EU will decide if it extends the sanctions for the authorities in Mińsk.

There are 7 markedly positive sementic prosodies in the 2007 set including:

- To właśnie hodowcom przeżuwaczy i rolnikom uprawiającym rośliny energetyczne Unia Europejska będzie od teraz dopłacać do ich działalności.//These are the breeders of ruminants and the farmers planting energy crops who are going to be subsidised by the European Union.
- Unia daje pieniądze, by bezrobotni mogli się szkolić.//The EU gives money so that the unemployed can undergo training.
- Unia chce solidarności.//The EU wants solidarity.

Strikingly, the preponderance of these revolve around financial profits, i.e. support the EU provides or is ready to provide. Being benefited by the EU will be close to the "good" pole but here again the body emerges as superior to the entities that are weaker and thus need to be aided. The positive marking is even more noticeable in the 2009 subcorpus where there are as many as 14 decidedly positive constructions, again based on the frame of pecuniary input:

- Skorzystać chcą prawie wszyscy zwalniani. Zapłaci Unia Europejska.//Almost all of those who are losing jobs want to use it. The EU will pay.
- Kolejne miliardy na drogi obiecuje Unia Europejska.//The EU promises more billions for Road (to be built)
- Unia Europejska poparła budowę rurociągu Nabucco i dała na to dwieście milionów euro.//The EU supported the construction of the Nabucco pipline and gave for this two hundred million euro.
- Unia dała także pieniądze na sztandarowy projekt Ministerstwa Spraw Zagranicznych.//The EU also gave money for the flagship project of the Ministry of Foreign Affairs.

Also other sorts of positive construals are to be found in the 2009 partition:

- Z pomocą Ukrainie przyjdą Unia Europejska i zachodnie banki.//The EU and the western banks will come to Ukraine's aid.
- Donald Tusk broni strategii rządu. Jego zdaniem Unia obroniła jedność. Nie będzie groźby protekcjonizmu.//Donald Tusk defends the government's strategy. In his opinion the EU has defended unity. There will be no threat of protectionism.
- Unia zawsze będzie popierała tych, którzy chcą urzeczywistniać zasadę unijnej solidarności.//The EU will always support those who want to put into practice the principle of the EU solidarity.

The remainder of occurrences in the two subcorpora are less explicitly evaluative. While a constituent like "Unia Europejska odlicza godziny do szczytu G20" [the European Union is counting down the hours to the G20 summit] could be viewed as conveying some sort of stance, these are the viewers and their perceptions that are of interest here and viewers would in most cases agree that in such a construction evaluation is not instantly detectable. However, a number of occurrences in the 2007 and 2009 sets carry features that could be axiologically categorised:

- Unia Europejska broni dziś polskiego lasu przed tym, co sami chcemy mu zrobić.//Today the EU defends the Polish forest against what we ourselves want to do to it.
- Wsparcie obrońców Rospudy zapowiada też Unia Europejska.//The EU also declared that it was going to support the defenders of Rospuda.
- Minister Szyszko nie przekonał Brukseli. Unia nie zgodzi się na drogę przez Rospudę.//Minister Szyszko did not convince Brussels. The EU will not consent to a road running through Rospuda.
- Plany zbyt ambitne w ciągu najbliższych kilkunastu lat mogą być z punktu widzenia Polski, kraju na dorobku, który musi gonić niejako przeciętną europejską. Niewykonalne. Unia uznała te argumenty.//The plans might be too ambitious in the course of the next dozen or so years from the point of view of Poland, a country working its way up, which, as it were, has to be catching up with the European average. Infeasible. The EU has accepted those arguments.
- Rząd pracuje jednak nad programem wspierania biopaliw. Musi go zaakceptować Unia.//The government are however working on a programme to support biofuels. It has to be accepted by the EU.
- Unia nie zgodziła się na protekcjonizm czyli lepsze traktowanie swoich.//The EU did not consent to protectionism, that is, better treatment of fellow countrymen.

Formations of this kind, even if only implicitly expressing stance, contribute to the picture of the EU as a decisive and influential actor who comes across as intransigent. Whether one views that actor positively or negatively relies on how the actor's attitudes or actions relate to the interpreter's position. On the other hand, constructions suggestive of a sort of weakness on the part of the EU are infrequent; the only instances are:

- Rozszerzona o Bułgarię i Rumunię Unia bardzo potrzebuje nowej konstytucji.//The EU extended by the accession of Bulgaria and Romania badly needs the new constitution.
- Zdaniem czołowych europejskich polityków bez nowej konstytucji Unia nie będzie zdolna do skutecznego działania.//In the opinion of the top European

politicians, without the new constitution the EU will not be able to operate efficiently.

In those concordances it is arguably the EU who is portrayed as a beneficiary but those constructions are rendered insignificant with the overwhelming number of those where the EU is framed conversely – as a benefactor.

6.2. The European Commission

The image obtained from the 2007 data appears to be relatively congruous in the sense that there is a tendency. Here are some of the representative agentive occurrences of the metonymy:

- chce wstrzymania tej inwestycji//wants the investment to be suspended
- zdecydowała się przyspieszyć działania przeciwko budowie obwodnicy//has decided to accelerate actions against building the ringroad
- zdecydowała się wysłać dwa wnioski do trybunału//has decided to send two motions to the Court of Justice
- zareagowała//has reacted [was critical towards Roman Giertych's views]
- rozpoczęła drugi etap procedury karnej przeciwko Polsce//has started the second phase of the punitive procedure against Poland
- jest gotowa zwrócić się do Trybunału Sprawiedliwości Unii Europejskiej o wydanie Polsce nakazu wstrzymania budowy//is ready to turn to the Court of Justice of the European Union to obtain an order to stop the building works
- skierowała do Trybunału Sprawiedliwości pozew przeciwko Polsce//has filed a lawsuit against Poland to the Court of Justice
- zażądała wstrzymania prac//has demanded that the works be stopped
- grozi nałożeniem na Polskę kar

In fact, all these personification-based constructions display to some extent an aura of negativity – either because the verb has a clearly negative illocutionary force or because what the verb collocates with is negative in relation to the plans/actions of the speaker and thus of Poland. For example, "chce" [wants to] is unlikely to have a strong negative tinge but when it goes with "wstrzymanie inwestycji" [suspending the investment] the aura of meaning is extended and the cluster of lexemes assumes a negative overtone. This was partly the case with some of the uses of "Unia" – for example, in the case of Rospuda the overall axiological charge could be positive despite the apparent negativity around the Commission's actions as they are ultimately meant to benefit the environment. This would be supported by Puzynina's (2003: 30) claim that "what is significant in text analysis are not the values of individual words but the values of the entire syntactic and textual relations"[8].

The 2009 data seem to be confirming the 2007 tendency though the overall number of relevant occurrences of the Commission in the corpus is small:

- `Nie ma się co dziwić rozgoryczeniu stoczniowców. Kilka miesięcy temu Komisja Europejska skazała na upadłość polskie stocznie.//No wonder the shipyard workers are chagrined. A few months back the European Commission doomed Polish shipyards to bankruptcy.`
- `w czasie kryzysu finansowego zarobki i odprawy w Komisji Europejskiej chyba na wszystkich robią wrażenie. Ale trzeba pamiętać, że reguły ustala Rada Unii Europejskiej, a zatem przedstawiciele wszystkich krajów członkowskich. No chyba, że Komisja wyśle sygnał, że chce zmian. Na razie nie wysyła.//In the time of financial crisis the earnings and gratuities in the European Union seem to make an impression on everyone. But is has to be remembered that the rules are set by the Council of the European Union, that is, the representatives of all the member states. Unless the Commission sends a signal that it wants changes. It hasn't sent one yet.`
- `Komisja Europejska szuka dróg wyjścia z kryzysu finansowego, ale sama jakoś nie zaciska pasa.//The European Commission is looking for ways out of the financial crisis but it somehow does not tighten the belt itself.`
- `Komisja Europejska nie zgodzi się, by dopłaty dotyczyły tylko aut produkowanych w Polsce.//The European Commission will not agree to the subsidies being applicable only to the cars manufactured in Poland.`

8 „W analizie tekstu istotne są nie wartości poszczególnych wyrazów, ale całych związków syntaktycznych i tekstowych." (*translation*: M.D.)

6.3. Brussels

The 2007 data corroborate the claims put forward on the basis of the two other discursive forms because Brussels is here once more assured and pertinacious, if not ruthless or baleful (except for the last instance):

- Na odpowiedzieć czeka też Bruksela.//Also Brussels is waiting for an answer.
- Bruksela rozważa wprowadzenie całkowitego zakazu połowu ryb na Bałtyku.//Brussels is considering introducing a complete ban on fishing in the Baltic Sea.
- „Macie tydzień na przerwanie prac w dolinie Rospudy, potem sprawa trafia do sądu" - tak zagrzmiała dziś Bruksela.//"You have got a week to stop the works in the Rospuda Valley, then the matter goes to court" - that is how Brussels thundered today.
- Bruksela daje Polsce

That picture of Brussels could be getting muddied in the 2009 partition but with the low number of occurrences the very topic in the context of which Brussels is referred to bears too heavily on the use and thus could affect representativeness:

- Bruksela nie ma się co łudzić. Czesi nie ratyfikują Traktatu z Lizbony.//Brussels should not delude itself. Czechs will not ratify the Lisbon Treaty.
- Bruksela też ma ból głowy, bo z powodu kryzysu może się oddalić ratyfikacja Traktatu Lizbońskiego przez Pragę.//Brussels also has a headache because as a result of the crisis Prague's ratification of the Lisbon Treaty might be deferred.

7. Conclusions

Due to the inevitably selective character of the corpus, rather than coming up with a conclusive account the paper has intended to propose a framework pointing to certain axiologically assessable properties of the ontologically-construed European Union. The focus here is on the linguistic choices of speakers but because of the multi-semiotic character of the TV material where an array of information is encoded into the non-verbal layers, I refrain from suggesting definitive answers. The remarks proposed so far should thus be treated as an outline whose details will be mapped only after further study. Even so, the interpretation of the data presented above has already brought up certain salient and highly homogenous features of the personified EU. It emerges as strong-willed, purposeful and unswerving. It is potent, frequently superior to entities it interacts with, possibly even awe-inspiring. Singling out such characteristics can, in my view, be a stage on the way to putting forward some more definite claims about the axiological picture of the European Union as it is being constructed in broadcast news and in the mass media as such.

References

Bakhtin, M.M. (1981). *The Dialogic Imagination.* (trans. C. Emerson and M. Holquist). Austin: University of Texas Press.

Bierwiaczonek, B. (1993). "The axiological domain in the description of evaluative predications – an exercise in cognitive semantic". In: E. Górska (ed.). *Images from the Cognitive Scene*. Kraków: Universitas: 27–42.

Davies, N. (1996). *Europa.* (trans. E. Tabakowska). Kraków: Znak.

Fairclough, N. (1995). *Media discourse.* London: Arnold.

Horolets, A. (2006). *Obrazy Europy w polskim dyskursie publicznym*. Kraków: Universitas.

Kalisz, R. (1981). *The Pragmatics, Semantics and Syntax of the English Sentences with' that Complements and the Polish 'że' Complements. A Contrastive Study*. Gdańsk: Gdańsk University Press.

Kalisz, R. (1993). "White-black spectrum as an image schema and its axiology". In: E. Górska (ed.). *Images from the Cognitive Scene*. Kraków: Universitas: 109–115.

Kalisz, R. (2001). *Językoznawstwo kognitywne w świetle językoznawstwa funkcjonalnego*. Gdańsk: Gdańsk University Press.

Kalisz, R. and W. Kubiński (1993). "A speech act as a radial category". In: E. Górska (ed.). *Images from the Cognitive Scene*. Kraków: Universitas: 73–85.

Kleparski, G.A. (1990). *Semantic Change in English: A Study of Evaluative Developments in the Domain of HUMANS*. Lublin: The Catholic University of Lublin Printing House.

Krzeszowski, T.P. (1989). "The axiological parameter in preconceptual image schemata". Cognitive Linguistics Symposium in Duisburg.

Krzeszowski, T.P. (1990). "The axiological aspect of idealized cognitive models". In: J. Tomaszczyk and B. Lewandowska-Tomaszczyk (eds.). *Meaning and Lexicography*. Amsterdam: John Benjamins: 135–165.

Krzeszowski, T.P. (1997). *Angels and Devils in Hell: Elements of Axiology in Semantics*. Warszawa: Energeia.

Krzeszowski, T.P. (2003). "Jeszcze klika słów o wartościach, schematach i metaforach". In: J. Bartmiński (ed.). *Język w kręgu wartości*. Lublin: MCSU Press: 35–41.

Lakoff, G. (1996). *Moral Politics*. Chicago: University of Chicago Press.

Lakoff, G. and M. Johnson (1980/2003). *Metaphors We Live By*. Chicago: University of Chicago Press.

Libura, A. (2005). "Od znaczenia przestrzennego do aksjologii. Złożenia z cząstką *euro-*". In: J. Adamowski (ed.). *Przestrzeń w języku i w kulturze. Problemy teoretyczne. Interpretacje Tekstów Religijnych*. Lublin: MCSU Press: 189–198.

Martin, J.R. and P.R.R. White (2005). *The language of evaluation: appraisal in English*. London and New York: Palgrave MacMillan.

Montgomery, M. (2007). *The Discourse of Broadcast News: A linguistic approach*. London and New York: Routledge.
Puzynina, J. (1982). "Językoznawstwo a aksjologia". *Biuletyn Polskiego Towarzystwa Językoznawczego* XXXIX: 23–32.
Puzynina, J. (1992). *Język wartości*. Warszawa: PWN.
Puzynina, J. (2003). "Wokół języka wartości". In: J. Bartmiński (ed.). *Język w kręgu wartości*. Lublin: MCSU Press: 19–34.
Scannell, P. (1996). *Radio, Television and Modern Life*. Oxford: Blackwell.
Stubbs, M. (1996). "Towards a modal grammar of English: a matter of prolonged fieldwork". In: M. Stubbs (ed.). *Text and Corpus Analysis*. Oxford: Blackwell.
Voloshinov, V.N. (1995). *Marxism and the Philosophy of Language, Bakhtinian Thought – an Introductory Reader* (trans. Dentith, L. Matejka and I.R. Titunik). London: Routledge.
Williams, G. (2008). "Are we European? What verbs reveal about identity in *Le Monde* and elsewhere". In: B. Lewandowska-Tomaszczyk (ed.). *Corpus Linguistics, Computer Tools, and Applications – State of the Art*. Peter Lang: Frankfurt am Main: 503–517.
Winston, B. (2002). "Towards tabloidization? Glasgow revisited, 1975–2001". *Journalism Studies*, 3 (1): 5–20.
Zając, B. (2006). "Europa – sposoby definiowania pojęcia w tekstach zwolenników i przeciwników integracji". In: I. Dobosz, and B. Zając (eds.). *Polskie media w jednoczącej się Europie – szanse i wyzwania*. Kraków: Universitas.

Keywords and the Discourse of the Northern Ireland Peace Process, 1997–2007. A Case Study in the Election Manifestoes of the Democratic Unionist Party and Sinn Féin[1]

Katarzyna Fronczak

Abstract: The main aim of this paper is to conduct a textual analysis of language used in the election manifestoes of the Democratic Unionist Party and Sinn Féin, based on the period during the Northern Ireland peace process, 1997–2007. Specifically, the author pays attention to the development and changes in the usage of words significant for the peace process, which are selected after comparing the frequency lists of parties' manifestoes against each other and against the Written Informative Section of the British National Corpus Sampler. The program called 'Wmatrix' is used to carry out these comparisons.

It is also investigated how the NI peace process affected the language used by the DUP and SF in their election manifestoes. Such analysis enables one to find the ways and strategies which both parties used in the political arena to gain popularity and support from voters. It also makes it possible to find how each party's political stance changed during the period of the peace process.

Keywords: Democratic Unionist Party, IRA, Northern Ireland, republican/ republicans, Sinn Féin, unionist/unionists.

1. Introduction

1.1. Language in politics

Language is a phenomenon which only humans possess and use in everyday life to communicate, express feelings and emotions. It plays a significant role in various domains of daily life, however, we will concentrate on the relationship between language and politics. Taking politics into consideration, language can be treated as a powerful weapon as politicians use it to persuade, manipulate and encourage potential voters to support their party.

In addition to this, language plays a significant role in the process of manifesting a political will, preparing any political actions and putting them into practise (Schäffner 1996: 201). Political parties by means of language control and influence politics defined as the struggle for power.

---

1 This paper is a revision of part of the M.A. thesis of the author entitled "The discourse of the Northern Ireland peace process, 1997–2007".

This can be clearly visible on the example of Northern Ireland where long lasting conflict and peace process greatly influenced political arena. Each of the political parties had to fight for voters support. The most powerful weapon which they possessed was language. Hence, they used it in a careful and planned way in their election manifestoes. It seems to be very interesting how two main parties the Democratic Unionist Party and Sinn Féin changed and developed to new political situations. Textual analysis of the language used in the DUP and SF 1997–2007 election manifestoes enables us to find the ways and strategies which both parties used in the political arena to gain popularity and support from voters. Additionally, it allows one to find how each parties political stance changed over the period of the peace process.

1.2. Discourse analysis theories

The aim of this paragraph is to introduce a range of basic theoretical concepts that will be used in the analysis section.

van Dijk's manipulative theory

It is impossible to talk about Critical Discourse Analysis without mentioning "manipulation" which as van Dijk (2006: 359) argues "is one of the crucial notions of CDA." He (2006: 360) also claims that "a discourse analytical approach is warranted because most manipulation, as we understand this notion, takes place by text and talk." In order to recognise the true nature of manipulation and how it works we should refer to van Dijk (2006: 360) who points out that:

> manipulation not only involves power, but specifically *abuse* of power, that is, *domination*. More specifically, manipulation implies the exercise of a form of illegitimate influence by means of discourse: manipulators make other believe or do things that are in the interest of the manipulator, and against the best interests of the manipulated

van Dijk (2006: 362) focuses on the fact that politicians use political discourse to exercise their political power as well as confirm and reproduce this power.

One of the main aims of manipulation in political discourse is making people believe that political programs and political action proposed by a particular politician or political party offers the best program and consequently it is better to support them. There are various methods in manipulating public opinion and one commonly used way of changing voters attitudes towards a particular party and at the same time increasing its popularity is the "strategy of positive self-presentation and negative other presentation" by highlighting its owns advantages and positive sides and criticising "the Others" by emphasising their weaknesses, negative values and blaming all negative situations and events which can have a negative effect on their position in the political arena (van Dijk 2006: 373–374). In addition to this, some classical examples of manipulative strategies used in political discourses as van Dijk (2006: 379) points out are "emphasizing one's own power and moral superiority, discrediting one's opponents, providing details of the 'facts', polarization between Us and Them, negative Other-presentation, ideological alignment, emotional appeals."

van Dijk's racism theory

Discourse can be a powerful weapon which can have a big influence on everyday life, especially as it can be used to spread ethnic and "racial" domination and inequality, discrimination, prejudices, slavery because "text and talk play a vital role in the reproduction of contemporary racism" (van Dijk 2002: 145). Such discourse usage is typical for "symbolic elites" mostly those in high positions who "literally have everything "to say" in society" (van Dijk 2002: 146) and can affect the lives of minorities and immigrants to a high degree, mainly in such areas as entry, residence, work, housing, education, welfare, health care, knowledge, information, culture, religion (van Dijk 2002: 145). As van Dijk (1992: 245) suggests the us/them community building point is characteristic for a kind of racism where "us" refers to the elites and "them" to minorities. Such division of society into "us" and "them" is typical for the dominant classes who in this way highlight their own values as the majority group and the weaknesses of others.

Benoit's image restoration theory

It is commonly known that in the political arena there can always be some significant events which can threaten the reputation and popularity of a particular party. In such case, Benoit's (in O'Leary and El-Nawaway 2002: 6) theory of image restoration strategies which shows the need to project a positive image and restore their reputation after an alleged wrongdoing by a person or organizations should be taken into consideration. This as he states that a central goal of communication is maintaining a positive image. Benoit argues that[2] after an embarrassing incident people employ one or more of five strategies in order to restore their image. With reference to the first strategy, "the communicator can simply deny that the incident happened or shift the blame in hopes of absolution of 'culpability'."

2 The following discussion is based on O'Leary and El-Nawaway (2002, pp. 7–9).

The second strategy involves trying "to evade or to reduce responsibility through any of the four suggested ways:

1. to claim retribution on the provocateur
2. to admit not having full control or knowledge of a situation, thereby claiming not to have been fully responsible
3. to recognize that an accident or external event caused the impropriety
4. to justify that the intentions or motives were good, but failed or backfired."

The third strategy is "to reduce offensiveness with six options:

1. to bolster, or mitigate, the "negative effect on the actor by strengthening the audiences' positive effect on the rhetor"
2. to minimize the "amount of negative affects associated with the offensive act"
3. to differentiate, or distinguish the act from other similar but less desirable actions
4. to transcendent the act by suggesting that it occurred in a different context or frame of reference
5. to attack the accuser in an attempt to decrease both the credibility of accuser and the amount of tarnish on the accused person's reputation
6. to offer compensation to counterbalance the injury to the victims."

The fourth image restoration strategy is "to offer a corrective action by either attempting to restore the situation to the status quo just prior to the improper act, or to make changes to prevent recurrence of the incident."

Benoit calls fifth strategy as "mortification" and points out that "an individual who employs this strategy admits wrongdoing, expresses regret, and seeks forgiveness."

2. Data and Method

My data consisted of the general election manifesto of the Democratic Unionist Party and the Sinn Féin Party over the same period 1997–2007.[3] Firstly, I put the manifesto from each year into a separate file and as a result I obtained four Democratic Unionist Party files called "dup97", "dup01", "dup05", "dup07" and

3 The DUP and SF general election manifestoes were downloaded from the website URL: http://www.psr.keele.ac.uk/area/uk/man.htm (date: 04.07.2007).

four Sinn Féin files called "sf97", "sf01", "sf05", "sf07". Secondly, I joined all sample texts into each file, one called "dup97_07" (used for Democratic Unionist Party files) and second called "sf97_07" (used for Sinn Féin files). Then I have used 'Wmatrix'[4] to conduct a statistical analysis necessary to generate a list of keywords in the DUP corpus and SF corpus as compared with the reference corpus[5].

In the exploratory phase I have done the following comparisons "dup97_07" vs BNC Written Informative, "sf97_07" vs BNC Written Informative[6] and "dup97_07" vs "sf97_07".

Then I analysed the lists of keywords which I obtained from the earlier comparisons described above, and I focused on those words/categories which have LL values equal or greater than 15.13 ($p < 0{,}0001$; 99,99% confidence level) and frequency higher than 10 overall in at least one of the two parties. After reducing the set of words down to a manageable number by getting rid of those which do not appear to be interesting for my analysis, I have arrived at the following list:

IRA/Sinn Féin
IRA
Decommisioning
Unionist/Unionists
Republican/Republicans
Nationalist/Nationalists
We
Our
They
Their
Must
Should
All-Ireland
Six county
Northern Ireland
Ulster
Province

4 The program for corpus analysis and comparison, invented by Paul Rayson (available on the website URL: http://juilland.comp.lancs.ac.uk/wmatrix2/).

5 British National Corpus (BNC) has been used as the reference corpus.

6 BNC Written Informative, which has been chosen to carry out comparisons, includes roughly equal quantities of informative writing texts from "the fields of texts applied sciences, arts, belief & thought, commerce & finance, leisure, natural & pure science, social science, world affairs" (URL: http://www.natcorp.ox.ac.uk/corpus/index.xml). Some kinds of texts mentioned above are probably to be found in analysed election manifestoes and as a result this fact makes BNC Written Informative an appropriate choice of comparator.

Consideration of space limit in this paper prevents us from a detailed analysis of all the keywords presented above, therefore I have decided to concentrate on words unionist/unionists and republican/republicans.

In the analytical phase I ran each year, and each party, separately and I compared the following workareas in Wmatrix: "DUP97" vs "SF97", "DUP01" vs "SF01", "DUP05" vs "SF05", "DUP07" vs "SF07". Then I extracted from each workarea the percentage frequency of each key word that I picked out from the exploratory phase. Then I produce the graphs from them (one graph per word). Needless to say, I used a line graph which made me able to plot both parties on the same graph which were helpful to show some changes and some pattern of development during the period of 1997 to 2007.

The below presented Table 1 shows the relative frequency of the selected keywords in the 1997–2007 DUP and SF election manifestoes which I have chosen to compare and analyse.

Table 1. The relative frequency of keywords in the DUP and SF 1997–2007 election manifestoes

Keyword	**1997**		**2001**		**2005**		**2007**	
	DUP	**SF**	**DUP**	**SF**	**DUP**	**SF**	**DUP**	**SF**
unionist/ unionists	0.95	0.14	0.24	0.03	0.42	0.04	0.40	0.06
republican/ republicans	0.04	0.13	0.13	0.11	0.19	0.02	0.32	0.06

3. Results and Discussion

The key word unionist/unionists

Unsurprisingly the key word *unionist/unionists* is used relatively more frequently in each year of the Democratic Unionist Party manifesto as it is easily noticeable on the below presented Graph 1.

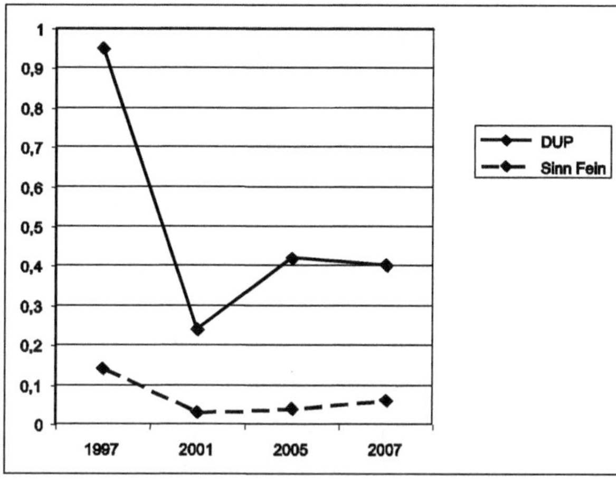

Graph 1. Frequency trends of key word *unionist/unionists* in DUP and SF data

We now turn to analyse the usage of this key word in more detail. In the election manifesto of 1997 *unionist/unionists* reaches a peak and is used 6.8 times relatively more frequently (0.95% compared to 0.14%) by the DUP and in its data we can find an overwhelming number of occurrences *the Official Unionists* (11 entries), *the Official Unionist Party* (3 entries).

The above mentioned collocations refer to the other unionist party being a strong rival of the DUP. In addition to this, a detailed analysis of concordance shows that the Official Unionist Party is presented in a rather negative way by mentioning their weaknesses and negligence. Besides that, the Democratic Unionist Party compares itself with the Official Unionist Party in order to present its own politics and actions as far better than its competitors. This hints at van Dijk's (2006: 373–374) theory of "positive own presentation and negative others presentation" (see section 1.2). This can be supported by the following sentences:

> In their Manifesto for the European election **the Official Unionists** attempted to deceive the people of Northern Ireland by claiming that they had succeeded in having the Order in Council procedure ended and Northern Ireland legislation dealt with by Bills as in the rest of the UK. This lie has been exposed – 88 Northern Ireland Orders in Council have been presented to Parliament since **the Official Unionists** made this dishonest claim. WE CHALLENGE THE OUP TO APOLOGISE TO THE ULSTER PEOPLE FOR THIS DECEPTION.

> When the DUP proposed that all Parties should put their proposals on the table for open debate **the Official Unionists** refused. The DUP has nothing to hide. It has

> faithfully represented the views of traditional unionism. You can trust us to safeguard Ulster's future within the United Kingdom.

Such a stance by the DUP suggests that there is a big division within the unionist parties which in fact should be united in their fight for a better future in Northern Ireland. However, this is politics and it should not surprise us that each unionist party wants to become the largest and the strongest unionist party of which the DUP uses all possible ways in criticising the Official Unionists. Using such methods may appear unfair but can be highly effective in persuading voters.

The highest usage of the key word *unionist/unionists* in 1997 can be explained by the fact that this was a difficult year preceding the signing of the Belfast Agreement which divided unionist parties as each of them has different strategies towards it. According to Simpson and Daly (2004: 167), "there is internal debate within the UUP, and in the wider unionist community, between those who want to accept the Good Friday Agreement and those who do not (represented by the recent defection of MP Jeffrey Donaldson to the DUP)."

Another explanation can be the fight between unionist parties who compete with each other to gain power and stick to their own stance in regards to the GFA. These suggestions sound sensible when we take into consideration the year 2001 when the relative frequency of this key word usage goes down sharply from 0.95% to 0.24% in the DUP election manifesto and from 0.14% to 0.03% in the SF election manifesto. The emotions calmed down after the Good Friday Agreement was signed and as a result each party had gained what it could and everything became more stable. We can assume that the DUP lacked interest in referring to the competitive unionist parties as *the Official Unionists* does not appear in its 2001 election manifesto. This can be explained by the fact that the strong opposition towards the Belfast Agreement which as Wilford and Wilson (2006: 8) describe was "a supposed conveyor-belt of concessions to republicanism", and at the same time toward the Unionist Party which supported it, expressed by the DUP was slightly neutralised by the IRA statement that had promised progress on disarmament. This finally allowed an agreement to be reached which had proved difficult before 1999.

On the other hand, as it is evidenced in the concordance, *unionist/unionists* is used in a different context, mainly in *the unionist people* (3 entries) and *the unionist community* (1 entry). Such collocations can be understood as if the party says *our people, our community* which is probably used to make ordinary people believe that they are really important for the DUP as it associates them with itself. When we know that someone takes care of us we feel more comfortable and secure. The DUP seems to choose the way of gaining support by creating a vision of one big unionist family in which members are guaranteed a better future. Conversely, the above mentioned collocations can be associated with the van Dijk's (1992: 245) theory of the us/them community building point characteristic of a kind of racism (see section 1.2). We may hypothesize that the Unionists consider themselves as better than others and try to create their own community consisting of shared opinions. Such a point of view may suggest that the sectarianism in Northern Ireland can be seen as a variant on racism. In case of NI the black victims are replaced by a minority group of Catholics whereas Protestants (represented by Unionists) are the elite group and the grassroots of the conflict is not the colour of skin but religion. Mitchell (2005: 113) argues that "in deeply divided society, religion is one of the key dimensions of difference." Opsahl (in Mitchell 2005: 114) concludes that "whilst many Protestants' attitudes to politics can be explained 'almost entirely in religious terms', Catholics do not have the same problem with Protestantism as a religion, and are more tolerant of Protestants as individuals."

Van Dijk (1992: 202) draws our attention to the fact that:

> in the increasingly multi-ethnic societies of Europe and North America, white people routinely engage in spontaneous talk about ethnic minorities, immigrants or refugees. White citizens in the inner cities often talk with each other about their minority or foreign neighbours, and about the changes newcomers have brought to the neighbourhood, the city or the country. Whether or not such changes are perceived to be negative, or even threatening, white ingroup members thus spread and confirm commonsense beliefs, if not ethnicist or racist prejudices, about the various outgroups.

This quotations in some way collocates with the situation in NI and as Bruce (in Mitchell 2005: 115) points out "religion has became a mark of belonging to a specific ethnic groups. What matters is not any individual's religiosity, but the individual's incorporation in an ethnic group defined by a particular religion. So conflict is ethno-religious."

It is worth mentioning that as in the previously analysed the 1997 DUP election manifesto, also in the 2001, 2005 and 2007 DUP election manifestoes the party uses similar ways to encourage support from potential voters as the only party which is able to take care of the people interests and finally clarify the uncertain and problematic case of the IRA and Sinn Féin. It means that the DUP tries to present itself in superlatives and as compared to its rivals by highlighting their disadvantages. We can assume that the DUP in order to increase the support of voters uses not only such manipulative policies which as van Dijk (2006: 374) points out involve "systematic negative representation of the Others in terms of negative values, characteristics and actions" but also applies the strategy of positive self-presentation by emphasizing owns values. This hypothesis can be supported by the following sentences:

> As a united and committed party only the DUP can deliver the full time vigorous and principled representation you deserve. Others are so badly divided they can not even unite themselves, never mind the **unionist** people. Unity is strength. The DUP has no division or dissension to distract from the vital task of defending and promoting your interests. (quoted from the 2001 DUP election manifesto)

> The DUP is the only party which can keep unionism number one at Westminster and it is the only party which can finish ahead of Sinn Féin /IRA both in terms of seats won and the number of votes cast across the Province. A vote for other **unionist** parties risks allowing Sinn Féin to top the poll. (quoted from the 2005 DUP election manifesto)

> The DUP... asserted from the outset of the Good Friday Agreement that it could secure a better arrangement for Unionists than David Trimble and the Ulster **Unionist** Party, and the DUPs stance has been largely vindicated.
> The DUP has reversed the failures of the UUP on the devolution of policing and justice and created the ideal position for unionism. (quoted from the 2007 DUP election manifesto)

The increase in the usage of the analysed keyword from 0.24% in 2001 to 0.42% in 2005 can be caused by the further problems which befell the Ulster Unionist Party. The DUP took advantage of its rivals difficulties such as the failure of IRA decommissioning which resulted in the suspension of the institutions in October 2002 and pushed the UUP into second position on during the election to the Assembly in 2003. Analysing its 2007 election manifesto we can notice the slight decrease in usage to 0.40% which suggests that the DUP is confident about its strong political position among unionist parties and continues its political strategy of criticising the UUP by mentioning its failures from previous years. Such a strategy is probably used to convince potential voters of their support.

Contrary to the DUP election manifestoes, in the Sinn Féin election manifestoes from the 1997, 2001, 2005 and 2007 we can observe that references to *unionist/unionists* are rather rare. It suggests that the party concentrates on its own politics and avoids comparing itself with the unionist parties. Additionally, detailed analysis of concordance in each election year shows that SF believes some changes in the political system should be taken in order to complete the peace process and improve the situation in Northern Ireland, as for instance the party draws attention to:

- inequality and injustice which are clearly visible in case of housing where unionists are in a much better position than nationalists who must face a number of obstacles, as in the sentences:

Housing Executive figures for Belfast show that in the allocation of housing, nationalists are underallocated by 16% while **unionists** are over-allocated by 21%. (quoted from the 2005 SF election manifesto)

Overall, nationalists are on housing waiting lists an average of one and a half times longer than **unionists**, and the rate of increase for nationalists on waiting lists is double that of unionists. (quoted from the 2007 SF election manifesto)

- the fact that the Unionist party did everything to delay the peace process. In this way Sinn Féin presents itself as the only party which takes care of the wider situation of the country and is ready to cooperate and negotiate with other parties in order to gain long lasting peace in Northern Ireland, as in the sentences:

Sinn Féin has also shown strong and creative leadership on the streets when it has been most needed over the last two years, particularly when the Orange Order, aided by a silent mutiny in the RUC, held the state to **unionist** ransom. Sinn Fein continues to work tirelessly on its peace project. Only last November Gerry Adams and John Hume but proposals to John Major which could have restarted the peace process. Major, working to a **unionist** agenda, rejected those proposals.(quoted from the 1997 SF election manifesto)

However, the potential to deliver the sort of fundamental changes still required is being threatened by the actions of the Ulster **Unionist** Party and the failure of the British Government to honour its commitments under the Good Friday Agreement. (quoted from the 2001 SF election manifesto)

- all-party negotiations which are indispensable in creating a devolved government and to understand each party politics, as in the sentences:

We will continue this engagement, and seek to promote dialogue with **unionists** at every possible opportunity. Our objective has been to build understanding of each other, and to build consensus based on respect for each others differences. (quoted from the 2007 SF election manifesto)

The *key word* republican/republicans

The next key word *republican/republicans* is strongly connected with the political ideology called republicanism which as Smyth (2005: 135–136) points out

has understood itself as a radical movement, committed to the idea of a United Ireland – a political entity based upon socialist principles. [...] Two dogmas of republicanism have been abandoned without significant protests: abstentionism and the rejection of, and refusal to be involved with, any form of British-sponsored administration in Northern Ireland.

Looking at the Graph 2 we can easily notice that the analysed key word is used 3.25 times relatively more frequently in the 1997 SF election manifesto (0.13% compared to 0.04%) and the context in which it appears suggests that Sinn Féin considers itself as a republican party with clearly defined aims of creating an all-Ireland, getting rid of British dominance and solving the existing long-term conflict between republicans and unionists/protestants. According to McGovern (2000: 133), "Sinn Féin represented the dominant voice of modern day Irish republicanism". This is supported by the following sentences:

> Now is the time for change Sinn Féin is an Irish **Republican** party. It is an activist, campaigning party. Our objective is to end British rule in Ireland.

> We commit ourselves to: reaching an accommodation with the unionist/protestant people of this island; overcoming the mistrust which exists between **republicans** and the northern unionist/protestant people.

The other collocation with *republican/republicans* from the 1997 SF data are *republican prisoners, republican political prisoners.* These expressions are used by SF in order to present discrimination in NI. The examples mentioned by the party in the following sentences show concrete evidences of inequality, injustice and harsher punishments for republicans:

> In June 1995 the British government released British paratrooper Lee Clegg after serving two years of a life sentence for murder – at the same time they refused to review the cases of **republican** prisoners who had served over 20 years; in November 1995 three **republican** lifers in Maghaberry prison were informed that they can expect to serve 50 years.

In the 1997 DUP election manifesto the key word *republican/republicans* occurs in a different context having a negative meaning and suggests the party's disapproval and condemnation for any action taken by republicans, as in the following sentence:

> This has always been the **republican** response to democracy - boycott and abstentionism.

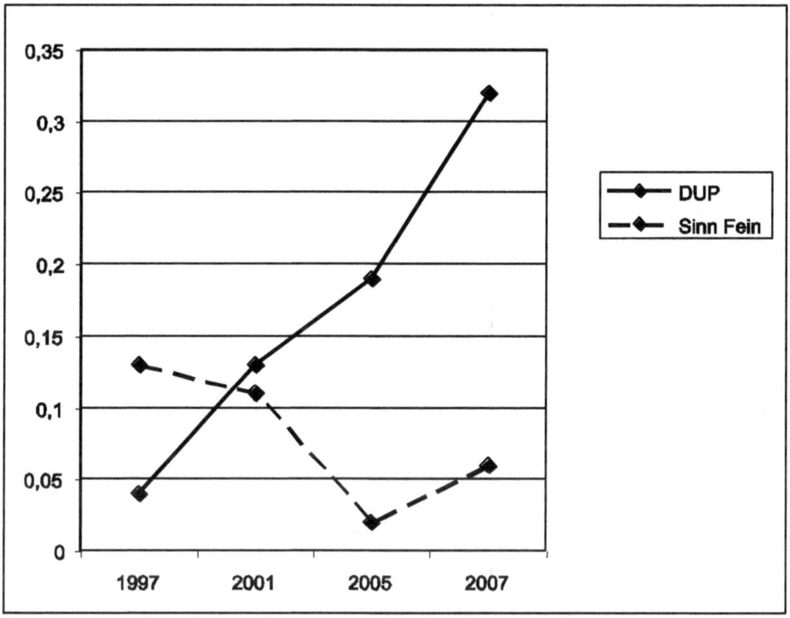

Graph 2. Frequency trends of key word *republican/republicans* in DUP and SF data

Analysing the Graph 2 above we can observe that the relative frequency of the key word *republican/republicans* in the DUP data rises from 0.04% in 1997 to 0.13% in 2001 and goes down slightly in the SF data from 0.13% in 1997 to 0.11% in 2001. The difference in this key word usage by the two parties is not so high as it is used 1.18 times relatively more frequently by the DUP. However, the context in which it appears is completely different, similarly to the 1997 election manifesto and also in the 2001 election manifesto, the Democratic Unionist Party presents republicans in a negative way. The party is appealing to its supporters and potential voters and reminding them of their British heritage which is under republican threat. Such a stance by the DUP aims to discourage potential voters of supporting those who are against British dominance or any other form of interference in NI which the DUP treats as indispensable and beneficial for the country. Besides that, the party does not hide its strong bonds with Britain and even considers itself as its offspring, as in the sentences:

> Day by day our British heritage and way of life is under attack. The symbols of the State, including even the National Flag and the image of Her Majesty, are being torn down. Everything Gaelic, **republican** and Irish is promoted while everything British, unionist or Orange is derided and reviled.

The rise in the usage of the analysed key word by the DUP may be caused by the fact that this party was a strong opponent of the Belfast Agreement and as a result mentions republicans in various negative contexts in order to assure NI citizens that its stance against this document has been proved accurate as the IRA did not end its violent actions after this deal, for example[7] the Omagh bombing in July 1998 where 29 people were killed, and the bomb attack on Fermanagh hotel on 6 February 2000. The DUP even criticises and accuses the other unionist party UUP for betraying unionism because it agreed to the signing of the Good Friday Agreement which as previously mentioned hints at van Dijk's (2006: 373–374) theory of political strategy of negative other presentation. This hypothesis can be supported by the following sentences:

> Unionism has paid a heavy price for the UUP endorsement of the **Republican** Agenda being delivered through the Belfast Agreement.

> Nationalist and **republicans** want you to vote for the UUP to bolster their position. Do not let them win. The UUP is trying to cut deals and make pacts with age-old enemies of unionism.

Interpreting the usage of *republican/republicans* in the 2001 SF election manifesto we can find that just as in the case of its 1997 data, the party considers itself as republican and highlights its aims to create an all-Ireland and guarantees better living conditions. This suggestion can be shown in the following sentences:

> Sinn Féin is a **republican** party. We are the only all-Ireland party. Our goal is to see a united Ireland which delivers real social and economic change.

The other context in which *republican/republicans* occurs shows that Sinn Féin wants to ensure its potential voters that it recognises the problems of Northern Ireland such as injustice, inequality, discrimination, poor living conditions and will do what it can to solve them. Mentioning obstacles which people have to meet every day make them believe that this party is really concerned about their lives and will improve their situation and in this way encourage them in voting for SF, as in the following sentences:

> Whether in Derry or Kerry, West Belfast or Dublin South-West, people have the opportunity to vote for **republicans**. We are the only party with a vision which looks beyond partition and inequality and towards a new, independent Ireland based on justice, equality and prosperity.

This hypothesis can be also supported by van Dijk (2006: 368) who argues that:

---

7 The following discussion is based on Dixon (2001: 275).

> if a political party wants to increase its popularity with voters, it will typically try to positively change voters' attitudes towards such a party (...) manipulation thus focuses on the formation or modification of more general, socially shared representations – such as attitudes and ideologies – about important social issues.

Another point to be made here is that after the year 2001 the frequency of *republican/republicans* usage increases in the DUP election manifestoes from 0.13% to 0.19% in 2005 and to 0.32% in 2007. On the other hand, it decreases in the SF election manifestoes from 0.11% to 0.02% in 2005 and then rises to 0.06% in 2007. Such development in frequency trends of this key word may be the result of the changes in each party politics over time.

Firstly, the more frequent usage in the DUP election manifestoes of each year can be evidenced by the party's belief that Sinn Féin is strongly connected with republican ideas of a military solution. Also the DUP is a strong opponent of British withdrawal which is one of the main aim of republicans. The differences in attitude towards the peace process in Northern Ireland can be the reason why the party uses *republican/republicans* more frequently in the ensuing manifestoes. As it is shown in the corpus data the context in which this key word occurs, similarly to the already analysed 1997 data, has a negative meaning and highlights weaknesses and drawbacks of republicans. This hypothesis can be supported by the following sentence:

> It is clear from recent events that **republicans** have proven themselves to be incapable of making the move to exclusively democratic means. (quoted from the DUP 2005 election manifesto)

This appears to be a political strategy to weaken the position of the Sinn Féin which in each election year gains more popularity among NI citizens and consequently becomes a strong political rival as Tonge (2006: 136) points out "the party moves from purported revolutionary Republican vanguardism towards becoming a competitive actor in a political marketplace." The Democratic Unionist Party just like in the 1997 election manifesto and also in later manifestoes mentions other unionist party and its leader Trimble as too weak and not strong enough to hold power. Such criticism of other UUP political actions aims to assure potential voters that the DUP is the only party worth voting for as only they can bring about tougher policies. The following sentences can support this hypothesis:

- quoted from the 2005 DUP election manifesto:

> In every negotiation **republicans** exploited the weakness of the UUP and were allowed to dictate their own terms.

> Keep the pressure on **republicans**. Do not let David Trimble do to unionism in 2005 what he did up until 2003.

- quoted from the 2007 DUP election manifesto:

> We can not afford to go back to the bad old days when UUP weakness was exploited by **republicans**, and Sinn Féin dominated the political agenda. Unionism needs a strong DUP.

> UUP took **republicans** on trust. Sinn Féin in Government without any requirement to decommission. Sinn Féin in Government despite paramilitary activity continuing. Sinn Féin in Government while criminal activity ongoing. Sinn Féin in Government despite opposing police and rule of law.

Another point to notice is that reaching the peak of frequency usage of the key word *republican/republicans* in the 2007 DUP election manifesto can be caused by the final IRA decommissioning on 28 July 2005 to which the party often refers and which treats as its own success because it was one of the party's condition to be fulfilled by republicans, as in the following sentences:

> Before the DUP became the largest unionist party neither the other parties nor the Government were prepared to insist that **republicans** totally end their illegal activity before they could enter Government.

Secondly, the decrease in usage of the key word *republican/republicans* in the 2007 SF data can be explained by the fact that Sinn Féin finally understands that the peace process cannot be completed and the solution cannot be achieved by the use of force. That is the reason why the party decides to change its previous stance and involves itself in constitutional politics. Also Smyth (2005: 137) draws our attention to the fact that "Gerry Adams, the Sinn Féin president, is shifting the movement's emphasis away from a military solution, and towards a rapport with constitutional nationalism." Bean (in Tonge 2006: 136) adds "'New' Sinn Féin seeks respect for its electoral mandate, co-operates with other parties and constructs its agenda primarily upon equality and rights rather than issues of sovereignty and territory." Shirlow and McGovern (in O'Leary and El-Nawaway 2002: 10–11) "traced Sinn Féin's decision to change its image from that of solely an anti-British and pro-united Ireland "propaganda machine which provided ideological support for the [republican's] ongoing military campaign to that of the legitimate political party." Additionally, the change in the Sinn Féin's stance hints at Benoit's theory (in O'Leary and El-Nawaway 2002: 6) of image restoration strategies (see section 1.2). It seems that Sinn Féin attempted to restore its image after a number of violent actions carried by its military wing the IRA and as Benoit (in O'Leary and El-Nawaway 2002: 9) points out "fourth strategy – to employ corrective action – is the course Sinn Féin took by making a conscious decision to change its image, or "mend one's ways"."

However, these modifying and deconstructing of Sinn Féin politics were viewed by the republicans as a fundamental betrayal of principle. Smyth (2005: 137) points out that in a letter to the *Irish News* (31 May 2004), a number of republicans bitterly attacked Sinn Féin and its leadership: "Today the ideas we fought for are never spoken of-and those who remember them are silenced. Our beliefs were traded for realities of the current process, a process that suits the interests of political parties and not the common people." Such a strained relationship between Sinn Féin and republicans are probably the reason why the party limited the usage of this key word in its 2005 manifesto in order not to intensify the recent conflict. Another corpus-based conclusion to be drawn here is that there are only two collocations with the describing key word:

> It has been a partisan, political, Protestant and paramilitary force which has been used in the main against Catholics, nationalists and **republicans**.

> Sinn Féin is the Irish **Republican** Party the united Ireland party. We are the party of radical social and economic change. We are the party of equality.

Taking into consideration the 1997, 2001, and 2005 SF election manifestoes we can find out that the usage of *republican/republicans* reaches its peak in 1997 when the party believed that the only way to achieve a solution was through military actions which is agreeable with republicanism ideas and principles. According to Smyth (2005: 142), "the political logic for the military campaign was based on premises that Britain would never leave Ireland voluntarily, and that political agitation alone-such as the constitutionals politics of the SDLP-would never achieve this end." However, frequency of *republican/republicans* usage goes down after the year 1997 until the year 2005. The significant issue which caused this decrease was the signing of the Belfast Agreement in 1998 and as Smyth (2005: 142) argues "when Sinn Féin signed up to the Great Friday Agreement, it effectively abandoned this position and accepted, at least publicly, that a military solution was not possible."

The rise in frequency usage of the analysed key word in the 2007 SF election manifesto can be explained by the already mentioned IRA final decommissioning in 2005 which was the undeniable evidence of an end to republican military actions. Therefore, there is no further need for the party to separate itself from the republicans as they no longer endanger Sinn Féin's position in the political arena. Also St Andrews Agreement of 2006 can be treated as a significant event which highly influences and dominates the character of both the 2007 DUP and SF election manifestoes.

4. Conclusion

As can be seen it is clear that both the DUP and SF changed their language to suit the political circumstances at the time. The most obvious factor for this change has to be the formulation of a peace process which began in 1997 with the signing of the Good Friday Agreement and ended with the historic deal taking place in May 2007 when Ian Paisley was sworn in as leader with Martin McGuinness of Sinn Féin as deputy leader.

Both parties had to radically change their use of words as each twist and turn of the process developed. In addition to this, both parties also had to compete with rival parties in its own political sphere which again altered the choice of words. For example both the DUP and SF were seen as outside the process by the end of 1990's. However, with the failure of both the UUP and SDLP to bring about peace it was left to the DUP and SF to move the process forward. This consequently had an affect on their language as both parties were at the forefront of the peace process. It was not always possible to continue rhetoric of an aggrieved nature which was in keeping of a party in protest of something. Once they were the main parties in the pace process it was not always possible to be so aggressive. It was also clear that over the years the public had become disillusioned with all the killings and had grown tired of no improvements in the economy. As Europe became richer Northern Ireland seemed to be stuck in past historically. Therefore the DUP and SF also had to be seen as showing a softer stance in later years in response to this growing dissatisfaction. In addition to this, another important factor which influenced the changes in the DUP stance towards the peace process was the change in the party's leader Ian Paisley who mellowed his tough policy.

It is these reasons which influenced both parties as it is clear to see that political parties in all countries have to change and adapt to new political situations.

References

Dixon, P. (2001). *Northern Ireland: the politics of war and peace.* Houndmills: New York: Palgrave.

McGovern, M. (2000). "Irish republicanism and the potential pitfalls of pluralism". *Capital and Class*, 71: 133–161.

Mitchell, C. (2005). "Catholicism and the construction of communal identity in Northern Ireland". *Irish Journal of Sociology*, 14.1: 110–130.

O'Leary, A. C. and M. El-Nawaway (2002). "A content analysis of image restoration in Northern Ireland: Public communication strategies of political parties". *Simile*, 2, 3.

Schäffner, Ch. (1996). "Editorial: Political Speeches and Discourse Analysis". *Current Issues in Language and Society*, 3: 201–204.

Simpson, K. and P. Daly (2004). "Politics and Education in Northern Ireland – An Analytical History". *Irish Studies Review*, 12: 163–174.

Smyth, J. (2005). "The road to God knows where: Understanding Irish Republicanism". *Capital and Class*, 86: 135–158.

Tonge, J. (2006). "Sinn Féin and 'New Republicanism' in Belfast". *Space and Polity*, 10: 135–147.

van Dijk, T.A. (1992). "Racism and argumentation: "Race Riot" Rhetoric in Tabloid Editorials". In: F.H. van Eemeren *et al.* (eds.). *Argumentation illuminated* (pp. 242–259). Dordrecht: Foris.

van Dijk, T.A. (1992). "Racism, elites and conversation". *Atlantis. Revista de la Asociacion española de estudios anglo-norteamericanos*, 14 (1/2): 201–257.

van Dijk, T.A. (2002). "Discourse and racism". In: D. Goldberg and J. Solomos (eds.). *The Blackwell Companion to Racial and Ethnic Studies* (pp. 145–159). Oxford: Blackwell.

van Dijk, T.A. (2002). "Political discourse and political cognition". In: P. A. Chilton and Ch. Schäffner (eds.). *Politics as Text and Talk. Analytical approaches to political discourse* (pp. 204–236). Amsterdam: Benjamins.

van Dijk, T.A. (2006). "Discourse and manipulation". *Discourse and Society*, 17(2): 359–383.

Wilford, R. and R. Wilson (2006). *The Trouble with Northern Ireland: the Belfast Agreement and Democratic Governance.* Dublin: New Island Press.

Correspondence Analysis in Discourse Studies

Joanna Kaim-Kerth

Abstract: Multidimensional statistical analysis is rarely used in discourse studies area. The aim of this paper is to show how those methods, particularly correspondence analysis, can be used in researching discourses focused on similar subject.

Research material is transcript of the parliamentary debate on prolonging maternal leave period. It was analyzed using computer software – coded in Max QDA and correspondence analysis was conducted using SPSS package.

Correspondence analysis not only enables objectification of the discourse analysis but also offers results visualization, what is useful in terms of their interpretation. In this particular analysis results show that different parliamentary fractions (understood here as different discourses) differ significantly in appealing to values and authorities as well as to visions of the family.

Keywords: discourse analysis, correspondence analysis, statistical analysis, maternity leave, Polish parliament.

1. Introduction

Application of the correspondence analysis to discourse studies originates from a need of structuring analysis techniques within this area.

Although discourse is a notion present in several fields – from social sciences to linguistics and each branch within them – apart from defining it differently – applies different techniques to researching it. Very rarely those studies are based on strict statistics. It is therefore very hard to achieve reliable results that could be repeated in next study in order to compare findings or check techniques on other material.

Most of the analysis is closer to phenomenology or heuristics, underlining interpretation and the need of re-reading texts continuosly until senses lying behind them become recognized.

Leo Spitzer's remarks on the philological circle as a method of text analysis seem to be very adequate to sum up this approach:

> Why do I insist it is impossible to offer the reader a step-by-step rationale to be applied to a work of art? For one reason, that the first step, on which all may hinge, can never be planned: it must already have taken place. This first step is the awareness of having been struck by a detail, followed by a conviction that this

> detail is connected basically with the work of art; it means that one has made an "observation" – which is the starting point of a theory, that one has been prompted to raise a question – which must find an answer. [...] the solution attained by means of circular operation cannot be subjected to a rigorous rationale because, at its most perfect, this is a negation of steps: once attained, it tends to obliterate the steps leading up to it (one may remember the lion of medieval bestiaries who, at every step forward, wiped out his footprints with his tail, in order to elude his pursuers!).
>
> (Spitzer 1948)

The question being asked in this paper is this: what to do in order not to wipe out the footprints of the analysis?

Corpus analysis based approach to discourse analysis gives some solutions to this problem, first of all allowing for application of statistical methods. However the need for large sets of data in order to apply corpus linguistics may often be an obstacle. Therefore adapting methods popular in social sciences may offer the solution for more reliable discourse analysis.

One of such techniques is correspondence analysis (CA) (Benzécri 1973).

Correspondence analysis is a method of data exploration in which relations that normally could be presented in a cross-table are analyzed. If one wants to find out how many blond people have blue eyes and how many dark-haired people have brown eyes, then a cross-tab is a helpful and simple method to present this information. However when it comes to relations between numerous variables and observations, the cross-table is no longer helpful. Making sense of it is simply too difficult. Then the graphical presentation of data relations offered by correspondence analysis becomes extremely helpful. The output of correspondence analysis is a scatter plot in which variables are demonstrated as one color and observations as the other (compare Romney *et al.* 2000). Depending on type of normalization conclusions may be drawn on relations between variables or observations only or – in case of symmetrical normalization – on relations between variables and observations (Singh 2007).

The axes of the scatter plot represent dimensions that help to make sense of data. Dimensions are often continuous phenomena that can be used as reference scales for data.

Another important feature of correspondence analysis is the possibility of estimating inertia. It is the equivalent of variance telling how much of the phenomenon was explained by the analysis. In this way it is known how meaningful the results are (Clausen 1998).

2. Aim and methodology

The aim of the study described below was to find out what are the similarities and differences between discourses that deal with the same topic and have the same objective but are still recognized as different. I used CA for the analysis of the maternity leave debate in Polish parliament in 2006. This particular topic was chosen as all the parties involved in the debate seemed to value the family and care for its wellbeing but employed very different arguments and communication strategies to prove their point. Therefore each party present in the parliament was treated as a separate discourse.

I assumed that the discourses even though focused on common objective will differ in terms of values and authorities as well as in terms of visions of the family considered as ideal.

Data for the analysis (transcription of the debate) was taken from the official website of the Polish parliament (Polish Parliament 2006). Then it was coded into categories describing values (i.e. life, family, democracy) authorities (i.e. research, normal people, European Union) and visions of the family and its members (i.e. traditional family, woman as mother / employee). The coding procedure was conducted using Max QDA software. After that the matrix of code frequencies (with discourses in rows and categories in columns) was exported to SPSS software where correspondence analysis was conducted.

3. Results

The results are presented on 3 scatter plots for more clarity. The general analysis explained almost half of the inertia (0,480).

The results shown at the general output (picture 1) will not be discussed here as the same phenomena are more clearly observable on latter scatter plots.

The analysis concerning values and authorities (picture 2) revealed two dimensions. The first one (horizontal axis) represents differences between conservative and liberal opinions about family. On the right hand side there are more liberal opinions – such as seeing gender equality and democracy as values or treating partnership-based families as a positive model as opposed to the traditional one. Values gathered on the left tend to be more conservative – underlining values such as Poland, life or future of the society, which seem to bring very elegiac concepts to the debate.

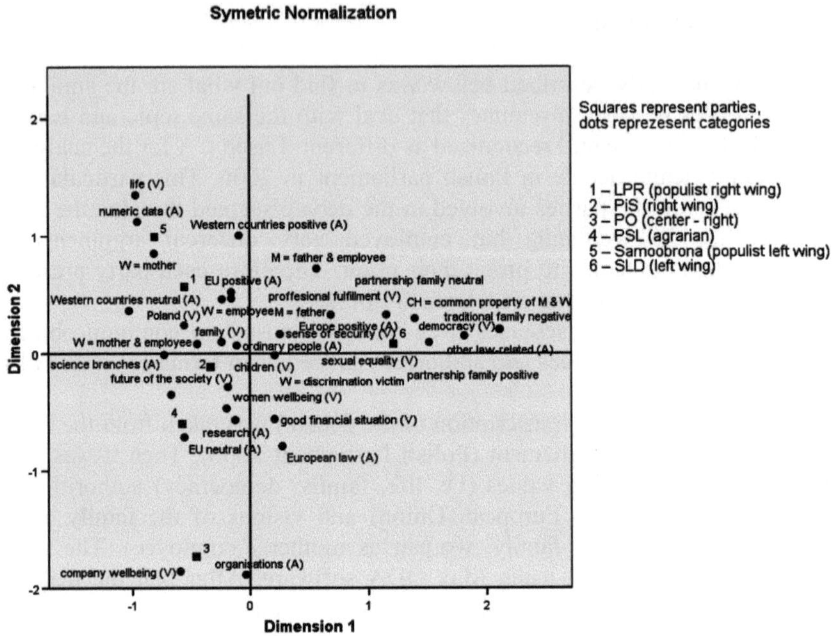

Picture 1. General results

As it may be easily observed most of the parties (all apart from the SLD – left wing party) share the same position in relation to the first dimension – all of them are positioned closer to the conservative end of the continuum.

The second dimension (represented by the vertical axis) differentiates between outer and inner world or outside and inside perspective. The top of the plot – inside perspective – gathers values such as life, family, sense of safety and normal people. Those values are more related to the home family life than those gathered at the opposite end where reference is made to organizations, European regulations and European Union as authorities and wellbeing of the company employing women is concerned as a value. The contrast between those two focus points is clear.

This dimension differentiated also the parties – the populist ones (LPR and Samoobrona) were both gathered quite high – close to the inside perspective. On the other hand agrarian (PSL) and center-right (PO) parties were closer to the outside perspective. There were also two parties positioned in the middle of the scale – left wing (SLD) and right wing (PiS, in government at the time of the debate).

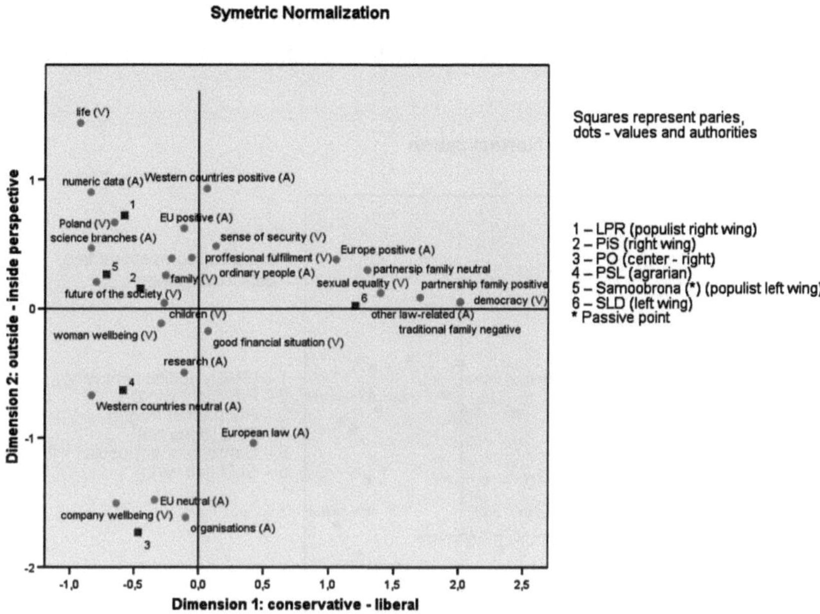

Picture 2. Values and authorities

Values presented in the centre are the ones shared by almost all the parties active in the debate – relation to them does not differentiate them. Those values are: family itself, children, wellbeing of the women and reference to the normal people as authority. Those notions were central for the topic of the debate – maternity leave so it is quite understandable that all discourses referred to them pretty often.

What is worth underlining is the fact that in both dimensions the populist parties are positioned very close to each other (although their official programs and approaches were not similar) what would suggest that the populist discourse is in fact very distinctive and has clear common features.

The second detailed analysis (picture 3) is less meaningful than the one described above. When it comes to visions of the family and its members (man, woman) only one dimension is valid. It is also very easy to interpret it – it distinguishes the situations when women were discussed from all the other instances analyzed (family as a whole, men). Again, as in the first dimension of the previous analysis all parties apart from one (SLD – left wing) were focused on discussing different roles of women in the debate. This shows that the context of maternity leave was perceived rather narrowly by most of the actors involved.

Although it was declared that the family and its wellbeing is the centre of attention, the focus was mostly on women and opposition of their professional and parental role.

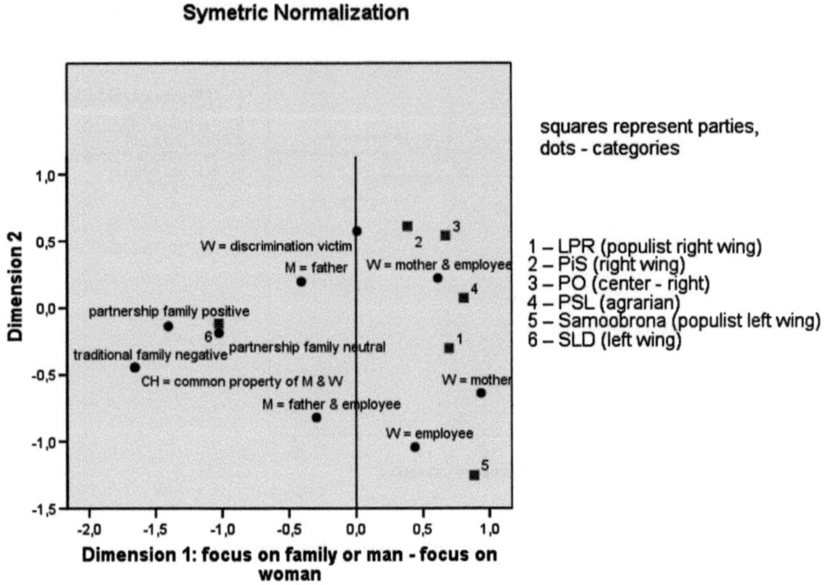

Picture 3. Visions of family and its members

4. Discussion

As it was shown above, correspondence analysis can be successfully used to discourse analysis. Different discourses present in the maternity leave debate differed in terms of values, authorities and visions of the family demonstrated in their representatives speeches. Correspondence analysis proved to be able to catch those differences and provided useful dimensions on which the similarities and differences could be analyzed. In the same time reliability of the analysis was assured as it was based on the statistical operations that can be checked or re-done at any moment.

However there is an element of subjectivity involved at the first step of the analysis – in code creation and text coding. Probably another researcher could design different categories as well as include into them different fragments of text. I would hesitate to call this a disadvantage as this limitation is accepted in the qualitative analysis within social sciences. However on the ground of linguistics corpus analysis tools could be employed to make sure that the criteria of text fragments selection are more objective. On the other hand in such situation some meaningful and in fact key fragments may be omitted by the mechanical browsing methods, what is not the case when the whole text is carefully read.

References

Benzécri, J.P. (1973). *L'Analyse des Données. Volume II. L'Analyse des Correspondences*. Paris, Dunod.

Clausen, S.E. (1998). *Applied Correspondence Analysis: an Introduction*, Sage: 14.

Polish parliament www.sejm.gov.pl, checked on October 15, 2006.

Romney, K.S. *et al.* (2000). *Statistical methods for characterizing similarities and differences between semantic structures*. PNAS (Proceedings of the National Academy of Sciences of the United States of America), vol. 97, no. 1.

Singh, K. (2007). *Quantitative Social Research Methods*. Sage: 219.

Spitzer, L. (1948). *Linguistics and Literary History. Essays in Stylistics*. Princeton University Press, Princeton: 26–27.

Selected Cognitive and Discoursal Aspects of the LSP of the Navy

Inga Massalina

Abstract: This article touches upon the cognitive and discourse aspects of the LSP of Navy. Taking into consideration L. Hoffmann's horizontal and vertical LSP stratification as a starting point there was an attempt to give the stratification of the LSP of Navy. As a result five strata with substrata were defined. The paper addresses the frame structure, and the main categories of this language. The means of cohesion are also reflected in the research. Two classifications of discourse markers – traditional and functional are given in the article.

Keywords: analysis, classification, concepts, discourse markers, LSP, research, stratification, study, text.

The interest in the study of Languages for specific purpose (LSP) has undeniably been on the rise and has constantly expanded a fact that has brought to light many illuminating features of the nature of these languages. They are necessary for communication in the special fields of knowledge, for the development of knowledge, for ability to transfer it from one generation to the next one.

This interest has also led to a growing industry that produces scores of theoretical and descriptive articles on LSP every year and in different languages all over the world. In fact, the results of the research are emerging as new and very distinct disciplines. Interest in the issue of LSP and lexical units related to them has grown not only in pragmatic and discourse analyses research, but also in other fields such as sociolinguistics or second language acquisition. However, and in spite of such interest in LSP, scholars do not seem to see eye to eye on several aspects regarding the nature.

The material of our research includes more than 200 articles of the naval magazines Jane's Navy International (1996–2008), All Hands (2007–2008) (it is a scientific popular discourse). We have analyzed the texts of some thesis reflecting academic discourse – A.N. Grainiceanu (2006), J. Rushton (2006), J. Russel (2007), J. Sudnic (2006), A. Tam (2006), A. Welch (2006). As for the dictionaries we dealt with Campaign Dictionary of Military Terms (2004); Dictionary of Military Terms by T.N. Dupuy, C. Johnson, G.P. Hayes (2003), Encyclopedia Britannica.

The scientific popular discourse reflected in the texts of Jane's Navy International turned out to be very interesting for the analysis of the LSP of

Navy. This journal informs readers about various things concerning the Navy. There are fleet reviews, program profiles, operations and training, technology developments, amphibious warfare, maritime aviation, maritime security issues, naval exercises, force structure and doctrine, defense industry updates e.t.c. [http://www.jane's.com]. With this global magazine readers can receive timely accurate and impartial coverage of key operations, technology and procurement issues as they affect maritime security.

With all this in mind we are going to focus on some features peculiar to the LSP of Navy in order to identify the stratification, frame structure, key concepts, conceptual fields, the main categories, terminology and non-terminological units constituting the LSP of Navy.

Different approaches to LSP have been revised and LSP has not been considered as homogeneous (Mentrup 1978: 48–77; Sager 1990; 1994; Savory 1988). Some attempts have been made to define **horizontal** and **vertical LSP classification** and to elaborate a taxonomy of the lexical units. In the **horizontal classification** researchers can differentiate the language of medicine, the language of mathematics, the language of physics etc. The **vertical classification** is considered to be more complex since it reflects the differentiation inside the science itself. Within the vertical LSP classification we can see the language of fundamental science, the language of experimental science, the language of applied science etc.

Within the theoretical contributions from a cognitive approach the work of L. Hoffman (Hoffmann 1981) should be mentioned since it is considered to be one of the most widely known analyses of LSP. L. Hoffmann's early interest in the function of LSP at a time when it was scantly known made his work a necessary point of reference for any researcher dealing with LSP. L. Hoffman's research is believed among one of the first attempts combining principles of horizontal and vertical LSP classification. In fact, many of the recent studies on the topic owe their insights in part to the model outlined in his research. L. Hoffman's horizontal and vertical LSP stratification has much potential for the analyses of great number of LSP regarding the field of knowledge and professional activity. First of all L. Hoffmann differentiates LSP relating the subject i.e. mathematics, physics etc. Then the four main criteria of LSP are outlined.

1) **the degree of abstraction**;
2) **the specification of linguistic means**;
3) **the sphere of functioning**;
4) **the users**.

As a result five LSP key strata or sublanguages are determined. Sublanguage is considered to be a specialized language or jargon associated with a specific group or context.

I. Sublanguage of theoretical fundamental science;
II. Sublanguage of experimental science;
III. Sublanguage of applied science and techniques;
IV. Sublanguage of material production;
V. Sublanguage of the sphere of consumption.

Taking into consideration L. Hoffmann's horizontal and vertical LSP stratification as a starting point of the research,the LSP of Navy can be broken down into five strata or sublanguages. Every stratum includes some substrata.

I. **Sublanguage of theoretical fundamental naval science**: 1. Navy science; 2. Navy education.
II. **Sublanguage of experimental naval science**: 1. Investigation; 2. Elaboration; 3. Testing.
III. **Sublanguage of applied naval science and techniques**: 1. Mathematics; 2. Physics; 3. Chemistry; 4. Automated systems of naval control; 5. Economics of Navy, 6. Justice; 7. Medicine; 8. Meteorology.
IV. **Sublanguage of naval material production and reconstruction.**

1. **Naval techniques and armament**:
1.1. Modern submarines, surface ships of main classes and aviation of US Navy and Royal Navy:

a) submarines: ballistic missile submarines (nuclear propulsion), multi-purpose nuclear propulsion submarines; b) surface ships of main types: nuclear aircraft carriers, aircraft carriers, (antisubmarine warfare) support aircraft carriers, Coast guard training ships; c) naval aviation: aircrafts, helicopters, free pilot aircrafts; d) Marine; e) naval shipbuilding; f) construction; g) repair(s); h) conservation; i) naval electronics; j) naval navigation systems;

1.2. **Naval armament**: a) missile armament, b) bomb armament, c) battery armament, d) torpedo armament, e) mine armament, f) anti-mine armament.

V. **Sublanguage of naval information system**: 1. Communication systems; 2. Search-rescue services; 3. Navy rear.

In our research there was an attempt to carry out frame analysis of the LSP of Navy. The frame analysis of the LSP of Navy addresses the processes and mechanisms of cognition reflecting the connections between explicit and implicit information. It is thought to gain in precision and clarity and will be able to present a non-biased description of the Navy.

There are five frames in our research: 1) "US Navy Administrative Organization", 2) "The Royal Navy", 3) "Navy", 4) "Naval activity", 5) "Space". The stratification of the LSP of Navy is seen in the first three frames (Frame 1, Frame 2 and Frame 3).

Frame 1

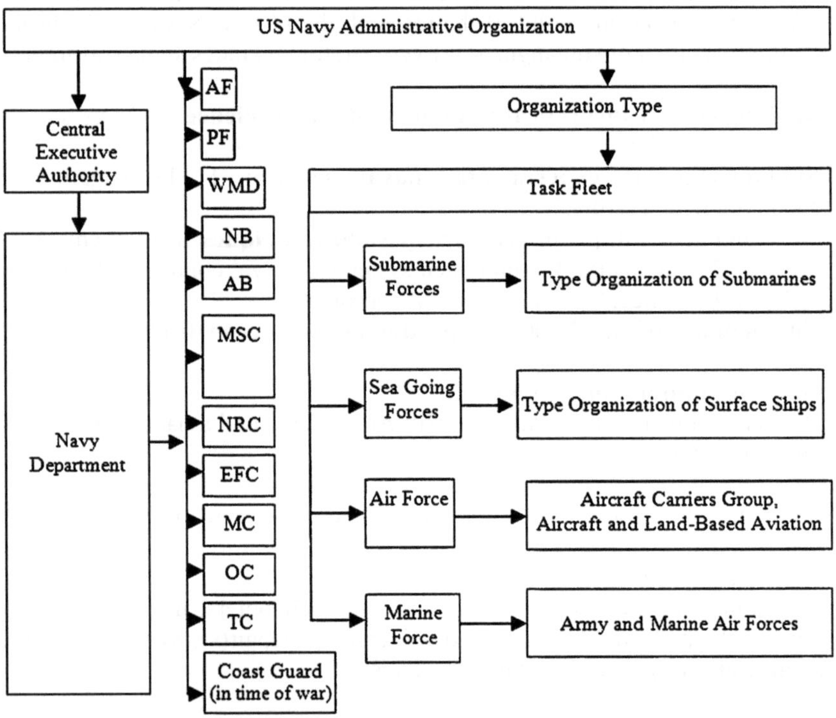

US Navy – United States Navy;
AF – Atlantic Fleet;
PF – Pacific Fleet;
WMD – Washington Maritime District;
NB – Naval Base;
AB – Aviation Base;
MSC – Military Sealift Command;
NRC – Naval Reserve Command;
EFC – Experimental Forces Command;
MC – Minesweeper Command;
OC – Oceanographic Command;
TC – Training Command.

Frame 2

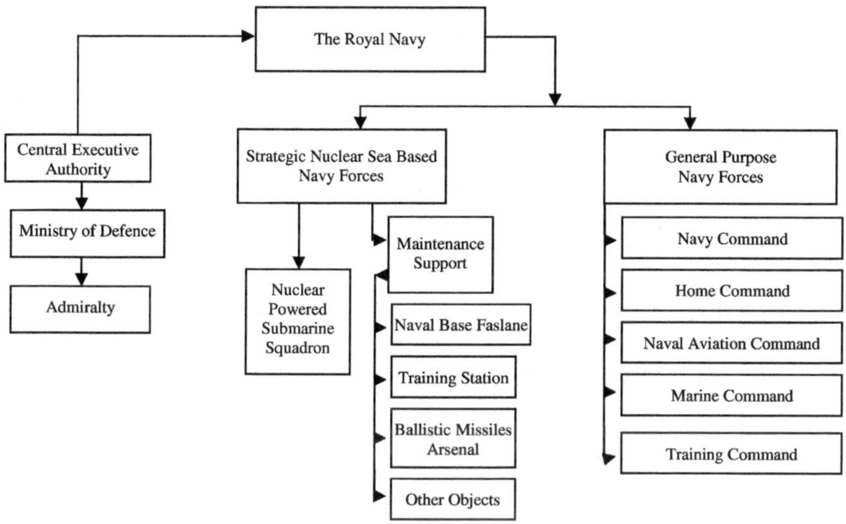

Frame 3

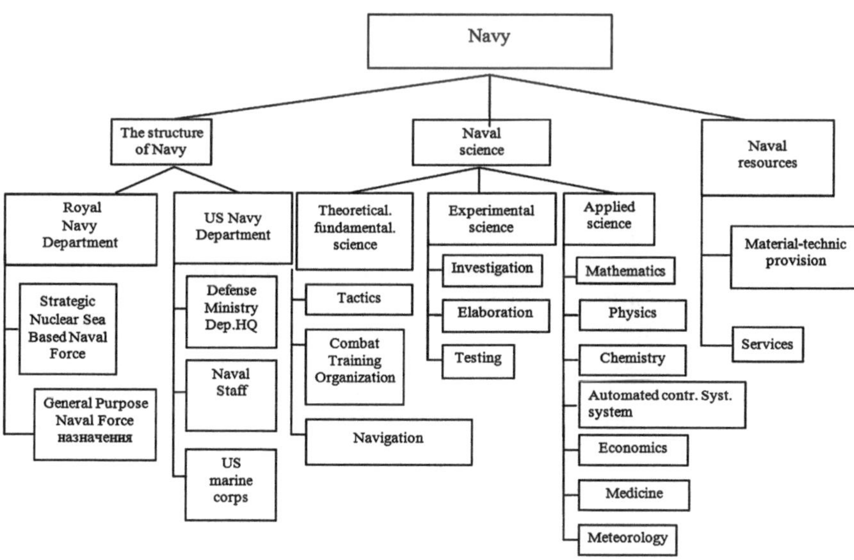

While observing the naval discourse there was an attempt to carry out conceptual analysis. As a result the following **key concepts** of the naval domain were identified: 1) **agens** (person, organization), 2) **state**, 3) **property**, 4) **place**, 5) **path** (way, trajectory), 6) **operation**, 7) **container**, 8) **parameter**, 9) **science**, 10) **concept** (scientific notion, conception), 11) **study** (field of knowledge, investigation), 12) **substance**, 13) **material**, 14) **space**, 15) **unit of measure**, 16) **quantity**, 17) **distance**, 18) **speed**, 19) **size**, 20) **time**, 21) **information**.

The prominence of the key concepts aids in the determination of the conceptual fields in this domain. So the picture of the concepts constituting this domain and its terminology is apparent.

1. **Naval science, its sections and applied science**: *tactics*, *battle training organization*, *navigation and others*.
2. **The structures of the Navy**: *submarine flotilla*, *Marine Corps and others*.
3. **Naval training and combat operations**: *training*, *amphibious assault landing*, *amphibious operation*, *attack*, *offensive action*, *defense*, *combat operation*, *combat action*, *fight*, *fighting*, *battle*.
4. **Persons in the Navy**: *admirals*, *officers*, *company officers*, *majors*, *captains*, *second lieutenants*, *first lieutenants*.
5. **Objects of the naval activity**: *aircraft carrier*, *submarine*, *missile*.
6. **Resources of the naval activity**: *logistics*, *facilities*.
7. **Means of the naval activity**: *timer*, *electronic device*, *electronic system*, *electromagnetic system*.
8. **Place of the naval activity**: *harbor*, *base*, *port*, *dock*, *plant*.

Frame 4 "**Naval activity**" illustrates the conceptual fields of the naval domain. Another important question in our research concerns the **categories** expressing different types of relations in the Navy. The following eight categories can be determined in the LSP of Navy: **1) naval space, 2) naval actions, processes, 3) qualities, parameters, 4) state, 5) objects in Navy, 6) units of measurement, 7) the categories of other sciences, 8) persons in Navy**.

The category "**Space**" is considered to be of great importance in the naval domain. Frame 5 "Space" illustrates the concept "space" with its subconcepts. The category "**space**" **(location)** (as it is illustrated in Frame № 5) consists of the following concepts: "**bodies of water**", "**aerial**", "**land**". The concept "**bodies of water**" includes the following subconcepts: "**surface**" and "**submarine**". The concept "**aerial**" has the subconcepts "**terrestrial**" and "**cosmic**". The concept "**land"** includes the subconcepts – "**forest**", "**plain**", "**mountain**", "**populated areas**" etc.

Frame 4

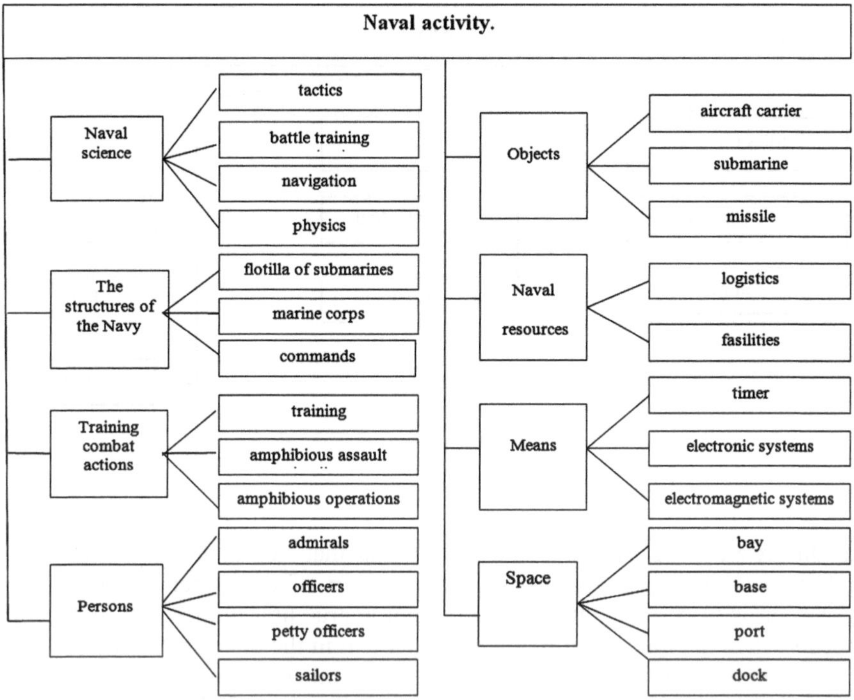

Among the identified categories in the LSP of Navy there is a category of **artifacts.** Artifacts are objects made by human being [Oxford Dictionary of English 2003]. The category of artifacts has been systematically organized and replenished. The following nominative classes of this category have been determined in the research: **1) security**, **2) service**, **3) material**, **4) architecture**, **5) space**, **6) channel**, **7) systems**, **8) information**, **9) technology**, **10) hardware**, **11) software**.

So the first part of the analysis dealt with some cognitive aspects of the naval terminology. In the second part we tried to focus on specific set of linguistic items linking the terminological and non-terminological units in the naval discourse.

Frame 5

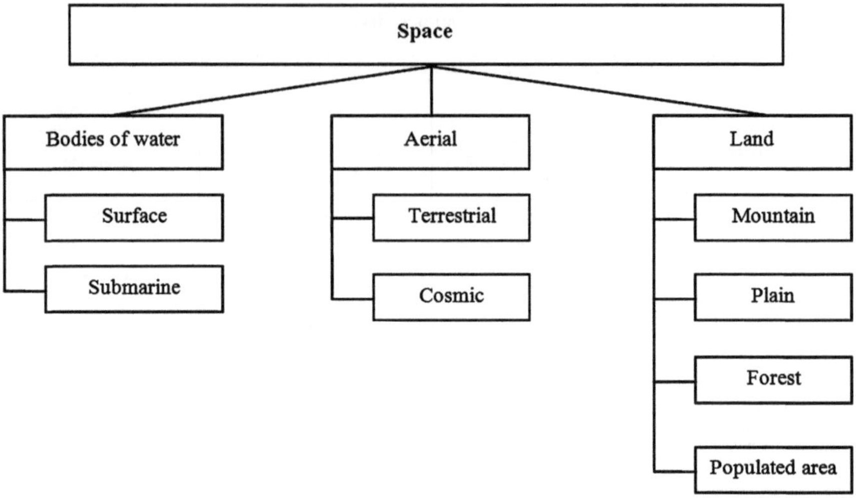

In this respect we start with the hypothesis that lies in the consideration of cohesion as a textual property and thus a part of the system of a language. Cohesion is also a semantic notion but not a structural property of texts, and it occurs when the interpretation of some element in the discourse is dependent on that of another, that is, the one presupposes the other and thus cohesion involves lexical and syntactic continuity in a text (Halliday and Hasan 1976: 4). The range and possibilities for linking something with what has gone before is the authors' main concern: the study of specific set of linguistic items and structures as semantic resources for linking a sentence. In our research we call the cohesive units **discourse markers**.

A discourse marker is a word or phrase that marks a boundary in a discourse. Discourse markers do not belong to the syntactic or semantic structure of an utterance. They can be understood as elements which have the function to connect utterances. In this sense they are equivalent to so-called connectives.
Diachronic data show that discourse markers often come from different word classes, such as adverbs (well) or prepositional phrases (in fact). So at first such units were analyzed in our research according to traditional part of speech classification. There were six groups: 1) conjunctions; 2) prepositions; 3) articles; 4) pronouns; 5) adverbs; 6) prepositional phrases. The table below shows these groups with their frequency in the naval texts.

conjunctions	prepositions	articles	pronouns	adverbs	nouns in prepositional phrases
3,4%	8%	6,6%	2,4%	0, 25%	0,1%

Traditionally, some of the elements considered discourse markers were treated as “fillers” or “expletives”, that is, elements whose function was that of not having any function at all. Nowadays they are assigned functions in different levels of analysis: topic changes, discourse planning, stressing, backchanneling, hedging or reformulations [Del Saz 2007]. Those functions can be classified into three broad groups: a) relationships among the parts of the utterances; b) relationships between the speaker and the message, and c) relationships between the speaker and the hearer.

There was an attempt in the research to carry out functional classification, consisting of 15 discourse markers groups.

1. MARKERS OF SIMILARITY: the, this, these, such, similarly, likewise, in the same way, equally: (*We call **these** shared resources **the** shared partition*) [Grainiceanu 2006: 7];
2. MARKERS OF DIFFERENCE: another, other (*Over the past roughly twelve years, NYC has been the target of two successful terrorist attacks and numerous **other** failed attempts*) [Sudnic 2006: 2];
3. ADDITIVE MARKERS: – *positive:* and, both … and, not only … but (also/as well), too, moreover, in addition to, furthermore, further, also, not to mention the fact that, besides *and* (*Most studies on civil-military relations in China have focused primarily on party military interactions with little regard for the effects of coercion (the key function of the military), economic development, legitimacy of the political system, **and** the influence of civil society **and** international actors*) [Tam 2006: 5];
   – *negative*: neither … nor, nor, neither, either;
4. CONTRASTIVE MARKERS: but, not … but, although, while, whereas, despite, even if, even though, on the other hand, in contrast, however, (and) yet, at the same time (*In chapter 5 we present P-ring, a new P2P index structure that reuses existing algorithms for some of the index components, **but** introduces new algorithms to handle data load balancing*) [Grainiceanu 2006: 148];
5. LOCAL MARKERS: where, wherever (*A P-Tree or Hierarchical Ring router of order D provides guaranteed 0 (log2P+m) range search cost performance in a stable 0 system of P pears, **where** M is the number of peers with data in required range*) [Grainiceanu 2006: 4];
6. TEMPORAL MARKERS: when, whenever, as, while, now (that), before, until, till, after, since, any time (*A pear can join a P2P system **at any time***) [Grainiceanu 2006: 7];

7. CONCESSIVE MARKERS: but, even so, however, (and) still, (and) yet, nevertheless, on the other hand, although, even though, despite/in spite of, regardless of, admittedly, whereas, while, nonetheless (***However**, in designing an index that supports range queries, the challenge is to devise a query router that is robust to failures while providing logarithmic search performance even in the presence of highly skewed data description*) [Grainiceanu 2006: 4];
8. MARKERS OF CAUSE / REASON: as, because, because of, since, on the grounds that, seeing that, due to, in view of, owing to for, now that, so (*Traditional techniques developed for equality queries are not applicable in this case **because** they distribute data items based on their hash value since hashing*) [Grainiceanu 2006: 4];
9. MARKERS OF PURPOSE: so that, so as (not) to, in order (not) to, in order that, for fear (that), in case (*In a P2P index data items or information about localization of data items are assigned to peers **so that** they can be late found by the users by using the query routing algorithms*) [Grainiceanu 2006: 4];
10. MARKERS OF MANNER: as, (in) the way, how, the way in which, in the same way (as), as if, as though (*The challenge is to distribute data items among peers **in a such way** that range queries could be answered efficiently*) [Grainiceanu 2006: 4];
11. MARKERS OF CONDITION: if, in case, on condition that, unless, in the event (that), in the event of, as/so long as, whether, whether … or, only if, even if, otherwise, or (else), in case of (*We assume there is some underlying network protocol that can be used to send messages from one peer to another, **once** the address of the destination peer is known*) [Grainiceanu 2006: 7];
12. CLARIFICATIVE MARKERS: that is to say, specifically, in other words, to put it another way, I mean (***Moreover**, this thesis undertakes an extensive review of the various explanations and theories advanced in the literature of civil-military relations*) [Tam 2006: 5];
13. MARKERS OF EFFECT / RESULT: such/so … that, consequently, for this reason, as a consequence, thus, therefore, so then, under those circumstances, if so, if not, so, in that case, otherwise, thus (***Finally**, in the leave phase, peers are killed at the specific rate*) [Grainiceanu 2006: 138];
14. REPLACIVE MARKERS: this, those, he, she, one (*Chapter 4 presents the P-Tree and chapter 5 presents Hierarchical Ring, two fault-tolerant routing structures **that** provide support for range queries*) [Grainiceanu 2006: 3];

15.CHRONOLOGICAL (LISTING) MARKERS:

– *beginning*: initially, first…, at first, first of all (*There are two reasons for this: **first**, since we start and end with no data items, the average number of items is very low at the beginning and end*) [Grainiceanu 2006: 128];

– *continuing*: secondly …, after this/that, second…, afterwards, then, next, before this;

– *concluding*: finally, at last, in the end, eventually, lastly, last but not least.

It is seen in the functional classification that words of different parts of speech fall into this classification reflecting different types of cohesion in the naval texts. For example, the first group "Markers of similarity and difference" includes the definite article *the*, the pronouns (*this*, *these*, *another*, *other*), adverbs (*likewise*, *equally*), the noun with the preposition (*in the same way*).

In conclusion it could be said that the cognitive approach to the LSP of Navy study provides the description of the professional sphere of communication. First of all, it is connected with the specific features of the naval domain – with its structure, function, national traditions, history etc. Then, it deals with the specific items of the LSP of Navy, with its terminology that reflects the professional activity and with the cohesive units – discourse markers – linking the words and sentences and marking the boundaries in the discourse. The functional classification is considered to be more convenient for the text analysis because different relationships in the text structure are reflected.

References

All Hands. The Magazine of U.S. Navy, 2007–2008.

Del Saz, M.M. (2007). *English Discourse Markers of Reformulation*. Bern: Peter Lang AG: 237.

Campaign Dictionary of Military Terms (2004). Macmillan ELT: 288.

Dupuy, T.N., Johnson, C., and G.P. Hayes (2003). *Dictionary of Military Terms*. 2nd edition. US Washington: 276 /www.militerms.com/

Encyclopedia Britannica. 32 Volumes Print Set. London /www.britanicashop.britannica.co/.

Hoffmann, L.A. (1981). *A cumulative analysis of scientific texts* // AILA 81. Proceedings. Lund.

Grainiceanu, A.N. (2006). *Answering Complex Queries in Peer-to-peer Systems*. A Dissertation to the Faculty of the Graduate School of Cornell University in Partial Fulfillment of the Requirements for the Degree of Doctor of Philosophy. Cornell University: 171 http://www.nps.edu.

Halliday, M.A.K. and R. Hasan (1976). *Cohesion in English*. London: Longman: 374.

Mentrup, W. (1978). *Überlegungen zur lexikographischen Erfassung der Gemeinsprache und der Fachsprachen* // Interdisziplinäres deutsches Wörterbuch in Diskussion. Düsseldorf: 48–77.

Rushton, J. (2006). Operationalizing Dissuasion. Master's Theses. Naval Postgraduate School. Monterey. California: 103 http://www.nps.edu.

Russel, J. (2007). Ideas and Foreign Policy. The Future of US relations with the Middle East. Europe and the Gulf. Instituto Per CLI Studi di Politica Internationale, Milan. Italy. May, 2007. http://www.nps.edu.

Russel, J. (2007). Whither Regional Security in a World Turned Upside Down. / MESA Roundtable: Mutual Threat. Preception in the Gulf. Middle East Policy Council. Journal Compilation. Vol. XIV, № 2: 141–148. http://www.nps.edu.

Sager, J.C. (1990). *A practical course in terminology processing*. Amsterdam, Philadelphea: Benjamins: 214.

Sager, J.C. (1994). *Language engineering and translation: consequences of automation*. Amsterdam, Philadelphea: John Benjamins publ. company: 346.

Savory, G. (1988). *The language of science*. London: Andre Deutsch: 173.

Sudnic, J. (2006). "Dirty Bomb" Attack: Assessing New York City's Level of Preparedness from a First Responder's Perspective. Master's Theses. Naval Postgraduate School. Monterey. California: 119 http://www.nps.edu.

Tam, A. (2006). Coercion and Governance in China: Analyzing Civil-Military Relations in the Post-Deng Era Using Multiah Alagappa's Analytical Framework. Master's Theses. Naval Postgraduate School. Monterey. California: 103 http://www.nps.edu.

Welch, A. (2006). Terrorism Awareness and Education as a Prevention Strategy for First Responders. Master's Theses. Naval Postgraduate School. Monterey. California: 129 http://www.nps.edu.

Oxford Dictionary of English. Second edition (2003). Oxford. Oxford University Press: 2088.

Jane's Navy International 1996–2009 /http://www.jane's.com/.

Part Six

ACADEMIC DISCOURSE

Corpora and EAP: Specificity in Disciplinary Discourses

Ken Hyland

Abstract: The emergence of community-oriented views of literacy in recent years has led to greater research attention being devoted to the specific contexts of language use and this is particularly evident than in the field of English for Academic Purposes. Corpus studies have become invaluable here in revealing how language choices help construct both arguments and disciplines and showing how texts are successful only when they employ conventions that other members of the community find familiar and convincing. In this paper I draw on my own work conducted over several years into student and research genres to show how some familiar conventions of academic writing are employed by different fields. More specifically, I will use corpus and interview data to not only show how language differs across disciplines, but what these differences can tell us about the epistemological understandings and social practices of those fields.

Keywords: Bundles, Citation, directives, Discipline, Discourse community, EAP, Genre, Hedges, Reporting verbs, Self-mention, Specificity.

Corpora and EAP are perfect companions. What we know of genre structures, disciplinary variation, and lexico-grammatical uses in academic communication are largely a result of corpus studies conducted over the past ten years. Essentially, corpora bring evidence of typical patterning and salient features to the study of academic discourse, providing data which represent a speaker's experience of language in a restricted domain. In other words, it is a method which moves away from individual preferences to focus on community practices, dematerializing texts and approaching them as a package of specific linguistic features employed by a particular group of users.

This makes corpus analysis particularly valuable in research into academic discourse (e.g. Biber 2006; Hyland 2004; Swales 2004) where intuition and impression guided teaching for many years. Instead we now have evidence of the ways language works in particular contexts and how it varies across disciplines, genres, modes, and languages. Alone, however, corpus analysis is insufficient. As Baldry (2000: 36) observes, for example, corpus linguistics treats language as a self-contained object, 'abstracting text from its context', so that corpus studies also require a focus on 'action' to balance the focus on 'language'. This necessitates rematerializing these features to understand how and why writers make the choices they do when they write, moving us beyond description to explanation. This kind of qualitative interpretation is greatly assisted by interviews with text users, grounding patterns of text meanings in the conscious choices of writers and readers. This is the approach I will take in this paper to reveal something of the contribution that corpus research has made to the study of academic discourse. In particular, I will draw on my own research to examine a key concept in language teaching and discourse analysis today, that of specificity.

1. Dimensions of specificity

Specificity, however, appears in numerous guises. Corpus studies undertaken by Biber (1988), for example, have confirmed Halliday's (1989) observations regarding the *specificity of mode*, finding greater nominalization, impersonalisation and lexical density in written compared with spoken texts. There is also a high degree of *specificity in the kinds of writing* that students are asked to do. In fact, because different fields value different kinds of argument and set different writing tasks, even students in fairly cognate fields, such as nursing and midwifery, are given very different writing assignments (Gimenez 2009). Similarly, corpus research in contrastive rhetoric (e.g. Hinkel 2002) has pointed to cultural *specificity in rhetorical preferences*. While we can't simply predict the ways people are likely to write on the basis of assumed cultural traits, students' first language and prior learning come to influence ways of organising ideas and structuring arguments when writing in English at university.

Perhaps most research into specificity has attended to *genre*, where particular purposes and audiences lead writers to employ very different choices (e.g. Hyland 2008). Table 1, for example, compares frequencies for different features in a corpus of 240 research articles and 56 textbooks.

Table 1. Selected features in Research articles and textbooks (Hyland 2005)

per 1,000 words	Hedges	Self-mention	Citation	Transitions
Research Articles	15.1	3.9	6.9	12.8
University Textbooks	8.1	1.6	1.7	24.9

We can see considerable variation in these features across the two genres. The greater use of *hedging* underlines the need for caution and opening up arguments in the research papers compared with the authorized certainties of the textbook, while the removal of *citation* in textbooks shows how statements are presented as facts rather than claims grounded in the literature. The greater use of *self-mention* in articles points to the personal stake that writers invest in their arguments and their desire to gain credit for claims and the higher frequency of transitions, which are conjunctions and other linking signals, in the textbooks is a result of the fact that writers need to make connections far more explicit for readers with less topic knowledge.

Overwhelmingly, however, it is *disciplinary* variation which underlies most specificity and this is what I want to focus on here. Research into differences in academic practices and the texts that these produce is relatively new, partly because the notion of discipline, and its underlying reliance on the idea of community, has been difficult to pin down, and partly because of our fixation with genre in recent years. While genre has provided a significant way of understanding situated language use, its power of harnessing generalisations has led us to over-emphasize resemblances between texts at the expense of variation. But, as Swales made clear in 1990, we need to see community and genre *together* to offer a framework of how meanings are socially constructed by forces outside the individual. Research on language variation across the disciplines is rapidly becoming one of the dominant paradigms in EAP (e.g. Hyland 2004; Flottem *et al.* 2006; Hyland and Bondi 2006).

Specificity here refers to what I hope is a fairly uncontroversial idea: that we communicate as members of social groups and that different groups use language to conduct their business, define their boundaries, and manage their interactions in particular ways. For EAP teachers this means focusing on communicating, and learning to communicate, as a disciplinary insider.

2. Disciplinary specificity

The idea of discipline has become important in EAP as we have become more sensitive to the ways genres are written and responded to by individuals acting as members of social groups. Ideas such as *communicative competence* in applied linguistics, *situated learning* in education, and *social constructionism* in the social sciences have contributed to a view which places community at the heart of writing and speech. This draws on Faigley's (1986: 535) claim that writing 'can be understood only from the perspective of a society rather than a single individual' and Geertz's (1973) view that knowledge and writing depend on the actions of members of local communities. Essentially, we can see disciplines as language using communities and the term helps us join writers, texts and readers together. Communities provide the context within which we learn to communicate and to interpret each other's talk, gradually acquiring the specialized discourse competencies to participate as group members.

The notion of discipline, however, is not an altogether happy one and under the challenge of post modernism, which sees intellectual fragmentation at every turn, and institutional changes such as the emergence of practice-based and mix-and-match modular degrees, it is increasingly questioned (e.g. Gergen and

Thatchenkery 1996; Gilbert 1995). It is certainly true that local struggles, intellectual developments and institutional convenience ensure that boundaries are never stable nor objects of study immutable. New disciplines spring up at the intersections of existing ones and others decline while, more prosaically, political and economic factors often determine what is recognised as a discipline.

It is, however, a notion with remarkable persistence and the distinctive existence of disciplines can be informed by study of their rhetorical practices (Hyland 2009). This is because successful academic writing does not occur in an institutional vacuum. Instead, it largely depends on the individual writer's projection of a shared professional context as they seek to embed their writing in a particular social world which they reflect and conjure up through approved discourses. So we can see disciplines as particular ways of doing things – particularly of using language to engage with others in certain recognised and familiar ways. Academic texts are about *persuasion* and this involves making choices to gain support, express collegiality and resolve difficulties in ways which fit the community's assumptions, methods, and knowledge. This is how Wells (1992) sees matters:

> Each subject discipline constitutes a way of making sense of human experience that has evolved over generations and each is dependent on its own particular practices: its instrumental procedures, its criteria for judging relevance and validity, and its conventions of acceptable forms of argument. In a word each has developed its own modes of discourse.

To work in a discipline, then, we need to be able to engage in these practices and, in particular, in its discourses.

So disciplines structure the work we do within wider frameworks of beliefs and provide the conventions and expectations that make texts meaningful. We can see this if we picture the disciplines as spread along a cline, with the 'hard' sciences at one end and the 'softer' humanities at the other.

SCIENCES	SOCIAL SCIENCES	HUMANITIES
◄	———	►
Empirical and objective		Explicitly interpretive
Linear and cumulative growth of knowledge		Dispersed knowledge
Experimental methods		Discursive argument
Quantitative methods		Qualitative methods
More concentrated readership		More varied readership
Highly structured genres (IMRD)		More fluid discourses

Figure 1. Continuum of academic knowledge (after Coffin, Swann, Lillis and Hewings 2003)

In the sciences new knowledge is accepted by experimental proof. Science writing reinforces this by highlighting a gap in knowledge, presenting a hypothesis related to this gap, and then reporting experimental findings to support this. The humanities, on the other hand, rely on case studies and narratives while claims are accepted on strength of argument. The social sciences fall between these extremes. While they have partly adopted methods of the sciences, in applying these to human data they have to give more attention to explicit interpretation. In other words, academic discourse helps to give identity to a discipline. This means that we need to understand the distinctive ways they have of asking questions, addressing a literature, criticizing ideas, and presenting arguments, so we can help students participate effectively in their learning.

3. Some example differences

I want to turn now to these disciplinary differences and look at a series of studies I've done over the past decade or so into the features of a 1.5 million word corpus of research articles in 8 disciplines and 4 million words of student dissertations together with interviews with 30 academics. I will briefly highlight a few of the disciplinary differences in these corpora.

3.1. Citation practices

One of the most striking differences in disciplinary uses of language is in citation practices. The inclusion of references to the work of other authors is obviously central to academic persuasion. This is because it not only helps establish a persuasive framework for the acceptance of arguments by showing how a text depends on previous work in a discipline, but also as it displays the writer's credibility and status as an insider. It helps align him or her with a particular community or orientation and confirms that this is someone who is aware of, and is knowledgeable about, the topics, approaches, and issues which currently interest and inform the field. But because discourse communities see the world in different ways they also write about it in different ways, with Table 2 showing that two thirds of all the citations in the article corpus in the philosophy, sociology, marketing and applied linguistics papers, twice as many as in the science disciplines (Hyland 1999).

Table 2. Rank order of citations by discipline

Discipline	per 1000 words	Discipline	per 1000 words
Sociology	12.5	Biology	15.5
Philosophy	10.8	Electronic Engineering	8.4
Applied Linguistics	10.8	Mechanical Engineering	7.3
Marketing	10.1	Physics	7.4

Basically, the differences reflect the extent writers can assume a shared context with readers. In Kuhn's (1962) 'normal science' model, natural scientists produce public knowledge through cumulative growth. Problems tend to emerge on the back of earlier problems as results throw up further questions to be followed up with further research so writers don't need to report research with extensive referencing. The people who read those papers are often working on the same problems and are familiar with the earlier work. They have a good idea about the procedures used, whether they have been properly applied, and what results mean. In the humanities and social sciences, on the other hand, the literature is more dispersed and the readership more heterogeneous, so writers can't presuppose a shared context but have to build one far more through citation.

This rather neat hard-soft discipline explanation is spoilt somewhat by the fact that biology has the highest citation count per 1000 words. Interestingly, this is largely due to a very high proportion of self-citation with 13% of all citations to the current author compared with about 6% overall. There does, in fact, seem to be a considerable emphasis given to recognising the ownership of ideas in Biology and showing how current research builds on the work of others which makes it unusual among the sciences (Hyland 2004).

3.2. Reporting verbs

There are also major differences in the ways writers report others' work, with results suggesting that writers in different fields draw on very different sets of reporting verbs to refer to their literature (Hyland 1999). Among the higher frequency verbs, almost all instances of *say* and 80% of *think* occurred in philosophy and 70% of *use* in electronics. It turns out, in fact, that Engineers *show*, philosophers *argue*, biologists *find* and linguists *suggest*. The most common forms across the disciplines are shown in Figure 2.

Discipline	Most frequent forms		
Philosophy	say, suggest, argue, claim	Biology	describe, find, report, show,
Sociology	argue, suggest, describe, discuss	Elec Eng.	Show, propose, report, describe
Applied Ling.	suggest, argue, show, explain	Mech Eng.	show, report, describe, discuss
Marketing	suggest, argue, demonstrate, propose	Physics	develop, report, study

Figure. 2. Most frequent reporting verbs

These preferences seem to reflect broad disciplinary purposes. So, the soft fields largely used verbs which refer to writing activities, like *discuss*, *hypothesize*, *suggest*, *argue.* These involve the expression of arguments and allow writers to discursively explore issues while carrying a more evaluative element in reporting others' work:

(1) Weinstein (1993) **suggests** that the critical thinking movement may well…
Davidson **defends** this claim on the grounds that …
Stayman and Deshpande (1989) **argue** that an individual's ethnicity…

Engineers and scientists, in contrast, preferred verbs which point to the research itself like *observe*, *discover*, *show*, *analyse*, and *calculate*, which represent real world actions.

(2) Carrington and Firn, 91) **showed** that differential growth involved complete…
Sliwinsky and Salisbury (18) **restrained** Xanthium stems for 48 h, which when released…
Michel et al. (1989) **subdivided** group II introns into two categories based on …

This emphasis on real-world activities helps scientists represent knowledge as proceeding from impersonal lab activities rather than from the interpretations of researchers. Two scientist informants commented on this kind of use:

Of course, I make decisions about the findings I have, but it is more convincing to tie them closely to the results.

(Physics interview)

You have to relate what you say to your colleagues and we don't encourage people to go out and nail their colours to the mast as maybe they don't get it published

(Biology interview)

The conventions of impersonality in science articles thus play an important role in reinforcing an objective ideology by portraying the legitimacy of hard science knowledge as built on socially invariant criteria. Again, it removes the author from the text to give priority to the unmediated voice of nature itself.

3.3. Hedges

Devices like *possible*, *might*, *likely*, and so on, collectively known as hedges, also diverge across fields. These function to withhold complete commitment to a proposition, implying that a claim is based on plausible reasoning rather than certain knowledge. They indicate the degree of confidence the writer thinks it might be wise to give a claim while opening a discursive space for readers to dispute interpretations (Hyland 1996).

Because they represent the writer's direct involvement in a text, something that scientists generally try to avoid, they are twice as common in humanities and social science papers than in hard sciences. So, we tend to find more statements like this:

(3) The existence of such networks did not go unnoticed by contemporaries (see, Rocke 1989), and it **seems** sensible **to assume** the men concerned **were probably** not unreflective about this patterned conduct either.

(Soc)

With hindsight, we **believe** it **might have been** better to have presented the questionnaire bilingually.

(AL)

One reason for this is there is less control of variables, more diversity of research outcomes, and fewer clear bases for accepting claims than in the sciences. Writers can't report research with the same confidence of shared assumptions so papers rely far more on recognizing alternative voices. Arguments have to be expressed more cautiously by using more hedges. In the hard sciences positivist epistemologies mean that the authority of the individual is subordinated to the authority of the text and facts are meant to 'speak for themselves'.

This means that writers often disguise their interpretative activities behind linguistic objectivity. They downplay their personal role to suggest that results would be the same whoever conducted the research. The less frequent use of hedges is one way of minimising the researcher's role, and so is the preference for modals over cognitive verbs. This is because modal verbs can more easily combine with inanimate subjects to downplay the person making the evaluation. So we are more likely to find examples like (4) in the sciences and those with cognitive verbs in the soft discipline fields (5):

(4) For V. trifidum, ANOVA showed a significant increase from L to L' and FI, which **could be interpreted** as reflecting the dynamics of fungal colonization.

(Bio)

it may be argued that the ratios obtained are high because the limit moment …

(ME)

(5) **I think** this would be a mistake.

(Soc)

We suspect that the product used in this study may have contributed to the result

(Mkt)

Scientists tend to be concerned with generalisations rather than individuals, so greater weight is put on the methods, procedures and equipment used rather than the argument. Two scientist informants commented on this kind of use:

Of course, I make decisions about the findings I have, but it is more convincing to tie them closely to the results.

(Phy interview)

You have to relate what you say to your colleagues and we don't encourage people to go out and nail their colours to the mast as maybe they don't get it published

(Bio interview)

Modals, then, are one way of helping to reinforce a view of science as an impersonal, inductive enterprise while allowing scientists to see themselves as discovering truth rather than constructing it.

3.4. Self mention

Self mention is another important feature which varies across disciplines. This concerns how far writers want to intrude into their texts though use of '*I*' or '*we*', or to use impersonal forms. Presenting a discoursal self is central to the writing process, and we can't avoid projecting an impression of ourselves and how we stand in relation to our arguments, discipline, and readers. To some extent we have to see this as a personal preference determined by seniority, experience, confidence, personality, and so on, but the presence or absence of explicit author reference is a conscious choice by writers to adopt a particular community-situated authorial identity. However, my 240 research articles, once again, show broad disciplinary preferences with 2/3 of cases in the social sciences and humanities papers (Hyland 2001).

Table 3. Self-mention in research articles (per 1,000 words)

Philosophy	5.5	Physics	4.1
Sociology	4.3	Biology	3.4
Applied Linguistics	4.5	Mechanical Engineering	1.0
Marketing	5.5	Electrical Engineering	3.3
Average	**5.0**		**2.9**

Now it's clear that writers in different disciplines represent themselves, their work and their readers in different ways, with those in the humanities and social sciences taking far more personal positions than those in the sciences and engineering. The reason for this is again that the strategic use of self-mention allows writers to claim authority by expressing their convictions, emphasizing their contribution to the field, and seeking recognition for their work (Hyland 2001; Kuo 1999). It sends a clear indication to the reader of the perspective from which statements should be interpreted and distinguishes the writer's own work from that of others. Successful communication in the soft fields depends far more on the author's ability to invoke a real writer in the text, emphasizing their own contribution to the field while seeking agreement for it.

(7) **I argue** that these critics partly misread Thompson's cultural materialism. (Soc)

I bring to bear on the problem **my own experience**. This experience contains ideas derived from reading **I have done** which might be relevant to **my puzzlement** as well as **my personal contacts** with teaching contexts.

(AL)

So self-mention can help construct an intelligent, credible, and engaging colleague by presenting a confident and authoritative authorial self:

Using 'I' emphasizes what you have done. What is yours in any piece of research. I notice it in papers and use it a lot myself.

(Soc interview)

The personal pronoun 'I' is very important in philosophy. It not only tells people that it is your own unique point of view, but that you believe what you are saying.

It shows your colleagues where you stand in relation to the issues and in relation to where they stand on them. It marks out the differences.

(Phil interview)

In the hard sciences, as I noted earlier, researchers are generally seeking to downplay their personal role in the research to highlight the phenomena under study, the replicability of research activities, and the generality of the findings. Scientists, then, try to distance themselves from interpretations in ways that are familiar to most EAP teachers. Either using the passive voice (8), dummy 'it' subjects (9), or by attributing agency to inanimate things (10):

(8) Splicing of an entirely different set of chloroplast introns **appears to be** dependent on chloroplast ribosomes.

(Bio)

(9) **It was found that** a larger stand-off height would give a smaller maximum shear strain when subjected to thermal fatigue…

(ME)

(10) **The images** demonstrate that the null point is once again well resolved and that diffusion is symmetric

(Phy)

By subordinating their voice to that of nature, scientists rely on the persuasive force of lab procedures rather than the force of their writing. As this biologist told me:

I feel a paper is stronger if we are allowed to see what was done without 'we did this' and 'we think that'. Of course we know there are researchers there, making interpretations and so on, but this is just assumed. It's part of the background. I'm looking for something interesting in the study and it shouldn't really matter who did what in any case. ... In theory anyone should be able follow the same procedures and get the same results.

(Bio interview)

In contrast, in the humanities and social sciences, the first person allows writers to strongly identify with a particular argument and to gain credit for an individual perspective:

Using 'I' emphasizes what you have done. What is yours in any piece of research. I notice it in papers and use it a lot myself.

(Soc interview)

> *The personal pronoun 'I' is very important in philosophy. It not only tells people that it is your own unique point of view, but that you believe what you are saying. It shows your colleagues where you stand in relation to the issues and in relation to where they stand on them. It marks out the differences*
>
> *(Phil interview)*

By marking your views with the first person, you leave readers in no doubt of your stance while claiming credit for what you are saying. It is a powerful way of demonstrating an *individual contribution* and establishing a claim for *priority*. It is also worth pointing out that these differences are not only found in research articles but are repeated in undergraduate essays, post graduate theses and dissertations, and in textbooks. This means that they influence what students read, write and are assessed on and so permeate their perceptions and understandings, as can be seen in these comments from masters students in Hong Kong:

> *I don't think the use of "I" is appropriate as it gives personal opinions.*
>
> *(CS MSc Interview)*

> *I think it's not necessary to emphasize "self" in the report, "self" is not important. What is important is what I did in the research. After all, I think the study of science is not a human-oriented thing.*
>
> *(EE MSc Interview)*

3.5. Directives

Another feature which supports the idea of specificity is directives. These are devices which instruct the reader to perform an action or to see things in a way determined by the writer (Hyland 2002). They are largely expressed through imperatives (e.g. *consider*, *note*, *imagine*) and obligation modals (such as *must*, *should*, and *ought*). Overall, they direct readers to three main kinds of activity: Textual, physical and cognitive.

- **textual acts**: direct readers to another part of the text or to another text (e.g. *see Smith 1999*, *refer to table 2*, etc.)
- **physical acts** direct readers how to carry out some action in the real-world (e.g. *open the valve*, *heat the mixture*).
- **cognitive acts** instruct readers how to interpret an argument, explicitly positioning readers by encouraging them to *note*, *concede* or *consider* some argument or claim in the text.

Generally, explicit engagement is a feature of the soft disciplines, where writers are less able to rely on the explanatory value of accepted procedures, but directives are a potentially risky tactic as they instruct readers to act or see things in a way determined by the writer (Hyland 2002). As a result, most directives in the soft fields are textual, directing readers to a reference or table rather than telling them how they should interpret an argument. So examples like these are common in the social sciences:

(11) *see Steuer* 1983 for a discussion of other contingencies' effects. (Mkt)

Look at Table 2 again for examples of behavioristic variables. (Mkt)

For transcription conventions *please refer to* the Appendix. (AL)

Two of my soc sci respondents noted this in their interviews:

> *I am very conscious of using words like 'must' and 'consider' and so on and use them for a purpose. I want to say 'Right, stop here. This is important and I want you to take notice of it'. So I suppose I am trying to take control of the reader and getting them to see things my way.*
>
> *(Soc interview)*

> *I am aware of the effect that an imperative can have so I tend to use the more gentle ones. I don't want to bang them over the head with an argument I want them to reflect on what I'm saying. I use 'consider' and 'let's look at this' rather than something stronger.*
>
> *(AL interview)*

Argument in the hard knowledge fields, in contrast, is formulated in a highly standardised code. Succinctness is valued by both editors and scientists and directives allow writers to cut directly to the heart of matters. Because of this we find a high proportion of cognitive directives here which explicitly position readers by leading them through an argument or emphasising what they should attend to:

(12) What **has to be recognized** is that these issues…….. (ME)

Consider the case where a very versatile milling machine of type M5... (EE)

A distinction **must be** made between cytogenetic and molecular resolution. (Bio)

My informants noted this in their interviews:

> *I rarely give a lot of attention to the dressing, I look for the meat – the findings – and if the argument is sound. If someone wants to save me time in getting there then that is fine. No, I'm not worried about imperatives leading me through it.*
>
> *(EE interview)*

> *I'm very conscious of how I write and I am happy to use an imperative if it puts my idea over clearly. Often we are trying to work to word limits anyway, squeezing fairly complex arguments into a tight space.*
>
> *(ME interview)*

3.6. Bundles

The final example of disciplinary specificity I want to mention is lexical bundles, or frequently occurring word sequences. These are a key way of shaping text meanings and contributing to our sense of distinctiveness and naturalness in a register. So collocations like *as a result of* and *it should be noted that*, help identify a text as belonging to an academic register while *in pursuance of*, and *in accordance with* mark out a legal text. Using a corpus of 120 research articles and 120 post-graduate dissertations in four disciplines I found that the most common bundles in this academic corpus of 3.5 million words were *on the other hand*, *at the same time* and *in the case of*, all of which occurred over 100 times per million words (Hyland 2008).

There are, however, some interesting disciplinary differences. The Electrical engineering texts contained the greatest range of high frequency bundles with 213 different 4-word strings, and also the highest proportion of words in the texts occurring in 4-word bundles. Biology, on the other hand, had the smallest range of bundles, the fewest examples, and the lowest proportion of texts comprised of words in bundles. So the electrical engineering texts were most dependent on prefabricated bundles and used many sequences not found in the other disciplines, perhaps because of the fact that technical communication is relatively abstract and graphical. This means that language constructs an argument by linking data or findings in routinely patterned, formulaic ways with the same forms used repeatedly.

There are also considerable differences across disciplines in the 4-word bundles. The top 20 most common ones are shown in Table 4 with items that occur in all four disciplines marked in bold and those in three disciplines shaded (Hyland 2008).

Table 4. Most frequent 4-word bundles in 4 disciplines (bold = 4 disciplines/ shaded = 3 disciplines)

Biology	Electrical Eng	Applied Ling	Business Studies
in the presence of	**on the other hand**	**on the other hand**	**on the other hand**
in the present study	as shown in figure	at the same time	**in the case of**
on the other hand	**in the case of**	in terms of the	at the same time
the end of the	is shown in figure	on the basis of	at the end of
is one of the	it can be seen	in relation to the	on the basis of
at the end of	as shown in fig	**in the case of**	as well as the
it was found that	is shown in fig	in the present study	the extent to which
at the beginning of	can be seen that	the end of the	the end of the
as well as the	can be used to	the nature of the	significantly different from zero
as a result of	the performance of the	in the form of	are more likely to
it is possible that	as a function of	as well as the	the relationship between the
are shown in figure	is based on the	at the end of	the results of the
was found to be	with respect to the	the fact that the	the hang seng index
be due to the	is given by equation	in the context of	the other hand the
in the case of	the effect of the	is one of the	in the context of
is shown in figure	the magnitude of the	in the process of	as a result of
the beginning of the	at the same time	the results of the	the performance of the
the nature of the	in this case the	in terms of their	hong kong stock market
the fact that the	it is found that	to the fact that	is positively related to
may be due to	the size of the	in the sense that	are significantly different from

The table clearly shows the extent of disciplinary specificity with just two forms in all four disciplines (*on the other hand* and *in the case of*) and a handful in three fields. In fact, over half of all items in the top 50 bundles in each discipline don't occur in the top 50 of any other discipline. Perhaps unsurprisingly, the greatest similarities are between cognate fields, so that business studies and applied linguistics share 18 items in the top 50 with *on the basis of*, *in the context of*, *the relationship between the*, and *it is important to* exclusive to these two fields. Similarly, biology and electrical engineering have 16 bundles in common, with *it was found that*, *is shown in figure*, *as shown in figure*, *is due to the*, and *the presence of the* not in the social science lists at all.

The functions of these sequences also reveals disciplinary specificity, with a broad split across the hard and soft fields. Table 5 shows that ***research-oriented bundles***, which refer to real world activities, make up about half of all bundles in the sciences and ***text-oriented bundles,*** which focus on argument, comprise half those in the social sciences. ***Participant bundles***, which focus on the writer or reader of the text, provide a structure for interpreting a following proposition, conveying the writer's individual stance and personal engagement with readers, and these are twice as common in the more discursive fields social science fields.

Table 5. Distribution of functions of bundles by discipline (%)

Discipline	**Research-oriented**	**Text-oriented**	**Participant-oriented**	**Totals**
Biology	48.1	43.5	8.4	100
Electrical Eng	49.4	40.4	9.2	100
Applied Linguistics	31.2	49.5	18.6	100
Business Studies	36.0	48.4	16.6	100
Overall	41.2	45.5	13.2	100

Once again, these uses reflect the argument patterns in the two domains. So we can see how text-oriented examples function to connect aspects of argument (11) while those in the sciences point to research and findings (12):

(11) The term 'linguistics' might be too narrow *in terms of the* diverse knowledge-base and expertise that is required.

(AL)

The *purpose of this paper* is to investigate the perceptions of consumers in the Hong Kong market toward fast food.

(BS)

(12) *The structure of the* coasting-point model can be divided into three areas

(EE)

The DNA was precipitated *in the presence of* 2.5 volumes of ethanol and 0.1 volume of 3.0 M sodium acetate pH.

(Bio)

The relatively substantial presence of these items in the hard sciences reflects the fact that these disciplines place considerable emphasis on precision, particularly to ensure the accurate understanding of procedures and results. In contrast, the text-oriented string which were particularly marked in the soft fields reflects a more discursive and evaluative patterns of argument, where persuasion is more explicitly interpretative and less empiricist.

4. Conclusions

Corpus studies reveal that the features I have presented here all occur and behave in dissimilar ways in different disciplinary environments. The ways that we use language are situated in domains of knowledge and ways of talking about knowledge, so that labels like reports, articles and conference presentations are not universals but just names that give our work a shorthand convenience. There are clear pedagogical implications of these studies in that the findings suggest that EAP is not an activity concerned with training students in generic language skills, but a way of developing new kinds of literacy. Language education at university is a means of equipping students with the communicative skills to participate in particular academic cultures.

The fact that writers in different fields draw on different resources to develop their arguments, establish their credibility and persuade their readers means that EAP teachers need to take the disciplines of their students, and the ways these disciplines create texts, into account in their classroom practices. The results therefore provide evidence for impressions about language use which have been around for some years, and Ballard and Clanchy's (1991) point from nearly three decades ago is worth repeating:

> *Just as modes of analysis vary with disciplines and with the groups that practise them (physicists, psychologists, and literary critics), so too does language. For the student new to a discipline, the task of learning the distinctive mode of analysis... is indivisible from the task of learning the language of the discipline...One area of development cannot proceed without the other.*

The value of corpus research in this endeavour then, is not that it produces a list of the features of disciplinary discourses, but that it can uncover more sophisticated understanding of disciplinary communities. Corpus studies provide a richer picture of what it means to be a member of an academic discourse community and the ways members work together to understand the world. The research I've presented points to just a few of the ways that communities are constituted through discourse and the different resources members draw on to develop their arguments, establish their credibility and persuade their readers.

References

Baldry, A. (2000). *Multimodality and multimediality in the distance learning age.* Campobasso: Palladino.

Ballard, B., and J. Clanchy (1991). "Assessment by misconception: cultural influences and intellectual traditions". In: L. Hamp-Lyons (ed.). *Assessing second language writing in academic contexts*. Norwood, NJ: Ablex.

Biber, D. (1988). *Variation across speech and writing*. Cambridge: CUP.

Biber, D. (2006). *University language: a corpus-based study of spoken and written registers*. Amsterdam: Benjamins.

Coffin, C., Curry, M., Goodman, S., Hewings, A., Lillis, T., and J. Swann (2003). *Teaching academic writing: A toolkit for higher education*. London: Routledge.

Faigley, L. (1986). "Competing theories of process: a critique and a proposal". *College Composition and Communication*, 48: 527–542.

Fløttum, K., Dahl, T. and T. Kinn (eds.) (2006). *Academic Voices – Across languages and disciplines.* Amsterdam/Philadelphia: John Benjamins.

Geertz, C. (1983). *Local knowledge: Further essays in interpretive anthropology*. New York: Basic Books.
Gergen, K.J. and T.J. Thatchenkery (1996). Organisational science as social construction: postmodern potentials. *The Journal of Applied Behavioral Science*, 32 (4): 356–377.
Gilbert, S.F. (1995). Introduction: Postmodernism and Science. *Science in Context 8*: 559–561.
Gimenez, J. (2009). Beyond the academic essay: Discipline-specific writing in nursing and midwifery. *Journal of English for Academic Purposes* 7 (3): 151–164.
Halliday, M.A.K. (1989). *Spoken and written language*. Oxford: OUP.
Hinkel, E. (2002). *Second language writers' texts*. Mahwah, NJ: Earlbaum.
Hyland, K. (1996). Writing without conviction? Hedging in scientific research articles. *Applied Linguistics* 17 (4): 433–454.
Hyland, K. (1999). Academic attribution: citation and the construction of disciplinary knowledge. *Applied Linguistics* 20 (3): 341–267.
Hyland, K. (2001). Humble servants of the discipline? Self-mention in research articles. *English for Specific Purposes* 20.3: 207–226.
Hyland, K. (2002). Directives: power and engagement in academic writing. *Applied Linguistics* 23: 215–239.
Hyland, K. (2004). Disciplinary discourse*s*. Ann Arbor, MI: University of Michigan Press.
Hyland, K. (2008). "As can be seen: Lexical bundles and disciplinary variation". *English for Specific Purposes* 27 (1): 4–21.
Hyland, K. (2009). *Academic discourse*. London: Continuum.
Hyland, K. and M. Bondi (eds.) (2006). *Academic discourse across disciplines*. Frankfort: Peter Lang.
Kuhn, T. (1962). *The Structure of Scientific Revolutions*. Chicago: Chicago University Press.
Kuo, C.-H. (1999). The use of personal pronouns: Role relationships in scientific journal articles. *English for Specific Purposes*, 18.2: 121–138.
Swales, J. (2004). *Research genres*. Cambridge: Cambridge University Press.
Wells, G. (1992). "The centrality of talk in education". In: K. Norman (ed.). *Thinking voices: the work of the national oracy project*. London: Hodder and Stoughton.

Keywords and Key Lexical Bundles as Cues to Knowledge Construction in RAs in Economics

Silvia Cacchiani

Abstract: Numerous studies have recently focussed on lexical bundles, or extended collocations which we encounter in specific genres more frequently than expected by chance. As such, they help characterize disciplinary discourses. Using the tools of corpus linguistics, we explore a 2.7 million word corpus, focussing on discourse signalling devices, and 5-word, 4-word, and 3-word bundles in particular. This enables us to identify the basic means of knowledge construction in research articles in economics as against research articles in history and business/marketing. Data analysis provides compelling evidence for seeing discourse signals in RAs in economics as realizing conditional prediction and empirical hypothesis within the macro-speech acts of hypothesis, analysis/interpretation/generalization, and prediction.

Keywords: analysis/interpretation/generalization, (conditional) prediction, (empirical) hypothesis, disciplinary variation, discourse signals/discourse signalling, key bundles, keywords, knowledge construction, (macro-)speech acts, RAs in economics.

1. Reasons, aims, methodology

Research articles (RAs) have long been a major concern for EAP researchers. Corpus compilation and query tools have increasingly enabled researchers to detail lexico-grammatical and organizational features of different genres, and shifting the focus on other genres and on cross-disciplinary, cross-generic, and cross-linguistic variation has brought new insights into the whys and wherefores of RAs.

While corpus research has gone a long way in recording and identifying points of overlap and dissimilarities across genres, languages and disciplines, one point that has not received much attention so far is providing quantitative evidence for discourse analytical investigation carried out manually within the framework of speech act theory. In the light of this, we shall use the tools of corpus linguistics in order to provide clear evidence for the claim that knowledge construction in RAs in economics amounts to the complex interplay of the macro-speech acts of *hypothesis*, *analysis/generalization*, and *prediction* (cf. Merlini Barbaresi 1983). Indeed, economists (Brandis 1968) see *prediction* as a distinctive feature of their disciplinary discourse, and *hypothesis*, *analysis* and *generalization* as ancillary to it. Evidence for this comes from Merlini Barbaresi's (1983) manual investigation of RAs in economics, which enables her to assess the relevance of *prediction* within the genre, categorize more and less frequent and distinctive speech acts, and also highlight relevant lexico-grammatical and organizational devices.

We therefore address the issue of discourse signalling in English RAs in economics in order to concentrate on knowledge construction within the genre. To this purpose, Section 2 verifies our working hypothesis: if *prediction* is a distinctive feature of the discourse of economics and economics RAs in particular, then cross-disciplinary comparison within the humanities will bring to the fore the related linguistic devices variously realizing this macro-speech act. We use the HEM-corpus of research articles[1], a collection of around 2,700,000 tokens equally distributed among the HEM-Economics (HEM-E), HEM-History (HEM-H), and HEM-Marketing (HEM-M). As a first step, we download a keyword list (Mike Scott's 1997 and following) of individual words (§ 2) in the HEM-E as against the HEM-H and HEM-M. Specifically, banking on research on lexical bundles, genre- and disciplinary variation (Biber *et al.* 1999, Biber 2006, Cortes 2006, Hyland 2008), we assume that whereas keywords for individual words might give us some cues to the disciplinary-specific discourse practices of research articles in economics, these are closely mirrored by key 5-word, 4-word, and 3-word bundles. We therefore adapt to our purposes previous classifications of the discourse functions of lexical bundles (§ 3), and in § 3.1 we provide an overview and discussion of the main functions by key lexical bundles in the discourse in economics. Some conclusive remarks and suggestions for future research follow in § 4.

2. Keywords in economics

In this section we compare wordlists from the HEM-E and the HEM-H subcorpora to test whether discourse-signalling devices clearly marking prediction and related macro-speech acts are "key" (cf. Scott 1997) in the HEM-E, i.e. unusually frequent in comparison with the HEM-H. The HEM-M is also used as a reference corpus in order to validate the results. Table 1 and Table 2 give a breakdown of the most salient one-word keywords in the HEM-E,

1 The HEM corpus of research articles was built and is currently held at the University of Modena and Reggio Emilia. The texts were downloaded from a panorama of academic journals in order to cover a good range of subdisciplines within economics (*HEM-Economics*: HEM-E), history (*HEM-History*: HEM-H), and business/marketing/ management (*HEM-Marketing*: HEM-M) in the years 1999–2000. For more on this point: http://www.cla.unimo.it.cofin/.

respectively contrasted with the HEM-H and the HEM-M. We use italics for the words present in both frequency lists.

Table 1. Keywords (keyness) [HEM-E; HEM-H]

N	WORD	FREQ.	HEM-E. LST %	FREQ.	HEM-H. LST %	KEYNESS
1	*is*	44.683	1,71	18.537	0,76	9.526,10
4	*are*	19.918	0,76	6.697	0,27	6.015,50
7	model	6.575	0,25	594	0,02	5.443,30
11	*table*	4.405	0,17	329	0,01	3.900,20
15	*results*	4.242	0,16	341	0,01	3.663,7
19	we	11.833	0,45	4.293	0,18	3.173,80
26	variables	2.640	0,1	94		2.800,10
46	*variable*	1.821	0,07	83		1.839,70
47	*if*	7.728	0,3	3.037	0,12	1.806,3
48	data	2.749	0,11	417	0,02	1.765,30
53	sample	1.997	0,08	162		1.718,60
59	will	5.794	0,22	2.051	0,08	1.613,40
65	can	6.663	0,26	2.756	0,11	1.414,00
73	*probability*	1.467	0,06	107		1.307,30
92	*estimated*	1.227	0,05	77		1.115,10
103	estimates	1.157	0,04	75		1.069.5
111	models	1.527	0,06	219		1.013,70
135	*assume*	1.225	0,05	156		868,3
141	hypothesis	1.146	0,04	138		835,7
146	may	4.838	0,19	2.228	0,09	816,2
171	be	16.541	0,63	0,5243	0,46	740,4
179	*implies*	948	0,04	105		719,5
203	*case*	3.341	0,13	1.453	0,06	639,7
218	*follows*	1.012	0,04	171		605,8
246	analysis	2.109	0,08	784	0,03	542,1
252	hence	1.180	0,05	283	0,01	530,8
263	*assumption*	993	0,04	209		503
330	due	1.014	0,04	277	0,01	397,9
353	therefore	1.854	0,07	793	0,03	367,4

N	WORD	FREQ.	HEM-E. LST %	FREQ.	HEM-H. LST %	KEYNESS
360	*assumed*	905	0,03	243		362
377	findings	503	0,02	70		339,1
383	*denote*	379	0,01	28		336,3
384	*suppose*	492	0,02	67		335,7
384	mean	879	0,03	246	0,01	335,5
402	shows	1.091	0,04	374	0,02	318,7
409	*then*	3.252	0,12	1.828	0,07	312,4
423	expectations	593	0,02	123		304,1
437	conditional	313	0,01	19		294,7
439	*denotes*	259		6		292,9
449	likely	1.245	0,05	494	0,02	268,8
454	find	1.320	0,05	543	0,02	282,7
460	analyse	340	0,01	33		273,3

Table 2. Keywords (keyness) [HEM-E; HEM-M]

N	WORD	FREQ.	HEM-E. LST %	FREQ.	HEM-M. LST %	KEYNESS
3	the	198.074	7,58	334.918	6,04	6.723,90
5	*is*	44.683	1,71	59.130	1,07	5.574,10
11	fig	1.912	0,07	42		3.980,70
32	*if*	7.728	0,3	8.888	0,16	1.515,50
37	*table*	4.405	0,17	4.114	0,07	1.407,90
75	*case*	3.341	0,13	3.364	0,06	910,3
95	since	2.369	0,09	2.190	0,04	772,3
131	*then*	3.252	0,12	3.836	0,07	584,5
136	*suppose*	492	0,02	132		578,2
150	*assume*	1.225	0,05	966	0,02	526,7
167	*hence*	1.180	0,05	948	0,02	494,1
168	*implies*	948	0,04	662	0,01	488,8
172	*probability*	1.467	0,06	1364	0,02	472,7
201	*follows*	1.012	0,04	411	0,01	298,7
220	*assumed*	905	0,03	724	0,01	381,5

N	WORD	FREQ.	HEM-E. LST %	FREQ.	HEM-M. LST %	KEYNESS
233	expected	2.340	0,09	2.904	0,05	361,6
236	*estimated*	1,227	0,05	1.250	0,02	361,8
247	*assumption*	993	0,04	886	0,02	346,4
272	*denote*	379	0,01	170		314,7
349	there	4.710	0,18	7.432	0,13	246,7
379	*are*	19.918	0,76	36.996	0,67	227,03
493	shall	206		88		178,1
495	*denotes*	259		142		178, 1

The keywords in Table 1 and Table 2 can be further grouped on the basis of their meaning and function. Specifically, the following categories can be identified:

1. Keywords used to instantiate or name the relevant (macro-)speech act:
   i. hypothesis (HEM-E; HEM-H: *assume* [863,3], *assumption* [503], *suppose* [335,7]; HEM-E; HEM-M: *suppose* [578,2], *assume* [526,7], *assumed* [381,5], *assumption* [346,4]);
   ii. analysis/interpretation/generalization (HEM-E; HEM-H: *estimated* [1.115,10], *estimates* [1.069,5], *analysis* [542,1], *find* [282,7], *analyse* [273,3]; HEM-E; HEM-M: *estimated* [361,4]);
   iii. prediction (HEM-E; HEM-H: *expectations* [304,1]; HEM-E; HEM-M: *expected* [361,6]).

2. Keywords which point to different degrees of certainty, possibility, and probability in hypothesis, analysis and prediction:

   i. modals (HEM-E; HEM-H: *will* [1.613,40], *can* [1.414], *may* [816,2], *likely* [268,8]; HEM-E; HEM-M: *x*);
   ii. other verbs (HEM-E; HEM-H: *denote* [336,3], *shows* [318,7], *implies* [719,5]; HEM-E; HEM-M: *implies* [488,8], *denote* [314,7]);

3. Markers of hypothesis or cause and reason relations (cf. Siepmann 2005) between elements within the clause or sentence (HEM-E; HEM-H: *if* [1.806,3], *case* [639,7], *hence* [530,8], *due* [397,9], *therefore* [367,4], *then* [312,4]; HEM-E; HEM-M: *if* [1.515,50], *case* [910,3], *since* [772], *then* [584,5], *hence* [494,1], *follows* [298,7]);

4. Self-reflexive markers pointing to the disciplinary-specific reliance on visuals (HEM-E; HEM-H: *table* [3.900,20]; HEM-E; HEM-M: *fig* [3.980,70]), *table* [1.407,90]);

5. Keywords used to describe and present data (HEM-E; HEM-H: *results* [3.663,7], *data* [1.765,30], *findings* [339,1]; HEM-E; HEM-M: *x*), and statistics (HEM-E; HEM-H: *model* [5.443,30], *variables* [2.800,10], *variable* [1.839,70], *sample* [1.718,60], *probability* [1.307,30], *models* [1.013,70], *hypothesis* [835,7], *mean* [335,5], *conditional* [294,7]; HEM-E; HEM-M: *probability* [472,7]).

What these preliminary keyword lists seem to suggest is a high saliency of items related to hypothesis (*if*, *assum**, *suppose*, *case*) and data analysis/interpretation/generalization in the discourse of economics.

3. Classifying lexical bundles

Lexical bundles (Scott 1997: clusters) are word strings that (a) appear in a genre more frequently than expected by chance, and (b) occur in multiple texts in that genre (Biber *et al.* 1999). Given corpus size and research purpose, we set our frequency cut-off point at 2 hits per million word.

If scientific *prediction* in the discourse of economics is *conditional*, or, in other words, bears on a set of factors or variables and on their interaction, then *prediction* follows from and overlaps with the speech acts of hypothesis and data analysis/generalization, based on the application of a given model within a main argumentative text type (Werlich 1976). Most importantly, there must be some lexical bundles that are key in this respect, also pointing to the writer's different degrees of commitment to the truth of his proposition (in the sense of Searle and Vandervecken 1985; see Hyland's 2008 *stance signals*).

Although lexical bundles are identified on the basis of frequency across texts, they can serve different functions and subfunctions. Slightly adapting Hyland (2008: 13–19), a development from Biber (2006) and Biber *et al.* (2004), we set forth a restricted number of categories and subcategories which bring together insights from research in speech-act theory, genre analysis and discourse studies:

1. *Research-oriented* bundles, which comprise markers of *location*, *procedure*, *quantification* and *identification*, *description*, and *focus*:
   a) *Location* bundles indicate time and place also in analyses and process descriptions (*in the first period*, *in the long-run*). *Text deixis* (*in Table 2*),

a subset of *referential expressions* (term from Biber *et al.* 2004), can be also seen as belonging here;

b) *Procedure* bundles point to research methodology and purpose. We include here also preliminary definitions, assumptions, and parameters and variables setting, e.g. *is defined as the*, *it is assumed that*;

c) *Quantification* bundles comprise Hyland's (2008) quantification bundles which specify quantity, identifying a position on a scale of quantity (cf. Biber *et al.*'s 2004) or pointing to a movement along the scale (*is the number of*, *an increase in the*, *more than # of the*). They comprise Biber *et al.*'s (2004) *referential expressions* which serve as *quantity specification*, but are extended in this study to include classificatory adjectives clearly pointing to an objective measure of frequency (*not significantly different*, *negative and significant*), and existential *there* and other forms exclusively used to introduce data description or exposition (cf. Biber *et al.*'s 2004 *identification* bundles), e.g. *that there is no*, *there exists a*, *there are a number of*);

d) *Description* bundles cover a wide range of vocabulary used to present data, usually for the possible outcomes of the application of a model. They make reference to physical or abstract entities. Some clusters here are *the first-order condition for*, or *the dependent variable is*. Inclusion into the class is not always straightforward, and marginal members of the category clearly point to quantification. One such example is *the probability of*: while it is used to describe the data presented in detailed statistics tables, it provides a quantitative description of the likely occurrence of a particular event. We also group here bundles which specify more general tangible and intangible attributes and features which do not point to a scale of quantity (*the nature of the*);

e) *Focus* bundles (in the sense of Hyland 2008)[2]: they provide information on the subject under investigation within a given research field (*of central bank independence*, *the inflation tax*, *Morck et al.*), which are not relevant to our investigation, are not listed in the tables;

2. *Text-oriented* bundles help organize the text and structure its meaning as a message or argument:

a) *Transition signals*: they explicitate additive and contrastive relations between elements (*on the other hand*), and, we may want to add, coherence relations that do not seem to fit under the following subsets;

b) *Resultative signals*, or markers of inferential or causative relations (*this is due to the*, *these results suggest that*);

2 The term *focus* is not taken here to cover Biber *et al.*'s (2004) *focus* bundles, which comprise *discourse organizers* which serve a *topic introduction* function (*if you look at*, *in this chapter we*) and *referential expressions* used to signal *identification* (*is one of the*).

c) *Structuring signals*, or text-reflexive cues that organize stretches of discourse or direct the reader elsewhere (*paper is organized as follows*, *table # and table #*, *as shown in table*);
d) *Framing signals*, which delimit an argument by specifying cases, circumstances of application of models and variables within the model. Some examples are *in the presence of the*, *if and only if*, *if the number of*[3];

3. *Participant-oriented* bundles, which focus on personal and impersonal (terms from Biber *et al.* 2004) stance and engagement features:
   a) *Stance features*, i.e. writer's attitude and evaluation (*are more likely to be*, *may be due to*);
   b) *Engagement features*, directly addressing the reader (*it can be seen that*, *it is straightforward to show*).

Since stance and engagement features may overlap to some extent, keeping in mind that the main purpose of this paper is to provide evidence for equating disciplinary knowledge constructions with the speech acts of hypothesis, analysis/generalization and prediction, no attempt is made at this stage to set them apart.

Strictly speaking, these categories are not mutually exclusive. Quite the contrary, bringing together features pertaining to various levels of analysis, they may overlap to different extents. To take one example, procedure bundles used for preliminary definitions, assumptions, and parameters and variables setting may also show engagement or stance features (*can be interpreted as*, *can be thought of as*, *I estimate the model using*). This, however, does not seem to detract from the ability of the above-mentioned categories to serve as a framework for distinguishing key discourse-signalling lexical bundles.

3.1. Key lexical bundles in economics

Tables 3 and 4 below provide a breakthrough of 5-word, 4-word and 3-word lexical bundles. The following data are given for the top ten bundles in each category: ranking, lexical bundle, frequency in the HEM-E, keyness. 4-word and 3-word lexical bundles are not included when they can be subsumed under one or more 5-word lexical bundles with similar keyness value. Single underlining is used for the top 25 5-word, 4-word, and 3-word items in the respective frequency list. As will be seen, inclusion within categories is not always

3 Note that Hyland's (2008) *framing signals* represent a small fraction of Biber *et al.*'s (2004) *intangible framing attributes*, a subset or their *referential expressions* which, the other way round, cut across Hyland's (2008) transition, resultative and framing signals.

straightforward. Most importantly, some lexical bundles do not seem to serve one single function at a time (e.g. *when there are* [quantification; framing signal], *purpose of this paper is* [procedure signal; structuring signal], *results are consistent with the* [resultative signal; procedure]), might serve different functions within different contexts (*can be thought of as* [procedure signal or stance signal], *in the form of a* [description or structuring signal]), or can only be assigned a specific function on the basis of their collocational behaviour within larger bundles (*of this paper is* in *the purpose of this paper is* [procedure and structuring signal], or *is beyond the scope of*, but not *the scope of this paper*, in *is beyond the scope of this paper* [structuring signal]).

Table 3. Keywords (keyness) for 5-word, 4-word, and 3-word bundles [HEM-E; HEM-H]

RESEARCH-ORIENTED

LOCATION

5-word: **7 in table # and table [58; 80,3]; 21 panel B of table # [38; 51,4]**; 50 the left-hand side of [29; 38,2]; 74 in columns # and # [25; 33]; 88 on the right-hand side [24; 31,6]; 101 column # of table # [22; 30,3]

4-word: 42 in the second period [74; 97,6]; 208 in table # are [37; 48,8]; 498 a model in which [24; 31,6]; 499 in section # and [24; 31,6]

3-word: 40 in the model [207; 272,9]; 59 in our model [166; 218,8]

PROCEDURE

5-word: **10 we assume that the [133; 175,5]; 11 is assumed to be [130; 171,4]; 17 it is assumed that the [50; 52,7]**; 37 the null hypothesis of no [32; 42,2]; 108 are summarized in table # [31; 28,7];

4-word: **11 is assumed to be [130; 171,4]; 24 it is assumed that [114; 116,1]**; 35 is defined as the [78; 108,2]; 45 can be written as [70; 92,3]; 50 is a function of [94; 87,3]; 71 the change in the [90; 78,6]; 92 is the number of [65; 70,6]; 117 is the sum of [21; 27,7]; 140 can be used to [87; 59]; 219 the hypothesis that [131; 111,3] ...

3-word: 341 I assume that [67; 88,3]

QUANTIFICATION

5-word: 114 more than # of the [21; 27,7]

4-word: **1 an increase in the [326; 354,4]; 3 significant at the # level [102; 134,5]**; 26 significantly different from zero [86; 113,4]; 30 the # level of significance [35; 46,1]; 62 of an increase in [61; 80,4]; 47 is equal to the [81; 90,8]; 89 to an increase in [74; 71,8]; 92 is the number of [65; 70,6]; 193 the total amount of [38; 50,1]

3-word: 208 is less than [118; 116,3]; 220 the higher the [97; 11,2]; 222 magnitude of the [106; 111,2]; 245 is higher than [81; 106,8]; 246 equal to # [98; 106,6]; 463 is lower than [58; 76,5]

DESCRIPTION

5-word: 70 the relative size of [26; 34,3]; 72 the standard deviation of the [25; 33]; 73 the present value of the [25; 33]; 79 the dependent variable is the [24; 31,6]; 100 the first-order condition for [23; 30,3]; 103 the short-run Phillips curve [22; 29]; 58 is a decreasing function of [28; 36,9]; 59 is a function of the [37; 36,9]; 69 is an increasing function of [26; 34,3]; 102 an increasing function of the [22; 29]; 124 there is a continuum of [20; 26,4]; …

4-word: **7 as a function of [184; 192,7];** 33 the distribution of the [80; 105,5]; 61 the effect of a [73; 80,7]; 63 the standard deviation of [61; 80,4]; 71 the change in the [90; 78,6]; 73 the coefficient on the [59; 77,8]; 74 the first-order conditions [59; 77,8]; 92 is the number of [65; 70,6]; 94 the effect of the [56; 70,3]; 99 the probability that the [52; 68,6]; 104 as a percentage of [51; 67,2]; 112 the probability of a [50; 65,9]; …

3-word: 375 probability of a [64; 84,4]

TEXT-ORIENTED

TRANSITION SIGNALS

4-word: 77 on the other hand [562; 281]

RESULTATIVE SIGNALS

5-word: 26 table # reports the results [36; 47,5]; 44 these results are consistent with [30; 39,5]; 49 table # presents the results [29; 39,5]; 77 results are presented in table [25; 33]; 78 table # shows the results [24; 33]; 84 this is due to the [24; 31,6]; 111 this result is consistent with [21; 27,7]; 128 does not depend on the [20; 26,4]; 129 leads to an increase in [20; 26,4]

4-word: 66 results are consistent with [61; 80,4]; 87 is determined by the [66; 71,9]; 110 the reason is that [66; 65,9]; 157 these results suggest that [42; 55,4]; 166 this implies that the [41; 54]; 170 the results of this [55; 53,3]; 179 is due to the [61; 52,3]; 458 may be due to [25; 33]

3-word: 38 depends on the [281; 282,9]; 89 implies that the [195; 184,5]; 232 so that the [196; 108,3]; 381 such that the [88; 84,3]

STRUCTURING SIGNALS

5-word: **1 table # and table # [184; 242,6]; 2 paper is organized as follows [102; 134,5]; 4 the paper is organized as [77; 101,5]; 5 are presented in table # [78; 101,5]; 8 are reported in table [56; 76,5]; 9 of this paper is to [60; 64,3]; 13 purpose of this paper is [42; 55,4]**; 26 table # reports the results [36; 47,5]; 49 table # presents the results [29; 38,2]; 51 are given in table # [29; 38,2]; …

4-word: 38 table # reports the [76; 100,2]; 422 as shown in the [26; 34,3]

FRAMING SIGNALS

5-word: **23 in the presence of the [112; 124,2]**; 48 with respect to the [164; 90,6]; 67 if and only if the [26; 34,3]; 109 in the case of a [45; 28,7]

4-word: **5 if and only if [150; 197,7]**; 155 the case in which [42; 55,4]; 157 for the case of [42; 55,4]; 165 the case where the [41; 54]; 457 if the number of [25; 33]; 478 other things being equal [24; 31,6]

PARTICIPANT-ORIENTED

STANCE AND ENGAGEMENT FEATURES

5-word: **12 can be thought of as [43; 59,3]; 20 are more likely to be [38; 50,1]**; 31 it can be shown that [48; 46,1]; 40 is easy to see that [31; 40,9]; 89 it can be seen that [24; 31,6]; 139 it is easy to see that; 146 can be interpreted as a [19; 25]; 161 is straightforward to show that [19; 25]

4-word: 188 it can be shown [56; 50,3]; 458 may be due to [25; 33]

3-word: 186 may not be [199; 123,1]; 318 consider the case [83; 93,4]; 471 we consider the [88; 76,2]

Table 4. Keywords (keyness) for 5-word, 4-word, and 3-word bundles [HEM-E; HEM-M]

RESEARCH-ORIENTED

LOCATION

5-word: **4 at the end of the [85; 193,5]; 5 are presented in table # [78; 177,6]; 6 at the beginning of the [62; 141,2]; 11 in table # and table [58; 132]; 18 the right-hand side of [45; 104,5]**; 40 panel B of table# [37; 84,2]; 65 the second half of the [31; 70,6]; 76 the left-hand side of [29; 66]; 106 in columns # and # [25; 56,9]; 134 in the rest of the [23; 52,4]; 184 in the second half of [20; 45,5]; ...

4-word: 343 in the present model [21; 30,4]; 348 the model presented in [21; 30,4]

3-word: 466 in our model [166; 54,3]; 494 in panel A [37; 53,5]

PROCEDURE

5-word: **14 it is assumed that the [50; 111,6]; 25 can be thought of as [43; 97,9]**; 37 is a function of the [37; 84,2]; 159 is the sum of the [21; 47,8]; 203 can be interpreted as a [19; 43,3]; 220 as a measure of the [18; 41]; 225 I estimate the model using [18; 41]

4-word: 15 is assumed to be [130; 91,5]; 17 it is assumed that [114; 89,1]; 38 it is shown that [49; 68,8]; 79 we assume that the [133; 53,5]; 91 is the ratio of [36; 52,1]; 264 where T is the [23; 33,3]

3-word: 44 the null hypothesis [233; 150,6]; 153 suppose that the [84; 89,6]

QUANTIFICATION

5-word: 46 to an increase in the [36; 82]; 50 the # level of significance [35; 79,7]; 61 the rate of growth of the [31; 70,8]; 133 there are two types of [23; 52,4]; 147 there are a number of [22; 50,1]; 156 more than # of the [21; 47,8]; 159 is the sum of the [21; 47,8]; 198 to the size of the [19; 43,3]; 450 increase in the rate of [13; 29,6]; 452 at the # level in [13; 29,6]

4-word: **3 an increase in the [326; 251,4]; 5 the growth rate of [135; 195,2]; 8 significant at the # [145; 127,5]; 9 the size of the [322; 127,3]; 14 significantly different from zero [86; 97,0]**; 250 is equal to # [24; 34,7]; 401 there is some evidence that [14; 31,9]

3-word: **21 is equal to [215; 208,1]**; 34 the increase in [223; 166,8]; 251 rise in the [73; 71,1]

DESCRIPTION

5-word: **8 as a function of the [77; 175,5]**; 37 is a function of the [37; 84,2]; 52 effect of a change in [34; 77,4]; 74 percentage change relative to the [30; 68,3]; 81 the probability of success of [29; 66]; 86 is a decreasing function of [28; 66]; 100 is an increasing function of [26; 59,2]; 121 in the form of a [24; 54,6]; 113 the standard deviation of the [25; 56,9]; 122 the first-order conditions for [24; 54,6]; …

4-word: 48 the present value of [65; 64,5]; 63 a positive relation between [40; 57,8]; 66 the distribution of the [80; 57,7]; 91 is the ratio of [36; 52,1]; 94 the opportunity cost of [77; 51,8]; 131 probability of success of [31; 44,8]; 132 the real value of [31; 44,8]; 139 the coefficient on the [59; 44,1]; 140 the ratio of the [72; 44,1]; 148 percentage change relative to [30; 43,4]; 157 the elasticity of substitution [29; 41,9]; …

3-word: 131 long-run equilibrium [94; 94,4]; 163 present value of [163; 86,6]; 256 a positive relation [49; 70,6]; 273 the variance of [117; 68,1]; 276 the symmetric equilibrium [47; 68]; 500 the critical value [50; 53,2]

TEXT-ORIENTED

TRANSITION SIGNALS

5-word: 353 as is the case with [14; 31,9]; 354 as well as in the [14; 31,9]; 357 such a way that the [14; 31,9]; 427 in the same way as [13; 29,6]

4-word: **7 on the other hand [152; 150,9]**

RESULTATIVE SIGNALS

5-word: **10 as a result of the [59; 134,3]; 23 due to the fact that [44; 100,2]**; 45 table # reports the results [36; 82]; 34 the results in table # [38; 86,5]; 45 table # reports the results [36; 82]; 48 on the basis of the [35; 79,7]; 70 these results are consistent with [30; 68,3]; 82 table # presents the results [29; 66]; 95 is due to the fact [26; 59,2]; 11 results are presented in table # [25; 56,9]; 116 this is due to the [24; 54,6]; …

4-word: 84 in such a way that [29; 66]; 400 it follows that the [31; 28,5]

STRUCTURING SIGNALS

5-word: **1 table # and table # [184; 418,9]; 2 is organized as follows [102; 232,2]; 5 are presented in table # [78; 177,6]; 12 are reported in table # [56; 127,5]**; 26 purpose of this paper is [42; 95,6]; 43 the remainder of the paper [36; 82]; 44 are shown in table # [36; 82]; 62 are summarized in table # [31; 70,6]; 64 as shown in table # [31; 70,6]; 170 table # shows that the [20; 45,5]; …

4-word: 137 as shown in fig [31; 44,8]

3-word: 412 the basic model [77; 56,9]

FRAMING SIGNALS

5-word: **19 in the context of the [45; 102,5]; 20 in the case of a [45; 102,5]; 25 as in the case of [44; 100,2]**; 29 from the point of view [41; 93,3]; 55 in the context of a [33; 75,1]; 94 if and only if the [26; 59,2]; 210 in the sense that the [18; 41]; 221 the extent to which the [18; 41]; 278 in the absence of any [16; 36,4]; 298 in the presence of a [15; 34,1]; 343 if the probability of success [14; 31,9]; 345 if this is the case [14; 31,9]

4-word: **6 if and only if [150; 151,3]**; 152 in the first case [48; 42,9]
3-word: 98 with respect to [594; 108,3]

PARTICIPANT-ORIENTED

STANCE AND ENGAGEMENT FEATURES

5-word: **16 it can be shown that [48; 109,3]; 21 it should be noted that [45; 102,5]; 25 can be thought of as [43; 97,9]**; 33 it is important to note [39; 88,8]; 49 it is easy to see [35; 79,7]; 66 is easy to see that [30; 68,3]; 87 it is clear that the [28; 63,7]; 88 it is not possible to [28; 63,7]; 99 it is well known that [26; 59,2]; 108 it is interesting to note [25; 56,9]; 112 it is possible that the [25; 56,9]; …

Setting aside text-oriented structuring signals which clearly mark organization or purpose of the paper (e.g. HEM-E; HEM-H: *paper is organized as follows, the paper is organized as*, *purpose of this paper is*), it is easy to see that the remaining discourse signals point to knowledge construction within RAs in economics as the complex interplay of the macro-speech acts of hypothesis, analysis/interpetation/generalization, and (though less represented) prediction. In other words, economic analysis is characterized by the use of models and recurrence to exogenous and endogenous variables as specified by the model. The model enables the analyst to make claims and predictions in the form of hypotheses based on facts. Specifically, the following features are brought to the fore:

1. Hypothesis is a distinctive feature of RA in economics (e.g. HEM-E; HEM-H: *we assume that the, it is assumed that the, is assumed to be, it is assumed that*; HEM-E; HEM-M: *it is assumed that the*).
2. Other procedural signals clearly mirror the reliance of RAs in economics on definitions and parameter settings, which are functional to data analysis and discussion (e.g. HEM-E; HEM-H: *is a function of the, is the sum of the*; HEM-E; HEM-M: *can be thought of as, is the ratio of*).
3. Frequent and highly salient items comprise quantification, description, location and structuring bundles. Quantification markers mirror the dependence of Economics rhetoric on statistics and numeric representation. Related to this, the density of location, description and structuring signals clearly mirrors the reliance of Economics rhetoric on visual representation of numeric data, which enables the writer to identify a reliable basis for his/her inferences and assertions. Some examples: quantification markers such as *an increase in the, significant at the # level, significantly different from zero, the # level of significance* (HEM-E; HEM-H), and *to an increase in the, the # level of significance, an increase in the*, *the size of the, significantly different from zero* (HEM-E; HEM-M); location, as in *in table # and table, panel B of table #, the left-*

hand side of (HEM-E; HEM-H), and *at the end of the, at the beginning of the, in table # and table* (HEM-E; HEM-M); description markers such as *the standard deviation of the, the present value of the, the dependent variable is the* (HEM-E; HEM-H), and *percentage change relative to the, the probability of success of* (HEM-E; HEM-M); structuring markers such as *table # and table #, are presented in table #, are reported in table* (HEM-E; HEM-H and HEM-E; HEM-M).

4. Applying a model to data analysis also calls for setting and testing individual variables in turn. Specifying cases, particular instances and conditions under which a statement can be accepted and pointing to limitations within the argument is a function of framing devices, which score high among the top 25 key bundles in all frequency lists. Some examples: *in the presence of the, with respect to the, if and only if the, if and only if, the case in which, other things being equal* (HEM-E; HEM-H), and *in the context of the, in the case of a, as in the case of, if and only if* (HEM-E; HEM-M).
5. Data interpretation and generalizations based on reliable inferences are introduced by resultative signals that help discuss research processes and outcomes: *table # reports the results, these results are consistent with, this is due to the, leads to an increase in, is determined by the, the reason is that, these results suggest that, this implies that the* (HEM-E; HEM-H); *as a result of the, due to the fact that, on the basis of the, these results are consistent with, explained by the fact that, these results suggest that the* (HEM-E; HEM-M). Different degrees of certainty can combine with generalizations and data interpretation. Salient stance and engagement bundles are: *it can be shown that* (HEM-E; HEM-H), *can be thought of as* (HEM-E; HEM-H and HEM-E; HEM-M), *it is easy to see* (HEM-E; HEM-M). Whereas prediction is not widely represented, stance bundles clearly marking this speech act are *are less likely to be*, *is more likely to be, can be shown that the*, *must be the case that* (HEM-E; HEM-H), and, among the top 25 key bundles, *are more likely to be* (HEM-E; HEM-M).

4. Conclusions

The results presented above provide compelling evidence for seeing knowledge construction in RAs in economics as resulting from the complex interplay of the macro-speech acts of *hypothesis, analysis/generalization*, and *prediction*. Specifically, such speech acts account for the presence of a number of keywords and key bundles which, the other way round, flesh out prediction in the relevant expository–argumentative text type. Whereas, however, the discourse signals we identified are clearly amenable to hypothesis, analysis, generalization and interpretation, prediction seems to be relatively underrepresented.

Conditional prediction and empirical hypothesis are precisely a good place to start when looking at RAs in economics from the point of view of genre and (second language) writing[4]. Whereas EAP textbooks essentially cover the language of definitions, data analysis, description of visuals and data interpretation to different extents (see e.g. Swales and Feak 2004, a multidisciplinary course), prediction has not received much attention in the EAP textbooks, possibly because of its highly disciplinary-specific nature. One preliminary question for further consideration, therefore, is expansion of the present analysis to explore conditional prediction in RAs in economics, which amounts to an empirical hypothesis, or a claim, supported by data analysis and bearing on a set of controlled factors and variables. Once we posit a premise-conclusion coherence relation as variously marking prediction, investigation can cover a number of discourse signals, also labelling devices (in the sense of Francis 1994, Moreno 2004), comprising, but not restricted to, the ones identified here (e.g. *if, then, assum**, *therefore, thus, suggest**, *denote*, *impl**, *due, follow**, *hypothes**, *estimat**, *result**, *find**, *likely, in the context of the*, *if and only if, these results suggest that*, *the results show that*, *it is easy to show that*, *this implies that the*).

References

Brandis, R. (1968). *Principles of Economics*. Homewood, Illinois: Irwin.

Biber, D. (2006). *University Language. A Corpus-based Study of Spoken and Written Registers*. Amsterdam: Benjamins.

Biber, D., Conrad, S. and V. Cortes (2004). "*If you look at* ...: lexical bundles in university teaching and textbooks". *Applied Linguistics*, 25 (3): 371–405.

Biber, D., Johansson, S., Leech, G., Conrad, S. and E. Finegan (1999). *Longman Grammar of Spoken and Written English*. Harlow: Pearson.

Francis, G. (1994). "Labelling discourse: an aspect of nominal-group lexical cohesion". In: M. Coulthard (ed.). *Advances in Written Text Analysis*. London: Routledge: 83–101.

Hyland, K. (2008). "*As can be seen*. Lexical bundles and disciplinary variation". *English for Specific Purposes*, 27: 4–21.

Merlini Barbaresi, L. (1983). *Gli atti del discorso economico: la previsione. Status illocutorio e modelli linguistici nel testo inglese*. Parma: Edizioni Zara.

4 See, in this respect, Neugeboren's (2005) concise and accessible set of guidelines (not an EAP textbook) for students writing essays in economics. Note, however, that whereas it takes the student through the stages of planning, revising and editing essays and other term assignments, it does not provide extensive coverage of the language of economic analysis.

Moreno, A.I. (2004). "Retrospective labelling in premise-conclusion metatext: an English-Spanish constrastive study of research articles on business and economics". *Journal of English for Academic Purposes*, 3: 321–339.

Neugeboren, R. (2005). *The Student's Guide to Writing Economicsi*. London: Routledge.

Scott, M. (1997). *Wordsmith Tools*. Oxford: Oxford University Press.

Searle, J.R. and D. Vandervecken (1985). *Foundations of Illocutionary Logic*. Cambridge: Cambridge University Press.

Siepmann, D. (2005). *Discourse Markers across Languages. A Contrastive Study of Second-level Discourse Markers in Native and Non-native Text with Implications for General and Pedagogical Lexicography*. London: Routledge.

Swales, J.M. and C.B. Feak (2004) [2nd ed.]. *Academic Writing for Graduate Students. Essential Tasks and Skills*. Michigan: Michigan University Press.

Werlich, E. (1976). *A Text Grammar of English*. Tübingen: Quelle und Meyer.

Conceptualising Spatial Relationships in Academic Discourse: a Corpus-Cognitive Account of Locative-Spatial and Abstract-Spatial Prepositions

Christoph Haase and Josef Schmied

Abstract: Prepositions form closed lexical classes in English which provide direct and metaphorical cognitive access to complex scenes and events. In texts from the natural sciences, these lexical items help build conceptualisations of abstract relationships that cannot be perceived directly, i.e. as phenomena occurring in any given observer's space-time. The separation of the perceivers from their objects thus demands semantic extensions (Hooper 2004) that is often grammaticalized in satellites, i.e. prepositional phrases (Slobin 1996, Schmied 2002). However, image-schemata provide a systematic motivational basis for extensions of prepositional senses from a prototypical spatial sense to a less representative, more abstract spatial sense.

Keywords: abstractness, academic English, cognitive linguistics, conceptualisation, corpora, image schema, metaphor, prepositions, popular science, spatial.

1. Introduction

This contribution looks into distributional properties of prepositions as heads of prepositional phrases that negotiate a mapping function between direct/literal and extended/metaphorical meaning when dealing with abstract concepts. If metaphor is an initial expansion of an identity relation then the lexicalization of the metaphor establishes some sort of imagery identity which depends on the discrete abstractness of the concepts.

Data is based on the Corpus of Specialised and Popular ACademic English (SPACE), which focuses on different sub-disciplines from the natural sciences and contains a wide spectrum of prepositions, as the following example illustrates:

> **0033AX** ***Measuring the Small-Scale Power Spectrum of Cosmic Density Fluctuations***
> ***Through 21 cm Tomography Prior to the Epoch of Structure Formation***
> [...] An unavoidable collisionless component **of** the cosmic mass budget beyond CDM, is provided **by** massive neutrinos (see [16] **for** a review). Particle physics experiments established the mass splittings **among** different species which translate **into** a lower limit **on** the fraction **of** the dark matter accounted for **by**

neutrinos **of** f. > 0.3%, while current constraints based **on** galaxies **as** tracers **of** the small scale power imply f. < 12% [17]... […]

Obviously, the prepositional meanings vary between “literal”, topological/ directional, and “abstract”, metaphorical senses. Contrary to expectation, the example above shows that either none of the spatial-core prepositions refer to concrete entities (*into a lower limit*) or, if they do, they have no spatial meanings (*on galaxies*). Instead, the systematic use of metaphor facilitates the building of abstract event frames.

We try to apply conceptualizations to the interpretation of corpus data. We hypothesize that quantitative arguments provide the tools for automatising said mapping function as plottable image schemata that enable more coherent and direct access to texts with high degrees of abstraction. The information necessary for the image schemata can be obtained from parallel texts in which the more direct and literal mappings occur in the “softer” sciences like biology as opposed to “hard” sciences like physics. An investigation of PPs and an assignment of roles to the parts of the construction (commonly: landmark, localizer and modalizer) will render a complex picture of prepositional use. The landmarks (usually NPs) will serve as locative or abstract complements with peripheral or direct import (cf. Lopez Rúa 2005).

Thus, a quantitative corpus-based profile of spatial-abstract mappings can generate comparable text-type specific signatures. We can compare usage of different prepositions (in particular *at*, *on* and *over*) in different text-types (according to sub-discipline or readership). We can also show that a continuum of abstractness exists on which concrete and purely abstract notions form the poles and hypothetical-concrete and imperceptible-concrete notions occupy middle ground. Thus a corpus-cognitive approach provides new insights into academic discourse.

2. Rationale and methodology

2.1. Aims

The aims of this study are to discuss (simple) prepositions in academic discourse, to present complementary empirical methodologies taken from cognitive linguistics (theory-wise) and corpus-linguistics (methodology-wise). For the linguistic material, a top-down cognitive analysis of spatial prepositions is presented which is complemented by a bottom-up quantitative analysis of prepositions in texts. We will compare different academic domains from the hard sciences (physics) and the soft sciences (biosciences and genetics) in order to test hypotheses on conceptualization specifics. Further, we will attempt to debunk some myths of spatial prepositions that are usually associated with their conceptual-metaphorical import.

2.2. Methodology

Data material

All samples were extracted from the Corpus of Specialised and Popular Academic English (SPACE), compiled from 2007 at Chemnitz University of Technology and available for registered users in the 2009 version online.

The corpus was compiled and structured according to discourse communities.

The corpus has a transparent binary structure: part 1 is comprised of the academic texts, part 2 of the popular texts. The corpus is parallel in the sense that a text in part one corresponds to a particular text in part 2. We started out with the observation that articles in popular science publications such as *Scientific American* or *New Scientist* commonly based on one current publication in an academic journal. The findings there are routinely put into a form accessible to a general-interest reader who has an academic background but is not necessarily an expert in the field of the article. As the original article is usually referenced in the popular article, we started compiling both original and popularized versions of the articles.

The academic texts were retrieved from 3 preprint servers for academic publications.

First, there is a set of 46 articles from *arXiv.org* which specializes in physics and astrophysics. The second set is comprised of 61 articles from the *Proceedings of the National Academy of Sciences* (pnas.org), usually biochemistry and genetics. The third part has 50 medical texts from the *Public Library of Science – Medicine* (PLoS). An equal number of corresponding articles were taken from the *New Scientist* magazine which routinely publishes popular summaries of the latest results in science.

Table 1. Corpus content and structure

subcorpus	descriptors	word count
arXiv	physics, astrophysics, computer science, quantum mechanics	161,864
New Scientist – physics	physics, astrophysics, Computer science, quantum mechanics	40,694
Proceedings of the National Academy of Science (PNAS)	biochemistry, genetics, genetical engineering, microbiology	267,105

New Scientist - biosciences	biochemistry, genetics, genetical engineering, microbiology	30,499
Public Library of Science – Medicine (PLoS), New England Journal of Medicine	medicine, virology, clinical psychology, public health	217,254
New Scientist – medicine	medicine, virology, clinical psychology, public health	17,050
total		**734,466**

Substructure and academic readership

The components of the corpus correspond to different readerships. For the study on prepositions, a 2x3x2 matrix was used in order to capture the subdomains in the two sciences (three subdomains each) and in readerships (two readerships in total)

Table 2. Word counts and readership-specific ratio

readership	**specialised**	**popular**	**popular : special**
domains	**words**	**words**	**%**
physics	**arXiv**	**NS**	
quantum physics	115,981	15,327	13
particle physics	26,384	4,574	17
astrophysics	167,553	18,119	11
bioscience	**PNAS**	**NS**	
biochemistry	53,212	7,114	13
genetics	183,312	19,101	10
microbiology	53,139	5,176	10
average	99,930	11,568	12

The table shows that the specialized texts in the sample are on average 12 times longer than their popularized counterparts.

2. Concepts & Methods

2.1. Conceptualization universals

Current research on academic language reflects a transition phase from the study of readership-oriented application towards efficient distribution of research results. Whereas the former is evidenced by numerous publications e.g. Barass, 2002 and other “guides to better writing for scientists, engineers and students”, (as in Day 1995 or Guess, 1997 in several current editions), research on information distribution is a domain of linguistic inquiry, e.g. Daston and

Galison 2007. A research question related to psycholinguistics and to cognitive linguistics is what makes academic texts (in principle) understandable. The markup in the following text shows that prepositions go a long way to establish coherence and cohesion between abstract concepts:

> 0033AX Measuring the Small-Scale Power Spectrum of Cosmic Density Fluctuations Through 21 cm Tomography Prior to the Epoch of Structure Formation
> [...] An unavoidable collisionless component **of** the cosmic mass budget **beyond** CDM, is provided **by** massive neutrinos (see [16] **for** review). Particle physics experiments established the mass splittings **among** different species which translate **into** a lower limit **on** the fraction **of** the dark matter accounted **for by** neutrinos **of** f. > 0.3%, **while** current constraints based **on** galaxies **as** tracers **of** the small scale power imply f. < 12% [17]... [...]

This text appears to be – for laypersons – rather impenetrable, if only for lexical and terminological reasons. However, the question arises, why is this text – in principle – understandable for academic laypersons? As this study shows, prepositional configurations can help readers to understand relationships between concepts, even though these concepts themselves may be opaque or unknown. From a cognitive linguistic point of view, it could be argued that speakers parse prepositions into Venn diagrams and flowcharts, as shown in Figure 1.

The prepositional sketch enables readers to establish a spatial, processual and set-inclusion/exclusion view on the text segment presented. This is also related to the conventional view in cognitive linguistics, in which speakers conceptualize prepositions as extensions of image schemata (Figure 2).

The question remains open then whether speakers employ a gestalt-like strategy of conceptualizations as in figures 1 and 2 and in what way this helps to map cognitive conceptualizations onto texts of difficult or abstract content.

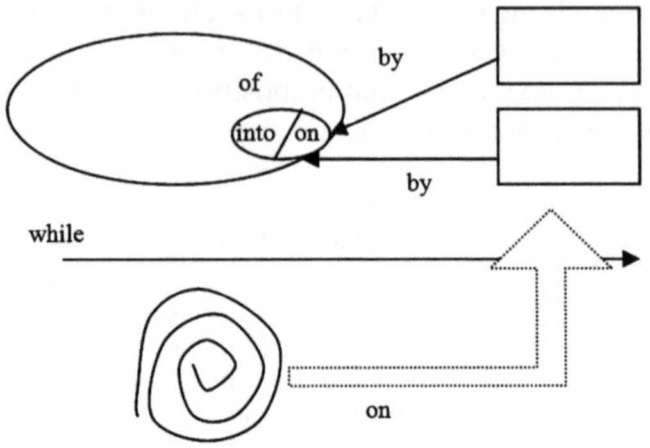

Figure. 1. Sketch of spatial configurations in 0033AX

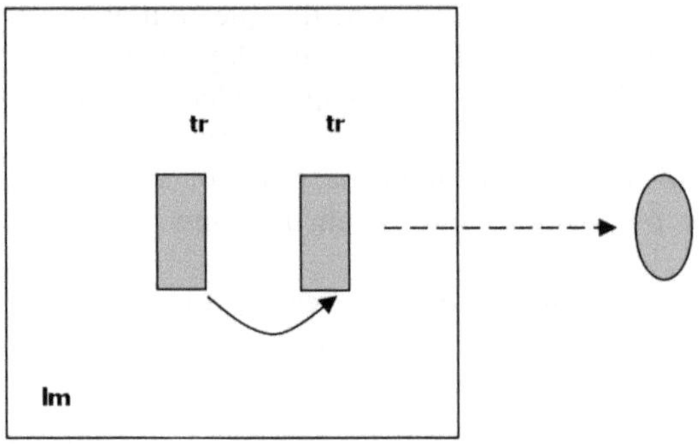

Figure 2. Landmark/trajectory image schemata in 0033AX

2.2. Conventionalized knowledge transfer

The diffusion of knowledge in academic texts bases on the conventional view that between author/speaker A and reader/listener B persists a contract into which both, A and B, enter and in which both share the knowledge that A knows that B does not know everything that A knows (about subject X). Therefore, in a cognitive linguistic view, A uses strategies of conventionalized conceptualization to express him/herself comprehensibly, i.e. A uses gestalt-like universals and up to a large extent metaphor because A relies on a shared cognitive endowment with B – both communication partners have nearly analogue instruments of bodily perception.

The academic discourse situation can be defined from a pragmatic point of view as a contract of diffusing knowledge which author/speaker and reader/listener enter into and in which both, the author A and the reader B, share the knowledge that A knows that B does not know everything that A knows. A therefore uses conventionalized strategies to express him/herself comprehensibly, which means in practice that semantic means such as metaphor and hedging are used to enable B to make the "transition from 'dubbing' to 'epistemic access'" (Kuhn 1993: 536). As a consequence, A relies on the shared cognitive endowment with B: both possess instruments of bodily perception so that any phenomenon that can be hypothesized or measured in the natural sciences can be mediated and transferred into comprehensible processes. As most of these phenomena (especially in the physical sciences concerned with phenomena at the quantum level of nature) are completely removed from any bodily experience, these linguistic markers are important and can be made subject of systematization. The separation of the perceivers from their objects thus demands semantic extensions (Hooper 2004: 1742). The systematization can be studied in the figurative uses of verbs of perception.

2.2. Diffusion of Knowledge in Academic Texts

The transfer processes mentioned above can be systematized with two principal linguistic strategies, the use of hedge expressions and the use of metaphor. The author A of an academic text knows that the research space in reality has more than 'ideal' cases of e.g. Newtonian mechanics but is blurred at the deepest levels of description, especially when microphysical phenomena are considered. Any formulation of natural laws is based on this. In describing these phenomena it is common to hedge an utterance by saying "Ideally,…". A caveat is that the intended listeners (of a related academic background) share this knowledge and do not need the explicit hedge marking. However, the author B of a popular academic text (who at the same time is an informed reader of A knows that his/her readers (of a general academic background) do not share the knowledge of A. In this case the gradient precision of the hedge expression has a different function.

A different way to represent phenomena is the verisimilar representation in which physically plausible schemata stand in for the abstract laws at work. A third way is the systematic use of metaphor in which the shareability of source domains between A and B facilitates communication (Jackson and Michon 1992: 352).

Metaphor and hedging are thus used as simplification strategies. They act as cues for the reader to stage the unknown and abstract elements within a referential structure that is graspable and offers an internal logic (Coulson and

Oakley 2000: 176). We can therefore extend the schema of diffusion of knowledge and state that the reader C of the texts of B enters into a contract that academic contents will be processed and force-fed via hedges and metaphors. The procedure in this contract is that C knows that C does not know what either A or B know so C expects lexicalization patterns that coincide with C's knowledge by the transformation of specific knowledge (target domain) to generic knowledge (source domains). This is the cognitive core of metaphorization and can be paraphrased as having implicit similes in perception. If metaphor is an initial expansion of an identity relation (e.g. Gibb and Wales 1990: 200) then the lexicalisation of the metaphor establishes some sort of imagery identity which depends on the discrete abstractness of the concepts. In that sense, the relation is also a simile relation because the direct perception works like: 'look at X like look at a representation/reification of X'.

The problem of the research space in reality is that the researcher is not really 'looking' and the data is not really 'there' to be looked at. Making abstract measurements accessible for bodily perceptions means that the results have to be transformed into representations of data which are generally metaphors for the 'real thing' and which curbs propensity even further. The metaphorical approach is thus a strategy of finding a cause-effect isomorphism in which representations of causes and representations of effects become perceivable gestalts.

3. Core hypotheses

3.1. The Cognitive Linguistic stance

The conventional view in Cognitive Linguistics emphasises that aspects of grammaticalization are metaphorical extensions of spatial experience (e.g. Langacker 2000). This means for the spatial use in language for phenomena removed from experience that this is a metaphorical use because space can be experienced. As Trim notes, one of the reasons why different historical periods produce large numbers of items from similar conceptual metaphors is due to the way we perceive our environment. The very essence of our forms of perception appears not only to be figurative in nature but also inevitably so… (Trim 2007: 7)

Recently, this has led to embodied meaning concepts (in the framework of Fauconnier and Turner 2002) in which mappings of image-schemata occur and a trajector (TR) moves in some spatial relationship to a landmark (LM) cf.

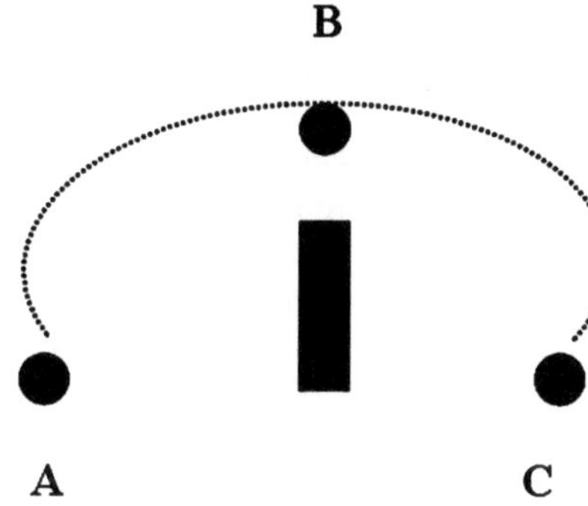

Figure 3. The cat jumped over the wall, Tyler and Evans 2003: 71

For the discussion of spatial phenomena in scientific texts this means that the source domains are selected from the field of conventional, bodily perception, whereas the primarily interesting and therefore lexicalised target domains are merely spatial, abstract configurations of entities. In this sense, Vandeloise (2006: 139) asks, "whether space is conceived as an abstract entity described by geometry or topology or as an indispensable host for our experience of the world".

3.2. The reductionist challenge

In this study, we offer a reductionist challenge to this conundrum by noting that

a) most spatial experience is never "close-range", i.e. concerning the direct and immediate spatial vicinity of the speaker, therefore it is mostly abstract anyway, and
b) wherever in an academic context it is close-range, i.e. concerning the immediate spatial vicinity of the experimentator, it concerns the representations of phenomena in the form of pieces of data, screen-readouts, diagrams or scales.
c) Thesc representations can be experienced directly.

Setting out from these observations we felt the need for a terminological split of the term metaphor when applied to prepositions. We call therefore those prepositions abstract-spatial in which the phenomena are abstract-perceptible and are based on conventional (1st order) metaphor. We call another group of prepositions locative-spatial for close-range lexicalisation and for representations of abstract phenomena. These are based on 2nd order metaphor. This enables us to formulate the following hypotheses:

1) The representational level makes academic texts comprehensible
2) No metaphor is involved where representations of abstract phenomena are concerned
3) Two types of metaphor need to be isolated:
   1st order metaphor: from perceptible to abstract
   2nd order metaphor: from representational-perceptible to abstract
4) Academic discourse is largely based on 2nd order metaphor

Whereas hypotheses 1–3 are largely overarching frames of research which have the character of axioms, hypothesis 4) can be verified or falsified using corpora.

4. Data discussion

The following segment from specialised academic discourse was taken from the SPACE Corpus (0036AX arXiv:astro-ph/0402584 v125Feb 2004) in order to illustrate the distribution of first-order and second-order metaphor in spatial prepositions (first-order in **bold**, second-order *italics*):

AN OBSERVATIONAL SIGNATURE OF EVOLVED OCEANS ON EXTRA-SOLAR TERRESTRIAL PLANETS

> *For* Lyman a, we assume Gaussian line profiles *with* .0 = 8.23 × 109 Hz and .0 = 4.11 × 1010 Hz, corresponding to 1 km s-1 and 5 km s-1, respectively. *With* the column densities given above then t (0) 14 (V = 1 km s-1) and t (0) 0.5 (V = 5 km s-1). As discussed below, such lines are detectable if the velocity shift **of** the star is sufficiently different **from** that **of** the interstellar matter *in* the line-of-sight. Higher order Lyman lines **in** the circumstellar gas might be detectable even if observations *at* the stellar Lyman a velocity are dominated *by* intervening interstellar absorption. We also note that the absorption lines produced **by** the wind **from** the planet are likely to be narrower than any structure *in* the Lyman emission lines that are produced *in* the chromospheres *of* main sequence G-type (Combi and Smythe 1988, Redfield et al. 2002) where the gas temperature is typically greater than 10,000 K and even the thermal width *of* the hydrogen emission is greater than 10 km s-1. We now consider how different levels *of* stellar activity can affect the observability **of** the planet's wind. The mass loss rate *of* hydrogen **from** the planet (.ZH) scales *with* LEUV and thus there is a tendency **for** more active stars to drive a stronger planetary wind and produce a larger projected column density *of* hydrogen. However, an increase in the stellar activity also leads *to* an increase *in* the neutral hydrogen ionization rate (JH) and thus a decrease *in* the size **of** the neutral cloud **around** the planet (R0). To assess these

> combined affects, we compute the value <u>of</u> the equivalent width *of* an absorption averaged **over** the disk **of** the star when the planet lies **toward** the very center **of** the star. We ignore any limb brightening or darkening **of** the stellar atmosphere. Because there are so many uncertainties, we consider Doppler broadening parameters equal *to* the assumed outflow speeds *of* either 1 km s-1 or 5 km s-1. Considering main sequence stars *of* age, t*, and following Ayres' (1997) study of photo-ionization rates and Wood et al.'s (2002a) study **of** stellar winds, we assume that both JH and LEUV scale as t-2

The differentiation between two types of metaphorical use can be sketched with this extract from the sample:

> matter **in** the line-of-sight. Higher order Lyman lines **in** the circumstellar gas

Clearly, the first occurrence of *in* concerns a visible phenomenon (*line-of-sight*) of the representation of something abstract (objects arrayed in a special relationship for an observer) whereas the second *in* concerns a concrete phenomenon (*circumstellar gas*) which is conceptualised as a container, therefore a conventional, first-order metaphor applies.

Within the text, we can observe that the prepositions are taken from a small lexical range with 8 types of P in 375 words. The two hypothesized classes of prepositions can be expanded into the following top-down ontology:

Table 3. Sample prepositions in ontological classification

locative-spatial, 2nd order metaphor		**abstract-spatial, 1st order metaphor**	
item	**type**	**item**	**type**
for	abstract direction	*from*	locative direction
with	abstract inclusion - inside	*in*	locative inclusion
of	abstract inclusion – outside	*around*	locative motion
over	abstract motion	*toward*	locative direction
by2	abstract causal	*by1*	abstract correlating

The ontology can be mapped onto the distribution of prepositions in the entire corpus. This enables us to introduce a second parameter: The corpus is structured into specialized and popular academic texts. A research question that arises is therefore, is there a distributional difference of first-order and second-order metaphor between specialized and popular texts of the same or nearly the same content. The full distribution shows some remarkable frequencies for popularised texts:

Table 4. Prepositions frequencies in the POS-tagged SPACE corpus ranked (high-frequency and low-frequency items in grey)

Prep	specPhys	specBio	popPhys	popBio	total
of	8,258	10,199	1,330	1,097	20,884
in	3,563	5,557	577	619	10,316
for	2,145	2,195	208	202	4,750
with	1,513	2,056	144	173	3,886
by	1,489	1,845	162	144	3,640
at	1,118	1,221	204	164	2,707
over	129	118	16	20	283
under	74	114	16	8	212
across	11	56	17	10	94
behind	13	6	7	3	29
past	6	1	9	1	17
up	7	2	6	4	19
down	5	0	1	1	7
beneath	0	3	5	0	8

In detail, all texts show prepositions of either metaphorical type. In the study however, it made sense to separate the high-frequency items from the low-frequency items and leave an interesting middle ground of mid-frequency items as shown in the following table:

Table 5. Corpus examples for 6 hi-freq, 5 low-freq, 3 mid-freq items

Prep	Example
of	010PN The dynamics of agent-based simulations are sensitive to the fraction **of** types in the population and …
in	014AX The obtained results are shown to be **in** good agreement with a complete theory taking into account …
for	037PN the non-linguistic numerosity system is supplemented by the acquisition of symbols **for** quantities ...
with	022AX black holes can form with TeV masses through nuclear interactions of particles **with** PeV and greater energies
by	107PN Experiments were approved **by** the French ethical committee for biomedical research, and subjects gave … consent
at	015AX These investigations are aimed **at** the identification of the characteristic mass scale of the first stars
over	019AX The basic concept is simple; **over** a given time period, more probable events happen more
under	054PN The question is always, is group selection important **under** plausible conditions?
across	013AX as a result, there is a substantial correlation between the frequency of cooperation and punishment **across** groups

behind	054PN However, … , the ultimate mechanisms **behind** the difference must be the mechanisms of development
past	053PN A steeper slope indicates a steeper approach for slicing …tough foods as opposing occlusal surfaces slide **past** one another
up	004AX2 ... and in both cases the motion of the particle will indicate spin **up** the z -axis.
down	031NS ... starting with galaxy clusters and rapidly moving **down** the scale to galaxies, stars, planets and atoms.
beneath	063PN the whole swarm activity was explained in terms of northwestward migration of underground magma from **beneath** Miyakejima

The two mid-frequency items, under and across, were selected out of three mid-frequency items because they represent a reasonable intersection of ontological membership and number of occurrence. Whereas the prepositions with the highest frequencies in the corpus (like *of*, *in* with 20,000 and resp. 10,000 occurrrences) have detailed and often strongly idiomatized meanings, *over*, *under* and *across* represent compromise candidates for which we designed an ontology partly adapted from the LDOCE (Longman Dictionary of Contemporary English). The following table shows seven main meanings for *across* and *under*:

Table 6. LDOCE Ontology for 7 main meanings of *across, under*

across	**1**	**2**	**3**	**4**	**5A**	**5B**	**6**
LDOCE definition	*from one side to the other*	*toward sth on the other side*	*exists from one side of an area to the other*	*opposite side of sth*	*in every part*	*in every part*	*show how wide sth is*
code thematic relation	A2B directio n	2B direction	A-B loc.span	onB location	evLoc location	evCat spatial	wid quant.
metaphor order	**2nd**	**2nd**	**2nd**	**2nd**	**2nd**	**1st**	**2nd**
under	**1**	**2**	**3**	**4**	**5**	**6**	**7**
LDOCE definition	*below*	*less than*	*having sth done to it*	*affected/ influenc ed*	*under… condition s*	*law/ agree-ment*	*in power*
code thematic relation	bel location	<qu quantity	done (/prog) theme	aff patient	cond circumst.	agr circumst.	pow agent
metaphor order	**2nd**	**1st**	**2nd**	**2nd**	**1st**	**2nd**	**1st**

Subsequently to these conceptual preparations, all corpus files were manually tagged for membership in these semantic ontologies. Our expectation was that striking patterns would occur when different sciences as well as different readerships were compared. Furthermore, in the ontologies, there was an uneven distribution of first-order and second-order metaphor: in the ontology for *across*, only type 5B (evCat) is filled by first-order metaphor, whereas *under* is semantically more conventional with 3 types out of 7 first-order metaphor: types 2 (<qu), 5 (cond), and 7 (pow). The following tables summarise these findings in quantitative detail:

Table 7/8. Ontology text-type distribution of *across* and *under*, 1st/2nd order

across	**A2B**	**2X**	**A-B**	**onB**	**evLoc**	**evCat**	**wid**
specPhys	3	2	2	0	0	0	1
popPhys	5	0	5	1	0	0	7
specBio	9	3	12	7	3	25	0
popBio	1	1	4	0	1	1	3
overall	**18**	**6**	**23**	**8**	**4**	**26**	**11**

under	**bel**	**<qu**	**done**	**aff**	**cond**	**agr**	**pow**
specPhys	0	0	11	38	19	7	6
popPhys	3	0	7	5	2	0	0
specBio	4	5	18	34	49	3	7
popBio	0	0	3	2	1	0	1
overall	**7**	**5**	**39**	**79**	**71**	**10**	**14**

The highest overall counts were found for the ontological types of A–B (something spans from one side of the area to the other), evCat (existence in every part of something), done (having something done to something) and aff (patient affected). Three of these types are processes, two are telic and occur in passive voice lexicalisation patterns.

This 2x2 comparison of science domain and text-type enables us to compare the singular counts with the respective parameter. The metaphor view on the data accounts for the following figures:

Table 9. LDOCE Ontology by 1st-order and 2nd-order metaphors

across	**18**	**6**	**23**	**8**	**4**	**26**	**11**
under	**7**	**5**	**39**	**79**	**71**	**10**	**14**

The dearth of 1st order metaphors accounts for a total of 116 occurrences, whereas the overall 10 out of 14 types of 2nd order metaphors account for 214 occurrences in total.

In the domain-specific view, these trends show an even stronger leverage towards the dominance of second-order metaphor in academic texts:

Table 10. LDOCE Ontology by text-type

text-type	words	1st order	2nd order	1st order per 100k	2nd order per 100k
specPhys	161,864	25	64	15.44	39.54
popPhys	40,694	2	33	4.91	81.09
specBio	267,105	89	90	33.32	33.69
popBio	30,499	2	14	6.56	45.9

In this table, the interesting figures are highlighted in grey: The first observation is that second-order metaphor dominates overall, but a look at the ratios shows that it is especially dominant in the popularised versions in the respective science domains. There is no significant difference between first order and second order in the specialized biosciences but striking ratios for specialized physics, where second-order is more than double but almost 20 times the amount in popular physics (4.9 to 81) difference.

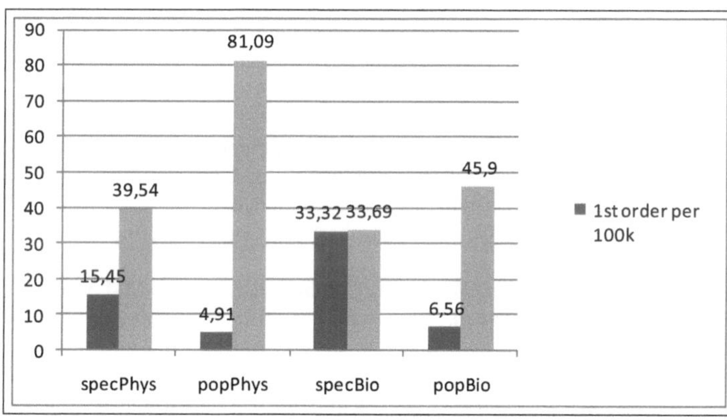

Figure 4. LDOCE Ontology 1st and 2nd order metaphors by ac. Community

The graphs in Figure 4 show the distribution in dependence on the different domains. We obtain impressively different signatures for all domains that invite substantiation (or refinement) with data from different (and larger) corpora.

5. Conclusion

The wealth of prepositional expressions in academic texts that refer to the spatial representations of abstractness in comparison to the relatively low indication of the use of conventional metaphor (in the cognitive linguistic sense) allows some tentative conclusion about the nature of argumentation in academia and a clearer statement concerning the hypotheses.

Hypothesis 4) can therefore be confirmed: Academic discourse is primarily based on 2nd order metaphor. This trend is more marked in popularised than in specialised academic discourse. The question remains, why are specBio texts exceptional? Here, 1st and 2nd order metaphor figures are extremely similar (33.32 and 33.69 per 100,000 words). Furthermore, more research is necessary to buttress claims that popularised academic texts are characterised by other markers, as in some successful case studies in the past concerning hedging, modality, cohesion, etc., cf. Haase and Schmied 2008. It is therefore necessary to expand the data base in sub-disciplines and timeframes, to extend the range of linguistic variables and possibly to develop teaching applications that raise awareness of the EAP spectrum for authors.

Corpora can therefore answer linguistic questions concerning conventions specific to scientific sub-disciplines and specific to discourse communities (as captured in the specialised – popular distinction).

References

Ahmad, K. (2006). "Metaphors in the Languages of Science?". In: M. Gotti and V. Bhatia (eds.). *New Trends in Specialized Discourse Analysis*. Bern: Peter Lang: 197–220.

Barass, R. (2002). *Scientists must write*. London: Routledge.

Coulson, S. and T. Oakley (2000). "Blending basics". *Cognitive Linguistics 11*, (3/4): 175–196.

Daston, L. and P. Galison (2007). *Objectivity*. Cambridge, MA: The MIT Press.

Day, R. A. (1995). *Scientific English. A guide for scientists and other professionals*. Phoenix: Oryx Press.

Fauconnier, G., and M. Turner (2002a). "Metaphor, metonymy, and binding". In: R. Dirven, and R. Pörings (eds.). *Metaphor and metonymy in comparison and contrast*. Berlin: Mouton de Gruyter: 469–487.

Fauconnier, G. and M. Turner (2002b). *The way we think*. New York: Basic books.

Gibb, H. and R. Wales (1990). "Metaphor and simile. Psychological determinants of the differential use of each sentence form". *Metaphors and Symbolic Activity* 5 (4): 199–213.

Guess, J. C. (1997). *Professional English in science and technology. A learner's essential companion with German equivalents*. München: Oldenbourg.

Haase, C. and J. Schmied (2008). "Clause linking in specialized and popular academic English: An investigation into scientific texts from the space corpus". In: B. Lewandowska-Tomaszczyk (ed.). *Corpus Linguistics, Computer Tools, and Applications – State of the Art*. Frankfurt, New York: Lang: 381–399.

Hooper, R. (2004). "Perception verbs, directional metaphor and point of view in Tokelauan discourse". *Journal of Pragmatics* 36: 1741–1760.

Hyland, K. (2006). *English for academic purposes. An advanced resource book* (1st ed.). London: Routledge.

Hyland, K. (2009). *Academic discourse. English in a global context*. London: Continuum.

Jackson, J. L. and J. A. Michon (1992). "Verisimilar and metaphorical representations of time". In: F. Macar, V. Pouthas, and W. J. Friedman (eds.). *Time, action and cognition. Towards bridging the gap.* Dordrecht: Kluwer: 349–360.

Kuhn, Th. S. (1993). "Metaphor in science". In: A. Ortony (ed.). *Metaphor and thought. 2nd ed.* Cambridge: Cambridge University Press: 533–542.

Langacker, R. W. (2000). *Grammar and conceptualization*. Berlin: Mouton de Gruyter.

Lopez Rúa, P. (2003). *Birds, Colours and Prepositions. The Theory of Categorization and its Applications in Linguistics*. München: LINCOM.

Schmied, J. (2002). "Prototypes, transfer and idiomaticity: an empirical analysis of local prepositions in English and German". In: L. I. Rabade and S.M.D. Suarez (eds.). *Studies in Contrastive Linguistics.* Universidade de Santiage de Compostela: 947–959.

Slobin, D. I. (1996). "Two Ways to Travel: Verbs of Motion in English and Spanish". In: Shibatani, M. and S.A. Thompson (eds.). *Grammatical Constructions: Their Form and Meaning*. Oxford: Clarendon Press.

Talmy, L. (1985). "Lexicalization patterns". In: T. Shopen (ed.). *Language typology and syntactic description III: Grammatical categories and the lexicon*. Cambridge: Cambridge University Press: 57–149.

Trim, R. (2007). *Metaphor networks. The comparative evolution of figurative language* (1st ed.). New York: Palgrave Macmillan.

Tyler, A. and V. Evans (2003). *The semantics of English prepositions. Spatial scenes, embodied meaning and cognition*. Cambridge: CUP.

Vandeloise, C. (2006). "Are there spatial prepositions?". In: M. Hickman and S. Robert (eds.). *Space in language. Linguistic systems and cognitive categories*. Amsterdam: Benjamins: 140–154.

Part Seven

TRANSLATION

Translation Memory and Textuality: Some Implications

Margaret Rogers

Abstract: The use of computer tools in the production of translations has become a popular topic for both practising professionals and scholars of translation over the last two decades. The subject has been addressed from a number of perspectives, often with a focus on issues of quality and cost. But another theme has also been emerging, namely, the relationship between the tools and the nature of the artefact which they help to fashion, text. This paper aims to explore this relationship in the context of the most popular translation tool, translation memory (TM), by asking whether the nature of the interface between the translator and the tool is helping to shape translation decisions. A discussion of the changing landscape of translation sets the scene for a brief review of translation and technology, and of aspects of the nature of text. Selected data from two TMs demonstrating a range of segmentation patterns (from phrase to paragraph) are then analysed focusing on one aspect of textuality, namely, cohesion. It is acknowledged that longer segments facilitate translation decisions relating to cohesion but concluded that other factors such as situationality and translation purpose can also shape textual patterns. Recommendations are made for future research projects using TM data.

Keywords: cohesion, peep-hole translation, Translation Memory.

1. Introduction

The central aim of this paper is to explore the use of computer-based tools in the translation of LSP (language for special purposes) texts and to consider whether this has any implications for the nature of textuality: more specifically, are modern and increasingly widespread methods of translation influencing the 'grammar' of text i.e. the way in which texts including translations are shaped? The question will be approached by looking first at the way in which modern translation practice has been developing in a professional context. This will lead to a discussion of the changing relationship between translation, translators and technology, before aspects of the nature of text itself are considered. Data from one of the most widely used tools, Translation Memory, will then be presented and analysed focusing on one aspect of textuality, namely, cohesion. Finally, some tentative conclusions are presented in terms of selected features of textuality, intertextuality and cohesion, and some suggestions are made concerning future research.

2. The changing landscape of translation

Translation as a textual practice has undergone significant changes since the days of the 19th century gentleman [*sic*] translator seeking an engaging pastime. In many areas of the world, the 20th century heralded the onset of the professionalisation of translation with the emergence of professional associations, codes of conduct, professional newsletters and journals, high-level training courses and recognised university qualifications (see, for instance, Woodsworth 1998: 42–43). This development has been accompanied by an explosion in the demand for the translation of often ephemeral *Gebrauchstexte* such as multilingual instructions for use, manuals, product descriptions, and so on. In the latter part of the last century, translation moved from being a kind of kitchen-table activity to a global business, with smaller and medium-sized companies being taken over by large international businesses offering an ever-expanding range of document services, of which translation is only one. With the business model changing to one of outsourcing to 'translation suppliers', i.e. freelancers working remotely, the use of technology is now crucial to effective collaborative working methods. The global nature of the business has also led to the need to manage large multilingual projects, with technology facilitating the management and re-use of data, including terms and their translation equivalents as well as full-text translations. So translators are now increasingly likely to work in teams (often virtually) not only with other translators but with project managers, terminologists, technical writers, desk-top publishing experts, web designers, and many others. And texts are increasingly likely to be published in non-print media for electronic dissemination, including the world wide web, mobile phones and PDAs, word processing and other software. Not only have these developments led to changes in working practices, they have also begun to challenge the nature of what we regard as 'text': communication is now increasingly fragmented in on-screen messages, menus and dialog boxes, only to be reconstituted and re-configured in many cases using software such as content management systems, with 'content' (as opposed to format) being the new text. Whilst 'text' in its fullest sense always incorporates the possibility of non-verbal components such as diagrams, drawings, illustrations, photographs, pictograms and so on, these components have taken on even more significance in the new media, owing to their functional role as navigation aids or design features of the emerging genres in which they appear.

The workflow pattern of many translators, particularly those who act as so-called 'suppliers' to large translation or document management companies, has consequently changed to reflect these developments. The practice of translation has moved from what Garcia (2000: 58) calls the 'artisan-like workflows' of a single translator working with one reviser to teams of translators working on text fragments such as Translation Memory segments extracted from source texts which, according to Pym (2008), may themselves be composites of previous multi-author texts and which have no real beginning or end. The 19th century Marxist concept of alienation, introduced to characterise the fragmentation of the industrial production of material goods through assembly lines, hovers as a spectre over the profession, raising questions about a resulting lack of pride and satisfaction of 'line workers'. In modern-day translation research and practice, the focus is less on the effect that the fragmentation of text and text-production processes may have on the translator-worker (although this is certainly worth pursuing), than on the nature and quality of the text thereby produced. Garcia (2008: 50) goes so far as to suggest that, from the perspective of 'localising' text to suit local cultural and linguistic expectations, the technology used to produce translations actually shapes the way in which texts, including translations, are written:

> ...beyond the client and the end-user, translating (and writing) for localisation is required to serve an additional and completely new type of text consumer – the TM [translation memory] itself, as the embodiment of [...] standards of consistency, repeatability and reuse.
>
> Garcia (2008: 50)

This is the perspective that I would like to explore in this contribution.

3. Translation and technology: A changing relationship

Electronic technology was first introduced into the daily practice of professional translators in the form of word processors around the 1980s, with multilingual functionality gradually becoming more common. During this period, the distinction between human and machine translation started to blur, as reflected in the terms current at that time: MAHT (machine-aided/assisted human translation) and HAMT (human-aided/assisted machine translation) (for further discussion see Quah 2006: 6–13). The 1990s saw the introduction of CAT (computer-aided/assisted translation) tools, including notably Translation Memory (TM), which allowed translators to accept translation proposals based on the matching of segments from previously translated source texts – usually sentences stored in a database of source and target texts – with segments in the new source text[1]. Translators therefore had to start working with isolated sentences on screen, one by one, sometimes only being presented with the previously untranslated segments, rather than with a full text. Two decades later,

1 TMs are usually created in one of two ways: automatically by aligning existing translations with their source text, or manually, by a human translator populating the memory database with translations, segment by segment.

this technology is well known, widely used and features prominently in many university translator training courses. To give an idea of how such matching works, an example from a TM[2] (Figure 1) shows how the new source text (ST) (in the second column) cannot be matched for segment 31 (shaded in column 3) but is partially 'translated' (i.e. pattern-matched) by the TM software in segment 33. Segment 31 has to be translated by the translator and then added to the TM database. In segment 33, just one new part or 'sub-segment' (shaded) is left to be translated by the translator[3]:

Segment number	**New Source Text**	**Target Text proposal from TM**
31	LATERAL THINKING	LATERAL THINKING
33	So you've decided you want a new Xxxxx3? But then which model do you go for: Base, Touring, Touring Plus or Sport? Each is superbly equipped. Choices, choices, choices...	So you've decided you want a new Xxxxx3? Et pour quel modèle opterez-vous: le modèle d'entrée de gamme, Touring, Touring Plus ou Sport? Ils sont tous dotés d'une abondance d'équipements. Vous avez vraiment l'embarras du choix...

Figure 1. Example of a non-match (segment 31) and a partial (sub-segment) match (segment 33) from a Translation Memory tool

Among the arguments voiced in favour of TM software are consistency (identical ST segments are always translated in the same way) and speed of working (the translator focuses on those segments for which a translation proposal is not available or only partially available from the memory). Consistency is usually related to quality (but see Rogers 2008 for a modified view), and time with cost savings. But an alternative perspective is now emerging, as noted in the previous section, namely, that the language technology may be influencing the way texts (including translations) are written. Anguished cries from translators could be heard on this topic as long as a decade ago: '...language is now being changed to fit the tools, instead of the other way round' (Mogensen 2000: 29). Examples cited by Mogensen include restrictions on the translator's freedom when creating a new TM to combine separate

2 I am grateful to an anonymous source for these data; the name of the car/model has also been anonymised for commercial reasons. This example is taken from Data Set 1: see Section 5 below. The view presented in Figure 1 is *not* the user-interface view, which only displays one segment on screen at any time.

3 I will not elaborate here on types of match and sensitivity thresholds for so-called 'fuzzy matches': for more details see Bowker 2002: 96–106.

sentences in the ST into, for example, one sentence with subordinate clauses in the target text (TT) as this would reduce the re-usability of the memory: the number of potential matches for a longer, complex sentence is likely to be lower than that for shorter simple sentences, which can more easily be re-configured. Textual decisions are therefore said to be made in some cases to suit the functioning of the TM software rather than the appropriateness of the language structures used. Mogensen describes the effect on her native Danish as producing 'machine-gun sentences', leading to, she goes on to argue, the emergence of 'a kind of simplified Danish' (2000: 30).

Other writers have been equally critical of the effect which the use of TM is said to have on the quality of TM-based translations. Bédard (2000: 45) speaks of a 'salade de phrases' (e.g. 'discontinuités terminologiques, erreurs de déictique'). Merkel (1998) has also pointed out that tensions arise between a perceived need for terminological consistency and the decontextualised nature of TM segments (e.g. in body text, headings, table cells). Along similar lines, Biau Gil and Pym (2006: 9) have suggested that '[t]ranslation memories change the way translators work', as translators are expected to 'follow the terminology and phraseology of the segment pairs included in that [memory] database rather than write the text using [their] own terminological decisions and style', possibly leading to 'a translation with no cohesive style'. A useful overview of some of the issues surrounding the use of Translation Memory tools and 'text' is given in Bowker (2006).

However, to date little empirical research has been conducted to add substance to the intuitively appealing claims made about the effects of technology on translation practice from a textual or cognitive point of view. One exception is Dragsted's work on the possible effects which the design of TM systems have on the cognitive task faced by translators (e.g. Dragsted 2008). She concludes that in her small study of English-Danish business translation, the sentence is not the professional translator's preferred unit of translation; rather it is the phrase or the clause. She proposes that paragraph segmentation may suit translators' needs better (2008: 251), avoiding what could be called a kind of tunnel vision and presumably providing a broader context for decisions relating to the preferred translation units.

4. Text: What manner of artefact is this?

Traditional models of textuality such as that of Beaugrande and Dressler (1981) are modelled on genres of text which emerged and developed largely in a paper-based communicative environment[4] in which linearity is a clear constraint on

4 Some attention is also given to spoken text.

text construction. Many new genres of text such as blogs, emails and homepages, however, are much less subject to this constraint as their primary medium is electronic, allowing quite different navigation patterns through hypertext links, e.g. embedded within texts linking to different texts, or at the end of the 'teasers' on webpages leading to the full text (see Schiller 2008 for a discussion of the implications for text authoring and translation). Teasers are also a good example of how fragments of text (here the opening few lines) can be designed to function as 'stand-alone' pieces, thus setting rather different constraints on text authoring. 'Fragmentation' – or more positively, segmentation – is also the very essence of new authoring systems such as content management systems (CMS) which allow the user to re-use ('leverage') pre-stored sections of text in new configurations. All these factors have implications for conventional definitions of key features of textuality, such as intertextuality and cohesion.

Intertextuality, according to Beaugrande and Dressler (1981: 10) 'concerns the factors which make the utilization of one text dependent upon knowledge of one or more previously encountered texts'. In electronic media, intertextuality takes on a different significance in at least two ways. First, the integration of the verbal and the visual becomes particularly productive in multimodal texts within so-called 'intertextual sets' (Baldry and Thibault 2005: 55). And second, texts are virtually linked *for* the reader, and this link is *forward* rather than backward looking from that perspective.

Users of TMs or rather, project managers, need to anticipate the nature of the intertextual relationship, making a judgment about how close a new source text is in terms of content and formulation to existing previously translated source texts already in the memory database; this is normally done to my knowledge on the basis of the verbal text alone through a pre-translation run through an existing TM. If the new source text is an update of a previously translated text, then using an available TM is likely to benefit from the close relationship – or intertextuality – of the two source texts (see Figure 2). Translations themselves also, of course, exhibit a strong intertextual relationship with their source texts, as they are dependent from the translator's rather than the reader's perspective, on knowledge of a 'previously encountered text'[5] (Beaugrande and Dressler 1981: 10).

5 I realise that there are interesting discussions to be had here about the nature of a 'translation' and whether a source text is pre-supposed (see, for instance, Malmkjær 2003).

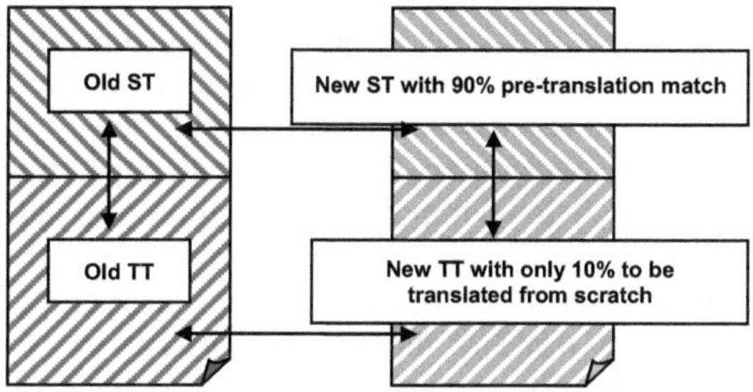

Figure 2. Source texts and their translations both as intertexts (ST: source text; TT: target text)

In other cases, however, where no suitable TM exists, managers need to make judgments about future texts, evaluating whether potential repeat business will make investment in the creation of a new TM worthwhile. Whilst this is at root a commercial decision, it is predicated *inter alia* on judgments about (future) degrees of intertextuality, i.e. the likelihood of the customer returning with linguistically *closely related* texts in the future.

Cohesion has been conventionally described as 'the ways in which the components of the surface text i.e. the actual words we see or hear, are mutually connected within a sequence' (Beaugrande and Dressler 1981: 3). Elsewhere, the talk is of connections to 'predecessors' and 'successors' (Hoey 1991: 3–4). Linearity is therefore crucial to conventional understandings of cohesion, but much less appropriate or useful when applied to certain new genres, particularly those which exhibit multimodal features and in which reading paths may be much looser than the typical left-right, top-bottom patterns (see Baldry and Thibault, 2005: 26). Of particular interest here is the combination of linguistic and visual content to form a textual whole, a common feature of LSP texts, including those translated using a TM such as manuals of various kinds. However, graphics are stripped out of texts before processing by the TM, thereby removing one important component of textuality, i.e. links between the linguistic and visual content. This makes the translator's decision-making even harder, as crucial aspects of meaning-making are removed. As Baldry and Thibault note:

> These [different semiotic] resources are not simply juxtaposed as separate modes of meaning making but are combined and integrated to form a complex whole which cannot be reduced to or explained in terms of the mere sum of its separate parts
>
> (Baldry and Thibault, 2005: 18)

An example of a meaning-making relationship of this kind would be the elaboration of condensed verbal information appearing in the cells of tables in the surrounding verbal text (Baldry and Thibault, 2005: 64).

Even in relation to cohesion in the traditional page, it has been argued (Baker, 1992: 206) that '[i]t is impossible to reproduce networks of lexical cohesion in a target text which are identical to those of the source text' and further that '[s]ignificant shifts do occur, *even* in non-literary texts' (*emphasis added*). If this is the case, it means that even if satisfactory solutions are found to the problems of establishing cohesion at a lexical level in texts which are created, for example, using a CMS or by multiple authors, then this pattern cannot necessarily be reproduced in the target text. In fact, it is quite possible that the choice of cohesive ties by both text authors and by translators may be different when creating text in CMSs or TMs: this much has already been mooted by Heyn (1998: 135) in relation to translation, who suggests that '… since retrieved translation units normally require fewer changes if they do not contain anaphoric and cataphoric references, translators are tending to avoid the use of such devices'. Whether they do remains to my knowledge an open empirical question.

It seems therefore that in the case of competing features of textuality, in CAT as opposed to human translation, intertextuality (and its future instantiations) is likely to trump cohesion in the name of re-usability. In the following section, some sample data from two TMs are considered from the point of view of cohesion, as a preliminary and necessarily limited attempt to explore some of the issues raised above.

5. Textuality, Translation Memory and translation behaviour

In this section, some TM extracts will be analysed in order to start exploring some of the claims made about the effects of segmentation in TM systems on aspects of textuality, particularly cohesion, including lexical cohesion, one of the most important devices for establishing textual links.

Two sources of data[6] are used, both in the domain of automotive engineering. Data set 1 consists of *circa* 7,000 words of web text for owners and potential car owners, with English as source, translated into Austrian German, French, Italian and Spanish. Data Set 2 is from a much larger corpus of which to date only 150 segment pairs have been analysed (a small sub-set is discussed here). The text is a workshop manual, with English as source and German as target language.

6 In both cases, the sources have requested anonymity. I am very grateful for their co-operation in providing me with these data for research purposes.

5.1. Data set 1

Four examples will be presented for the same segment in each target language, focusing on lexical cohesive patterns (Figures 3–6), showing the proposal made by the TM system (column 2), based on previously stored translations which are then retrieved by the system as TT proposals. Previously untranslated sub-segments are shaded and each item in the chosen lexical chain – or putative chain as new target sub-segments remain in the source language (SL) – is underlined. Cases of ellipsis are marked by 'Ø'.

New Source text	**Target text: Proposal from TM**
The only parts made with the same care and passion as your Xxxxx itself. Manufactured to the highest quality, **they** are carefully engineered for a perfect fit and faultless performance and **Ø** are competitively priced. Naturally, **they** are covered for 12 months from the date of fitting.	**The only parts** made with the same care and passion as your Xxxxx itself. Bei der Herstellung wird auf höchste Qualität geachtet. Dank gewissenhafter Konstruktion passen **die Teile** ideal und **Ø** erfüllen ihren Zweck perfekt. Und als Sahnehäubchen sind **sie** auch noch preisgünstig. Naturally, **they** are covered for 12 months from the date of fitting.

sub-segment not in TM
ST sentence split into three TT sentences
nominal phrase in TT instead of ST pronoun
elliptical structure in ST becomes pronoun in TT
sub-segment not in TM

ST lexical chain showing 3 sub-segments:
[the only parts]$_1$ –> [they–>Ø]$_2$–>[they]$_3$
TT lexical chain showing 5 sub-segments:
[the only parts]$_1$–>[[impersonal construction]$_{2.1}$–>[die Teile–>Ø]$_{2.2}$–>[sie]$_{2.3}$]$_2$–>[they]$_3$

Figure 3. Example of segment from Data set 1 (TL: Austrian German)
Lexical chain for 'the only parts'

The first example is from the English-Austrian German TM. In a number of ways, it presents the most complex picture of the four target languages (TLs) discussed for the given segment. The German TM proposal includes, for instance, five sub-segments (including two untranslated sub-segments), whereas the French, Italian and Spanish mirror the ST segmentation into three parts.

First, it is clear that the nominal phrase 'the only parts' in the introductory sub-segment of the new ST must have some kind of co-referential item outside the segment stating or showing which parts are meant. This could be verbal e.g.

a heading, or alternatively an image of some kind[7]. This initial sub-segment is new to the English-Austrian German TM. The second and central sub-segment of the English ST is, however, already in the existing German part of the TM and therefore showing a partial match for the segment, but with three TT sentences instead of one ST sentence. The apparent explicitation in this sub-segment of the English pronominal 'they' by the nominal German *die Teile* arises because in the existing TM, there is no immediately preceding nominal expression with which a pronoun could co-refer, as sub-segment 1 is new. There is therefore no antecedent for a pronominal co-reference within the segment. The translator would, when reviewing the TM proposal, presumably consider the possibility of changing *die Teile* to *sie*, since a nominal phrase – *die einzigen Teile* – would be part of the translation of the initial new sub-segment. This kind of adjustment would be far less likely to occur if the segmentation were finer grained, as the translator would only be expected to translate new segments and would not necessarily take time to look across segments, especially if they had already been translated. It is the rather unusual segmentation of this TM – large 'chunks' consisting of more than one sentence in several sub-segments – which facilitates the translator's decision about the shape of the lexical chain.

In the English-French TM (see Figure 4), it is again the middle ST segment which shows the most re-structuring in the TM proposed translation.

New Source text	**Target text: Proposal from TM**
The only parts made with the same care and passion as your Xxxxx itself. Manufactured to the highest quality, **they** are carefully engineered for a perfect fit and faultless performance and **Ø** are competitively priced. Naturally, **they** are covered for 12 months from the date of fitting.	**Ces pièces** sont fabriquées avec le même soin et la même précision que votre Xxxxx. **Elles** répondent aux plus hauts critères de qualité et **Ø** ont été conçues pour assurer un montage parfait avec des performances irréprochables et des prix concurrentiels. **Elles** sont naturellement couvertes par une garantie de 12 mois à partir de la date de montage.

nominal phrase repeated in TT

non-finite structure in ST becomes finite clause in TT: subject pronoun appears in TT

subject pronoun 'they' in ST elided in TT

ST co-ordinated clause nominalised in TT

subject pronoun in TT as in ST

ST lexical chain showing 3 sub-segments:
[the only parts]$_1$ –> [they–>Ø]$_2$–>[they]$_3$
TT lexical chain showing 3 sub-segments:
[ces pièces]$_1$–>[elles–> Ø]$_2$–>[elles]$_3$

Figure 4. Example of segment from Data set 1 (TL: French)
Lexical chain for 'the only parts'

7 In fact, the current published version begins: 'Genuine Xxxxx Parts are the only parts made …'. The preceding segment in the TM ('Genuine Xxxxx Parts and Genuine Xxxxx Accessories') appears to have been truncated and blended with the segment discussed here.

New Source text	Target text: Proposal from TM
The only parts made with the same care and passion as your Xxxxx itself. Manufactured to the highest quality, **they** are carefully engineered for a perfect fit and faultless performance and **Ø** are competitively priced. Naturally, **they** are covered for 12 months from the date of fitting.	**I soli ricambi** costruiti con la stessa cura e la stessa passione della tua Xxxxx. Prodotti secondo standard della massima qualità, dimensionalmente perfetti, garantiscono prestazioni impeccabili e hanno un prezzo competitivo. **I ricambi originali Xxxxx** sono coperti per 12 mesi dalla data di installazione.

mirrors ST pattern

restructuring of ST sentence minimal

no subject pronoun in TT finite clause – Italian linguistic system

nominal phrase in TT replaces ST pronoun

ST lexical chain showing 3 sub-segments:
[the only parts]$_1$ –> [they–>Ø]$_2$–>[they]$_3$
TT lexical chain showing 3 sub-segments:
[i soli ricambi]$_1$–>[pro-drop structure–> pro-drop structure]$_2$–>[i ricambi originali Xxxxx]$_3$

Figure 5. Example of segment from Data set 1 (TL: Italian)
Lexical chain for 'the only parts'

The English and French lexical chains in the middle sub-segment appear identical in their patterning of pronominal and elliptical choices, but they do not actually map: the ST non-finite structure ('Manufactured…') has been made into a finite structure necessitating a subject pronoun, *elles* (co-referential with the earlier *ces pièces*), allowing a subsequent ellipsis of the French subject pronoun in the following co-ordinated clause: '...**they** are carefully engineered for a perfect fit...' / *et **Ø** ont été conçues pour assurer un montage parfait...* The restructuring of the cohesive patterns within this short sub-segment clearly indicate a human hand in the creation of the TM. In both the ST and the TT, the absence of a full nominal phrase in the middle sub-segment is predicated on the preceding co-referential item 'the only parts' / *ces pieces* in the opening subsegment. A different pattern emerges in both the Italian and the Spanish TTs.

As in the German and French examples, the Italian[8] also re-structures the middle ST sentence but to a lesser extent, leaving intact two co-ordinated main clauses. No subject pronoun is present in either finite clause as Italian is a pro-drop language (*garantiscono*, 'they guarantee'; *e hanno*, 'and they have'); the change from subject pronoun in the English to zero pronoun in the Italian is due entirely to the linguistic system. However, the final sentence features what appears to be an explicitation from a subject pronoun to a nominal phrase: 'they' *–> i ricambi originali Xxxxx* ('the original Xxxxx parts'). A plausible explanation here is that the cohesive link has already been weakened by an intervening sentence with no explicit link in the lexical chain because of the pro-drop: the lexical link is therefore explicitly restored with a nominal phrase in the third sub-segment. Some variation is also introduced by comparison with the

8 I am grateful to Davide de Leo for his expert advice. Any errors remain my own.

first sub-segment: *i soli ricambi* ('the only parts'), then *i ricambi originali Xxxxx* ('the original Xxxxx parts'). As with the French, the cohesive patterns indicate that the TM was created from an existing TT which had been translated 'manually', or that the decision to create a TM based on longer segments facilitated the translator's task when creating the TM segment by segment.

In the Spanish[9] TT, synonymous expressions are used to link sub-segments 1 and 2: *las únicas piezas del mercado* ('the only parts of-the market') followed by *los recambios y accesorios de Xxxx* ('the spares and accessories of Xxxx'), rather than the pattern of nominal phrase → pronoun exhibited by the English lexical chain. Where the Italian uses a nominal phrase in the last sentence, arguably to strengthen the lexical chain, Spanish (also a pro-drop language) inserts a quantifier (*todos*, 'all'). Different solutions have therefore been found in the Italian and the Spanish, although the grammatical systems function similarly in this area.

New Source text	**Target text: Proposal from TM**
The only parts made with the same care and passion as your Xxxxx itself. Manufactured to the highest quality, **they** are carefully engineered for a perfect fit and faultless performance and **Ø** are competitively priced. Naturally, **they** are covered for 12 months from the date of fitting.	**Las únicas piezas del mercado** fabricadas con el mismo esmero y pasión que tu Xxxx. Creados con los niveles más exigentes de calidad, **los recambios y accesorios de Xxxx** están diseñados con el máximo cuidado, para ofrecer un ajuste y rendimiento perfectos, a precios competitivos. Por supuesto, **todos** están cubiertos con una garantía de 24 meses desde la fecha de instalación.

mirrors ST pattern

subject pronoun in ST becomes full noun phrase in TT, using synonym phrase

finite clause in ST (co-ordinated main clause) becomes non-finite clause in TT

subject pronoun in ST replaced by quantifier in TT

ST lexical chain showing 3 sub-segments:
[the only parts]$_1$ –> [they–>Ø]$_2$–>[they]$_3$
TT lexical chain showing 3 sub-segments:
[las únicas piezas del mercado]$_1$–>[los recambios y accesorios de Xxxx –> non-finite structure]$_2$–>[todos]$_3$

Figure 6. Example of segment from Data set 1 (TL: Spanish)
Lexical chain for 'the only parts'

Each target language therefore maintains the lexical chain in a different way. This pattern is consistent with Baker's (1992: 206) assertion relating to human translation i.e. that lexical chains cannot be exactly reproduced in translation. The segmentation in this particular data set does not, however, follow what is

9 I am grateful to María Montserrat Rodríguez Márquez for her expert advice. Any errors remain my own.

commonly held to be the case for TMs, i.e. sentence by sentence alignment, wherever possible[10]. It therefore potentially reduces the possibilities for re-using the content in other combinations as each segment consists of several sub-segments which do not necessarily map on a sentence-by-sentence basis across language pairs.

The brief analysis above has shown that the lexical chains for 'the only parts' have been carefully fashioned in each case in the TT in ways which are motivated by the different constraints on each language. The human translators who first fashioned these patterns were able to take language-specific constraints on cohesion into account. And cohesion with any new sub-segments is easier to create in a larger segment.

5.2. Data set 2

The second data set conforms much more closely to the more common sentence-based segmentation. Three examples of contiguous segment pairs are presented below, in all cases from an English-German TM, showing a range of ST-TT cohesion patterns: a similar ST-TT pattern (Figure 7), differing ST-TT patterns (Figure 8), and a possible case of changing patterns (Figure 9).

Source text	**Target text in TM**	
On vehicles with transponder starter keys (increased theft protection), **the starter key has also been verified and approved.**	Bei Fahrzeugen mit Transponder-Zündschlüsseln (erweiterter Diebstahlschutz) **wurde der Zündschlüssel ebenfalls überprüft und bestätigt.**	similar link ('also' / *ebenfalls*) to preceding segment
This applies to vehicles with extended theft protection (with transponder starter keys) and vehicles without extended theft protection (with starter keys without transponder).	**Dies** gilt für Fahrzeuge mit erweitertem Diebstahlschutz (Transponder-Zündschlüssel) und für Fahrzeuge ohne erweiterten Diebstahlschutz (Zündschlüssel ohne Transponder).	ST pattern of deixis repeated in TT

Figure 7. Example of contiguous segments from Data set 2 (TL: German): Similar pattern in ST and TT (underlining and bold added)

10 The length of the segment discussed here is replicated many times in the data.

Source text	Target text in TM
You tried to read the result before the test was finished.	Es wurde versucht, das Ergebnis vor Abschluß der Prüfung auszulesen.
The [*sic*] may be due to the voltage from the vehicle being too low.	Möglicherweise war die Spannung vom Fahrzeug zu niedrig.

2nd person pronoun avoided in German TT

English ST attempts cohesive link ('The' in error for 'This'?); no cohesive link in German TT

Figure 8. Example of segment from Data set 2 (TL: German): Different pattern in ST and TT

The pattern of ST cohesion in Figure 7 is mirrored exactly in the TT, with an equivalent link ('also'/*ebenfalls*) back to the previous segment (not shown in Figure 7) and an initial demonstrative pronoun ('this'/*dies*), i.e. also an item with co-reference outside its own segment (shown in Figure 7). The first segment shown is therefore tied cohesively to the following segment, as well as to the preceding segment. So in this case, the translators who first created the TM seem not to have considered future TM-generated texts from the perspective of possible re-configuration.

In Figure 8, the personal, direct style of address in the English ST – using the 2nd person – changes to an impersonal construction in the TT (*Es wurde versucht, das Ergenbnis vor Abschluß der Prüfung auszulesen*, 'It was tried to read the result before completion of the test'). The nominal form chosen in the TT (*Abschluß* for the verbal 'finish') also re-inforces the more formal style of the TT. In contrast to the previous example (Figure 7), there is no repetition of the ST link with the previous segment, making the German TT more amenable to re-use in other textual configurations. But whether this is due to an awareness of the capacity for re-configuration in future use of the TM is doubtful: an observance of differences in genre conventions is a more likely explanation.

Source text	Target text in TM
Check **the status of the coordinator**.	**Status des Koordinators** prüfen.
The status of the coordinator is not correct.	**Der Status des Koordinators** ist nicht korrekt.
Check **the status of the engine control unit**.	**Status des Motorsteuergeräts** prüfen.
The status of the engine control unit is not correct.	**Der Status des Motorsteuergeräts** ist inkorrekt.

Figure 9. Example of contiguous segments from Data set 2 (TL: German): Changing patterns of cohesion?

The four consecutive segments in Figure 9 – each pair of segments repeating the same pattern of 'check' followed by an error message – show a repetition of the full nominal phrase in each case in both languages. This explicit approach could be regarded as a potential overspecification of the referent in the error message in each pair, as the reference should be quite clear from the juxtaposition of these simple sentences. However, it is not clear from the data provided[11] how the text is actually presented to the user, taking into account the situation i.e. performing tasks in a workshop. When referring to instructions of this kind (which could also be presented graphically as a flowchart in the original document), the user needs to take his/her eyes away from the text at frequent intervals, and then relocate the right place to continue. It could therefore be argued that another feature of textuality, situationality, influences patterns of cohesion in both ST and TT, in this case favouring explicitation in the form of a lexical chain consisting of nominal phrases, i.e. nominal–>nominal rather than nominal–>pronominal.

An alternative explanation would be that each segment has been translated to ensure the maximum manoeuvrability of segments in future translations, as lexical repetition obviates the need to take into account particular sequences needed for interpreting co-reference, as would be the case for pronouns and quantifiers, for example. But this suggestion, i.e. that the pattern is due to the awareness of the translator of the constraints of 'peep-hole translation' in future use of the TM, is less likely in my view than the constraints of genre conventions, shaped by the nature of the task to be performed by the reader.

6. Concluding remarks

The analysis of the examples of TM segments presented here has shown that in a number of cases it is problematic to isolate possible TM effects from expected ST-TT shifts, either for system-related or genre-related reasons. The literature on the use of TM indicates that intertextuality (understood here as a relationship to potential future texts) may override normal patterns of cohesion by reshaping cohesive ties, although no clear evidence of this has been found so far in the limited data discussed here. Indeed, Dragsted suggests that most professional translators in her study introduced 'a fair amount of sentence structure alterations when they used a TM' (2008: 251).

From the small samples of data analysed here, it is clear that segment length can vary considerably. In the first data set (the web text), segments varied from phrases to paragraphs, although only one paragraph-like segment was analysed here. The project manager who supplied data set 1 reported that the varied

11 The data were provided in a text file with html markers.

segmentation was due to the very specific requirements of each country to localise the text, leading mainly to longer segments: shorter segments would, in her view, have made it harder to re-use segments in future localised texts, a view which goes against the grain of conventional TM wisdom. In the second data set (the workshop manual), the segmentation was much more even, usually being sentence-based. This difference between the data sets suggests that segmentation is influenced by contextual factors, including text genre and future use of the TM related to the purpose of the translation.

In order to move forward with the central question addressed here, namely whether TM reshapes translation decisions, it is clear that a much larger study needs to be undertaken. Such a study could take the form of a think aloud protocol study based on translations using a TM, or a corpus-based study extending the kind of analysis undertaken here and comparing the TM with the published text in which the linguistic and the visual aspects of the text are integrated on the printed or web-based page. The study would also need to be contextualised in terms of the brief given to the translators using the TM tool and the provenance of the TM. Such information is needed in order to facilitate the interpretation of the TM data and to help pinpoint conclusions about the possible influence of TM on aspects of textuality aside from other more well-documented effects.

References

Baker, M. (1992). *In Other Words. A coursebook on translation*. London and New York: Routledge.

Baldry, A. and P. J. Thibault (2005). *Multimodal Transcription and Text Analysis*. London/Oakville, CT: Equinox.

Beaugrande, R. de and W. Dressler (1981). *Introduction to Text Linguistics*. London and New York: Longman.

Bédard, C. (2000). "Mémoire de traduction cherche traducteur de phrases". *Traduire*. Number 186: 41–49.

Biau Gil, J. R. and A. Pym (2006). "Technology and translation (a pedagogical overview)". In: A. Pym, A. Perekrestenko and B. Starink (eds.). *Translation Technology and its Teaching*. Tarragona: Servei de Publicacions. Carrer de l'Escorxador s/n: 5–19.

Bowker, L. (2002). *Computer-Aided Translation Technology*. Ottawa: University of Ottawa Press.

Bowker, L. (2006). "Translation Memory and 'Text'". In: L. Bowker (ed.). *Lexicography, Terminology and Translation. Text-based Studies in Honour of Ingrid Meyer*. Ottawa: University of Ottawa Press: 175–187.

Dragsted, B. (2008). "Computer-aided translation as a distributed cognitive task". In: I.E. Dror and S. Harnad (eds.). *Cognition Distributed. How cognitive technology extends our minds*. Amsterdam/Philadelphia: John Benjamins: 237–256.

Garcia, I. (2008). "Translating and Revising for Localisation: What do we know? What do we need to know?". *Perspectives: Studies in Translatology*, 16 (1–2): 49–60.

Heyn, M. (1998). "Translation memories: Insights and Prospects". In: L. Bowker, M. Cronin, D. Kenny and J. Pearson (eds.). *Unity in Diversity? Current Trends in Translation Studies*. Manchester: St. Jerome: 123–136.

Hoey, M. (1991). *Patterns of Lexis in Text*. Oxford: Oxford University Press.

Malmkjær, K. (2003). "Looking forward to the translation: On 'A dynamic reflection of human activities". In: G. Anderman and M. Rogers (eds.). *Translation Today*. Clevedon: Multilingual Matters: 76–85.

Merkel, M. (1998). "Consistency and variation in technical translation". In: L. Bowker, M. Cronin, D. Kenny and J. Pearson (eds.). *Unity in Diversity? Current Trends in Translation Studies*. Manchester: St. Jerome: 137–149.

Mogensen, E. (2000). "Orwellian Linguistics. How using computer-aided translation tools impacts the target language". *Language International*, 12(5): 28–31.

Pym, A. (2008). "Translation technology and training for intercultural dialogue: What to do when your translation memory won't talk with you". In: R. Dimitriu and K.-H. Freigang (eds.). *Translation Technology in Translation Classes*. Iasi: Institutul European: 12–27.

Quah, C. K. (2006). *Translation and Technology*. Basingstoke and New York: Palgrave Macmillan.

Rogers, M. (2008). "Consistency in terminological choice: Holy Grail or false Prophet?". In: I. Simmonæs (ed.). *Festskrift for Magnar Brekke*. Special Issue of *SYNAPS. Fagspråk, Kommunikasjon, Kulturkunnskap*, 21/2008: 107–113.

Schiller, A. (2008). *Aspects of cohesion in web site translation: a translator's perspective*. PhD thesis. Dublin City University.

Snell-Hornby, M. (2006). *The Turns of Translation Studies*. Amsterdam/Philadelphia: John Benjamins.

Woodsworth, J. (1998). "Geschichte des Übersetzens". In: M. Snell-Hornby, H. Hönig, P. Kussmaul, P. A. Schmitt (eds.). *Handbuch Translation*. Tübingen: Stauffenburg: 39–43 (Translated from the English by R. Geiser).

Corpus Encoding and Integration for English-Spanish MT

Alejandro Curado Fuentes and Martín Garay Serrano

Abstract: MT (Machine Translation) has come a long way since the advent of rule-based systems in the early 70s. MT may be developed more or less effectively by integrating specific resources and specialized discourse. In recent years, some techniques derived from the CBMT (Context-Based Machine Translation) approach may be described as the possibility to weave and interlock "infinite" sentences for MT. Carbonell *et al.* (2006) have undertaken this project with the premises of blocks and connectors, proposing to manage and to deal with a massive target corpus alone (i.e., to process the translated data from a bilingual dictionary in context). In our own project, we apply these premises to the translation of English to Spanish, describing the compilation and encoding of the Spanish corpus and its integration on the database with the bilingual dictionary. The collection is indexed as plain text and with UTF-code. The indexation does not require fully POS tagged corpora, but as much context text as possible so that the n-grams retrieved from the target corpus may contain many component options. This technique may be partially tested by working with a small specific corpus (academic Spanish from research papers and textbooks). This integration should enable the step called "flooding" for the scoring of best translation options (Carbonell *et al.* 2006).

Keywords: academic corpus, CBMT, discourse, encoding, indexing, massive corpus, MT, n-grams, translation.

1. Introduction

MT (Machine Translation) and MAHT (Machine-aided Human Translation) have become two realities for the human translator over the years. He / she may cope with either approach as more or less consistent and in accord with his / her expectations, usually depending on the text type and subject area encompassed (cf. Sin-wai 2004). In fact, as Wilks (2009) notices, it seems that MT has especially delivered good products in conjunction with other resources, such as on-line dictionaries, thesauri, and word processors. However, seldom mentioned in terms of general translation output is the linguistic theory relying on context from one corpus alone: CBMT (Context-based Machine Translation), with no need for parallel corpora, would chielfy work with linguistic chunks transferred to a massive target corpus in the form of inter-connected n-grams. Such features, explained by Abir *et al.* (2002) in their inital discussion of CBMT, then called the EliMT prototype after the system's inventor, involve infinite numbers of sentences, but "a finite number of discreet ideas" (Abir *et al.* 2002: 216). This limited amount of information would be linguistic and in the form of n-gram pairs regarded as "pieces of DNA" (Abir *et al.* 2002: 217). Then, a crucial process of connecting these DNA blocks would enable the weaving and interlocking of sentences along the translated text.

Abir's MT system seems to open up access to new experimental developments for MT. A chief requirement would be the construction of a massive corpus (between 50 GB and 1 TeraByte of electronic text), filtered and indexed accordingly. The second key feature would be a fully inflected bilingual dictionary for the source and target languages. With such resources and the aid of an optional smaller source language corpus for synonym finding implementations, Carbonell *et al.* (2006) seem to succeed in the implemention of a CBMT approach from Spanish to English, achieving high scores in the BLEU (Bilingual Evaluation under Study) scale for MT systems. In both the non-blind and blind tests, their CBMT system (called "MM" for "Meaningful Machines") outperform other MT systems based on rules and statistics (e.g., Systran). The different blind tests demonstrate that the bigger the target corpus becomes in MM, the higher the scores achieved.

Following this line of work with CBMT, our research group aims to produce English to Spanish MT for specific and general purposes. In this paper, we focus on the CBMT approach as the pivotal integration of corpus-based information in the form of both prefabricated language and free discourse (i.e., based on both idiom and free choice principles – cf. Sinclair 1991). At this stage we focus on written academic English to be taken as source text and to be translated into target Spanish text. The tool can then be provided with linguistic enhancements that may offer sound alternatives for the translated output via cache memories, approved n-gram information, and synonym finding alternatives.

2. Method

A fully inflected dictionary of English / Spanish (Lozano Palacios 2008) is searched for each word, compound, or phrase (if listed) contained within the source text n-grams (4 to 8 words), determined by a sliding window from left to right over the input text. A massive indexed corpus is built according to web-crawling techniques (cf. Boleda *et al.* 2006) and multi-layered inverted indexing for the dynamic identification of n-grams (cf. Badia *et al.* 2005), using a crawl of the .es domain (i.e., web pages in Spain, accepted and filtered only if they contain Spanish text). In addition, searching and crawling for appropriate texts are performed by using the webbootcat utility in Sketch Engine (Baroni *et al.* 2006). The txt files are downloaded from appropriate linked resources on the web (e.g., newspapers, reports, forums, etc.). The key words used to compile the text files are exclusively content words taken from frequency wordlists in Spanish. It is found that the most profitable amount of key words to be entered ranges between 6–8 words that include adjectives, verb forms, and nouns. Thus, a good number of texts is obtained with these key words, and the sources can be managed as txt conveniently for MySql indexation by segmenting text at web address markers. In addition, both the wikipedia and the link www.urumedia.org /formarse have been used to download various academic writing sources, also filtered and indexed conveniently in the numerical corpus database.

By constrasting the inflected dictionary equivalences with the linguistic information in the corpus, words and / or multi-word units are managed as numbers on the databases. Thus, the word *give*, for instance, receives one of the Spanish equivalences in the dictionary database as *dar*, but, for example, in the collocation *give a call* the translation is *hacer una llamada*. *Dar* and its conjugations receive matching numbers to be labeled for all their occurrences over the corpus, while the unit *hacer una llamada* has entirely different numerical insertions. As the resources (dictionary and corpus databases) may grow exponentially, new information may result that "contradicts" already stored words. For instance, if the idiom *raining cats and dogs* is introduced with its dictionary translation *llueve a cántaros*, the old date when the texts with this expression were inserted will determine that those previous numbers for *llueve* followed by *cántaros* must be replaced on the corpus with the new assigned numbers for the idiom and its variants. As a result, the dictionary database updates will serve to revise the linguistic corpus information indexation. That way we may prevent multi-word number assignment from missing previously unfound expressions in the corpus.

Unlike statistical approaches like Badia *et al.* (2005), the corpus indexation does not require fully POS tagged corpora, but as much context / text as possible so that the n-grams retrieved from the target corpus may contain the dictionary component words. The aim is to find the information in n-grams through a step called "flooding" by Carbonell *et al.* (2006). In flooding, various n-gram candidates can be retrieved for each flood (up to hundreds, depending on the size of the corpus) derived from the segmented source n-gram. Then, as a subsequent computational step, the system should enable target lattice overlapping maximization, i.e., the computation of the best overlapping option based on more word overlaps between one flood of n-grams and another (e.g., for "he gave his mother a call at home" or "he gave a call to his mother at home", the flooding should take place by sliding the overlapping tool one word or multi-word unit at a time: *hizo una llamada a su madre / a su madre en / su madre en la / madre en la casa /* and so forth). Figure 1 shows an example of a search of some n-gram words on the corpus; the many sentences where the words appear are retrieved and the number of items as well as the distance between them are recorded.

Figure 1. An example of an n-gram search in the corpus

3. Preliminary testing with a small corpus

In written English, co-occurring lexical items often signal attributes of academic stance (e.g., impersonal statements with "seem", or nominal phrases as subject with "consequence", etc. – cf. Biber *et al.* 2004). This academic register is often determined by means of collocational strength degrees – i.e., in terms of content, grammatical-discursive position, semantic space, and text-item relationships (cf. Hoey 2005). Academic Spanish discourse operates similarly, given the findings from a selection of academic texts (as part of our larger general corpus). This type of discourse is chosen to conduct some preliminary tests with the MT system.

CBMT may yield the availability of significant resources for the identification of specific linguistic-discoursive traits (e.g., in academic discourse). The target corpus and fully inflected bilingual dictionary can be linked via different database tables with key linguistic information approved and stored as cache, similarly to how TM (translation memories) would store tranlation units or segments. The MT system would thus retrieve such data from the database as a first step in the case of translating pair existence, much in the line proposed by Abir *et al.* (2002) originally.

The linguistic information may be stored according to academic language co-occurrence, i.e., in the form of collocations, colligations, semantic associations, textual collocations, and textual colligations (cf. Hoey 2005). Some examples of lexical items in these categories are displayed in Table 1, derived from a corpus-based analysis of Academic Spanish.

Table 1. Examples of lexical items collected from the academic Spanish sub-corpus

Collocations	***Colligations***	***Semantic associations***	***Textual collocations***	***Textual colligations***
razón por la cual	*¿por qué no* + present simple	*La mayor parte de* + 'people'	. *En la medida en que*	. *A continuación* + future tense & impersonal clause
lo que se denomina	*necesidad de* + infinitive	'collected' + *en la tabla #*	. *Por lo que respecta a*	. *Teniendo en cuenta* + NP
hay que tener en cuenta que	*en el proceso de* + noun-*ción*	*en el marco* + 'institution'	. *Contrariamente a lo que*	. *Desde el punto de vista* + adjective

In this analysis, word co-occurrence is measured as percentages according to proportional frequencies related to one of the content words in the construction. Such items also appear in the BNC Sampler (Burnard and McEnery 1999) as frequent combinations, but not necessarily with the same lexical, grammatical or textual status. For example, in Academic Spanish, the pattern of the marker *a continuación* ("then") is characterized within an impersonal statement clause that has a verb in the future tense and occurs at the beginning of sentences. In English, the pattern for "then" is not like that, given the information from the BNC.

The items stand out as key when a total of 1540 Spanish texts (6,898,481 running words) are compared with the larger general corpus (nearly 400 million words). In addition, lexical density is higher in these academic texts (40.21 words as the standard rate per 1000 words) when contrasted with the general corpus. This vocabulary use is in fact similar to the one calculated for the academic English texts, in the BNC Sampler: 41.54. Given these initial similarities, it seems that the academic register of the Spanish texts can parallel English discourse proportions of word use. It should be found, then, that the five types of lexical co-occurrence described above, abundant in specialized discourse, are significant in academic texts. Specific discourse is, to a large extent, represented by such features, as being competent in a given academic discipline is closely related to having "mastery of collocations, colligations and semantic associations of the vocabulary (...) of the domain-specific and genre-specific primings" (Hoey 2005: 182). These items should provide enriching alternatives in the English-to-Spanish translation. The combinations are often easy to record and label for the provision of fitting translation options. For example, the construction *al mismo tiempo* (*at the same time*) is produced in 80 percent of the cases of *al mismo* (actually, a very close figure to *at the same time* in relation to *at the same* in the BNC sampler texts – 79.1 percent).

Because the CBMT system is based on a segmenting tool that takes n-grams (4 to 8 words / multiword units) and sends them to the linguistic / text resources, in the process, collocations and other combinations can work as basic items on which this system may rely to find alternatives in the form of prefabricated language. These items are inserted as approved items in the cache database to complete information before the CBMT segmentation analysis takes place or even when some lexical items may not be found in the bilingual dictionary. For instance, when the system encounters *at the same time*, the cache database should offer *al mismo tiempo*, given the approved information stored (at the same time¬al mismo tiempo). The collocation would then be selected even if it is not in the dictionary database, once approved candidates have been stored. Other examples include several colligations where the adjacent item is grammatical: *al objeto de* + infinitive verb (86.6 percent) (*with the objective of*), *una vez* + past participle (73 percent) (*once...*), *si no se* + present simple indicative (86.6 percent) (*should he /it / she...*), etc – see others in Table 1 above –. In such cases, the information to be held should be labeled as lexico-grammatical features that must be invoked (e.g., if a specific verb tense is favored, the system should check and select it from lists / tables of conjugations). In the case of possible textual collocations and textual colligations found, the system would operate via potential changes in the arrangement of the translated sentences. For instance, the item *en este trabajo* (*in this paper*) should be re-positioned at the beginning of the sentence and followed by a comma. This rearrangement would be done after checking the information regarding this item, where it appears as a textual collocation with 72 percent of its occurrences at sentence initial position (i.e., *En este trabajo*,). Among other aims, the purpose is double-fold: to retrieve the best possible lexico-grammatical equivalent, and to reduce computational cost by establishing direct relationships among items.

Thus, the dictionary, as mentioned, should already contain the various suitable translation options for each word unit in the source text n-grams. Because there may be x number of n-gram words / multi-word units found across the whole corpus, the different possible combinations among them can be many (see Figure 2).

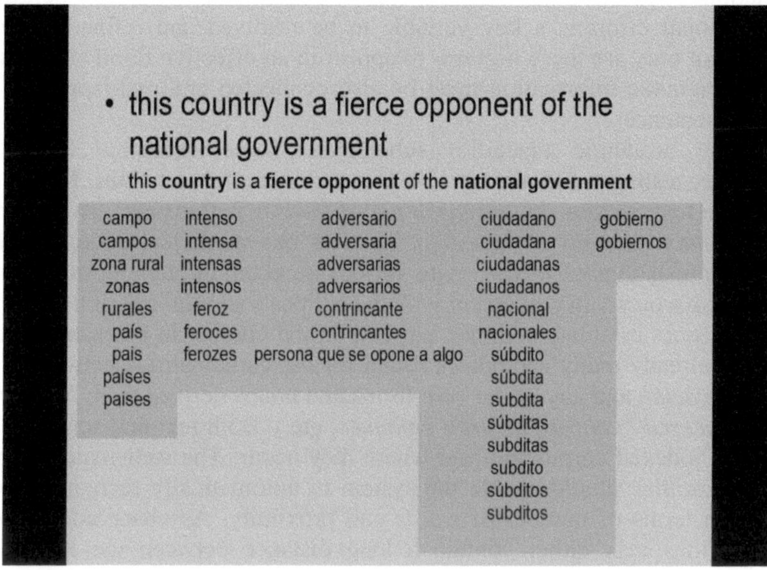

Figure 2. Possible translations from n-gram to be transferred to the corpus

The classification of best translation options should be done according to statistical formulae that contain number of words in the given n-grams, co-occurrences within the 4-to-8 word spans, and distances among such words. Suitable options are taken from the numerical corpus to match equivalences within the n-grams. The addition of number of words found + the number of words found together minus the distance among those words may be a sound basis to start from. This operation is done so that we can obtain a good score for most suitable n-grams. In the process, the system only works with content words (nouns, verb forms, adjectives, and adverbs). The main purpose is to establish and test linguistic co-occurrence throughout the texts and sentences.

In Figure 2, there are five word units to be searched in the Spanish corpus within n-grams. Undoubtedly, the first option would be one that contains all five words in close proximity (order is given less importance because of the likely structural differences between languages). Disambiguation would mainly take place as a result of such word interrelated frequencies and proximity. For instance, so that *country* be resolved as *país* ("state") and not *campo* ("field"), its inter-relations in the n-grams with items like *gobierno* or *nacional* constitute a high priority. Since the corpus is managed numerically (i.e., each word unit corresponds to one unique number assigned according to the dictionary information), and, e.g., only for *country* there are nine numbers to be identified in relation to all the other numbers for the content words, as can be guessed, computational effort is a key variable to be resolved and refined, especially because not only are these n-grams to appear in an effective flood classification, but the linguistic information must be also connected and overlapped to make coherent sentences.

In the academic (specific) sub-corpus, some examples found from preliminary testing could already hint at possible implementations. For instance, the source text n-gram *this research paper focuses* is translated as two units in the dictionary: *trabajo de investigación* with one numerical code, and all the possible translations of *focuses* with various numbers throughout the corpus. In academic discourse, in agreement with the collocational information above, such co-occurrences establish common patterns in the corpus. In our sample corpus, there are already many candidates found for the combinations between *trabajo de investigación* and any of the verb forms and nouns derived from *focuses* (e.g., *enfoca / acerca / centra / centre / enfoques*, etc.). Both text and sentence labels (#) in the indexed corpus indicate where they occur. The statististical formulae in the algorithm should enable the system to automatically recognize the best options in terms of number of words and proximity. As observed in Table 2, some options may either contain a long distance between the items in the sentences (e.g., 7 or 8 words in the second line) or may only include one of the items (e.g., third line). These options should be given less priority. In this process, preliminary machine-based results should be tested against the human eye to discern best translated options so that the weights determined in the statistical formulae can be rounded up (e.g., 0.1 / 02, etc in terms of number of words – distance – found in-between).

Table 2. Some n-gram options found for the source n-gram *research paper focuses*

7772#9# Para Bwin , - trabajo de investigación - - enfoque - muestra - verdadera
19393#14# - trabajo de investigación - - - perfectamente clara - - - enfoques alternativos
11171#19# - wagner , - - - instrumento internacional avala - trabajo de investigación - -
8763#17# - - - ocurrencia principal - - trabajo de investigación, enfocado - - servicio -
17612#23# pielografía - - - - inyectado oxígeno - - pelvis renal neumoquisis - centra
11334#17# aclimatación conjunto – centran - incluidos - - selección - adaptación , - - - -
19952#13# - objetivo - - monografía - - - - - - - trabajo de investigación - enfoca - -

The higher scores correspond to the last and first lines (0.98 and 0.86 respectively). After the scoring of content items, the ranking must be cross-examined with the insertion of functional items that fill in the n-grams. The hyphens (–) between the words point to such function / grammatical words, which must be retrieved from the tables in the system (based on frequency lists). For instance, in the last line, the word missing is the reflexive form *se*, while in the first line, the two spaces point to the need to insert *tiene el* ("has the"). The first option would be given a higher score because of a better fitting functional item: *el trabajo de investigación se enfoca* matches the source n-gram better (in number of words and proximity) than *el trabajo de investigación tiene el enfoque*.

The connection of this n-gram with subsequent ones should also be done according to matching priorities with the source n-grams. This phase seems intricate, and the support of well tested statistical formulae is crucial: the accurate measurement of the word units found, sentence structure, and text type where the n-grams occur, is important so that appropriate connections based on these labels can be made computationally. In these terms, the bigger the corpus, as Carbonell *et al.* (2006) claim, the better possibilities to find suitable matches. For instance, given an x number of texts dealing with a specific topic, the amount of favorable matches among n-grams and their connections within sentences should be facilitated by using translation options from similar sources (e.g., if text # 19952 in Table 2 appears in those matches for various options, it is likely to score high in the n-gram matching rank).

4. Conclusions and future work

CBMT seems to favor the inclusion of multi-word units in the system to obtain specific linguistic correspondences in the corpus. The corpus encoding with this information from the dictionary may disambiguate many instances of lexical-grammatical choices (e.g., *give a call* as *hacer una llamada*). Recent scholarship on MT tends to acknowledge the fact that the use of web-based tools is already producing effective results for specific text types. In our system, this view may be confirmed. For instance, in argumentative discourse, an item like *There is no need for* or *There is no point in*, when translated as *No se trata de* followed by infinitives, becomes effective for Spanish academic writing. These approved n-grams are stored on the main cache memory for the MT system because both (English and Spanish) suit the co-textual information obtained, i.e., they appear in more than 80 percent of the instances at the beginning of sentences in the same type of argumentative texts. The n-gram information derived from our very early tests, may already speak about the salience of such lexical-rhetorical features, fundamental for the comprehension (and cohesion) of text type and specialized discourse. The targeted range of lexical items may differ not only depending on the types of texts used, but also even topic or subject area. After all, as Sin-wai (2004: 233) claims, "conventions of highly conventionalized text types should be observed in the translation because readers expect to read texts in a recognizable form".

Nonetheless, the CBMT project proves to be both labor-consuming and intricate. At our current stage, the corpus is 4 GB in size and growing, but the amount of text information to be indexed (recommended by Carbonell *et al.* 2006) is up to 1 TB. The approach must be able to cope with as many candidate translations as possible, and these must be retrieved effectively from the huge resources, as described. For certain types of text / discourse, the linguistic information derived can support complementary search tools such as stylesheets and synonym finders. The lexical connections can be made possible or at least aided in their processing thanks to much input data favored, playing a crucial role for the organization of discourse. In this paper we have only described the very initial prototype for the CBMT approach. The formulae in the algorithms will have to be tuned up in such a way that the system may be capable of discerning among very similar candidates. This task will become a great challenge for open translation, i.e., when specific / academic language (e.g., lexical bundles) does not appear: then, complex factors such as corpus size, computational cost, n-gram choice and matching, and synonym finding alternatives may have to play the key roles for disambiguation and translation scoring.

References

Abir, E., Klein, S., Miller, D. and M. Steinbaum (2002). "Fluent Machines' EliMT system". *Association of Machine Translation in the Americas*, 2002: 216–219.

Badia, T., Boleda, G., Melero, M. and A. Oliver (2005). "An n-gram approach to exploiting a monolingual corpus for Machine Translation". Paper prepared for the Proceedings of the Second Workshop on Example-based Machine Translation, MT Summit X, Phuket, Thailand, 16 September 2005. [Accessed on 20th September, 2008: http://mutis.upf.es/glicom/Papers/gboleda/MTsummit2.pdf].

Baroni, M., Kilgarriff, A., Pomikálek, J. and P. Rychly (2006). "WebBootCaT: Instant domain-specific corpora to support human translators". Paper prepared for the Proceedings of EAMT 2006 - 11th Annual Conference of the European Association for Machine Translation, Oslo: The Norwegian National LOGON Consortium and The Deparments of Computer Science and Linguistics and Nordic Studies at Oslo University. [Accessed on 16th September, 2008: www.sketchengine.co.uk].

Biber, D., Csomay, E., Jones, J. K. and C. Keck (2004). "A corpus linguistic investigation of vocabulary-based discourse units in university registers". In: U. Connor and T. A. Upton (eds.). *Applied Corpus Linguistics. A Multidimensional Perspective*, Amsterdam: Rodopi: 53–72.

Boleda G. S., Bott, S., Castillo, C., Meza, R., Badia, T. and V. López (2006). "CUCWeb: a Catalan corpus built from the web". Paper prepared for the Proceedings of the Second Workshop on the Web as a Corpus at EACL'06. Trento, Italy, April 2006. Accessed on 17th October, 2008: http://www.citeulike.org/bibtex_options/user/ChaTo/article/501628.

Burnard, L. and T. McEnery (1999). *The British National Corpus Sampler*. Oxford: Oxford University Press.

Carbonell, J., Klein, S., Miller, D., Steinbaum, M., Grassiany, T. and J. Frey (2006). "Context-based Machine Translation". *Association of Machine Translation in the Americas*, 2006: 19–28.

Hoey, M. (2005). *Lexical Priming. A New Theory of Words and Language*. London: Routledge.

Lozano Palacios, A. (2008). *Diccionario Inglés – Español*. Granada: Servicio de Publicaciones.

Sinclair, J. (1991). *Corpus, Concordance, Collocation*. Oxford: Oxford University Press.

Sin-wai, C. (2004). *A Dictionary of Translation Technology*. Hong Kong: The Chinese University Press.

Wilks, Y. (2009). *Machine Translation. Its Scope and Limits*. New York: Springer.

Localisation, Centre for Next Generation Localisation and Standards

Dimitra Anastasiou

Abstract: Localisation is the adaptation of a product to a language-culture combination, called target *locale*. Software and website localisation are the two most common types of localisation; many industries and particularly, language service providers (LSPs) offer such services.

In this article, though, we will focus on localisation in Academia and particularly on a project called "Centre for Next Generation for Localisation" which currently runs in Ireland.

The second part of the article will describe standards in terms of localisation. The standard XLIFF will be described in more detail in section 5.2.

Keywords: Centre for Next Generation for Localisation, globalisation, internationalisation, locale, localisation, Localization Industry Standards Association, Localisation Research Centre, standards, XLIFF.

1. Introduction

Localisation, internationalisation and globalisation are terms which will appear throughout the article and thus we define them in Section 2. We provide the definitions given by Localization Industry Standards Association[1] (LISA) and describe them by focusing on the individual words included in the definitions.

Section 3 refers to the Localisation Research Centre (LRC) which is based at the University of Limerick in Ireland and is the educational centre for the localisation industry. In section 4 we describe one of the projects of the LRC, the Centre for Next Generation for Localisation (CNGL) and the three main challenges which are commonly faced within a localisation project and are addressed by CNGL, i.e. access, volume and personalisation. Section 5 is about localisation standards and more precisely, we refer to two standards developing organisations, namely LISA and OASIS and some of their certified standards.

---

1 http://www.lisa.org/, 27/09/09

2. Definition of terms

In this section we provide the definitions of localisation, internationalisation and globalisation according to the Localization Industry Standards Association (LISA). LISA consists of over 200 corporate clients and their globalization solutions partners and provides business guidelines and multilingual information management standards (see section 5).

We start by the definition of localisation:

> Localisation involves taking a product and making it linguistically and culturally appropriate to the target locale where it will be used and sold.

If we analyse each word of the aforementioned definition, localisation deals with products. Product can be either a software, a tool or a market item in general. Apart from products, localisation also deals with services, such as websites, e-mails, instant messages and so on.

"Making the product linguistically appropriate" essentially means translation. However, there are other linguistic aspects to consider here. To mention only one example, the source text has to be linguistically correct in order for the translation to be performed smoothly in terms of quality, volume, cost and time, i.e. high volume in high quality with low cost in low time. This linguistically appropriate source text should be prepared by authors who are specialised in authoring and technical documentation. Controlled Language plays also a significant role here. According to Muegge (2007), a controlled language has the two following essential characteristics:

> The grammar of the controlled language is typically more restrictive than that of the general language, and the vocabulary of the controlled language typically contains only a fraction of the words that are permissible in the general language. This means that authors who write in a controlled language have fewer choices available when writing a text.

We will now discuss the second part of the definition: "making the product culturally appropriate". This means that the images, the symbols, the colours and generally the visualisation of the product shall be in accordance with the culture of the target locale. It is not an uncommon situation that different colours, icons and even the alignment of text are changed, when one switches to a website from one available language to another.

We now describe the third and last part of the definition: "appropriate to the target locale where it will be used and sold". Target locale, as aforementioned, is the combination of language and culture. Locale is not necessarily a country, as in one country there can be more than one languages (official and spoken) and accordingly, more than one culture. In this target locale the product will not be only used, but also sold. That implies a plethora of marketing enterprises behind the localisation concept. This is exactly where globalisation comes into play.

All these parts of the definition that we just analysed are indispensable in order to accomplish a successful localisation project.

Now we focus on internationalisation which is the step before localisation. LISA provides the following definition for internationalisation:

> Internationalisation is the process of enabling a product at a technical level for localisation.

The important part of this definition is "enabling a product at a technical level". This is the engineering and designing stage of a product. Localisation engineers are responsible for correctly engineering localised content in software applications, help systems, websites and documentation. Each type of content presents its own unique challenges. For example, engineering localised software involves compiling and executing the application, resizing and the rearrangement of user interface elements, while engineering localised help systems involves compiling and executing the help system, checking the page layout, text formatting and validating navigation elements such as table of contents, index, browsing sequence and hyperlinks.

As far as globalisation is concerned, it is a process that includes both localisation and internationalisation and not only these. LISA defines it as follows:

> [Beyond localisation and internationalisation], globalisation encompasses global and local marketing, local after-market support, the establishment of local business presence, and many other aspects of global business.

We see that marketing and business are keywords in this definition. A product which has been successfully designed – task of internationalisation – and come to the target locale – task of localisation – has not necessarily become global. In order to become global, it has firstly to be attractive and catchy to gain the attention of the locals, secondly to be sold in amounts that returns a profit to the selling company and thirdly to remain among the selling product preferences at the target market. The target locale should have their needs and wants satisfied by the localised products and services and also pay for them establishing them as a standard preferred market item; this is the task of globalisation.

3. Localisation Research Centre

In 1995 the Localisation Research Centre[2] (LRC) was established as the Localisation Resources Centre at University College Dublin (UCD). In 1999 it was re-constituted as the Localisation Research Centre (LRC) and moved to the University of Limerick (UL). The LRC comprises a director (Reinhard Schäler), faculty members, staff and research students.

It is regarded as the information, research and educational centre for the localisation industry, as its activities include development and evaluation of localisation tools, the establishment of a Localisation Tools Library, consultancy services, education and training. Since 2009 the LRC has offered a Master about Global Computing and Localisation[3]. It also annually publishes a journal called "Localisation Focus – The International Journal of Localisation[4]" which is the only peer reviewed and indexed academic journal focusing exclusively on localisation and the localisation industry.

The LRC cooperates with worldwide digital publishers and their partners who are interested in future technologies and processes for Globalisation, Internationalisation, Localisation and Translation (GILT); it also co-operates with researchers and students, the media, consultancy firms, government agencies, and the European Commission.

A number of EU projects have been managed by the LRC, such as IGNITE, Transrouter and CLP[5] (The Certified Localisation Professional programme). CLP has been successfully implemented by The Institute of Localisation Professionals (TILP) and was officially launched in 2004 at the annual LRC Localisation Conference. CNGL (Centre for Next Generation for Localisation) is the most up-to-date project and we will describe it in section 4.

4. Centre for Next Generation for Localisation

Here we present the Centre for Next Generation Localisation[6] (CNGL), a dynamic Academia-Industry partnership project which was established in 2007. There are over 100 researchers developing novel technologies which address the localisation challenges of volume, access and personalisation. We would like to address these three issues in detail in subsection 4.1.

The director of the CNGL project is Josef Van Genabith. There are four academic Irish university partners: Dublin City University (DCU), Trinity

2 http://www.localisation.ie/, 23/08/09
3 http://www.csis.ul.ie/course/LM632/, 23/08/2009
4 http://www.localisation.ie/resources/locfocus/index.htm, 23/08/09
5 http://www.localisation.ie/resources/Research/clp/index.html, 23/08/2009
6 http://www.cngl.ie/, 23/08/2009

College Dublin (TCD), University College Dublin (UCD) and University of Limerick (UL). The industrial partners are the following: Alchemy, DNP, IBM, Microsoft, SDL, SpeechStorm, Symantec, Translan, VistaTEC. All industrial partners listed as well as more information about the CNGL project can be found in the CNGL annual report 2008[7]. In the following paragraphs we summarize the research tracks within CNGL.

The CNGL research is based on the four following technologies:

1. Integrated Language Technology,
2. Digital Content Management,
3. System Framework and
4. Localisation.

Research into the Integrated Language Technology (ILT) includes Machine Translation (MT), Speech Technologies and Text Analytics. The examination and improvement of the quality of the state-of-the-art MT systems with focus on hybrid and syntax-based MT systems, word alignment and controlled language are some of the goals of the ILT research group. MATREX (Du *et al.* 2009) is a multi-engine MT system, developed at DCU, which combines example-based with statistical MT aspects.

As for the Speech Technologies, the major focus is to intelligently access digital content in a flexible, eyes-busy and hands-busy scenarios. Text analytics includes among other things, text classification, alternative category labels and datasets.

The Digital Content Management group focuses on the combination of Adaptive Hypermedia and Information Retrieval and Extraction. The user queries should be tailored according to the users' requirements, e.g. their goals, abilities, interests, knowledge and so on. The dynamic adaptation of ad hoc queries for Next Generation Localisation, the automated generation of metadata and the dynamic composition of intelligent responses are some of the research areas.

The System Framework group combines Integrated Language Technology and Digital Content Management. They deal with the demonstrators of the system and aim to create a framework for evaluation of core technologies. The researchers develop a workflow management system that supports the adaptive integration and operation of services and define an architecture within various components can be dynamically integrated with user applications.

As far as the localisation research track is concerned, the LRC (see section 3) which is based at the UL has divided the research into three sub-tracks: i) multilingual digital content development, ii) translation, adaptation and

7 http://www.cngl.ie/Press/CNGL_Annual_Report_2008.pdf, 23/08/2009

evaluation and iii) localisation workflows. The first one, multilingual digital content development, focuses on the design of the original content having localisation in mind as well as the creation and maintenance of the digital content right from the design stage. It has been working on a Localisation Knowledge Repository (LKR) (see Ryan and Anastasiou 2009), where internationalisation guidelines are incorporated into the content development process. The LKR consists of a Digital Library, Test Area and Virtual Community. The Test Area facilitates automating elements of the authoring, enabling and pre-translation testing processes. The Virtual Community enables users to connect with other content developers, upload and download resource files, and post discussion forums. Also, a localisation taxonomy, which defines the file formats of localisation relevant data, is currently built.

The second research group works on translation, adaptation and evaluation by focusing on the current tools and technologies and exploring whether they cover the requirements of the localisers. The third group is about localisation workflows and examines localisation scenarios with workflow ranging from bulk to personalised localisation.

4.1. Challenges

The three main challenges which are addressed within CNGL are volume, access and personalisation. All interrelate with each other and thus localisers have to find the balance between these challenges in order to have the desired result. We describe these essential challenges in the following paragraphs.

Access relates with the personalised multilingual social networking. Social networking is the grouping of individuals who are connected with each other through friendship, professional relationship, shared knowledge or common interests about an activity, such as sports, arts, etc. The social networking sites which gained ground the last years are these ones where the people can write articles in a free encyclopaedia (www.wikipedia.org), upload pictures and share them with their friends (www.flickr.com), upload own videos (www.youtube.com) and so on, i.e. the user ceases to be a passive recipient, but becomes an actor instead. All these are included under the umbrella of "Web 2.0". The concept of "Web 2.0" began with a conference brainstorming session between O'Reilly and MediaLive International. According to the Web 2.0 map presented at the O'Reilly Media, Inc.[8], the Web is used as a platform and the users can control their own data. Nowadays services replace packaged software and collective intelligence is harnessed.

8 http://oreilly.com/web2/archive/what-is-web-20.html#mememap, 23/08/2009

Another term which was first coined by Jeff Howe in June 2006 *Wired* magazine article[9] is *Crowdsourcing*. The term has become popular with business authors who wanted to achieve business goals by leveraging the mass collaboration enabled by Web 2.0 technologies. More information can be found in Howe's (2008) book "Why the Power of the Crowd Is Driving the Future of Business".

As for the second challenge, personalisation, it deals with the personalised production content for informal learning. It takes into account the user requirements and thus the user interfaces should be designed in not only a functional, but also in a more friendly and catchy way and should be adapted to the user needs and preferences.

Volume is the challenge which is mainly addressed by bulk localisation, i.e. localisation for big publishers and corporate institutions. The content nowadays is localised in ever more languages and this should be necessarily considered in relation to the volume.

The objective of CNGL is to counterbalance these challenges, access, volume and personalisation by examining the state-of-the-art and developing new localisation technologies.

5. Localisation and Standards

The existence of standards in localisation is necessary and fundamental. Tool providers shall agree on a certified standard, so that localisation industries have the flexibility to change their tools. Also, freelance translators shall not depend on a specific tool or tool provider; thus the standards should be flexible and open.

5.1. LISA/OSCAR Standards

The Localisation Industries Standards Association (LISA) hosts a special interest group called Open Standards for Container/Content Allowing Re-use (OSCAR). LISA/OSCAR develops technical standards[10] for the globalization process. Some of them are the following:

a. Term Base eXchange (TBX): it is the open, XML-based standard for exchanging structured terminological data that has been approved as an international standard by LISA and ISO. TBX, assuring controlled

9 http://www.wired.com/wired/archive/14.06/crowds.html, 23/08/2009

10 http://www.lisa.org/Standards.30.0.html, 23/08/2009

terminology, improves the quality of the localised text, reduces localisation cost and brings the products faster to market.

b. Translation Memory eXchange (TMX): the vendor-neutral open XML standard for the exchange of Translation Memory (TM) data created by Computer Aided Translation (CAT) and localisation tools. The organizations are not dependent on a specific tool or tool provider any longer.
c. Global information management Metrics eXchange (GMX): it is a family of standards of globalisation and localisation-related metrics with three main components, i) volume, ii) complexity and iii) quality (proposed). These metrics provide standard definitions to assess the quantity, textual complexity and quality requirements for globalisation tasks.

5.2. OASIS and Standard XLIFF

In this chapter we turn our attention to another Technical Committee called Organization for the Advancement of Structured Information Standards (OASIS)[11] Technical Committee[12]. This committee is a non-profit consortium that develops, converges and adopts open standards for the global information society.

One of the open standards is XLIFF[13] (XML Localisation Interchange File Format). Generally, XLIFF is mainly a format for exchanging localisation data. XLIFF could be used to exchange data between companies, such as a software publisher and a localisation vendor, or even between localisation tools, such as Translation Memory (TM) systems and Machine Translation (MT) systems; thus it is tool or partner-independent.

XLIFF is developed by representatives of all aspects of the translation industry and has standardised methods for automating workflow, translation word counts, TM and segmentation. It is intended to give any software provider or technical communicator a single interchange file format that can be understood by any localisation provider.

The benefit of XLIFF is that it enables translators to concentrate on the text to be translated. It provides tags and attributes for review comments (metadata) as well as the translation status of individual strings. It also separates localisable text from formatting. However, the most important advantage of XLIFF is that it allows many separate tools to work on files. While working on source file formats, it is not easy for users to run both a MT and a TM on the same files. Moreover, during review it would be difficult to distinguish which part of text

11 http://www.oasis-open.org/who/, 23/08/2009
12 http://www.oasis-open.org/committees/tc_home.php?wg_abbrev=xliff, 23/08/2009
13 http://docs.oasis-open.org/xliff/xliff-core/xliff-core.html, 23/08/2009

came from the MT tool, the TM tool, or a human translator. By contrast, if the tools, MT and TM, read the XML-based standard XLIFF, they could be run sequentially.

Summarising, XLIFF enhances localisation research by coping easily with localizing different types of source files, providing a common platform for localisation tools vendors and facilitating the localisation process through its commenting features and metrics.

6. Summary

In this article we introduced and explained the definitions of localisation, internationalisation and globalisation given by LISA. Then we referred to the main activities of an educational centre based at the University of Limerick, the Localisation Research Centre (LRC). The current project, CNGL, in which the LRC together with three other Irish Universities is involved, was highlighted and the various technologies researched were described. Within CNGL, it has been examined how the three main challenges which are faced within a localisation project, i.e. access, volume and personalisation can be counterbalanced. The last part of the article briefly explained the importance of standards in localisation and referred to two standards developing organizations, i.e. LISA and OASIS and some of their certified standards.

References

Du, J., He, Y., Penkale, S. and A. Way (2009). "MATREX: The DCU MT System for WMT 2009". *Proceedings of the 4th Workshop on Statistical Machine Translation*. EACL 2009. Athens, Greece: 95–99.

Howe, J. (2008). *Crowdsourcing, Why the Power of the Crowd Is Driving the Future of Business*. Crown Business.

Muegge, U. (2007). "Controlled language: the next big thing in translation?". *ClientSide News Magazine* (ClientSide Publications) 7 (7): 21–24. http://www.translationdirectory.com/articles/article1359.php.

Ryan, D. and D. Anastasiou (2009). "Developing Digital Content for Global Audiences". *tcworld Conference Proceedings*. Wiesbaden, Germany.

Making the Most of the Data: Old Church Slavic and the PROIEL Corpus of Old Indo-European Bible Translations

Hanne Eckhoff, Dag Haug and Marek Majer

Abstract: This article reports on ongoing work on the PROIEL corpus of old Indo-European New Testament texts, consisting of the New Testament in its Greek original and its earliest translations. In particular, the article looks at the corpus' usefulness as a resource to Old Church Slavic (OCS). Since the corpus is of such a modest size, it has been possible to give it rich, multilayered annotation, and each of the translated versions is aligned at token level with the Greek original. We illustrate the possibilities of the corpus with a preliminary case study of animacy as an emergent grammatical category in OCS, letting the corpus data shed light on the correlation between Greek definiteness and the OCS nominative-accusative and genitive-accusative.

Keywords: alignment, information structure, Old Church Slavic, parallell corpus, syntax.

1. Background: The PROIEL project

Pragmatic Resources in Old Indo-European Languages (PROIEL) is a project based at the Department of Philosophy, Classics, History of Art and Ideas, University of Oslo. The main objective of the project is to investigate what morphological and syntactic resources the project languages employ for expressing categories related to information structure, contrastively and language-specifically. In particular we look at word order, definiteness, anaphoric expressions, participial constructions and discourse particles across the different languages.

In order to carry out the studies, we have developed a richly annotated corpus of texts in older Indo-European languages. The corpus[1] currently includes texts in Ancient Greek, Latin, Gothic, Old Church Slavic and Classical Armenian. The core of our material is the text of the New Testament (NT) – the Greek original of the NT and its translations into the remaining languages (Jerome's Vulgate for Latin, Wulfila's translation for Gothic, the Old Church Slavic translation as found in the Codex Marianus, and the oldest version of the Classical Armenian translation). These NT texts constitute a naturally occurring parallel corpus, as well as covering the oldest texts of substantial length written

---

1 The corpus is available at http://foni.uio.no:3000, the project website is at: http://www.hf.uio.no/ifikk/proiel/index.html

in Germanic, Slavic and Armenian and thus provides the most suitable material available for such research. However, we have also started work on adding texts from outside the NT in order to provide diachronic depth (particularly for the Greek and Latin), stylistic variation, and, for the translation languages, original texts as close as possible to the translations in time and geography, in order to separate native features from Greek influence. This is certainly a wish for the Slavic part of the corpus. So far, the corpus only includes one text apart from the NT material (Julius Caesar's *Commentaries on the Gallic War*); the addition of further original texts is planned.

Even though the structure of the corpus is designed so as to fit the needs of the PROIEL project, its potential uses are far greater. The rich annotation our corpus involves makes it of interest to both historical linguists – Indo-Europeanists as well as specialists in the respective languages – and to scholars interested in purely synchronic issues concerning any of the languages. What is more, the data may be of interest to researchers interested in Bible scholarship, translation studies, computational linguistics and numerous other fields. For this reason, the structure of the corpus is at all times open – there always exists a possibility of adding further layers of annotation should it be required for a given purpose. Given that all the translations are aligned at token level with the Greek original, the corpus is an especially valuable resource to OCS, as well as to Gothic, since these languages are (virtually) only attested in translation, making a contrastive glance at the Greek essential in any study.

3. Corpus design

This section provides a brief overview of the design of the PROIEL project. For more details, especially on the technical issues, we refer to Haug *et al.* (2009).

3.1. The texts used

Since the availability of electronic editions of ancient material is relatively good for most of the project languages, not least when it comes to the NT, we have resolved not to conduct any digitisation work within the project, but rather to employ already existing resources. Needless to say, various editions of the Greek NT are available; we decided to use Tischendorf's 8th edition (1869–1872), previously digitised by Ulrik Sandborg-Petersen. Among the advantages of this text is the fact that it strikes a reasonable balance between a modern edition and a version resembling those we used for the languages other than

Greek; furthermore, it is in the public domain. As regards Old Church Slavic,[2] we decided to use the Codex Marianus, the largest extant manuscript; our text is a digitisation of Jagić's edition (1883) carried out by Jouko Lindstedt for the Corpus Cyrillo-Methodianum Helsingiense.[3]

Our approach implies a vast oversimplification of the editorial situation, not least in that the Armenian, Latin, Gothic and OCS translations are linked to the same Greek original, but it offers considerable practical advantages: a corpus aiming at a representation of the textual tradition of the Greek NT and its translations would demand its own, much larger project. For scholars who study rare forms or individual passages of the NT, consultation of modern editions remains indispensable; however, for the investigation of more frequent phenomena as well as various kinds of statistical analysis of the texts, the PROIEL corpus is fully adequate.

3.2. Parsing

For statistical research to yield interesting results, much more than a simple electronic version of the text is required: we need structured markup of the text with linguistic information. In the PROIEL corpus, we employ a number of distinct layers of such annotation:

- lemmatisation
- morphological analysis
- syntactic analysis
- information structure analysis

Moreover, we use a range of additional semantic tags, which are atomic attribute-value features (ie. full or partial categorisations) of lemmata and/or tokens.

Linguistic markup of ancient texts is not nearly as well developed as pure text corpora, but there is good lemmatisation and morphological analysis already available for the Greek text. For the other texts, less data were available, but we have profited from morphological analyses provided by the Perseus project (Latin), LALT (Armenian), the Wulfila project (Gothic) and the USC South

2 As for the remaining languages, the choice of editions was relatively straightforward: we use the digitised edition of Streitberg (1919) compiled by the Wulfila project for Gothic (http://www.wulfila.be), the electronic version of Kunzle (1984) prepared by the Leiden Armenian Lexical Textbase for the Armenian text (http://www.sd-editions.com /LALT/home.html), and the Perseus project version of the Latin Vulgate (http://www.perseus.tufts.edu/hopper/).

3 See http://www.slav.helsinki.fi/ccmh/

Slavic Corpus.[4] Still, the situation for OCS was not ideal: a great deal of the lemmata and morphology had to be entered manually by the annotators.

All texts had to be preprocessed and fitted to our own needs. They were converted to Unicode 5.1, which provides adequate support for Old Church Slavic. For syntactic annotation, we also needed to break the texts up in syntactic units, ie. sentences. Since the style of the NT is rather paratactic, and sentence-initial *kai* "and" is extremely frequent, the division into sentences will to some extent be arbitrary. Our approach was to use the punctuation in Tischendorf's edition to determine sentence boundaries in the Greek text, and then to transfer this to the other versions using an implementation of the Gale-Church algorithm (Gale and Church 1993).

3.3. The corpus application

A corpus is essentially a collection of data that can be stored and distributed in various ways, as a flat text file, a structured XML file, or as a relational database. Our approach has been to create a web application which uses a relational database to store data, but also generates export files in various standard formats which can be browsed with tools such as TIGERSearch.[5] The corpus web site and application is therefore essentially a tool for *annotating* texts and not primarily for retrieving data.

The web application has allowed us to use student assistants from various countries to annotate our texts and save their analyses, as described in the next section. Once sentences have been reviewed by project members, the morphological and syntactic annotation can also be browsed, but for the moment, morphological and syntactic queries must be done using external tools. However, the interface does allow queries (with wild cards) for word forms and lemmata, and the lemma pages show concordances and statistics on the morphological forms of that lemma found in the corpus.

As a complement to the current application which focuses on annotation, we are currently developing a web based query interface which will also be linked to the database. This will allow searches in the syntactic structures (combined with other layers of the annotation) using the Tiger graph description language.

4 http://www-rcf.usc.edu/~pancheva/ParsedCorpus.html

5 http://www.ims.uni-stuttgart.de/projekte/TIGER/TIGERSearch/

3.4. Workflow

The parsing of the corpus is the joint effort of a team of project members and collaborators – annotators, reviewers and administrators. The process of annotating a sentence comprises several stages.

When starting the annotation of a "raw" sentence, the annotator is first asked is to check and possibly correct the sentence boundary. The annotator then proceeds to enter the morphological data. This is done by manually marking each item using the relevant grammatical categories as well as providing the lemma. However, the annotation is usually based on what the system application guesses relying on the already existing reviewed annotations and/or specially written rules. The accurateness of the guesses varies from language to language and from sentence to sentence. Since comparatively little work had been done on the OCS text beforehand, the annotators had little to rely on in the early phase of the annotation: most of the lemmata and morphological annotation had to be entered by hand. In the annotation of Greek, on the other hand, morphological annotation mostly involves making distinctions that were not made in Sandborg-Petersen's original text.

Afterwards, the annotator proceeds to enter the syntactic annotation. This is carried out by creating a syntactic dependency tree. (cf. section 4). The structure of the tree is created entirely manually, by marking a head and clicking on its dependent. The application then provides a guess on the label of that relation, based on the morphology of head and dependent (ie. accusatives dependent on verbs are guessed as objects). The decision to rely on manual procedures for the generation of the tree structure is dictated by the fact that no reliable parsers are currently available for any of the project languages.

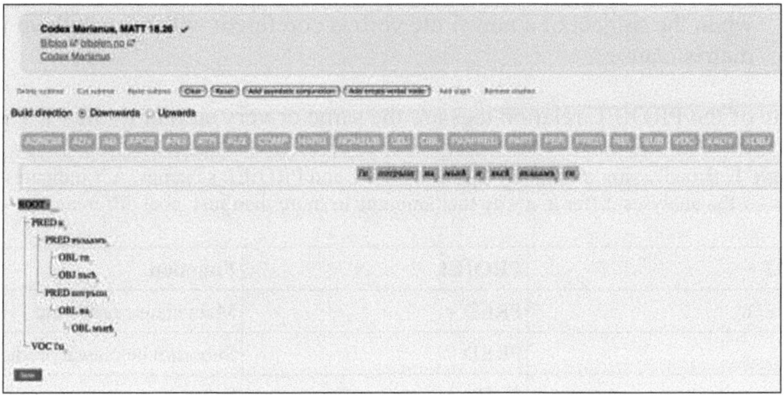

Figure 1. The syntactic annotation interface

After the morphological tags have been entered and the dependency tree has been created, the sentence is marked as "annotated". At a later stage, it is analysed and if necessary corrected by an independent reviewer. The sentence is flagged as "reviewed" and becomes publicly available. The reviewers are members of the PROIEL project and specialists in the respective languages. In particularly difficult or important cases, the reviewers discuss the annotation together in order to keep the annotation policy for the different languages as consistent as possible. The rules agreed upon after such consultations are then added to the annotation guidelines and applied consistently throughout the corpus.

4. The syntactic model

The model of syntactic annotation employed in our corpus is based on dependency grammar (DG), similar to and inspired by the syntactic annotation employed in the Prague Dependency Treebank (PDT).[6] Such an approach is both computationally attractive and very suitable for the project languages: All of them have 'free' or pragmatically conditioned word order, which makes it necessary to represent syntactic dependencies and word order in separate layers, especially given the project's focus on interactions between pragmatics/ information packaging and syntax. There are three main differences between our scheme and the PDT's:

- the PROIEL set of relation tags is more granular (cf. table 2)
- we allow a limited set of empty nodes (null verbs and null conjunctions)
- we have introduced secondary edges to capture structure sharing, i.e. when the subject of a non-finite verb is coreferent with a constituent in the matrix clause

Many of the PROIEL relation tags are the same or very similar to the PDT tags.

Table 1. Broadly similar relation tags in the PDT and PROIEL schemes. A * indicates that the analyses differ in a way that amounts to more than just label differences

PDT	**PROIEL**	**Function**
PRED	PRED	Main clause predicate
*	PRED	Subordinate clause predicate
SBJ	SUB	Subject

6 See http://ufal.mff.cuni.cz/pdt2.0/.

ADV	ADV	Adverbial
ATV	XADV	Free predicative
PNOM	XOBJ	Subject complement
OCOMP	XOBJ	Object complement
COORD	*	Coordinator
APOS	APOS	Apposition
Aux*X*	AUX	Auxiliary
ExD	*	External dependency
ExD	VOC	Vocative

Table 2. Added granularity in the PROIEL scheme

PDT	**PROIEL**	**Relation**
OBJ	OBJ	Object
	OBL	Oblique
	ARG	Argument (supertag)
	AG	Agent
	XOBJ	Open complement
ATR	ATR	Attribute
	NARG	Nominal argument
	PART	Partitive

We have added granularity to our annotation scheme because syntax is at the core of the PROIEL research interests, and we believed it to be feasible to achieve consistent annotation even with finer distinctions than those found in the PDT. There is evidence that e.g. OBJs, OBLs and AGs behave differently with respect to e.g. definiteness in Greek. We therefore distinguish between arguments of verbs that require particular cases, and arguments that can become subjects when the sentence is passivised. Thus we get two different analyses for sentences (1) and (2):

(1) г҃ъ трѣбоуоутъ его
"the Lord needs him" (Luke 19: 34)

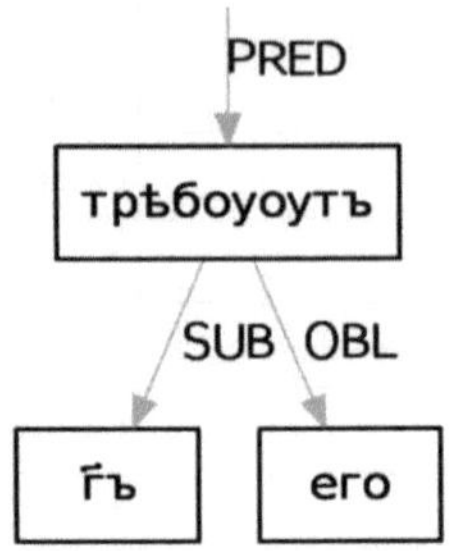

(2) самъ бо отецъ любитъ в?
"for the father himself loves you" (John 16: 27)

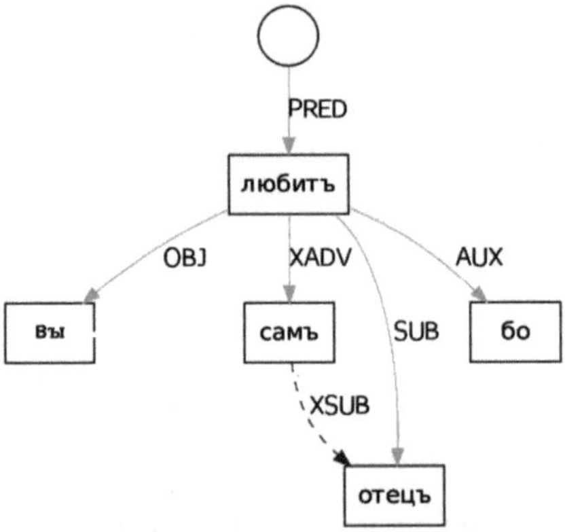

In section 8 we give a fuller example on how the more granular set of adverbal relations can be exploited to give a good representation of the marking of animacy in OBJs in OCS.

The decision to include a limited set of empty nodes and add secondary dependencies to the annotation scheme was based on a wish to include relationships that are in principle impossible to express in classical dependency grammar. The following example illustrates most of the uses:

(3) никтоже благъ тъкъмо единъ б҃ъ
"no one is good, only God alone" (Mk. 10: 18)

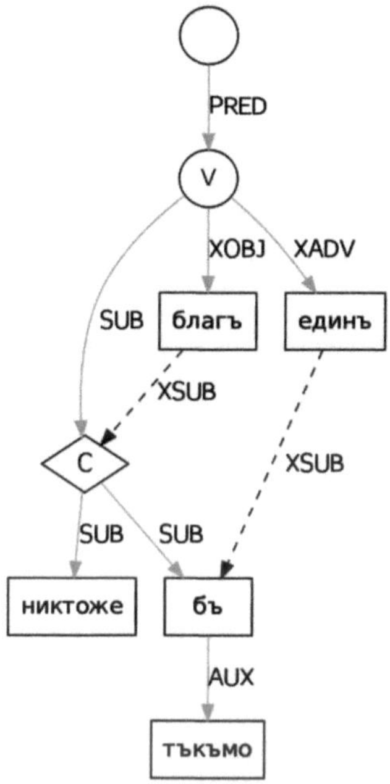

The empty nodes allow us to deal with missing heads, such as the null copula which is the PRED of this sentence and the missing conjunction in the asyndetic coordination of the two subjects никтоже and богъ. The example also shows us an important use of secondary edges, namely, to indicate structure sharing: богъ is both the subject of the null copula and the subject of the XADV (free adverbial) единъ.

In example (4) we see that the secondary edges can also be used to express elided constituents: the edge then indicates a shared dependent, such as the subject они in this sentence, which also, in its turn, is the subject of the XOBJ въпросити. We do not, however, allow the secondary edge to go directly from въпросити to они, instead we have an edge to the PRED on which въпросити depends. This edge tells us that we should look for the subject of въпросити in the argument structure of боѣахѫ:

(4) они же не разоумѣшѧ г҃ла. ? боѣахѫ сѧ въпросити и
“but they did not understand the saying, and were afraid to ask him” (Mk. 9:32)

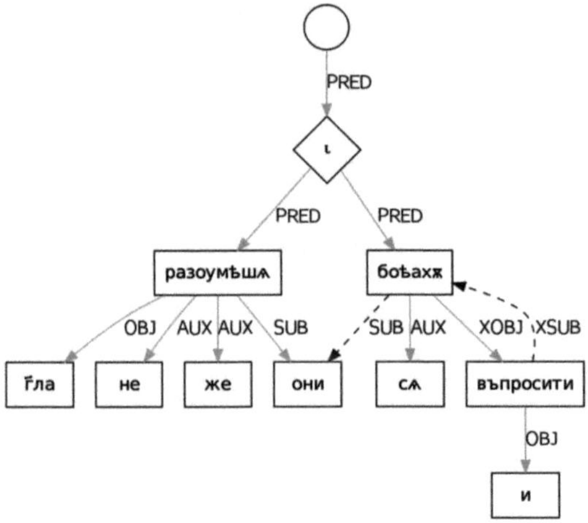

5. Token alignment

To profit fully from the fact that we have at our disposal the same text in several languages, it is essential to align the versions in such a way that it becomes possible to compare the different texts versions computationally. The advantages of doing so are numerous: For OCS and the other translation languages, it is essential that the user should be able to single out constructions in the translation languages that differ from the Greek and thereby to shed light on their native syntax. However, this solution also lets us use the various translations to cluster subgroups of Greek constructions which appear unitary on the surface.

A unique advantage of the text of the NT is that all versions are marked up with Robert Estienne’s division of the text into verses. While this system is by no means perfect – the units are not always syntactic units, and numerous divergences in its application among the different translations are apparent – it does in most cases provide a correct and reasonably fine-grained alignment. Furthermore, this ‘chunk alignment’ can be exploited to automatically create alignments at the word level.

To achieve this, we first generated a dictionary of candidate translation pairs by looking at the frequency of their co-occurrence in the same Bible verse. In principle, each word in the Old Church Slavic text of e.g. Mark 6: 38 may possibly be the direct translation of each word in the Greek Mark 6: 38 :

ὁ δὲ λέγει αὐτοῖς· πόσους ἄρτους ἔχετε; ὑπάγετε ἴδετε. καὶ γνόντες λέγουσιν· πέντε, καὶ δύο ἰχθύας.

онъ же г҃ла имъ. колико имате хлѣбъ. ?дѣте и видите. ? оувѣдѣвъше г҃лашѧ. пѧть хлѣбъ и дъвѣ р?бѣ

"and he said to them: How many breads do you have? Go and see. And when they had found out, they said: Five, and two fishes."

It is, however, to be noted that words that are actual translation equivalents are likely to co-occur in the same verse with more than chance frequency. Therefore we construct 2x2 contingency tables for each pair of lemmata and calculate the significance of each collocation using Fisher's Exact Test.

Table 3. Contingency table for *ryba vs. ikhthús* cooccurrences

	р?ба	no р?ба
ikhthús	17	0
no ikhthús	6	3529

As we see from this table, the Greek ikhthús "fish" is much more likely to occur in a verse if р□ ба occurs in the corresponding verse than to occur without it, and vice versa. (The most likely outcome is that neither of them will occur at all.) We use these relative frequencies of cooccurrences to rank pairs of Greek and Slavic lemmata according to their likelihood of being translation equivalents. The best matches for р□ ба by this measure turn out to be *ikhthús* "fish" and *opsárion* "fish"; the next two candidates are *ártos* "bread" and *díktuon* "net" – which are of course wrong, but also clearly cooccur with р□ ба with above chance frequency.

Notice that the dictionary generation only makes use of the lemmatisation: the remaining types of linguistic information are retrieved in the next step, where likely translation equivalents inside each verse are ranked using the morphological and syntactic annotation as well as the linearisation. The latter is of particular significance, since, as is well known, the early Bible translators aimed at preserving the basic order of words.

The token alignments are thus created entirely automatically. In order to evaluate the procedure, we have manually aligned a single chapter and used the resulting data as a benchmark. In the course of the test, the alignments created by the automatic procedure have proved to be about 97% correct. This means that they may safely be used for linguistic research without altering the data in any significant way.

6. Information structure: givenness and anaphoric distance

Given the research interests of the PROIEL corpus, a layer of information structure annotation is essential. There are, however, several problems in annotating ancient texts for information structure. The theoretic field of information structure is difficult in itself, with many controversial notions that are not necessarily easy to apply to actual data. Some of them also rely crucially on intonation and/or are subtle and require native speakers' intuitions to be applied properly. In dealing with ancient texts, of course, neither prosody nor native speakers are available. Our annotation schemes must therefore be devised to make the most of bad data and concentrate on the information-structural categories most objectively available to us in such a material. The corpus will therefore be annotated for a) givenness, b) anaphoric distance and c) contrast. The annotation of contrast is at an experimental stage and will not be discussed in this article; instead we will give a brief overview of our approach to givenness and anaphoric distance.

6.1. Givenness

Our approach to givenness is to find the answer to the question "How does the hearer establish the referent of an NP?" In our case, the hearer would be a member of the first intended audience of the New Testament: a first-century AD Hellenised Jew holding the current religious beliefs and with a fair knowledge of the geography of the areas where the NT takes place.[7]

Most approaches to givenness use a fundamental tripartition into new – mediated/accessible – old (as in Prince's classical 1981 article, for corpus annotation schemes see Nissim *et al.* 2004 and Dipper *et al.* 2004), where each group is generally divided into various subgroups, especially the accessible/mediated group. We decided to base our subdivisions on the insights in Riester and Lorentz's (2009) annotation scheme, which draws on Discourse Representation Theory (DRT) (Kamp and Reyle 1993) and its notion of different contexts where discourse referents may be identified by the hearer: Referents can be retrieved from the discourse (OLD), from the speech situation (ACC-sit), they may be inferred from other available discourse referents (ACC-inf) or be found in the interlocutors' encyclopaedic knowledge. Only when the referent has no context is it tagged as NEW.

7 This is not the only possible approach, other options include looking for the referent's discourse status (has it been mentioned in the text?) or assessing its state of cognitive activation (cf. Gundel *et al.* 1993).

Table 4. Givenness tags in the PROIEL corpus

Context	Tag
Discourse (anaphora)	OLD
Situation (deixis)	ACC-sit
Scenarios (inferences)	ACC-inf
Encyclopaedic knowledge	ACC-gen
No context (no extra-NP information)	NEW

6.2. Anaphoric links

Illustration 2 shows a sample sentence with givenness tags (red for OLD, green for ACC-gen, yellow for NEW) and anaphoric links. Unlike the givenness annotation, where a high degree of intersubjective agreement is quite difficult to achieve, anaphoric distance can be tagged and measured with relative objectivity. In every case where a referent (overtly realised or prodrop) has been mentioned within the 13 last sentences, we set an anaphoric link from anaphor to antecedent. The limit of 13 sentences is to some extent arbitrary, and may be adjusted as the work proceeds. For referents with a last mention outside this limit, but which seem not to be "reintroduced" but simply picked up again, we use the tag OLD-inactive.

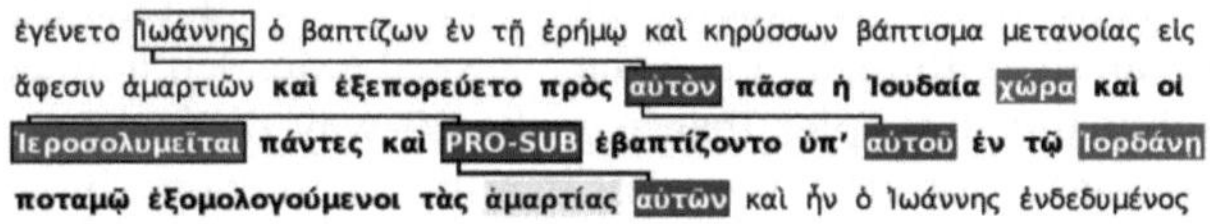

Figure 2. Givenness and anaphoric links in the corpus application

The anaphoric links can be used to calculate not only exact distances between anaphors and antecedents, but also the length and density of entire anaphoric chains, and thus also the relative saliency of individual discourse referents. Several pilot studies have shown that anaphoric distance may be an equally or even more important predictor than givenness in many cases, and it is a tool that is well suited to the special style of the NT, where so many of the discourse referents are old due to the small circle of main participants and the repetitive and somewhat formulaic narrative.

As we will see in section 7 on animacy annotation, the anaphoric links can also be useful devices to transfer lemma-level information from antecedent tokens to anaphors.

7. Semantic annotation: animacy

The corpus application allows customised tagging by individual researchers working on specific problems. Even the detailed annotation of morphology, syntax and information structure that the corpus provides does not suffice for all kinds of research. Project members and others will want to classify nouns for animacy or relationality, verbs for aktionsart and so on. To make these data, too, available to other researchers in the interests of replicability and further research, the database allows for customized tagging where scholars can define their own attribute-value features and mark up linguistic material. Such tags can be set at the lemma level and overridden at the token level, a system which allows for efficient, but accurate tagging. So far, these tags have mainly been used for semantic classifications, but are not restricted to semantics. We will exemplify this annotation layer by describing our approach to animacy annotation.

Animacy is a semantic category that has been shown to have impact on and interact with a series of grammatical phenomena cross-linguistically, such as argument realisation, word order and definiteness, all areas of interest to the PROIEL project. In Slavic, animacy has developed into a grammatical category outright. In OCS, we only see this category at an emergent stage, which made animacy annotation essential to the PROIEL corpus.

We wanted an animacy annotation scheme that was sufficiently detailed to give interesting distinctions, but simple enough to make it easy to apply. We therefore chose a slightly simplified version of the annotation scheme in Zaenen *et al*. 2004, see table 5. The scheme is considerably more detailed than a simple human:non-human dichotomy and e.g. the classical extended animacy hierarchy (Dixon 1979), but much simpler than e.g. the 20-way distinction employed in the Russian National Corpus.[8] We consider the distinctions between various kinds of inanimates to be important: in particular we expect there to be interesting differences between concrete and non-concrete inanimates. We can also retrieve nominals denoting time and space by way of the animacy annotation.

Table 5. Animacy annotation scheme

Animacy tag	Brief description
human	things that look and act like humans, including deities and spirits
org	a collectivity of humans with some degree of group identity
animal	non-human animates

8 See their guidelines for semantic annotation at http://ruscorpora.ru/en/corpora-sem.html

veh	vehicles
concrete	"prototypical" concrete objects or substances, excluding intangibles
nonconc	anything that is not prototypically concrete but clearly inanimate, e.g. events
time	expressions referring to periods of time
place	nominals that will normally serve as locations for human actions

For a maximally efficient annotation, we started by annotating all Greek nouns for animacy at lemma level. The annotation was done by one project member and then reviewed by another. In most of the cases the two agreed on the annotation. The tags are meant as token-level tags, so the annotator and reviewer kept an eye on what would be the most common meaning among the tokens actually represented in the corpus, not on the lemma's "basic meaning". For example, none of the occurrences of *kardía* "heart" referred to a physical heart, but always to the minds of opinions of people. The lemma was therefore annotated as nonconc, not concrete. The annotation will still need adjustment at token level, but the non-adjusted annotation is also of good quality.

The animacy annotation also provides a good example of how the various components of the corpus can be put to use. Naturally, it is not sufficient to have animacy annotation only for nouns: we want it for other referential expressions too, for pronouns and even for prodrops. However, it is not necessary to do manual annotation of all referring expressions, instead the anaphoric links in the information structure annotation (see section 6.2) can be put to work. Every member of an anaphoric chain will necessarily have the same animacy as the end point of that chain.

Similarly, there is no need to do separate animacy annotation for each of the project languages: since the OCS, Latin, Gothic and Armenian texts are all close translations of the Greek original, we can use the token alignments (see section 5) to do an automatic transfer of the annotation to the other languages. A test transfer to OCS showed over 95% success for this method.

8. Combining the layers: Animacy and definiteness

In this section we would like to demonstrate how the many layers of annotation can be employed, first in establishing a sound annotation practice in dealing with a complex morphosyntactic phenomenon, and then in a contrastive case study of that same phenomenon. Our example will be the differential case marking of OCS human masculine singular OBJs.

8.1. Animacy and syntax: fine-grained relations and detailed morphology

As is well known, all Slavic languages have developed a grammatical category of animacy to a greater or smaller extent. In OCS this category is only emergent: OBJs in the singular referring to (adult, high-status) males are sometimes genitive-marked and sometimes accusative-marked (see e.g. Klenin 1983, Huntley 1993). The verbs involved are regular transitives, and the OBJs can be nominative SUBs in the passive. (In the following, these two realisations will be referred to as the genitive-accusative and the nominative-accusative, respectively.)

The tagging of the OCS genitive-accusative was a challenge to the PROIEL annotation scheme. Since the category is only emergent and obviously a good candidate for further analysis based on the PROIEL data, we wanted to impose as few assumptions as possible on the annotation.

We rejected the idea of tagging all such genitive-accusatives as accusatives because of their function, and leaving it to the semantic animacy tagging (see section 7) to single out the ones that might be genitive-shaped – there are too many unambiguously accusative-marked human referents for this to be a practical solution: it would over-simplify the data. It is also not obvious to us that the genitive-accusative is yet an accusative proper in its emergent OCS state. Nor did we want a separate tag for the genitive-accusative. The main reason to avoid a separate tag is the high number of ambiguous cases of genitive-marked arguments in OCS, due to the many genitive-triggering environments in OCS syntax:

- A good number of verbs require the genitive, and many of these have uncertain valency and are attested with both unambiguous accusatives and unambiguous genitives (e.g. perception verbs)
- Negated verbs mostly take genitive objects
- Regular transitives can take partitive objects in the genitive

Consequently, when a candidate for the genitive-accusative appears in the genitive after a negated verb or a verb with uncertain valency, we cannot be certain why it is genitive-marked. (Human singulars will not be partitive objects, though.) We have therefore decided to base our annotation on the interplay between several layers of annotation:

- All genitive-formed tokens are tagged as morphological genitives
- Regular transitive verbs take OBJs, also when genitive-marked (due to animacy, negation, partitivity), since such sentences can be passivised
- Verbs consistently requiring the genitive take OBLs

- Verbs with uncertain valency take the supertag ARG for genitive-marked objects

Consider examples (5) and (6):

(5) посълавъ оусѣкнѫ иоана вь темьници
"by sending someone he beheaded John in the prison" (Matt. 14:10)

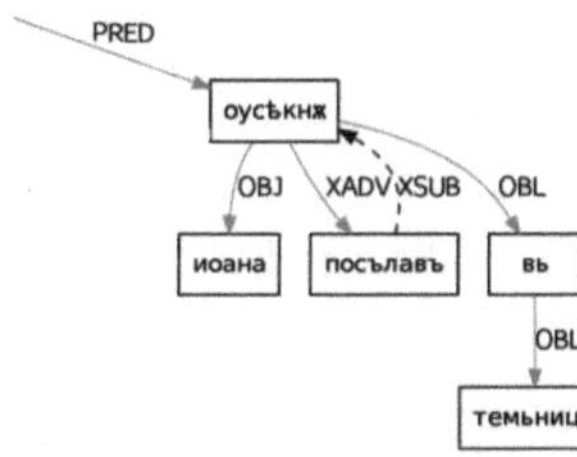

In this example, we see that иоана is an OBJ, since оусѣкнѫти "chop down" regularly takes the accusative. In the morphology, on the other hand, it is tagged as a genitive. In example (6), on the other hand (repeated from section 4), его must be analysed as an OBL, since трѣбовати "need, demand" regularly occurs with the genitive.

(6) г҃ъ трѣбоуоутъ его
"the Lord needs him" (Luke 19: 34)

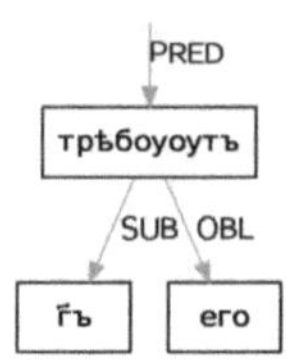

(7) оузьрѣ и҃са грѧдѫшта
"he saw Jesus coming" (John 1: 36)

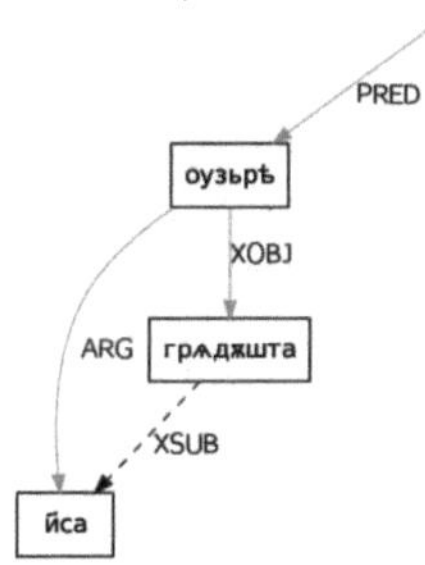

Verbs of perception generally have uncertain valency, sometimes adhering to the old Indo-European tendency for such verbs to take genitives and sometimes taking regular accusative. Therefore, we cannot tell whether Исоуса is a genitive-accusative OBJ or a genitive OBL in example (7). Consequently, it gets the supertag ARG in the syntax layer, but is a genitive in the morphology.

By combining this policy with the animacy annotation (see section 7), we can retrieve all the interesting categories, which would not have been possible without the extra adverbal relations.

Table 6. Genitive-marked human masculine singulars

Valency	Negated	Syntactic tag	Morphological tag	Genitive-accusative
transitive	no	OBJ	genitive	yes
transitive	yes	OBJ	genitive	uncertain
uncertain	no	ARG	genitive	uncertain
uncertain	yes	ARG	genitive	uncertain
requires genitive	no	OBL	genitive	no
requires genitive	yes	OBL	genitive	no

8.2. The animacy category and Greek definiteness: a preliminary case study

The possibility to combine information from several annotation layers into complex queries means that the corpus can be used to verify statements in the literature very quickly. We want to take a look at the following claim by Huntley (1993: 137–138): "There is a strong tendency for the genitive-accusative to refer to a definite object, and for the nominative-accusative to refer to an indefinite object." Huntley's claim is not contrastive: he does not make reference to the (in)definiteness of the corresponding Greek objects. Instead he counts the percentage of *semantically* definite objects (without giving a precise definition of what this means).

With a combination of information from several layers of the PROIEL corpus, we can get a quick answer to this question.[9] To get at the unambiguous genitive-accusative candidates and their Greek equivalents, we compose the following query:

9 The answers we obtain must be considered preliminary only, since the corpus is not as yet fully reviewed. There is every reason to believe that the main tendencies hold, though.

- Morphology: masculine singulars (excluding a-stems)
- Syntax: OBJs, excluding OBJs that are daughters of negated verbs
- Semantics: the animacy tag must be human
- Token alignment: find the Greek equivalent and check for presence or absence of definite article

The data we thus obtain show us that there is certainly something in Huntley's statement. Indefinite Greek objects are significantly less likely to be translated into OCS genitive-accusatives than definite ones, but it seems a bit of an overstatement to call this a strong tendency for indefinite objects to be realised as nominative-accusatives.

Table 7. OCS masculine singular human OBJs, corrected for negation, a-stems omitted, and their Greek token alignments

Greek token alignment	OCS accusative	per cent	OCS genitive	per cent
definite	20	10.60%	168	89.40%
indefinite	23	21.90%	82	78.10%

(P – value, Fischer's exact test: 0.0099)

However, given that Huntley looks at "definite reference", not at the presence or absence of a definite article in the Greek, it is clearly relevant to distinguish between proper nouns, which are often considered inherently definite, and common nouns. Thus we need to include the part of speech in our query. This is also important since the use of definite articles with NT Greek proper nouns clearly follows different rules than with common nouns. A significant difference between the realisation of definite and indefinite proper nouns would be a very interesting finding, as this would imply that the distribution of the article with proper nouns is conditioned by some of the same factors as the distribution of the OCS genitive-accusative.

Table 8. Masculine singular human OBJs, corrected for negation, a-stems omitted, token alignments by noun type

Greek object	OCS accusative	per cent	OCS genitive	per cent
proper definite	0	0%	57	100 %
proper indefinite	0	0 %	45	100 %
common definite	20	15.3 %	111	84.7 %
common indefinite	23	37.5 %	37	62.5 %

However, this is not what we find. In fact, all proper nouns, regardless of article use, occur in the genitive-accusative. It is in the common nouns that we find a distinction, indefinite common nouns are significantly less likely to be translated as nominative-accusatives (P-value 0.0007). Note that most indefinite common nouns in this group are still translated as genitive-accusatives, so Huntley's "strong tendency" does not really hold.

These findings point to the fact that at the OCS stage, the distribution of the genitive-accusative was not regulated by animacy and social prominence alone, but also by discourse prominence. Since the PROIEL corpus also includes information structure annotation (see section 6), we can also take out the givenness status of our data set. So far, only the Gospel of Mark and the first five chapters of the Gospel of Luke are annotated for information structure, so this data set is quite small, but even now the preliminary data set gives us statistically significant differences between genitive-accusatives and nominative-accusatives when it comes to givenness (p-value = 0.0188). Old or easily accessible objects are more prone to get the genitive-accusative than new ones are.

Table 9. Genitive-accusative candidates by givenness status (common nouns only)

	nominative-accusative		genitive-accusative	
old or accessible	4	13.80%	25	86.20%
new	9	47.40%	10	52.60%

When we have more text annotated for information structure, we will surely get even more interesting results.

9. Conclusions

In this article, it was our intention to present the possibilities offered by the PROIEL corpus, in particular its usefulness as a resource to a language such as OCS, where contrastive work against the Greek is indispensable. The distinguishing feature of our modestly-sized corpus is its detailed, multilayered annotation – with a coverage spanning morphology, syntax, information structure and semantics – and the possibility for individual scholars to add customised annotation. Crucial to the OCS part is also the high-quality token alignment with the Greek original, making it possible to compare the different language versions directly and accurately. Hence, the PROIEL corpus is a tool specifically designed and ideally fit for contrastive work: combining information from various annotation layers and exploiting the alignments gives rich research opportunities in many different fields. Our brief and preliminary sample study of the correlation between Greek definiteness and OCS incipient animacy marking may serve as an illustration of the corpus' potential for interesting work on OCS: we believe that the corpus opens both for entirely new findings and for new and accurate answers to old questions.

References

Dipper, S., Götze, M. and S. Skopeteas (2007). *Information Structure in Cross-Linguistic Corpora: Annotation Guidelines for Phonology, Morphology, Syntax, Semantics, and Information Structure.*
Available at http://www.sfb632.uni-potsdam.de/~d1/sfb632_guidelines/.

Dixon, R. (1979). "Ergativity". *Language*, vol. 55, n° 1: 59–138.

Gale W.A. and K.W. Church (1993). "A Program for Aligning Sentences in Bilingual Corpora". *Computational Linguistics*, vol. 19, n° 1: 75–102.

Gundel, J.K., Hedberg, N. and R. Zacharski (1993). "Cognitive status and the form of referring expressions in discourse". *Language* 69: 274–307.

Haug, D.T.T., Jøhndal, M.L., Eckhoff, H.M., Welo, E., Hertzenberg, M.J. and A. Müth (2009). "Computational and linguistic issues in designing a syntactically annotated parallel corpus of Indo-European languages". *Traitement automatique des langues* (à paraître).

Huntley, D. (1993). "Old Church Slavonic". In: B. Comrie and G.G. Corbett (eds.). *The Slavonic languages*. London and New York: Routledge.

Jagić, V. (1883). *Quattuor evangeliorum versionis palaeoslovenicae Codex Marianus glagoliticus.* Berlin: Weidmann.

Kamp, H. and U. Reyle (1993). *From Discourse to Logic. Introduction to Modeltheoretic Semantics of Natural language, Formal Logic and Discourse Representation Theory.* Dordrecht: Kluwer Academic Publishers.

Klenin, E. (1983). *Animacy in Russian: A New Interpretation*. Columbus, Ohio: Slavica.

Künzle B. (1984). *Das altarmenische Evangelium.* Bern: Peter Lang.

Nissim M., Dingare, S., Carletta, J. and M. Steedman (2004). "An Annotation Scheme for Information Status in Dialogue". Proceedings of *Language Resources and Evaluation*. Lisbon.

Prince, E.F. (1981). "Toward a taxonomy of given-new information". In: P. Cole (ed.). *Radical pragmatics*. New York: Academic Press: 223–255.

Riester, A. and D. Lorenz (2009). *Richtlinien zur Annotation von Informationsstatus (Gegebenheit) in Projekt A1, SFB 732*. 2009.

Streitberg, W. (1919). *Die gotische Bibel.* Heidelberg: Carl Winter.

Tischendorf, C. v. (1869–1872) *Novum Testamentum Graece*. 8th ed. Leipzig: Hinrich.

Zaenen, A., Carletta, J., Garretson, G., Bresnan, J., Koontz-Garboden, A., Nikitina, T., O'Connor, M.C. and T. Wasow (2004). "Animacy Encoding in English: why and how". In: B. Webber and D.K. Byron (eds.). *ACL 2004 Workshop on Discourse Annotation*. Association for Computational Linguistics, Barcelona, Spain: 118–125.

Parallel Corpora for Translation Teaching and Translator Training Purposes

Cécile Frérot

Abstract: Over the past decade corpora – and comparable corpora in particular – have proved a useful aid in the translation classroom and most studies have focused on using this type of corpora for translation teaching. The aim of our study is to explore the use of corpora – especially parallel corpora – in designing a corpus-based translation course that is relevant from a translational standpoint and that is best suited to future professional translators, especially in terms of corpus-based translation tools.

Keywords: corpus-based translation tools, concordances, comparable corpora, parallel corpora, professional translators, terminology, translation memory, translation teaching, translator training, translation strategies.

1. Introduction

Over the past decade there has been a growing interest in using corpora and concordancers for translation teaching. Comparable corpora have received most attention and have proved of great value in the translation classroom (Zanettin 1998; Bowker 1999; Zanettin 2001). As for parallel corpora, they have not been so much explored in the translation classroom (Pearson 2003; Granger 2003) even though this type of corpus is commonly used in Computer-Aided Translation (CAT) tools under the form of translation memories and is usually part of translator training.

Besides, while corpora and concordancers can be of considerable interest for translation teaching – which most studies have focused on – the question arises as to what extent these tools meet the needs of professional translators and consequently, in what respect and under what conditions they have to be integrated in translator training (Frérot 2009).

In this paper, we will show that parallel corpora can be a useful resource for translation teachers and translator trainers whose concerns are to raise student awareness of translation strategies and provide them with evidence of such strategies using corpora as well as to provide students with the skills needed to use corpus-based translation tools that are of valuable help for translation problem solving.

Section 2 provides some major references on using comparable and parallel corpora for translation teaching. Section 3 sheds some interesting light on the use of corpora by professional translators. The core of the paper is dedicated to designing a corpus-based translation course that encompasses both translation teaching and translator training purposes using parallel corpora. The pedagogical objectives and the teaching material are defined in section 4 while section 5 provides the course content with a focus on integrating parallel corpora in the translation classroom.

2. Corpora in Translation Teaching and Translator Training

2.1. Comparable Corpora

The references mentioned in this section refer specifically to the work that has been done on the benefits of using comparable corpora for translation teaching – and *not* language teaching. Comparable corpora are usually defined as "a collection of texts composed independently in the respective languages and put together on the basis of similarity of content, domain and communicative function" (Zanettin 1998: 614).

Comparable corpora have proved to enhance the understanding of the source language text and target language production (Zanettin 1998). Zanettin (2001) has also shown that comparable corpora help students produce more natural-sounding translations and gain insights in the languages and cultures involved as well as develop reading and writing skills.

An experimental study carried out by Bowker (1998) has shown that monolingual-native corpora help enhance translations by providing information missing from dictionaries, especially regarding term selection and idiomatic expressions. They can also help promote language awareness (Bowker 1999) and help students become better language service providers (Wilkinson 2005). Finally, in their pedagogically-oriented guide on using corpora (Bowker, Pearson 2002) have shown how to use LSP corpora as a translation resource.

2.2. Parallel Corpora

Parallel corpora – defined as having "components in two or more languages, consisting of original texts and their translations" (Aston 1999: 290) – remain largely underexplored in translator education though they are increasingly applied to translation research and language teaching (Pearson 2003).

The literature on using parallel corpora for translation purposes shows that this type of corpus can be a useful resource for terminology (Danielson, Ridings 2000; Pearson 2000) as well as a valuable tool to raise student awareness of translation strategies (Johansson, Hofland 2000; Pearson 2003). Williams (1996) has shown that parallel corpora can help retrieve correct equivalents compared with bilingual dictionaries and Fernandes (2007) has found that they can provide evidence of how professional translators transform the source text in the translation process.

2.3. Translation Memory as Parallel Corpus

A very specific type of parallel corpus widely used on the translation market is that produced by a Translation Memory (TM). TMs are well known in the translation industry and are part of the skills identified for professional translators. They are usually taught in CAT courses as such and are not integrated in the translation classroom.

In conventional TM tools, the aligned texts are divided into sentence-level source and target translation units for storage in a database. Each sentence of a new source text is compared with the units stored in the database, and the tool proposes matches that are exact or similar.

Conventional TMs have drawbacks due to the sentence-based approach which according to Bédard (2000) turns professional translators into mere "*traducteurs de phrases*". It has also been shown that professional translators tend to lose sight of the notion of "*text*" while using TMs.

Because of these drawbacks, another approach known as the character-string-within-a-bitext-based approach has been developed (Gow 2003). It is based on full source and target text pairs. It involves storing those text pairs in the database and identifying identical character strings of any lenght. Tools that fall into that category make it possible to search full aligned texts just as bilingual concordancers do, so these tools combine conventional TM functionalities and corpus-browsing facilities.

2.4. Corpora and Academic Use

Overall, corpora have proved to be useful in the classroom. Mastering corpora as a translation resource should be part of the curriculum of future translators (Zanettin 2002; Maia 2003; Varantola 2003). However, the use of corpora in the classroom is far from being systematic (Bernardini, Castagnoli 2008) and "if corpora are to play a role in the translation professions of tomorrow, it is important that they impact on the education of students today" (Benardini, Castagnoli 2008: 40).

Therefore, the preliminary question that should be addressed before designing a corpus-based translation course is to what extent translators use corpora in their professional environment and under what conditions corpora should be integrated in the translation classroom.

3. Are Corpora used by Professional Translators?

3.1. National Surveys

Surveys conducted over the past few years shed some interesting light on the use of corpora by professional translators. While a UK survey (Fulford, Granel-Zafra 2005) mentions neither corpora nor corpus analysis tools, a Canadian survey conducted by (Bowker 2002) shows that professional translators are more interested in TMs than in corpora even though they know that corpora exist.

3.2. European Survey

A survey conducted in Europe – which was part of a larger European study on Multilingual eLearning in Language Engineering (MeLLANGE 2006) – shows that corpora are not common practice among professional translators but it also highlights the particular interest of the participants to the survey in *(i)* using software that provide domain and language specific corpora tailored to their needs, *(ii)* using tools for extracting terms from a domain specific corpus and *(iii)* learning about the potential of corpora.

While going into greater details on the results would take more space than is available here[1], it should be mentioned that overall the results show how necessary it is to disseminate the potential corpora provide as well as to integrate tools that make corpus building and querying easier and faster (Bernardini 2006).

4. Designing A Corpus-Based Translation Course

4.1. Pedagogical Objectives

The corpus-based translation course is aimed at undergraduate students in their third year who are French-native speakers learning two languages including English. The course that has been designed aims to encompass both translation

1 For further details on the results, see (MeLLANGE 2006).

teaching and translator training purposes providing students with linguistic and technical skills.

The linguistic purpose is to help students gain insights into the usage of words in context and to raise student awareness of corpora as a translation resource. The technical purpose is to teach students how to use corpus-analysis tools for translation purposes, starting with comparable corpora and monolingual concordancers to gradually move on to parallel corpora and corpus-based translation tools. The aim is to integrate the best suited tools that meet the needs of professional translators so ideally work with tools that combine TM functionalities and corpus-building and corpus-browsing facilities.

4.2. Teaching Material

In order to get acquainted with corpora and concordances, students also use online corpora – namely the British National Corpus (BNC) and the Corpus of Contemporary American English (COCA).

Students use a comparable corpus made up of French-English popular-science texts dealing with volcanology (Josselin-Leray 2005) as well as parallel corpora: *(i)* English texts and their French translations for the *Global Fund*[2] and *(ii)* French extracts from *Le Monde* and their translations in *Guardian Weekly* – which are part of the Intersect Corpus[3]. Students use a monolingual concordancer (AntConc[4]) as well as a corpus-based translation tool (Multitrans) to browse these corpora.

The course is divided into three parts. The first part introduces key concepts to corpora and students get acquainted with concordances using the online BNC and COCA while in the second part students learn how to use a comparable corpus as a translation ressource. The last part of the course is dedicated to using parallel corpora in the translation classroom and this is the major focus of the current paper.

---

2 Both source and target texts have been manually extracted from the website http://www.theglobalfund.org/en/

3 The Intersect Corpus was built by Raphaël Salkie (Salkie 2000); I am very grateful to him for making the corpus available to me.

4 Freely available at http://www.antlab.sci.waseda.ac.jp/

5. Corpus-Based Translation Activities

5.1. Introducing Corpora and Concordances

Key concepts are introduced in the classroom in order to provide students with some basic knowledge on corpora – definitions, corpus types for instance – and key issues such as corpus building are outlined. As searching for words in context is essential for translators, students get acquainted with concordances. They are trained on how to produce and interpret concordance lines using the BNC and the COCA.

The BNC is a 100 million word collection of samples of written and spoken language from a wide range of sources, designed to represent a wide cross-section of current British English. Students use the free interface available at http://www.natcorp.ox.ac.uk/. Basic activities provided to students consist in searching for words – the word *rise* for instance – skimming through the occurrences and distinguishing the different parts of speech. Another activity involves working on collocates in order to show students which words typically belong together. For instance, students are asked to search for the verbs that collocate with the noun *findings* or to search the best natural ways of expressing in English that *prices fall* or *rise*. Students find out a whole range of verbs – such as *reduce*, *drop*, *decrease*, *decline*, *rise*, *increase*, *range*, *plummet* or *soar* – which are used in context and they learn how to combine those verbs with the right preposition or adverb (e.g. *decline by*, *increase dramatically*, *drop steeply*).

Students also use the COCA[5] which contains 20 million words in each year from 1990 to the present, with five genres of spoken, fiction, popular magazines, newspapers, and academic (Davies 2009). The COCA offers a wide range of possibilities to query the corpus and the main activity given to the students involves searching for words in context using the part of speech list – since the corpus is POS tagged – and comparing the corpus-based results with the results they have produced with their own intuition. For instance, students have to find out which verbs typically collocate with the noun *research* or which prepositions are most used with the verb *come*. This activity usually helps students produce more naturally-sounding English and it raises their awareness on using corpora as a language resource.

5 Freely available at http://www.americancorpus.org

5.2. Using a Comparable Corpus as a Translation Resource

At that point of the course, students are familiar enough with corpora and concordances so they can start using the concordancer AntConc and a comparable corpus as a translation resource.

The translation-related tasks that have been designed involve comparing the information found in dictionaries with the information in corpora. As mentioned earlier, I will not go into great details on using a comparable corpus as a translation resource since the current paper focuses on using parallel corpora in the translation classroom; so I will very briefly mention some of the corpus-based activities given to the students. For a more thorough description of the comparable corpus-based activities see (Frérot 2009).

The translation-related tasks involve comparing the data in the comparable corpus with the data in dictionaries given that "the obvious way in which corpora can help translators is as reference tools, as complements to traditional dictionaries and grammars" (Aston 1999). This activity shows students that dictionaries may not be as accurate and reliable as expected and students investigate usage through the corpus in order to discover new corpus-based translations. They look for words in context using the advanced search[6] in AntConc. By studying a term in context, students learn what other words typically collocate with that term. Identifying new corpus-based translations raises student awareness of corpora as a relevant complement to dictionaries and students also use the comparable corpus to find explanatory contexts likely to provide useful information in order to find new translations. Another corpus-based learning activity given to students involves analysing verb patterns. Students compare the information provided by dictionaries with the data found in the corpus and use the corpus to discover unknown patterns dictionaries do not provide.

Overall, these corpus-based activities illustrate how a comparable corpus can be used in the classroom as a translation resource. Using a concordancer such as AntConc allows students to see how a search in not one but several contexts gives critical information about the usage of words and phrases, insights that one is unlikely to find in such detail in dictionaries.

6 It enables users to specify a word that must appear within a certain number of words of another word *i.e.* in the vicinity of the search pattern.

6. Integrating Parallel Corpora in the Translation Classroom

The last part of the course is dedicated to using parallel corpora with a corpus-based CAT tool for translator training (6.1) and translation teaching (6.2) purposes.

6.1. Translator Training and Professional Needs

Translator training should be designed in order to meet the needs of professional translators. It should therefore integrate tools that can compete with TMs and bring an added value – since TMs are widely used in the translation industry – make corpus building and querying easier and faster as well as extract and process terminology as shown by the results of the MeLLANGE survey on the use of corpora by professional translators.

As mentioned by (Bernardini 2006: 21) when underlining the challenges that lie ahead for the use of corpora in translator education and practice:
Widespread use of corpora and corpus construction and search facilities is likely to depend on their integration with Computer-Aided Translation (CAT) technology.

As a result (Bernardini, Castagnoli 2008) suggest that corpus construction and corpus searching should ideally be integrated with CAT tools. Actually, this form of integration has somehow been performed in a corpus-based translation tool that has been introduced in our translation course.

6.1.1. Multitrans

Multitrans (http://www.multicorpora.com/) is a corpus-based translation tool that features both powerful corpus-browsing facilities and functionalities of TMs which distinguish it from other CAT tools available on the market such as bilingual concordancers on the one hand and TMs on the other hand. It is a commercial package of next-generation CAT tool that has been increasingly used in a variety of companies as well as in international and European organizations.

6.1.2. Translation-Related Tasks using Multitrans

Multitrans has been integrated in the translation classroom to show students how such a corpus-based translation tool can help translators solve terminology and phraseology problems – which is essential for translators especially for those who translate texts that do not contain a large number of repeated segments and for which TMs with a sentence-based approach are not the best suited tools (Bowker 2002).

Students use the English to French translations for the *Global Fund* mentioned earlier (see 4.2) and learn how to quickly create and enrich an aligned corpus. In Multitrans, such a task is made possible with a *TextBase Agent* and students are easily guided throughout the whole automatic process. The next task involves creating a terminology database using the *TermBase Agent* and enriching it by searching the previously built corpus with the *TextBase Agent.*

Figure 1 displays the *TextBase Agent* whose most relevant corpus-browsing facility is to search for strings of any length and display the number of occurrences together with their translations in full-text context. For instance here, students were asked to retrieve the English term *antimalarial drugs*, identify the most frequent French translation in the corpus (namely *antipaludique*) and store it in the *TextBase Agent* by creating automatically a terminology entry as shown in figure 2.

A greater emphasis is put on training students on how to search through the aligned corpus during the translation process making the best of the automated search functions provided by the *TextBase Agent* as well as saving any relevant information from the corpus in the *TermBase Agent*. Actually, Multitrans enables translators who use popular editors to interactively work with both the *TextBase Agent* and *TermBase Agent* in order to enhance their translations by retrieving accurate terminology dictionaries fail to provide. This is the case for the term *tuberculosis patient* students had to translate in the following sentence: *tuberculosis patients, whether undergoing treatment or already cured, will be essential participants in the disease awareness network.*

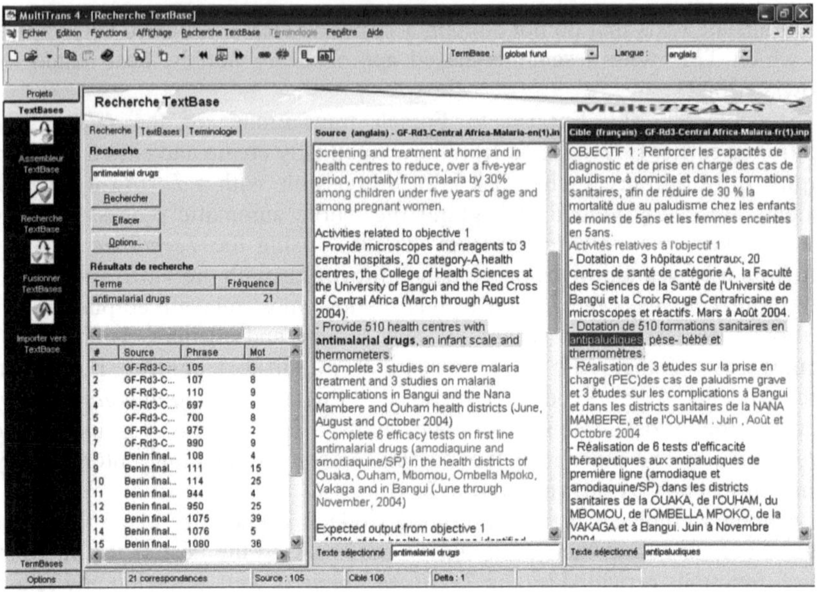

Figure 1. *TextBase Agent*

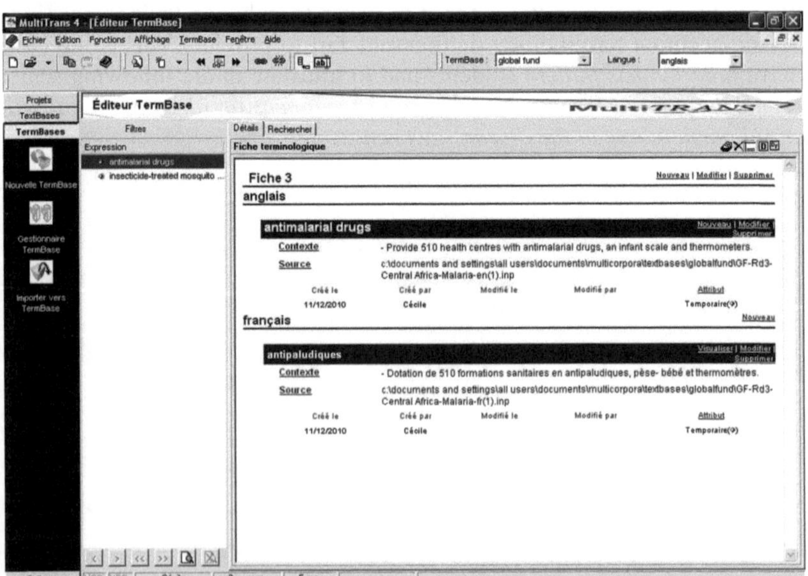

Figure 2. *TermBase Agent*

Students found out that the most frequent French translation was *patient tuberculeux* (10 occurrences) while the dictionary-based translation *tuberculeux* provided by the well-known *Grand Dictionnaire Terminologique*[7] occurred only once in the corpus and the second most frequent corpus-based translation – *malade de la tuberculose* (5 occurrences) – was not provided by the above-mentioned specialised dictionary. Overall, comparing the information found in the corpus with the information found in dictionaries has proved to help students raise their awareness of parallel corpora as a useful complement to dictionaries.

Training students on how to easily and quickly build a corpus, extract terminology and search the corpus to solve translation problems – meeting therefore the needs of professional translators – has been achieved by integrating a leading-edge corpus-based translation tool: Multitrans. In addition to integrating such a tool in translator training, we also used it for translation teaching purposes by providing students with translation case-studies. Our aim is to provide evidence for translation strategies, raise student awareness of language differences and improve their target language production thanks to the wide and rich set of accurate and idiomatic possible translations found in the corpus.

6.2. Case-studies for Translation Teaching: Translating the Verb "Say" into French using a Parallel Corpus

The case-studies students work on are based on translation errors and a lack of idiomaticity identified in the English to French translation course which is part of the undergraduate translation programme. Contrary to the course on using corpora for translation purposes the current paper is based on, the translation course takes place in the first term and it mainly consists in putting into practice some translation strategies students started to learn during their second year by translating English newspaper texts into French.

As a translation teacher, I have identified common translation errors as well as a lack of idiomaticity in the French translations made by the students over the years. More specifically, I have noticed lexical choices made by the students, among which the overuse of the word "*dire*" to translate *say* into French in direct and indirect speech as shown by sentences (1) and (2), while there is a wider set of appropriate and idiomatic French translations as put forward by the search made in the parallel Intersect corpus.

7 Available at http://www.granddictionnaire.com

(1) "We've had zero federal assistance," **says** Ron Stimmel.
(2) Consider the Nokia 6680 mobile phone, **says** Adam Greenfield.

Based on this evidence, I have designed a case-study whose aim is to show students how a parallel corpus can contribute to provide appropriate translations.

6.2.1. Aligning and Querying a French-English Parallel Corpus

As students have learned previously how to align a parallel corpus using Multitrans, they use the French extracts from the daily *Le Monde* and their translations in *Guardian Weekly* to build the parallel corpus. The next step is to use the corpus-browsing facilities in Multitrans to query the corpus and search the verb *say* and its conjugated forms – *i.e. say*, *says*, *said* and *saying*. Students skim through the occurrences and retrieve those in active voice occurring in direct and indirect speech – which excludes the passive voice as in sentence (3):

(3) Bosnian President Alija Izetbegovic, who was opposed to signing the agreement, **is said to** have given in slightly to French and British pressure to agree to negotiations.

6.2.2. Analysing the French Source Corpus

6.2.2.1. Overall Results

As students find out a total of 192 occurrences matching the verb *say* and its conjugated forms in active voice, they analyse the results and identify which French words match the English translation *say* in the French source corpus. The results are displayed in figure 3.

	Lexical verb – *dire*	**Other lexical verbs**	**Ø**	**Adverb**
Number of occ.	39	**111**	30	12
%	20.31	**57.82**	15.62	6.25

Figure 3. Results in the French corpus

As mentioned earlier, students overuse the verb *dire* to translate the verb *say* and consequently, they fail to provide more natural-sounding and native-like translations. When looking at the results, students were striked by the great variety of verbs used in the French source corpus. Actually, other lexical verbs –

apart from *dire* – are used in more than 57% of the total occurrences in the source texts while the verb *dire* accounts for only 20% of the total occurrences. Besides, students found out that in more than 6% of the occurrences an adverb was used (namely the French adverb *selon*) – a choice that hardly occurs to students even though they acknowledged that it sounded very idiomatic and natural. Finally, it should be noticed that in 15% of the occurrences the choice made by the translators is to add the verb *say* while in the French source texts there is neither mention of the verb *dire* nor of any other word. This is the case in the example (4B) where the translator's choice is to use the indirect speech and to reintroduce the proper noun *Sahnoun*:

(4A) Cette aide a commencé à être acheminée au mois de janvier. Les Nations unies, elles, ne sont intervenues de manière notable qu'à partir du mois de mars.

(4B) The aid, **said Sahnoun**, began to be sent in January, while the United Nations began making a significant contribution only in March.

A thorough analysis of the sentences occurring before sentence (4B) in the parallel corpus shows that this choice is part of the whole translator's strategy to use the indirect speech (5B) while in French the journalist has used the direct speech as shown in (5A):

(5A) – Mohamed Sahnoun, représentant spécial du secrétaire général des Nations unies en Somalie (…) « **Quel jugement portez-vous sur la situation actuelle en Somalie?** » On s'imagine (…)

(5B) – (...) according to Mohamed Sahnoun, the United Nations secretary general's special representative there.
Asked what he thought of the present situation in Somalia Sahnoun said: You imagine (...)

6.2.2.2. French Source Verbs

As the great variety of lexical verbs was unexpected to most students – even though they acknowledged it was a relevant and natural-sounding alternative to the verb *dire* – they further investigated those verbs and recorded 49 different lexical verbs accounting for a total of 111 occurrences. The results are displayed in Figure 4.

French non neutral verbs	Frequency
affirmer	22
déclarer, expliquer	8
assurer, estimer	5
confier, constater, résumer, souligner	3
ajouter, écrire, indiquer, lancer, noter, raconter, rapporter, répondre, se dire, se prononcer	2
annoncer, avouer, commenter, considérer, décrire, donner peu d'indications, être le révélateur, faire valoir, insister, ironiser, lâcher, observer, poursuivre, préciser, prévoir, rappeler, réaffirmer, reconnaître, regretter, réitérer, renchérir, répéter, reprocher, révéler, s'insurger, se taire, soupirer, soutenir, voter	1

Figure 4. French non neutral verbs in the source corpus

Those preliminary results show that the 49 non neutral verbs in the French corpus have been translated by the verb *say* – one "neutral reporting verb" (Thompson 1994). Furthermore, the French most literal translation of say – *dire* – was not recorded among the results. This corpus-based information gives students straightforward evidence of the wide and rich set of possible verbs they can use in their translations.

6.2.3. Discovering Translation Strategies

6.2.3.1. Lexical modulation

This corpus-based case-study provides students with further evidence on translation strategies and raises their language-awareness. Students are faced with real data that highlights what is usually taught in the translation classroom as modulation, *i.e* "a variation of the form of the message obtained by a change in the point of view" (Vinay *et al.* 1995: 36) that "presents a same reality in a different light" (Vinay *et al.* 1995: 88). The translation strategy used by the translators – known as lexical modulation as it operates at the lexicon level – shows a semantic "delete" in the English translations; there are non neutral verbs in the French source texts translated by the same neutral reporting verb in English. A set of examples is given below:

(6A) « Les Cubains ont essayé de traiter directement avec les Russes » **explique** un expert.

(6B) "The Cubans tried to negotiate directly with the Russians," **says** an insider.

(7A) « Je vais sans doute envoyer mes garçons, mais moi je resterai », **avoue** un ingénieur d'une cinquantaine d'années.
(7B) "I think I'll probably send my boys off, but I myself will stay here," **says** a 50-year-old engineer.
(8A) « C'est la première fois, **souligne**-t-on à la FORPRONU, qu'un de nos soldats a été délibérément tué ».
(8B) "It's the first time one of our soldiers has been deliberately killed," **said** a UNPROFOR spokesman.

For instance, in the example (6A), students notice the use of the lexical verb *expliquer* – whose most literal translation is *explain;* in the examples (7A) and (8A), the lexical verb *avouer* – which could be rendered in English by *acknowledge* or *admit* – and *souligner* – whose most straightforward translation could be *underline* – have a heavier semantic load than the neutral verb *say* chosen consistently by the translators.

This corpus-based approach used in the classroom enables students to collect real data from a parallel corpus by using Multitrans and to put forward the translation strategy used by the translators known as "lexical modulation" and termed here as "semantic delete". Besides, they become more fully aware of the differences in French and English regarding the translation of French declarative verbs by a single neutral reporting verb in English – a main feature in French to English translation as studied by (Nita 2006; Poncharal 2006).

As students are guided throughout the data, they also notice that the translators have chosen to compensate[8] for the lack of straightforward verb equivalent in the target language by adding a word to the verb *say* – be it an adjective (example (9B)) or an adverb (example (10B)):

(9A) « Notre oppression a commencé en 1939, lorsque Hitler a annexé les territoires des Sudètes (nord de la Bohême), pas en 1948 ! », **s'insurge** Tomas Kraus.
(9B) "We first began to suffer oppression in 1939, when Hitler annexed the Sudeten territories in northern Bohemia, not in 1948!" **says an angry** Kraus.
(10A) « Si seulement il ne s'était montré à ce point caractéricl, les choses auraient pris un tour bien différent », **soupirent**, l'air désolé, les autorités tunisiennes.
(10B) "IF ONLY HE hadn't been such a problem case, things would've turned out very differently," **said** the Tunisian authorities **regretfully**.

8 This has been studied by (Nita 2006) who talks of "semantic compensation".

6.2.3.2. Transposition

Among the translation strategies used by translators, students find evidence of what is commonly taught as transposition, *i.e.* a change in grammatical category between the source language and the target language (Vinay *et al.* 1995). In the following examples, the French adverb *selon* is used (11A, 12A) while the translators used the verb *say* (11B, 12B):

(11A) **Selon** un groupe d'économistes cubains, le recul du produit intérieur brut.
(11B) One group of Cuban economists **says** the island's gross domestic product
(12A) A Londres, M. John Major a placé "le SME au cœur de sa stratégie économique", **selon** l'expression de l'hebdomadaire The Economist
(12B) British prime minister John Major has placed the "EMS at the heart of his economic strategy", **says** the weekly Economist.

7. Conclusion

Corpora – and parallel corpora in particular – can undoubtedly be relevant to students specialising in translation and introducing parallel corpora in the translation classroom requires to integrate corpus-based translation tools that are best suited to translation problem solving. Using the leading-edge corpus-based translation tool Multitrans in our translation programme has proved of valuable interest for translator training as Multitrans makes it possible to easily and quickly create aligned corpora, search through them and extract terminology – some of the major needs identified by professional translators.

From a linguistic standpoint, designing case-studies based on parallel corpora can be of great relevance for translation teaching purposes, making it possible to teach translation strategies by providing straightforward evidence of strategies such as transposition and lexical modulation as illustrated here. Furthermore, as students investigate the corpus and query it, they are faced with real data through an inductive approach that provides them with wide and rich sets of possible translations and raises their language-awareness as demonstrated here with the translation of the verb *say* into French.

Future work involves working with a bi-directional parallel corpus therefore complementing the French-English translations with an English-French corpus made up of newspaper texts which should enable us to refine the case-study just presented.

References

Aston, G. (1999). "Corpus use and learning to translate". *Textus*, 12: 289–314.

Bédard, C. (2000). « Mémoire de traduction cherche traducteur de phrases… ». *Traduire*, n°186.

Bernardini, S. (2006). "Corpora for translators and translation practices. Achievements and challenges". *Proceedings of the Language Resources and Evaluation Conference*: 17–22.

Bernardini, S. and S. Castagnoli (2008). "Corpora for translator education and translation practice". In: Y. Rodrigo, Elia (ed.). *Topics in Language Resources for Translation and Localisation*: 39–55.

Bowker, L. (1998). "Using Specialized Monolingual Native-Language Corpora as a Translation Resource: a Pilot Study". *Meta*, 43 (4): 631–651.

Bowker, L. (1999). "Exploiting the potential of corpora for raising language awareness in student translators". *Language Awareness*, 8: 160–173.

Bowker, L. (2002). *Computer-Aided Translation Technology: A Practical Introduction*. University of Ottawa, Ottawa Press, Didactic of Translation Series.

Bowker, L. and J. Pearson (2002). *Working with Specialized Language. A practical guide to using corpora*. London and New York: Routledge.

Danielson, P. and D. Ridings (2000). "Corpus and Terminology: Software for the Translation Program at Göteborgs Universitet, or Getting Sutdents to do the Work". In: S.P. Botley, A. M. McEnery, and A. Wilson (eds.). *Multilingual Corpora in Teaching and Research*: 65–72.

Davies, M. (2009) "The 385+ Million Word Corpus of Contemporary American English (1990-present)". *International Journal of Corpus Linguistics*.

Fernandes, L. P. (2007). "On the Use of a Portuguese-English Parallel Corpus of Children's Fantasy Literature in Translator Education". *Cadernos de Tradução* (UFSC), vol. 20: 141–163.

Frérot, C. (2009). "Designing a Corpus-based Translation Course for Translation Teaching and Translator Training". *International Journal of Translation*, 2 (1–2): 133–147.

Fulford, H. and J. Granell-Zafra (2005). "Translation and Technology: a Study of UK Freelance Translators". *The Journal of Specialised Translation*, 4: 2–17.

Gow, F. (2003). Metrics for Evaluating Translation Memory Software. Thesis under the supervision of L. Bowker, School of Translation and Interpretation. University of Ottawa.

Granger, S. (2003). "The corpus approach: a common way forward for Contrastive Linguistics and Translation Studies". In: S. Granger, J. Lerot and S. Petch-Tyson (eds.). *Corpus-based Approaches to Contrastive Linguistics and Translation Studies*. Amsterdam and Atlanta: Rodopi: 17–29.

Johansson, S. and K. Hofland (2000). "The English-Norwegian Parallel Corpus: Current Work and New Directions". In: S.P. Botley, A.M. McEnery, and A. Wilson (eds.). *Multilingual Corpora in Teaching and Research*: 134–147.

Josselin-Leray, A. (2005). Place et rôle des terminologies dans les dictionnaires généraux unilingues et bilingues. Etude d'un domaine de spécialité : volcanologie. Thèse de doctorat, Université Lyon II.

Maia, B. (2003). "Some languages are more equal than others. Training translators in terminology and information retrieval using comparable and parallel corpora". In: F. Zanettin, S. Bernardini and D. Stewart (eds.). *Corpora in Translator Education*. Manchester and Northampton: St. Jerome: 55–70.

MeLLANGE Corpora and E-learning Survey Results (2006). ITI Bulletin, Available at http://www.iti.org.uk/uploadedFiles/surveys/Mellange_Survey_Updated(05-06).pdf

Nita, R. (2006). « … » *ironise un professeur* vs « … » *says a teacher* ou sur les dérives du discours direct dans la traduction de verbes introducteurs. Etude contrastive français, anglais, roumain. In: C. Delesse (ed.). *Collection Traductologie, Artois Presses Université. Discours rapportés, Approches linguistiques et/ou* traductologiques: 173–195.

Pearson, J. (2000). "Teaching terminology using electronic resources". In: S.P. Botley, A.M. McEnery, and A. Wilson (eds.). *Multilingual Corpora in Teaching and Research*: 92–105.

Pearson, J. (2003). "Using Parallel Texts in Translation Training Environment". In: F. Zanettin, S. Bernardini and D. Stewart (eds.). *Corpora in Translator Education*. Manchester and Northampton: St. Jerome: 15–24.

Poncharal, B. (2006). « *Say* un verbe à part – analyse contrastive anglais/français ». In: C.Delesse (ed). *Collection Traductologie, Artois Presses Université. Discours rapportés, Approches linguistiques et/ou traductologiques*: 127–141.

Salkie, R. (2000). « Corpus Linguistics ». *Cahiers AFLS*, 01/00: 44–50.

Thompson, G. (1994). *Collins Cobuild English Guides, 5, Reporting.* Londres, HarperCollins Publishers.

Varantola, K. (2003). "Translators and Disposable Corpora". In: F. Zanettin, S. Bernardini and D. Stewart (eds.). *Corpora in Translator Education*. Manchester and Northampton: St. Jerome: 55–70.

The Combination of Comparable and Translation Corpora and How Translators May Benefit from IT[1]

Marlén Izquierdo

Abstract: This paper deals with the combination of comparable and parallel corpora in the descriptive, functional analysis of languages in contrast and its positive impact for extending applications to translation. It draws on the results obtained from a project where a corpus-based contrastive analysis and a descriptive translation study have been carried out on English gerund-participle constructions (G-P) and Spanish gerund constructions (G). Combining different types of corpora in an attempt at bridging the gap between theoretical language contrast and the application of results is proving to be feasible for the language pair English-Spanish, as the research endeavour carried out by the ACTRES group is showing. There are two main features which back up this feasibility: the usefulness and the usability of the results. The former accounts for the advantageous alliance of different types of corpora and the latter shows how fruitful this can be. The results obtained are not only applicable in the field of translation but also in the teaching of English and/or Spanish as a foreign language.

Keywords: ACTRES[2], applied extensions, contrastive linguistics, linguistic corpora, translation studies, usability, usefulness.

1. Introduction

This piece of research has been prompted by a social need whereby translators require help to tackle problem-trigger grammatical phenomena when translating from English into Spanish. The problem in mind is of a communicative nature, for it relates to grammatical resources that are assumedly cross-linguistic equivalents but may convey partially divergent meanings. Thereby, they pose a problem for the translator, who might risk rendering an infelicitous translation which either fails to get across the original meaning or deviates from the normal way of communicating such a meaning in the target language. As such, this study is to be described as functional, application-oriented and cross-linguistic.

---

1 This paper was funded by the research grant LE025A09 from the regional government of Castilla y León (Spain).

2 Análisis Contrastivo y Traducción English-Spanish [English-Spanish Contrastive Analysis and Translation] http://actres.unileon.es.

It is functional because it adheres to a theory of language which centres on meaning, as being its primary function or means of communication. It is application-oriented because it seeks to enable an application of language, namely, translation, and it is cross-linguistic because two languages are involved: English and Spanish. The three features are interrelated, for the application, i.e., translation, entails a cross-linguistic practice which is based on functional equivalence.

Whenever this practice is jeopardised due to the problematic nature of the linguistic resources involved in the translation, such phenomena are relevant for research with an applied goal because their description might clear the way towards the application. In other words, the problem occurs between a given pair of languages in actual situations of cross-linguistic communication. In order to find a solution, the problem-trigger resources have to be described independently as well as in the contact situation where such a problem occurs. This is the reason why such a descriptive procedure requires authentic data of the functionality of the grammatical resources which challenge translation as well as evidence of the cross-linguistic situation where the problem arises. The need for empirical data demands the use of linguistic corpora, which adds another feature to the study: empirical or "usage-based". All in all, the main features of this piece of research frame it within the field of applied linguistics and demand the tenets of two interrelated disciplines, namely, contrastive linguistics and translation studies. Corpus linguistics is the methodological approach for the analyses are based on the data provided by two different types of corpora, i.e., one comparable and one parallel, the combination of which is believed to favour English-Spanish acceptable translation by yielding useful and usable insights on contrastive and translation terms as will be shown.

2. Corpus-based cross-linguistic, applied research

A way of satisfying the social need underlying this piece of research can be attained if translators are aware of the correct usage of certain linguistic resources and their degree of translatability. The process of translation is a directional activity where the starting point is a functional resource in the original text (OT), whose meaning is to be expressed in the target one (TT) in the most normal way, which urges knowledge of the expressive means to convey such a meaning. Therefore, the translator is expected to acknowledge the existence of at least an assumed equivalent resource in the target language, on the assumption that all languages are able to express the same meanings even though they differ in how they do so. Thus, being aware of the correct usage of at least, these phenomena requires a contrastive analysis between the language resources involved in the translation. Along with the functional correspondences identified between the OT resource and its assumed equivalent through contrast, translators might resort to other translational options, different from the assumed one, which preserve functional equivalence too. These options, which would make a repertoire of functional equivalents, are to be found in authentic translations. Hence, a descriptive translation pertains. The translational options observed are of paramount importance for cross-linguistic research, for not only do they meet the need of a choice on the part of the translator (Köller 1989), but also hint at how "...la lingüística contrastiva se nutre de la traducción para poder llevar a cabo el contraste entre lenguas" (Ramón García 2001: 620).

In order to deal with all these phenomena, both linguistic correspondences between the original resource and its assumed equivalent as well as other functional equivalents involved in an actual instance of translation, it is a must to *observe* them in accurate communicative contexts as are exemplified by language corpora.

It is believed that the combination of comparable and parallel corpora in the contrastive, descriptive analysis of language usage has a positive impact for extending applications to translation for two main reasons; first, all the possible Spanish equivalents of the English resource are not established *a priori*. Second, limiting the linguistic correspondence to just one resource in the target language (TL) (the assumed equivalent) would disallow a compilation of various translational options. Either type of corpora belongs with one of two complementary analyses, so that the comparable corpus is the tool for a contrastive analysis whereas the parallel corpus is suitable as a repository of examples for a descriptive translation study. Therefore, an accurate procedure would imply a first step whereby the degree of equivalence between the ST resource and its assumed equivalent is established so as to observe differences and similarities, among which problem-triggers for translation can be observed. All this is achieved by means of a comparable-corpus-based contrastive analysis. A second step would include a) the observation of other resources which are possibly used as translational options, hence, functional equivalents, and b) the verification of whether or not the translated use of the assumed equivalent deviates from native-like use, which can only be attained by comparing it with comparable-corpus-based contrastive information. This second stage involves working with a translation or parallel corpus.

Summing up, if one embarks on a descriptive project within the field of translation studies, there should be a contrastive analysis that ascertains the degree of translatability between source language (SL) and target language (TL) phenomena prior to extending applications to translation. As Rabadán asserts: "En este sentido cabe preguntarse si el análisis contrastivo [...] no es un nivel, posiblemente el más básico e inmediato, de la teoría de la traducción, y el que proporciona la transición real entre teoría y práctica" (2005). To put it differently, contrasting both resources is the way of raising awareness of how equivalent they are in terms of the functions or meanings they convey, commonly as well as independently. In this way, contrastive analysis unveils similarities and differences of usage, contributing *useful* information for the applied purpose in mind. In addition, there is further information for the translator to achieve successful translation from English into Spanish more efficiently. The insights gained from the contrastive analysis and the functional relations identified in the descriptive translation study prove to be *usable* if formulated as "descriptively prescriptive guidelines" (Rabadán 2008: 114) for future translation tasks, as the present study attempts to do. In this way, the complementation of results might lead the way to applied extensions as Rabadán (2008) advocates.

3. Case study: English *-ing* constructions in contrast and translation into Spanish

The case study reported upon here focuses on an English resource whose complex functionality challenges the language user, be it a translator or a student of English as a foreign language alike. The grammatical phenomenon under analysis is the so-called *-ing* constructions, for which I refer to those functional resources whose main constituent is a gerund-participle (G-P) (Huddleston and Pullum 2002) surrounded by co-textual elements which contribute to its function or meaningful behaviour as a whole. There are two main reasons why the G-P triggers a problem in English-Spanish translation: first, it is a multifunctional resource which has to be analysed in co(n)text so as to determine the meaning to translate into the TL, which implies the search for an equivalent target resource. Second, this resource of English has been long associated with the Spanish gerund (G), correspondence which has been so much generalised that their equivalence is taken for granted irrespective of the fact that they do not always express the same meanings. Moreover, this overgeneralization hinders the search for other, possibly better, equivalents. In short, the assumed similarity between the English G-P and the Spanish G constructions might lead translators to misuse the Spanish resource, giving into translationese, which might call the acceptability of the TT into question. Therefore, in order to solve this problem, a thorough analysis of the functionality of these constructions is in order so as to identify common grounds and divergences, which would hint at the degree of equivalence, and therefore translatability, between them. A comparable-corpus-based contrastive analysis seeks to provide a useful solution to this problem, as explained below.

3.1. Comparable-corpus-based contrastive analysis

To begin with, it is important to keep in mind that this is a contrastive *functional* analysis (from here on *cfa*) which focuses on meaning, which is arrived at by observing a given expressive resource in context. This requires the consideration of the four building blocks of language function, i.e., form, meaning, frequency and co(n)text. The first one is given, for this is the starting point, namely, English G-P and Spanish G constructions. Along with the various resources made up of the English G-P and Spanish G and the meanings conveyed by each of them in context, a complete functional description ought to consider how frequent the realisation of each meaning is and how relevant co(n)textual support is. These are the criteria looked at in the descriptive stage of the *cfa*.

3.1.1. The data

I have used two monolingual corpora from where a sample of each key resource in context is extracted. The corpora used are BoE[3] from Cobuild and CREA[4]. Due to the fact that these corpora have been built independently, a custom-made subcorpus has been isolated in each of them according to certain criteria which preserve comparability. These criteria are genre (books), domain (written), time-span (from 2000 onwards) and geographical variety (both European). By checking word frequency lists[5] the top ten gerund-participles (G-Ps) and gerunds (Gs) were chosen as the input word for searches in the corpora. A first search retrieved far too many concordances (see table 1), so a statistical formula was applied to narrow the initial population into a more manageable sample, which resulted in 6,676 concordances altogether. Table 1 illustrates the G-Ps and Gs selected and the number of concordances per form, both the initial population and the sample obtained after applying the formula:

Table 1. Sample of G-P/G concordances to analyze

ENGLISH			SPANISH		
G-P	POPULATION BoE	SAMPLE	G	POPULATION CREA	SAMPLE
Being	5,460	367	Siendo	8,456	382
Going	3,539	357	Haciendo	6,230	376
Having	1,822	328	Mirando	3,065	354
Using	781	264	Hablando	3,244	356
Making	1,522	316	Dando	3,722	361

3 Bank of English. Online access previous subscription.

4 Corpus de Referencia del Español Actual. http://corpus.rae.es/creanet.html

5 Leech *et al.* (2001) and Alameda & Cuetos (1995).

Looking	1,568	320	Pensando	2,498	345
Taking	1,263	304	Esperando	2,101	336
Doing	1,455	314	Dejando	2,259	340
Working	1,103	298	Buscando	2,194	338
Getting	1,039	288	Viendo	1,944	332
TOTAL	**19,552**	**3,156**	**TOTAL**	**35,713**	**3,520**

The actual extraction of the concordances has been done using the search facilities with which each corpus is equipped. BoE enables the extraction of the exact number of concordances whereas CREA does not. Instead, the initial population has had to be filtered as many times as necessary so as to get the closer, but bigger, sample, discarding the superfluous ones.

3.1.2. Functional description

This stage in the analysis aims at interpreting and classifying the concordances semantically. The description of the English and Spanish sample has proceeded according to the same criteria so that all the concordances are analysed in an individual but parallel way (James 1980). These criteria are bound up with the functionality of the resources and, as such, they are not fixed and have been adapted when necessary so as to depict the reality under examination. Moreover, these criteria are easily embedded in any corpus approach. The guidelines followed are:

a. relevance of co-text: surrounding elements might contribute directly to the realization of a given meaning;
b. the interdependence of lexis and grammar: the lexical nature of the G-P and/or G might be highly related to the function of the whole construction;
c. the flexible nature of meaning: there are various ways of expressing the same meaning, even within one given language. Thus, the possibility of rephrasing any G-P or G construction has been a criterion for deciding on their semantic classification.

The observation of the G-P and G constructions has revealed a range of meanings conveyed by each of them which confirm their complex functionality. Overall, the insights derived from the descriptive phase show four different uses of the English resource, namely, periphrastic, non-periphrastic, fossilized and independent. The periphrastic use refers to those G-P constructions which behave as verb phrases. The non-periphrastic use is represented by G-P constructions which realize functions common to grammatical categories other than verbs. The fossilized use of the G-P refers to cases where the G-P has become a full noun or adjective in the language, as their modification by determiners, intensifiers or variability of number (singular/plural) indicate. A hundred and fifty-two fossilized G-Ps have been found and discarded from the analysis, along with a hundred and seventy-seven of a given G-P which has undergone a process of grammaticalization becoming a semi-modal verb, namely, "be going to". In relation to the independent use of the English resource, a small number of concordances do not convey functions usually associated with either verbs or any other word class. Concerning the Spanish resource, three different uses have been observed: periphrastic, non-periphrastic and independent. As can be seen, the contrastive analysis has brought to light a clear difference of use between both resources. In turn, every use displays a fairly wide range of meanings or semantic functions, which increases the functional complexity of either resource as well as affecting their degree of linguistic correspondence and, therefore, functional equivalence or translatability.

The ensuing stage of the analysis juxtaposes both inventories so that it is easier to observe their degree of correspondence, showing commonalities as well as *lacunae* (Ø), as illustrated by table 2 (Juxtaposition of semantic functions realized by G-P&G constructions[6]).

The juxtaposition of the functionality of the resources is prior to the contrast proper.

Table 2. Juxtaposition of semantic functions realized by G-P& G constructions

	G-P CONSTRUCTIONS	**MEANING**	**G CONSTRUCTIONS**	
Periphrastic use	Be + V-*ing*	**Progression**	Estar + G Periphrasis G	Periphrastic use
	Be + V-*ing*	**Temporary habit**	Ø	
	Be + V-*ing*	**Gradual Progression**	Estar + G Periphrasis G	
	Be + V-*ing*	**Future intention**	Ø	
	Be + V-*ing*	**General Validity**	Ø	
	Be + V-*ing*	**Iteration**	Estar + G Periphrasis G	
	Be + V-*ing*	**Temporary state**	Ø	
	Be + V-*ing* Aspectual V + V-*ing*	**Inchoation**	Estar + G Periphrasis G	
	Be + V-*ing*	**Continuation**	Estar + G	

6 GPO stand for Gerundio Predicativo de Objeto, GPS stand for Gerundio Predicativo de Sujeto and GD stand for Gerundio Descriptivo (Izquierdo 2008).

	Aspectual V + V-*ing*		Periphrasis G	
	Be + V-*ing*	**Result**	Ø	
	Aspectual V + V-*ing*	**Cessation**	Periphrasis G	
Non-periphrastic use				Non-periphrastic use
	Adjunct	**Time**	Adjunct	
	Adjunct	**Process**	Adjunct	
	Adjunct	**Elaboration**	Adjunct	
	Adjunct	**Cause**	Adjunct	
	Adjunct	**Contrast**	Adjunct	
	Adjunct	**Result**	Adjunct	
	Adjunct	**Purpose**	Adjunct	
	Adjunct	**Condition**	Adjunct	
	Adjunct	**Illocution**	Adjunct	
	Adjunct	**Place**	Adjunct	
	Verb object Subject	**Reference**	Ø	
	Verb object Verb complement	**Characterization-Time**	GPO	
	Verb object Verb complement	**Characterization-Description**	Ø	
	Verb object Verb complement	**Characterization-Manner**	GPS	
	Adjacent	**Specification**	Ø	
	Characterizer	**Description**	GD	
	Characterizer	**Class**	Ø	
	Characterizer	**Designation**	Ø	
Independent				Independent
	G-P Independent	**Reference-description**	Ø	
	G-P Independent	**Progression-description**	G Independent	
	Ø	**Progression-subjectivity**	G Independent	
	Connector	**Addition**	Ø	

3.1.3. Contrast: differences and similarities of usage

As observed, the resources under study are not always equivalent since the English realization of certain meanings lacks an equivalent G construction. Yet, this does not mean that such a meaning cannot be expressed or even translated into Spanish. In actual fact, there are other possibilities which would broaden the repertoire of translational options from which the translator might choose. The contrastive stage focuses, though, on those meanings which are shared by the English and Spanish constructions, for it is on the basis of this common ground that idiosyncrasies of realization can be noticed.

In relation to the periphrastic use, the English G-P construction is more versatile than its Spanish counterpart. Whereas it ranks first in English, the G constructions are more frequently used in non-periphrastic contexts. Periphrastic G-P conveys up to eleven meanings, six of which match with a G construction. The actual realization of these common functions differs in form, frequency and co(n)text.

The non-periphrastic use displays a great variety of G-P/G functional resources in either language, the range being wider in English. The greatest degree of equivalence is found between G-P and G adjuncts, which are those constructions conveying meanings of an adverbial nature. Both resources share a repertoire of ten semantic functions whose realization is pretty similar in terms of frequency; their three central functions coincide although certain divergences have been observed in the expression of a couple of functions, probably due to the lexical nature of the G-P/G. There is, on the other hand, an outstanding difference of form, which is bound up with co-textual support. The English adjunct resorts quite often to an introductory particle which overtly reinforces the meaning, whereas this is rare in Spanish.

Concerning other non-periphrastic G-P and G resources as well as independent constructions, these seem to share the lowest degree of equivalence, as the great number of *lacunae* indicates. In addition, the Spanish resources occur much less frequently in relation to the overall functional behaviour of the G.

All in all, the awareness raised through a contrastive analysis is useful information for the translator because the differences observed, even if they do not prevent equivalence, they might condition it in such a way that the translator ought not to ignore them for the sake of idiomaticity. By considering these contrastive insights the translator knows what he is expected to do or not to do so as to render an acceptable translation. More importantly, he becomes aware of which areas are more problematic and why, which lets them consider a solution, be it a careful use of the assumed equivalent or the choice for another option. The question, though, is how to control the use of the assumed equivalent in translation and what other options exist if only the assumed one has been examined in contrast. Working with translation corpora might provide an answer to these new questions.

3.2. Parallel-corpus-based, descriptive translation study

Due to the vast range of functions conveyed by both resources, the second analysis focuses on the adverbial G-P and G constructions alone, because they display a higher degree of equivalence. The parallel-corpus-based, descriptive study aims at revealing new functional relations between English G-P and Spanish, providing translators with a choice. Furthermore, it analyses the actual usage of the G as a translational option, which can be checked against its native usage, as portrayed by the descriptive contrast previously undertaken.

3.2.1. The Data

The data analyzed consist of 3,475 parallel concordances taken from P-ACTRES, an English-Spanish translation corpus which has been compiled for English-Spanish, corpus-based, cross-linguistic research[7]. P-ACTRES contains over 2.5 million words distributed in five different subcorpora. The corpus is aligned at the sentence level and POS-tagged (Izquierdo *et al.* 2008). The tool used to browse the corpus is Corpus Workbench[8], which enables searches of strings of up to three words, truncated options or full words, either specifying their grammatical category or not. The input query for the study has been "any verb ending in *-ing*", which retrieved over 12,000 concordances taken from the subcorpora of fiction and non-fiction books. These concordances were managed manually so as to discard those where the G-P did not belong with an adjunct, yielding the final sample for analysis.

3.2.2. Functional description

The first stage of the analysis is devoted to the functional description of the OTs (cf. 3.1.3.) so as to classify their TTs in terms of expressive resources per function. According to the analysis, up to fifteen resources might hold a functional relation with the English G-P adjunct, which are unevenly used. Table 3 illustrates an example of each of these options and their frequency of realization in the translated sample:

---

7 http://actres.unileon.es/

8 A demo of the corpus and browser is available at the ACTRES website.

Table 3. Spanish translational options of English G-P Adjuncts

Option	% use	Example
G Adjunct	39.3	Remojó las flores sumergiéndolas en la pila…
AdvSub	25.1	Después de haber agotado todos los demás recursos, sólo quedaba
Simple clause	14.3	…siguen creciendo a razón del 6 al 100 anual, y en un momento cualquiera más del 3 por 100 de la población del Reino Unido…
PP	6.6	Mediante el proceso de trazar símbolos de tinta en una página, enviaba ideas
Relative clause	3.6	Harkenss, que ya se había lazado, no estaba dispuesto a dejarse…
Nominal Sub clause	2.5	La forma de animar a Rusia a firmar el Protocolo de Kioto ha sido ofrecerle una ayuda condicionada a su ratificación
Adverbial Phrase	2.1	Cuando Trevor regresó directamente a su casa a la salida del restaurante, las cinco
Adjectival Phrase	1.7	Ahí permanecen al accho, listos para resurgir en cuanto tengan la oportunidad
No translation	1.3	Ø
Characterising G	1.2	Me marché con un montón de ideas <u>rondándome</u> ya en la cabeza y todo…
NP	0.9	…decenas de grandes maestros tibetanos descansando en un estado trascendente, una escena que cautivó la atención de Matthieu
Infinitive	0.6	La primera es conserver la rebeldía juvenal (fumar hierba, tomar copas…)
Adversative clause	0.3	Hace años que deberías habernos dado otro heredero, pero preferiste marcharte a ese campo de brujas y echar raíces
Participle clause	0.3	Una vez completada la secuenciación del genoma humano es muy probable que..
Locution	0.2	En términos generales, la condena general de la dirección judía que hace Arendt mostró poca comprensión
	100%	

Four of these resources stand out as frequent translational options: the G adjunct, the adverbial subordinate clause (AdvSub), a simple clause and the prepositional phrase (PP), three of which belong to the paradigm of adverbial, expressive means in Spanish. The remaining functions are marginal for two main reasons: first, they are not very frequent and second, some of them deviate from the original function, even though the content is lexically preserved. This repertoire shows that even though real practice proves why the G Adjunct is an assumed equivalent, it is not the only possibility.

A thorough analysis of the G adjuncts found is in order to determine whether this resource has been misused. The process, which considers the functionality patterns observed in native-usage contexts, requires both qualitative and statistical information, which is obtained from CREA, here used as a control corpus. The former demands the observation of meanings realized by the G patterns found. The realization of functions such as illocution and result by the translated G exceeds the realization of other functions which are more frequent in native usage. Any Spanish G adjunct conveying illocution belongs to a specific lexical field, i.e., verbs of speech, whereas the instances found in translations deviate from this regularity. Hence, they are prone to exemplify translationese. The function of "result" is a tricky issue. This function implies the notion of "time after", which is somehow related to the so-called *gerundio de posterioridad.* Thus, the fact that this function is more frequently realized in the translated sample than in the native one broadens the controversy around the *gerundio de posterioridad*, which is considered agrammatical and unacceptable in Spanish. However, the contrastive analysis has revealed that the G adjunct can well convey result, and it actually does it more frequently than its English counterpart. Thus, the deviation in frequency of use seems not to be motivated by the frequency of realization in English.

Due to the fact that the samples compared are not equal in size, a statistics package has been used so as to contrast their frequency of realization on comparable parameters. The package used is the so-called Chi-Square test. This check has revealed instances of translationese in the realization of nine out of ten functions, with "process" being the function which is mainly overused in translation. On the contrary, on quantitative terms "result" does not seem to deviate from its native usage, which strengthens the argument mentioned before, that is, there is no translationese irrespective of the fact that the qualitative distribution of functions in translated language differs from the native one.

Overall, the comparison of native and translated usage of the Spanish G adjunct has not shown drastic or recurrent deviations.

A further analysis would concentrate on the translation of G-P constructions, other than the adjunct, so as to cover the *lacunae* identified. The insights derived from another parallel-corpus-based study (Izquierdo 2006) reveal a group of translational options for those G-P resources which do not behave as adjuncts, as table 4 illustrates:

Table 4. Some translational options which could fill in the *lacunae* identified

Resource	**Options**			
Periphrastic G-P	VP	Estar + G	G Periphrases	Others
G-Pcomplement/ subject	Infinitive	NP	Gerund	Others
G-P Characterizer	Adjective Phrase	Relative clause	PP	Others

The number of translational options per resource is considerably high, but the ones mentioned above are particularly frequent. How acceptable and functionally equivalent these options are is to be determined by means of a comparable-corpus-based contrastive study, which remains to be done. Yet, this analysis shows, not only how intertwined contrastive analysis and translation studies are, but also how the functional relation between languages is *one-to-many*, for there are various ways of expressing one particular meaning.

4. Usefulness and usability of corpus-based insights: the benefit

The relevance of contrastive results for translation has been debated upon for quite some time already. Likewise, translation has been considered "one of the ways in which the contrast of two languages is acted out. It is one of the ways in which linguistic contrast exists in social reality" (Mauranen 2002: 165). Yet, not always have researchers managed or even dared to show why and how such results are relevant. Thanks to corpus linguistics and to the combination of comparable and parallel corpora, it is possible to observe how fruitful the alliance of contrastive analysis and translation studies has turned out to be. The analysis undertaken comprises two stages, each of which builds on the other so as to provide beneficial results for the translator and (possibly) other language users. In actual fact, the benefit that this combination represents takes shape as the usefulness and usability of the results obtained in a corpus-based, contrastive and translation descriptive study. Being useful means providing a solution to a problem, whereas being usable implies the possibility of improving translator's performance or efficiency by applying newly-discovered insights (Rabadán 2008).

All the insights drawn from the study can be rephrased as guidelines for the translator, such as the following:

1. The *lacunae* detected should prevent from translating a G-P construction expressing reference, characterization or specification by means of a G construction. These meanings are not typical of the Spanish resource as ascertained by an empirical observation of its functionality;

2. Translational data provide alternatives, which override the *lacunae* observed: the noun phrase, infinitives, or adjectival phrases seem to hold a functional relation with G-P constructions conveying reference, characterization or specification. Therefore, translators may use these options;
3. G-P progressive constructions are equivalent to G (semi)periphrases for expressing certain meanings but not all of them, so translators should not consider that any semiperiphrasis can do as an equivalent of the G-P verb phrase.
4. Any meaning realised by means of a G-P Adjunct can be translated into Spanish by means of a G Adjunct, an adverbial subordinate clause or a PP, for these options hold the greatest degree of equivalence;
5. English G-P Adjuncts are characterised as semantically indeterminate, which can be overridden in translation by means of a simple clause, which simplifies the OT but renders an acceptable, communicative TT;
6. It is common practice not to translate a given G-P construction which is not easily classified semantically. Yet, due to the wide range of translational options observed, the translator is advised to translate the OT by using a suitable, idiomatic option instead of ignoring it altogether.

All these guidelines, far from imposing a way of approaching translation, are meant to help translators tackle problem-trigger phenomena.

5. Conclusions

The need of making cross-cultural communication possible through translation assumes the communicative function of language. Thereby, to satisfy this need, a description of the usage of the linguistic codes involved, both independently as well as in an actual relation of translation, pertains. As such, it is necessary to analyse authentic instances of language usage, which are to be found in a corpus. Whereas a comparable corpus provides data about the individual functionality of either language, which can be later on juxtaposed and contrasted for differences and similarities, revealing linguistic correspondents or translation equivalents, a translation corpus shows actual instances of how the problem-trigger has been tackled and "rephrased" into the target language.

Such a combination has rendered a solution to the problems posited and a way of tackling challenging and new situations by rendering a list of useful and usable guidelines for researchers, translators or translator trainers as well as FL teachers.

The case study that is described here reflects a way of bridging the gap between theory and application of language as a science, for which its description plays an important role. Contrastive analysis and descriptive translation studies provide results which can solve problems earlier identified in translation. When the results obtained are formulated in how to tackle translation for the sake of successful communication, an application of language is carried out, which implies extending, not only the applied branch of the translation theory, but the science of translation as a whole, for the results obtained come from their description branch, uniting theory and practice. All in all, the combination of *cfa* and a descriptive translation study (*dts*) is useful as long as it produces usable guidelines which make applied extensions such as translation happen.

References

Alameda, R. and F. Cuetos (1995). *Diccionario de frecuencias de las unidades lingüísticas del castellano*. Oviedo: Universidad.

Huddleston, G. and G.K. Pullum (2002). *The Cambridge Grammar of the English Language.* Cambridge: Cambridge University Press.

Izquierdo, M. (2006). *Análisis contrastivo y traducción al español de la forma -ing verbal inglesa*. León: Universidad de León (Unpublished Master's dissertation).

Izquierdo, M. (2008). *Estudio contrastivo y de traducción de las construcciones de -ing inglesas y sus equivalentes en español*. León: Universidad de León (Unpublished PhD Thesis).

Izquierdo M., Hofland, K. and Ø. Reigem (2008). "The ACTRES Parallel Corpus: an English-Spanish Translation Corpus". *Corpora*, vol. 3 (1): 31–41.

James, C. (1980). *Contrastive Analysis*. Singapore: Longman.

Köller, W. (1989). "Equivalence in translation theory". In: A. Chesterman (ed.). *Readings in translation theory*. Helsinki: Oy Finn Lectura Ab.: 99–104.

Leech, G. *et al.* (2001). *Word Frequencies in Written and Spoken English: based on the British National Corpus*. Longman, London.

Mauranen, A. (2002). "Will 'translationese' ruin a CA?". *Languages in contrast* 2(2): 161–185.

Rabadán, R. (2005). "Niveles de teorización en traducción. La transición entre teoría y práctica". In: A. Álvarez Lugris and J Yuste Frías (eds.). *Estudios sobre Traducción: Teoría, didáctica, profesión.* Vigo: Universidad de Vigo: 21–34.

Rabadán, R. (2008). "Refining the idea of 'applied extensions' ". In: A. Pym, M. Shlesinger and D. Simeón (eds.). *Beyond Descriptive Translation Studies. Investigations in homage to Gideon Toury*. Amsterdam/Philadelphia: John Benjamins Publishing Company: 103–117.

Ramón García, N. (2001). "Lingüística contrastiva y traducción". In: B. Anne, Mª R. Martín Ruano and J. Torres del Rey (eds.). *Últimas corrientes teóricas en los estudios de traducción y sus aplicaciones.* Salamanca: Universidad de Salamanca: 617–623.

Translation of Eurojargon as a Source of Neologisms in Polish – a Corpus-Based Study

Marta Kajzer

Abstract: Language used at the EU institutions makes extensive use of neologisms coined to denote specifically European concepts which are absent at a national level, yet must be rendered in the target language. This paper presents a corpus-based analysis of Eurojargon translation as a potential source of neologisms in Polish. The analysis aims at verifying how the translators handle the influx of novel Eurojargon terminology; what translation strategies they apply; whether they use Eurojargon neologisms eagerly in the Polish renditions of the original texts. It is also shown which types of lexical innovations seem to be most frequently used in Polish translations. All these issues are discussed on the basis of data derived from a parallel corpus of English Press Releases and their Polish translations issued by the major EU institutions. Translator's choices are further analysed in the light of two corpora of the Polish language: PWN Corpus and IPI PAN Corpus.

Keywords: borrowings, calques, corpus-based study, Eurojargon, neologisms, parallel corpus, translation strategies, translators' role.

1. Introduction

As the nations of Europe unite joining their efforts in the spirit of integration, the translators face a new challenge: the language of the European Union i.e. Eurojargon. As any kind of jargon, Eurojargon has its lexical characteristics: a barrage of names, neologisms, and abbreviations coined to denote specifically European concepts – absent at a national level. Translators need to catch up with the dynamic process of European integration and facilitate the communication between the nations, governments, high EU officials and grass root citizens. The process of European integration is constantly developing; EU officials speak of new policies, strategies, agendas etc., which need to be translated in all official EU languages causing an influx of lexical innovations.

The aim of this paper is to examine the translation of Eurojargon as a potential source of neologisms in Polish. The analysis will focus on verifying how the translators handle the influx of novel Eurojargon terminology; what translation strategies they apply, whether or not they 'welcome' Eurojargon neologisms in their mother tongue and use them in their renditions of the original texts.

2. Eurojargon – name and definition

The language used at the European Union institutions is depicted by a number of names but it is most frequently referred to as Eurojargon or Eurospeak. Eurojargon may be perceived from various perspectives, which is why scholars developed a few slightly different definitions of the phenomenon (Boylan (2001), Kosecki (2002: 235), Vitkuvienė (2005), Wagner (1999)). To avoid confusion, it is vital to clarify that in this paper the phenomenon in question is referred to as Eurojargon, defined as a variety of language, augmented by the terms used specifically in the EU context and terms that in the EU context acquire a new meaning; a variety, which is open to lexical and phraseological innovations and is strongly influenced by EU official languages. It is also assumed that the scope of Eurojargon users and authors of Eurojargon terms expands beyond the walls of the European Union institutions.

3. Eurojargon – lexical characteristics

Several characteristic traits of Eurojargon are enumerated in literature on the subject: Eurojargon employs a great number of new terms, which are either entirely new word forms or semantic neologisms; many EU terms are compounds; names of various European Union institutions or programs are abbreviated or denoted by acronyms; EU texts are also full of metaphors and metonyms. For the translators, however, it is the novel terminology that constitutes the biggest difficulty. Many Eurojargon terms are completely new words e.g. *comitology*, *communitisation*, *co-decision*, *eurotarrif*, *flexicurity*, or semantic neologisms i.e. terms that acquire new, specific meaning such as *cohesion* or *subsidiarity*, whose understanding requires effort also on the part of the EU translators (Wagner1999). Compounds also constitute a significant part of Eurojargon and *euro-* is the predominant prefix in their structure. Prefix *euro-* is always the defining element, visible also in the term Eurojargon itself. Kosecki (2002: 236–240) notices that in the Polish version of Eurojargon, most of the compounds are borrowings and calques from other languages, especially from English.

4. Eurojargon vs. official languages in the EU member states – the example of Polish

Eurojargon affects all official languages of the EU member states, including Polish. Poland's accession to the European Union resulted in a variety of political and economic changes; Poland belongs to European structures, applies regulations of the European law etc. These processes result in emergence of novel concepts and elements in the Polish reality, which necessitate also new forms of linguistic description. This need has been quickly fulfilled mostly (but not exclusively) by means of borrowings (Ryzza-Woźniak 2000: 312), the number of which is constantly increasing.

Polish Eurojargon develops in a very dynamic way entering gradually not only other professional jargons e.g. legal language, but also the everyday language of Polish citizens. This dynamic development is achieved mainly by the contribution of three groups of professionals that engage in the EU issues on daily basis. It is EU officials and politics on international, national and regional level, translators and journalists, who, with their involvement in the EU current affairs, coin new expressions and terms and popularise them.

Polish Eurojargon is used mainly by Polish politicians and EU officials, who remain, however, under constant influence not only of Euro-English, but also other official EU languages. Since English is at present the lingua franca of the EU, most of the borrowings derive from this language and the jargon spoken by politicians and EU officials employs a vast number of English borrowings. The EU officials, on the other hand, have a huge bearing on the contamination of national languages. The effect of this process is that the native speakers use a lot of French or English loan words as well as very unusual grammatical structures. Journalists constitute the second group that contributes to the development of Eurojargon. They deliver relevant information about current issues at the EU directly to the public thus disseminating the knowledge of Eurojargon among the Polish citizens. According to Majkowska and Satkiewicz (1999: 195), although the variety of the Polish language presented in the media is not the paragon of correctness, it contributes substantially to the development of certain standards due to the omnipresence of the media in everyday life.

The professionals, who seem to use Eurojargon carefully due to their linguistic awareness, are translators. It is translators' task to, on the one hand be extremely cautious with the use of unnecessary borrowings that may 'litter' the Polish language, and on the other, respect the needs of all parties to the communication process and adjust to novel phenomena (Chmiel, Paskal 2005: 89–97). Paprocka (2002: 129) claims that translators should share the responsibility for the quality of the Polish language, since it is also heavily influenced by the constantly increasing number of translations into Polish.

5. Eurojargon and translator's impact on national languages

As has already been stated, translators play a certain role in shaping national languages and exert influence on national versions of Eurojargon. They may either propagate Eurojargon and incorporate new terminology in the outcome of their translation activity, or use all available strategies to protect national languages from the flood of novel terms.

That translators do have the power to influence national languages was proved in the course of history: translations have always had an effect on the target languages and indeed 'many languages owe their first literary written text to a translation' (Swallow 2003: 104). Translators of EU texts may exert a great influence on the target language for two major reasons: texts devoted to the issues of the EU are produced in large numbers and they are related to many different aspects of everyday life.

Considering translators' influence on a national language one needs to address another important issue – the 'size' of the language in question i.e. whether the language has a greater or smaller number of native speakers. In the case of 'small' languages, such as Greek:

> ... the translations in the European Parliament and other EU institutions represent an enormous number of structured, written, rigorous texts running into tens of thousands pages per year, these texts, inevitably have an influence on the Greek language spoken in the homeland.
>
> Swallow 2003: 104

Bearing this in mind translators should be extremely cautious while translating EU texts, especially, when facing the problem of finding appropriate equivalents of neologisms. The use of unnecessary borrowings may 'litter' the target language, but one also has to respect the needs of the parties to the communication process.

According to Swallow (2003: 105), translators encountering neologisms in their work may adopt two approaches and become either language 'guardians' or 'hosts'. First, they may act as 'guardians' of language and react sceptically to introduction of novel, foreign terminology to the target language. This attitude may be perceived as closed and conservative. On the other hand, translators may also act as 'hosts' and, in justified cases, welcome neologisms perceiving them as 'new blood for the language'. The two attitudes are mutually exclusive and thus demand that the translators make a choice that will affect their work. The question arising in this context is: which of the two approaches is dominant in the case of translation of EU texts.

6.Translation strategies

Translators' approach may be analysed on the basis of the strategies they apply in translation. Intrusive translation strategies involve any kind of translator's intrusion in the target language i.e. creating neologisms either in the realm of lexis and phraseology or semantics. As defined by Pisarek (1999, as cited in Smółkowa 2001: 11–12) a neologism is a linguistic innovation, a new element in a language i.e. a new word, expression, grammatical form, meaning or syntactic construction. Neologisms demonstrate new communicative needs of the language users. They denote novel concepts, objects or state of affairs in technology, industry, politics, culture, science or to describe concepts that are novel not in general, but only to the target culture. As such, neologisms are likely to be applied by the translators, who frequently have to transfer the meaning of texts concerning such novel developments from one language into another. There are several intrusive translation strategies: translation with the use of a loan word or a loan word plus explanation (Mona Baker 1992), calque (Vinay and Darbelnet 2000), creation of neologisms by affixation, semantic extension.

Encountering a term with no equivalent in the target language, the translator does not necessarily have to intrude into the target language by borrowing new words or changing meanings, but may also apply other, non-intrusive strategies, such as generalisation, omission, paraphrase etc. The aforementioned strategies are rarely adopted alone. Usually intrusive translation strategies are accompanied by non-intrusive strategies e.g. if a new term is borrowed, a gloss or a paraphrase of a fragment of the text may be necessary. Combination of strategies needs to be adjusted to a particular translation situation.

Table 1. Intrusive and non-intrusive translation strategies

Intrusive translation strategies	Non-intrusive translation strategies
Translation using a loan word or a loan word plus explanation (Mona Baker 1992) Calque (Vinay and Darbelnet 2000) Creation of neologisms by affixation Semantic extension	Generalisation and particularisation (Vinay and Darbelnet 1958) Dilution and concentration (Vinay and Darbelnet 1958) Translation by paraphrase using a related and unrelated word (Baker 1992) Translation by omission (Baker 1992) Translator's intervention: notes, additions, glosses (Newmark 1988)
Combination of procedures	

7. Organisation of the corpus-based study

The examination of how the translators handle non-equivalent terms in Eurojargon, and how eagerly they resort to neologisms is based on a set of procedures. First, a compilation of equivalents of the original term in question, provided by five different sources, is analysed. Secondly, the Polish equivalents are examined in terms of their status in the Polish language, by means of analysing the meaning of the proposed Polish equivalent provided by the dictionaries of the Polish language, or its occurrence in the Polish language corpora, or both. Next, the translation strategies and solutions applied in the case of key Eurojargon terms are analysed on the basis of the parallel corpus of Press Releases. Finally, translators' solutions are verified against the corpora of the Polish language

a) Consulted glossaries and term bases

In the introductory stage of the analysis, equivalents proposed by five different sources are compared and examined. The sources vary in form, year of publishing and the issuing authorities. Analysis performed on five sources allows to examine whether suggested equivalents of particular terms are consistent vary to a greater extent.

b) Corpora of the Polish language

Two corpora of the Polish language Korpus Języka Polskiego Wydawnictwa Naukowego PWN (2008) (henceforth PWN Corpus) and Korpus IPI PAN (2007) (henceforth IPI PAN Corpus) are used as a reference in determining the use of particular terms in the Polish language as well as the frequency and context of their occurrence. The corpora are also used to determine whether the application of a given equivalent is limited to the EU-related context only, or not.

c) RAPID Press Releases Translation Corpus

RAPID Press Releases Translation Corpus is a compilation of two language versions (English and Polish) of 72 Press Releases available from RAPID Service, which is run by Directorate General for Communication. RAPID service constitutes one of the information dissemination services of the Directorate concerned with collection, processing and publishing of Press Releases. The two language versions are aligned on the sentence level. English texts in the corpus contain 149,101 words, whereas the Polish version consists of 135,537 words. The disproportion between the number of words may result from the fact, that certain part of the English Press Releases were sometimes left untranslated.

d) Concordancing tool

RAPID Press Releases Translation Corpus has been compiled and aligned in ParaConc (Barlow 1996). It is a concordancer for parallel texts, which offers similar search options to typical concordance software.

8. Sample analysis – *subsidiarity*

Due to space limitations it is necessary to present the full analysis on the example of one term only, followed by a review of results of other analyses.
In the case of *subsidiarity* the consulted sources distinguish two equivalents i.e. *pomocniczość* and *subsydiarność*. Both alternatives are neologisms in the Polish language. *Pomocniczość* is a morphological neologism, a noun formed from the adjective *pomocniczy*. *Subsydiarność*, on the other hand, is an adopted loanword i.e. a borrowing whose form has been adjusted to the morphological requirements of the target language. Data gathered in Table 2 suggest that both equivalents collocate with the term *zasada*, which may result from the fact that in English the expression *principle of subsidiarity* is often used.

Table 2. Equivalents of subsidiarity in the consulted sources

PLGE[1]	GTUE[2]	IATE[3]	BDTKIE[4]	STUE[5]
pomocniczość / zasada pomocniczości	pomocniczość, zasada subsydiarności / pomocniczości	pomocniczoś ć	zasada pomocniczoś ci	zasada subsydiarnoś ci

Both *pomocniczość* and *subsydiarność* rarely appear in the dictionaries of the Polish language. Whereas a separate entry for *pomocniczość* cannot be found in any of the major dictionaries of the Polish language, an entry for *subsydiarność*

1 PLGE – *A plain language guide to Eurojargon*, (http://europa.eu/abc/eurojargon/index_en.htm) (date of access: 2 Apr. 2008).
2 GTUE – Misztal-Kania, A. (2004), *Glosariusz terminów Unii Europejskiej*, Warszawa. (http://1markoz.webpark.pl/glosariusz.htm) (date of access: 2 Apr. 2008).
3 IATE – *Inter Active Terminology for Europe*, (http://iate.europa.eu/) (date of access: 12 Jan. 2008).
4 BDKIE – *Baza danych terminologicznych Komitetu Integracji Europejskiej* (http://www.ukie.gov.pl/dtt.nsf) (date of access: 2 Apr. 2008).
5 STUE – Kienzler, I. (2001), *Słownik terminologii Unii Europejskiej*, Gdynia: IVAX

was included in two dictionaries issued by one publishing house i.e. PWN in 2005. One of the dictionaries, suggested the term *pomocniczość* as a synonym of *subsydiarność*. Both dictionaries provide a similar definition of the term:

> zasada uznająca, że każdy szczebel administracji publicznej powinien przejmować tylko te zadania, które nie mogą być skutecznie realizowane przez szczebel niższy; pomocniczość[6]
>
> Bańko 2005: 1189

This meaning corresponds to the meaning of subsidiarity provided in *A plain language guide to Eurojargon:*

The "subsidiarity principle" means that EU decisions must be taken as closely as possible to the citizen. In other words, the Union does not take action (except on matters for which it alone is responsible) unless EU action is more effective than action taken at national, regional or local level.

It seems therefore that both terms: *pomocniczość* and *subsydiarność* are fairly new in the Polish language, that their meaning is directly imported from Eurojargon, and that they have not acquired any other meanings yet.

In RAPID Press Translation Corpus the translators visibly preferred not to resort to borrowings but chose the more 'Polish-sounding' neologism. The term *subsidiarity* as such occurred 21 times and on 15 occasions in expression *principle(s) of subsidiarity*. *Pomocniczość* was used as a translation of subsidiarity 18 times, whereas *subsydiarność* appeared only 3 times. It is worth mentioning that in all 21 cases, regardless of the fact whether in English the word *principle* preceded *subsidiarity* or not, the Polish rendition included the term *zasada*, as a pre-modifier of the chosen equivalent. As a result neither of the terms appeared in Polish alone but always as *zasada pomocniczości* or *zasada subsydiarności*.

A search for *pomocniczość* in the whole PWN Corpus yields only 20 concordances, 15 of which come from the Rzeczpospolita sub-corpus (compiled of daily issues of a national newspaper). The search in IPI PAN Corpus results in 354 hits altogether. Analogical search for *subsydiarność* produced 7 concordances in the whole PWN Corpus and only one in Rzeczpospolita sub-corpus. The number of occurrences of the term *subsydiarność* in IPI PAN Corpus amounted to 130. It may be concluded that the term *pomocniczość* occurs in both corpora on average 3 times more frequently than *subsydiarność*. Thus the translators' choice of strategy seems to be justified.

---

6 Principle according to which each level of public administration should handle only those tasks, which cannot be effectively completed at a lower level; *pomocniczość* [translation: MK]

9. Most frequently and most consistently applied strategies

As it has been shown, *subsidiarity* is always rendered in Polish with the use of neologism. It is, however, difficult to distinguish any strong regularities in application of translation strategies. The study only confirms that each translation situation needs to be approached individually. Although it is not possible to make any generalisations, certain tendencies in translation of Press Releases can be observed. These tendencies have been indicated in the Table 3. Calque was the most frequently and the most consistently applied strategy in translation of collocations. Almost all analysed collocations rendered as calques were translated with great consistency and were hardly ever paraphrased or rendered in any different way (c.f. Table 3).

The translators of Press Releases rarely created Eurojargon neologisms by means of borrowings. Any equivalent of a term rendered as a simple loanword e.g. *flexicurity* or *acquis* was used inconsistently. Therefore, despite the fact that the term *flexicurity* was borrowed in the 71% of cases, in the remaining 29% it was rendered by various translation strategies and even more varied equivalents. In the case of *acquis* a borrowing was one of many futile attempts to find an efficient and productive equivalent, and in the end, the term was paraphrased most of the time. *Presidency*, which was rendered by means of adopted loanword i.e. *prezydencja* was translated extremely consistently (in 99% translated by the same equivalent) but this situation is more complex. The fact that the term was actually once present in the history of the Polish language[7], with only slightly different meaning, might have an influence on its current application in the Polish language.

It seems that the equivalents rendered by means of semantic extension are used relatively consistently. *Spójność*, the equivalent of *cohesion*, ranks the highest, since it was applied in 100% of cases. *Przystąpienie* serves as an equivalent of *accession* in 80% of cases (another 20% is rendered with *akcesja* which is also a semantic extension). *Konwergencja* was used to translate *convergence* in 61% of cases. It is worth noticing that the translators of Press Releases seem to favour semantic extension of more general and Polish sounding terms.

The inclination towards Polish-sounding terms is visible also in creation of neologisms by means of affixation. This strategy is not used in case of a great number of terms, but was consistently applied to render equivalents of *subsidiarity* and *co-decision*. *Pomocniczość*, a neologism made by affixation,

7 Doroszewski (1964: 1470) refers to the term as archaic and provides the following definition: 'przewodnictwo w zebraniu, w obradach, prezydowanie; stanowisko prezydenta, prezydentura' [chairmanship in a meeting, proceedings, presidency; the position of a president, presidency]. He also provides examples of usage, which can be traced back to the period between the years 1788–1924.

was used to render the meaning of *subsidiarity* in 86% of cases, compared to the borrowing *subsydiarność* 14%. *Współdecyzja*, a neologism transferring the meaning of *co-decision* into Polish was also used very consistently (87%).

As regards translation strategies, which do not introduce any lexical innovations into language it seems that paraphrase and a consequent dilution of meaning are applied most frequently. It is highly possible that this situation may be ascribed to the fact that many Eurojargon equivalents (e.g. borrowings) are not fixed. Thus, translators, who are not eager (or allowed) to introduce neologisms violate language economy for the sake of precision and language purity and opt for a paraphrase. It is also due to precision that translators of Press Releases rarely resorted to omission.

As visible in Table 3, translation strategies were rarely used alone. Most commonly, especially, when no linguistic innovation was introduced, the translators combined generalisation, paraphrase and dilution of meaning. Non-intrusive translation strategies were also often used when a term was rendered by a neologism, whose meaning was not self-explanatory e.g. as in the case of *flexicurity*.

Table 3. Frequency of applied strategies: No. – number of the term's occurrences in the RAPID Press Releases Corpus, B (B+e) – borrowing (borrowing plus explanation), C – calque, N–a – neologism made by affixation, SE – semantic extension, G (P) – generalisation (particularisation), D (C) – dilution (concentration), P – paraphrase, O – omission, NAG – notes, additions, gloss

Term	No.	B (B+e)	C	N–a	SE	G (P)	D (C)	P	O	NAG
flexicurity	53	58% (13%)	11%				28%	5%	2%	13%
acquis	17	18%	5%			(5%)	59%	65%	5%	
presidency	79	99%					1%	1%		
cohesion	91				100%					
agenda	79				39%	15%	16%	27%	6%	
convergence	13				62%			38%		
accession	110				100% [8]					
subsidiarity	21	14%		86%			23%			
co-decision	8			100% [9]			12%	12%		25%
transnational	8		50%			25%		25%		
financial	13		100%							

8 Two different equivalents: *przystąpienie (80%)* and *akcesja (20%)* have been used as a result of the same strategy

9 Two different equivalents:*współdecyzja (87%)* and *współdecydowanie (13%)* have been used as a result of the same strategy

perspective										
framework programme	8		100%							
enhanced cooperation	19		89%					11%		
third country	18		100%							
cohesion policy	43		100%							
social cohesion	20		100%							
territorial cohesion	10		100%							
accession negotiations	7		85%					14%		
principle of subsidiarity	15		100%							

Notes, additions and glosses were not too frequently used by the translators of press releases. It seems that these translators were not in favour of overt or covert translator's intervention.

The analysis of translation strategies adopted by the translators of Press Releases also allows one to observe whether they have eagerly resorted to lexical innovations or not, whether they tended to be 'guardians' treating lexical innovations cautiously or 'hosts', who perpetuate all lexical innovations. It seems that the translators of Press Releases cautiously treat all neologisms which experiment on form. It can be illustrated with the example of *flexicurity*, which was translated with the use of a borrowing in 71% of cases but was also accompanied by explanations, additions or paraphrases. In case of *acquis communautaire* the translators did not arrive at any successful rendition in Polish, and therefore the term was translated very inconsistently. Even in such a case, translators of Press Releases have limited themselves to a borrowing on only three occasions. This attitude is especially surprising, since both corpora of the Polish language provide examples of *acquis communautaire* used in the form of direct loanword in Polish.

Translators of Press Releases prefer to resort to a semantic extension or a familiarly sounding neologism made by affixation rather than a borrowing. The examples of *spójność*, *kohezja*, *akcesja*, *przystąpienie*, *agenda* and *konwergencja* show that, whether an equivalent, rendered by means of semantic extension became a widely used translation of a given term may have been dependent on one or more of three factors. First, whether the term to be subject to semantic extension was highly specialised and limited to one domain. Second, whether its current meaning was widely recognised. Third, whether the term looked or sounded like a borrowing or a calque or as a truly Polish term. Therefore, it seems that *spójność* is a more viable equivalent of *cohesion* because it is a general term, with no specialised meaning and it does sound very Polish. *Kohezja* on the other hand, which was initially suggested by some sources, is a highly specialised scientific term resembling English *cohesion* in terms of phonology and morphology and therefore may be also perceived as a calque. It is possible that *kohezja* did not manage to remain a recognised translation of cohesion for these reasons. Consequently, similar factors may have influenced the choice of *przystąpienie* over *akcesja* as a prevalent equivalent of *accession*. In its original, specialised meaning akcesja has a very limited application and it sounds foreign. *Agenda* is applied as an equivalent of the English *agenda* only in names, or with reference to a particular EU agenda and in no other context. The reason for this situation may be the fact that *agenda*, in Polish, is extremely often used to denote a branch of an institution. The term *konwergencja* stands out among other discussed Eurojargon terms because it sounds foreign and is used in a scientific context. Perhaps it is the fact that its application is not restricted to one domain only that contributed to the extension of meaning of the term to yet another area: the EU. It is worth noticing, however, that in the group of terms whose meaning has been extended, *konwergencja* is used as an equivalence of convergence in 61% only.

10. Conclusions

In the final analysis, it seems that Polish translators try to avoid foreign and foreign-sounding complex word formations that could stand out from the text and be incomprehensible. Surprisingly, the translators freely import Eurojargon collocations and transcode them into Polish in form of calques. Such lexical innovations are perhaps less striking, but still involve incorporation of foreign patterns into the target language.

References

A plain language guide to Eurojargon. 2008,
Available at: http://europa.eu/abc/eurojargon/index_en.htm (2 April 2008).

Baker, M. (1992). *In other words, A coursebook on translation*. New York: Routledge.

Bańko, M. (2005). *Wielki słownik wyrazów obcych PWN*. Warszawa: Wydawnictwo Naukowe PWN.

Barlow, M. (1996/2001). *ParaConc* – BETA Version 1.0.

Baza danych terminologicznych Komitetu Integracji Europejskiej
(http://www.ukie.gov.pl/dtt.nsf) (date of access: 2 Apr. 2008).

Boylan, P. (2001). "Cross-cultural accommodation through a transformation of Consciousness". In: M. Koch (ed.). *Globalisation, foreign languages and intercultural learning*. Proceedings of the 1st SIETAR-UK conference, South Bank University, London, 9–10.2.2001.

Available at: http://host.uniroma3.it/docenti/boylan/text/boylan11.htm (10 Dec. 2006).

Chmiel, A. and I. Paskal (2005). „Europolszczyzna i Euroangielszczyzna czyli o tłumaczeniu tekstów hybrydowych". In: J. Lewandowski and M. Kornacka (eds.). *Języki specjalistyczne 5, Teksty zawodowe w kontekstach zawodowych i tłumaczeniach.* Warszawa: Katedra Języków Specjalistycznych: 89–98.

Darbelnet, J. and J.-P. Vinay (2000). "A methodology for translation". In: L. Venuti (ed.). *The translation studies reader*. New York: Routlege: 85–93.

Darbelnet, J. and J.-P. Vinay (1958/1995). *Comparative stylistics of French and English: A methodology for translation.* (Edited and translated by Juan C. Sager and Marie-Josée Hamel), Amsterdam: John Benjamins.

Community Interpreting in a Blended Environment – Student and Teacher Assessment

Maria Tymczyńska

Abstract: This study presents and discusses the application of Moodle, a free open-source online course management system, in the creation and implementation of practical interpreting courses in the Post-Graduate Programme in Community Interpreting offered at the Adam Mickiewicz University in Poznań, Poland. The rationale for choosing a blended environment for teaching community interpreting is given, and an overview of the most useful features of Moodle is provided. Subsequently, the data obtained from oral interviews conducted with course instructors as well as from the questionnaires completed by students are used to evaluate the usefulness of Moodle in the learning and teaching of community interpreting in a blended environment. It emerges that while the general learning and teaching experience was useful and rewarding for both students and instructors alike, the specific nature of the interpreting classes solicited more in-class than online participation so that only selected features of Moodle were used.

Keywords: blended learning and teaching, Community Interpreting, course assessment, Course Management Systems, Moodle, postgraduate education.

1. Introduction

Information and communication technologies (ICT) have had a sizeable impact on the way teaching and learning take place in higher education institutions. In different courses, including translation and interpreting, the use of on-line learning components has been encouraged (Samson 2005; Gómez and Weinreb 2002; Gran, Carabelli and Merlini 2002):

The opportunities offered by multimedia tools are extremely stimulating and challenging for interpreting teachers. Though direct contact between teacher and students in the classroom is obviously a sine qua non for successful training, the possibility of supplementing information, suggestions and material offered during classes … is of invaluable help (Gran *et al.* 2002: 278).

Various course management solutions have been designed to enable both students and instructors to benefit from the most recent online learning and teaching tools.

2. Background

2.1. Course Management Systems

Course Management Systems (CMS), also known as Learning Management Systems (LMS) and Learning Content Management Systems (LCMS), help to create, manage, control, retrieve and package a variety of learning resources (Weller 2007: 64). CMS products may be used either to support and complement face-to-face instruction (the so-called "blended" learning approach), or to deliver fully online web-based courses (Osguthorpe and Graham 2003). In fact, there is evidence that CMS solutions are increasingly being used to enhance face-to-face courses (Ioannou and Hannafin 2008).

Course Management Systems have to a large extent become an established part of the higher education landscape in the United States (Sloan Consortium 2008, 2006) and Great Britain (Browne, Jenkins and Walker 2008, 2005). In Poland, rapid advances are being made in the provision of blended and fully web-based courses (Runiewicz-Wardyn 2008). Despite some faculty resistance connected with the time and effort needed to launch and manage such courses, student demand as well as educational considerations seem to be the main factors driving the growth of CMS use (Mason and Rennie 2006; Weller 2007; Runiewicz-Wardyn 2008).

2.2. Moodle

There is a wealth of both commercial and open source CMS solutions available in the market nowadays (a community-driven comparison of CMS products is available at http://www.edutools.info). Moodle (i.e. Modular Object-Oriented Dynamic Learning Environment) is a free, open-source online course management system which offers a variety of tools to streamline course administration and delivery, improve course communication and productivity, and enhance student involvement. Moodle, originally created by Martin Dougiamas, supports a social constructivist framework and promotes discussion and collaboration between Moodle developers and users. The Moodle website (http://www.moodle.org) provides links to the Moodle book, the Moodle manuals, and to a variety of video tutorials assisting the course developer. There is also an online demonstration site (http://demo.moodle.org/). Over 36 000 validated Moodle sites from 202 countries have been registered by August 2009 (the latest statistics are available at http://moodle.org/stats/). Moodle runs without modification on most operating systems that support PHP like Unix, Linux, Windows, or Mac OS X.

2.3. Community Interpreting at the AMU

Community interpreting, also known as public services interpreting, liaison interpreting, or dialogue interpreting, is a type of interpreting offered to people who are not fluent speakers of the official language(s) of a country to enable them to communicate with public services providers (Valero Garcés and Martin 2008; Wadensjö, Englund Dimitrova and Nilsson 2007; Hale 2007; Niska 2002). Community interpreting is mostly conducted in institutional settings and it customarily involves the interaction of three parties: the service provider, the immigrant, and the interpreter (the so-called triadic exchanges). Community interpreting is usually done in the short consecutive mode but other modes are also possible: long consecutive, simultaneous, whispering, sight translation. This type of interpreting is characterised by bidirectionality and varying register (from very formal to very informal). There are often sharp differences in participants' social status. In addition, community interpreters are sometimes viewed as advocates or culture brokers who go beyond the traditional neutral role of the interpreter as conduit (cf. Roberts 1994; Niska 2002; Tryuk 2006; Hale 2007).

The one-year Postgraduate Community Interpreting Programme was launched in 2007/2008 by the Department of Translation Studies at the Adam Mickiewicz University (AMU) in Poznań, Poland. The Programme is unique in Poland in that it offers training for community interpreters intending to serve the needs of the Polish immigrant community abroad. The programme comprises a total of 120 hours, and includes, among other things, four practical interpreting courses: Economy, Legal Issues, Education and Social Issues, and Health Care. The interpreting courses are structured around problem-based case scenarios featuring a community interpreter, an English-speaking services provider, and a Polish immigrant.

Given the relatively short duration of the practical interpreting courses (ten in-class meetings of 1.5 hours in the academic year) and the fact that the students enrolled in the community interpreting programme had no prior interpreter training, it was necessary to design and combine online and in-class activities in such a way as to facilitate the acquisition and development of community interpreting skills while at the same time motivating the students to complete the necessary background and follow-up readings and to develop the course-specific vocabulary and phraseology. With those considerations in mind, Moodle was adopted in the creation and implementation of the practical interpreting courses offered.

2.4. Blended learning and teaching environment

In order to take a full advantage of the benefits of the online and in-class instruction modes, a blended environment was deemed well-suited for the teaching and learning of community interpreting, since in a blended environment there is "a systematic combination of co-present (face-to-face) interactions and technologically-mediated interactions between students, teachers and learning resources" (Bliuc, Goodyear and Ellis 2007: 234). It is important to note at this juncture that while the term *blended learning* continues to be in widespread use, its conceptual integrity has been called into question (Oliver and Trigwell 2005). The term *blended* (*learning and teaching*) *environment* therefore refers to contexts where both learning and teaching are combined.

Blended environments demand that both the synchronous and asynchronous contexts be carefully integrated (Garrison and Vaughan 2007; Buttaroni and Sobczak 2008). Coherence across the two contexts may be achieved by the students and instructors focusing on the same intended learning outcomes (Ellis and Calvo 2007). It remains unclear, however, "how much, or how little, online learning is inherent to blended learning" (Garrison and Hanuka 2004: 96–97).

The proportions between the online and offline components may vary depending on individual course characteristics and student needs (Steen 2008). In the practical interpreting courses three distinct stages may be distinguished: (i) the pre-class preparation stage, (ii) the in-class practical interpreting activities, and (iii) the post-class follow-up stage. In the pre- and post-class stages Moodle was used. The following section presents an overview of the options available to course instructors and students using Moodle 1.9.

3. Features of Moodle

The latest Moodle version provides instructors with a set of tools and a framework that enable a relatively easy creation of course content (also from existing resources), and allow to streamline the management and presentation of that content in an interactive manner.

Moodle is organised into blocks which may be defined by topic or by week. Blocks include dropdown resource and activity menus. The resource menu enables instructors to compose text or web pages, create links to files or websites, and display directories with course materials. The activity menu comprises about twenty different customisable activities such as adding online or offline assignments (various submission formats being supported, like PDF, image, audio/video), and quizzes (including true-false, multiple choice, short answer or matching questions). Chats and threaded discussion boards allow synchronous and asynchronous communication with students. Instructors can create questions with a number of answers for students to choose from using the Choice function. The Database function allows both instructors and students to create and manage a bank of entries about a given topic. All activities, sections and blocks can be moved around easily thanks to the drag-and-drop feature.

Regarding course administration, students can be enrolled manually or given a special course enrolment key. Moodle enables instructors to organise course participants into groups, monitor their activity (logs can be accessed from the 'Reports' section), manage grades in a spreadsheet resembling a gradebook (customisable grading scales), and keep a course calendar alerting to different colour-coded course events.

From the student's perspective, Moodle provides a 24-hour access to course materials as well as instant email notifications of course updates or information. Students may also receive email copies of all new messages in forums they subscribed to (anonymous forum participation is possible) and see their grades and activity logs. They are offered various communication tools such as messaging, blogs and forums. They can also create a personal profile page and include a picture. Finally, the navigation bar displays hyperlinks showing where the user is in relation to the main site so that it is possible to return to the previous screen at any time.

While listing all the specific features of Moodle is beyond the scope of the present article, it is evident that that Moodle is a very robust software. Its numerous resources, activities and features can easily be customised, reused and improved with time to meet different educational needs. The following section presents and discusses the results of a case study designed to evaluate the usefulness of Moodle in the blended learning environment of the practical interpreting courses at the AMU.

4. Study

4.1. Purpose

The purpose of the study reported here was twofold: first, it was undertaken to determine the existing blend proportions between the in-class and online course components in the practical community interpreting classes using Moodle; secondly, it was carried out to evaluate those proportions from the students' and instructors' perspective. This was done with a view to enhancing the learning experience and facilitating the transfer of knowledge in the subsequent editions of the Community Interpreting Programme.

4.2. Methodology

In order to evaluate the role of Moodle in the practical community interpreting courses, data collection proceeded in two stages i.e. interviews with course instructors and student questionnaires.

First, semi-structured interviews were conducted with the instructors of the practical interpreting courses who were asked for their opinions about course planning and organisation, online resources and activities including communication tools, course administration and management, and student learning.

Course evaluation questionnaires were then constructed and administered to all students (n = 21) towards the end of the Programme during formally scheduled class time. In addition to a range of opinion questions with a Likert response scale about in-class and online course components, the respondents were invited to provide answers to open-ended questions and assess their overall degree of satisfaction with the blended learning environment using Moodle in the community interpreting courses. A demographic profile of the respondents is reported in Table 1.

Table 1. Respondent demographics

Respondents	**n= 21**
Gender	Male 19%
	Female 81%
Age	22– 29% 24 25–27 46% 28–31 25%

The relevant interview and questionnaire data are presented and analysed in the following section.

5. Results

5.1. Interviews

This section presents the results of semi-structured interviews carried out with the instructors of the four practical interpreting courses: Economy, Legal issues, Education and Social issues, and Health Care. The interviews focused on course planning and organisation, online resources and activities, communication with course participants, course administration and management (with particular attention to the technical aspects), and student learning. Additionally, the instructors were asked to indicate their degree of satisfaction with the blended environment and assess the usefulness of implementing Moodle in their courses. All instructors were unanimous in emphasising that Moodle helped them to organise class materials "in a neat manner." They also agreed that it proved to be "a good return on investment" in the second edition of the Programme since it enabled them to import course materials from the previous year. Two instructors mentioned they no longer had to copy in-class materials as students accessed them online and came to class with the relevant printouts.

When asked about the range of online resources and activities they used on Moodle, the instructors mentioned uploading links to websites as well as files with vocabulary lists and interpreting case scenarios (as .doc, .rtf, and .pdf). One instructor reported using image, audio and audiovisual files in the lesson preparation and follow-up stages, while the remaining course developers saw "no real need to include audiovisual aids or any other multimedia materials" in their respective courses. An attempt was made by one instructor to create online quizzes to be completed by students in the pre-class stage. However, this feature was discontinued when the students said they preferred the traditional pen-and-paper format.

Moodle is claimed to be particularly well-suited to foster collaborative learning and facilitate an exchange of ideas between course participants and instructors. However, with regard to using Moodle for communication, one instructor said: "I do not use Moodle to communicate with students. I tell them in class what materials to prepare for the next meeting. The procedure is always the same." There was one instructor who reported trying the course forum and course news but the level of student participation was low. Two instructors added short text or web pages into the respective thematic blocks on Moodle with guidelines for students concerning individual class preparation and follow-up.

The instructors were largely satisfied with the course enrolment procedure (enrolment key). They also said they monitored student activity logs regularly. Two instructors used the course calendar feature and found it communicated course events (e.g. quizzes and tests) in a clear manner. When asked about the technical aspects, one instructor complained about *Safari* compatibility problems which "ended after switching from Mac to Windows." No other major problems were reported. The instructors said they turned to the platform administrator for support with problem-solving and troubleshooting.

The instructors agreed that thanks to Moodle students knew exactly what was expected of them and were made directly responsible for accessing course materials and preparing for classes. Class preparation and follow-up stages involved vocabulary study (mostly text files or scanned vocabulary lists in PDF files) and background readings (a list of recommended websites). By way of preparation for two courses students were expected to translate short texts (e.g.

parts of the maternity allowance application form) which were later discussed in-class. One instructor asked students to watch short introductory video files with transcripts online before the start of each thematic block. In two courses there were 10-minute vocabulary quizzes at the start of every second class.

When asked about their overall course satisfaction, all instructors responded positively. They said they appreciated the face-to-face interaction with students both in terminology discussions and in problem-based case scenarios. Additionally, the instructors said that Moodle enabled them to use in-class time "more efficiently." Thanks to moving most of content delivery online, valuable in-class time was saved for interpreting practice. They also reported satisfactory feedback from students who were able to interpret and practice all roles in class thanks to that arrangement.

Interestingly, in their assessment of the necessity of Moodle for their particular course on a scale from 1 (useless) to 7 (indispensable), the instructors gave an average response of 4.66 and justified their ratings by saying that, although Moodle was of great help in organising and managing their courses and constituted a constant motivating factor for improving them, it was not indispensable (two instructors said that they "could easily live without it").

Summing up, the instructors appreciated selected features of Moodle pertaining to course organisation and management as well as student learning. They also emphasised it created more in-class opportunities for students to practice their community interpreting skills. The various Moodle resources and activities were found to have been put to a rather limited yet goal-oriented use. Despite the limited number of in-class meetings, face-to-face communication with students was the preferred choice over chats or the course forum. Interestingly, students were reported to favour pen-and-paper rather than online quizzes.

5.2. Questionnaires

Students were asked a range of opinion questions with a Likert response scale about such aspects of the blended environment as class preparation, skills development, the usefulness of online resources for learning, the technical aspects of Moodle use, knowledge organisation and final exam preparation.

Most students (69.9%) said that Moodle played a major role while 20.6% said that it played a moderate role in preparing for the in-class meetings. Few students thought Moodle played a small role in class preparation (7.9%). Moodle was found by 52.4% of students to shorten the time necessary to prepare for classes (33.3% of students disagreed with that opinion, and 9.5% had no opinion on that subject).

The majority of students (79.8%) thought that the in-class meetings had a big influence on the development of community interpreting skills. Fewer said that influence was moderate (13.1%).

When asked to evaluate the usefulness of the online resources for learning, the majority of students (90.5%) pointed to text files as the most useful for learning. Internet sites, graphics files and audiovisual files were considered either definitely useful or useful. Details are presented in Figure 1.

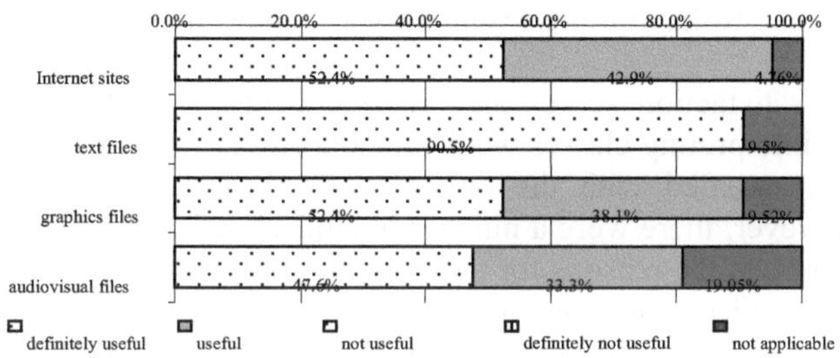

Figure 1. The usefulness of Moodle resources for learning

As regards technical difficulties, 33.3% of students reported problems with course enrolment while 47.6% of students had difficulties with access to text files (no specific reasons were given). Course navigation, access to websites and graphics files did not present any problems to 14.3% of students.

In their assessment of the online and in-class learning contexts in organising knowledge, students indicated that Moodle played a big (54%) to moderate (17.5%) role in the process of knowledge organisation. Moodle was slightly outperformed by the in-class meetings in this respect: students indicated that the in-class meetings played a big (58.7%) to moderate (36.5%) role in knowledge organisation.

As regards the preparation for the final exam consisting of community interpreting performance (students acted out selected case scenarios), the majority pointed to the in-class meetings (79.4%) rather than Moodle (44.5%) as being the most helpful in this respect.

Additionally, the respondents were invited to provide comments on the practical interpreting courses in an open-ended item. In general, students were satisfied with the practical interpreting courses in the following aspects: well-prepared (85.7%) and professional (90.5%) instructors, well-organised classes (80.9%) and a range of useful (95%), authentic (71.4%) materials. They also appreciated the short translation assignments (76.2%) and vocabulary quizzes (38.1%). Some of them said that interpreting in front of the rest of class was stressful for them (28.6%) and that they would prefer having additional training in interpreting strategies (14.3%) and stress management (4.8%). Several students indicated that too much time was devoted to homework discussions (19%) and that the entry quizzes should be eliminated (19%). Some said that there were too many links to websites on Moodle, and they would prefer PDF or text files (38.1%). Half of the students indicated they would appreciate having ready-made vocabulary lists for each class (47.6%). There were also some who thought there was too much vocabulary to prepare (38.1%) and too many background readings to be completed (28.6%). A few students mentioned that they would like to have more visual aids and multimedia materials on Moodle (23.8%).

Student satisfaction scores are reported in Table 2. Overall the students thought the interpreting classes were valuable and effective. They were also to a large extent satisfied with the online platform and its integration with the classes. However, there were a number of students who felt dissatisfied in those respects. Some of the reasons for their dissatisfaction could be inferred from the comments provided in the open-ended item: too many background readings and too much vocabulary to prepare. Additionally, some students said ready-made vocabulary lists, a selection of background readings in text files rather than website links, as well as more multimedia materials would be appreciated.

Table 2. Student satisfaction level

Specification	definitely satisfied (%)	satisfied (%)	dissatisfied (%)	definitely dissatisfied (%)	not applicable (%)
satisfaction with the practical interpreting classes	33.3	61.9	-	-	4.8
satisfaction with Moodle	38.1	42.86	14.29	-	4.75
satisfaction with the integration of Moodle with the practical interpreting classes	28.6	57.1	9.5	-	4.8

6. Discussion

It was the goal of the present study to explore and evaluate the proportions between the in-class and online course components in the practical community interpreting classes using Moodle. The results seem to indicate that both students and instructors appreciated the advantage of being able to focus on in-class discussions, problem-solving and interpreting as a result of most of the content delivery having been moved online. In this respect, the blended environment was found to streamline the learning and teaching processes.

Instructors appreciated Moodle in the areas of course organisation and management as well as student learning; yet, their use of the platform was mainly restricted to the dissemination of course materials. Attempts at using online quizzes and the course forum were also made but were subsequently abandoned as a result of low student uptake. In addition, the instructors did not see the need to integrate the more advanced Moodle functionalities into their courses. This may have been partly due to a lack of awareness or familiarity with ICT technologies, and combined with a reluctance to explore the more advanced features of the system. At the same time, instructors may have felt there was no need to change their teaching habits in view of a heretofore generally positive student feedback.

Students mostly appreciated the facilitating role of Moodle in preparing for classes though some felt overwhelmed with the amount of course materials, which may have contributed to over 30% of them stating that Moodle lengthened the time needed to prepare for classes. This, however, from an instructor's standpoint, is a positive aspect. It emerged that the in-class meetings slightly outperformed Moodle in their usefulness for organising knowledge. Moreover, in student assessment the in-class meetings surpassed Moodle considerably from the point of view of exam preparation. Those results seem to indicate that community interpreting courses were rather specific in that they demanded considerable in-class participation while not necessarily encouraging online collaboration. Despite the limited number of in-class meetings, students were reluctant to avail themselves of online communication tools. However, online collaboration was not rewarded. Students were also reported to prefer pen-and-paper to online vocabulary quizzes, which could be related to a certain level of anxiety towards using Moodle for assessment purposes. That final conclusion seems to be corroborated by the finding that a significant proportion of course participants reported difficulty with access to text files online, with only a few students indicating they would prefer more multimedia materials.

7. Conclusions

Based on the positive responses from faculty interviews and student questionnaires, the present study has shown that Moodle aided course developers most effectively in course organisation, administration and management while helping students to prepare for classes and to organise knowledge. However, the specific nature of the community interpreting courses does seem to demand more in-class than online participation. As a result, the online platform was used mainly for disseminating class materials and assisting students in their preparation for classes and knowledge consolidation. While not providing an optimum level of student engagement in online communication, Moodle was nevertheless shown to have its indisputable merits, a more efficient use of in-class time being its greatest asset.

The results of the present study may not necessarily be adaptable readily to other courses. However, the tendency of course instructors to use course management systems to distribute and access course materials rather than to engage in creating interactive and collaborative activities is certainly not an isolated case (Blin and Munro 2008). Some of the possible reasons for the relatively low uptake of Moodle features were suggested: an understandably greater focus on the in-class than on online participation in the community interpreting courses, lack of student demand combined with a limited awareness of the more sophisticated resources and activities, as well as a certain degree of ICT anxiety on the part of both the faculty and course participants.

It should be emphasised that, while the specific nature of the interpreting classes solicited more in-class than online participation resulting in a limited use of Moodle features, the general learning and teaching experience gathered in the blended environment was found to be highly useful and rewarding for both students and instructors alike.

References

Blin, F. and M. Munro (2008). "Why hasn't technology disrupted academics' teaching practices? Understanding resistance to change through the lens of activity theory". *Computers and Education*, 50: 475–490.

Bliuc, A.-M., Goodyear, P. and R.A. Ellis (2007). "Research focus and methodological choices in studies into students' experiences of blended learning in higher education". *Internet and Higher Education*, 10: 231–244.

Browne, T., Jenkins, M. and R. Walker (2005). "VLE surveys: A longitudinal perspective between March 2001, March 2003 and March 2005 for higher education in the United Kingdom". Retrieved April 1, 2009 from: http://www.ucisa.ac.uk/~/media/groups/tlig/vle_surveys/vle_survey_2005%20pdf.ashx.

Browne, T., Jenkins, M. and R. Walker (2008). "2008 Survey of Technology Enhanced Learning For Higher Education in the UK". Retrieved April 1, 2009 from: http://www.ucisa.ac.uk/publications/~/media/groups/tlig/vle_surveys/TEL%20survey%2 02008%20pdf.ashx.

Buttaroni, S and E. Sobczak (2008). "Blended Language Learning in European Educational Institutions – Discrete Requirements". *Vienna English Working Papers*, 17 (3): 57–64.

Ellis, R.A. and R.A. Calvo (2007). "Minimum Indicators to Assure Quality of LMS-supported Blended Learning". *Journal of Educational Technology and Society*, 10 (2): 60–70.

Garrison, D.R. and H. Kanuka (2004). "Blended learning: Uncovering its transformative potential in higher education". *Internet and Higher Education*, 7 (2): 95–105.

Garrison, D.R. and N.D. Vaughan (2007). *Blended Learning in Higher Education: Framework, Principles, and Guidelines.* San Francisco, CA: Jossey-Bass.

Gómez, M.A. and S. Weinreb (2002). "An Alternative Instructional Model: Teaching Medical Translation Online". *META*, 47 (4): 643–648.

Gran, L., Carabelli, A. and R. Merlini (2002). "Computer-assisted Interpreter Training". In: G. Garzone and M. Viezzi (eds.). *Interpreting in the 21st Century: Challenges and Opportunities*. Selected Papers from the 1st Forli Conference on Interpreting Studies, 9–11 November 2000, Amsterdam: John Benjamins: 277–294.

Hale, S.B. (2007). *Community Interpreting*. Basingstoke/New York: Palgrave Macmillan.

Ioannou, A. and R.D. Hannafin (2008). "Course Management Systems: Time for Users to Get What They Need". *TechTrends*, 52 (1): 46–50.

Mason, R. and F. Rennie (2006). *Elearning. The key concepts*. London: Routledge.

Niska, H. (2002). "Community interpreter training: past, present and future". In: G. Garzone and M. Viezzi (eds.). *Interpreting in the 21st Century: Challenges and Opportunities*. Selected Papers from the 1st Forli Conference on Interpreting Studies, 9–11 November 2000, Amsterdam: John Benjamins: 133–144.

Oliver, M. and K. Trigwell (2005). "Can *Blended Learning* Be Redeemed?". *E–Learning*, 2 (1): 17–26.

Osguthorpe, R.T. and C.A. Graham (2003). "Blended learning environments: Definitions and directions". *The Quarterly Review of Distance Education*, 4(3): 227–233.

Roberts, R.P. (1994). "Community Interpreting Today and Tomorrow". In: P. Krawutschke (ed.). *Proceedings of the 35th Annual Conference of the American Translators Association*. Medford, NJ: Learned Information: 127–138.

Runiewicz-Wardyn, M. (2008). *Towards building an eLearning environment in Poland.* Warsaw. Academic and Professional Press.

Samson, R. (2005). "Computer-assisted translation". In: M. Tennent (ed.). *Training for the New Millennium: Pedagogies for Translation and Interpreting*. Amsterdam: John Benjamins: 101–126.

Sloan Consortium (2008). "The Sloan survey of online learning, Staying the Course: Online Education in the United States, 2008". Retrieved May 4, 2009 from http://www.sloan-c.org/publications/survey/pdf/staying_the_course.pdf.

Sloan Consortium (2006). "The Sloan survey of online learning, Making the grade: Online education in the United States, 2006". Retrieved from http://www.sloan-c.org/publications/survey/pdf/making_the_grade.pdf

Steen, H.L. (2008). "Effective eLearning Design". *MERLOT* Journal of Online Learning and Teaching, 4 (4): 526–532. Retrieved May 4, 2009 from http://jolt.merlot.org/vol4no4/steen_1208.htm.

Tryuk, M. (2006). *Przekład ustny środowiskowy: mity i rzeczywistość* [Community Interpreting: Myths and Reality].Warszawa: PWN.

Valero Garcés, C. and A. Martin (2008). *Crossing Borders in Community Interpreting: Definitions and Dilemmas*. Amsterdam: John Benjamins.

Wadensjö, C., Englund Dimitrova, B. and A.-L. Nilsson (2007). *The critical link 4: professionalisation of interpreting in the community*, Selected papers from the 4th International Conference on Interpreting in Legal, Health and Social Service Settings, Stockholm, Sweden, 20–23 May 2004, Amsterdam: John Benjamins.

Weller, M. (2007). *Virtual Learning Environments*. London: Routledge.

Part Eight

LEXICOGRAPHY

New XML-encoded Swahili-Polish Dictionary: Micro- and Macrostructure

Piotr Bański and Beata Wójtowicz

Abstract: The paper describes the structure of a new Swahili-Polish electronic dictionary. The dictionary is at the planning stage – it will be extracted from a corpus of Swahili once we collect the appropriate funds. Its electronic format, however, is being tested on a small Swahili-English dictionary constructed by hand – this is why in what follows, we sometimes switch from talking about what the Swahili-Polish dictionary *will be* to describing what the test Swahili-English dictionary already *is*. We first discuss the microstructure (citation forms for particular parts of speech, additional elements present in the entry), moving next to the lumping vs. splitting debate concerning the status of derivatives, which we treat as a surface issue of presentation. Finally, we briefly discuss the mechanisms that allow us to construct a modern versatile dictionary with the properties outlined here.

Keywords: electronic dictionary, lexicography, macrostructure, microstructure, Polish, Swahili, TEI, XML.

1. Introduction

80 million speakers of Swahili make it the most widespread language of Sub-Saharan Africa (on the entire continent, it is second only to Arabic). It serves not only as official and national language but also as a *lingua franca* for many millions of African citizens. Although numerous bilingual Swahili dictionaries exist, the only publication of this kind targeting Polish is the small (3.5 thousand entries) Swahili-Polish / Polish-Swahili dictionary by Stopa and Garlicki (1966), out of stock for years now and criticized, e.g. by Ohly (1967), for the choice of headwords and the underlying grammatical assumptions.

Given the growing interest in learning Swahili among Polish students, the fact that Swahili dictionaries are not available for purchase in Poland, and that the only Swahili-Polish dictionary is now simply outdated, the compilation of a new Swahili-Polish (and Polish-Swahili) dictionary becomes a must. The present paper describes a project aiming at creating a new dictionary, in electronic form, encoded in XML, accessible both locally and via the Internet, with possibly a printed version as well. The focus here is on its Swahili-Polish part – the reverse will at first be handled by a structured index, as is standard in this type of resources. The primary target audience for the dictionary are learners of Swahili and tourists; therefore, the dictionary will be of the descriptive type, with additional grammatical information supplied beyond what is minimally necessary, in a user-friendly way. Most of these features are discussed in section 2.

All derivatives will by default have the status of main entries. In order to maintain a system whereby derivatives have the status of headwords (ordered alphabetically) and at the same time, the derivational and semantic relationships between particular lexemes are preserved, the dictionary will use an extended mechanism of cross-entry references. We discuss the decision to split word-families in section 3, and the system of cross-entry references and the role it plays in the dictionary in section 4. Section 5 presents an example of the TEI XML format of the dictionary, and section 6 summarizes and concludes the paper.

At present, the dictionary exists in a 'toy' form of, at the time of writing, over 300 main entries that incorporate almost the entire pronominal system of the language as well as specific cases meant to illustrate the most notorious problems of Swahili lexicography and our way of approaching them. It is encoded in XML conformant with the TEI P5 0.6 specification of March 2007 (Sperberg-McQueen and Burnard 2007) and all the XML fragments used here are drawn from it. The examples of entries are as seen in the browser, with minimal adjustments.

2. Microstructure

Apart from the basic grammatical information provided in most of Swahili dictionaries (part of speech, noun class number, transitivity or type of derivation), the dictionary will also indicate various grammatical features that the beginning student may find helpful. This means information such as explicitly marked class prefixes on nouns and pronouns, irregular plural forms of nouns, animacy of nouns from non-human classes or irregular verbal forms. The most frequently used words will also be indicated, in order to stress their importance to the student. Most entries will feature examples, either short, meant to illustrate e.g. the relevant agreement pattern, or long, drawn from the Helsinki Corpus of Swahili, pre-processed fragments of which we demonstrate in section 2.1 below. After that, we proceed to elaborate on the shape of headwords (section 2.2) and the content of entries (section 2.3).

2.1. Source of the dictionary

The content of the dictionary proper will be the sum of the toy dictionary and one derived from the extended form of the Helsinki Corpus of Swahili (HCS 2004), the largest corpus of Swahili, containing over 20 million words and growing. Some of the decisions concerning what is to be included in the dictionary will be determined by the dictionary-building system, which is part of SALAMA (Swahili Language Manager), a multi-purpose language management environment created and maintained by Arvi Hurskainen of the University of Helsinki (Hurskainen 2007). A sample of the output of SALAMA follows, courtesy of Arvi Hurskainen.[1]

(1)

Noun:
{afisa} N 9/6 {officer} ENG HUM
[afisa] Alihoji Afisa [afisa] huyo.

(2)

Verbs:
a. {ajiri} V [ajiri] {employ, hire, engage, retain} AR
[ajiri] Aidha, Tarimba alishangazwa na kauli za baadhi_ya wanachama wa Yanga kutaka eti waonyeshwe vyeti vya Mintjens vinavyomwezesha kufanyakazi ya ushauri Yanga, wakati klabu haijamwajiri [ajiri].
b. {ajiriwa} V [ajiri] {employ, hire, engage, retain} AR PASS
[ajiriwa] Yeye Liundi kaajiriwa [ajiriwa] na Serikali.

(3)

Adjective, inflected:
{bivu} ADJ A-INFL {(kwa matunda) ripe}
[bivu] Ukijiandaa vizuri leo, utavuna mbivu [bivu] kesho.

"ENG" and "AR" signal English and Arabic origin of borrowings, HUM signals [+ human] nouns, and PASS – passive forms of verbs. As can be seen in the examples, the occurrences of the particular inflected forms are indicated by their lemmatised form (e.g. *ajiri* for *haijamwajiri* in 2a). For derivatives, the information on their base form is provided (cf. *-ajiriwa* in 2b). All of these features (and more) are translated into the underlying XML format of the corpus, to which we turn in section 5.

---

1 This is a version of early 2007. Currently, SALAMA equips entries with information on what subcorpus the given example came from, on the frequency of occurrence of the given lexeme, and on its synonyms. Examples illustrating frequent contexts are additionally indicated.

2.2. The form of headwords

Swahili is a Bantu language and as such, it is characterised by agglutinative morphology and a noun class system, whose reflexes are manifested both lexically, on the noun, and syntactically, via agreement. This is demonstrated in the six sentences below, where the only crucial lexemic variable is the initial noun, with which all other elements have to agree (cl stands for a class marker).

(4)

a. M-tu huyu m-zuri m-moja a-li-ye-anguka
cl1.man this.cl1 cl1-nice cl1-onecl1-past-cl1.rel-fall
'this one nice man who fell down'

b. Wa-tu hawa wa-zuri wa-tatuwa-li-o-anguka
cl2.people these.cl2 cl2-nice cl2-three cl2-past-cl2.rel-fall
'these three nice people who fell down'

c. M-ufko huu m-zuri m-moja u-li-o-anguka
cl3.bag this.cl3 cl3-nice cl3-onecl3-past-cl3.rel-fall
'this one nice bag which fell down'

d. Ma-chungwa haya ma-zuri ma-tatu ya-li-yo-anguka
cl6.oranges these.cl6cl6-nice cl6-three cl6-past-cl6.rel-fall
'these three nice oranges which fell down'

e. Ki-tu hiki ki-zuri ki-moja ki-li-cho-anguka
cl7.thing this.cl7 cl7-nice cl7-onecl7-past-cl7.rel-fall
'this one nice thing which fell down'

f. Kalamu hizi n-zuri tatu zi-li-zo-anguka
cl10.pens these.cl10 cl10-nice cl10.three cl10-past-cl10.rel-fall
'these three nice pens which fell down'

Each nominal lexeme is classified as belonging to one of 15 classes, and each of these classes has a default mapping onto the agreement pattern that holds of most of the other elements of the sentence. Note that both noun-class membership and the resulting agreement are in most cases manifested by prefixal means (in the above examples only the demonstrative pronoun breaks this rule). This is also visible in (5) below, in the present-tense paradigm of the verb *kuanguka* 'to fall down'.

(5)

a. ku-anguka 'to fall down'
inf-fall.down

b. ni-na-anguka 'I fall down' e. tu-na-anguka 'we fall down'
1sg-pres-fall.down

c. u-na-anguka 'you fall down' f. m-na-anguka 'you (pl) fall down'
d. a-na-anguka 'he/she/it falls down' g. wa-na-anguka 'they fall down'

All infinitives in Swahili begin with *ku-* (or *kw-*), and practically all verbal stems could be substituted for the stem *-anguka* in the paradigm above. Prefixes change depending on the grammatical context, and the only element that remains unchanged is the stem.

Note that if the traditional lexicographic practice used e.g. for European languages were followed here in citation form selection and verbs were cited in their infinitival forms, most of the space in Swahili dictionaries (and that is also true of many other Bantu languages) would be taken by the letter "k" – all verbs would end up there, which is hardly user-friendly or sensible. A similar problem concerns adjectives: listing their fully inflected forms would result in distributing most of them under the letters of alphabet that their agreement prefixes begin with, which is completely predictable and fully regular. As in the case of inflected verbs (cf. the paradigm in 5), using the full, inflected forms would result in massive redundancy.

The solution to this that is fairly standard in Swahili lexicographic tradition is to ignore the prefixes and list the stems alone. This applies to verbs, numerals, possessive pronouns and inflected adjectives, as illustrated in the sketchy entries below.[2]

(6)

a. **-anguka** *v stat* [< -anga] 1. fall down 2. fail

b. **-zuri** *adj* beautiful, pretty, nice; good: *mtu m~* a good man; *wasichana wa~* beautiful girls; *kitu ki~* a nice thing [> uzuri, vizuri]

c. **-tatu** *num* three: *watu wa~* three people; *miaka mi~* three years; *kalamu ~* three pens

The fragment "[< -anga]" in (6a) specifies the root from which the verb derives and in the Web version of the dictionary, it is a hyperlink pointing at the entry of *-anga*. Similarly, the fragment "[> uzuri, vizuri]" in (6b) contains links to the derivatives of *-zuri*: the noun *uzuri* 'beauty' and the adverb *vizuri* 'correctly; beautifully'. We return to this issue in section 4.

In the case of possessive pronouns, we include both the stem form and all the inflected forms, pointing back to the stem:

2 Nouns and a few other grammatical (sub)classes, due to morphological and semantic idiosyncrasies, are typically exempt from this treatment. See Kiango (2000) for extensive discussion.

(7)

a. **-angu** *pron poss 1 sg* my, mine [> wangu, yangu, langu, changu, vyangu, ...]

b. **w|angu** *pron poss 1 sg* (agrees with 1 2 3 11, an sg) form of -angu: my, mine: *mtoto* ~ my child; *mfuko* ~ my bag; *mbuzi* ~ my goat[3]

2.3. Additional information present in entries

In accordance with the established practice (see e.g. Kiango 2000), nouns will be listed as complete words, together with their class prefixes, in the singular form, if that form is available.[4] As in the case of possessive pronouns, the class prefix is explicitly separated from the stem, cf. (8).

(8)

a. **m|toto** *n 1/2* (wa-) child
b. **ki|tabu** *n 7/8* (vi-) book
c. **kaa** *n 5/6* (ma-) crab
d. **jambo** *n 5/6* (mambo) matter

The purpose of this is to identify the noun stem clearly to the user for the purpose of turning it into the plural form by means of the appropriate prefix. The plural is identified in two ways: traditionally – by means of the second class specification provided at the beginning of the entry (after the slash), and apart from that, by listing either the actual plural nominal prefix, as in (8a–c) or the entire irregular plural, as in (8d).[5] Irregular plural forms will be listed as separate headwords that refer the user to the singular form.

---

3 Because the dictionary exists currently in the electronic form only, the rendering of entries is performed by CSS stylesheets that operate on a version of the dictionary that has been transformed by XSLT scripts. This obviously means freedom in shaping entries whichever way we like (in the future, it will be customisable for the user) and is in no way considered final at the moment. The tildes are expanded to full forms whenever the user points at them with the mouse, and the reference to the root *-angu* in (7b) is a hyperlink, which we artificially mark with an underline and keep to this practice in later examples.

4 Some abstract/mass nouns only occur in what is traditionally called the plural form.

5 Although, given the explicit plural class number specification, the plural prefixes in examples (8a–c) are redundant, they are relevant to students, for whom the dictionary is primarily meant: not every learner of Swahili will remember the shape of the plural class morpheme given the class number, and conversely: the class number, needed for establishing agreement relations with other elements in the clause, is not always recoverable from the shape of the singular or plural prefix, as in the case of (8d).

Moreover, animate nouns from non-human classes will be identified as such, because animacy in this case has direct influence on the agreement pattern within a sentence. That is demonstrated in the following example, on the noun *ndege*, which has animate and inanimate senses – 'bird' and 'plane', respectively.

(9)

a. ndege huyu m-zuri a-li-ruka
cl9.bird this.cl1 cl1-nice cl1-past-fly
'this nice bird flew away'
b. ndege hii n-zuri i-li-ruka
cl9.plane this.cl9 cl9-nice cl9-past-fly
'this nice airplane departed'

An example entry for *ndege* follows.[6]

(10)

ndege[1] *n 9/10* (–) 1. *an* bird: ~ *huyu mzuri aliruka* this nice bird flew away 2. aeroplane, airplane, plane: ~ *hii nzuri iliruka* this nice airplane departed. Syn: **eropleni**

A different kind of additional grammatical description is also present in verbal entries. For example, we list irregular verbal inflections both in the entry of the base form, as shown below in (11a), and also as main entries, each with a reference pointing to the base form, as in (11b).

(11)

a. **-ja** *v ku-* (imp. njoo) come, turn up
b. **-njoo** *v* imp. of -ja

The entry in (11a) indicates the irregular imperative form of *-ja* as well as the fact that, as a monosyllabic verb, it needs prosodic support in some of its forms, and uses the augment *ku-* for this purpose.[7]

6 The superscript number after the headword is a standard indicator of multiple homographs. In this case, *ndege*2 is a class 9/10 noun meaning "omen, sign". This touches upon the interesting issue of discrimination between homographs, to which we have a rather uninteresting, practical answer: in most cases, the SALAMA tools will make a decision for us.

7 Hypertext links need not be restricted to words. They may also point from grammatical descriptions to e.g. paradigms illustrating them, which is a feature that we plan to implement soon.

As we have already mentioned, information on high frequency words, etymology of borrowings and synonyms is also provided, as well as examples of use. For all derivatives, the type of derivation is indicated and a reference to the derivational root is provided (cf. 6a, where *-anguka* is marked as a stative verb that derives from the root *-anga*); that is further discussed in sections 3 and 4.

3. Macrostructure: the treatment of derivatives

The most important issue with respect to macrostructure concerns the handling of derivatives, sometimes referred to as the "lumping vs. splitting" debate, which we describe below in section 3.1 and then proceed to present our approach to it in section 3.2. In brief, while in the default arrangement of entries, we assume the splitting approach, in fact we are able to abstract away from this issue, by delegating it to the presentational level.

3.1. Lumping vs. splitting

Bantu derivational word-families can be extremely numerous, especially those based on verbal roots – for example, De Schryver and Prinsloo (2001: 225ff) count over 140 regular derivatives of the root *reka* 'buy, purchase' in Sepedi.

We begin this section by looking at the verb *-anguka* 'fall down', introduced in examples (4) through (6). This verb derives from the root *-anga* 'fly', via the reversative *-angua* 'throw down'. There are many other derivatives of *-anga*, a selection of which is shown below.[8]

(12)

-anga *v* 'fly'
-angama *v* 'hang, hover'
-angika *v caus* 'hang up'
-angua *v rev* 'throw down'
-anguka *v stat* 'fall down'
-angukia *v stat appl* 'fall into/on'
-angukiana *v stat appl res* 'fall into each other'
anguko *n* 'drop, fall'
-angusha *v caus* 'drop'
-jiangusha *v refl caus* 'lie down'

---

8 It will be noted that some verbs in (12) are described in the same fashion, cf. *-angika* and *-angusha*, the latter being in fact a causative derived from the reversative *-angua*. This is because we do not treat all derivational steps as equally significant and e.g. indicate reversative forms only if the reversative step was the most recent in the derivation.

-angulia *v appl* 'burst out'
kiangushio *n* 'parachute'
mwangushi *n* 'one who lets sth drop, one who destroys'
mwanguko *n* 'fall'

These words can be easily expected to be found in Swahili texts or broadcasts. The problem that we look at in this section deals with presenting them to the user, and the basic question is whether to lump them all into the entry of the root, or whether to distribute them across the dictionary.

Radical lumping means cramming all the information into a single entry, often denying independent status to the most commonly used words only because they happen to be derivatives; additionally the user is required to know the word-formation mechanisms (which are always less transparent than the inflectional system) in order to identify the base form of the given derivative, which means searching for e.g. *utumishi* 'civil service' in the entry for *-tuma* 'assign/give work to sb', which e.g. in Johnson's (1939/1985) dictionary takes half a page. De Schryver and Prinsloo (2001: 224) report on a similar case in a Sepedi–Afrikaans–English dictionary, where the entry for *reka* and its derivatives takes an entire page of dense print. Partial lumping of only the regular forms, as recommended by e.g. Kiango (2000) does not help if it is the regular forms that happen to have high frequency and that should therefore be presented to the user in separate entries.

The choice of the splitting strategy may be considered primarily practical – as Zgusta (1971: 16) notes, "[...] we must not forget that the lexicographer is doing scientific work, but that he publishes it for users whose pursuits are always more practical, at least as regarded from his own point of view." Given this, a user-friendly dictionary of Swahili should list the broadest possible range of derivatives as separate entries. It is not without reason, as Herms (1999) notes, that students of Swahili praise the "friendly" dictionary of Baba Malaika (1994), who adopts this kind of distributed approach to derivatives, while De Schryver and Prinsloo (2001) note the lack of popularity of dictionaries that group words on etymological grounds and/or under verbal or nominal roots.

The lumping approach has one undeniable virtue – it keeps word families together. In agglutinative languages, it can even show how the particular members are derived (see Bosh *et al.* 2007, building on Weber 2002). Scattering derivatives across the entire dictionary (admittedly not so drastically evident in example (12), where not many frequently used non-verbal derivatives exist; this is a fairly exceptional case, though) means severing the lexical and semantic ties between closely related lexemes and practically hiding some of them from the user looking up the root form.

Evidently, both approaches have their virtues and their disadvantages, and both of them have been suggested in the literature and used in practice: Bosch *et al.* (2007) argue for lumping (in South Bantu languages), and that is what e.g. Johnson (1939/1985) did for Swahili. De Schryver and Prinsloo (2001) argue for splitting and this is what, among others and to various limits, Sacleaux (1939) and TUKI (2001) have implemented. Madan (1903/1992) and Abdulla *et al.* (2002) represent mixed approaches, where derivatives representing the same part of speech as the derivational base are placed inside the entry of that base form, while derivatives representing different parts of speech are listed separately.

3.2. Lumping and splitting as a surface issue of presentation

Our initial decision regarding the new dictionary was to follow the path of radical split between members of word-families and to list each derivative word separately. However, in the process of implementing the structure in the form of XML, we realised that what we should do is treat the lumping vs. splitting debate not as a deep issue of structuring the data, but rather as a surface issue of presenting data to the user.

What we do now is use one of these options as the default for constructing the dictionary, but leave the final choice open and subject to the user's choice. The underlying format of the data is modular and it is easier for us to maintain a dictionary where each entry-sized element has independent status, though some such elements are marked as derived, and some of them as roots. At the user's click we can embed all (or even only some of) the derivatives under their roots (or, more generally, base forms) or scatter them across the dictionary, leaving behind only hypertext references as run-on entries.

4. Cross-entry references

In the previous section, we mentioned hypertext references as the condition for our abstracting away from the "lumping vs. splitting" debate. In this section, we first discuss the state of affairs in this respect, as reported in the literature, i.e. flat derivational trees (section 4.1) and then we move on to discuss our proposal for greater explicitness in how derivational relationships are encoded (section 4.2).

4.1. The flat reference system

Recall example (6a), where the derivative *-anguka* points at its root, *-anga*. Such textual references have been in use in lexicography for a long time. Nowadays, in electronic dictionaries, they are often replaced with hyperlinks and/or pop-up information. This offers one way to restore the severed word-family links. Such rather standard backward-references are often complemented with forward-references, so-called run-on entries, that start at the root. In various forms, this has been implemented by Sacleaux (1939) and TUKI (2001), as well as Madan (1903/1992) and Abdulla *et al.* (2002), who only split derivatives that differ from the root in the part of speech. The large online Swahili-English dictionary, *Kamusi*, at Yale University [http://www.yale.edu/swahili/], uses hypertext pointers in both directions.

A sketch of such a system is presented below. Example (13) contains schematic entries of derivatives in (a) and (b), followed by the root in (z).

(13)

a. **-anguka** *v stat* [< -anga] 1. fall down, crash 2. fail

b. **-angua** *v rev* [< -anga] throw down

…

z. **-anga** *v* fly, float [> angama, angika, angua, anguka, …]

This system results in a flat derivational tree shown in (14).

(14)

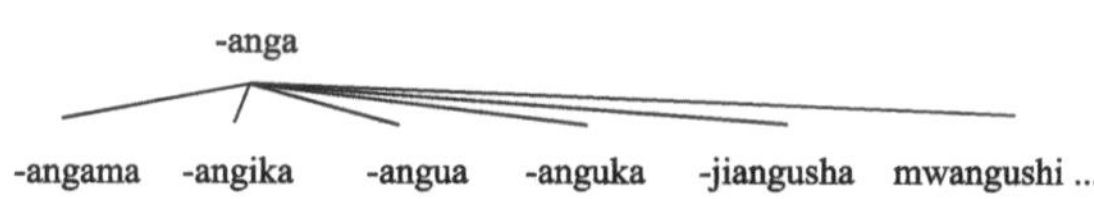

While this represents a serious step towards re-establishing word-family links among entries scattered across the dictionary, it is only a partial remedy. We discuss an improved solution in the next section.

4.2. The hierarchical reference system

What the lumping approaches (somctimes implicitly) offer is presenting the internal structure of word-families: an entry will begin at the root and often proceed through subsequent layers of derivatives. The system described in section 4.1 only partially recreates this situation, by creating flat trees of the sort presented in (14) above.

Traditional cross-entry references, especially among word-families, offer one-sided view of derivational relationships (derivative → root). Run-on entries offer a view from the opposite side (root → derivatives). Typically, however, word-families feature more than two generations of words, and quite often the link between the ends of the chain (root ↔ ultimate derivative) is either unclear to the average speaker or at least not as important as the relationship between the immediately related lexemes.

As an example, consider the English word *establishmentarian*: while the information on the root, *establish*, may in some way be helpful to the dictionary-user, it is more critical for them to know that the word has a lot to do with the intermediate form, *establishment*, because *establishmentarian* derives its meaning only very indirectly from the root and crucially depends on the semantic drift that resulted in the lexicalised meaning of *establishment*. The semantic connection between *establish* and *antidisestablishmentarianism* is even thinner.

A case somewhat similar in nature is shown below, on the example of the verb *-timilizishiana* 'cause to carry out for each other's benefit' that derives from *-timu* 'be complete' (Schadeberg 1992).[9] In the case at hand, the root *-timu* underwent complicated valence changes, as evidenced by two applicative morphemes surrounding two causative ones, topped off with the reciprocal *-an-* (the final *-a* is a native Bantu verbal closing suffix; the root in this case is a borrowing from Arabic).

(15)

-tim-il-iz-ish-i-an-a	< -timu
-tim-appl-caus-caus-appl-rec-a	
'cause to carry out for each other's benefit'	'be complete'

Notice that apart from the semantic problem of recreating the changes in the meaning of the root at each step, the shapes of each of the causative and applicative morphemes are different and it is not at all obvious how a learner will identify the shape of an intermediate form when all that is known is the shape of the root. Being able to identify each consecutive form is naturally not a must, but we treat this as a learner-oriented feature on the one hand, and on the other, as a detail that brings the dictionary closer to the status of electronic language resource for computational purposes.

Other problems with identifying the root given a derivative, or identifying the intermediate derivational steps, attested also in teaching practice, are shown below.

(16)

a. la 'eat' – lisha 'feed' – mlisha 'waiter'

---

9 It also demonstrates one of the reasons why in Swahili it is possible to derive so many lexemes from a single verbal root, as it features multiple occurrences of the same derivational operation.

b. oga 'timid, coward' – ogopa 'fear' – ogofya / ogofisha 'frighten' – ogofyo 'threat'
c. anga 'fly' – angua 'drop' – anguka 'fall down'

While case (16a) appears to be quite regular, teaching practice has shown that beginning students only rarely realise that *mlisha* 'waiter' derives from *-la* 'eat'. Example (16b) presents another version of the problem of morphophonological idiosyncrasies and segmentation, already seen in (15). Finally, the very existence of reversative derivations of the type illustrated by *-anga* 'fly' vs. *-angua* 'drop' in (16c) can also easily confuse users, when they are told that *-anguka* 'fall down' derives from *-anga* 'fly'. "Regularity" is one of the keywords here: each step of the derivation presents a pattern that the learner should internalise, because it is highly regular and it may reapply at a later stage of the derivation. Making students aware of the structure of the hierarchy in one case reinforces their knowledge of the possible derivational patterns that can be productively applied in other cases: to the creation of new forms or to the analysis of newly encountered words, which need not be present in the dictionary due to their low text frequency.

The evidence above points to the need for reestablishment and refinement of hierarchical relationships in word-families, and that means further elaboration on the flat-tree approach. The modification that we propose is for run-on entries to point to the next level of the derivational hierarchy only, and for derivatives to point to their derivational bases, which, crucially, need not be the same as their roots. This yields entries of the sort presented immediately below and hierarchical trees such as that sketched in (18).

(17)

a. **-anguka** *v stat* [< -angua] 1. fall down, crash 2. fail [> -angukia, anguko, mwanguko]
b. **-angua** *v rec* [< -anga] throw down, knock down [> -angulia, -angusha, -anguka]
z. **-anga** v fly [> -angama, -angua, -angika]

Recall that backward-references to the base form are enclosed in "[<]", while forward run-on references are marked by "[>]".

(18)

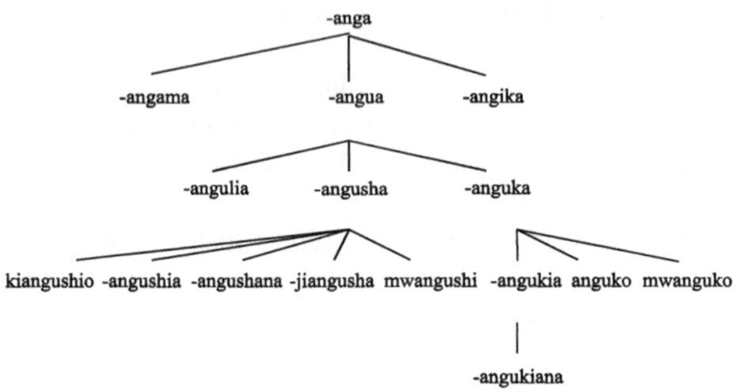

It is possible to equip the dictionary with enhancements of various sorts in order to visualize such trees and let the user navigate across them in e.g. a pop-up window. This is the ultimate step in restoring and improving the information on the relationships within word-families.

Naturally, it is not always possible to establish the correct hierarchy, due to many diverse factors. Sometimes, the intermediate forms may be missing from the dictionary because they do not exist or are below the frequency threshold that would qualify them for inclusion in the dictionary. In such cases, the lexicographer may fall back to the safe system of flat relationships for the more problematic parts of the derivational tree. Crucially, modifying such trees and updating them with new information is made extremely easy by the underlying format of the dictionary, which is the topic of the following section.

5. Underlying format: TEI P5 XML

The dictionary is encoded in XML conformant with the TEI P5 Guidelines of March 2007 (Sperberg-McQueen and Burnard 2007). The virtues of this decision are extensibility, interchangeability, manageability, ease of maintenance, and possibility to create virtually any kind of output. Below, we provide an example XML fragment – the entry for the verb *-anguka*, cf. (17a), copied below for convenience.

(17)

a. **-anguka** *v stat* [< -angua] 1. fall down, crash 2. fail [> -angukia, anguko, mwanguko]

(19)

```
<entry type="derived" n="anguka">
   <form type="stem"><orth>anguka</orth></form>
   <gramGrp>
    <pos>v</pos>
    <gram type="deriv">stat</gram>
   </gramGrp>
   <xr type="derived_from">
    <ref target="#angua">-angua</ref>
   </xr>
   <sense n="1">
    <trans>
     <tr>fall down</tr>
     <tr>crash</tr>
    </trans>
   </sense>
   <sense n="2">
    <trans><tr>fail</tr></trans>
   </sense>
   <xr type="run-on">
    <ref target="#angukia">-angukia</ref>
    <ref target="#anguko">anguko</ref>
    <ref target="#mwanguko">mwanguko</ref>
   </xr>
  </entry>
```

The entry is almost self-documenting and encodes the information presented in a more human-readable form in (17a).[10] First, the orthographic representation is provided, with an indication that the headword is a stem and should have a hyphen prepended. What follows is grammatical information, which is the content of the <gramGrp> element, and the first hypertext reference, to the derivational base (both instances of the <xr> element, which is responsible for cross-references, are boxed for convenience). Below that, senses are specified, followed by another hypertext reference, this time to the forms that derive from -*anguka*. Note that turning the sequence of references into a sequence of nested subentries is only a matter of running the appropriate XSLT script – all the necessary data is there, and all we need to take care of is how to best present it to the user.

---

10 This is an entry on which XSLT scripts operate in order to supply, among others, real XML hypertext references, which are only marked with the "target" attributes in the basic form.

Apart from the various formats that the dictionary can be translated into for the purpose of presentation, publication, or data exchange, another obvious virtue is the sorting/selection options that it makes possible, especially in the context of an XML database. A database is naturally where the dictionary in the final form will be stored.

6. Conclusion

The modern electronic learner dictionary presented here (at the time of writing still in the closed, testing stage) is meant to fill a serious gap: it will be the first electronic dictionary of Swahili available to Polish learners, and the second Swahili-Polish dictionary after the obsolete and out-of-print dictionary of Stopa and Garlicki (1966). Subject to financing, it will be larger than its predecessor that contained only 3.5 thousand entries (we plan to at least double that amount), and it will be based on a balanced subcorpus of the Helsinki Corpus of Swahili, with living language examples.

We have presented an overview of its formal and learner-oriented features: extended information in entries (section 2), the default splitting approach to the status of derivatives (section 3), which can be turned into the lumped view thanks to consistent XML encoding (section 5). XML encoding of the data is what allows us to switch between presentation modes easily, with run-on references in the splitting mode acting as placeholders for information that can be put in their place in the lumping mode (section 4). We have also touched upon the importance of multi-level hierarchical presentation of derivational families (section 4.2).

References

Dictionaries and corpora

Abdulla, A., Halme, R., Harjula, L. and M. Pesari Pajunen (2002). *Swahili-Suomi-Swahili sanakirja*. Helsinki: Suomalaisen Kirjallisuuden Seura.

Baba Malaika (1994). *Modern Swahili Modern English*. Tanzania: MS Training Centre for Development Cooperation.

(HCS) Helsinki Corpus of Swahili (2004). Compilers: Institute for Asian and African Studies (University of Helsinki) and CSC – Scientific Computing Ltd. See http://www.aakkl.helsinki.fi/cameel/corpus/intro.htm

Johnson, F. (1985) [1939]. *A Standard Swahili-English Dictionary (founded on Madan's Swahili-English Dictionary)*. Oxford: Oxford University Press.

Madan, A.C. (1992) [1903]. *Swahili-English Dictionary*. New Delhi: Asian Educational Services.

Sacleux, Ch. (1939). *Dictionnaire Swahili-Français*. Paris: Institut d'Ethnologie.

Stopa, R. and B. Garlicki (1966). *Mały słownik suahilijsko-polski i polsko-suahilijski.* Warszawa: Wiedza Powszechna.
(TUKI) Taasisi ya Uchunguzi wa Kiswahili (2001). *Kamusi ya Kiswahili-Kiingereza. Swahili-English Dictionary.* Dar es Salaam: Chuo Kikuu cha Dar es Salaam.

Other works

Bosch, S.E., Pretorius, L. and J. Jones (2007). "Towards Machine-Readable Lexicons for South African Bantu languages". *Nordic Journal of African Studies* 16(2). Available at http://www.njas.helsinki.fi. Accessed on 10 July 2007.
De Schryver, G.M. and D.J. Prinsloo (2001). "Towards a Sound Lemmatisation Strategy for the Bantu Verb through the Use of Frequency-based Tail Slots – with special reference to Cilubà, Sepedi and Kiswahili". In: J.S. Mdee and H.J.M. Mwansoko (eds.). *Makala ya kongamano la kimataifa Kiswahili 2000.* Dar es Salaam: TUKI, Chuo Kikuu cha Dar es Salaam: 188–215.
Herms, I. (1999). "Swahili Lexicography: The Swahili-German Dictionary". In: H.E. Wolff (ed.). *Contributions to Bantu Lexicography.* Vol. 10: 1–8. Leipzig: University of Leipzig Papers on Africa, Languages and Literatures.
Hurskainen, A. (2007). "SALAMA Dictionary Compiler". Helsinki: University of Helsinki. Available at http://www.transtechno.fi/dict-examples.pdf. Accessed on 10 July 2007.
Kiango, J.G. (2000). *Bantu lexicography: a critical survey of the principles and process of constructing dictionary entries.* Tokyo: Institute for the Study of Languages and Cultures of Asia and Africa, Tokyo University of Foreign Studies.
Ohly, R. (1967). "Roman Stopa, Bolesław Garlicki, Mały Słownik Suahilijsko-Polski i Polsko-Suahilijski, Kamusi Dogo ya Kiswahili-Kipolanda, Kipolanda-Kiswahili, Warszawa 1966. s. 126". *Przegląd Orientalistyczny* 3(63): 265–268.
Schadeberg, T.C. (1992). *A sketch of Swahili Morphology.* Köln: Rüdiger Köppe Verlag.
Sperberg-McQueen, C.M. and L. Burnard (eds.) (2007). "TEI P5: Guidelines for Electronic Text Encoding and Interchange". Available at http://www.tei-c.org/P5. (10 July 2007).
Weber, D.J. (2002). "Reflections on the Huallaga Quechua dictionary: derived forms as subentries". Available at http://emeld.org/workshop/2002/presentations/weber/emeld.pdf. Accessed on 10 July 2007.
Zgusta, L. (1971). *Manual of Lexicography.* Praha: Academia.

Insights into Selected Scientific and Technical Dictionaries Currently Available on the Polish Publishing Market

Piotr Burmann

Abstract: This paper aims at evaluating five scientific and technical dictionaries chosen from those currently available on the Polish publishing market. The dictionaries are intended for professionals for whom English is either a tool at work or the subject of work. The author, therefore, carefully examines the dictionaries not only from the viewpoint of the ESP learner, but also the engineer who needs to communicate in the international circles and the translator dealing with specialized texts. This "triple" approach results in detecting many imperfections of dictionaries in question and proposing a number of improvements aimed at designing a dictionary, which could acquire the status of being a user-friendly and practical resource. The framework for such a discussion is the standard and quality introduced by contemporary dictionaries created due to the achievements of corpus linguistics. At the same time, this paper is intended to present a set of assumptions needed to design and compile a specialized bilingual corpus for applications in lexicography and translation of scientific and technical language.

Keywords: bilingual dictionary, comparable corpus, dictionary, e-dictionary, entry quality, lexicography, LSP, phraseology, scientific and technical language, specialized language.

1. Introduction

In today's world, where working with a foreign language is an everyday issue, the dictionary has become more important than ever. Today electronic print competes with traditional paper books, but the art of designing and compiling a reliable and useful dictionary is still a difficult and time-consuming process regardless of the medium.

Studies on general language and specialized sublanguages have been conducted for many years, but scientific and technical register is still neglected. The number of publications for this sublanguage is limited and their content does not provide sufficient number of answers in this field. Before any new resource is proposed, it is reasonable to have a critical look at the present publications to draw appropriate conclusions.

Development of corpus linguistics and its practical application, e.g. in lexicography, led to new era; new standard and higher quality have been

introduced. In view of this and the fact that there are differences between general and specialized language, the author chose five dictionaries and analyzed the quality of their entries as well as other minor aspects of the dictionaries which influence the usefulness of this kind of publication.
Since this review is not only intended as a pure assessment, but also as preparation for further work devoted to the scientific and technical register, description of given elements is extended in some places.

This work cannot be treated as an exhaustive source of information on those dictionaries as well as the subject, but it should be considered as introductory insight in the problem of scientific and technical dictionaries.

2. Initial assumptions

To maintain clear line of argumentation and avoid misunderstanding, which may occur in a review, a few initial assumptions are provided.

Achievements of corpus linguistics in lexicography which led, among others, to publication of such dictionaries as Oxford Advanced Lerner's Dictionary (Hornby) and PWN-OXFORD Dictionary (The PWN-Oxford English-Polish Polish-English Dictionary) forced the author to think why we cannot have the same quality of entries in case of scientific and technical dictionaries, or more generally, in specialized dictionaries.

Deep belief in the power of the dictionary has led many learners and beginning translators to many mistakes. The dictionary is not an exhausting source of information and a set of dictionaries and appropriate references should be used in daily work, not to mention appropriate experience. The quality of the dictionary and range of information depends on the user. This means that not every lexicographic publication must be as extensive as possible. Nonetheless, one should not resign from adequate quality when it is possible to provide it at sufficient level, especially, if there is such a need. In other words, we may say that the prime aim of lexicography is to show the direction, rather than foreseeing every possible context in which a given entry may occur.

In many works devoted to the subject of specialized language there is a clear distinction between two poles of specialized language: linguistic competence and field-specific knowledge. Unfortunately, most often only the first one is paid attention to. It is understandable to some degree, but when we discuss the final product which is intended to be a rich and practical resource, also the second pole should be maintained in the discussion on scientific and technical dictionaries. For this reason, the author will analyze both types of information.

Further, the scientific and technical language, as specialized language, is understood as language which has its peculiarities, but it is based on general language which means that there is the same grammar (but distribution of grammatical phenomena is different) and frame vocabulary, which constitute a kind of base on which specialized language (and its terminology) is structured.

The author hesitates from using the words "good" or "bad" in reference to the dictionaries in question. Each of them represents a different type of the dictionary and situations when they are helpful are different. Therefore, the dictionaries should not be compared to one another. They are taken into consideration at the same time to outline the general situation. Instead of a direct assessment, the author prefers to think about "quality" and "functionality" as was done by Swanepoel (2001).

3. Users – triple approach

Creation of a user profile is an inherent element of any dictionary-making process. Similarly, when assessing a dictionary the understanding of the user is vital. The profile, however, is prepared before entry-writing process begins, which is why the author prepared his own brief analysis of the potential user with the aim to learn the basic characteristics of the user. To begin with, any user of specialized language can be categorized as a member of the following groups:

ESP learner

Any learner of specialized language with lower linguistic competence then the translator and smaller field-specific knowledge compared to the engineer should be included in this group. The learner who belongs here has in fact the most difficult task since s/he attempts to acquire both poles of specialized language. On the other hand, the ESP learner is not required to gain full field-specific knowledge and linguists-like competence. Nonetheless, a given resource should help the ESP learner with both aspects of specialized language.

engineer

The difference between the ESP learner and the translator is not clear-cut at first. Of course, the engineer faces the same linguistic competence issues, but s/he has filed-specific knowledge, which puts him/ her in a slightly better position than the ESP learner. Despite this advantage the engineer should be provided with a tool which would assists his linguistic problems indicating non-linguistic aspects of specialized language as e.g. differences in notations, conventions etc.

translator

In opposition to the previous users the translator is meant here as an educated linguists who was trained to perform translation professionally. Here linguistic competence is not an issue; we assume that the translator is fully capable of working not only with language as a tool, but also with language as the subject of work. For this reason, the translator is able to adjust to new situations due to his/ her extensive experience with working on language. Nonetheless, the need to understand the subject of work is essential for success and the translator often faces the lack of appropriate assistance. The translator is required to search and verify constantly on his/ her own.

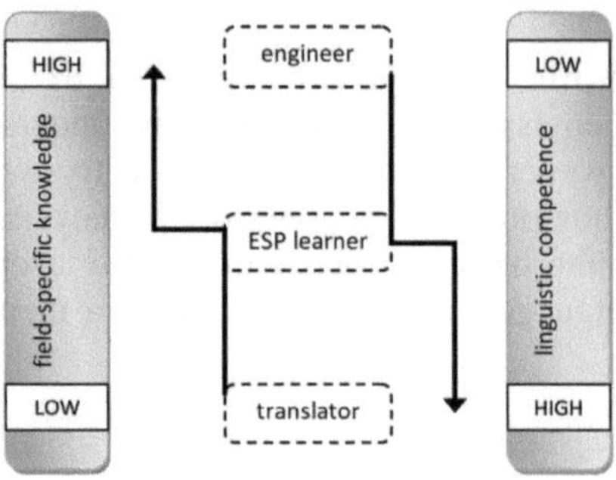

Figure 1. Relationship between the two poles of specialized language and its users

Even such a brief discussion of the potential user shows that any attempt to outline the user profile, and consequently any attempt to apply the conclusions in practice, is quite complicated. The range of information to be provided in a dictionary is considerably wide. This leads to the question whether different users should have different sources adjusted to their needs. The idea of separate dictionaries for field-experts and translators is not new (cf. Pieńkos 2003). However, financial and economic reasons, which underline every publication, force us to remain with the idea of one single volume. Again one single volume, which would aspire to include both linguistic and technical information, is in danger of becoming something more than a dictionary e.g. a handbook.

To summarize, both poles of specialized language are paid with equal attention in this paper. Although this review was mainly intended to concern those linguistic aspects, the second pole will be sustained visible due to the above-mentioned arguments.

4. The dictionaries (general introduction)

The choice of the dictionaries was not accidental. First, these dictionaries are well known on the Polish publishing market (considering their presence in bookshops and easy access to them). Further, the dictionaries can be treated as representatives of other dictionaries of this kind, which are similar in form and/ or content. Below general overview of the dictionaries is presented, and then more information is provided.

a) general description

	Name	Publisher/ year	Range/ type	Size (entries)
1	Słowniki angielsko-polskie i polsko-angielskie naukowo-techniczne, specjalistyczne i ogólne	LexLand	scientific and technical, general, bilingual	372 000
2	Wielojęzyczny Słownik Terminologiczny Elektryki	Stowarzyszenie Elektryków Polskich	electrical engineering, multilingual	1600 (EN-PL)
3	Słownik techniczny angielsko-polski, polsko-angielski. Technical dictionary English-Polish, Polish-English.	Rea	technical, general, bilingual	90 000
4	Angielsko-polski słownik specjalistyczny elektronika	Kanion	electronics, bilingual, EN-PL only	16 000
5	Angielsko-polski i polsko-angielski słownik terminów, pojęc i zwrotów z dziedziny elektroenergetyki.	Wydawnictwo Politechniki Śląskiej	power engineering, bilingual	NA

b) overview based on authors'/ publishers' information

[1] It is an electronic dictionary composed of four smaller dictionaries (scientific and technical, chemical, computer science and general dictionary) with a dictionary of acronyms. All of that is delivered with System TL+7.0 software. Wydawnictwo Naukowo-Techniczne originally published the dictionaries as separate books. The publisher informs that besides numerous terms and their equivalents from different disciplines there is a great number of examples of how words are used in sentences. A very important property

is that a dictionary of general language was also included. The dictionaries can be used separately or all-in-one option.

[2] The second biggest scientific and technical dictionary available on the Polish publishing market. The information on the cover says that the dictionary answers in detail all the questions rising during reading and translating specialized scientific and technical texts. It is intended for scientists, engineers, technicians and students of technical faculties.

[3] The author's writes that it is practical help in work of electronic engineer, computer scientists, and English translator of specialized texts. Then the publisher adds that the dictionary is not intended for an English linguist.

[4] The author says that some entries were based on entries from other dictionary.

The fact that the publishers try to convince the potential users that their publications are sufficient for success in foreign language communication, if we take into consideration further part of this review, is disturbing. On one hand, it is dictated by marketing. On the other hand, it may be bad understanding of true complex nature of S&T language.

c) additional remarks

Besides the quality of entries, we should analyse other more down-to-earth aspect of the dictionaries in question. Below additional information on given dictionaries describe other factors that influence the whole shape of the publications.

dictionary	property	comment
Leksykonia	software	The dictionary is delivered with TL+7 software; it makes the publication very comfortable in use with many options possible to be adjusted by the user. The software allows to create own dictionaries. The software can cooperate with MS Word.
	repeated entries	Since the sub-dictionaries are separate items, some of the entries are screened separately with different pieces of information. It lowers the level of functionality as it may cause some inconvenience.
REA	form	Nice, concise edition. Thumb index is present. Head entries distinctly marked in bold and colour.
SEP	source of data	The main source of information included in the

		dictionary comes from norms and standards. This ensures accuracy of chosen terminology and additional information.
	arrangement of entries	Anything given in Polish part is given in English as well.
	form	The dictionary is delivered in non-searchable PDF file. Looking up for an entry is preceded by finding tree-part identification number and then following it to the entry.
WPS	arrangement of entries	Clear and nice arrangement. Entries found in English-Polish part are mirrored in Polish-English part.
	source of data	This dictionary includes highly professional terminology, difficult to be found somewhere else.
Kanion	form	Very clear and easily searchable. Thumb index is present.
	language	The dictionary is only English-Polish.

ii) supplements which are absent

The author expected the dictionaries to include at least some supplements considering S&T language. Unfortunately, there are no such supplements. Of course, the main aim of the dictionary is to provide information on meaning and grammatical behaviour, but since there are no sufficient studies devoted to S&T language it is reasonable to include so-called topic pages. An example of such a supplement may be the ones included by the nautical dictionary compiled by Ratajczak and Lotko (2004) which contains the following supplements: Beaufort scale, Douglas sea scale, visibility scale, International Code of Signals, weather symbols and sailing points. In case Oxford's Advanced Learners Dictionary we may find supplements such as: maps, vocabulary pages, basic grammar, examples of written forms, symbols of IPA and other. The author believes that contemporary dictionary of specialized language should be equipped with similar basic supplements with suitable topics. It is difficult to find correct examples of e.g. report on experiment or list of standard expressions used in scientific register (for instance examples of written forms were included in An English-Polish Dictionary of Legal and Economic Terms (Jaślan and Jaślan). In addition, a table of unit conversion, lists of visual symbols of elements and devices used on e.g. rate plates and similar elements would constitute great help to the user regardless his/her linguistic competence and field-specific knowledge. Such addition would significantly improve the functionality of the dictionary.

5. Entries and their quality

A review of a number of items, belonging to the same subject group, has to be organized and followed according to a common procedure of assessment to obtain reliable results and conclusions. Bearing in mind the above discussion the author prepared a list of properties (further a list of parameters) according to which the review in conducted. The list is based on Koren's work (2009), but it was adjusted to the dictionaries in question. It must be mentioned that the choice and arrangement of the following parameters in not final and they can be reorganized and supplemented. In author's opinion, however, the chosen set should work as tool to observe presence and quality of various parameters. Also importance of given parameters is not equal which is why there will be additional remarks despite just determination of presence or absence of a given parameter.

The selection criteria for global and local parameters used in this section are the following:

global parameter: if a property is typical for an every single entry; if a property is vital for basic understanding of an entry (meaning); if a property is vital for basic determination of grammatical behaviour

local parameter: if a property is not typical for every single entry; if a property is vital for correct use in S&T context, if a property serves as additional help to the user

Marks used in the tables stand for:
++ parameters is present and its quality is good
\+ parameters is present and its quality is questionable
– parameter is absent
n/a not applicable

1) global parameters

a) meaning

	WNT	SEP	REA	KANION	WPŚ
explanation/ definition	-	++	-	-	-
contextual examples	-	-	-	-	-
equivalent(s)	+	++	+	+	++
polysemy	++	+	+	n/a	-
synonyms/ antonyms	+	-	+	+	-

Explanation/ contextual example/ equivalent. In specialized language, precise and adequate determination of meaning in decoding, encoding and translation is of high priority. For this reason, simple equivalent is not enough. The entry should provide a range of properties, which allow determining the meaning by different means. Even terms, which undergo standardization, cannot be always said to be fully understandable without support from parameters such as a definition, contextual example or other ones discussed latter. Regarding the general component of S&T language, it is also not always possible to find appropriate information, suitable for S&T context, in general dictionaries, which leads to the need of extending this group of parameters.

Polysemy/ synonyms/ antonyms. If we sustain the argument of precise determination of meaning we have to remember that submeanings of an entry accompanied with their synonyms and antonyms also have a great impact on how the user construe the information.

b) grammar

	Leksykonia	SEP	REA	KANION	WPŚ
part of speech	+	-	+	-	-
coutability/ transitivity	-	-	-	-	-
irregular forms	++	-	-	-	-
complementation/ patterns	-	-	-	-	-

Along with previous group, these parameters contribute to both active and passive processing of information included in an entry. Grammatical parameters can be often verified in general dictionaries. However, if we take into consideration naturalness of utterance, which we aim to achieve, we cannot be sure which patterns and which complementation is the most common and acceptable in S&T context compared to the information given in general dictionaries.

c) other

	Leksykonia	SEP	REA	KANION	WPŚ
register	-	-	-	-	-
pronunciation	+	-	-	-	-
syllable division	-	-	-	-	-
phrasal verbs	+	-	+	-	-

It is suprising that dictionaries of specialized language, which contain rarer and more difficult words (often borrowed) then general dictionaries, do not inform the user about pronunciation (lack of phonetic transcription). In case of Lexland only entries from general sub-dictionary are provided with their phonetic transcription.

Due to different levels of formality of scientific and technical language, appropriate stylistic information and e.g. phrasal verbs should be included, especially with their more formal equivalents. Syllable division is of second importance, but still the author is not sure whether it should be excluded completely.

2) local parameters

a) linguistics

	Leksykonia	SEP	REA	KANION	WPŚ
phraseology	+	-	+	-	++
discipline	++	++	++	++	++
related terms	+	++	+	-	+
long/ short form	++	-	+	++	-
abbreviation/ acronym	++	-	+	++	-

Phraseology. In this review, we are interested in phraseology of S&T language as well. General dictionaries often do not provide the user with sufficient number of (most frequent) phraseological expressions typical for S&T register, which is understandable due to their purpose. For this reason, the S&T dictionary is expected to inform the user about those expressions since wrong choice of phraseological expressions is one of the most common errors in encoding and translation. Phraseology is the second most important aspect of specialized language just after terminology. Even correctly chosen terms will not guarantee full success as wrong phraseology can introduce vagueness and imprecision of meaning. Consequently lack of sufficient phraseological assistance together with unclear explanations (if at all) of entries and their equivalents constitute the main flaw of the dictionaries.

Related term/ cross references have double function. First, all they make it easier to move around one given group of concepts. Second, they suggest other entries, which may be important for the user since they are associated with the entry being used.

Long/ short form. It is common for S&T language that some terms have both long and short forms (e.g. gwint_PL >> (screw) thread_EN). Of course there is no difference in meaning; it just the form (generally). In more specialized context, the short form is fully acceptable, whereas in more general context the long form would be required as it avoids misunderstanding/ provides precision.

Abbreviation/ acronym. Generally, the only problem with abbreviations and acronyms lies in determination of their meaning. Abbreviations and acronyms are quite popular in S&T context due to their function. Quite often one abbreviation or acronym stands for two or more objects (e.g. AD >> air-dried_EN, AD >> average deviation_EN, AD >> Anno Domini_EN). Also not always, this shorter form can be used in foreign language in the same way as in source language.

b) non-linguistic

	Lexland	SEP	REA	KANION	WPŚ
notation/ unit	-	++	-	-	-
formula	-	++	-	-	-
illustration/ picture	-	+	-	-	-

What makes S&T language different from other sublanguages is, among others, high content of elements such as units, notations, formulae and graphical representations. In addition, those elements differ between languages (countries) despite some standardization procedures. Therefore, there is a need to have access to a source, which includes such information. If it is a dictionary, then there is no obstacle to include it right within an entry. For the ESP learner and engineer such elements often constitute more powerful source of information then its equivalent written form. As far as the translator is concerned, s/he is also required to inform about such changes even if s/he is not competent enough to interfere into text content alone as a person who is responsible for the final shape of a translated text.

6. Possible improvement

Possible improvement of the current situation must consider application of corpus linguistics. A type of corpus, which could serve appropriate assistance to this activity, is a comparable corpus. Although compilation of comparable corpora may cause problems, due to lack of examples of this kind of corpora, the benefits, which would be gained, enhance to work with it.

Comparable corpora, compiled according to carefully prepared procedures, would allow to determine terms which are typical for every subject module (in case given disciplines have their own subcopora). What is more, comparable corpora would make it possible to analyse phraseology in a comparative approach.

Further, it would result in a study of other aspects then only terminology. For instance, we could study this "general" component of specialized language to determine its frame in terms of general vocabulary and grammar used in S&T context. This would be another solution, which would help to obtain data important for increasing naturalness.

Such bilingual specialized comparable corpus causes, however, many obstacles. First, access to appropriate literature may not be difficult, but determination of representative samples is surely a time-consuming process. Then digitalization of scientific and technical texts is difficult because of high content of equations, signs, Greek letters and many illustrations.

On the other hand, this undesired content may be used to build corpus of non-linguistic elements to study mentioned differences in notations, signs etc. One more remark concerns the need of cooperation between linguists and experts from a given discipline. The first group would process the sources provided by the experts, who would be familiarized with the idea of the corpus, and then the second group would help to verify the results.

Despite the fact that this corpus would be intended for working in specialized lexicography, translators of specialized texts could use it during their daily work. In addition, the comparable corpora could be split into two independent corpora for separate use if necessary.

Finally, the shape of the whole dictionary must be carefully designed and its content once again reconsidered according to the user profile. It can be anticipated that the most convenient form for such a dictionary would by an electronic version due to its size and advanced searching options needed. One cannot forget about adequate supplements for the user with additional information, which normally cannot be included in entries e.g. examples of different written forms, table of most frequent concepts and scientific notations etc.

Summary

Due to the above discussion, it is possible to draw the following conclusions on current dictionaries of scientific and technical dictionaries available on the Polish Publishing market.

- Lack of extensive studies on scientific and technical language, compared to studies on e.g. legal or business language, significantly hinders any work devoted to this register.

- The study of scientific and technical language cannot be limited just to terminology. Appropriate attention has to be paid to phraseology, general vocabulary and grammar.
- The user of S&T language requires additional materials, which present and describe the nature of different written forms, conventions and different aspects of S&T language vital for successful communication in both professional and non-professional circumstances.
- Prior to design and compilation of a dictionary, the nature of potential user has to be well understood to adjust the tool to the needs and requirements of the user.
- Today's state of art allows designing and creating tools whose quality and user-friendliness are close to requirements and expectations of the users.
- Development and achievements of corpus linguistics should be the base for any dictionary-making activity nowadays.

Once again, we cannot forget about keeping balance between quality and functionality of such a dictionary. If the quality and informative power of an entry is too high then probably the functionality may decrease. If we want to create, however, an extensive reference dictionary, then the design has to be carefully planned.

References

Hornby, A.S. *Oxford Advanced Learner's Dictionary of Current English*. Ed. Sally Wehmeier. 7th. Oxford University Press, n.d.

Jaślan, J. and H. Jaślan (2009). *An English-Polish Dictionary of Legal and Economic Terms.* IX. Warszawa: Wiedza Powszechna.

Koren, S. (2009). *Quality versus Convenience: Comparison of Modern Dictionaries from the Researcher's, Teacher's and Learner's Points of View.*

Pawluk, K. and J. Sawicki (2008). *Wielojęzyzczny słownik terminologiczny elektryki.* Warszawa: Stowarzyszenie Elektryków Polskich, Centralny Ośrodek Szkolenia i Wydawnictw.

Pieńkos, J. (2003). *Podstawy przekładowznastwa. Od teorii do praktyki*. Kantor Wydawniczy Zakamycze.

Ratajczak, P. and W. Lotko (2006). *Słownik żeglarsko-morski, angielsko-polski, polsko-angielski*. Zielona Góra: Kanion Net.

Ratajczak, P. (2004). *Angielsko-polski słownik specjalistyczny elektronika.* Zielona Góra: Kanion Net.

Seidel, K.-H. (2008). *Technical dictionary, English-Polish, Polish-English.* Trans. Grzegorz Jaśkiewicz and Krzysztof Nycz. Warszawa: Rea.

Słowniki angielsko-polskie i polsko-angielskie naukowo-techniczne, specjalistyczne i ogólne (2007). Knurów: Lexland s.c.

Swanepoel, P. (2001). *Dictionary quality and dictionary design : a methodology for improving the functional quality of dictionaries : contemplative article.*

Szewc, B. (2005). *Angielsko-polski i polsko-angielski słownik terminów, pojęć i zwrotów z dziedziny elektrotechniki.* Gliwice: Wydawnictwo Politechniki Śląskiej.

The PWN – Oxford English-Polish Polish-English Dictionary (2008). Wydawnictwo Naukowe PWN.

Research in Historical Lexicography: Can Google Books Collection Complement Traditional Corpora?

Mirosława Podhajecka

Abstract: The aim of the present paper is to show that the Google Books collection, a non-specialized textual resource available from <http://books.google.com>, can be applied successfully for research in historical lexicology and lexicography. I argue that the collection offers to researchers extremely rich material which can help, *inter alia*, to antedate OED3 headwords. To verify this hypothesis, I use a handful of headwords from the third edition of the *Oxford English Dictionary*, which have been checked against the evidence of Google Books. Importantly, the collection is immense, free and available at the click of a button, but – unlike traditional corpora and lexical databases – it is not a neat and tidy corpus of machine-readable texts. Because of its atypical form, searches are inevitably full of obstacles, which will be presented here in some detail. The problems, referring primarily to Google Books digital format, the quality of metadata, the search procedures and the interpretation of data, will be illustrated with practical examples drawn from my study.

Keywords: analysis, antedating, corpus, Google Books, headword, historical lexicology, lexicography, quotation, research, search.

1. Introduction

In the present paper I examine the usability of Google Books, a huge, non-specialist collection of texts, for research in historical lexicology and lexicography. Since a project of this kind can become genuinely overwhelming in terms of time, it had to be narrowed to allow a detailed analysis of data. Having considered various possibilities, I decided to look for additional evidence for the *Oxford English Dictionary* (henceforth, OED3) headwords pertaining to dancing. Dances have always been an important element of social and cultural histories of nations – their names being on everybody's lips at specific periods – so I was interested to see how they would be reflected in this substantial (albeit disparate) corpus of English texts. As the Goggle Books collection (henceforth, the GBC) is far from a neat and tidy corpus, however, using the framework of my research I focus on presenting a range of obstacles that a researcher working with the collection is bound to face.

It may be necessary to ask at this juncture whether the GBC can be treated as a corpus. Traditionally, a corpus has been defined as a computer-held collection of pieces of language, selected and ordered according to explicit criteria (like size, quality or time-span) in order to be used as a sample of the language (EAGLES qtd. in Tognini-Bonelli 2001: 53, cf. Sinclair 1991: 15–21). According to Greenbaum (1984: 193), the basic function of a corpus is "to supply examples that represent language beyond that corpus", so a well-structured corpus which allows investigation of patterns of language use should be, above all else, representative and balanced (cf. Ooi 1998: 53, Leech 2007: 135).

Still, recent advances in corpus linguistics and corpus lexicography have begun to move away from issues such as the composition of a corpus (and, hence, representativeness) towards the new challenges of how best to extract relevant information from large text databases (Rundell 2002: 140). In the era of information technology, producing corpora that would include hundreds of millions of words is no longer a problem, technically or materially, access to machine-readable texts being far easier than ever before. It comes as little surprise that even the World Wide Web, with its massive volume of multilingual text that cannot be controlled or monitored in any way, has now come to be treated as a corpus (cf. Kilgarriff 2001, Grefenstette 2002, Kilgarriff & Grefenstette 2003).

In line with these developments I decided to take a flexible approach to the definition of a corpus, based on the premise that "[I]n statistical NLP, one commonly receives as a corpus a certain amount of data from a certain domain of interest, without having any say in how it is constructed. In such cases, having more training data is normally more useful than any concerns of balance, and one should simply use all the text that is available" (Manning and Schütze 1999: 120). Consequently, however atypical the GBC may seem as a professional textual resource – the documents are not tagged, raw frequency cannot be taken as statistically significant and the generated concordances often do not provide the required context – I will treat it as an historical corpus. I strongly believe that despite its deficiencies, the GBC can be successfully "harnessed" for lexicological and lexicographic purposes, providing insight into rich documentation material.

2. Research materials

2.1. The *Oxford English Dictionary*

The *Oxford English Dictionary*, now in its third edition, is a prestigious historical dictionary which provides a record of the development of the English language from the Anglo-Saxon times to the present day. Although the objectives of its editors today remain practically the same as a hundred years ago, with growing access to materials previously unknown, every new edition of the dictionary is, unsurprisingly, a benchmark of language change (cf. Mugglestone 2009).

The first edition of the dictionary, originally called *A New English Dictionary on Historical Principles* and later renamed *Oxford English Dictionary* (henceforth, OED1), was published in fascicles between 1884 and 1928 under the general editorship of James Murray. OED1 was followed by one-volume Supplement published in 1933, and, several decades later, four additional volumes of Supplement were edited by Robert Burchfield (1972–1986). In 1989, the whole dictionary material, i.e. OED1, approximately 5,000 entries that were not recorded in Burchfield's Supplement, and the three-volume *Oxford English Dictionary Additions Series* (1990–1997), was edited by John Simpson and Edmund Weiner as the second edition of the dictionary (henceforth, OED2). The electronic version of the dictionary came out in 1994. Over the last decade a revision of OED2 has been in progress (the revised draft entries so far being treated in the alphabet range M-Q), which is the first fully-fledged attempt to update all the previously published dictionary material (Gilliver 2005: 241, Durkin 2002a: 66). The revision process has not only helped improve the entries, but it has also affected significantly the dictionary wordlist. OED3, compiled under the editorship of John Simpson, does not demonstrate a wider policy of inclusiveness – in fact, more occurrences of a word are now required to consider its inclusion into the dictionary – but it integrates both the evidence missing from the previous editions and the new vocabulary that has been pouring into English for the last several decades.

As for the inclusion procedure, OED3 lexicographers select headwords from collections of printed sources, mainly their own directed reading programme conducted both in Britain and in America, as well as from electronic corpora and databases, like the *Making of America* digital library or *Eighteenth Century Collections Online* (cf. Gilliver 2005, Brewer 2006, Durkin 2004). The combination of historical files, material from the current reading programmes, as well as contemporary corpora and databases means that OED3 editors have a huge body of interrelated resources at their disposal. No wonder it is claimed that "while each of these individually has its shortcomings, taken together they bring to the department approximately a quarter of a million of quotations per annum, providing a substantial body of evidence that allows close monitoring of the language as it evolves" (Paton 1995: 81).

While it is generally true, the fact remains that some information categories in OED3 may be missing, antedating being a case in point (cf. Podhajecka in press). This issue received much attention after the publication of Schäfer's seminal books (1980, 1989), in which the author claimed that nearly 30% of the OED headwords could be antedated. Alerted by Schäfer's findings, which have indeed been confirmed by other researchers (e.g. McConchie 1997, Brewer

2007), OED3 lexicographers now make sure that every headword in the third edition be thoroughly revised, updated and, if possible, antedated. However, even vast dictionary documentation will turn out to be patchy when faced with a gigantic textual resource which, judging on the basis of my research alone, promises a rich yield in antedatings.

2.2. The Google Books collection

The Google Books collection, first named Google Print, was made available in 2005[1]. It covers two major groups of materials, i.e. (1) texts in the public domain, which are available for download, and (2) texts protected by copyright, either unavailable or available in the forms of text snippets. The texts scanned and published online come from several renowned public and university libraries, such as the Bodleian Library in Oxford, the Stanford University or the Public Library of New York. Importantly, many of the textual sources are rare documents that the digitization process has, quite literally, brought back to daylight. In my view, it is the major reason which accounts for the unexpected percentage of antedatings in my research.

At present, the collection encompasses approximately 7 million books and is growing, so in the future it is expected to cover many more texts, both English and multilingual ones[2]. To English researchers this multilingual aspect of the GBC is without doubt a handicap – one has to search through masses of texts in several languages – but, at the same time, it is also a godsend, particularly in historical research, as word origins are best traced in a comparative perspective.

1 The revision of OED2 was announced in the 1990s and initiated in 2000, which explains why OED3 lexicographers could not make use of the riches of Google Books from the beginning of their project.

2 It may be important to add that the publishing of international library resources by Google brought about a conflict over copyright, which has now turned into a huge legal case concerning such issues as privacy, security, competition and pricing. The so-called "Google Books Settlement", a proposed legal settlement agreement between Google and a group of publishers and authors, would allow Google to provide greater access to even more books and to offer new services. It is claimed that such a settlement would have a profound influence on future digitization projects, the marketplace for books, the role of libraries, scholarly research, etc. Opponents of the settlement do not agree to giving sole ownership of this unique resource to a single corporation, which may in the future charge universities for the use of this resource in an unrestrained way. Whatever the terms of the final settlement, I hope (optimistically) that scholars worldwide will be granted full access to the corpus in line with the principle of fair use, which will provide a solid basis for their research. More information on the ongoing debate over Google Books Settlement is available from Professor Mark Liberman's Language Log <http://languagelog.ldc.upenn.edu/nll/?p=1698#more-1698>.

For instance, searching for attestations of *waltz*, a word of German provenance, one can also look for its counterparts in other languages (e.g. French *valse*). Arguably, some loans are taken from different donor languages, so juxtaposing word-forms and dates may occasionally contribute to new etymological discoveries (cf. Durkin 2002b).

Obviously, the value of the GBC lies in the fact that it is operated by a search engine. To retrieve words and expressions one can use simple search as well as advanced search, which offers additional criteria like time span, language or text genres. One can also conduct searches using Boolean expressions (such as "milonga" AND "tango"). The search engine provides the number of hits to each query as well as brief context and bibliographic record. By clicking on the title of the source one obtains access to either full text or snippets of text. What remains to be done, then, is to ascertain that the retrieved data has been interpreted properly.

3. Research methodology and results

My study is based on a group of dance names selected from the revised letter sections (M-Q) of OED3. The words were extracted automatically from OED3 by means of the "search in definitions" facility, "dance" being used as the query key word. However, some of the extracted words (e.g. *miller*, *pipe* or *pole*) date back even to the Old English period, whereas most materials in the GBC date back to the second half of the 18th century. Therefore, to arrive at reliable results, I excluded all the words and senses with the first recorded occurrence before 1750, and I took into account nouns only, as typical of dance names. In consequence, my final research sample covered 115 words and senses denoting dances, dance movements as well as dance participants (*macabre*, *Macarena*, *Madison*, *makossa*, *malagueña*, *mambo*, *Manipuri*, *marabi*, etc.).

Speaking of the results obtained, 76 headwords have been antedated (66%), and earlier occurrences in the GBC have not been found for only 39 headwords (34%). As some of the evidence is available in the form of full-text versions and some in the form of text snippets, the latter being questioned as doubtful evidence, I decided to take into account the reliability factor. With the proviso that at least a handful of the excluded examples may be fully eligible, there are 39 antedating citations extracted from full-text versions, which accounts for 34% of my research sample[3]. Some of my findings are presented below.

3 I would like to thank Professor Mark Davies of Brigham Young University for the information that the texts which are not accessed from Google Books may be available from the website <www.archive org>. This Internet archive allowed the verification of 33 additional quotations.

Table 1. Range of antedatings in selected examples

macabre	1851>1841	nautch	1789>1750
Macarena	1995>1993	nayaka	1967>1933
Madison	1962>1960	nayika	1948>1871
makossa	1985>1976	New Beat	1988>1964
malagueña	1853>1810	ngoma	1905>1859
mambo	1948	Noh	1871
Manipuri	1957>1911	Northern Soul	1971
marabi	1933	nritta	1835>1833

This reduced percentage, too, points to the value of the GBC and the usefulness of such research. It goes without saying that OED3 lexicographers have put a lot of effort into filling the gaps in the former editions, but even so corrections and changes to OED3 historical documentation seem a matter of time. It is evident that to ensure the infallibility of the dictionary they would need to consult **all** [emphasis mine] texts produced in the language, inasmuch as "[T]he results are only as good as the corpus" (Sinclair 1991: 13). Suffice it to say that access to all texts in English is, at least at this stage, completely unfeasible.

To show that the range of antedating is not accidental, as one might claim, I collected a few antedating quotations for the headwords whenever possible. The examples cited below come from full-text versions available from Google Books or, alternatively, from the Internet text archive at <www.archive.org>.

Table 2. Antedating citations for *malaqueña* and *Molly dancer*

Malagueña	
1853>1810	"Tonadillas, seguedillas, boleros and tyranas are the general national songs, but there are many provincial styles, such as the **Malaguena**, &c. These dances though sometimes met in Spanish America, are not those generally used in society; they have adopted the waltz, besides the Spanish country dance, which is extremely graceful, and more complicated, but not so monotonous as our own, though the type is slower.", *Present State of the Spanish Colonies*
1853>1834	"The lower classes are also addicted to gambling, but their chief amusements are playing the guitar, singing and dancing. Their principal dances, are *las seguidillas*, *las* ***malagueñas***, and what they call *las folias*.", *Letters from the Canary Islands*
Molly dancer	
1903>1881	"The name of **molly dancers** was used some 46 years ago. The name contains two very significant corruptions of very common Christian names in Lancashire-Mary and Elizabeth. The two personages were respectively called Dirty Moll and Lazy Bet.", *Advertiser Notes and Queries,* vol. 1

1903>1882	"I have heard the dancers who attended the rush cart had two persons who were distinguished from the rest, who were called **molly dancers**.", *Cheshire Notes and Queries,* vol. 1-2
1903>1891	"The morris-dancers (or "**molly-dancers**," as they are now often called by the ignorant), were led by the fool, who bore the title of "King Coffee" inscribed on his hat.", *Rush-bearing: Carrying Rushes to Church; the Rush-cart; Garlands in Churches; Morris-dancers; the Wakes; the Rush*

As a matter of fact, multiple antedatings are not that infrequent, because at least two citations antedating OED3 headwords have been retrieved for 55 words, or 72% of the antedated sample. A more comprehensive description of my documentation material will be presented elsewhere, so I will now go on to illustrate drawbacks of researching the GBC.

4. Research problems

4.1. Original versus derivative sources

One of the challenges is that the same or similar passages can be found in different, variously dated texts, so the researcher's task is to look for the original source. In doing so, one should remember that the earliest text found may as well be derivative, because the GBC, as any other corpus of texts, is inevitably limited in scope.

Table 3. Identical passages found in variously dated sources

The journal of the Royal Geographic Society of London
Strona 56 autor: Royal Geographical Society (Great Britain) – 1859

At the Ngoma Ku, or great dance, which celebrates every event in these realms of revelry, only the Diwans may perform the morris with drawn swords before **...**
Pełny widok – Informacje o tej książce – Dodaj do mojej biblioteki

The lake regions of Central Africa: a picture of exploration
Strona 30 autor: Sir Richard Francis Burton – 1860 – Liczba stron: 572

At the ngoma ku, or great dance, which celebrates every event in this land of revelry, **...**
Pełny widok – Informacje o tej książce – Dodaj do mojej biblioteki

Livingstone lost and found: or Africa and its explorers ...
Strona 338 autor: Josiah Tyler – 1873 – Liczba stron: 782

At the ngoma ku, or great dance, which celebrates every event in this land of

revelry, only the diwan may perform the morris with drawn sword before the ... Widok krótkiego opisu – Informacje o tej książce – Dodaj do mojej biblioteki

Interestingly, the unavailability of the originals is also an obstacle that OED3 lexicographers must have faced. For example, the first attestation of *monkey dance* recorded in the dictionary comes from a poem by G. Croly, dated to 1821, but the same poem was published in *The Quarterly Review* as early as 1817. Discrepancies in the documentation material notwithstanding, thanks to one of the sources in the GBC, *The Voyage to the Cape of Good Hope, Towards the Antarctic Polar Circle, and Round the World* [...], the headword has now been antedated to 1786.

4.2. Dating of sources

Problems with the dating reflect a broader category of inaccurate metadata, particularly bibliographic information, provided to the GBC sources.

Some of the texts, primarily magazines, journals and other multi-volume publications (e.g. dictionaries), are dated erroneously by Google Books, which means that the bibliographic record provides the publication date of the first rather than the needed volume. For instance, the expression *mosh pit* (though thematically irrelevant for my research) is claimed to be found in the first volume of *Dictionaries*: *Journal of the Dictionary Society of North America* (1979). As has turned out, *mosh pit* is recorded in volume 16, published in 1995.

Difficulties in dating sources refer to other types of publications as well. For instance, Google dates a novel entitled *Sierra Leone* to 1817, while it is in fact 1847. In this case, the error has resulted from incorrect match of the Optical Character Recognition software (see 4.3).

Table 4. Information on a selected source dated incorrectly

Sierra Leone: The Principal British Colony on the Western Coast of Africa - Strona 9 autor: William Whitaker Shreeve – 1817 – Liczba stron: 114 **...** quadrilles, or **polkas**, I shall not attempt a description of the most fashionable steps and figures, fearing that I might lead some of my fair readers **...** Pełny widok – Informacje o tej książce – Dodaj do mojej biblioteki

To mention another example, *Roland Cashel* by Charles Lever is dated to 1801. This date is shown on the title page, so it appears in the bibliographic record, but a leaf inside the full-text version proves that the book, dedicated to G.P.R. James, Esq., comes from 1849. Similarly, searching for the earliest recorded instances of the word *quadrille* I came across *Catalogue of Rare Books* dated to 1728 (the first occurrence of *quadrille* in OED3 is 1773). Encouraged by this promising result, I looked into the full-text version only to realize that the dating was wrong again: the book came out as late as 1825, and it was the publishing house that was established in 1728. Clearly, such errors do not invalidate the use of the textual resources, but they are a great disadvantage for historical lexicologists, for whom proper dating is of utmost importance.

The dates in the full-text versions can usually be quickly verified, but there are also more complicated cases. For instance, I found a source that could possibly antedate *mazurka* (*The Dramatic Works of John O'Keeffe*, 1798), but, under closer scrutiny, it turned out to be useless. The date on the title page is indeed 1798, but going through the text (or, more exactly, scrolling down) I noticed that the book was a compilation of various works by O'Keefe, including *The son-in-law*, performed at the Theatre-Royal in 1827.

While full-text versions are usually fairly user-friendly, working with snippets is far less reliable. When merely a snippet of text is provided, one of simple yet fairly effective ways to check whether the publication is dated properly is keying various dates into the "search in this book" slot.

Table 5. A snippet of text with a "search in this book" slot

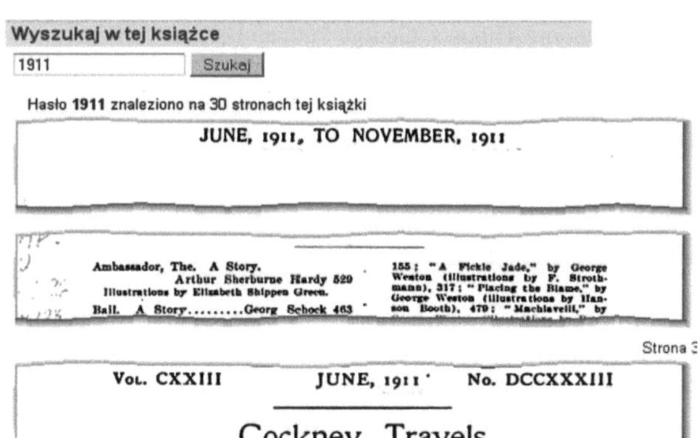
Wyszukaj w tej książce

1911 Szukaj

Hasło **1911** znaleziono na 30 stronach tej książki

JUNE, 1911, TO NOVEMBER, 1911

Ambassador, The. A Story. Arthur Sherburne Hardy 529
Illustrations by Elizabeth Shippen Green.
Ball. A Story.........Georg Schock 463

155; "A Fickle Jade," by George Weston (illustrations by F. Strothmann), 317; "Placing the Blame," by George Weston (illustrations by Hanson Booth), 479; "Machiavelli," by

Strona 3

VOL. CXXIII JUNE, 1911 No. DCCXXXIII

Cockney Travels

If any later date is found in the source, then the GBC dating is clearly wrong. The method suggested above, however, is merely commonsensical, so it does not guarantee full reliability in determining proper dates.

4.3. Quality of Optical Character Recognition (OCR)

Optical Character Recognition is a technique used by OCR software, which consists in converting the scanned image of text into a machine-readable form through a process of pattern matching. The point is that in the character-recognition process there is scope for error (Bowker 2002: 26). In other words, the OCR software often makes incorrect matches, e.g. "a" can be mistakenly identified as "e", while "c" and "l" can be combined into "d", particularly when the quality of the hard copy is not good enough. Such matches were apparently at play in OCR-ing some of the older sources in the GBC.

Problems encountered here are related to several major categories. Firstly, the queried forms can be recognized as components of longer words. For instance, in most cases *ork* 'an orchestra; *spec.* a jazz or dance band' was identified as part of *York* or *work*, while *mento* 'a traditional Jamaican dance in duple time, or a song, often anecdotal or topical in content, sung to accompany this; (later also) the style of folk music associated with this dance' appeared to be part of *monumento*, *momento*, etc.

Table 6. Error in OCR-ing ("mento" AND "dance" search)

Theodore Thomas, a Musical Autobiography: Concert programmes. - Strona 254
autor: Theodore Thomas, George Putnam Upton – 1905
... Onda," from "Il Giura- **mento**," Mercadante (Mme. **...** to the **Dance**," Weber; Ballet divertissement, "Henry VIII.," **...**
Widok krótkiego opisu – Informacje o tej książce – Dodaj do mojej biblioteki – Więcej wydań

Secondly, the query key word and the retrieved word-form may differ significantly. For example, I retrieved a number of texts where irrelevant words, such as *police*, *folks* or *pollen*, were mistakenly recognized optically as *polka*. There are also cases when the searched word turns out to be written in another alphabet, like Greek.

Table 7. A word in Greek alphabet recognized optically as *polkas*

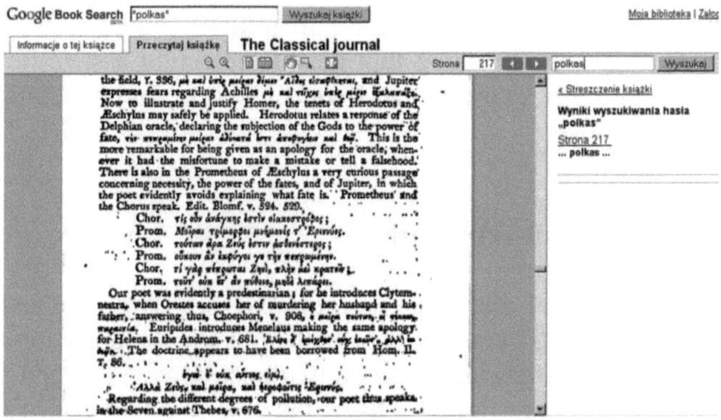

Thirdly, many of the hard copies contain old-fashioned characters, which are hard, not to say impossible, to query successfully in OCR-ed documents. To mention one specific instance, traditional Gothic fonts, especially "s", may bring failure to searches even if the given word is in the text.

4.4. Refining searches

Searches in the GBC are extremely time-consuming because, to avoid mistakes, one has to go through a number of passages manually. Refining searches is an inevitable consequence of the substantial volume of data, and the most crucial criterion in limiting the sample is selecting the time-span. Depending on how many years one hopes to antedate the given headword, the time-span can be wider or narrower. For instance, searching for *nritta*, according to OED3 first recorded in 1835, it is reasonable to select the span 1800–1835, but one can also check results for a more remote period, e.g. 1700–1800. In my study, most words (62) have been antedated by up to 50 years, but for several headwords antedating quotations have pushed the first recorded occurrence by more than 50 years.

Additionally, in the case of frequent words (like *pop*, for example), it is recommended to use a Boolean expression to refine the search (e.g. "pop" AND "dance"). Sometimes a few Boolean expressions have to be used one by one to obtain a number of hits that can be handled (e.g. "pop" AND "dancing", "pop" AND "danced", "pop" AND "dances", "pop" AND "steps", "pop" AND "craze", etc.). Components of Boolean expressions are best selected intuitively, so that the search yields the best results.

As for the most difficult examples, *pop* was retrieved in 56,200 texts, while the word-form *No*, a variant form of *Noh* ‘a traditional Japanese masked drama with dance’, appeared in three and a half million source texts. Given so many occurrences, it is not surprising that despite selecting a specific time-span and using various Boolean expressions, I was unable to find antedating citations for either of these words.

4.5. OED3 meaning discrimination

OED3, as an historical dictionary, arranges senses chronologically, i.e. a sense first recorded in the 18th century is presented inside the entry before one attested in the 19th century. There are a few situations, however, when the ordering of OED3 senses can be questioned. This is the case of *mambo*, two senses of which are probably derived from two different languages (see Table 8 below).

Table 8. OED3 entry *mambo* (first citations only)

mambo, n. *Brit.* /mamb≅Y/, *U.S.* /mAmb□Y/ Forms: 19- **mambo**, 19-**manbo**. [In sense 1 < Cuban Spanish *mambo* modified form of rumba, and in sense 2 < its probable etymon, Haitian Creole *mambo*, the name of a voodoo ritual dance, a kind of voodoo priestess. Compare French *mambo* (1951).] **1.** A modified form of rumba, of Latin American origin; (a piece of) music for this dance or in its rhythm; (also, occas.) the dance rhythm itself. **1948** *San Francisco Call-Bull.* 17 Sept. 11/1 Tony De Marco predicts the new dance fad will be ‘The Mambo’, which was introduced..last week. A zingier form of rhumba. **2.**A voodoo priestess. **1964** R. SEVERN *Blood & Gold* x. 102 She must be a *Mambo..*, a *Voodoo* priestess.

Although I did not find any texts that would help me antedate sense 2, I came across materials suggesting that sense 1 had apparently been attested earlier, chronologically speaking, than sense 2.

Table 9. Sample GBC documentation for sense 2 of *mambo*

mambo	
1964>1939	“He smoked a cigar, and in his free hand held a bottle of rum. The drums began again on a signal from the *houngan*, and the visiting *mambos* ("priestesses") and *houngans* […]”, *Haiti Singing*
1964>1952	“And so on that first visit I met not only a mambo (priestess) but a houngan (priest) as well.”, *Haiti: Highroad to adventure*

Another problem derives from the discrimination of meanings and forms in OED3. For example, two headwords, *pastourelle* and *pastorale*, illustrate differences in lexicographic treatment, i.e. in the entry *pastourelle* both words are shown as analogues (words introduced by "cf."), whereas in the entry *pastorale* they are apparently viewed as synonyms[4].

Table 10. Different treatment of *pastourelle* and *pastorale* in OED3

pastourelle, *n. Dance.* One of the figures of a quadrille, likened to a dance of shepherds and shepherdesses. Cf. **PASTORALE** *n.* 2. Now *hist.*
pastorale, *n.* **2.** *Dance.* = **PASTOURELLE** *n.* 1. *Obs. rare.*

As a result, researchers may be at a disadvantage trying to somehow relate the recorded forms, among which there can also be some "intermediary" ones like *pastoral dance*, as in the following quotation: "A Pastoral Dance commences the various implements of the Mintage, with ribbons and flowers, made use of in a gay fanciful arrangement." (*Yes, Or No? A Musical Farce in Two Acts*, 1809). It may be important to add that *pastoral dance* is not in OED3, which suggests that *pastoral* is treated as a qualifying adjective, but is not part of a dance name.

To mention another example, it is unclear why only the first sense of *myal* in OED3 is supported with a quotation that is also relevant for sense 2. Despite *myal dance* being mentioned in the 1774 quotation, sense 2 is dated to 1868.

Table 11. Overlooked citation (1774) for sense 2 in OED3

myal, adj. 1 and n. A. *adj.*[1] (*attrib.*). Designating a person or thing involved in or associated with the practice of myalism. Freq. in ***myal-man***. **1774 E. LONG** *Hist. Jamaica* II. III. iii. 416 Not long since, some of these execrable wretches in Jamaica introduced what they called the *myal dance*, and established a kind of society, into which they invited all they could. The lure hung out was, that every Negroe, initiated into the myal society, would be invulnerable by the white men. **1774 E. LONG** *Hist. Jamaica* II. III. iii. 417 One of these myal men..gave him a wonderful account of the powerful effects produced by the myal infusion. **B.** *n.* Myalism; a dance associated with this cult or belief. **1868 T. RUSSELL** *Etymol. Jamaica Gram.* 6 Myal Excitement bordering on madness. African. **1952** M. KERR *Personality and Conflict in Jamaica* 141 It is interesting that myal now means dancing with a spirit in a trance. **1961 F. G. CASSIDY** *Jamaica Talk* xi. 241

4 The same inconsistency has been noticed in the entries *oberek* and *obertas* in OED3.

The revision of OED3 is no doubt an enormous undertaking, which requires the coordination of many efforts, yet such instances as overlooked citations seem to call for more caution on the part of the lexicographers and proof-readers alike.

4.6. Sense disambiguation in the GBC

As has already been mentioned, searching through hundreds of hits is extremely time-consuming, and so is the analysis of contexts to interpret the retrieved data. Still, it is an inevitable element of research, because without checking the samples for consistency in meaning, one would be collecting irrelevant language data, all the more because a number of contexts are fairly ambiguous.

One quandary concerns the status of words that derive from native English resources, e.g. *massive*, *old time*, *one step*, *modern dance* or *new beat*, and which also have (or whose constituent elements have) general meanings. Particularly in the case of *modern dance* (OED3 1933) interpreting the hundreds of quotations was extremely labour-intensive, because for the older generation who practiced "dances of polite society" any dance that came into fashion later was always classified as a modern dance.

Table 12. Obscure citations for *modern dance*, *new beat* and *one step*

Whether any motions like those of the **modern dance** were intended in these passages is, to say the least, very doubtful.", *The Ladies' Repository: A Monthly Periodical Devoted to Literature and Religion*, v. 15 (1855)
At that moment of truth, which is not far off if it is not already upon us, music educators as a profession had better know the new steps and tune in on the **new beat**. They can only do this for themselves.", *Source Readings in Music Education History* (1982)
"I shan't dance **one step** with you until you take that dreadful thing off," said she, indicating his dangling sabre, and utterly ignoring his protest […]. Is this the name of a dance, or just a metaphor?", *The Story of Fort Frayne* (1895)

Moreover, it is occasionally difficult to differentiate between formally convergent but semantically and etymologically divergent forms (cf. *matachin 1* and *matachin 2* in OED3). Distinguishing different senses of the same word, particularly when both of them are found in one quotation, is equally troublesome.

Table 13. Ambiguous citation for the word *Mazurka*

"I shall never forget the pretty sprightly *Shenkerka* (barmaid) at Gdov, nor the grace with which she led us, her two evening guests, to the dance, a gay **Mazurka**, played by two Slovaks. Nothing can be more pretty or graceful than Polish girls when dancing.", *Austria, Vienna, Hungary, Bohemia and the Danube, Galicia, Styria, Moravia, Bukovina, and the Military Frontier* (1843)

Speaking of the last example, should this usage be related to *mazurka* as a dance, a piece of music, or both?

4.7. Variant forms unrecorded in OED3

Searching for antedatings one has to take into account all the variant spellings recorded in the dictionary, both in the singular and plural, which have been diligently collected in OED3. With a little luck, however, one will come across additional word-forms; part of my success, so to say, in antedating headwords is that some variants have apparently been overlooked. For example, OED3 does not include such spellings as *Polsk* (OED3 *polska*), *mazurek* (OED3 *mazurka*) or *Matchiche* / *Machiche* (OED3 *maxixe*), all of which are attested in the GBC (sometimes new variants are only recorded in the plural form). Importantly, as the search engine treats the spellings *quickstep* and *quick step* as two different word-forms, they have to be retrieved separately.

It is useful to add that homographic forms can be a notorious obstacle throughout the research, which means that one has to check carefully whether the given usage reflects the correct meaning. To provide a practical example, *Mentos* or *Maringa* are also place names; *milonga* denotes a palaver; the term *pachanga* refers, among others, to the Pachanga Indians; *Pascola* is a place name and trademark, etc.

Table 14. Examples of homographic forms

"These tops, or "**puntas**," as they are now termed, are, as a rule, loaded into carabao carts and taken to some convenient spot […].", *Hawaiian Planters' Record* (1911)
"As the work is carried on incessantly day and night, the miners are divided into parties called **puntas**, each party working for twelve successive hours.", *Travels in Peru: During the Years 1838–1842* (1847)
"[…] which is divided into decimal fractions which are called by the natives tăt, and by the linguists **puntas**, from the Portuguese, thus: 10 *tăt* make a *touick*, or covid.", *Voyage to Cochin China* (1824)
"**PUNTAS**, a mountain thus called, also on the s. coast of the Straits of Magellan.", *Geographical and Historical of America and the West Indies* (1814)

The sample above shows the word-form *puntas* with four different meanings. It should be noted that, no matter how exhaustive OED3 entries are, not all the senses encountered in the GBC will be found in the dictionary, as some of them have probably been peripheral to the lexical system of English.

5. Conclusions

To recapitulate, however imperfect the Google Books collection as a corpus must be to a professional lexicographer, this resource is unprecedented in terms of new language data, including antedatings, variant forms unrecorded in OED3 and new illustrative quotations. Nonetheless, to what extent the obtained material is fully reliable depends on the form of the GBC textual sources. In other words, while full-text versions can be treated as verifiable evidence, there are practically no benefits of using snippets of texts, which are comparable to "peeks in the keyhole". Clearly, the GBC is far from an ideal corpus because of its limited access to some sources, but the digital format and the quality of metadata also need to be improved to facilitate the searches and enhance the credibility of the findings.

Interestingly, in contrast to standard databases and corpora applied by OED3 lexicographers, the GBC is not representative and balanced in **any** [emphasis mine] way, which is, somewhat paradoxically, indicative of the fact that its chaotic and uncontrollable composition should not necessarily be taken as a drawback. Obviously, a considerable proportion of OED3 headwords may never be antedated at all, but there are reasons to think that for many words, such as those denoting cultural phenomena, the GBC will turn out to be a gold mine of linguistic facts. It is to be expected that, with the collection growing steadily, even more surprises will come to the fore in the future.

With easy access to this tremendous (though, admittedly, labour-demanding) corpus from home, chances are the term "armchair research" will take on a completely new meaning. For the time being, however, the riches of the GBC still await to be exploited and duly appreciated by historical linguists, lexicologists and lexicographers.

References

Bowker, L. (2002). *Computer-Aided Translation Technology: A Practical Introduction*, Ottawa: University of Ottawa Press.

Brewer, C. (2007). "Reporting eighteenth-century vocabulary in the OED". In: J. Considine and G. Iamartino (eds.). *Words and Dictionaries from the British Isles in Historical Perspective*. Newcastle-upon-Tyne: Cambridge Scholars Publishing: 109–135.

Durkin, P. (2002a). Changing documentation in the third edition of the *Oxford English Dictionary*: Sixteenth-century vocabulary as a test case'. In: T. Fanego, B. Méndez-Naya, and E. Seoane (eds.). *Sounds, Words, Texts and Change. Selected Papers from 11 ICEHL, Santiago de Compostela, 7–11 September 2000*. Vol. 2. Amsterdam/Philadelphia: John Benjamins: 65–81.

Durkin, P. (2002b). "'Mixed' etymologies of Middle English items in OED3: Some questions of methodology and policy". *Dictionaries: Journal of the Dictionary Society of North America*, 23: 142–155.

Durkin, P. (2004). "Loanword etymologies in the third edition of the *OED*: Some questions of classification'. In: C. Kay *et al.* (eds.). *New Perspectives on English Historical Linguistics: Selected Papers from 12 ICEH, Glasgow. 21–26 August 2002*. Vol. 2. *Lexis and Transmission*. Amsterdam/Philadelphia: John Benjamins: 79–90.

Gilliver, P. (2005). "Materials and methodologies for the new *Oxford English Dictionary*". In: H. Gottlieb, J.E. Mogensen, and A. Zettersen (eds.). *Symposium on Lexicography XI. Proceedings of the Eleventh International Symposium on Lexicography May 2–4, 2002 at the University of Copenhagen*. Tübingen: Max Niemeyer Verlag: 241–248.

Grefenstette, G. (2002). "The WWW as a resource for lexicography". In: M.-H. Corréard (ed.). *Lexicography and Natural Language Processing. A Festschrift in Honour of B. S. T. Atkins*. EURALEX 2002: Göteborg University: 199–215.

Greenbaum, S. (1984). "Corpus analysis and elicitation tests". In: J. Aarts and W. Meijs (eds.). *Corpus Linguistics – Recent Developments in the Use of Computer in English Language*. Amsterdam/New York: Rodopi: 193–201.

Kilgarriff, A. (2001). "The web as corpus". In: P. A. Rayson *et al.* (eds.). *UCREL Technical Papers 13. Special Issue. Proceedings of the Corpus Linguistics 2001 Conference*. Lancaster: Lancaster University: 342–344.

Kilgarriff, A. and G. Grefenstette (2003). "Introduction to the special issue of web as corpus'. *Computational Linguistics*, 29(3): 333–348.

Landau, S. (2001). *Dictionaries. The Art and Craft of Lexicography*. Cambridge/New York: Cambridge University Press.

Leech, G. (2007). "New resources, or just better old ones? The Holy Grail of representativeness". In: M. Hundt, N. Nesselhauf and C. Biewer (eds.). *Corpus Linguistics and the Web*. Amsterdam/New York: Rodopi: 133–150.

Manning, C. and H. Schütze (1999). *Foundations of Statistical Natural Language Processing*. Cambridge (MA): MIT Press.

McConchie, R. W. (1997). *Lexicography and Physicke: The Record of Sixteenth-Century English Medical Terminology*. Oxford: Clarendon Press.

Mugglestone, L. (2009). "The Oxford English Dictionary". In: A.P. Cowie (ed.). *The Oxford History of English Lexicography*. Vol. 1. *General-Purpose Dictionaries*, Oxford: Clarendon Press: 230–259.

OED3. *Oxford English Dictionary* (2000–). *The Oxford English Dictionary Online*. Third Edition. J. Simpson (ed.). Oxford: Oxford University Press. Online at < http://www.oed.com>.

Ooi, V. (1998). *Computer Corpus Lexicography*. Edinburgh: Edinburgh University Press.

Paton, B. (1995). "New-word lexicography and the OED". *Dictionaries: Journal of the Dictionary Society of North America*, 16: 79–89.

Podhajecka, M. (in press). "Third edition of the OED and lexical transmission: Towards a consistent research methodology". In: J. Considine (ed.). *Webs of Words: New Studies in Historical Lexicology*. Newcastle-upon-Tyne: Cambridge Scholars Publishing.

Towards the Creation of a Belarusian Grammatical Dictionary

Igor V. Shevchenko, Natalia Kotsyba and Kiryl Kurshuk

Abstract: The article describes the process of creation of the Belarusian grammatical inflexion dictionary on the basis of linguistic similarities with the existing Ukrainian grammatical dictionary. The grammatical dictionary is developed to enable morphological mark-up of Belarusian texts and is the first tool of the kind for this language. The notions of the inflexion parameter and the inflexion class are introduced and explained. Cases of similarity and discrepancy in inflexion classes of the closely related languages are considered.

Keywords: Belarusian grammatical dictionary (BGD), grammatical dictionary (GD), highly inflected languages, part of speech (POS), Slavic languages, Ukrainian grammatical dictionary (UGD), word-inflexion class (WIC).

1. Introduction

Grammatical dictionaries that provide description of the word-declension and word-formation are of great importance for inflecting languages. Creation of an exhaustive set of lexemes' variants, as well as rules of word formation, belongs to the most significant tasks in natural language processing as they enable lemmatization of word forms, i.e. the identification of their citation form available in dictionaries; morphological analysis and synthesis; grammatical tagging of text corpora.

2. Prototypes and the theoretical background

A grammatical dictionary, as we understand it, deals with declension and has to contain all forms of inflected words of a language with their grammatical features. The great variety of such forms in Slavic languages makes such a task far from trivial. Talking about grammatical dictionaries we should first of all mention the fundamental work by Andrey Zaliznyak (Zaliznyak 1967) that was the first thorough and systematic attempt to present a uniform and exhaustive description of the word-declension in a Slavic language. Even though the dictionary was not designed for computer-aided processing (back in the 1960's), it appeared to be quite applicable for it when computers became a bread-and-butter tool for linguists.

The Grammatical dictionary of the Ukrainian language (UGD) developed in the ULIF NANU (Shevchenko *et al.* 2005) provides by now a division of the lexemes fixed in dictionaries into 2456 inflexion grammatical classes (WIC), each of them presenting a set of lexeme endings according to their grammatical meanings, unique and uniform inside a class, and therefore contains all the types of inflexion in Ukrainian (Shevchenko 1996). The UGD has been one of the main tools supporting the first integrated Ukrainian lexicographical system "Dictionaries of Ukraine" that has already seen eight CD-ROM editions (2001–2008) (Shirokov *et al.* 2007).

The uniformity of inflexion inside a WIC means, in terms of the computer processing of written texts, that all the words belonging to a WIC have the same set of the grammatical meanings and in each of the grammatical meanings (as well as their variants, if any) the same number of characters counting from the right is replaced with the same line of characters. Thus, words belonging to the same WIC differ in their invariable parts only.

As a matter of fact, a WIC is a set of words with the same type of inflexion, which is characterized by a set of values of the inflexion parameters (Shevchenko 1996, 2008). The conformity of inflexion for many lexemes that are different in meaning and form allows to specify the following grammatical inflexion parameters.

1. Part of speech (or as its inflexion generalization – inflexion type)
2. Type of word stem
3. Conjugation pattern
4. Type of changes
5. Paradigm incompleteness
6. Aspect (for verbs)
7. Reflexivity (for verbs)
8. Imperative form (for verbs)
9. Passive participle suffix
10. Gender (for nouns)
11. Denotatum type (for nouns)
12. Form of the genitive case for masculine nouns
13. Form of the locative for masculine and neutral nouns
14. Form of the dative for masculine nouns
15. Form of the accusative case in plural (for nouns)
16. Atypical word-form features in certain grammatical meanings
17. Type of the accent distribution in the inflexion paradigm.

A WIC is determined by a combination of the parameter values, for example, all masculine nouns of the second declension that indicate human beings, end in a soft consonant, drop the vowel *-e-* in oblique cases and do not have atypical features in their inflexion belong to the same WIC (in our classification #1540), examples are: “vyborec’” (“voter”), “irlandec’” (“Irishman”).

Table 1. Examples of feature dictribution in WICs

lexeme	part of speech	declension	basis	change	animacy	genitive	WIC
vyborec’ vydavec’ promyslovec’	n	2dec	soft	-e	person	a	1540

lexeme	part of speech	conjugation	basis	final suffix	aspect	reflex	change	WIC
kompensuvaty likviduvaty normalizuvaty	v	1dec	iota	-aty	imperf+ perf	–	–	382

lexeme	part of speech	declension	basis	change	animal coord	pecul	WIC
Vitalijiv zmijiv nencijiv	a	possessive	hard	ji-je	+	–	2335
vsjakyj dekotryj žodnyj	pron	general	hard	–	+	–	1145

The citation form of a word recorded in a dictionary as a word entry is the object of identification. A inflexion parameter makes sense only for certain groups of words according to their grammatical function. For example, there is hardly any use considering the option “form of the genitive” and the “gender” for a verb (if we deal with gender in general as a characteristic feature of a lexeme); likewise, the parameter “aspect” or “form of imperative” with respect to a noun or an adjective. Thus, a parameter is characterized within its domain. The inflexion parameter can be regarded as a discrete function with a limited range of possible values (the value area). As an example, the well-known list of parts of speech can be given. The parameter “type of the word stem” can get one of 5 values: hard, soft, combined, iotacized and r-type. The parameter ”gender” has potentially 10 different values for a lexeme (three genders, their six combinations by the order of two and, besides, one combination of all three genders), while the form of the genitive for masculine nouns has three values: *-a* (or *-ja*, depending on the word ending), *-u* (*-ju*), or both *-a* (*-ja*) and *-u* (*-ju*) are possible.

Each of the inflexion parameter values can be implemented only for words that possess a certain form. For example, Ukrainian verbs can end only in *-ty*, or *-tysja*. No word entry with a different form can be considered as a candidate for a verb in the process of grammatical identification[1]. At the same time, the word that ends in *-mu* is not necessarily a verb. For example, it can be a *pluralia tantum* noun, for example: *graty* ("bars"). Thus, the words with the ending *-ty* and *-tysja* set a domain for the parameter. Belonging to a domain does not imply that the parameter value of the word is really implemented. In such cases it is logical to talk about an optional parameter since a word that ends in *-ty* can be but is not necessarily a verb. There are, however, some cases when a word is determined by a parameter value unconditionally. For example, any Ukrainian feminine noun whose last stem consonant is *-k* changes it into *-c* in the dative and locative cases. Thus, for this very productive group of words, the above value of the change is mandatory and one can talk about an area of mandatory implementation for the parameter value.

3. The material basis for the Belarusian Grammatical Dictionary

The problem of full and explicit descriptions of the inflexion exists for other Slavic languages as well. For most of them it has been already resolved in one way or another. However, this cannot be said about the Belarusian language yet. The problem of the creation of the Belarusian grammatical dictionary is being solved by us with the help of an electronic version of the *Dictionary of the Belarusian Language. Spelling. Orthoepy. Accentuation. Inflection.* ("Slounik belaruskaj movy. Arfahrafija. Arfaepija. Akcentuacyja. Slovazmjanenne") that deals first of all with the spelling and some elements of orthoepy (BelOrthDict 1987). The dictionary contains the main stock of the Belarusian vocabulary in its state by the end of the 20th century covering the material from *The Belorussian-Russian Dictionary* (Moscow, 1962), *Explanatory Dictionary of the Belarusian Language* ("Tlumačal'ny slounik belaruskaj movy", vol. 1–5, 1977–1984), as well as the materials of the lexical card file of the Yakub Kolas Institute of Linguistics. The inflexion in the dictionary is given in an abridged form, typical for a spelling dictionary of Slavic languages, so that the non-initial word-forms are presented starting from the last letter common to all forms followed by other spelling forms in different grammatical meanings.

1 Perhaps with the exception of expressions like *spatky*, *jiston'ky*, ("to sleep", "to eat") which are classified as predicatives in the UGD. However, they are treated as diminutive forms of the infinitive in the UGTag, see (Kotsyba, Mykulyak, Shevchenko 2009) in the same volume and (Derzhanski, Kotsyba 2008) for the discussion about predicatives.

abvjaz**a**c' *zak.*, abvja**žu**, abvj**a**žaš, -ža, -žam, -žace, -žuc'
kac**i**c' *nezak.*, ка**ču**, k**o**ciš, k**o**cic', k**o**cim, k**o**cice, k**o**cjac'
v**y**h**a**n *s.-g.*, -nu, -ne, -nau; *(dzejanne)* -nu, -ne
nas**e**nne [n'ne] -nni
svjakr**u**xa -usje, -ux

The dictionary presents options for certain grammatical forms and meanings:

druk**a**rnja -rni, -ran' *i* -rnjau

mad**e**l' -llu [l'lu], -lej *i* -ljau

The volume of a paradigm presentation varies depending on the rolling accent:

knot kn**o**ta, -oce, *mn.* knat**y**, -t**o**u
les l**e**su, l**e**se, *mn.* ljas**y**, ljas**o**u
svat sv**a**ta, sv**a**ce, *mn.* svat**y**, -t**o**u
sklep -pa, -pe, *mn.* skljap**y**, -p**o**u

The dictionary specifies the position of the accent for all the word forms.

Given all the information contained in the orthographic dictionary, it can be an invaluable source of grammatical information that can be used for morphological analysis. For this purpose, the content of the paper dictionary had to be brought to a electronic form.

4. Digitalization as a preparatory stage of creating a grammatical database

The paper dictionary containing over 900 pages with words presented in three columns at each page was scanned and OCRed with the use of the Fine Reader 8.0 program for optical character recognition. The specifics of the dictionary text and its layout demanded a careful and painstaking post-OCR correction. The insufficient quality of the dictionary text recognition, including improper splitting of the text into paragraphs, excessive bolding etc., presented a serious problem while dealing with its electronic form, making it impossible in many cases to automatically identify word entries' limits. One of the biggest problems was the lack of recognition sets for the characters of accentuated Cyrillic letters, which strongly distorts the original text and significantly increases the time for its correction.

Due to the inadequacy of recognition software for Belarusian texts and the poor quality of scanned pages the scanning and recognition of the dictionary text by computer programs generated a lot of mistakes. During the correction of the dictionary text after its OCR we found some regular and irregular errors and inadequacies. Regular errors could be corrected by the AutoCorrect editing function in the MS Word, the rest of the errors were to be corrected manually, which required a lot of time and still did not guarantee a hundred-percent accuracy.

The most frequent regular text recognition errors include:

1. u (u under stress) was recognized as the letter ŭ (u semivowel): abahač**u** → abahačŭ.

This problem was partially solved by replacing through the AutoCorrect the combination of "a consonant + 'ŭ'" by "a consonant + 'y'".

2. o (o under stress) was misrecognized as follows: abl**o**ki → abl**b**ki

To correct these errors we also used the AutoCorrect function of the MS Word: the combination of "a consonant + 'b' + a consonant" (this combination is almost never found in the Belarusian language) was replaced by "a consonant + 'o' + a consonant". However, here we needed to replace separately each combination of letters: "rbk", "lbs", "lbp" and many others. For example, when using the AutoCorrect function on the combination "rbm" to change it into „rom" the program returns about 250 substitutions. Here one should be very careful as the combination of the type "a consonant + b + a consonant" can be, even though only occasionally, found in the Belarusian language, e.g. in the word "adbrakavany" ("rejected"). That is why this procedure had to be controlled.

3. e (e under stress) in some cases was transformed into *ë*: sm**e**cce → smëcce.
4. In some cases the character „y" was misrepresented by the combination "'i".

Apart from spelling errors, after the recognition the text lost its paragraphs' layout, which made it problematic to separate word entries automatically.
An example of a dictionary text distorted by the recognition program:

ablbki -kau, *adz.* vbblaka, *častej* vbblaki
vbblaka -ku, *mn.* v**o**blaki *i* ablbki, vbblakau *i* ablbkau
vbblaki -kau, *adz.* v**o**blaka *i* ablbki

5. Grammatical forms and lexemes to be reconsidered

It should be noted that some of existing word-formation models that are present in the orthographic dictionary are regarded presently by Belarusian linguists as Russisms, and some corrections will have to be introduced into the BGD later, cf. also (Lomtev 1956, Pivtorak 1997).

For example, the suffix of the Russian origin *-cel'* is to be replaced by other Belarusian specific suffixes: dubicel' → dub**i**l'nik ("tanning agent"), akisl**i**cel' → akislj**a**l'nik ("oxidizer"), zbav**i**cel' → zb**a**uca ("saviour"), natxn**i**cel' → nathnj**a**l'nik ("inspirer"), vyxav**a**cel' → vyxav**a**l'nik ("tutor").

The adjective suffix *-jonn-*, considered unnatural for the Belarusian language, is being replaced with more relevant ones: pensij**o**nny → pensijny (adj. "pension"), sesij**o**nny → sesijny (adj. "session") and the suffix *-ann-* with *-avy*: firmenny → firmavy (adj. "brand-name"), darefo**r**menny → darefo**r**mavy ("pre-reform").

Therefore, the dictionary published in 1987 contains some words with suffixes that are not recommended for use anymore.[2]

6. Mapping Belarusian WICs on the Ukrainian Grammatical Dictionary

The idea of creating a Belarusian grammatical dictionary is based on a wide parallelism in inflexion of the two closely related languages – Ukrainian and Belarusian. The proximity in lexical composition and the apparent parallelism in the inflexion systems of both languages, and in some cases non-flexion modifications (change proper, insertions, omissions) are easy to notice (Pivtorak 1997). Thus, it is assumed that nouns of neuter gender in *-nne*: "staj**a**nne" ("standing"), "abohatvar**e**nne" ("idolizing"), "ab**y**hravanne" ("playing up"), and others are similar in their inflexion to the Ukrainian WIC 2108 covering *singularia tantum* nouns of neuter gender ending with *-nnja*: "stoj**a**nnja" ("standing"), "maljuv**a**nnja" ("drawing"), while those ending with *-sc'*: "lehal'nasc'" ("legality") „lehkavažnasc'" ("light-mindedness") and many others meet the Ukrainian WIC 2143 covering singular nouns of the 3rd declension with the change *o-i* in some cases: "aktyvnist''" ("activity"), "rapt**o**vist''" ("suddenness"). Adjectives ending with *-y* "b**e**ly" ("white"), "ah**u**l'ny" ("general") obviously have the Ukrainian corresponding WIC 2302 "bilyj" ("white"), "spil'nyj" ("common") that brings together adjectives with the hard ending. In the verb ending with *-ac'* "dbac'" ("take care"), "spac'"

2 The problem is not crucial at the initial stage of our work. Most probably both russified and authentic forms will be necessary in the grammatical dictionary to correctly identify as many forms as possible that occur in texts. This is a sociolinguistic issue and needs further research.

("sleep") we recognize the Ukrainian WIC 697 "db**a**ty" ("take care"), "sp**a**ty" ("sleep"), i.e. verbs of the 1st conjugation with iotacized endings in the present tense and without passive participle in the paradigm. Similarly, the infinitive form ending in *-acca*: "abahašč**a**cca" ("get rich"), "zžyv**a**cca" ("get used") roughly corresponds to the WIC 700 "vyhyn**u**tysja" ("bend"), "zupyn**y**tysja" ("stop"), and so on.

Table 2. Comparison of some Belarusian and Ukrainian WICs

language	lexeme	part of speech	declension	basis	change	animacy	genitive	WIC
Ukr.	**stojannja**	n	2dec	hard	–	person	a	2108
Bel.	**abahravanne**	n	2dec	hard	–	animate	a	2108
Ukr.	**raptovist'**	n	2dec	hard	i-o	inanimate	a	2143
Bel.	**lehal'nasc'**	n	2dec	hard	–	inanimate	a	2143

language	lexeme	part of speech	declination	basis	change	animal coord	pecul	WIC
Ukr.	**bilyj**	adj	general	Hard	–	+	–	2302
Bel.	**ahul'ny**	adj	general	Hard	–	+	–	2302

language	lexeme	part of speech	conjuga-tion	basis	final suffix	aspect	reflex	change	WIC
Ukr.	**dbaty**	v	2dec	iota	-aty	imperf	–	–	697
Bel.	**dbac'**	v	2dec	iota	-ac'	imperf	–	–	697
Ukr.	**zupyniatysja**	v	2dec	iota	-jaty	imperf	+	–	700
Bel.	**abahaščacca**	v	2dec	iota	-acca	imperf	+	–	700

Such analogies allow us to make the first rough division of the Belarusian dictionary entries into specific inflexion proto-classes that require further differentiation. We can ascribe WIC numbers to a large part of the lexemes presented in the dictionary through a series of global replacements based on the ending of forms, as well as elements of inflexion paradigms available in the dictionary. Further refinement of the word stock, as well as detection of rare classes, are to be carried out manually.

7. Further differentiation of Belarusian WICs

We should note that the existence of far-going analogies between WICs of the Ukrainian and Belarusian languages does not mean a total coincidence of the endings or their inflexion parameters. For example, in Belarusian there is no vowel change in the feminine nouns ending in *-asc'*: "tv**o**rčasc'" ("creativity"), "pramysl**o**vasc'" ("industry"), which is inherent for similar Ukrainian nouns ending with *-ist'*: "vlučnist' – vlučnosti'" ("marksmanship") in a number of oblique cases.

Let us consider the process of differentiation of Belarusian inflexion classes. For example the WIC 1607 covers masculine nouns of the 2nd declension with stems ending in a hard consonant and *-a* flexion in the genitive without vowel change, designating inanimate objects, e.g., Ukr. "hryb" ("mushroom"). The closest counterpart to this Ukrainian WIC can be found in similar, vowel-invariable, Belarusian entries like "mar**o**z" ("frost"). At the same time, there are some types of change for this group of Belarusian nouns that are not founf in the Ukrainian inflexion, for instance, the change *t – c* "abanem**e**nt" – loc. "abanem**e**nce" ("season ticket"), *d – dz* „pad'j**e**zd" – loc. "pad'j**e**zdze" ("doorway"), as well as the double change of the lexeme "sneh" ("snow") with the locative "sneze" and the nominative plural "snjah**i**". The WICs 1615, 1627 and 1635 respectively are differentiated on the basis of these lexemes. Similarly, the Ukrainian WIC 2134, represented by the lexeme "p**o**vist'" ("novel"), corresponds in the Belarusian inflexion system at least to two classes: the WIC 2134 "ap**o**vesc'" ("novel") and the WIC 2137 "kosc'" ("bone"), the latter having the change of the stem vowel in oblique cases *o – a* (kosc' – kasc**i**).

Table 3. Further differentiation of Belarusian WICs

language	lexeme	part of speech	declension	basis	animacy	genitive	change	WIC
Ukr.	**hryb**	n	2dec	hard	inanimate	a	–	1607
Bel.	**maroz**	n	2dec	hard	inanimate	a	–	1607
Bel.	**abanement**	n	2dec	hard	inanimate	a	t-c	1615
Bel.	**pad'jezd**	n	2dec	hard	inanimate	a	d-dz	1627
Bel.	**sneh**	n	2dec	hard	inanimate	a	h-z, je-ja	1635
Ukr.	**povist'**	n	3dec	soft	inanimate	a	–	2134
Bel.	**apovesc'**	n	3dec	soft	inanimate	a	–	2134
Bel.	**kosc'**	n	3dec	soft	inanimate	a	o-a	2137

In some cases we have noticed phonetic phenomena that are not typical for the Ukrainian language like the appearance of the prothetic *v-* in some grammatical forms. This also predetermines further differentiation of inflexion classes. For example, the Ukrainian WIC 1991, which combines nouns of neuter gender with hard endings, corresponds to several Belarusian WICs. In addition to the obvious WIC 1991 "haspad**a**rstva" ("economy"), which reflects the main type of the inflexion in the neuter gender, we have also lexemes like "akn**o**" ("window", WIC 2001) and "v**o**zera" ("lake", WIC 2002). In the first case we can observe the appearance of the inserted *v-* in the plural (akn**o** – v**o**kny), in the second case it is the omission of the same *v-* (v**o**zera – azj**o**ry).

Table 4. Variation of WICs 1

language	lexeme	part of speech	declension	basis	gender	anim	genitive	change	WIC
Ukr.	**hospodarstvo**	n	2dec	hard	n	inanimate	a	–	1991
Bel.	**haspadarstva**	n	2dec	hard	n	inanimate	a	–	1991
Bel.	**akno**	n	2dec	hard	n	inanimate	a	+v	2001
Bel.	**vozera**	n	2dec	hard	n	inanimate	a	-v	2002

The Ukrainian verbal class 490 represented by "ohorn**u**ty" ("embrace") in its basic version corresponds to the Belarusian WIC 490 represented by the lexeme "nedacjahn**u**c'" ("fail to hold out"), but also to the WIC 491, the inflexion paradigm with the change of *e-*: abamkn**u**c', -ne, -nješ, -n**u**, -njem, -njac**e**, -n**u**c' ("surround"), and the WIC 494 with a stem change *a-o* (abharn**u**c', abharn**e**, abh**o**rneš ("embrace").

Table 5. Variation of WICs 2

language	lexeme	part of speech	conjugation	basis	final suffix	aspect	change	WIC
Ukr.	**ohornuty**	v	1conj	hard	uty	perf	–	490
Bel.	**nedacjahnuc'**	v	1conj	hard	uc'	perf	–	490
Bel.	**abamknuc'**	v	1conj	hard	uc'	perf	e-ë	491
Bel.	**abharnuc'**	v	1conj	hard	uc'	perf	a-o	494

Meanwhile, some Ukrainian inflexion parameters are not found in the Belarusian language: such a WIC as 1628, whose peculiarity is in the change *k-č* in the vocative case: "čolovi**k**" ("man") – voc. "čolovi**č**e" ("o, man!"), has no counterpart in the Belarusian language since the modern literary language does not have this case at all. Therefore, the Belarusian counterparts of the Ukrainian lexemes from the WIC 1628 like "čalavek" ("a man") correspond to the more general class of masculine nouns ending in a *-к*, which is the WIC 1788 represented by "mistyk" (mystic"), where the change in the vocative case is not observed.

Let us have a look at another example of the same phenomenon. In the Ukrainian language there are different types of inflexion for nouns designating people and those for animals because the accusative plural case of words designating animals is realized in two optional ways. One of them equals the nominative plural and the other coincides with the genitive: "pasty koni" and "pasty konej" ("to graze horses"). In the case of human beings, only the form coinciding with the genitive is acceptable: "zustrity divčat", not "*zustrity divčata" ("to meet girls"). For the Belarusian language such a differentiation does not exist. Therefore, the Belarusian counterparts like "zajčyk" ("little hare") or "vožyk"("hedgehog") of Ukrainian nouns from the WIC 1789 ("zajčyk") and 1629 ("jižak") belong in the Belarusian inflexion system to the same WIC 1788.

Table 6. Unification of WIC

language	lexeme	part of speech	declension	basis	vocative change	animacy	genitive	WIC
Ukr.	**mistyk**	N	2dec	hard	–	person	a	1788
Bel.	**mistyk**	N	2dec	hard		animate	a	1788
Ukr.	**zajčyk**	N	2dec	hard	–	animal	a	1789
Bel.	**zajčyk**	N	2dec	hard		animate	a	1788
Ukr.	**čolovik**	N	2dec	hard	k-č	person	a	1628
Bel.	**čalavek**	N	2dec	hard		animate	a	1788
Ukr.	**jižak**	N	2dec	hard	k-č	animal	a	1629
Bel.	**vožyk**	N	2dec	hard		animate	a	1788

In this case in fact we have a convergence of at least four different Ukrainian WICs in one Belarusian. Or, from another point of view, differentiation of one Belarusian inflexion class into several Ukrainian ones.

At the same time we can see here an opposite example where one Ukrainian inflexion class is split in the Belarusian inflexion: the Belarusian word "junak" ("young man") corresponding to the Ukrainian word with the same spelling and meaning from the WIC 1788 falls into a different inflexion class (in our classification it is the WIC 1787) due to the changed ending *-ou* in the genitive plural: "junakou", unlike the more conventional *-au* (čalavekau, vožykau). Such a differentiation is unknown in Ukrainian: "junakiv", "čolovikiv", "jižakiv".

Table 7. Variation of WICs 3

language	lexeme	part of speech	declension	basis	plural change	anim	genitive	WIC
Bel.	**čalavek**	n	2dec	hard	–	animate	a	1788
Bel.	**vožyk**	n	2dec	hard	–	animate	a	1788
Bel.	**junak**	n	2dec	hard	a-o	animate	a	1787

8. Conclusions and further work

Nowadays, the importance of common tools and formats in the NLP is stressed by many scholars. This enables easier convergence, alignment and reuse of natural language resources. The presented here mapping method of developing new ones, especially for less-resourced languages like Belarusian, can help to catch up with better-resourced languages in shorter time and with less effort. At the same time, the common format and conceptual apparatus is preserved and the existing tools and expertise are reused.

The controlled compiling of a dictionary described above is connected with discovering the grammar of a language in detail on a large (and, hopefully, exhaustive) amount of language material and can be compared to a corpus-driven approach to grammar study. Ideally, it should be projected on existing grammar descriptions to serve as their complementation. Further check-up on large corpora data is necessary as well, of course.

The described analysis can also give an account about the comparative morphology of Belarusian and Ukrainian and serve as a material basis for a comparative grammar of these languages.

Apart from the additional advantages for language description brought by the mapping method of creating a grammatical dictionary, its direct usage cannot be overestimated.

To sum up, grammatical dictionaries present a number of merits:

- GDs can be used in a variety of ways, e.g. the statistics of usage given by a GD can help us trace more common patterns of inflexion in similar classes of words, which can be useful for recommendations on standardization, considering the current variability of existing forms in both Ukrainian and Belarusian. Statistics of WICs can be of use in disambiguation of grammatical homonymy disambiguation.
- GDs can be a powerful tool for comparative studies too, an area much neglected by computational linguistics so far.
- GDs are corpus-driven, so they help us reveal information about a language that is not covered in grammars, or is not covered consistently or clearly enough for the users.

Thus, creating a Belarusian Grammatical Dictionary allows us, on the one hand, to obtain a detailed inflexion classification of the Belarusian language, and on the other hand, to study and summarize the differences in the inflexion systems of closely related languages. At the moment we have in our classification about 400 inflexion classes for Belarusian. The work on the Belarusian grammatical dictionary is going on and will lead to the creation of a morphological analyzer and tagger for the Belarusian language.

References

BelOrthDict (1987). *Slounik belaruskaj movy. Arfahrafija. Arfaepija. Akcentuacyja. Slovazmjanenne*. Minsk: "Belaruskaja Savetskaja Encyklapedyja" imya P. Brouki.

Derzhanski, I. and N. Kotsyba (2008). "The category of predicatives in the light of the consistent morphosyntactic tagging of Slavic languages". *Lexicographic Tools and Techniques: Proceedings of the MONDILEX First Open Workshop*, pages 68–79, Moscow: IITP—RAS.

Kotsyba, N., Mykulyak, A. and I.V. Shevchenko (2009). "UGTag: morphological analyzer and tagger for Ukrainian language" (in this volume).

Lomtev, T.P. (1956). *Grammatika belorusskogo jazyka*. Moscow.

Pivtorak, H. (1997). *Bilorus'ka mova*. Kyiv: Lybid: 240.

Shevchenko, I.V. (1996). "Algorytmična slovozminna klasyfikacija ukrajins'koji leksyky". *Movoznavstvo*. Vol. 4–5. Kyiv: 40–44.

Shevchenko, I.V., Shirokov, V.A., and A.G. Rabuletc' (2005). "Elektronnyj grammatičeskij slovar' ukrainskogo jazyka". *Proceedings of the international conference „Megaling'2005. Prikladnaja lingvistika v poiske novyx putej", 27.VI–2.VII 2005*. Meganom, Crimea, Ukraine: 124–129.

Shevchenko, I. (2008). "Parametryzacija jak osnova hramatyčnoji identyfikaciji slovnykovyx odynyc' ukrajins'koji movy". *Prykladna lingvistyka ta lingvistyčni texnolohiji. Megaling-2007. Zbirnyk naukovyx prac'*. Kyiv: Dovira: 393–402.

Shirokov, V.A. (1998). *Informacijna teoria leksykohrafičnyx system*. Kyiv: Dovira: 16, 152–174, 274–288.

Shirokov, V.A., Rabulec', O.H., Shevchenko, I.V., Kostyshyn, O.M., and K.M. Yakymenko (2007). *Intehrovana leksykohrafična systema „Slovnyky Ukrajiny"*, version 3.1. Kyiv. CD-edition.

Zaliznyak, A.A. (1967). *Russkoje imennoje slovoizmenenije*. Moscow: Nauka: 370.

Part Nine

LANGUAGE TEACHING AND LEARNING

Data-Driven Learning: the Perpetual Enigma

Alex Boulton

Abstract: Many uses have been found for corpora in language teaching and learning, most radically perhaps where learners explore the data themselves. Such procedures are especially associated with Tim Johns, who proposed what he called 'data-driven learning' over 20 years ago. While he described his techniques in detail in a number of papers, researchers and practitioners over the years have adapted Johns' procedures and invented new ones of their own, with the result that it can be difficult to pin down exactly what DDL is.

In a tribute to Johns, this paper traces the evolution of DDL through his work from 1984 up until his death in 2009, as well as in DDL studies by other researchers. The enormous variety of activities possible with corpora means it is difficult if not impossible to identify any single element which is either necessary or sufficient for an activity to qualify as DDL. This paper therefore defends a prototype definition of DDL: the further an activity is from the central, prototypical core, the less DDL-like it is, but any cut-off point beyond which we might like to say 'this is no longer DDL' seems likely to be arbitrary rather than empirically grounded or based on a coherent, hermetic definition.

Keywords: authentic, concordancing, corpus, Data-driven learning, DDL, induction, language learning, Tim Johns.

1. Introduction

In recent decades, electronic corpora have transformed linguistic study almost beyond recognition, in particular enabling vastly improved descriptions of language varieties. In the field of language teaching and learning, a number of researchers (e.g. McCarthy 2008: 564) have hailed this as a truly Kuhnian paradigm shift in many areas, from dictionaries and other resources to syllabus design, course contents and examinations, and even increasing numbers of coursebooks and other materials for both general and specific purposes.

Corpora have multiple potential uses or "affordances", to use the term popularised in applied linguistics by Hafner and Candlin (2007). One of the more controversial of these is as a language resource for learners themselves. This approach is particularly associated with Tim Johns, who started developing it in the 1980s. He first used the term 'data-driven learning' (DDL) in print in the seminal collection of papers co-edited with his colleague, Philip King, in 1991.[1] The introduction has a clear statement:

All the papers in this issue... describe an application of computers to language-learning that has come to be known as 'classroom concordancing' or 'data-driven learning' (DDL) – the use in the classroom of computer-generated concordances to get students to explore the regularities of patterning in the target language, and the development of activities and exercises based on concordance output. (Johns and King 1991: 3)

Nonetheless, the term remains controversial to this day, with researchers applying the label 'DDL' almost at random to a range of activities. This paper is an attempt to clarify the field and associated concepts, and try to answer the question of what constitutes DDL. We begin by looking at Johns' work to see in greater detail what he intended it to mean, then move on to other studies to see how it has been adopted or rejected in different cases. Finally, we discuss the term itself and its implications for a coherent field of research. The title of this paper is a tribute to Johns' 2002 article, "Data-driven learning: the perpetual challenge", in recognition of the inspiring work of this unceasingly innovative researcher and teacher, who died in March 2009.[2]

2. Background to DDL

The term 'data-driven learning' derives from computer science, describing software which can learn from new data. Because it was Johns who first adopted it to describe the uses of corpora in language learning in 1991, any discussion of DDL will inevitably rely heavily on his work. However, he was not the first to be interested in the concept. McEnery and Wilson (1997: 12) attribute the first applications of corpora to language teaching to Peter Roe at Aston University in 1969, while Johns himself (1986: 159) refers to work by Antoinette Renouf at Birmingham University in the early 1980s using *COBUILD* concordances in the language classroom. The earliest paper Johns (1986) cited along these lines is by Ahmad *et al.* (1985), who report giving learners access to corpora so they can find multiple examples of language phenomena themselves. But a far earlier publication seems to have come from an entirely different source: in 1980, Sandra McKay in San Francisco published an article in *TESOL Quarterly*

1 Actually, one of his papers in the volume (Johns 1991b) which included the term had previously appeared in *CALL Austria* in 1990. Several of his articles were reprinted in various forms, or translated to other languages (Johns 1988b was a French version of Johns 1988a). More interested in teaching than academic research, he was not the most prolific of writers.

2 Tributes can be found on the homepage of his centre at the University of Birmingham (http://www.eisu.bham.ac.uk/timjohns.shtml), in the *International Journal of Corpus Linguistics* (Scott 2009), and elsewhere.

describing the uses of corpus data for teaching verb usage. The learners in her study are provided with multiple extracts (full sentences) along with instructions to list the types of item that occur before and after the key words, categorising them and observing their behaviour, comparing and contrasting patterns, and so on. DDL thus has a number of roots, coming together in the work of Johns as the main populariser.

Nowhere does Johns provide a single, concrete definition of DDL – or rather, he provides many, defining different aspects and elements of it, along with a tremendous variety of activities. This is inevitable given the multiple affordances of language corpora: Johns and King (1991: iii) describe concordancers as being "as useful a tool in their own way as the Swiss army knife", opening up a "wide range of approaches". Johns himself was certainly not dogmatic about what constituted DDL, and particularly concerned that it should be "integrated with older and more familiar methods" (1991a: 3). Indeed, for him "reasoned eclecticism is a perfectly tenable theoretical position", and any instantiation of DDL (or indeed any other approach) is necessarily "dependent not only on the social, cultural and political setting of a particular society at a particular point in time and the development of education within that setting but also on the technology available in the classroom" (Johns 1988a: 13).

At the University of Birmingham[3] from 1971 until his retirement in 2001, Johns had been in contact with the many researchers working on the *Bank of English* monitor corpus and associated *COBUILD* projects (Sinclair 1987). Working with a concordancer convinced him that it was "one of the most powerful tools that we can offer the language user" (Johns 1988a: 15), inspiring the "classroom use of concordances" which:

> represents rather more than a 'teaching technique' and… can be the basis of a distinctive methodology characterised by the central importance given to the development of the ability of learners to discover things for themselves on the basis of authentic examples of language use.
>
> (Johns 1993: 4)

The corpus and concordancer allowed him to "cut out the middleman as far as possible and to give the learner direct access to the data" (Johns 1991b: 30) – one of the most widely quoted phrases he ever wrote. It is therefore largely an inductive approach (Johns 1991b: 29), replacing the traditional 'presentation, practice, production' paradigm (the 'three Ps' so familiar to trainee language teachers in the early communicative era) with a new trilogy which he variously named *identification*, *classification*, *generalisation* (Johns 1991a: 4) or *research*, *practice*, *improvisation* (Johns 1997a: 101). Other researchers have since come

3 Specifically the English for Overseas Students Unit (now the English for International Students Unit).

up with different labels to characterise the learner's use of language corpora, most famously perhaps the 'three Is' of *illustration*, *interaction*, *induction* (Carter and McCarthy 1995: 155; McEnery *et al.* 2006: 99).

Clearly aware of the radical shift in the underlying philosophy of language teaching, Johns frequently resorted to metaphors to explain them: "The central metaphors embodying the approach are those of the learner as 'linguistic researcher'[4], testing and revising hypotheses, or as a 'language detective', learning to recognise and interpret clues from context ('Every student a Sherlock Holmes')" (Johns 1997a: 101). This gives rise to another of his widely-quoted passages, that "research is too serious to be left to the researchers"[5] (1991a: 2). Unfortunately, perhaps, the term 'data-driven learning' did little to clarify matters.

3. A hermeneutic approach to data-driven learning

Johns wrote on a number of topics before concentrating on DDL, notably in the fields of reading English for specific or academic purposes, and various CALL applications (Johns 1976, 1980, 1981; Johns and Davies 1983; Johns and Dudley-Evans 1985). Although unconnected to DDL, these papers are helpful in understanding his main concerns in language teaching, with repeated reference to concepts such as induction, problem-solving, puzzling it out, learning by doing, communication and collaboration, as well as the importance of authentic language. A number of later papers are also only tangentially related to DDL, especially describing software (Johns 1996, 1998; Johns and Lixun 1999). In total, Johns' legacy of DDL-related publications resides mainly in nine articles (Johns 1986, 1988a, 1991a, 1991b, 1993, 1997a, 1997b, 2002; Johns *et al.* 2008), a co-edited collection (Johns and King 1991), a number of on-line collections[6], and a short discussion in a co-edited book (Higgins and Johns 1984). For reasons of space it is not possible to go into details of all his papers here; a summary of each individual paper can be found on the present author's homepage.[7]

---

4 Johns (1988: 13-14) attributes this metaphor to Seliger (1983).

5 Based on the French statesman Clémenceau (*Letters and Diaries* 1935: 6): "La guerre! C'est une chose trop grave pour confier à des militaires." (War is too serious a thing to be left to the military.)

6 *Virtual DDL Library*. http://www.eisu2.bham.ac.uk/johnstf/ddl_lib.htm; *EAP page*. http://www.eisu2.bham.ac.uk/johnstf/timeap3.htm; *Ustí nad Labem DDL Workshop*. http://www.eisu2.bham.ac.uk/johnstf/unl_ddl.htm.

7 Boulton (n.d.), *Tim Johns' Data-Driven Learning: Summaries*, http://arche.univ-nancy2.fr/course/view.php?id=967.

Johns briefly referred to the potential uses of corpora in language learning in Higgins and Johns (1984), but it was not until his first major paper on the topic that he gave it any kind of name. This article included the term "classroom concordancing" in the title, but also referred to "data-based learning" in the text (Johns 1988a: 24). "Classroom concordancing" was kept as the title to the 1991 collection of papers. The introduction to this volume also introduced a newer term: "an application of computers to language-learning that has come to be known as 'classroom concordancing' or 'data-driven learning' (DDL)" (Johns and King 1991: iii), with the term 'data-driven learning' also featuring in the titles of both of Johns' own papers in this volume (Johns 1991a, 1991b). If the two terms thus seem to be interchangeable, Johns later (1993: 4) attempted a clarification: "The earlier term Classroom Concordancing described the technique; the new term Data-Driven Learning was coined to emphasise the methodology." However, he was clearly not entirely happy with it: over ten years later (Johns 2002: 107), he referred to it as "an approach... that I have, *for want of a better term*, named data-driven learning" (emphasis added). Finally, in his last paper (Johns *et al.* 2008: 495) he referred to "corpus-based language learning". While the concepts were presumably clear in his own mind, finding an appropriate label was more difficult: if Johns had his own doubts, it was perhaps not without reason.

Nonetheless, DDL is the term that has stuck in relation to his work, so merits some discussion. The choice of the word **data** is provocative: "what is distinctive about the DDL approach... is the principle that the data is primary" (Johns 1991a: 3). 'Data' here crucially refers to corpus data; one might then wonder why he chose 'data' over 'corpus', especially as the former sounds perhaps colder and more scientific. The choice could have been deliberate if he originally wanted to shake others in their complacency, but as corpus linguistics gained ground, he did come back to the more neutral term later (Johns *et al.* 2008).

The word **driven** is similarly controversial, especially given that he used 'data-*based* learning' in an earlier publications (1988a: 24) and 'corpus-*based* learning' in the last (Johns *et al.* 2008: 495). The crucial difference from the Birmingham perspective was that a corpus-*driven* approach to language meant trying to put aside all one's previous intuitions and preconceptions in order to look at language afresh only from the evidence of the data, while a corpus-*based* approach meant using corpus data to test existing ideas (cf. Tognini-Bonelli 2001). Whether in language analysis or pedagogy, the term 'driven' is clearly intended to be more radical – the data are primary and everything else has to bend to that; the more nuanced 'based' means taking what one wants from a corpus but not being strait-jacketed by it.[8] As McCarthy and Carter (2003: 338) put it, "the pedagogic process should be informed by the corpus, not driven or controlled by it," although it is difficult to see Johns disagreeing with this position. In the end, one is forced to agree with McEnery *et al.* (2006: 8) that "the distinction between the corpus-based vs corpus-driven approaches is overstated." Again, we can only presume that Johns' choice was not arbitrary, and in a typically Sinclairean (2004) 'trust the text' frame of mind he wrote of his:

> obstinate belief that even the most refined expert system would here, at best, come a poor second to the teacher's imperfect human system in selecting examples that truthfully reflect the patterning of an item in the corpus, and that students can work with and learn from. (Johns 1997a: 114)

However, it is clear from the many activities he proposed that the teacher's role was crucial in guiding the learner, scaffolding the activities, and mediating the data. He always admitted his print-outs involved "a degree of 'rule-hiding' in the selection of citations, the categories adopted, and the sequencing of citations within each category" (Johns 1991a: 4), and even accepted "editing of concordance data" (Johns 1997a: 114). This is scarcely the radical approach one might expect from the term 'data-driven', and one wonders if the terminological choice was not deliberately provocative: pedagogy would still prevail over ideology.

The concept of **learning** was very much at the centre of Johns' priorities, generating some quite abstract discussion in his 1988a paper. Learning here is thus contrasted with teaching, though this did not mean DDL could not be used "proactively… in a more traditional teacher-centred setting" (Johns 1991b: 31). He was also convinced that DDL would help students to "learn how to learn" (Johns 1991a: 1) and hence to "become better language learners outside the classroom" (Johns 1991b: 31). In many ways, then, the emphasis is less on the language than on the learner. Furthermore, learning was not his only concern, as he also experimented with using corpora as a reference source for translation (2002) or for helping students to correct their own writing (Johns 1986: 61), culminating in his 'kibbitzers' (Johns 1997b). Learning may or may not happen, but is incidental and not the main goal when using corpora (or dictionaries, or any other reference resource) in this way for specific inquiries as and when they arise.

8 Confusingly, McCarthy (e.g. 2008: 566) makes a similar distinction, but with 'corpus-based' as the radical term, and 'corpus-informed' as the more flexible.

4. Empirical research: corpora and language learners

So far we have been looking at what Johns seems to have meant by DDL, on the assumption that, as the inventor of the term in this context, his word is final. That said, the essence of the field of corpus linguistics is to describe common usage and meaning rather than to prescribe it *ex cathedra*. To avoid the trap of etymological fallacy, what it seems to mean to the majority of users has to be taken into consideration.

To identify how the approach has been used by others, this section draws on 61 separate studies looking at some aspect of corpus use for language learners.[9] The definition adopted is necessarily broad, as the aim is to capture the variety of techniques, tasks and procedures used by different researchers, whatever the explicit terminology they use. The survey is limited to empirical evaluations, which tend to provide at least a minimum of background information. The studies were all published in English subsequent to the popularisation of the term DDL in 1991, excluding Johns' own work, and divide into three relatively even-sized groups:

- Type A studies: 19 with a more or less explicit claim to being DDL;
- Type B studies: 23 with at least some reference to Johns' work and/or DDL;
- Type C studies: 19 with no reference at all to Johns or DDL.[10]

The objective then is to compare the three types of study to see what they share and where differences may lie. The first section of Table 1 below provides some background information on the context of the studies. Clearly not all elements are relevant: the fact that the majority of all studies featured English as the target language should not be taken as an indication that English is the 'best' language for DDL (though as a language with comparatively few inflections, it may be more suitable than some). Similarly, the overwhelming majority of studies are conducted among students in higher education, but this is presumably in large part simply because that is where the researchers work rather than due to any inherent limitation of DDL. Other cases are less clear-cut: most studies concern learners at relatively advanced levels of language ability, and it has been argued

9 An evolving list of studies can be found on the author's homepage: *Empirical Research in Data-Driven Learning: A Summary*, http://arche.univ-nancy2.fr/course/view.php?id=967.

10 There is of course no way of knowing whether the lack of reference to Johns' work or DDL means that the authors were unaware of it, or felt it irrelevant to their present paper, or rejected it outright. Similarly, some of the B Studies mention DDL only to dismiss it or suggest an alternative approach. The discussion is intended only to bring out tendencies.

that DDL is not appropriate at lower levels. Johns (1986: 161) designed *MicroConcord*:

> for a particular type of student (adult: well motivated: a sophisticated learner with experience of research methods in his subject area) with particular needs (fairly closely specifiable in terms of target texts) in a particular learning/teaching situation (in which a great deal of emphasis is placed on developing students' learning strategies and on their responsibility for their own learning).

However, DDL should not be ruled out automatically at lower levels, and Johns (1997a) himself reported using DDL in a 'remedial grammar' course for lower-level international students. A number of other studies do attempt it – especially, as Table 1 shows, among those with a stronger claim to follow Johns' work – and a number of arguments have been put forward (e.g. Boulton 2009a, 2009b).

The most obvious difference between the three types of study lies in the learners' specialisation, with those citing Johns tending to work more with students majoring in areas other than the target language, with an emphasis on English for specific or academic purposes. The importance of this is reflected in the second part of the table, which shows the main focus of the studies: those presenting it as a separate corpus linguistics course; those focusing on one or more specified language areas (e.g. phrasal verbs, connectors, etc.); those using it for written production (including translation and error-correction) or reading; and a small number of others with mixed aims. There are a number of differences between the three types of study, but two stand out: type A studies are more likely to focus on learning ('language'), while type C ones are more frequently interested in corpus use as a reference resource ('writing' or 'reading'). Although these two different uses of corpora rarely receive explicit discussion or differentiation (though see Landure and Boulton 2010), it is possible that some researchers might shy away from claiming to be DDL if their main interest is not learning as such.

Table 1. Overview of 61 empirical studies

		A studies (*n* = 19)	B studies (*n* = 23)	C studies (*n* = 19)	average (*n* = 61)
background	English	89%	78%	79%	82%
	HEI	89%	87%	89%	88%
	advanced	42%	65%	53%	54%
	intermediate	47%	26%	47%	39%
	low	11%	9%	0%	7%
	specialists	37%	42%	53%	48%
	non-specialists	52%	30%	37%	40%
main focus	corpus linguistics	16%	30%	0%	16%
	language	68%	35%	47%	49%
	writing	0%	22%	42%	21%
	reading	0%	9%	11%	7%
	miscellaneous	16%	4%	0%	8%

support	hands-on	47%	74%	79%	67%
	program	11%	22%	21%	18%
	paper	42%	4%	0%	15%

The final part of the table lists the main type of support or interface used. Type B and C studies are more likely to require learners to interact with corpus data on computer, either directly or via a software package that includes one or more corpora. Type A studies, on the other hand, are more likely to be providing the learners with printed DDL materials. Looking at the table as a whole, this could be because these studies tend to use corpora for learning (with general language items relevant to the entire class) rather than as a resource (with specific language points generated by individual learners), and the learners are probably in greater need of guidance, due both to their lower overall levels of language proficiency and (possibly, given that they are not language specialists) motivation and sophistication.

It is important to bear in mind that these differences reflect general trends only: any of these elements can feature in any of the study types, thus making any hard-and-fast classification or separation difficult. The same can be said of the corpora and tools involved, and the approaches adopted. Both A and C studies make use of the web as corpus, on-line corpora, locally-built corpora of particular language varieties for specific purposes, large multi-purpose corpora such as the BNC, monolingual and bilingual corpora, and they use the same concordancers. Similarly, both types may introduce corpus consultation: as a separate course or integrated to an on-going course; in class, in the computer laboratory or outside; for individual use, pair-work or whole-class activities; proactively in teacher-controlled activities or reactively in response to individual learner queries; using selected samples or an entire corpus; inductively or deductively; in a highly controlled or almost entirely open 'serendipitous' manner; and so on. To summarise: different researchers do different things with corpora, but the differences are at most tendencies, as virtually every type of activity can be found in various studies whether they call themselves DDL or something else.

5. Defining data-driven learning

It is apparent that DDL means different things to different people, sometimes in contradiction with Johns' own work. Virtually the only aspect that is transparently essential in all cases is the use of *corpus* data, and even this is not enough to define DDL. For example, corpora have been used as the basis for course materials such as *Touchstone* (e.g. McCarthy *et al.* 2006), but the authors' "mediation" makes the corpus origins completely invisible: "Teachers and learners should expect that, in most ways, corpus informed materials will look like traditionally prepared materials" (McCarthy 2004: 15). Few would argue that this is an example of data-driven learning (Boulton forthcoming). DDL may include working with whole texts extracted from a corpus (e.g. Flowerdew 2005), but using whole texts alone is not what most people would understand by DDL – although Johns *et al.* (2008) based DDL activities on the use of a single novel, *Swallows and Amazons*[11]. DDL is frequently associated with truncated concordance lines or KWICs (key words in context), but may feature whole sentences – as used for example by Schmitt and Schmitt (2005) in their self-proclaimed DDL course *Focus on Vocabulary*. While there are typically several contexts at a time, in some cases there are only two – again, an absolute minimum requirement seems difficult to justify: Johns' examples of the "one item, many contexts" paradigm (e.g. 1997a: 102) frequently featured as few as three lines. In all of these cases, it seems, to qualify as DDL, corpora must not only be present, but must also have a high profile.

The position taken here is that it is simply not possible to identify any element which is both *sufficient* and *necessary* to define an activity as DDL. Certainly it has no monopoly on such apparently key features as induction (Schaffer [1989] presents an intriguing study of induction using full texts, in no way an instantiation of DDL) or authentic materials (recommended extensively in the communicative approach, among others). Watertight definitions are often difficult or impossible to establish in the real world; an alternative is to provide a 'prototype' (Aitchison 2003: ch3), an example which is generally perceived as a good exponent of the class; other instantiations may differ in one or more aspects, but the greater the differences, the less likely they are to be considered members of that class. Gilquin and Gries (2009: 6) apply this approach to the concept of a corpus itself, identifying "several criteria that, if met, define a prototypical corpus, but the criteria are neither all necessary nor jointly sufficient."

In the case of data-driven learning, we might propose a prototype such as the following:

- The hands-on use of authentic corpus data (concordances) by advanced, sophisticated foreign or second language learners in higher education for inductive, self-directed language learning of advanced usage.

Yet virtually any part of this description might be absent in a particular case:

- **Hands-on**: Johns (e.g. 1991a, 1991b), like many other researchers, made extensive use of paper-based materials for DDL, and encouraged the use of

11 Johns had been working on a biography of the author, Arthur Ransome, during his retirement: http://www.allthingsransome.net/.

generic, reusable "ready-made DDL materials" (1991b: 36) to reach a wider audience (as in the examples on his own websites). He even (Johns 1993) mentioned the practice of "blackboard concordancing", getting learners to identify target items from a page of text and write the concordances on the board – no technology required for learners or teachers. Paper-based materials can provide a gentle "way in" (Johns 1993: 7), and "the amount of help on offer can be gradually reduced until students can be presented with concordance output to investigate independently and unaided" (Johns *et al.* 2008: 495), rather than imposing the new approach (DDL), new materials (corpora), and new technology (software) all at once (Boulton forthcoming). Furthermore, while hands-on DDL may be a long-term goal to promote autonomous corpus investigation for those with strong specific needs (e.g. Johns 1997b), it is not obvious that this is true for all learners.

- **Authentic**: some (notably Widdowson [e.g. 1998]) have claimed that any texts removed from their original context and function should be considered inauthentic in themselves for teaching purposes; even rejecting this extreme position (e.g. Mishan 2004), one might doubt the authenticity of isolated concordance lines chosen by the teacher, especially if they are graded, and possibly even edited, or the use of learner corpora (also envisaged by Johns [1986: 158–159]). Furthermore, despite Johns' repeated insistence on the "overriding importance of authentic text" (Johns and King 1991: iv), corpora of simplified data (e.g. of textbooks, exam papers or simplified novels) might still be used in a DDL approach (e.g. Allan 2009).
- **Corpus data**: some research focuses on whole texts extracted from corpora (e.g. Braun 2005), or a single large text such as a novel (e.g. Johns *et al.* 2008) or short story (Cobb *et al.* 2001). As discussed above, the language used also has to be *overtly* extracted from a corpus.
- **Concordances**: in addition to longer texts, or paragraph- or sentence-length extracts, DDL activities may also include study of frequencies, distributions, collocates lists, and so on (e.g. Boulton 2010). The aim is still to generalise from corpus data.
- **Advanced, sophisticated**: the majority of research to date has focused on advanced learners, a common objection being that it "may be all very well for students as intelligent, sophisticated, and well-motivated as ours..., it would not work with students as unintelligent, unsophisticated and poorly-motivated as theirs" (Johns 1991a: 12). But Johns goes on to say, "what I suspect, however, is that most students given the opportunity to show what they are capable of might be (almost) as remarkable." While noting the prevalence of work with advanced learners, Johns and King (1991: iv) wonder: "How far back towards the beginning could this approach be used?" Yoon and Hirvela (2004) find DDL even more successful with intermediate

than with advanced learners, and others report benefits with even lower levels (e.g. Boulton 2008a).

- **Foreign / second language learners**: there seems no obvious reason why DDL should not be applied to learning one's first language, such as in work by Sealey and Thompson (2004). It might also be used by language professionals such as translators who do not consider themselves to be 'learners' as such.
- **Higher education**: occasional studies have been conducted outside formal education (Cobb *et al.* 2001), independently via the Internet (Smith *et al.* 2008), in language centres (Allan 2006) and in secondary education, including work by Johns *et al.* (2008).
- **Inductive**: induction is certainly a central component of DDL (Johns 1991b), but cannot be considered an ultimately defining element. Cresswell (2007) is among those to mention potential deductive uses, comparing corpus data against known or supposed rules to test or refine them, an approach earlier suggested by Johns (1986: 159) himself. However, even in its deductive form it does remain firmly constructivist in outlook, as the learners are not simply given the rules and then told to practise drills.
- **Self-directed**: the freest form of corpus consultation, where learners take on complete responsibility for their learning, has since come to be called "serendipity" learning, most closely associated with Bernardini (2000).[12] But there is "a scale from free to controlled" (Johns and King 1991: iii): for learners at lower levels or with fewer specialist needs, the teacher might usefully retain control over some of the decisions, although in a new guise as "research director and research collaborator rather than transmitter of knowledge" (Johns 1988a: 14). Johns produced CALL software and activities that were "'closed' in the sense that the result is known to the teacher in advance" (Johns 1997a: 101), on the principle that "the more complex the program, the more inaccessible it may become" (Johns 1986: 156), and made extensive use of prepared materials for 'proactive' whole-class use (e.g. 1991a, 1991b).
- **Language learning**: corpus data can also be used as a resource or "informant" (Johns 1991a: 1) as well as explicitly for learning, especially for error-correction or written production in general. Johns mentioned such possibilities early on (1986: 161), developing them into his "kibbitzers" (1993, 1997a) which enable an observer (as in chess [Johns 2002: 111]) to examine the interactions between himself, the concordancer, and learners who came to individual sessions for help with their writing. He developed a

12 Johns had himself used the expression "serendipity learning", but referring to a specific activity where pairs of learners are provided with print-outs of different concordances "with the instruction to find as many things as possible in ten minutes that are worth reporting back to the rest of the class" (Johns 1988: 21).

parallel concordancer specifically for DDL work for translation as well as for learning (Johns 1993: 7), and made use of translation for "reciprocal learning" (Johns 2002), where learners are paired so that each is a native speaker of the other's target language and collaborate to work on parallel corpora, as well as in his final paper (Johns *et al.* 2008). It can also be used for testing purposes, particularly in the form of multiple blanked concordances, whether on paper (e.g. Stevens 1991) or in CALL software (e.g. Johns 1997a).

- **Advanced usage**: DDL is often associated with "what is normally untaught and possibly unteachable" (Johns 1991b: 28), on the "'collocational border' between syntax and lexis… [which is where] DDL methods seem to be most effective" (Johns 2002: 109). But DDL has also been used to help with skills work (mainly writing and reading), and the activities proposed in Johns (1991b) include making sentences from fragments for increased coherence, inferring meaning from context, guessing the background situation, constructing new dialogues, and so on. It has frequently been used for vocabulary learning (e.g. Cobb 1999), occasionally for wider grammatical patterns (e.g. Johns 1997a; Boulton 2008b), and even pronunciation (Gut 2006).

To allow for all these exceptions, the only hard-and-fast definition would have to be something like 'language users exploiting language corpora', so vague as to be nearly useless – hence the relevance of a prototype definition. One important corollary of all this is that DDL is not an all-or-nothing affair: its boundaries are fuzzy, and any identifiable cut-off point will necessarily be arbitrary. With first-time users, especially given lower levels of language proficiency, sophistication and motivation, it might well be appropriate to start with a relatively 'weak' form of DDL (near the boundary), gradually moving on to a more 'hard-core' version (at the prototypical centre) as and when necessary.

In many cases, the teacher is likely to remain the centre of attention at the start, deciding the language points to study, the corpora and tools to use, the activities, progression, and so on; as the learners become familiar with all of this, they can gradually take on more responsibility for their own learning by deciding these issues for themselves. Such a gradual changeover from a proactive to a reactive approach is truly 'autonomising' in the classic sense intended by Holec (e.g. 1981). It might be easier to adopt a deductive approach initially, testing rules or hypotheses against the data rather than trying to work them out unaided. Carefully-designed activities with known outcomes can give way to more open-ended exploration, especially as learners move from fixed materials (e.g. print-outs) to hands-on corpus consultation. This can also be a way to make the data more accessible as an alternative to simplifying the corpus itself, as concordance lines can be selected, graded and organised in advance.

6. Conclusion

Johns frequently referred to DDL as an 'approach', outlining a number of associated techniques; it is not a 'method' in its own right, but can be integrated into various types of courses each with their own methods. In their classic textbook, Richards and Rodgers (2001: 19) make the following distinctions:

> *Approach* is the level at which assumptions and beliefs about language and language learning are specified; *method* is the level at which theory is put into practice and at which choices are made about the particular skills to be taught, the content to be taught, and the order in which the content will be presented; *technique* is the level at which classroom procedures are described. [emphasis added]

In other words, an approach does not give rise to "a specific set of prescriptions and techniques" but "a variety of interpretations as to how the principles can be applied", meaning it can be "revised and updated over time" (Richards and Rodgers 2001: 245). The spirit inherent in the DDL approach is clear: empowering learners to explore language corpora and come to their own conclusions. An enormous variety of techniques can be used within this approach: the absence of any can not be taken to mean that an activity is not DDL – precisely because it is not a method and avoids the dogmatism associated with the level of method. Such criticism is therefore not only unfounded, but also does a disservice to the field as a whole.

One might wonder whether the name one applies is of any real importance, but it has been argued here that the term 'data-driven learning' may in itself be off-putting for some: 'data' sounds cold and clinical (whereas DDL is highly learner-centred), 'driven' sounds uncompromising (whereas DDL is anything but dogmatic), and 'learning' is only one aspect (DDL can also refer to corpus use as a resource for writing or translation, for example). If no label is generally accepted, then the approach as a whole cannot assume a coherent identity, essential if the "'trickle down' from research to teaching" is to turn into the torrent confidently predicted by Leech over a decade ago (1997: 2). A readily-identifiable brand name helps to increase marketability in any sphere, and language pedagogy is no exception: without it, research is perceived as fragmented, reducing its overall visibility. 'Data-driven learning' might or might not be the phrase to take the field further, only time will tell. Other proposals have included '(classroom) concordancing', 'corpus consultation', and 'corpus-based language learning' among others, each also with its relative merits and disadvantages.

This is not to denigrate the potential of the approach itself. Johns (1993: 8) claimed it "mirror[ed] the Zeitgeist of the 1990s", but it fits just as well with the post-communicative movement of the present day which, even in caricature, "turns the school into a house of personal learning and discovery, task-based, collaborative, with process-input, the teacher as guide, and the like" (Decoo 2001: n.p.). The eclectic and non-dogmatic nature of DDL (by whatever name) is fully compatible with communicative language teaching; discovery learning and learning by doing; autonomisation and learning to learn; learner-centredness and individualization; collaborative learning and creativity; task-based and process as well as product orientations; form and meaning in constructivism; with an emphasis on the authentic language of discourse by register / genre. It can be particularly useful in language for specific purposes (including content and language integrated learning), making full use of information and communication technology, and thus promoting computer skills.

It seems reasonable then to hope for a bright future where DDL can integrate ordinary classroom practice.

References

Ahmad, K., Corbett, G. and M. Rogers (1985). "Using computers with advanced language learners: an example." *The Language Teacher* (Tokyo), 9 (3): 4–7.

Aitchison, J. (2003). *Words in the Mind: An Introduction to the Mental Lexicon*. Oxford: Blackwell.

Allan, R. (2006). "Data-driven learning and vocabulary: investigating the use of concordances with advanced learners of English." Centre for Language and Communication Studies, Occasional Paper, 66. Dublin: Trinity College Dublin.

Allan, R. (2009). "Can a graded reader corpus provide "authentic" input?". *ELT Journal*, 63: 23–32.

Bernardini, S. (2000). "Systematising serendipity: proposals for concordancing large corpora with language learners." In: L. Burnard and T. McEnery (eds.). *Rethinking Language Pedagogy from a Corpus Perspective*. Frankfurt: Peter Lang: 225–234.

Boulton, A. (2008a). "Looking for empirical evidence for DDL at lower levels." In: B. Lewandowska-Tomaszczyk (ed.). *Corpus Linguistics, Computer Tools, and Applications – State of the Art*. Frankfurt: Peter Lang: 581–598.

Boulton, A. (2008b). "DDL is in the details… and in the big themes." In: M. Davies, P. Rayson, S. Hunston and P. Danielsson (eds.). *Proceedings of 4th Corpus Linguistics Conference*. Available at: http://ucrel.lancs.ac.uk/publications/CL2007/

Boulton, A. (2009a). "Testing the limits of data-driven learning: language proficiency and training." *ReCALL*, 21 (1): 37–51.

Boulton, A. (2009b). "Data-driven learning: reasonable fears and rational reassurance." *CALL in Second Language Acquisition: New Approaches for Teaching and Testing. Indian Journal of Applied Linguistics*, 35 (1): 81–106.

Boulton, A. (2010). "Data-driven learning: taking the computer out of the equation." *Language Learning*, 60 (3).

Boulton, A. (forthcoming). "Data-driven learning: on paper, in practice." In: T. Harris and M. Moreno Jaén (eds.). *Corpus Linguistics in Language Teaching*. Bern: Peter Lang.

Braun, S. (2005). "From pedagogically relevant corpora to authentic language learning contents." *ReCALL*, 17 (1): 47–64.

Carter, R. and M. McCarthy (1995). "Grammar and the spoken language." *Applied Linguistics*, 16: 141–158.

Cobb, T. (1999). "Breadth and depth of lexical acquisition with hands-on concordancing." *Computer Assisted Language Learning*, 12 (4): 345–360.

Cobb, T., Greaves, C. and M. Horst (2001). "Can the rate of lexical acquisition from reading be increased? An experiment in reading French with a suite of on-line resources." In: P. Raymond and C. Cornaire (eds.). *Regards sur la Didactique des Langues Secondes*. Montréal: Editions Logique. 133–135.
Available at: http://www.er.uqam.ca/nobel/r21270/cv/BouleE.htm

Cresswell, A. (2007). "Getting to "know" connectors? Evaluating data-driven learning in a writing skills course." In: E. Hidalgo, L. Quereda and J. Santana (eds.). *Corpora in the Foreign Language Classroom*. Amsterdam: Rodopi: 267–287.

Decoo, W. (2001). "On the mortality of language learning methods." L. Barker lecture. Brigham Young University, 8 November.
Available at: http://www.didascalia.be/mortality.htm

Flowerdew, L. (2005). "An integration of corpus-based and genre-based approaches to text analysis in EAP/ESP: countering claims against corpus-based methodologies." *English for Specific Purposes*, 24 (3): 321–332.

Gilquin, G. and S. Gries (2009). "Corpora and experimental methods: a state-of-the-art review." *Corpus Linguistics and Linguistic Theory*, 5(1): 1–26.

Gut, U. (2006). "Learner speech corpora in language teaching." In: S. Braun, K. Kohn and J. Mukherjee (eds.). *Corpus Technology and Language Pedagogy: New Resources, New Tools, New Methods*. Frankfurt: Peter Lang: 69–86.

Hafner, C. and C. Candlin (2007). "Corpus tools as an affordance to learning in professional legal education." *Journal of English for Academic Purposes*, 6 (4): 303–318.

Higgins, J. and T. Johns (1984). *Computers in Language Learning*. London: Collins.

Holec, H. (1981). *Autonomy in Foreign Language Learning*. Oxford: Oxford University Press.

Johns, T. (1976). "The communicative approach to language teaching in the framework of a programme of English for academic purposes." In: E. Roulet and H. Holec (eds.). *L'Enseignement de la Compétence de Communication en Langues Secondes*. Neuchâtel: Institut de Linguistique de l'Université de Neuchâtel: 94–112.

Johns, T. (1980). "The text and its message: an approach to the teaching of reading comprehension for students of development in administration." In: H. Faber and A. Maley (eds.). *Leseverstehen im Fremdensprachenunterricht*. Munich: Goethe Institut.

Johns, T. (1981). "The uses of an analytic generator: the computer as teacher of English for specific purposes." *ESP Teacher: Role, Development and Prospects. ELT Documents*, 112. London: British Council.

Johns, T. (1986). "Micro-Concord: a language learner's research tool." *System*, 14 (2): 151–162.

Johns, T. (1988a). "Whence and whither classroom concordancing?" In: P. Bongaerts, P. de Haan, S. Lobbe and H. Wekker (eds.). *Computer Applications in Language Learning*. Dordrecht: Foris: 9–27.

Johns, T. (1988b). "Implications et applications des logiciels de concordance dans la salle de classe." *Les Langues Modernes*, 82 (5): 29–45.

Johns, T. (1991a). "Should you be persuaded: two examples of data-driven learning." In: T. Johns and P. King (eds.). *Classroom Concordancing. English Language Research Journal*, 4: 1–16.

Johns, T. (1991b). "From printout to handout: grammar and vocabulary teaching in the context of data-driven learning." In: T. Johns and P. King (eds.). *Classroom Concordancing. English Language Research Journal*, 4: 27–45.

Johns, T. (1993). "Data-driven learning: an update." *TELL&CALL*, 2: 4–10.

Johns, T. (1996). "If our descriptions of language are to be accurate... A footnote to Kettemann." *TELL&CALL*, 4: 44–46. Available at: http://www.eisu2.bham.ac.uk/johnstf/ifbeto.htm

Johns, T. (1997a). "Contexts: the background, development and trialling of a concordance–based CALL program." In: A. Wichmann, S. Fligelstone, T. McEnery and G. Knowles (eds.). *Teaching and Language Corpora.* Harlow: Addison Wesley Longman: 100–115.

Johns, T. (1997b). "Kibbitzing one-to-ones." Paper prepared for the *BALEAP meeting on Academic Writing.* University of Reading, 29 November. http://www.eisu2.bham.ac.uk/johnstf/pimnotes.htm

Johns, T. (1998). *Multiconcord: The Lingua Multilingual Parallel Concordancer for Windows.* http://www.eisu.bham.ac.uk/johnstf/lingua.htm

Johns, T. (2002). "Data–driven learning: the perpetual challenge." In: B. Kettemann and G. Marko (eds.). *Teaching and Learning by Doing Corpus Analysis.* Amsterdam: Rodopi: 107–117.

Johns, T. and F. Davies. (1983). "Text as a vehicle for information: the classroom teaching of reading in ESP." *Reading in a Foreign Language*, 1 (1): 1–19. Available at: http://nflrc.hawaii.edu/rfl/PastIssues/rfl11johns.pdf

Johns, T. and A. Dudley–Evans (1985). "An experiment in team–teaching of overseas postgraduate students of transportation and plant biology." In: J. Swales (ed.). *Episodes in ESP.* Oxford: Pergamon.

Johns, T., Hsingchin, L. and W. Lixun (2008). "Integrating corpus-based CALL programs in teaching English through children's literature." *Computer Assisted Language Learning*, 21 (5): 483–506.

Johns, T. and P. King (eds.) (1991). *Classroom Concordancing. English Language Research Journal*, 4.

Johns, T. and W. Lixun (1999). "Four versions of a sentence–shuffling program." *System*, 27 (3): 329–338.

Landure, C. and A. Boulton (2010). "Corpus et autocorrection pour l'apprentissage des langues." *Asp*, 57: 11–30.

Leech, G. (1997). "Teaching and language corpora: a convergence." In: A. Wichmann, S. Fligelstone, T. McEnery and G. Knowles (eds.). *Teaching and Language Corpora.* Harlow: Addison Wesley Longman: 1–23.

McCarthy, M. (2004). *Touchstone: From Corpus to Coursebook.* Cambridge: Cambridge University Press. http://www.cambridge.org/us/esl/Touchstone/teacher/images/pdf/CorpusBookletfinal.pdf

McCarthy, M. (2008). "Accessing and interpreting corpus information in the teacher education context." *Language Teaching*, 41 (4): 563–574.

McCarthy, M. and R. Carter (2003). "What constitutes a basic spoken vocabulary?" *Cambridge University ESOL Examinations Research Notes*, 13: 5–7.

McCarthy, M., McCarten, J. and H. Sandiford (2006). *Touchstone 4* (teacher's edition). Cambridge: Cambridge University Press.

McEnery, T. and A. Wilson (1997). "Teaching and language corpora." *ReCALL*, 9 (1): 5–14.

McEnery, T., Xiao, R. and Y. Tono (2006). *Corpus-Based Language Studies: An Advanced Resource Book.* London: Routledge.

McKay, S. (1980). "Teaching the syntactic, semantic and pragmatic dimensions of verbs." *TESOL Quarterly*, 14 (1): 17–26.

Mishan, F. (2004). "Authenticating corpora for language learning: a problem and its resolution." *ELT Journal*, 58 (3): 219–227.

Richards, J. and T. Rodgers (2001). *Approaches and Methods in Language Teaching* (2nd edition). Cambridge: Cambridge University Press.

Schaffer, C. (1989). "A comparison of inductive and deductive approaches to teaching foreign languages." *Modern Language Journal*, 73: 395–403.

Schmitt, D. and N. Schmitt (2005). *Focus on Vocabulary: Mastering the Academic Word List*. London: Pearson.

Scott, M. (2009). "In memory of Tim Johns." *International Journal of Corpus Linguistics*, 14 (3): 271–274.

Sealey, A. and P. Thompson (2004). "What do you call the dull words? Primary school children using corpus–based approaches to learn about language." *English in Education*, 38 (1): 80–91.

Seliger, H. (1983). "The language learner as linguist: of metaphors and realities." *Applied Linguistics*, 4 (3): 179–191.

Sinclair, J. (1987). *Looking Up: An Account of the COBUILD Project in Lexical Computing*. London: Collins.

Sinclair, J. (2004). *Trust the Text: Language, Corpus and Discourse*. London: Routledge.

Smith, S., Chen, A. and A. Kilgarriff (2008). "A corpus query tool for SLA: learning Mandarin with the help of SketchEngine." In: B. Lewandowska-Tomaszczyk (ed.). *Corpus Linguistics, Computer Tools, and Applications – State of the Art*. Frankfurt: Peter Lang: 673–686.

Stevens, V. (1991). "Concordance–based vocabulary exercises: a viable alternative to gap–filling." In: T. Johns and P. King (eds.). *Classroom Concordancing. English Language Research Journal*, 4: 47–61.

Tognini-Bonelli, E. (2001). *Corpus Linguistics at Work*. Amsterdam: Benjamins.

Widdowson, H. (1998). "Context, community, and authentic language." *TESOL Quarterly*, 32 (4): 705–716.

Yoon, H. and A. Hirvela (2004). "ESL student attitudes toward corpus use in L2." *Journal of Second Language Writing*, 13 (4): 257–283.

Anticipatory 'It' in English Abstracts: a Corpus-Based Study of Non-Native Student and Published Writing

Carmen Dayrell

Abstract: This paper explores the use of anticipatory *it* patterns (such as *it is found that* and *it is necessary to*) in English abstracts written by Brazilian graduate students from the disciplines of physics, pharmaceutical sciences and computing as opposed to abstracts of published papers from the same disciplines. The primary purpose is to investigate potential differences between the two corpora with respect to the forms (lexical and grammatical patterns) and rhetorical functions of anticipatory *it* patterns. The data are drawn from two separate corpora of English abstracts. One corpus is made up of 189 abstracts (40,278 words) written by Brazilian graduate students from the abovementioned disciplines. These abstracts were collected in nine courses on English academic writing offered between 2004 and 2009 by the relevant departments of a Brazilian university. The other corpus consists of 1,086 abstracts (187,619 words) taken from papers published by various leading academic journals. It has been designed to match the specifications of the corpus of students' abstracts in terms of disciplines and percentages of texts in each. Striking differences were found between the two corpora in relation to both the lexical and syntactical features of *it*-patterns and the rhetorical motivations behind their selection. The study also indicates that different disciplines draw on different variations of the pattern but, in many cases, students do not seem to comply with disciplinary conventions.

Keywords: abstracts, anticipatory *it* patterns, corpus linguistics, English for academic purposes, foreign language teaching, foreign language writing, learner corpora, lexico-grammatical patterning, materials design, phraseology.

1. Introduction

With the predominance of English as the lingua franca of research and scholarship, a good command of the language has now become a basic academic skill for researchers, lecturers and students worldwide (Hyland 2009: 4–5). However, acquiring communicative competence in a field of study is not a simple task. In fact, it may be a challenge for students and novice researchers, particularly those operating in a foreign language.

Within the context of English for Academic Purposes (EAP), the identification of underlying lexical and syntactical regularities in academic prose is usually regarded as highly relevant for teachers and material writers who wish to help the apprentice to achieve fluent linguistic production. This is mainly because gaining control of a new genre involves developing some sensitivity towards the preferences of expert users for certain sequences of words over others which may be equally possible (Haswell 1991: 236; Hyland 2008a, 2008b). As Hyland (2004: 143) puts it, 'raising students' awareness of general features helps them to see how academic fields are broadly linked and how language both helps construct and is constructed by features of its context'.

The present study focuses on one grammatical feature which is said to be highly prominent in English academic discourse, namely, anticipatory *it* patterns (Biber *et al.* 1999: 996–997, Carter and McCarthy 2006: 286–287). For convenience, the term *it*-patterns is used here to refer to anticipatory *it* patterns. These are sequences of words, such as *it has been shown that* and *it is important to*, in which *it* is used as dummy subject, preceding a finite or a non-finite clause (Biber *et al.* 1999: 155, 332, 660, Hunston and Francis 1999: 50, 156–157, Sinclair *et al.* 1990: 411–414). In this type of construction, '*it* is not referential and the complement clause functions as logical subject of the main clause' (Biber *et al.* 1999: 660). The pattern enables writers to conform to the principle of end-weight in English, according to which long and heavy elements, typically carrying a high information load, tend to be placed in the end of the sentence (Hewings and Hewings 2002, Hyland and Tse 2005, Sinclair *et al.* 1990: 411).

It-patterns are particularly useful to writers of academic texts for creating an impersonal structure in which the author can avoid explicit commitment to a proposition by remaining in the background (Carter and McCarthy 2006: 286, Groom 2005, Hewings and Hewings 2002). For instance, rather than using a first person pronoun (*I/We suggest that*), authors can distance themselves by using an impersonal structure (*It is suggested that*) (Carter and McCarthy 2006: 283, Hewings and Hewings 2002). Similarly, adjective phrases (*it is important that*) can also be used to disguise the subjective nature of a stance or evaluation (Biber *et al.* 1999: 660, Groom 2005). A third way of hedging propositions is to attribute them to other, unnamed experts, such as in *it has been claimed that* or *it is generally agreed that* (Carter and McCarthy 2006: 283).

However, when it comes to non-native speakers of English, *it*-patterns are said to cause problems (Hewings and Hewings 2002). In their investigation of MBA dissertations written by non-native speakers of English, Hewings and Hewings (2002) have found grammatical errors as well as inadequate lexical choices associated with the use of *it*-patterns. Our previous work (Dayrell 2009, 2010) has also suggested that Brazilian graduate students do not seem comfortable to employ the sequences *it BE shown that* and *it BE found that* when writing English abstracts of research papers.

This paper explores the use of *it*-patterns in English abstracts of research papers written by Brazilian graduate students from the disciplines of physics, pharmaceutical sciences and computing. The primary purpose is to investigate potential differences between the forms (lexical and syntactical features) and rhetorical functions of *it*-patterns in student abstracts as opposed to abstracts of published papers from the same disciplines. The comparison is first made in general terms, that is, by considering all disciplines together, and it then goes on to examine disciplinary variations.

English abstracts are of special interest for their relevance in most academic contexts, even where English is not the official language. This is the case in Brazil, where they are expected to be part of dissertations as well as research papers written in Portuguese, be it for academic journals or conference proceedings. However, as Swales and Feak (2009: xiii) point out, constructing an efficient, clear abstract is a fairly difficult task, even for experienced and widely published writers. Abstracts are 'highly polished and condensed texts' (Gledhill 2005: 41) in which authors have to capture readers' interest and convince them about the relevance and main claims of the paper (Hyland and Tse 2005). They serve as the gatekeeper for a number of academic activities. As Swales and Feak (2009: 2) suggest, an abstract usually function as a summary of the study in question. Not only do abstracts help readers decide whether to read the whole paper but also allow reviewers to obtain a general picture of the paper they are about to review. Conference organizers may also be inclined to accept or decline a given study for presentation on initial impressions gained from the abstract (Swales and Feak 2009: 43).

Before describing the data analysed in this paper, an overview is given of previous related corpus-based studies. These studies provide the grounds for establishing the categorisation of the rhetorical functions of *it*-patterns adopted here. Section 3 details the methodology used to retrieve and manipulate the data and is followed by a discussion of the findings. The paper concludes with some considerations on the pedagogical implications of the study.

2. Anticipatory *it*-patterns in academic texts

Corpus-based studies on *it*-patterns have paid special attention to the rhetorical motivations behind their use in a particular context. For example, Groom (2005) examines the use of *it*-patterns with adjective complementation (such as *it is clear that* and *it is important to*) across two academic genres (research articles and books reviews) and two disciplines (history and literary criticism). The study looks into their distribution and rhetorical functions in relation to their syntactical structure: whether the complement clause is a *that* or a *to*-infinitive clause. *That*-clauses are found to be more closely associated with the writer's evaluation of the likelihood of a proposition (*it is clear that*) while *to*-infinitive-clauses tend to be related to the writer's indication of the importance (*it is important to*), difficulty (*it is difficult to*) or desirability (*it is appropriate to*) of a proposition. The findings indicate that the selection of a *that*-clause or a *to*-infinitive clause as the complement clause after an adjectival predicate depends on the communicative purposes of the genres and disciplines analysed.

Most closely related to the present research are studies which have focused on the comparison of texts produced by non-native speakers of English vis-à-vis texts produced by native or expert speakers. For instance, Hewings and Hewings (2002) examine the use of *it*-patterns with interpersonal function in MBA dissertations written by non-native speakers of English studying at a British university as opposed to research papers published by three different journals from the field of Business Studies. Selected *it*-patterns were categorised according to the following four meta-discoursal functions: (i) hedges, (ii) attitude markers, (iii) emphatics and (iv) attribution. Hedges are divided into two categories: (a) the writer's assessment of the probability, importance or necessity of a proposition (e.g. *it is likely*) and (b) the writer's indication that it is an assumption, suggestion or argument (*it could be argued*). Attitude markers indicate either that the writer finds the information worthy of attention (*it is worth pointing out*) or his/her epistemic judgement of it (*it is interesting*). Emphatics includes all cases in which the writer wants to place emphasis on a proposition. They can be of three types: a) indicates that a conclusion should be reached (*it is evident*); b) draws the reader's attention to a point (*it is important to stress*); and c) expresses a strong conviction of what is possible, important, necessary, etc. (*it is clear*). Last but not least, attribution is used to attribute a proposition to unnamed experts (*it has been proposed*). Hewings and Hewings (2002) find that *it*-patterns figure prominently in student writings, especially attitude markers and those indicating emphasis or attribution. Hedges are the only category which shows a lower proportion of instances in student in comparison with published texts.

In Hyland's (2008a, 2008b) study of academic writing, *it*-patterns are found to be among the 10 most frequent structural patterns of four-word lexical bundles. Hyland (ibid.) examines a 3.5-million-word corpus of MA/MSc and PhD dissertations written by Cantonese speakers studying at five Hong Kong universities, contrasting them with published research articles. The focus is on the following four disciplines: electrical engineering, biology, business studies and applied linguistics. *It*-patterns largely occur in participant-oriented functions, which may indicate: (i) the writers' evaluation or attitude towards a proposition (*it is possible that*) or (ii) the writers' attempt to address readers directly (*it should be noted that*). The pattern may also be used as a resultative marker to express the writers' interpretation and understanding of research processes and findings (*it was found that*). In line with Hewings and Hewings (2002), Hyland (2008a) also finds that, overall, *it*-patterns are far more frequent in student than in published writing. In terms of disciplinary variations (Hyland

2008b), science writers (electrical engineers and biologists) show the highest number of *it*-patterns. In these two disciplines, devices for disguising authorship are mainly used to either discuss results and graphs or address readers directly. In the social sciences texts, *it*-patterns are particularly prominent to express the writer's opinion or evaluation.

3. Corpora

The data analysed in this paper are drawn from two independent and separate corpora of English abstracts. One corpus comprises abstracts written by Brazilian graduate students (EA-STS), thus native speakers of Portuguese, from the disciplines of physics, pharmaceutical sciences (pharmacology, chemistry and biology) and computing. The EA-STS contains 189 abstracts (40,278 tokens) which were collected in nine courses on academic writing offered between 2004 and 2009 to graduate students (master's and PhD) from a Brazilian university. The main reason for working with these three disciplines specifically is the fact that these are the only departments that offer such courses. These courses are intended to help students to decide on the content and structure of a research paper. All abstracts included in the EA-STS were written at the very beginning of the courses, before any correction or inclusion of comments and suggestions by instructors, supervisors and/or colleagues. Another point to be made here is that the students' level of English varies considerably, ranging from lower intermediate to very advanced levels (further details in Genoves *et al.* 2007).

The size and composition of the corpus are determined by the number of abstracts handed in by students and their field of research (Table 1). The higher number of texts in physics is explained by the fact that this department runs these courses annually and has had the largest number of students in each. The department of pharmaceutical sciences also runs them on an annual basis but, thus far, solely with small groups of students. Computer science has run only two courses to date.

The other corpus is made up of abstracts taken from published papers from the same disciplines (physics, pharmaceutical sciences and computing). It contains 1,086 abstracts (187,619 words) published by leading academic journals in the disciplines in question. For the purposes of this study, I have opted for designing the corpus of published abstracts (EA-PUB) to match the specifications of the EA-STS in terms of percentages of texts by discipline (Table 1).

Table 1. Composition of the corpus of English abstracts written by Brazilian graduate students (EA-STS) and the corpus of English abstracts of published papers (EA-PUB)

	Disciplines	EA-STS			EA-PUB		
		Number of abstracts	Percentage of abstracts	Tokens	Number of abstracts	Percentage of abstracts	Tokens
1.	Physics	110	58%	25,613	630	58%	93,707
2.	Pharmaceutical Sc.	53	28%	10,743	304	28%	67,552
3.	Computing	26	14%	3,922	152	14%	26,360
	TOTAL	189	100%	40,278	1,086	100%	187,619

It is also important to mention that abstracts included in the EA-PUB are not necessarily written by native English speakers. Although an attempt has been made to select authors affiliated to universities in English speaking countries, what is valued here is that papers have been accepted by a recognized scientific body for publication and hence presumably meet the required textual quality. This is in line with Swales and Feak's (2009: xi) suggestion that with the emergence of English as the lingua franca of research and scholarship, the number of people who do not have English as their first language has rapidly increased and 'the traditional distinction between native speakers and non-native speakers (NNS) of English is collapsing'[1]. For Swales and Feak's (ibid.), the more 'valid and valuable distinctions' are now either between senior and junior researchers or between those who are proficient in academic English as opposed to those with a limited command of it.

For convenience, preference has been given to abstracts of published papers available online. Most abstracts in the EA-PUB come from papers of multiple authorship. Given that the abstracts included in the EA-STS are, at least in principle, written by one single student, an attempt has been made to diversify the EA-PUB as much as possible in terms of authors included.

4. Retrieving and categorising *it*-patterns

It-patterns are identified by first retrieving all occurrences of *it* in the two corpora and then sifting through the concordance lines and examining the surrounding context of the item. These procedures are carried out by means of the *Concord* tool of the software package *WordSmith Tools*, version 5.0 (Scott 2007). The following have been discarded from the analysis[2]:

1 See Williams (2006), for a discussion on the various issues around the concept of native speaker.

2 All examples presented below come from the two corpora used in this study.

(i) *It* as a dummy object:

```
the data in a form that makes it easier to explore and find
 incidents; (iii) how to make it possible the interoperability
```

(ii) Referential *it* (both as a subject and as an object):

```
Results show that it might be used as an alternative to carry out
ylene) (MEH-PPV). It is a semiconducting luminescent polymer with a

space group P21 and compare it with the other reported structures
ses of items chosen to load it. The constrained compartimentalized
```

(iii) Structural problems. These occurred in student abstracts only and represented 25% of all instances of *it* in the EA-STS. Most inadequacies (86%) were related to the misuse of *it* as a dummy subject such as in:

```
It has been analyzed 172 financial statements of agricultural
It was tested 100 individuals, in 20 different localities and 200
process, it was evaluated the influence of delay in the compaction
```

This error is most probably due to the influence of students' mother tongue; fronting the main verb and placing the subject at the end of the clause is an unmarked structure in Portuguese.

```
ctricity, what it is not easy.
ese properties it is very difficult.
d states, i.e. it's dispersion, in
```

Although lexico-grammatical errors are not the focus of this study, these instances are worth special attention given their relevance for pedagogical practice.

The remaining 14% of ill-formed sentences in the EA-STS referred to (i) instances in which *it* is included where it is not needed and (ii) instances in which *it's* is used for *its*:

```
which was used to produce this electricity, what it is not easy.
l problem, that to lead measurement these properties it is very.
and excited states, i.e. it's dispersion, in ruby (Al2O3:Cr3+), in
```

Once all instances of *it*-patterns have been identified, they are categorised according to two approaches: grammatical structure and rhetorical function. This study focuses on the two types of grammatical structure which are said to be particularly salient in academic English (Biber *et al.* 1999: 1019–1020), namely, *it* + verb phrase (*it is shown that*) and *it* + adjective phrase (*it is necessary to*). In both cases, *it* fills the slot preceding the main clause verb and the complement clause occurs after a main clause verb or an adjectival predicate (Biber *et al.* 1999: 660).

The categorisation of rhetorical functions has been developed from the classification systems proposed by Hyland (2008a, 2008b), Groom (2005) and Hewings and Hewings (2002). Here, categories have been established taking into consideration the five rhetorical 'moves'[3] which are usually associated with abstracts (Swales and Feak 2009: 5): (i) background, (ii) purpose, (iii) methodology, (iv) results and (v) discussion and conclusion. This is mainly because, as Milton and Hyland (1999: 159) suggest, in addition to the lexical and grammatical features of the target language, language learners also need 'guidance in order to recognise the semantic and pragmatic contexts of the target genre'. Thus, for the purposes of this study, five rhetorical categories have been established: (1) expressing an opinion or evaluation; (2) presenting findings; (3) attributing a proposition to unnamed experts; (4) non-factual propositions; and (5) indicating a gap in the literature.

(1) *Expressing an opinion or evaluation* includes all instances in which writers comment on or evaluate a given proposition, indicating their attitude, assessment or epistemic judgement on the content of the complement clause. A distinction is made between comments on methodological procedures and on findings. The former indicates writers' evaluation of the methods, models and approaches related to their own research. These instances fell into three main subcategories: (a) comments on the importance or necessity of a proposition, in which writers justify the relevance of adopting a given methodological procedure (examples 1–3); (b) writers' evaluation of how feasible a given methodological procedure is (examples 4–6); and (c) writers' epistemic judgement of a procedure (examples 7–9).

(1) rpose, **it is necessary to** select reference methods for the
(2) Hence, **it is essential to** use suitable computational
(3) Therefore, **it is crucial to** predict these characteristics as

(4) mplication **it is possible to** verify with reasonable precision
(5) ironments, **it was possible to** quantify the dipolar coupling
(6) ases where **it is difficult to** discriminate between the

3 A *move* is 'a stretch of text that does a particular job' (Swales & Feak 2009: 5).

(7) vailability, **it should be appropriated [*sic*] to** use form VIII
(8) ols. In practice **it is common to** perform shallow evaluations
(9) ata effectively, **it is unsurprising that** data-mining

The other type of evaluation refers to writers' assessment or interpretation of their own findings. A distinction is made between instances in which writers wish to indicate that a conclusion should be drawn (examples 10–12) and instances in which writers express their assessment of the contributions of their research results (examples 13–15):

(10) y distribution. **It seems that** alpha is sensitive to the width
(11) ncomplete, **it is evident that** the polypropylene with
(12) was 149,27 U/L. **It can be concluded that** the most added

(13) manner, **it is hoped that** software with more usability can be
(14) **it is likely that** the necessary petaflop computing technology
(15) **It is noteworthy that,** since the approach …, it can be applied

(2) *Presenting findings*, as the name indicates, refers to writers' descriptions of their own results. The category includes only instances in which findings are presented in a clear, straightforward way, with no assessment on the content of the proposition.

(16) programs. **It is showed that** the robust formulations trade off
(17) In conclusion, **it was found that** organic milk can be used as
(18) the mobility. **It was observed that** the weight of

(3) The third category refers to instances in which writers attribute a proposition to other, unnamed experts:

(19) mainly CO. **It is known that** bimetallic catalysts based on
(20) eral. While **it has been widely argued that** it makes sense to
(21) In general, **it is understood that** a well-characterized and

(4) *Presenting a non-factual proposition* refers to instances in which writers indicate that the complement clause is a suggestion, assumption or argument:

(22) **It is argued that** such a design will result in fewer errors
(23) Consequently, **it is suggested that** the direct substitution of
(24) **It is assumed that** the reaction follows a Michaelis-Menten-type

(5) *Identifying a gap in the literature* groups all instances in which writers pinpoint issues and questions which call for clarification or investigation (examples 25–27).

```
(25)   However, it has been unclear whether IL-18 is involved in the
(26)   fection, it remains uncertain how this control occurs. We
(27)   However, it is not known which of the membrane-bound (HLA-G 1-
```

Table 2 shows a summary of the categorisation of rhetorical functions used in this study:

Table 4: Categorisation of rhetorical functions used in this study

	Rhetorical functions	Examples
1.	Opinion or evaluation:	
	1.1 Methodological procedures	
	(a) Importance or necessity	it is necessary to, it is important to, it is crucial to
	(b) difficulty	it is possible to, it is infeasible to, it is difficult to
	(c) epistemic	it should be appropriated to, it is common to, it is unsurprising that
	1.2 Findings	
	(a) Conclusion	it can be concluded that, it seems that, it is evident that
	(b) Contribution	it is hoped that, it is likely that, It is noteworthy that
2.	Findings	it is shown that, it was found that, it has been demonstrated that
3.	Attribution of propositions to unnamed experts	it is know that, it has been argued that
4.	Non-factual propositions	It is argued that, it is suggested that, it is assumed that
5.	Gap in the literature	it has been unclear whether, it remains uncertain how, it is not known which

For comparison, all frequencies are normalised per 10,000 words. The analysis first takes into consideration the general differences between student and published writing irrespective of the discipline and then goes on to examine disciplinary variations.

5. Data analysis and discussion

Taking into consideration the occurrences of *it*-patterns in the EA-STS and EA-PUB, the present analysis reveals that students resort to *it*-patterns as often as writers of published abstracts do (Table 3). In other words, students are clearly aware of the pattern. However, when frequency counts are calculated by discipline, student and published abstracts reveal different tendencies. For physics, *it*-patterns are far less frequent in student than in published abstracts: 42% difference. In pharmaceutical sciences, it is the other way round; students use 65% more *it*-patterns per 10,000 words than published writers do. The tendency continues to hold for computing, students use 39% more *it*-patterns per 10,000 words.

Table 5. Frequencies of *it*-patterns in the student (EA-STS) and published (EA-PUB) corpora

	Frequencies in the EA-STS		**Frequencies in the EA-PUB**	
	Raw	**Normalised**	**Raw**	**Normalised**
Physics	20	7.8	104	11.1
Pharmaceutical sciences	11	10.2	42	6.2
Computing	6	15.3	29	11.0
Overall frequency	**37**	**9.2**	**175**	**9.3**

In terms of grammatical structure, students do seem aware of the two *it*-pattern constructions most frequently used in academic writing (Table 4). However, while verb phrases figure prominently in published abstracts, students use the two structures in a fairly similar proportion. If we assume that structural patterns are strongly connected with discourse strategies (Groom 2005, Hyland 2008a, Hyland and Tse 2005), it is reasonable to conclude that this difference may be interpreted as an indication that students and published abstracts resort to *it*-patterns for different rhetorical reasons.

Table 6. Grammatical structure of *it*-patterns: overall frequencies in the student (EA-STS) and published (EA-PUB) corpora

Grammatical structure of *it*-patterns	**Frequencies in the EA-STS**		**Frequencies in the EA-PUB**	
	Raw	**Normalised**	**Raw**	**Normalised**
It + verb phrases	20	5.0	125	6.7
It + adjective phrases	17	4.2	50	2.7
Overall frequency	**37**	**9.2**	**175**	**9.3**

Differences between student and published abstracts still hold true when the structural patterns are examined by discipline. For physics, verb-patterns are nearly twice more frequent in published than in student abstracts (Table 5). Abstracts from pharmaceutical sciences show a fairly similar proportion of verb-patterns in the two corpora. In contrast, computer science students employ 43% more verb-patterns per 10,000 words than published writers do. As regards adjective phrases, their proportion is consistently higher in student abstracts from all disciplines, particularly in the field of pharmaceutical sciences where its frequency in the EA-STS more than doubles its frequency in the EA-PUB.

Table 7. Grammatical structure of *it*-patterns by discipline

Grammatical patterns	**Disciplines**	**Frequencies in the EA-STS**		**Frequencies in the EA-PUB**	
		Raw	**Normalised**	**Raw**	**Normalised**
It + verb phrases	Physics	12	4.7	84	9.0
	Pharmaceutical sc.	5	4.7	27	4.0
	Computing	3	7.6	14	5.3
It + adjective phrases	Physics	8	3.1	20	2.1
	Pharmaceutical sc.	6	5.6	15	2.2
	Computing	3	7.6	15	5.7

Substantial differences are also found between the two corpora with respect to the rhetorical motivations behind the selection of *it*-patterns. Due to constraints of space, the discussion will be restricted to the main differences between the two corpora and the dominant features of each subcorpus and discipline.

As shown in Table 6 below, students seem to draw more heavily on *it*-patterns to signal their opinion or evaluation of propositions whereas published writers tend to employ them to present findings. Although published writers also use the pattern to express an opinion or evaluation, this tendency is far more marked in student abstracts: in the EA-STS, there are 67% more *it*-patterns per 10,000 words for this specific purpose. This overall higher proportion of *it*-patterns in the EA-STS seems, at least in principle, to support the idea that student tend to be reluctant to take full responsibility for an opinion or evaluation (Hyland 2008a, 2008b, Hyland and Tse 2005).

In contrast, when it comes to presenting findings, published writers employ 59% more *it*-patterns per 1000 words than students do. This is interesting to note because our previous studies (Dayrell 2009, 2010) have indicated that, when describing findings, Brazilian students seem to avoid placing themselves in the spotlight and tend to rely on impersonal writing. However, *it*-patterns did not seem to be the most obvious choice made by Brazilian students. Instead, students opt for non-human subjects such as in *results SHOW/DEMONSTRATE (that)* and *analysis/tests/experiments SHOW (that)*.

It-patterns occur with similar overall frequencies in the two corpora both when writers attribute propositions to unnamed experts and when they indicate that the complement clause is a suggestion, assumption or argument (Table 6, items 3 and 4). Last but not least, only published writers resort to impersonal *it* to refer to a gap in the literature.

Table 8. Rhetorical functions of *it*-patterns: overall frequencies in the student (EA-STS) and published (EA-PUB) corpora

	Rhetorical functions	**Frequencies in the EA-STS**		**Frequencies in the EA-PUB**	
		Raw	**Normalised**	**Raw**	**Normalised**
1.	Opinion or evaluation	20	5.0	57	3.0
2.	Findings	11	2.7	81	4.3
3.	Attribution of propositions to unnamed experts	4	1.0	19	1.0
4.	Non-factual proposition	2	0.5	11	0.6
5.	Gap in the literature	-	-	7	0.4
	TOTAL	**37**	**9.2**	**175**	**9.3**

As explained in the previous section, instances within the first category (expressing an opinion or evaluation) fall into two groups depending on what was being evaluated: methodological procedures or findings. Interestingly, the main difference between the two corpora is seen in relation to comments on methodological procedures. For this specific purpose, students employ 3.7 *it*-patterns per 10,000 words while published writers use the construction twice per 10,000 words. Perhaps even more interesting is that the student subcorpus displays a considerably higher proportion (170%) of instances in which writers evaluate how difficult or feasible a given methodological procedure is. Instances in which writers highlight the importance or necessity of a proposition and those in which they make an epistemic judgement of it appear with the same relative frequency in both corpora.

In terms of interpreting findings, students exhibit a higher proportion (43% more) of instances in which writers wish to indicate that a conclusion should be drawn. Assessment of the contributions of their research results occurs with similar frequency in both corpora.

Table 9. Frequencies of the subcategories of the rhetorical function *expressing an opinion or evaluation* in the student (EA-STS) and published (EA-PUB) corpora

Expressing an opinion or evaluation		**Frequencies in the EA-STS**		**Frequencies in the EA-PUB**	
		Raw	**Normalised**	**Raw**	**Normalised**
Methodological procedures	Importance or necessity	3	0.7	14	0.7
	Difficulty	11	2.7	19	1.0
	Epistemic	1	0.3	6	0.3
Findings	Conclusion	4	1.0	13	0.7
	Contribution	1	0.3	5	0.3
TOTAL		**20**	**5.0**	**57**	**3.0**

In line with other studies which have dealt with the use of *it*-patterns in academic texts (Groom 2005, Hyland 2008a, Hyland and Tse 2005), the present analysis found the abovementioned rhetorical functions to be closely associated with certain lexical and grammatical features.

Opinions and evaluations are expressed in both corpora by means of adjectival phrases mainly. When evaluating methodological procedures, *to*-clauses are the most frequent in both corpora. In both corpora, *it BE necessary to* is the most frequent phrase for evaluating the importance or necessity of a proposition and *it BE possible to* for expressing how difficult or easy a given methodological procedure is. In contrast, when it comes to assessing findings, only *that*-clauses are employed in both corpora. The sequence *it BE concluded that* figures prominently when writers wish to indicate that a conclusion should be drawn. Published writers also employ *it appears/seems that*; these sequences are not used by students. No lexical items stand out when writers make an epistemic judgement of a methodological procedure or express their opinion about the contributions of the study.

For presenting findings, both corpora rely solely on the structure *it* + passive voice + *that* (e.g. *it is shown that*). What is interesting to note here is that students do not seem to be aware that the pattern tends to occur with certain specific verbs. In the EA-STS, we find seven different verbs out of 11 instances of *it*-patterns. The most frequent verb is *observed* (27%), followed by *showed/shown* (18%) and *found* (18%). The remaining four verbs (*presented, seen, spotted* and *verified*) appear only once (9% each). In the EA-PUB, there are also seven different verbs but out of 81 instances of the pattern. These are: *shown* (53% of all instances), *found* (27%), *demonstrated* (9%), *observed* (8%) and the remaining three verbs (*seen, proved* and *revealed*) account for 1% each.

As regards attribution of propositions to unnamed experts and expression of a suggestion, assumption or argument, both corpora rely heavily on the structure *it* + passive voice + *that*. Various verbs are used for attribution purposes. Following Hyland and Tse (2005) terminology, these refer to either research (*shown, demonstrated, reported, noted*), discourse (*argued, said, postulated, speculated*) or cognitive acts (*known, thought, understood*). In terms of non-factual propositions, students employ *it*-patterns to present either a hypothesis (*it was hypothesized that*) or a proposal (*it was proposed that*). In published abstracts, on the other hand, *suggested* and *argued* are the most frequent verbs and all others occur only once (*assumed, expected, estimated, suspected, proposed, determined*).

Finally, for stressing that some questions remain unanswered in the literature, published writers use adjectival phrases with a negative meaning – either *it is not clear* or *it LINK-VERB unclear/uncertain* –, followed by a *wh*- or *if*-clause.

Differences in rhetorical functions also cut across disciplines. These are summarised in Table 8 and discussed below.

Table 10. Rhetorical functions of *it*-patterns by discipline

Rhetorical functions	Disciplines	Frequencies in the EA-STS		Frequencies in the EA-PUB	
		Raw	Normalised	Raw	Normalised
Opinion or evaluation	Physics	9	3.5	27	2.9
	Pharmaceutical sc.	6	5.6	13	1.9
	Computing	5	12.7	17	6.4
Findings	Physics	7	2.7	68	7.3
	Pharmaceutical sc.	2	1.9	8	1.2
	Computing	2	5.1	5	1.9
Attribution of propositions to unnamed experts	Physics	3	1.2	4	0.4
	Pharmaceutical sc.	1	0.9	11	1.6
	Computing	-	-	4	1.5
Non-factual propositions	Physics	1	0.4	3	0.3
	Pharmaceutical sc.	1	0.9	5	0.7
	Computing	-	-	3	1.1
Gap in the literature	Physics	-	-	2	0.2
	Pharmaceutical sc.	-	-	5	0.7
	Computing	-	-	-	-
TOTAL		**37**		**175**	

As we shall see, students do not follow disciplinary conventions and tend to adopt discourse strategies which are not typically used by published writers from the same disciplines. The only exception in this case is for the category *presenting a non-factual proposition*, which is infrequent in both corpora and does not exhibit significant differences across disciplines. The last category (*identifying a gap*) is not discussed here because it appears in the EA-PUB only. The category *expressing opinion or evaluation* figures prominently in student writing irrespective of the discipline. This preference is particularly evident in abstracts by students from pharmaceutical sciences and computing.

In terms of *presenting findings*, the most striking difference between the two corpora is seen for the discipline of physics. Its frequency in the EA-PUB more than doubles its corresponding frequency in the EA-STS. By way of contrast, for pharmaceutical sciences and computing, student abstracts display a much higher proportion *it*-patterns.

Although *it*-patterns occurs with similar overall frequencies in the two corpora when writers attribute propositions to unnamed experts, if we examine the data by discipline, we find that most instances in the EA-STS are from physics students. However, the pattern is not as frequent in published abstracts from the same discipline. In contrast, for pharmaceutical sciences and computing, the frequencies of *it*-patterns are far higher in published than in student abstracts.

6. Final remarks

My main purpose in this paper has been to investigate the forms and rhetorical functions of *it*-patterns in English abstracts written by Brazilian graduate students from the disciplines of physics, pharmaceutical sciences and computing vis-à-vis published abstracts from the same disciplines. In spite of the fact that student writers use *it*-patterns, they do not always make the same linguistic and rhetorical choices as published writers do. This study also indicates that different disciplines draw on different variations of the pattern but, in many cases, students do not seem to comply with disciplinary conventions.

However, there are some reasons for caution. To start with, some differences between the two corpora may be related to the limited size of the student collection. Clearly, additional benefits could be gained from the analysis of a larger set of data. A robust corpus of student writing would allow the researcher to reach definite conclusions and obtain a clearer picture of the use of *it*-patterns in English abstracts written by Brazilian graduate students. Further achievements could also result from the examination of the possible influence of students' first language on their lexical choices. A large-scale corpus analysis of Portuguese abstracts is well worth pursing so as to clarify differences between the two language systems.

Although more work is still needed in order to support or refute the tendencies identified here, these findings can be an important contribution to pedagogic practice and offer useful insights for teachers and material writers.

Introducing students to *it*-patterns can help them overcome structural problems related to the use of dummy *it* subject and hence organize messages more appropriately. In addition, drawing students' attention to the main differences between their own and published writing can enhance their understanding of the ways *it*-patterns are used in English. Novice academic writers are also likely to benefit from consciousness raising tasks focusing on the preferred lexico-grammatical sequences of published writers and different meanings of *it*-patterns. A better understanding of the forms and functional uses of *it*-patterns can help them move beyond syntactical structure and into the rhetorical motivations behind their selection. In sum, raising students' awareness of the strict relation between form and function can improve their ability to use *it*-patterns more effectively.

Acknowledgements

I would like to thank FAPESP (Brazil) for providing the financial support needed in this research (2007/52405-3).

References

Biber, D., S. Johansson, G. Leech, G.. Conrad and E. Finegan (1999). *Longman Grammar of Spoken and Written English.* Harlow: Pearson Education.

Carter, R. and M. McCarthy (2006). *Cambridge Grammar of English: A Comprehensive Guide.* Cambridge: Cambridge University Press.

Dayrell, C. (2009). "Sense-related verbs in English scientific abstracts: A corpus-based study of students' writing". *ESP Across Cultures*, 6: 61–78.

Dayrell, C. (*forthcoming*). "Sense-related verbs in published and student writing: a corpus-based study of English and Portuguese abstracts". In: R. Xiao (ed.). *Using Corpora in Contrastive and Translation Studies*. Newcastle: Cambridge Scholars Publishing: 486–507.

Genoves, Jr., L., R. Lizotte, E. Schuster, C. Dayrell, and S. Aluísio (2007). "A two-tiered approach to detecting English article usage: an application in scientific paper writing tools". In: N. Nicolav and R. Mitkov (eds.). *Proceedings of the International Conference RANLP'2007*. Borovetz, Bulgaria, 26th Sep. 26 2007, European Comission: 225–239.

Gledhill, C. (2005). *Collocations in Science Writing*. Tübingen: Gunter Narr Verlag.

Groom, N. (2005). "Pattern and meaning across genres and disciplines: an exploratory study". *English for Academic Purposes* 4: 257–277.

Haswell, R. (1991). *Gaining Ground in College Writing: Tales of Development and Interpretation*. Dallas: Southern Methodist University Press.

Hewings, M. and A. Hewings (2002). "It is interesting to note that …': a comparative study of anticipatory 'it' in student and published writing". *English for Specific Purposes*, 21: 367–383.

Hunston, S. and G. Francis (1999). *Pattern Grammar: A corpus-driven approach to the lexical grammar of English*. Amsterdam: John Benjamins.

Hyland, K. (2004). *Genre and Second Language Writing*. Michigan: Michigan University Press.

Hyland, K. (2008a). "Academic clusters: text patterning in published and postgraduate writing". *International Journal of Applied Linguistics*, 18(1): 41–61.

Hyland, K. (2008b). "As can be seen: lexical bundles and disciplinary variation". *English for Specific Purposes*, 27: 4–21.

Hyland, K. (2009). *Academic Discourse*. London/New York: Continuum.

Hyland, K. and P. Tse (2005). "Hooking the reader: A corpus study of evaluative *that* in abstracts". *English for Specific Purposes*, 24: 123–139.

Milton, J. and K. Hyland (1999). "Assertions in students' academic essays: A comparison of English NS and NNS student writers". In: R. Berry, B. Asker and K. Hyland (eds.). *Language Analysis, Description and Pedagogy*. Hong Kong: Language Centre HKUST: 147–161.

Scott, M. (2007). *WordSmith Tools 5.0*. Oxford: Oxford University Press.

Sinclair, J. (editor-in-chief), S. Bullon, G. Fox, R. Krishnamurthy, E. Manning, J. Todd (1990). *Collins COBUILD English Grammar*. London and Glasgow: Collins Publishers.

Swales, J.M. and C.B. Feak (2009). *Abstracts and the Writing of Abstracts*. Michigan: University of Michigan Press.

Williams, G. (2006). "Challenging the native-speaker norm: A corpus-driven analysis of scientific usage". In: G. Barnbrook, P. Danielsson e M. Mahlberg (eds.). *Meaning Texts: The Extraction of Semantic Information from Monolingual and Multilingual Corpora*. London/New York: Continuum International Publishing Group: 115–127.

Analogy-Based Generation of Questions for E-Learning Platforms

Stefano Federici

Abstract: E-learning is getting increasing attention by educational institutions. The assessment of the knowledge acquired by students of e-learning courses is mainly achieved by means of multiple-choice tests that require the teacher to formulate a large number of questions/answers pairs. Several methodologies and tools for the automatic generation of questions have been proposed in the past. Now the challenge is to widen the domain of automatic question generation systems to non-technical subjects. In this paper I will describe the "E-generation in E-learning" project that aims to evaluate and improve automatic question generation methodologies by means of analogy-based techniques to implement an automatic question generation system that best suites the needs of today e-learning platforms such as Moodle.

Keywords: analogy-based techniques, automatic question generation, moodle, e-learning.

1. Introduction

E-learning is getting increasing attention by educational institutions and it is becoming a widespread methodology either for delivering online courses or associated to classroom lessons of already existing courses. One of the key points of e-learning, namely the assessment of the knowledge acquired by the student, is mainly achieved by means of multiple-choice tests. The creation of such tests requires to the teacher the formulation of a large number of questions/answers pairs and, for each question, the selection of a fair number of alternative wrong answers. Moreover, several different ways of formulating the same question are needed in order to re-evaluate the real understanding of students when feedback to wrong answers has been provided. During the past years, several methodologies and tools for the automatic generation of questions have been proposed. The majority of systems are mainly designed for technical subjects (mathematics, computer science, medicine, etc.). Now the challenge is to widen the domain of already existing systems to non-technical subjects. In this paper I will describe the "E-generation in E-learning" project that aims to evaluate which are the methodologies, among the ones already investigated in other research projects, that will better work with data coming from general e-learning materials and to hopefully provide a new way of automatically acquiring question/anwer patterns from real texts. The final outcome of the project will be an application integrated in the LMS e-learning platform Moodle (www.moodle.org) to provide automatic multiple-choice test generation for university courses held by a consortium of several Italian Universities. The work described in this paper is part of the "E-generation in E-learning" project (2009) of the University of Cagliari.

2. Automatic Question Generation

Automatic Question Generation (AQG) is a relatively new field. AQG is a subfield of Natural Language Generation, a branch of Natural Language Processing very important in learning environments, data mining, and information extraction. During the past years a handful of works in this field have been proposed, all basically centered on automatically creating questions of several different types (multiple choice questions, completion questions, strategy instructions, etc). Now, starting from 2008, two workshops organized under the auspices of the National Science Foundation (*Question Generation Shared Task and Evaluation Challenge, Arlington, USA, 2008; Brighton, UK, 2009*; Rus and Lester 2009) have paved the way to a better understanding of the subject field and to the application of advanced techniques for automatic question generation to a broader set of disciplines. In this paper we will concentrate on the problem of automatically generating multiple-choice tests. Multiple-choice tests are indeed a key component of today e-learning platforms (such as Moodle, ATutor, Learning Space, etc.).

As strategies from works focused on the automatic generation of alternative kind of tests can be successfully adapted to the generation of multiple choice tests, we will start by giving a brief overview of the general field of Question Generation. In the next section a first distinction between different classes of automatic question generation systems will be outlined and several interesting models for Automatic Question Generation will be described. In the final section of this paper a new system for AQG developed in the "E-generation in E-learning" project of the University of Cagliari will be illustrated, based on the principles of computational analogy.

3. Ten years of AQG systems

Preliminary works on Automatic Question Generation have been proposed starting from the beginning of this century (Prakash *et al.* 2000; Lemos *et al.* 2001; Mitkov and Ha 2003). AQG is indeed an evolution of the Question Answering research field. In Question Answering (QA) we are interested in finding in a knowledge base (either a database or a collection of texts) the answer to a given natural language question. For example, Kaisser and Becker (2004) do QA by searching large corpora. They make use of pattern matching, after showing how the usage of stop words cannot cope with structured natural language[1]. They do not search for questions, but only for answers. When a question matches a given pattern, the "targets" of the pattern are used to predict the linguistic structure of potential answers.

So, in QA systems, we need to understand as much as possible of the question by applying Natural Language Understanding techniques, looking for matching knowledge in the knowledge base and then (if the knowledge is stored in a formal way in the knowledge base) rephrasing the answer back to natural language by means of Natural Language Generation techniques (Reiterand Dale 2000). In AQG systems a few more steps are needed. First, questions are not readily available, but must be generated from the knowledge base. Second, when the knowledge base is a collection of texts, matching mechanisms between a natural language question and the sentences in the collection must be defined. Finally, when dealing with multiple-choice tests, distractors (i.e. wrong but, hopefully, plausible answers that must be submitted to the student together with the correct one) must be computed.

3.1. AQG systems for computational domains

Not all AQG systems need the full list of steps above to be performed. There is indeed a class of AQG systems that are tailored on *computational domains*, that is domains in which the answer to the question can be computed by the system by means of a given algorithm. In this way often a potentially infinite set of questions can be generated from a few question templates. The methodology applied in these works is centered on using algorithmic knowledge about a single domain (e.g. mathematics, physics, verb conjugations, etc.) and then creating questions and answers based on several pre-arranged templates, following an approach whose goal is to enhance the power of on-line and question-banking systems, so to ensure reliable and secure tests. For example, in the Vyasa system[2] (Prakash *et al.* 2000), starting from the following template[3]:

```
question(
       text: "An aircraft has enough fuel to fly :qTime1: hours when
             its tank is :qPers1:% full.  How long will it fly when
```

1 They show how finding the sentence "Franz Kafka was NOT born on July 3, 1884" is indeed not an answer to the question "When was Franz Kafka born?".

2 http://www.cdacmumbai.in/index.php/cdacmumbai/research_and_publications/research_groups/kbcs_artificial_intelligence/products/vyasa

3 http://www.cdacmumbai.in/design/corporate_site/override/doc-doc/example

```
            the tank is :@qPers2:% full?"

        vars: [
                qTime1(domain: 2#20 type:int)
                qTime2(domain: 2#20 type:int)
                qPers1(domain: 10#99 type:int)
                qPers2(domain: 10#99 type:int)
               ]

        ansVar: qTime2

        answerDomain: 2#20

        constraints:[distinct([qTime1 qPers1])]

        relations: [
                   proportion(qPers1 qTime1 qPers2 qTime2)
                  ]

        altSuffix: suffix(singular: "hour" plural: "hours")
        )
```

we can generate the following questions/answers:

```
Question A:
An aircraft has enough fuel to fly 13 hours when its tank is 39% full.
How long will it fly when the tank is 12% full?
$choice  4 hours $endchoice
$choice  9 hours $endchoice
$choice  12 hours $endchoice
$choice  2 hours $endchoice
#ans a

Question B:
An aircraft has enough fuel to fly 11 hours when its tank is 66% full.
 How long will it fly when the tank is 18% full?
$choice  7 hours $endchoice
$choice  3 hours $endchoice
$choice  5 hours $endchoice
$choice  10 hours $endchoice
#ans b
```

In this system (as defined in the “relations” field), simple arithmetic proportions among the qPers1, qTime1, qPers2, qTime2 terms are used to calculate the correct answer. Wrong answers are instead computed randomly on the base of the intervals defined in the "vars" field (domain). So, the structure remains constant and numeric values are changed from question to question.

From this early days proposal, other research has been carried out on computational domains. Jean-Daubias *et al.* (2009) suggest defining user profiles in order to propose to the learner activities that are tailored on her skills (PERLEA Project). The suggested exercises are generated from exercise structures that consist in an operational pattern with associated generation constraints. Their approach is tailored on computational domains such as mathematics and verb conjugations. Hirashima (2009) proposes to automatically generate simplified versions of an original problem to improve learner understanding for problems that involve computational relations, such as mathematics, physics, etc.

3.2. Ontological AQG systems

A second class of AQG systems is the class of ontological systems. The step of generating questions and answers in ontological AQG systems is almost trivial: they are directly generated from the knowledge stored in the ontology. Ou *et al.* (2008) make use of domain ontologies to generate RDF/XML triples that will be matched against semantically annotated user questions. The tricky step in this case is the one of selecting good distractors. Distractors are indeed not directly stored in the knowledge base. Mitkov and Ha (2003) use WordNet to retrieve hypernyms, hyponyms, and coordinates of the term contained in the answer as distractors. Papasalouros *et al.* (2008) list instead a comprehensive list of strategies based on the kind of ontological relation expressed in the question. For example, their "Strategy 10" states that:

Choose sibling classes of the direct superclass of a given class to substitute the subject of the correct answer. If class *A* is subclass of *B*, *B* is a direct subclass of *C*, *D* is another direct subclass of *C* then a distractor is: *D is a B*. Distractors differ from correct answers in the class used as subject. Example: 'Sovereigns are politicians' is the correct answer, since Sovereign is a subclass of Politician. 'Monks are politicians' is a distractor, since Monk is a sibling class of Politician [as Monk, such as Politician, is a subclass of Person in the ontology].

3.2. Linguistic AQG systems

The last class of AQG systems is the class that makes use of simple or complex linguistic strategies, thus applying several of the available tools for Natural Language Processing, such as regular expressions, tokenizers, stemmers, PoS taggers, chunkers and parsers. Using NLP tools is a necessary step when the domain is not a computational one or when a sufficient ontology is not available.

Mitkov and Ha (2003) describe a semi-automatic procedure by first identifying key terms by their frequency then extracting sentences containing simple pattern of those key terms such as [AN]+N or [AN]*NP[AN]*N[4]. Then sentences containing those key terms that match some grammatical patterns (such as, S V O, S V) are identified by using a FDG parser (that returns syntactic functions such as S, V, or O). Such sentences are then rearranged by using simple rules such as

> from a sentence with "SVO" structure derive a "Which HVO" question plus "S" as the correct answer

where H is an hypernym of S in Wordnet. Distractors, as already described in the previous section, are identified as concepts that are semantically close to S in WordNet and, when they are not available, the corpus is searched for noun phrases with the same head.

In Wang *et al.* (2007) question templates are automatically extracted from a corpus of texts on the selected topic. For example, the following template:

```
Question:"what is the symptom for <Disease>?"
Required Entries: symptom, disease;
Keywords: feel, experience, accompany
Related Answer:<symptom>.
```

allows the system to generate a question by replacing the <disease> with the specific terms found in sentences that matches this template. The corresponding answers are then generated by replacing the <symptom> with the specific symptoms found in the matching sentence.

Templates are created by automatically analyzing medical texts by assigning them ontological tags, such as:

```
There are three types of cough medications available OTC for the temporary relief of <Symptom> cough </Symptom> due to a <Disease>cold</Disease>. They are oral cough <Substance>suppressants</Substance>, <Substance>oral expectorants</Substance>, and <Medicine>topical (externally applied) medicines</Medicine>.
```

The parsed texts are then manually revised by domain experts that will take care of formulating the corresponding templates:

4 As suggested by Justeson and Katz (1996).

```
question: What medications are used in <Disease>?
required entities: <Medicine>, <Disease>
optional entities: <Substance>, <Symptom>
keywords: Nouns: drug, medicine, effect; Verbs: help, use,release, improve;
Adjectives: suitable, effective.
```

Gütl (2008) describes a (semi-)automatic tool for creating completion tests (that is tests in which gaps must be filled) from documents in several different formats (HTML, PDF, DOC, etc.). Applying an automatic summarizer, he identifies the most important sentences and then parses them with the GATE toolkit[5] to extract synonyms and antonyms of the nouns that will be replaced by gaps.

Mostow and Chen (2009) describe a system to generate "strategy questions", that is questions that a successful reader would ask herself in order to get a better understanding of the text she is reading. Obviously in their context the problem of generating the correct answer and the set of wrong answers is not taken into account. They start by identifying several patterns including discourse markers that indicate condition (by identifying several specific constructions), causal relationships (by using the ASSERT semantic role labeler and then filtering the extracted sequences by using simple regular expressions) and modality (by identifying several patterns based on specific auxiliary verbs). So, for example:

```
Conditional: what would happen if <x>?
Temporal: when would <x>? what happens <temporal-expression>?
Modality: why <aux verb> <x>?
```

Information is then extracted by means of "situation models". The approach based on words (if-constructions and auxiliary verbs), regular expressions (temporal expressions) and heuristics is not always ideal: if about 87% of the questions based on condition patterns and modality are judged as plausible, only 66% of questions extracted by means of temporal information are judged as plausible, extracting for example the question "What would happen when in a huge circle?" from the sentence "If the pressure changes over a large area it can cause [ARG1 winds] to [TARGET blow] [ARGM-TMP in a huge circle]".

Wyse and Piwek (2009) describe the usage of online materials from e-learning curses (OpenLearn) and describe the "Ceist" AQG system. Applying QG to educational material showcases an excellent practical application of the QG task: the material covers a wide range of categories authored by subject experts; the XML schema of OpenLearn's study units is valuable to retrieve

5 Last retrieved Nov. 29th, 2007 form http://gate.ac.uk/sale/gate-flyer/2007/gate-flyer-4-page.pdf

only the relevant parts of the content. They extract plain text from study units and parse them with a syntactic parser that generates a tree structure. Questions templates are manually created on the base of single keywords, PoSs and restrictions so that questions (and the corresponding answers) are found into the OpenLearn materials.

Forăscu and Drăghici (2009), by using a corpus-based approach, suggests to extract question taxonomies from actual questions (taken as models of general questions, minimally tokenized, POS-tagged and chunked) using a lexicalized model of the taxonomy and a set of pattern-rules (manually or automatically developed) that can also serve as a test set.

4. A new class of AQG systems

No strategy is perfect. Nonetheless, as the time necessary to validate a question is generally much less than the time necessary to compute it (Mitkov and Ha 2003), every strategy gives at least a first filter on the set of knowledge that is stored in the knowledge base. A perfect system would require a full understanding of natural language texts, but natural language understanding belongs to the class of AI-complete problems.

No strategy can be applied to all cases: AQG systems for computational domains cannot be applied to general subjects; ontology-based systems require an available ontology being developed; linguistic AQG systems require patterns, templates and rules to be developed, often ad hoc. As sometimes it is impossible to reduce our target domain to a computational one, and building a flexible and reliable ontology of a given domain it is very likely going to take much longer that developing a set of question/answer pairs, the class of AQG systems that is more likely to be usefully exploited in a general e-learning environment is the one that make use of (sophisticated) linguistics tools.

For this reason the “E-generation in E-learning” Project will start evaluating, in its initial phase, which among the strategies described so far will work better with data coming from general e-learning materials. The best results will represent a test bed against which newer techniques will be compared.

Finally, no strategy described so far is language-independent. All the necessary manual work to create templates, patterns, rules and ontologies is heavily language-dependent.

In order to avoid deep NLP processing and to overcome the need for a procedure that will evaluate the semantic distance of distractors (when a Wordnet is not available), Hoshino and Nakagawa (2005) propose an oversimplified approach by creating gaps in positions decided by standard classification methods and proposing gap filler randomly selected from words occurring in the article. Obviously, this can’t be the solution to the problems highlighted: this simple and quick approach gives raise to questions of poor quality.

What we want to suggest in this paper is a different methodology to create a question/answer generation system that will allow us to:

- avoid to manually create detection patterns for plausible questions
- avoid to manually create detection patterns for plausible answers
- avoid to manually create a domain ontology to select plausible distractors

and that will work on general subjects.

What we need to acquire is:

- general patterns to detect plausible questions
- general patterns to detect plausible answers
- a semantic network from which plausible distractors can be selected

To get this result we propose to use an analogy-based self-learning engine (Federici *et al.* 1996) that, combined with several tools for semi-automatic annotation (Federici and Wade 2007), will allow us to browse a general collection of texts from e-learning courses and to annotate those part of the sentences that represents plausible sources of questions and answers. The annotation will also contain the actual question/answer pair that will be added to the training set of manually created questions. The annotated parts will be stored in an analogy-based network that will allow us to:

1. match unseen, non annotated, parts of sentences that represent good candidates for new questions and answers
2. create a network of relations among answers so that plausible alternants of a given term or plausible fillers of a given relation can be automatically selected as distractors.
3. build new questions on the basis of the links between annotated parts that are stored in the network and their realizations as full questions/answers that are stored in the training set

The advantages of such a procedure are clear: the annotator must not know about grammars, sentences, regular expressions, templates, keywords, related entries. The annotator is asked to perform exactly as he would do by manually creating its question/answer pairs. She must only make explicit the relation between those parts of the text that are the source of a question/anwer pair and the pair itself.

The bootstrapping approach allowed by analogy-based systems (Federici and Wade 2007) will allow the annotator to automatically extract new question/answer pairs and new distractors on the basis of what it has learned from the annotator. After revising the automatically extracted questions, the annotator will be allowed to add them to the analogy-based network and to the training set in order to automatically select a second round of questions. And the cycle will be reapplied until the necessary number of questions has been extracted.

5. Expected results

What does it make us confident that the described methodology could work? Similar approaches have been applied in recent years to a variety of problems in Natural Language Processing at almost all levels of linguistic description: phonological level (Federici *et al.* 1996), morphological level (Federici 1998), syntactic level (Federici and Pirrelli 1997), semantic level (Federici *et al.* 1999, 2000; Gola e Federici 2009). To support these applications and to speed up the annotation process, a linguistic platform has been developed consisting of a tokenizer, a PoS tagger, a chunker and a KWIC visualizer and annotator (Federici and Wade 2007).

The analogy-based engine that has been modeled to perform the linguistic tasks described above is language- and application-independent in that it is not tailored on a particular order of the linguistic units nor it presupposes a particular and specific segmentation of the character sequence. The same engine has successfully coped with text-to-speech tasks for different languages such as English, French and Italian; morphological analysis of English and Italian texts; semantic analysis and classification of English and Italian word senses.

As to performances, the quality of the analysis performed by analogy-based systems has shown to be of an excellent level, especially when compared with the smaller size of the training set when compared with other example-based approaches such as statistical algorithms for linguistic analysis.

6. Conclusions

The automatic generation of questions, and in particular of multiple-choice questions, is an important step towards the successful usage of modern e-learning platforms. Several systems for AQG have been proposed so far, all lacking of general features that would make them fully usable and scalable to larger and diverse materials. In this paper I outlined a new methodology for automatically generating multiple-choice questions that would overcome the limitation of state-of-the-art AQG systems. The new system will be implemented in the "E-generation for E-learning" Project and will be made available as a module of the LMS platform Moodle (www.moodle.org).

Acknowledgements

The work described in this paper was fully supported by a grant from University of Cagliari (Project "E-generation in E-learning"), Fund for the Support of Base Research and Start-up of Young Researchers.

References

Federici, S. (1998). "An efficient algorithm for the automatic building of a lexicon from textual corpora". *Proceedings of EURALEX 98*. Liegi, Belgium.

Federici, S., Montemagni, S. and V. Pirrelli (1999). "SENSE: an analogy-based Word Sense Disambiguation system". *Natural Language Engineering*: 207–218.

Federici S., Montemagni, S. and V. Pirrelli (2000). "ROMANSEVAL: Results for Italian by SENSE". *Computers and The Humanities*, 34: 199–204.

Federici, S. and V. Pirrelli (1997). "Analogy, computation and linguistic theory". *New Methods In Language Processing*. Taylor and Francis Ltd. Bristol, United States.

Federici, S., Pirrelli, V. and F. Yvon (1996). "A dynamic Approach to Paradigm-driven Analogy". *Connectionist, Statistical, and Symbolic Approaches To Learning For Natural Language Processing*. Springer-Verlag, Berlin, Germany.

Federici, S. and J. Wade (2007). "Letting in the light and working with the Web – A dynamic corpus development approach to interpreting metaphor". *Proceedings of Corpus Linguistics 2007*. University of Birmigham, Birmigham (UK).

Forăscu, C. and I. Drăghici (2009). "Question Generation: Taxonomies and Data". *Proceedings of the 2nd Workshop on Question Generation, AIED 2009*. Brighton, UK.

Gola, E. and S. Federici (2009). "Words on the edge: conceptual rules and usage variability". Proceedings of the Workshop *Corpus Based Approaches to Figurative Language. CL2009*. University of Liverpool, 20 July 2009. British Library, ISSN 1368-9223.

Gütl, C. (2008). "Automatic Limited-Choice and Completion Test Creation, Assessment and Feedback in modern Learning Processes". *Proceedings of LRN 2008 Conference*. February 12–16, 2008, Guatemala.

Hirashima, T. (2009). "Increasing Problem Simplification as Scaffolding in Exercises". *Proceedings of the 2nd Workshop on Question Generation. AIED 2009*. Brighton, UK.

Hoshino, A. and H. Nakagawa (2005). "Real-time multiple choice question generation for language testing: a preliminary study". *Proceedings of the Second Workshop on Building Educational Applications using Natural Language Processing*. Ann Arbor, US: 17–20.

Jean-Daubias, S., Lefevre, M. and N. Guin (2009). "Generation of exercises within the PERLEA project". *Proceedings of the 2nd Workshop on Question Generation. AIED 2009*. Brighton, UK.

Justeson, J.S. and S.L. Katz (1996). "Technical terminology: some linguistic properties and an algorithm for identification in text". *Natural Language Engineering*, 3 (2): 259–289.

Kaisser, M. and T. Becker (2004). "Question Answering by Searching Large Corpora With Linguistic Methods." *TREC*. Vol. Special Publication: 500–261, National Institute of Standards and Technology (NIST).

Lemos, M., Muralidharan, R. and V. Kamat (2001). "Automatic Generation of Questions for On-line Evaluation". Technical Report of the Department of Computer Science and Tecnology of Goa University, as downloaded on 18 October 2008, http://www.cdac.in/html/pdf/Session4.2.pdf.

Mitkov, R. and L. Ha (2003). "Computer-Aided Generation of Multiple-Choice Tests". *Proceedings of HLT-NAACL 03*. Volume 2. Edmonton, Canada, May 27–June 1, 2003.

Mostow, J. and W. Chen (2009). "Generating Instruction Automatically for the Reading Strategy of Self-Questioning". *Proceedings of 14th International Conference on Artificial Intelligence in Education 2009*. Brighton, UK.

Ou, S., Orasan, C., Mekhaldi, D. and L. Hasler (2008). "Automatic Question Pattern Generation for Ontology-based Question Answering". *Proceedings of 21st FLAIRS Conference, Coconut Grove*. Florida, May 15–17, 2008.

Papasalouros, A., Kanaris, K. and K. Kotis (2008). "Automatic generation of multiple choice questions from domain ontologies". *E-Learning IADIS 2008*. Amsterdam, The Netherlands: 427–434.

Prakash, P.R., Sasikumar, M., Mhashilkar, P. and R. Vakil (2000). "Vyasa: A system for multiple-choice generative questions". *Proceedings of KBCS-2000*. Mumbai, India, December 17–19, 2000.

Rus, V. and J. Lester (2009). Proceedings of 2nd Workshop on Question Generation, the fourteen International Conference on Artificial Intelligence in Education, July 6–7, 2009, Brighton, UK.

Wang, W., Hao, T. and W. Liu (2007). "Automatic Question Generation for Learning Evaluation in Medicine". In: H. Leung *et al.* (eds.). *Proceedings of ICWL 2008*, Springer Verlag, Berlin.

Wyse, B. and P. Piwek (2009). "Generating Questions from OpenLearn study units". *Proceedings of the 2nd Workshop on Question Generation, AIED 2009*. Brighton, UK.

Reiter, E. and R. Dale (2000). *Building Natural Language Generation Systems*. Cambridge University Press.

Webcef – the Project, Deliverables and Status Quo

Przemysław Krakowian

Abstract: Following the completion of WebCEF, a Socrates Minerva project in which web-based environments can be used for assisting the teacher in the process of evaluating spoken performance of language learners, as well as for providing learners themselves with the opportunities to have their oral production evaluated, this article looks at some of the issues and obstacles the project partners dealt with while meeting the objectives described in the project outline. A number of interesting research question arose in the process of data analysis and annotation within the duration of the project, which could potentially shed light on the nature of oral performance and interaction. The insights gained in the process of online, collaborative assessment should allow a deeper understanding and a better grasp of the CEF scales, as well as offer interesting research directions for follow-up work outside the project.

Keywords: assessment, Communities of Practice, evaluation, oral assessment, oral performance, oral proficiency, Web 2.0, web based tools for evaluating oral performance.

1. Introduction

WebCEF is a Minerva EU project that aimed at enabling the collaborative assessment of oral language proficiency through a web-based environment. A language learner or language teacher was envisaged as being able to evaluate his/her own video and audio samples together with colleagues and peers across Europe. The assessment was conceived to be based on the descriptors of the Common European Framework of Reference (CEF).

The main objectives WebCEF were

- to bring teaching staff across Europe together;
- to provide them with a community where their assessments could be validated by their colleagues and;
- to be able provide them and their pupils with tools to provide and share annotated video and audio materials on the Internet.

The aim of this article is to sum up the efforts of the linguistic partners in collecting speech samples for the Showcase as well as to outline some developments in sample collection and annotation that fall outside the scope of the original project. This article also includes information on the efforts of the Bologna team (Italian late-joining partner).

2. Overview

The sample collection started with coordinated efforts to establish parameters for samples for the Showcase in English. Linguistic partners (Belgian, Dutch, Finnish, French, German, Polish) first pooled available, recorded prior to the project, audio and video samples in an attempt to moderate length, content (exposition, lecture, summary), type of interaction (monologue, dialogue) as well as domain (private, official, educational, leisure, work).

Altogether, the video and audio recordings, comprising hi fidelity/high resolution as well as low bandwidth flash media spanned four 4,7 GB DVD disks, of which several samples have been selected as a starting point for discussion and which have been included in the annotation tool prior to the Chambery Partner meeting (November 2007).

It was assumed that whatever the decisions were to be made concerning the Showcase in English, those would be replicated in the respective partner languages of the Showcase to guarantee comparability across languages.

During the Chambery meeting, the Belgian and the Dutch partners expressed dissatisfaction with the CEFR scales and their ease of use in evaluating some more diverse samples from different educational backgrounds, voicing concerns that factors not explicitly present in the CEFR descriptors may influence the perception of some samples thus producing undesired effects where satisfactory convergence cannot be reached (cf. section on convergence issues). The two partners additionally suggested assuming an alternative set of scales to include the missing descriptors of performance and allowing to account for the phenomenon of native-like performance.

While this discussion continued as a peripheral discussion throughout the project (cf. section on the phenomenon of the native speaker), the majority of the Linguistic partner believed that despite the shortcomings of the CEFR scales, the project deliverables demand that the Showcase needs to illustrate the CEFR scales as they are the centrepiece of the project, and whatever other outcomes of the process of sample collection, evaluation and annotation may be in terms of comparative research, the Showcase would primarily be concerned with explicating and illustrating the CERF scales through a selection of comparable, analogous and, if possible, equivalent samples.

As a result the major scales for the showcase were those of CEFR for monologue samples, all based on a selection of video clips with minimum language content and explicit situational content, and a short reading task for a dialogue/interaction.

The scales for monologue and dialogue/interaction were rendered in the annotation tool first in English, and when work was undertaken on Transfer to other Languages (WP6) also in respective partner languages.

The Dutch and Belgian partners, apart from contributing to the mainstream work on scales, continued their work on alternatives to CEFR producing what in the annotation tool is now implemented as an Assessment Wizard, a customisable system for attaching weights to different aspects of oral performance, some of which are verbatim CEFR scales, some of which are categories not present in the CEFR descriptors such as intelligibility, fluency understood as a mere speed of talking (wpm) as well as pronunciation and intonation (cf. illustrations below).

3. The convergence issues

The discussion on convergence and discrepancies in evaluating samples was initiated in the project meeting on March 9, 2009. For parties interested in reviewing the discussion a live link to the recording http://fm.ea-tel.eu/fm/a76037-16318 is maintained by the Open University in the UK.

The topics that discussed included:

Possible sources of discrepancies in marking by different assessors such as:

- cultural differences in the perception of non-native speech such as:
  = phonetic accuracy,
  = speed of talking, and the ensuing perceived fluency,
  = range and;
  = accuracy of student vs. native speaker performance
- inter and intra rater variability affected by external factors as well as by the above

Inter rater variability is something that is partly affected by the fatigue and boredom/tediousness of the task, but also relates to the learning curve and the perception of the rating scales overtime, as it can be concluded that with greater understanding of the mechanics of scoring, the accuracy and reliability of the scorer increases until it reaches a plateau, and the variability there is beyond individual's control and impervious to training effects;

Intra rater variability may be attributed to a number of factors:

= generally the more complicated the rating scale, the larger the opportunity to make errors of judgment:

i) the overall scales for either of the tasks in our Showcase are complicated;

ii) they are supplemented by additional scales pertaining to different aspects of performance;
iii) the additional scales are complicated;
= perhaps less so in the case on national languages and partner Showcases, but definitely in the case of the Showcase for English, which was constructed based on efforts of individuals of different cultures, backgrounds and with different educational and evaluation histories, there is at least some effect of the intercultural communication and intercultural communication interference.

> (n.b.: Intercultural communication is a symbolic, interpretative, transactional, contextual process in which the degree of difference between people is large and important enough to create dissimilar interpretations and expectations about what are regarded as competent behaviours that should be used to create shared meanings
>
> (Lustig and Koester 1993: 51)

Sources of misunderstandings are numerous and have been pointed out by two separate theories:

= Psychological anthropology theory of intercultural interference (Barna 1994, Scollon and Scollon 1995) claims that interference emerges when: i) discourse participants (and in our case evaluators who interact with the samples) assume that all humans are essentially similar and therefore behave and interpret behaviour in a similar way; ii) discourse participants incorrectly interpret non-verbal clues and non verbal communication; iii) discourse participants read into their interpretation of discourse their pre-conceptions, stereotypes, and superstitions; iv) discourse participants assume a stance in which they judge and evaluate elements of the discourse according to their set of values and culture related norms of behaviour; v) additionally there is an element which is inherently connected with the language component, namely with the differences between any two or more languages and vi) ensuing tension, anxiety and other affective factors that appear when a language other than a native one is used by a speaker, a.k.a.: culture shock
= Dell Hymes, when outlining his model of communication and the concept of communicative competence (1967, 1972), used the acronym SPEAKING, where the individual letters stand respectively for: scene, participants, ends, act sequence, key, instrumentalities, norms, and finally genres, by which he understood where and how the act of communication is performed, what is the purpose and aim of it, how conventionally the communication unfolds, what is the degree of correctness /ceremoniality /detachement vs. casuality /familiarity /intimacy, how the communication is conveyed and what are the

overall, culturally sanctioned norms of communicating and interacting within the discourse and how they are to be interpreted, and finally what are the characteristics of different types of texts we produce and how they are constructed. The claim here is that the violation or misinterpretation of even one of the above will lead to intercultural interference.

- gender in the perception of speech: effeminate male language tends to be decidedly underscored by male raters and slightly, but statistically significantly overscored by female raters, but only of some nationalities (n.b.: looking for this trend, a manual search of the samples was performed which is inconclusive due to either insufficient metadata or too few samples of a particular kind, but points at least to the first of the findings (paper in print).
- the difficulty of the task, the resource intensity of the task: the effect the task has on the complexity of the discourse and range of linguistic resources that have been implemented in an effective and efficient achievement of the task. A task which is not demanding enough may leave the evaluator with the impression that the performance was of a lesser value and that the level of competence is lower when actually the examinee had no opportunity to spread the wings.
- the familiarity with the subject under evaluation: a tentative tendency to evaluate more favourably those who are known to us as opposed to those we are not familiar with (favouritism, a.k.a.: the teacher effect). Some examining bodies (e.g.: ESOL formerly UCLES) require that their oral examiners familiarise themselves with the names of the examinees before the exam and identify those whom they have taught in the last several years

4. The native speaker phenomenon

The work done in the Showcase can be described in relation to two separate phenomena: (i) work conducted in connection with the English Showcase and the discussion on convergence; and (ii) the work carried out in relation to the samples collected for the Polish Showcase. Before the samples for the Polish Showcase were selected, approximately 200 samples of monologues and dialogues involving non-native and native speakers were recorded, reviewed and analysed before consensus was reached. In an attempt to reach convergence the researchers looked at distinguishing features of good, fluent and proficient speech. This necessitated establishing some selection procedure and criteria and one of the premises used in the process was the notion of propositional and idea density, a notion which was postulated to be a distinguishing feature of samples that could be deemed native-like.

The notions of propositional density and idea density are an attractive premise in attempting to clearly define the rating scales for oral performance under various examination schemes. CPIDR (a Computerized Propositional Idea Density Rater, pronounced "spider") is a computer program that allows the researcher to establish the propositional idea density of a transcribed spoken text without human intervention (Brown, Snodgrass, Kemper, Herman and Covington 2008). The authors of the program claim that it has been validated against human raters and the convergence is sufficiently high to lead to further applications in machine aided assessment (MAA). Recent neurological studies (Caplan, Alpert and Waters 2008) of how people handle multiple propositions and how the mechanism changes both with age and when handling languages other than native, as well as studies dealing with propositional and idea density in the native speaker speech (Krakowian in print) tentatively suggest that there is perhaps another explanation accounting for the phenomenon of the native speaker and they point in the direction of the role of external context and implicature used by native speakers and more proficient non-native speakers, something which is not explicitly covered by CEF scales.

Propositional density, also known as proposition density, or P-density, but sometimes referred to as propositional idea density, and understood as in Kintsch (1974) and Turner and Greene (1977), can be determined by the total number of content words such as verbs (but not auxiliaries), adjectives, adverbs, prepositions, and conjunctions against by the total number of words (Snowdon *et al.* 1996). In a research study by Brown, Snodgrass, Covington, Herman, and Kemper (2007), a computer algorithm was conceived and perfected allowing the researchers to obtain accurate idea density measures. The implementation of this algorithm, the CPIDR program (or a Computerized Propositional Idea Density Rater, pronounced "spider") was vetted against human raters, and according to its creators, it *agrees with them better than they agree with each other, r = 0.97 vs. 0.82 respectively* (Brown, Snodgrass, Kemper, Herman and Covington 2008: 2).

Started by Kintsch and Keenan (1973) and Kintsch (1974), research into propositional density and idea density posits that propositions are the elements of the utterance involved in the process comprehending and recall of texts, both spoken and written. Following the Kintsch's paradigm (Kintsch and Keenan 1973; Kintsch 1974), with subsequent revisions of Turner and Greene (1977), the verb of the main clause alongside the subject, object, indirect object, and any other elements present form a single proposition. Additional descriptive elements such as modifiers in the form adjectives, adverbs which qualify the main verb, and qualifier phrases need to be seen as additional propositions.

The authors of the CPIDR program somewhat depart from Kintsch's ideas, as those differ from propositions in logic or logical semantics. The first, and probably most quantitatively important, point of departure concerns the fact that most of the information about the main verb in the main clause such as verb tense, aspect, and its modality is reduced in Kintsch's model of propositional density (Turner and Greene 1977). The second reason being that common nouns are not propositions in Kintsch's understanding of propositional density. As a result the model produces deflated measures of propositions as can be seen in the examples below. Following Kintsch's model both sentence (1) and sentence (2) contain the same number of propositions, namely three, and the propositional density measured in Kintsch's model, therefore, would respectively be 0.375 and 0.333 as the number of word in the examples is 8 and 9. Paradoxically, the sentence expressing a more complex meaning scores lower on the measure propositional density as it expresses the same number of propositions in more words.

(1) I would like to go to the cinema.
(2) I would like to have gone to the cinema.

The CPIDR algorithm accounts for the propositions differently:

```
CPIDR 3.2.2695.24633
"I would like to have gone to the cinema."
 002 PRP  W   i
 002 MD   W P would
 200 RB   W P like
 510 TO   W   to
 402 VB   W P have
 200 VBN  W P gone
 200 TO   W P to
 201 DT   W   the
 002 NN   W P cinema
 000 .        .
     6 propositions
     9 words
 0,666 density
"I would like to go to the cinema."
 002 PRP  W   i
 002 MD   W P would
 200 RB   W P like
 510 TO   W   to
 200 VB   W P go
 200 TO   W P to
 201 DT   W   the
 002 NN   W P cinema
 000 .        .
     4 propositions
     8 words
 0,500 density
```

The measures in CPIDR are obtained based on the notion of idea density, which the authors of the program tend to use over the term propositional density, which is understood as the number of expressed propositions divided by the number of words. In terms of semantics, idea density constitutes a gauge of the extent to which the speaker is making claims or for that matter making requests rather than just referring to entities. Propositions here include the notions of verb tense, aspect, and its modality, as well as account for the common nouns.

There exists a body of empirical research in the field of psychology looking at the connection between idea density to readability (Kintsch and Keenan 1973; Kintsch 1998), its relation to memory and retention (Thorson and Snyder 1984), evaluation of the writing by students, both native and non-native (Takao, Prothero, and Kelly 2002). A number of studies attempted to explain how propositions are handled depending on age (Kemper, Marquis, and Thompson 2001; Kemper and Sumner 2001) as well as various neurological conditions connected with old age (Caplan, Alpert and Waters 2008) and finally the role other languages play in relation to idea density (Altarriba and Heredia 2008).

Numerous attempts such as Voss (1979), Embretson and Gorin (2001), Takao, Prothero, and Kelly (2002), Milfont (2006), Sayeed (2007), to name but a few, have been made to ascertain the qualities of the native speaker in comparison with the L2 learners, some for evaluation and validation purpose, some to establish a uniform measure of oral proficiency and fluency, and some to dispel popular myths that native speakers speak faster, construct longer and more complex sentences, use longer, rarer and/or more sophisticated vocabulary and manage to involve a greater number of propositions in their speech.

In a recent research project, Krakowian (in print) claims that such empirical measures as those that were obtained in a corpus study of non-native speech, when compared with the performance of native speakers, contrary to popular beliefs, and what is more important to a evaluative study of speech perception by both native and non native speakers, do not indicate a greater rate of speech in native speakers. A small transcribed corpus of over 50 samples of speech by Polish speakers of English as a Second and Foreign language, amounting to nearly 17,000 words, indicates that the rate of speech of non-native speakers is approximately 20 per cent higher than that of native English speakers. Other indices seem to be pointing in a similar direction. From the point of view of mere word length, vocabulary sophistication understood as the proportion of words belonging to different frequency groups, native speakers are statistically significantly behind non-native users of the language. The same observation applies to sentence length and the number of embeddings.

The only exception lies in propositional and idea density measures, but it seems to be only statistically significant when they are obtained by hand rather than by the CPIDR algorithm. This could be owing to a rather striking observation made in the process of investigation concerning a commonsensical impression about some of the sentences analysed using the program. Consider the sentences below; sentence (3) is deemed in this mode of analysis to be more idea or propositional dense than sentence (4). The first of the sentences is a genuine sentence from a written task (an information brochure), the second one is prepared for the purpose of analysis by CPIDR.

(3) Conveniently located for outdoor sports, surrounded by picturesque green forests and within easy reach of the Lublinek airport, Lodz is definitely a place to go.
(4) Lodz is definitely a place to go as it is conveniently located for outdoor sports, and it is surrounded by picturesque green forests and lies within easy reach of the Lublinek airport.

The CPIDR calculations yield density of 0.520 based on 13 propositions in 25 words for the former and 0.469 based on 15 propositions in 32 words for the latter. The difference is negligible, and from a statistical point of view within measurement error, and based on the calculations the sentences may be considered comparable. Yet even a very superficial look at the sentences by a human rater will have to regard the first as a much more complex, mature and altogether more elegant and native-like. It would seem that the secret of the native speaker may lie somewhere else, or that automatic density measures are not necessarily yet the determining index to rely on.

WebCEF, a Socrates Minerva project involving a creation of a multimedia database of speech samples to be assessed within the Common European Framework of Reference for Languages offers sufficiently diverse material for analysis. Within the project a number of threads of discussion concerned the issue of convergence and adequate measures and criteria to be used in establishing valid instruments in language assessment (Krakowian in print). Principally, the samples were collected to build a showcase of samples to illustrate key concepts in CEF scales. With lack of consensus and convergence in the case of a large proportion of collected samples, several of the project partners investigated the issue of sample comparability with native oral performance on the same tasks.

The findings point to similar conclusions as were noted by Krakowian (in print) on the basis of the above mentioned small transcribed corpus, namely that while the differences in the rate of speech and language sophistication indices do sometimes favour native speakers in some of the selected samples in the analysis, there is no statistically significant difference between empirical measures between native and non-native oral language production. Native language production, however, is perceived, following the analytical scales of the CEF to be consistently and statistically significantly better than the selected upper-scale non-native performance used in the analysis.

It has been tentatively noticed that the source of such perception may lie in the fact which escapes the corpus methodology and is beyond the grasp of the CPIDR model, but which may be impressionistically acknowledged by the raters, even when they allegedly use the analytical CEF scales. At closer inspection at least some of the samples involving native speakers contain propositions which are not only implied, but implied in a manner that makes the inference by their interlocutors easy.

The samples under investigation consist of several types of interaction including (i) native speakers talking with other natives speakers; (ii) native speakers talking with non-native speakers; (iii) native speakers talking to native speakers; and (iv) native speakers talking to non-native speakers.

The implicature used when addressing other native speakers, either as part of a monologue or interaction, seems to be more frequent, which would reflect how propositions are handled by native speakers, as well as the recognition that a non-native speaker will have greater difficulties handling multiple prepositions and requires language adjustment (Altarriba and Heredia 2008), which apparently happens not only at the level of syntax, a phenomenon known as foreigner talk, but also at the level of propositional density both explicitly and through implicature.

Further research, preferably of quantitative type involving explicit marking to be included in the corpus of spoken language of comparable samples from native and non-native speakers is required to claim conclusively that implicature in native speech influences the perception of propositional density. Implicature, however, and more precisely the capacity for the quantitative control of implicature seems to be one of the factors distinguishing native and non-native speech

5. Conclusions

While the investigation of various phenomena characteristic of native as well as non-native speech were not the primary aim of the WebCEF project, and while the Showcase as well as the abundance of annotated and shared samples remain its central focus, it is well worth noticing that he WebCEF project will probably continue generating various research findings providing insights into the phenomenon of communicative oral performance.

References

Altarriba, J. and R.R. Heredia (2008). *An Introduction to Bilingualism: Principles and Processes*. Taylor and Francis LLP.

Anderson, R.C. (1982). "How to construct achievement tests to assess comprehension". *Review of Educational Research* 42: 145–170.

Brown, C., Snodgrass, T., Kemper, S.J., Herman, R. and M.A. Covington (2008). "Automatic Measurement of Propositional Idea Density from Part-of-Speech Tagging". *Behavioral Research Methods* 40(2): 540–545. L&B

Caplan, D., Alpert, N. and G. Waters (1998). Effects of Syntactic Structure and Propositional Number on Patterns of Regional Cerebral Blood Flow *Journal of cognitive nuroscience*, July 1998, Vol. 10, No. 4: 541–552. Massachusetts Institute of Technology

Embretson, S.E. and J.S. Gorin (2001). "Improving construct validity with cognitive psychology principles". *Journal of Educational Measurement* 38: 343–368.

Flesch, R. (1948). "A new readability yardstick". *Journal of Applied Psychology* 32: 221–233.

Freedle, R. and I. Kostin (1991). The prediction of GRE reading comprehension item difficulty for expository prose passages (ETS Research Report #RR-91-29). *Educational Testing Service*; Princeton, NJ.

Johnson, D.K., Storandt, M. and D.A. Balota (2003). "Discourse analysis of logical memory recall in normal aging and in dementia of the Alzheimer type". *Neuropsychology* 17: 82–92.

Kemper, S., Marquis, J. and M. Thompson (2001). "Longitudinal change in language production: Effect of aging and dementia on grammatical complexity and propositional content". *Psychology and Aging* 16: 600–614.

Kemper, S. and A. Sumner (2001). "The structure of verbal abilities in young and older adults". *Psychology and Aging* 16: 312–322.

Kintsch, W. and J. Keenan (1973). "Reading rate and retention as a function of the number of propositions in the base structure of sentences". *Cognitive Psychology* 5: 257–274.

Kintsch, W. (1998). *Comprehension: A paradigm for cognition*. Cambridge University Press: Cambridge, UK.

Kintsch, W. (1974). *The representation of meaning in memory*. Erlbaum; Hillsdalex, NJ.

Krakowian, P. (in print). A corpus study of L2 speech – in search of fluency determinants.

Milfont, T. L. (2006). "Native speaker biases". *PsycheD! – The University of Auckland PhD Newsletter of the Psychology Department*, 1(8): 3–4.

Perfetti, C. A. and M. A. Britt (1995). "Where do propositions come from?" In: Weaver C. A. III, Mannes, S., Fletcher, C.R. (eds.). *Discourse comprehension: essays in honor of Walter Kintsch*. Erlbaum; Hillsdale, NJ: 11–34.

Sayeed, S. A. (2007). "The Notion 'Native Speaker': A Philosophical Response". *Annual Review of South Asian Languages and Linguistics*.

Snowdon, D.A., Kemper, S. J., Mortimer, J. A., Greiner, L. H., Wekstein, D. R., and W. R. Markesbery (1996). "Linguistic ability in early life and cognitive function and Alzheimer' disease in late life: Findings from the Nun Study". *JAMA* 275: 528–532.

Takao, A.Y., Prothero, W.A. and G.J. Kelly (2002). "Applying argumentation analysis to assess the quality of university oceanography students' scientific writing". *Journal of Geoscience Education* 50: 40–48.

Thorson, E. and R. Snyder (1984). "Viewer recall of television commercials: Prediction from the propositional structure of commercial scripts". *Journal of Marketing Research* 21: 127–136.

Turner, A. and E. Greene (1977). *The construction and use of a propositional text base (Technical Report 63).* University of Colorado, Institute for the Study of Intellectual Behavior; Boulder, CO.

Voss, B. (1979). "Hesitation Phenomena as Sources of Perceptual Errors for Non-Native Speakers". *Language and Speech*, v22 n2 p129-44 Apr-Jun 1979

ŁÓDŹ
Studies in Language

Edited by
Barbara Lewandowska-Tomaszczyk

Vol. 1 Barbara Lewandowska-Tomaszczyk / Patrick James Melia (eds.): PALC'99: Practical Applications in Language Corpora. Papers from the International Conference at the Universtiy of Łódź, 15–18 April 1999. 2000.

Vol. 2 Lou Burnard / Tony McEnery (eds.): Rethinking Language Pedagogy from a Corpus Perspective. Papers from the third international conference on Teaching and Language Corpora. 2000.

Vol. 3 Barbara Lewandowska-Tomaszczyk / John Osborne / Frits Schulte: Foreign Language Teaching and Information and Communication Technology. 2001.

Vol. 4 Piotr Cap: Explorations in Political Discourse. Methodological and Critical Perspectives. 2002.

Vol. 5 Ewa Waniek-Klimczak / Patrick James Melia (eds.): Accents and Speech in Teaching English Phonetics and Phonology. EFL perspective. 2002.

Vol. 6 Barbara Lewandowska-Tomaszczyk / Kamila Turewicz (eds.): Cognitive Linguistics Today. 2002.

Vol. 7 Barbara Lewandowska-Tomaszczyk (ed.): PALC 2001: Practical Applications in Language Corpora. 2003.

Vol. 8 Corpus Linguistics by the Lune. A Festschrift for Geoffrey Leech. Edited by Andrew Wilson, Paul Rayson and Tony McEnery. 2003.

Vol. 9 Barbara Lewandowska-Tomaszczyk (ed.): Practical Applications in Language and Computers. PALC 2003. 2004.

Vol. 10 Imagery in Language. Festschrift in Honour of Professor Ronald W. Langacker. Edited by Barbara Lewandowska-Tomaszczyk and Alina Kwiatkowska. 2004.

Vol. 11 Seana Coulson / Barbara Lewandowska-Tomaszczyk (eds.): The Literal and Nonliteral in Language and Thought. 2005.

Vol. 12 Piotr Cap (ed.): Pragmatics Today. 2005.

Vol. 13 Jacek Waliñski / Krzysztof Kredens / Stanisław Goźdź-Roszkowski (eds.): Corpora and ICT in Language Studies. PALC 2005. 2007.

Vol 14 Krzysztof Kosecki (ed.): Perspectives on Metonymy. Proceedings of the International Conference "Perspectives on Metonymy", held in Łódź, Poland, May 6–7, 2005. 2007.

Vol. 15 Barbara Lewandowska-Tomaszczyk / Tomasz Płudowski / Dolores Valencia Tanno (eds.): The Media and International Communication. 2007.

Vol. 16 Krzysztof Kredens / Stanisław Goźdź-Roszkowski (eds.): Language and the Law: International Outlooks. 2007.

Vol. 17 Barbara Lewandowska-Tomaszczyk (ed.): Corpus Linguistics, Computer Tools, and Applications – State of the Art. PALC 2007. 2008.

Vol. 18 Barbara Lewandowska-Tomaszczyk / Katarzyna Dziwirek (eds.): Studies in Cognitive Corpus Linguistics. 2009.

Vol. 19 Barbara Lewandowska-Tomaszczyk / Marcel Thelen (eds.): Meaning in Translation. 2010.

Vol. 20 Łukasz Bogucki / Krzysztof Kredens (eds.): Perspectives on Audiovisual Translation. 2010.

Vol. 21 Piotr Stalmaszczyk (ed.): Turning Points in the Philosophy of Language and Linguistics. 2011.

Vol. 22 Stanisław Goźdź-Roszkowski: Patterns of Linguistic Variation in American Legal English. A Corpus-Based Study. 2011.

Vol. 23 Kamila Ciepiela (ed.): Identity through a Language Lens. 2011.

Vol. 24 Stanisław Goźdź-Roszkowski (ed.): Explorations across Languages and Corpora. PALC 2009. 2011.

www.peterlang.de